SO-CTN-241

American Constitutional Law

Volume II: Limitations on Government
By Paul C. Bartholomew

About the Author

1. Dr. Bartholomew was Professor of Government, University of Notre Dame. Sometime Visiting Professor at Northwestern University, Michigan State University, St. Mary's College, Loyola University (Chicago), the University of Tennessee, the University of Chicago, Southwest Texas State University, University of Texas at Austin, and the National University of Ireland, Dublin. Consultant: Department of the Navy, U.S. House of Representatives, State of Indiana, and the City of Chicago. Visiting lecturer at School of Public Administration, Dublin; Trinity College, Dublin; Queen's University, Belfast; University College, Galway; Chulalongkorn University, Bangkok.
2. Publications: *A Manual of American Government* (Burgess, 1936 and 1939); *A Manual of Political Science Research* (Notre Dame, 1940); *Public Administration* (Littlefield, Adams, 1959, 1967, 1972); co-author, *For Americans Only* (Nesterman, 1944); *American Government Under the Constitution* (Brown, 1947, 1949, 1956); *Leading Cases on the Constitution* (Littlefield, Adams, 9th ed., 1974); *Profile of a Precinct Committeeman* (Oceana, 1968); *The Indiana Third Congressional District, A Political History* (University of Notre Dame Press, 1970); *Ruling American Constitutional Law* (Littlefield, Adams, 1970); *The Irish Judiciary* (Institute of Public Administration, Dublin, 1971). He has written a number of articles and reviews for various journals in the field including "Constitutional Law," 1956 and subsequent editions, *Encyclopedia Americana*, as well as "Checks and Balances" and "Constitution," 1968 Edition. His annual analysis of the work of the Supreme Court appeared for a considerable number of years in the *Western Political Quarterly*; since, and including, the 1973-1974 Term of the Court, it has appeared in the *Emory Law Journal (Journal of Public Law)*.

About the Book

1. More cases are covered as "major cases" than in other leading casebooks. Adequate coverage of a case is combined with the minimum of quantity needed to present the pertinent parts of an opinion including concurring and dissenting opinions without loss of "flavor." Nothing that is essential is left out and little that is irrelevant is included.
2. The coverage of concurring and dissenting opinions is unexcelled in any other leading casebook.
3. Each "major case" is placed in its proper historical and political setting by a foreword and a concluding note.
4. Each "major case" is followed by a series of "Related Cases" in chronological order to indicate the development of the basic point or points involved in the "major case." For each such "related case" there is a brief summation of the point of law or contribution made by the case. This should prove to be of great help also in courses in constitutional history. For each case the name of the justice who wrote the opinion and the names of the dissenting justices, if any, are noted.
5. Page margins are wide to allow for notations.
6. Cases that have been overruled and are therefore no longer controlling are clearly indicated by boxing their names.
7. The Table of Cases at the rear of the book has cases arranged alphabetically by plaintiff, by defendant, and by popular name. No other major casebook at present has this very useful feature. Dates of decisions and official citations are supplied there also.
8. The Appendix contains a listing of members of the Supreme Court from 1789 to 1976 as well as the text of the Constitution.
9. Certain cases, valuable chiefly for their historical interest and not normally included in casebooks on constitutional law, are presented here and make the book especially valuable in courses in constitutional history.

AMERICAN CONSTITUTIONAL LAW

Volume II
Limitations on Government

by

PAUL C. BARTHOLOMEW

PROFESSOR OF GOVERNMENT

UNIVERSITY OF NOTRE DAME

Second Edition

LITTLEFIELD, ADAMS & COMPANY
TOTOWA, NEW JERSEY

Copyright © 1970, 1978

By

Littlefield, Adams & Co.

Library of Congress Cataloging in Publication Data

Bartholomew, Paul Charles, 1907-1976
  American constitutional law.

  (A Littlefield, Adams quality paperback; no. 240-241)
  First ed. published in 1970 under title: Ruling American constitutional law.
  Includes table of cases and index.
  CONTENTS: v. 1. Governmental organization, powers, and procedure—v. 2.
Limitations on government.
  1. United States—Constitutional law—Cases. I. Title.
KF4549.B33   1977   342'.73   76-56128
ISBN 0-8226-0240-7 (v. 1)
ISBN 0-8226-0241-5 (v. 2)

Printed in the United States of America

TO MY FAMILY

PUBLISHER'S NOTE

All material for this major revision was prepared by the author, Dr. Paul C. Bartholomew, prior to his death in 1976. The manuscript was copy-edited by Dr. Gladys Walterhouse. All of the work was reviewed and approved by Dr. Joseph F. Menez of Ball State University. It was the expressed wish of Dr. Bartholomew that his publishing projects should be continued by Dr. Menez.

PREFACE

This is a casebook distinctly and purposefully designed for students in political science. At the outset, it is important to understand that the objectives of a college or university course in government or political science differ markedly from those of a law school course in "Constitutional Law." In political science we are concerned with the rule of law involved in a case and we are equally concerned with the reasons for such a holding on the part of the Court and with the logical processes by which such a determination was reached. Moreover, we are involved with the points of view of both the concurring and the dissenting justices to a degree not appropriate to law school classes. We are properly interested in what the Court has said historically on the question basic to the case, and we only casually bear upon the technicalities of the legal process, a matter that is, of course, of much more concern to law students.

Constitutional law is evolutionary and incremental; one case is built upon another. Often one can understand the ruling or controlling case well only if one has previously read the older case, even if the latter has been overruled or reversed; hence the inclusion of certain overruled cases (indicated by boxes around their names and citations).

The schematic arrangement of this book attempts to bring out these desired points. For each case there is a presentation of excerpts in a much more abridged form than is normally true of casebooks. Carefully chosen to represent the basic matter of the case, these excerpts are followed by still briefer ones from the concurring and dissenting opinions. And to further extend coverage of the points of law involved, corollary cases are listed with a brief statement of the applicable rule of law enunciated. Sometimes there are pertinent statements from the concurring and/or dissenting opinions of these "related cases." Finally, a short note summarizes the situation to date, separating the ruling points of law from those that have been reversed or modified by the Court, so that for each section the reader will have a comprehensive view of current American constitutional law.

I am extremely grateful to a large number of persons who have either directly or indirectly influenced the makeup of this work, including the students in my classes at the various universities where I have taught. Also, special mention should be made of Nola Allen of the University of Notre Dame, Randall Bland of Southwest Texas State University, Charles Leonard of Western Illinois University, Joseph F. Menez of Ball State University, Walter F. Murphy of Princeton University, Louis A. Radelet of Michigan State University, and Thomas E. Woods, III, of Lansing, Michigan, for their help. To these and to others too numerous to mention I owe a deep debt of gratitude.

Paul C. Bartholomew

THE FIELD OF STUDY

Constitutional law is that law which deals with the contents of the Constitution and with the interpretation and construction of those contents. Included here are such matters as the organization of the government, i.e., its agents and agencies, how they are chosen, what terms they serve, and how they can be removed; the powers of the government including the distribution and mode of exercise of those powers; and the relations between the government and persons under its jurisdiction. The chief problems of constitutional law under the American system center on the basic matter of judicial review, on relations between and among the three departments of the government, on the federal system's distribution of powers between the federal and state governments, and on the restrictions or limitations on government in either a procedural or a substantive sense.

One of the truisms of American government is that ours is a government of laws and not of men. This sentiment is, in effect, emblazoned on the frieze of the Supreme Court Building—"Equal Justice Under Law." All that this means is that the ultimate measure of the legality of the use of force by our government is furnished by our system of a written constitution and not by a legally unlimited discretion of officials.

The study of constitutional law offers real persons sincerely confronting problems and offering reasoned justifications for their answers to the problems. This study emphasizes the point that all fields of knowledge are interrelated. It encourages the capacity to order facts, to note options, to foresee results, and to make morally and rationally justifiable decisions. This study also encourages flexibility in thinking and the ability to recognize the demands of the future while retaining basic principles.

As DeTocqueville noted, "Scarcely any political question arises in the United States that is not resolved, sooner or later, in a judicial question."

A Note on Citations

In the early days of this country, Supreme Court cases were reported by the Court Reporters, and their names are attached to the cases up to 1875—published in 90 volumes. Here is a list of the early reporters:

Years	Reporter	Abbreviation	No. of Vols.	Example
1780-1800	Dallas	Dall.	4	*Chisolm* v. *Georgia*, 2 Dall. 419 (1973)
1801-1815	Cranch	Cr.	9	*Marbury* v. *Madison*, 1 Cr. 137 (1803)
1816-1827	Wheaton	Wheat.	12	*Anderson* v. *Dunn*, 6 Wheat. 204 (1821)
1828-1842	Peters	Pet.	16	*American Insurance Co.* v. *Cantor*, 1 Pet. 511 (1828)
1843-1860	Howard	How.	24	*Ableman* v. *Booth*, 21 How. 506 (1859)
1861-1862	Black	Bl.	2	*Prize Cases*, 2 Bl. 645 (1863)
1863-1874	Wallace	Wall.	23	*Collector* v. *Day*, 11 Wall. 113 (1871)

Since 1875 the volumes are cited as 91 U.S. and so on. Thus *Chisholm* v. *Georgia*, 2 Dall. 419 (1793) means that the case, which took place in 1793, is found in Vol. 2 of Dallas, the Court Reporter, at page 419. A more recent case, such as *Coyle* v. *Smith*, 221 U.S. 559, means that the case is found in Vol. 221 of the *United States Reports*, at page 559.

There are three reporting services: *United States Reports*, published by the Government Printing Office (cited as U.S.), and two private ones, *Supreme Court Reporter* (cited as S.Ct.) and *Lawyer's Edition* (cited as L.Ed.).

In order to facilitate finding a reported case, all cases are usually reported under these three publications. Thus, *Coyle* v. *Smith*, 221 U.S. 559 can also be found in 31 S.Ct. 688 and in 55 L.Ed. 853.

Some additional abbreviations refer to geographical courts such as Atl. (Atlantic), N.E. (Northeast), S.E. (Southeast). Other abbreviations refer to legal items such as F. or Fed. (Federal), Stat. (Statute), and U.S.C. (United States Code). Sometimes this last item is U.S.C.A. (United States Code Annotated).

CONTENTS (Volume II)

V. Other Bill of Rights Guarantees 124

AMERICAN
CONSTITUTIONAL LAW

CHAPTER I

EX POST FACTO LEGISLATION

If there are any parts of the Constitution that immediately impress one as being outmoded or at least of no immediate application, they are the portions containing guarantees against *ex post facto* laws and bills of attainder. It is therefore surprising to find that both guarantees have been invoked very recently. The very rarity of the occasions, of course, makes them most interesting. These guarantees are contained in the original Constitution and are made applicable against both the federal and state governments. While there is some thought that the men who made the Constitution intended the prohibition to apply to both civil and criminal legislation, especially paper money or legal tender statutes, the Court in *Calder* v. *Bull* changed that, and the case is still ruling case law.

Calder v. Bull
3 Dallas 386; 1 L.Ed. 648 (1798)

(The dispute in this case involved the right to property under the will of Normand Morrison, a physician, dated March, 1793. The Probate Court of Hartford, Connecticut, had ruled against the will and in favor of the claims of Calder and his wife. In 1795 the state legislature passed a law under which a new hearing was held, the will was approved, and the right to the property transferred from Calder to Bull. This action by the legislature was attacked as being *ex post facto* in nature.)

Vote: Without dissent

Mr. Justice Chase delivered the opinion of the Court:

. . . I shall endeavor to show what law is to be considered an *ex post facto* law, within the words and meaning of the prohibition in the Federal constitution. The prohibition, "that no State shall pass any *ex post facto* law," necessarily requires some explanation; for naked and without explanation it is unintelligible, and means nothing. Literally, it is only that a law shall not be passed concerning, and after the fact, or thing done, or action committed. I would ask, what fact; of what nature or kind; and by whom done? That Charles I., King of England, was beheaded; that Oliver Cromwell was Protector of England; that Louis XVI., late King of France, was guillotined,—are all facts that have happened, that it would be nonsense to suppose that the States were prohibited from making any law after either of these events, and with reference thereto. The prohibition in the letter is not to pass any law concerning and after the fact, but the plain and obvious meaning and intention of the prohibition is this, that the legislatures of the several States shall not pass laws after a fact done by a subject, or citizen, which shall have relation to such fact, and shall punish him for having done it. The prohibition, considered in this light, is an additional bulwark in favor of the personal security of the subject, to protect his person from punishment by legislative acts, having a retrospective operation. I do not think it was inserted to secure the citizen in his private rights,

1

of either property or contracts. The prohibitions not to make anything but gold and silver coin a tender in payment of debts, and not to pass any law impairing the obligation of contracts, were inserted to secure private rights; but the restriction not to pass any *ex post facto* law, was to secure the person of the subject from injury or punishment, in consequence of such law. If the prohibition against making *ex post facto* laws was intended to secure personal rights from being affected or injured by such laws, and the prohibition is sufficiently extensive for that object, the other restraints I have enumerated were unnecessary, and therefore improper, for both of them are retrospective.

I will state what laws I consider *ex post facto* laws, within the words and the intent of the prohibition. 1st. Every law that makes an action done before the passing of the law, and which was innocent when done, criminal; and punishes such action. 2d. Every law that aggravates a crime, or makes it greater than it was, when committed. 3d. Every law that changes the punishment, and inflicts a greater punishment than the law annexed to the crime, when committed. 4th. Every law that alters the legal rules of evidence, and receives less or different testimony than the law required at the time of the commission of the offense, in order to convict the offender. All these, and similar laws are manifestly unjust and oppressive. In my opinion, the true distinction is between *ex post facto* laws and retrospective laws. Every *ex post facto* law must necessarily be retrospective; but every retrospective law is not an *ex post facto* law; the former only are prohibited. Every law that takes away or impairs rights vested, agreeably to existing laws, is retrospective, and is generally unjust, and may be oppressive; and it is a good general rule that a law should have no retrospect; but there are cases in which laws may justly, and for the benefit of the community, and also of individuals, relate to a time antecedent to their commencement; as statutes of oblivion, or of pardon. They are certainly retrospective, and literally both concerning, and after, the facts committed. But I do not consider any law *ex post facto*, within the prohibition, that mollifies the rigor of the criminal law; but only those that create, or aggravate, the crime; or increase the punishment, or change the rules of evidence, for the purpose of conviction. Every law that is to have an operation before the making thereof, as to commence at an antecedent time, or to save time from the Statute of Limitations, or to excuse acts which were unlawful, and before committed, and the like, is retrospective. But such laws may be proper or necessary, as the case may be. There is a great and apparent difference between making an unlawful act lawful, and the making an innocent action criminal, and punishing it as a crime. The expressions "*ex post facto* laws" are technical; they had been in use long before the Revolution, and had acquired an appropriate meaning by legislators, lawyers, and authors. The celebrated and judicious Sir William Blackstone, in his Commentaries, considers an *ex post facto* law precisely in the same light I have done. His opinion is confirmed by his successor, Mr. Wooddeson, and by the author of the "Federalist," whom I esteem superior to both, for his extensive and accurate knowledge of the true principles of government.

I also rely greatly on the definition, or explanation of *ex post facto* laws, as given by the convention, of Massachusetts, Maryland, and North Carolina, in their several constitutions, or forms of government. . . .

I am of the opinion that the decree of the Supreme Court of Errors of Connecticut be affirmed, with costs.

Judgment affirmed.

Mr. Justice Paterson concurred:

. . . The question, then, which arises on the pleadings in this cause, is, whether the resolution of the Legislature of Connecticut be an *ex post facto* law, within the meaning of the Constitution of the United States? I am of opinion, that it is not.

The words, *ex post facto*, when applied to a law, have a technical meaning, and, in legal phraseology, refer to crimes, pains and penalties. . . .

. . . The words of the Constitution of the United States are, "That no State shall pass any bill of attainder, *ex post facto* law, or law impairing the obligation of contracts." Article One, Section 10. Where is the necessity or use of the latter words, if a law impairing the obligation of contracts, be comprehended within the terms *ex post facto* law? It is obvious from the specification of contracts in the last member of the clause, that the framers of the Constitution did not understand or use the words in the sense contended for on the part of the plaintiffs in error. They understood and used the words in their known and appropriate signification, as referring to crimes, pains and penalties, and no further. The arrangement of the distinct members of this section necessarily points to this meaning. . . .

Mr. Justice Iredell concurred:

. . . Still, however, in the present instance, the act or resolution of the Legislature of Connecticut, cannot be regarded as an *ex post facto* law; for, the true construction of the prohibition extends to criminal, not to civil, cases. It is only in criminal cases, indeed, in which the danger to be guarded against, is greatly to be apprehended.

The policy, the reason and humanity of the prohibition, do not, I repeat, extend to civil cases, to cases that merely affect the private property of citizens. Some of the most necessary and important acts of Legislation are, on the contrary, founded upon the principle, that private rights must yield to public exigencies. . . .

Mr. Justice Cushing concurred:

The case appears to me to be clear of all difficulty, taken either way. If the act is a judicial act, it is not touched by the federal constitution: and if it is a legislative act, it is maintained and justified by the ancient and uniform practice of the state of Connecticut.

RELATED CASES:

Burgess v. Salmon: 97 U.S. 381 (1878). Opinion: Hunt, J. No dissent.

A seller of goods who makes a sale in the morning of a particular day may not be required to pay a tax on those goods authorized by a legislature on the afternoon of that day. To hold such an act applicable to such a sale would be to violate the *ex post facto* clause of the Constitution. This was held to be essentially criminal legislation. Burgess was a Collector of Internal Revenue and Salmon a tobacco dealer.

Hawker v. New York: 170 U.S. 189 (1898). Opinion: Brewer, J. Dissenting: Harlan, Peckham, and McKenna, JJ.

Hawker, a physician, was convicted of continuing to practice medicine after the passage of a statute in 1893 which forbade the practice to anyone who had ever been convicted of a felony. Hawker had been convicted of abortion in 1878. The Court held this not to be *ex post facto* but a determination of qualifications and of personal competence to practice medicine. The statute had no punitive intention and the felony involved must bear a substantial relationship to fitness to practice the profession, and the state could require good moral character.

Thompson v. Utah: 170 U.S. 343 (1898). Opinion: Harlan J. Dissenting: Brewer and Peckham, JJ.

A state constitution that provides for the trial in courts of general jurisdiction of criminal cases, not capital, by a jury composed of eight persons, is *ex post facto* in its application to felonies committed before the territory became a state. Thompson was the defendant on a grand larceny charge. The Court held that as applied to accused persons as a class, it is simply easier to get eight jurors to convict than twelve.

Thompson v. Missouri: 171 U.S. 380 (1898). Opinion: Harlan, J. No dissent.

A statute which does nothing more than admit evidence of a particular kind (here letters) in a criminal case upon an issue of the fact which was not admissible under the rules of evidence as enforced by judicial decisions at the time the offense was committed is not *ex post facto*. Such legislation merely regulates court procedure. Both the accused (here Thompson was on trial for murder) and the state have equal rights under the new rule. There was no impairment of the substantial guarantees of the defendant.

Johannessen v. United States: 225 U.S. 227 (1912). Opinion: Pitney, J. No dissent.

Because the *ex post facto* provision of the Constitution is confined to laws affecting punishment for crime and has no relation to retrospective legislation of any other description, an act of Congress permitting the cancellation of a certificate of citizenship obtained solely by fraud is not a punishment but simply nullifies that to which the party had no right. This was a civil and not a criminal proceeding. Johannessen, from Norway, did not have five years of residence in the United States.

Mahler v. Eby: 264 U.S. 32 (1924). Opinion: Taft, C. J. No dissent.

The inhibition of *ex post facto* laws applies only to criminal laws and not to a law for deporting aliens who by conviction of crime are shown to be undesirable as residents of this country. The deportation of Mahler was not punishment but was simply an exercise of governmental power.

Garner v. Los Angeles Board of Public Works: 341 U.S. 716 (1951). Opinion: Clark, J. Dissenting: Douglas, Black, Burton, and Frankfurter, JJ.

A city may require employees to file an affidavit disclosing past or present membership in the Communist Party and to take an oath that they had not, during the previous five years, belonged to any subversive organization. There was the presumption that scienter was implicit in each clause of the oath. This was held to be a violation of neither the *ex post facto* nor bill of attainder guarantees. Past conduct may well relate to present fitness. See p. 280, below.

Galvan v. Press: 347 U.S. 522 (1954). Opinion: Frankfurter, J. Dissenting: Douglas and Black, JJ.

The *ex post facto* guarantee does not apply to deportation. Thus, an alien can be deported for having joined the Communist Party at a previous date even though such membership was without knowledge of the Party's advocacy of violence. Galvan, from Mexico, had no vested right to remain in this country.

Rowoldt v. Perfetto: 355 U.S. 115 (1957). Opinion: Frankfurter, J. Dissenting: Harlan, Burton, Clark, and Whittaker, JJ.

One who is to be deported under the Internal Security Act of 1950 for membership in the Communist Party must have presented against him solid proof of meaningful association with the Party, and proof that he (in this case, Rowoldt) understood the "political implications" of membership. At least to some extent, this decision overruled the effect of *Galvan*.

DeVeau v. Braisted: 363 U.S. 144 (1960). Opinion: Frankfurter, J. Abstaining: Harlan, J. Dissenting: Douglas and Black, JJ., and Warren, C.J.

The New York Waterfront Commission Act of 1953 could constitutionally disqualify from holding office in a waterfront organization any person who had been convicted of a felony. This was held to be consistent with the supremacy clause, and not violative of the due process clause of the 14th Amendment, or prohibitions against *ex post facto* laws or bills of attainder.

Williams v. Florida: 399 U.S. 78 (1970). Opinion: White, J. Dissenting: Marshall, J. Abstaining: Blackmun, J.

A six-member jury in a noncapital case is valid. The real purpose of a jury—"the interposition between the accused and his accuser of the commonsense judgment of a group of laymen"—has no relation to the number on a jury. (399 U.S. at 100.) *Thompson* v. *Utah* (see above) was overruled.

NOTE:

Only criminal statutes can be voided as *ex post facto*. In general, an *ex post facto* statute is one that is disadvantageous to a criminally accused person. This provision in the Constitution applies only to legislative actions, not to executive acts or court decisions

A statute that is really criminal in nature cannot be saved by putting the matter in the form of a civil statute.

Habitual criminal statutes are regarded as simply imposing greater punishment for earlier crimes.

CHAPTER II

BILLS OF ATTAINDER

A bill of attainder is a legislative act—a bill—that convicts—attaints—a person of an offense and imposes a punishment without judicial process. If the punishment is less than death, such a legislative act is known technically as a "bill of pains and penalties." The guarantees against bills of attainder by either federal or state governments seem, like those against *ex post facto* laws, almost "prehistoric" in nature and out of place in a modern government's constitution. However, such is not the case, a very recent decision of the Court having held an act of Congress void on this ground.

United States v. Lovett
328 U.S. 303; 66 S.Ct. 1073; 90 L.Ed. 1252 (1946)

(Three persons, Lovett, Watson, and Dodd, were government employees and were accused by the House Committee on Un-American Activities of being subversives. Their work for the government had been satisfactory, according to their supervisors. In 1943 a rider was attached to an appropriation act which provided that these three men should not be paid any salary unless they were reappointed by the President and confirmed by the Senate. The reappointment did not take place, but the men continued to work and then they brought suit in the Court of Claims for their salaries. The action of Congress was challenged as being a bill of attainder.)

Vote: 8-0

Mr. Justice Black delivered the opinion of the Court:

[*First.*] . . . We hold that the purpose of Section 304 was not merely to cut off respondents' compensation through regular disbursing channels but permanently to bar them from government service; and that the issue of whether it is constitutional is justiciable. The Section's language as well as the circumstances of its passage which we have just described show that no mere question of compensation procedure or of appropriations was involved, but that it was designed to force the employing agencies to discharge respondents and to bar their being hired by any other governmental agency. . . . Any other interpretation of the Section would completely frustrate the purpose of all who sponsored Section 304, which clearly was to "purge" the then existing and all future lists of Government employees of those whom Congress deemed guilty of "subversive activities" and therefore "unfit" to hold a federal job. What was challenged therefore is a statute which, because of what Congress thought to be their political beliefs, prohibited respondents from ever engaging in any government work, except as jurors or soldiers. Respondents claimed that their discharge was unconstitutional; that they consequently rightfully continued to work for the Government and that the Government owes them compensation for services performed under contracts of employment. Congress has established the Court of Claims to try just such controversies. What is involved here is a Congressional proscription of Lovett, Watson, and Dodd, prohibiting their ever holding a Government job. Were this case to be not justiciable, Congressional action, aimed at three named individuals, which stigmatized their reputation and seriously impaired their chance to earn a living, could never be challenged in any court. Our Constitution did not contemplate such a result. . . .

[*Second.*] We hold that Section 304 falls precisely within the category of Congressional actions which the Constitution barred by providing that "No Bill of Attainder or *ex post facto* Law shall be passed." In *Cummings* v. *State of Missouri*, 4 Wall. 277, this Court said, "A bill of attainder is a legislative act which inflicts punishment without a judicial trial. If the punishment be less than death, the act is termed a bill of pains and penalties. Within the meaning of the Constitution, bills of attainder include bills of pains and penalties." . . . In an illuminating opinion which gave the historical background of the Constitutional prohibition against bills of attainder, this Court invalidated the Missouri Constitutional provision both because it constituted a bill of attainder and because it had an *ex post facto* operation. On the same day the Cummings case was decided, the Court, in *Ex parte Garland*, 4 Wall. 333, also held invalid on the same grounds an Act of Congress which required attorneys practicing before this Court to take a similar oath. Neither of these cases has ever been overruled. They stand for the proposition that legislative acts, no matter what their form, that apply either to named individuals or to easily ascertainable members of a group in such a way as to inflict punishment on them without a judicial trial are bills of attainder prohibited by the Constitution. Adherence to this principle requires invalidation of Section 304. We do adhere to it.

Section 304 was designed to apply to particular individuals. Just as the statute in the two cases mentioned it "operated as a legislative decree of perpetual exclusion" from a chosen vocation. This permanent proscription from any opportunity to serve the Government is punishment, and of a most severe type. It is a type of punishment which Congress has only invoked for special types of odious and dangerous crimes. . . .

Section 304, thus, clearly accomplishes the punishment of named individuals without a judicial trial. The fact that the punishment is inflicted through the instrumentality of an Act specifically cutting off the pay of certain named individuals found guilty of disloyalty, makes it no less galling or effective than if it had been done by an Act which designated the conduct as criminal. No one would think that Congress could have passed a valid law, stating that after investigation it had found Lovett, Dodd, and Watson "guilty" of the crime of engaging in "subversive activities," defined that term for the first time, and sentenced them to perpetual exclusion from any government employment. Section 304, while it does not use that language, accomplishes that result. The effect was to inflict punishment without the safeguards of a judicial trial and "determined by no previous law or fixed rule." The Constitution declares that that cannot be done either by a state or by the United States.

. . . When our Constitution and Bill of Rights were written, our ancestors had ample reason to know that legislative trials and punishments were too dangerous to liberty to exist in the nation of free men they envisioned. And so they proscribed bills of attainder. Section 304 is one. Much as we regret to declare that an Act of Congress violates the Constitution, we have no alternative here.

Section 304 therefore does not stand as an obstacle to payment of compensation to Lovett, Watson, and Dodd. The judgment in their favor is affirmed.

Mr. Justice Frankfurter concurred, along with Mr. Justice Reed:

. . . We are not faced inescapably with the necessity of adjudicating these serious constitutional questions. The obvious, or at the least, the one certain construction of § 304 is that it forbids the disbursing agents of the Treasury to pay out of specifically appropriated moneys sums to compensate respondents for their services. We have noted the cloud cast upon this interpretation by manifestations by committees and members of the House of Representatives before the passage of this section. On the other hand, there is also much in the debates not only in the Senate but also in the House which supports the mere fiscal scope to be given to the statute. That such a construction is tenable settles our duty to adopt it and to avoid determination of constitutional questions of great seriousness.

Accordingly, I feel compelled to construe § 304 as did Mr. Chief Justice Whaley below, whereby it merely prevented the ordinary disbursal of money to pay respondents' salaries. It did not cut off the obligation of the Government to pay for services rendered and the respondents are, therefore, entitled to recover the judgment which they obtained from the Court of Claims.

Mr. Justice Jackson took no part in the consideration or decision of these cases. (He was at Nuremberg at the War Crimes trials.)

RELATED CASES:

Cummings v. Missouri: 4 Wallace 277 (1867). Opinion: Field, J. Dissenting: Miller, J., Chase, C.J., and Swayne and Davis, JJ.

A provision of the state constitution that required all persons in certain professions such as here, a clergyman, to take an oath that they had not in any way, by act or word, aided the cause of the Confederacy, was held to be both a bill of attainder and an *ex post facto* law. ·

Ex parte Garland: 4 Wallace 333 (1867). Opinion: Field, J. Dissenting: Miller, J., Chase, C.J., and Swayne and Davis, JJ.

An act of Congress that required an oath by an attorney that he had not aided the Confederacy in any way before he could be admitted to practice before the Supreme Court was held to be both a bill of attainder and an *ex post facto* law.

United States v. Brown: 381 U.S. 437 (1965). Opinion: Warren, C.J. Dissenting: White, Clark, Harlan, and Stewart, JJ.

A statute that designates in no uncertain terms the persons who possess feared characteristics and therefore cannot hold union office without incurring criminal liability (here members of the Communist Party) is void as a bill of attainder. The opinion has a good historical summary and review of pertinent cases. See also p. 75, below.

NOTE:

The case of *United States* v. *Lovett* represents the principle of partial invalidity. When a portion of a statute is declared void, the remainder may be enforced if it can be separated from the invalid section.

Further, the case proves that the bill of attainder prohibition in the Constitution is not a dead letter.

Conceivably in *Lovett* the Court could have voided the provision of the statute as an attempt by Congress to exercise the removal power of the President in violation of the doctrine of separation of powers.

Cummings and *Garland* are sometimes referred to as the Test Oath Cases. In both cases the Court held that there was no relationship to the fitness of the individuals to perform the duties of their professions.

The President appears not to be hampered as Commander-in-Chief by the *ex post facto* prohibition. Franklin Roosevelt at Yalta and Truman at Potsdam agreed to the War Crimes Trials. These matters were not previously punishable under either international law or any other law.

CHAPTER III

THE FEDERAL BILL OF RIGHTS

THE APPLICABILITY OF THE BILL OF RIGHTS

Since the ratification of the first ten amendments of the Constitution—the so-called federal Bill of Rights—there has been raised intermittently the question of the application of these to the states and, almost continuously—particularly in recent years—the question of the specific meaning of the various amendments. John Marshall's decision in *Barron* v. *Baltimore* rather settled the first matter until the proclamation of the "Gitlow doctrine" in 1925. Since then the chief difficulty has been in the application of this doctrine along with the interpretation of specific guarantees.

Barron v. Baltimore
7 Peters 243; 8 L.Ed. 672 (1833)

(The city of Baltimore in the process of paving certain streets around the waterfront had diverted the course of some streams and the net result had been the deposit of silt and sediment around a wharf owned by Barron making the water so shallow as to preclude use of the wharf. In a suit for $4500 damages using the provision of the Fifth Amendment of the Constitution which forbids deprivation of property without just compensation as a basis for his claim, Barron lost in the lower courts.)

Vote: No dissent

Mr. Chief Justice Marshall delivered the opinion of the Court:

. . . The Constitution was ordained and established by the people of the United States for themselves, for their own government, and not for the government of the individual States. Each State established a Constitution for itself, and, in that Constitution, provided such limitations and restrictions on the powers of its particular government as its judgment dictated. The people of the United States framed such a government for the United States as they supposed best adapted to their situation, and best calculated to their interests. The powers they conferred on this government were to be exercised by itself; and the limitations on power, if expressed in general terms, are naturally, and, we think, necessarily applicable to the government created by the instrument. They are limitations of power granted in the instrument itself; not of distinct governments, framed by different persons and for different purposes.

If these propositions be correct, the Fifth Amendment must be understood as restraining the power of the general government, not as applicable to the States. In their several constitutions they have imposed such restrictions on their respective governments as their own wisdom suggested; such as they deemed most proper for themselves. It is a subject on which they judge exclusively, and with which others interfere no further than they are supposed to have a common interest.

The counsel for the plaintiff in error insists that the Constitution was intended to secure the people of the several States against the undue exercise of power by their respective State governments; as well as against that which might be attempted by their general government. In support of this argument he relies on the inhibitions contained in the tenth section of the first article.

We think that section affords a strong if not a conclusive argument in support of the opinion already indicated by the court.

The preceding section contains restrictions which are obviously intended for the exclusive purpose of restraining the exercise of power by the departments of the general government. Some of them use language applicable only to Congress; others are expressed in general terms. The third clause, for example, declares that "no bill of attainder or *ex post facto* law shall be passed." No language can be more general; yet the demonstration is complete that it applies solely to the government of the United States. In addition to the general arguments furnished by the instrument itself, some of which have been already suggested, the succeeding section, the avowed purpose of which is to restrain State legislation, contains in terms the very prohibition. It declares that "no State shall pass any bill of attainder or *ex post facto* law." This provision, then, of the ninth section, however comprehensive its language, contains no restriction on state legislation. . . .

If the original Constitution, in the ninth and tenth sections of the first article, draws this plain and marked line of discrimination between the limitations it imposes on the powers of the general government, and on those of the States; if in every inhibition intended to act on State power, words are employed which directly express that intent,—some strong reason must be assigned for departing from this safe and judicious course in framing the amendments, before that departure can be assumed.

We search in vain for that reason.

. . . In almost every convention by which the Constitution was adopted, amendments to guard against the abuse of power were recommended. These amendments demanded security against the apprehended encroachments of the general government, not against those of the local governments. . . .

RELATED CASES:

Hurtado v. California: 110 U.S. 516 (1884). Opinion: Matthews, J. Dissenting: Harlan, J. Abstaining: Field, J.

Any legal proceedings (here, use of the information) enforced by public authority in furtherance of the public good which have due regard for the principles of liberty and justice, must be held to be due process of law. See p. 234 below.

Maxwell v. Dow: 176 U.S. 581 (1900). Opinion: Peckham, J. Dissenting: Harlan, J.

The guarantees of the Fifth and Sixth Amendments are secured to all persons as against the federal government entirely without regard to citizenship. Therefore, these are not privileges or immunities of United States citizenship which the states are forbidden to abridge. Maxwell was defendant in a robbery case. Dow was Warden of the Utah State Prison.

(Mr. Justice Harlan's dissents in this case and in *Hurtado* are notable because of their extensive examination of the Fourteenth Amendment.)

Twining v. New Jersey: 211 U.S. 78 (1908). Opinion: Moody, J. Dissenting: Harlan, J.

The exemption from self-incrimination is not a privilege or immunity of United States citizenship which the states cannot abridge nor is it inherent in due process of law. This decision was overruled by *Griffin* v. *California*, 380 U.S. 609 (1965). Twining was the defendant in a charge of fraud.

Gitlow v. New York: 268 U.S. 652 (1925). Opinion: Sanford, J. Dissenting: Holmes and Brandeis, JJ.

The guarantees of freedom of speech and the press are among the fundamental liberties of which persons cannot be deprived by a state without due process of law, according to the Fourteenth Amendment. See p. 58, below.

Palko v. Connecticut: 302 U.S. 319 (1937). Opinion: Cardozo, J. Dissenting: Butler, J.

Only those provisions of the Bill of Rights are applicable to the states through the due process clause of the Fourteenth Amendment that are of the very essence of a scheme of ordered liberty. See p. 237, below.

Adamson v. California: 332 U.S. 46 (1947). Opinion: Reed, J. Dissenting: Black, Douglas, Murphy, and Rutledge, JJ.

This case, a reaffirmation of *Twining*, is interesting for Mr. Justice Black's dissent holding that the entire Bill of Rights should be applicable to the states through the Fourteenth Amendment. See p. 259, below.

NOTE:

Barron v. *Baltimore* is a remarkable and most interesting case. It represents nicely Marshall's logic at work, and it was his last decision on constitutional matters. It is still good law in principle. Only the extent of its application has been narrowed by *Gitlow*. It is still ruling case law that general provisions of the Constitution, without more, apply only to the federal government. The definition of "liberty" in the Fourteenth Amendment has been a matter of gradual expansion by the Court, but the principle of *Barron* remains.

Gitlow followed the precedent of the *Insular cases* in dividing the provisions of the Constitution into *formal* and *fundamental* categories. The Court in *Gitlow* said that only such rights in the Bill of Rights as are so basic to be necessary for any reasonable definition of liberty are to be applied to the states through the Fourteenth Amendment. These are the fundamental things. The others, not necessary or basic, are to be applied only in accordance with their original intent as expressed by the Court in *Barron*.

CHAPTER IV

THE FIRST AMENDMENT

The First Amendment has been regarded by the Court from time to time as possessing a certain priority among individual guarantees against governmental action when balanced against other rights, particularly property rights. While the First Amendment contains five specific guarantees, the Court has generally treated these as three basic rights: religion, speech and press, and assembly and petition. As already noted, the Court has held that certain of the Bill of Rights guarantees have been "absorbed" into the Fourteenth Amendment and thus applied to the states. This has been done by the Court defining "liberty " (which no state can deny to a person without due process) as including certain specific guarantees. The first portion of the Constitution to be so treated by the Court was the First Amendment, as first enunciated in *Gitlow* v. *New York* (268 U.S. 652, 1925), known commonly as the "Gitlow doctrine."

THE RELIGION GUARANTEES

There are really two specific restrictions on Congress (and now on the states also) in regard to religion. The first of these prohibits any law "respecting an establishment of religion" and the second prohibits any restriction on the free exercise of religion. These were originally restrictions only on Congress but with the "Gitlow doctrine" these began to be applied to the states. However, it was not until fifteen years after the *Gitlow* decision (involving speech and press) that the Court declared that the religion clause—the "first freedom"—of the First Amendment was likewise applicable to the states by the *Cantwell* decision. *Hamilton* v. *Regents* is sometimes cited in this connection, but the question of religious freedom was not basic to that decision.

Cantwell v. Connecticut
310 U.S. 296; 60 S.Ct. 900; 84 L.Ed. 1213 (1940)

(Certain members of the Jehovah's Witnesses [Jesse Cantwell and his two sons] went from house to house in Cassius Street in New Haven, Connecticut, selling books. Part of their procedure was to play a record that described the books. They were convicted of violating a statue that required a permit from the Secretary of the Public Welfare Council before solicitations were made for money for alleged religious purposes.)

Vote: 9-0

Mr. Justice Roberts delivered the opinion of the Court:

... We hold that the statute, as construed and applied to the appellants, deprives them of their liberty without due process of law in contravention of the Fourteenth Amendment. The fundamental concept of liberty embodied in that Amendment embraces the liberties guaranteed by the First Amendment. The First Amendment declares that Congress shall make no law respecting an establishment of religion or prohibiting the free exercise thereof. The Fourteenth Amendment has rendered the legislatures of the states as incompetent as Congress to enact such laws. The constitutional inhibition of legislation on the subject of religion has a double aspect. On the one hand, it forestalls compulsion by law of the acceptance of any creed or the practice of any form of worship. Freedom of conscience and freedom to adhere to such religious organization or form of worship as the individual may choose cannot be restricted by law. On the other hand, it safeguards the free exercise of the chosen form of religion. Thus the Amendment embraces two concepts,—freedom to believe and freedom to act. The first is absolute but, in the nature of things, the second cannot be. Conduct remains subject to regulation for the protection of society. The freedom to act must have appropriate definition to preserve the enforcement of that protection. In every case the power to regulate must be so exercised as not, in attaining a permissible end, unduly to infringe the protected freedom. No one would contest the proposition that a State may not, by statue, wholly deny the right to preach or to disseminate religious views. Plainly such a previous and absolute restraint would violate the terms of the guarantee. It is equally clear that a State may by general and non-discriminatory legislation regulate the times, the places, and the manner of soliciting upon its streets, and of holding meetings thereon; and may in other respects safeguard the peace, good order and comfort of the community, without unconstitutionally invading the liberties protected by the Fourteenth Amendment. The appellants are right in their insistence that the Act in question is not such a regulation. If a certificate is procured, solicitation is permitted without restraint, but, in the absence of a certificate, solicitation is altogether prohibited. . . .

Nothing we have said is intended even remotely to imply that, under the cloak of religion, persons may, with impunity, commit frauds upon the public. Certainly penal laws are available to punish such conduct. Even the exercise of religion may be at some slight inconvenience in order that the state may protect its citizens from fraudulent solicitation by requiring a stranger in the community, before permitting him publicly to solicit funds for any purpose, to establish his identity and his authority to act for the cause which he purports to represent. The State is likewise free to regulate the time and manner of solicitation generally, in the interest of public safety, peace, comfort or convenience. But to condition the solicitation of aid for the perpetuation of religious views or systems upon a license, the grant of which rests in the exercise of a determination by state authority as to what is a religious cause, is to lay a forbidden burden upon the exercise of liberty protected by the Constitution. . . .

The offense known as breach of the peace embraces a great variety of conduct destroying or menacing public order and tranquility. It includes not only violent acts but acts and words likely to produce violence in others. No one would have the hardihood to suggest that the principle of freedom of speech sanctions incitement to riot or that religious liberty connotes the privilege to exhort others to physical attack upon those belonging to another sect. When clear and present danger of riot, disorder, interference with traffic upon the public streets, or other immediate threat to public safety, peace, or order, appears, the power of the State to prevent or punish is obvious. Equally obvious is it that a State may not unduly suppress free communication of views, religious or other, under the guise of conserving desirable conditions. Here we have a situation analogous to a conviction under a statute sweeping in a great variety of conduct under a general and indefinite characterization, and leaving to the executive and judicial branches too wide a discretion in its application. . . .

The essential characteristic of these liberties is that under their shield many types of life, character, opinion and belief can develop unmolested and unobstructed. Nowhere is this shield more necessary than in our own country for a people composed of many races and many creeds. There are limits to the exercise of these liberties. The danger in these times from the coercive activities of those who in the delusion of racial or religious conceit would incite violence and breaches of the peace in order to deprive others of their equal right to the exercise of their liberties, is emphasized by events familiar to all. These and other transgressions of those limits the States appropriately may punish.

RELATED CASES:

Hamilton v. Regents of the University of California: 293 U.S. 245 (1934). Opinion: Butler, J. No dissent.

Requiring students at a state university to take a course in military science and tactics is not a deprivation of religious liberty without due process. Hamilton, the student, and his father were Methodists.

Jamison v. Texas: 318 U.S. 413 (1943). Opinion: Black, J. Abstaining: Rutledge, J. No dissent.

The right to distribute handbills on religious subjects on the public streets cannot be prohibited at all times, at all places, and under all circumstances. Here an ordinance of Dallas was held void. Mrs. Jamison was a member of Jehovah's Witnesses. The case represents a step in the evolution of the thought of the Court.

Largent v. Texas: 318 U.S. 418 (1943). Opinion: Reed, J. Abstaining: Rutledge, J. No dissent.

Requiring a permit for the distribution of religious handbills is prior restraint and void. In this case out of Paris, Texas, the permit was to be secured from the Mayor who could determine if it was "proper or advisable." This was held to be "administrative censorship." These handbills "seek in a lawful fashion to promote the raising of funds for religious purposes." Such handbills are to be distinguished from commercial handbills. Distribution of the latter can be regulated or prohibited. See also *Jamison v. Texas*, 318 U.S. 413 (1943).

Marsh v. Alabama: 326 U.S. 501 (1946). Opinion: Black, J. Dissenting: Reed, J., Stone, C.J., and Burton, J. Abstaining: Jackson, J.

One may remain on private property contrary to the will of the owner and the law of the state so long as the only objective of his presence is that he is exercising an asserted right to spread his religious views. Here was involved Chickasaw, a company-owned town, a suburb of Mobile, which the Court held was no different from any other city. Thus, the "company town" was held to be performing a function that was basically governmental. Therefore it was bound by constitutional guarantees. See p. 18, below.

Tucker v. Texas: 326 U.S. 517 (1946). Opinion: Black, J. Dissenting: Stone, C.J., and Reed and Burton, JJ.

One may remain on the streets of a government-owned town to distribute religious pamphlets even though the property had been posted to prohibit such solicitation. Tucker was a minister of Jehovah's Witnesses. See p. 20, below.

McGowan v. Maryland: 366 U.S. 420 (1961). Opinion: Warren, C.J. Dissenting: Douglas, J.

Sunday closing laws or "blue laws" are not laws respecting the establishment of religion within the meaning of the First Amendment since the legislation is not religiously motivated but simply to provide a uniform day of rest for all citizens. The legislation does not violate the equal protection clause of the Fourteenth Amendment since the classifications involved are reasonable. Statutes may impose on religious observances where no reasonable alternative is available. This was a "utiliarian decision." This and the following three cases are sometimes listed as the "Sunday Closing Cases."

Gallagher v. Kosher Supermarket: 366 U.S. 617 (1961). Opinion: Warren, C.J. Dissenting: Douglas, Brennan, and Stewart, J.J.

The Massachusetts Sunday closing statute did not violate the equal protection clause as applied to Orthodox Jews and was not contrary to the First Amendment's establishment clause.

Two Guys from Harrison-Allentown, Inc. v. McGinley: 366 U.S. 582 (1961). Opinion: Warren, C.J. Dissenting: Douglas, J.

Pennsylvania's Sunday closing statute was held not in violation of either the equal protection clause or the establishment clause of the First Amendment. The Court refused a federal injunction to enjoin prospective criminal prosecution under the statute.

Braunfield v. Brown: 366 U.S. 599 (1961). Opinion: Warren, C.J. Dissenting: Douglas, Brennan, and Stewart, JJ.

Pennsylvania's Sunday closing law was not a deprivation of equal protection or in violation of the establishment clause of the First Amendment or that Amendment's guarantee of the free exercise of religion as applicable to Orthodox Jews.

Engel v. Vitale: 370 U.S. 421 (1962). Opinion: Black, J. Dissenting: Stewart J. Abstaining: Frankfurter and White, JJ.

The provision of the First Amendment forbidding an "establishment of religion" is made applicable to the states by the Fourteenth Amendment and thus state officials may not compose an official state prayer and require that it be recited in the public schools of the state at the beginning of each school day. See page 48, below.

Walz v. Tax Commission of the City of New York: 397 U.S. 664 (1970). Opinon: Burger, C.J. Dissenting: Douglas, J.

Tax exemption of church property is not "establishment" under the First Amendment. It is "benevolent neutrality."

NOTE:

As noted, *Cantwell* was the first case to apply the "Gitlow doctrine" to religious guarantees in the First Amendment and to include these in the definition of "liberty" in the Fourteenth Amendment applicable to the states. Freedom of religion, like freedom of speech, cannot be made subject to prior restraint by governmental authority.

Cantwell was based on the clear and present danger test and was based as well on a matter of balance of interests, i. e., freedom of religion and the state's interest in preserving the peace. Here the Court held that the balance was on the side of religious freedom in the light of the unwarranted administrative censorship of religion provided by the statute in question.

Murdock v. Pennsylvania
319 U.S. 105; 63 S.Ct. 870; 87 L.Ed. 1292 (1943)

(The city of Jeannette, Pennsylvania, had an ordinance requiring all solicitors to secure a license with fee attached from the Treasurer of the Borough before beginning their activity. The Jehovah's Witnesses attacked this as an abridgment of religious freedom.)

Vote: 5-4

Mr. Justice Douglas delivered the opinion of the Court:

. . . The hand distribution of religious tracts is an age-old form of missionary

evangelism—as old as the history of printing presses. It has been a potent force in various religious movements down through the years. This form of evangelism is utilized today on a large scale by various religious sects whose colporteurs carry the Gospel to thousands upon thousands of homes and seek through personal visitations to win adherents to their faith. It is more than preaching; it is more than distribution of religious literature. It is a combination of both. Its purpose is as evangelical as the revival meeting. This form of religious activity occupies the same high estate under the First Amendment as do worship in the churches and preachng from the pulpits. It has the same claim to protection as the more orthodox and conventional exercises of religion. It also has the same claim as the others to the guarantees of freedom of speech and freedom of the press. . . .

We do not mean to say that religious groups and the press are free from all financial burdens of government. . . . We have here something quite different, for example, from a tax on the income of one who engages in religious activities or a tax on property used or employed in connection with those activities. It is one thing to impose a tax on the income or property of a preacher. It is quite another thing to exact a tax from him for the privilege of delivering a sermon. . . . Those who can tax the exercise of this religious practice can make its exercise so costly as to deprive it of the resources necessary for its maintenance. Those who can tax the privilege of engaging in this form of missionary evangelism can close its doors to all those who do not have a full purse. Spreading religious beliefs in this ancient and honorable manner would thus be denied the needy. Those who can deprive religious groups of their colporteurs can take from them a part of the vital power of the press which has survived from the Reformation. . . .

The fact that the ordinance is "nondiscriminatory" is immaterial. The protection afforded by the First Amendment is not so restricted. A license tax certainly does not acquire constitutional validity because it classifies the privileges protected by the First Amendment along with the wares and merchandise of hucksters and peddlers and treats them all alike. Such equality in treatment does not save the ordinance. Freedom of press, freedom of speech, freedom of religion are in a preferred position. . . .

. . . Plainly a community may not suppress, or the state tax, the dissemination of views because they are unpopular, annoying or distasteful. If that device were ever sanctioned, there would have been forged a ready instrument for the suppression of the faith which any minority cherishes but which does not happen to be in favor. That would be a complete repudiation of the philosophy of the Bill of Rights.

Jehovah's Witnesses are not "above the law." But the present ordinance is not directed to the problems with which the police power of the state is free to deal. It does not cover, and petitioners are not charged with, breaches of the peace. They are pursuing their solicitations peacefully and quietly. . . .

The judgment in *Jones* v. *Opelika* has this day been vacated. . . .

Reversed.

Mr. Justice Reed dissented with the concurrence of Mr. Justice Roberts, Mr. Justice Frankfurter, and Mr. Justice Jackson:

. . . Is subjection to nondiscriminatory, nonexcessive taxation in the distribution of religious literature, a prohibition of the exercise of religion or an abridgment of the freedom of the press?

Nothing has been brought to our attention which would lead to the conclusion that the contemporary advocates of the adoption of a Bill of Rights intended such an exemption. The words of the Amendment do not support such a construction. . . . A number of the states suggested amendments. Where these suggestions have any bearing at all upon religion or free speech, they indicate nothing as to any feeling concerning taxation either of religious bodies or their evangelism. This was not because freedom of religion or free speech was not understood. It was because the subjects were looked upon from standpoints entirely distinct from taxation.

The available evidence of Congressional action shows clearly that the draftsmen of the amendments had in mind the practice of religion and the right to be heard, rather than any abridgment or interference with either by taxation in any form. . . .

Is there anything in the decisions of this Court which indicates that church or press is free from the financial burdens of government? We find nothing. Religious societies depend for their exemptions from taxation upon state constitutions or general statutes, not upon the Federal Constitution. . . .

But whether we give content to the literal words of the First Amendment or to principles of the liberty of the press and the church, we conclude that cities or states may levy reasonable, non-discriminatory taxes on such activities as occurred in these cases. Whatever exemptions exist from taxation arise from the prevailing law of the various states. . . . These are the only exemptions of the press or church from taxation. We find nothing more applicable to our problem in the other constitutions. Surely this unanimity of specific state action on exemptions of religious bodies from taxes would not have occurred throughout our history, if it had been conceived that the genius of our institutions, as expressed in the First Amendment, was incompatible with the taxation of church or press. . . .

Mr. Justice Frankfurter dissented:

. . . The real issue here is not whether a city may charge for the dissemination of ideas but whether the states have power to require those who need additional facilities to help bear the cost of furnishing such facilities. Street hawkers make demands upon municipalities that involve the expenditure of dollars and cents, whether they hawk printed matter or other things. As the facts in these cases show, the cost of maintaining the peace, the additional demands upon governmental facilities for assuring security, involve outlays which have to be met. To say that the Constitution forbids the states to obtain the necessary revenue from the whole of a class that enjoys these benefits and facilities, when in fact no discrimination is suggested as between purveyors of printed matter and purveyors of other things, and the exaction is not claimed to be actually burdensome, is to say that the Constitution requires not that the dissemination of ideas in the interest of religion shall be free but that it shall be subsidized by the state. Such a claim offends the most important of all aspects of religious freedom in this country, namely, that of the separation of church and state.

The ultimate question in determining the constitutionality of a tax measure is— has the state given something for which it can ask a return? There can be no doubt that these petitioners, like all who use the streets, have received the benefits of government. . . . There is nothing in the Constitution which exempts persons engaged in religious activities from sharing equally in the costs of benefits to all, including themselves, provided by government. . . .

RELATED CASES:

Cox v. New Hampshire: 312 U.S. 569 (1941). Opinion: Hughes, C.J. No dissent.

An administrative board may be given very narrow discretion in the issuance of parade permits. This was simply a traffic regulation with no discrimination or interference with First Amendment freedoms. Here there was no exercise of arbitrary power. The permit involved a nominal, nondiscriminatory fee to cover the cost of policing for the parade. This was valid. This case out of Manchester, New Hampshire, *Chaplinski* out of Rochester, New Hampshire, and *Jones* from Opelika, Alabama, all involved Jehovah's Witnesses.

Chaplinksi v. New Hampshire: 315 U.S. 568 (1942). Opinion: Murphy, J. No dissent.

A state may forbid expressions that are outside the area of communication of information or opinion safeguarded by the Constitution. Abusive epithets are beyond the protection of the Constitution. Further, there was real danger of breach of the peace. Some words are "constitutional outlaws." There are words whose speaking constitutes a breach of the peace by the speaker including "classical fighting words," words in current use less "classical" but equally likely to cause violence, and other disorderly words, including profanity, obscenity, and threats.

Jones v. Opelika: 316 U.S. 584 (1942). Opinion: Reed, J. Dissenting: Stone, C.J., and Murphy, Black, and Douglas, JJ.

Nondiscriminatory taxes that impose no special burden on those who sold religious literature are not invalid. This was reversed by *Murdock,* after Rutledge had been appointed to the Court.

Kunz v. New York: 340 U.S. 290 (1951). Opinion: Vinson, C.J. Dissenting: Jackson, J.

When an administrative official is given administrative discretion to issue permits for speeches on religious matters "the ordinance is clearly invalid as a prior restraint on the exercise of First Amendment rights." See p. 102, below.

Cox v. Louisiana: 379 U.S. 536 (1965). Opinion: Goldberg, J. Dissenting: Black, White, Clark, and Harlan, JJ.

Local officials cannot be permitted unfettered discretion in regulating the use of streets for peaceful parades and assemblies although a state has the right to impose nondiscriminatory restrictions. In this case out of Baton Rouge there was "speech plus" —conduct—which is to be distinguished from "pure speech." However, the Court did not sustain the conviction because of police consent for the action.

NOTE:

In *Murdock* appeared for the first time in a majority opinion the concept of the guarantees of religion, speech, and press being in a "preferred position." Over the years and despite internal opposition on the Court, more often than not, the Court has upheld the notion that First Amendment freedoms do in fact have a preferred position. In the meaning attributed by the Court in this instance to that phrase, the Court was holding that statutes that restrict civil rights are not to be accorded a presumption of constitutionality as are other types of statutes.

Some other points should be mentioned. The Court might have approved a nominal license fee but here the fee was $1.50 for one day, $7.00 for a week, $12.00 for two weeks, and $20.00 for three weeks. Also, in spite of the fact that selling was involved here, the Court emphasized that this was a religious matter rather than a commercial venture. The selling activities were held to be no more commercial than passing the collection plate. The burden of proving that fees, such as here, are not excessive has been held to be on the government.

Marsh v. Alabama
326 U.S. 501; 66 S.Ct. 276; 90 L.Ed. 265 (1946)

(Chickasaw, Alabama, is a town owned by a private corporation, Gulf Ship-building Corp. A member of Jehovah's Witnesses had been warned not to distribute literature on the streets of the town. After she ignored this warning, she was arrested for violation of a state statute making it a crime to enter upon or remain on the premises of another after being warned not to do so.)

Vote: 5-3

Mr. Justice Black delivered the opinion of the Court:

. . . We do not agree that the corporation's property interests settle the question. The State urges in effect that the corporation's right to control the inhabitants of Chickasaw is coextensive with the right of a homeowner to regulate the conduct of his guests. We cannot accept that contention. Ownership does not always mean absolute dominion. The more an owner, for his advantage, opens up his property for use by the public in general, the more do his rights become circumscribed by the statutory and constitutional rights of those who use it. . . .

Many people in the United States live in company-owned towns. These people, just as residents of municipalities, are free citizens of their State and country. Just as all other citizens they must make decisions which affect the welfare of community and nation. To act as good citizens they must be informed. In order to enable them to be properly informed their information must be uncensored. There is no more reason for depriving these people of the liberties guaranteed by the First and Fourteenth Amendments than there is for curtailing these freedoms with respect to any other citizens.

When we balance the Constitutional rights of owners of property against those of people to enjoy freedom of press and religion, as we must here, we remain mindful of the fact that the latter occupy a preferred position. As we have stated before, the right to exercise the liberties safeguarded by the First Amendment "lies at the foundation of free government by free men" and we must in all cases "weigh the circumstances and . . . appraise the . . . reasons . . . in support of the regulation . . . of rights." *Schneider* v. *State*, 308 U.S. 147. . . . In our view the circumstances that the property rights to the premises where the deprivation of liberty, here involved, took place, were held by others than the public, is not sufficient to justify the State's permitting a corporation to govern a community of citizens so as to restrict their fundamental liberties and the enforcement of such restraint by the application of a State statute. In so far as the State has attempted to impose criminal punishment on appellant for undertaking to distribute religious literature in a company town, its action cannot stand. The case is reversed and the cause remanded for further proceedings not inconsistent with this opinion. . . .

Mr. Justice Jackson took no part in the consideration or decision of this case.

Mr. Justice Reed dissented, with the concurrence of Mr. Chief Justice Stone and Mr. Justice Burton:

Former decisions of this Court have interpreted generously the Constitutional rights of people in this Land to exercise freedom of religion, of speech and of the press. It has never been held and is not now by this opinion of the Court that these rights are absolute and unlimited either in respect to the manner or the place of their exercise. What the present decision establishes as a principle is that one may remain on private property against the will of the owner and contrary to the law of the state so long as the only objection to his presence is that he is exercising an asserted right to spread there his religious views. . . . This is the first case to extend by law the privilege of religious exercises beyond public places or to private places without the assent of the owner. . . .

As the rule now announced permits this intrusion, without possibility of protection of the property by law, and apparently is equally applicable to the freedom of speech and the press, it seems appropriate to express a dissent to this, to us, novel Constitutional doctrine. . . . While the power of this Court, as the interpreter of the Constitution to determine what use of real property by the owner makes that property subject, at will, to the reasonable practice of religious exercises by strangers, cannot be doubted, we find nothing in the principles of the First Amendment, adopted now in the Fourteenth, which justifies their application to the facts of this case. . . .

RELATED CASES:

Bunger v. Green River: 300 U.S. 638 (1937). Per Curiam. No dissent.

Appeal of this case to the Supreme Court was dismissed for want of a substantial federal question. The Supreme Court of Wyoming had held that an ordinance declaring uninvited visits to private residences by solicitors a nuisance punishable as a misdemeanor was not violative of the equal protection clause, the commerce clause, or the due process clause of the Federal Constitution. This was commercial soliciting. Ordinances of this sort since adopted by other cities have come to be known as "Green River ordinances." The original state case can be found at 50 Wyoming 52; 58 P. (2d) 456.

Lovell v. Griffin: 303 U.S. 444 (1938). Opinion: Hughes, C.J. No dissent. Abstaining: Cardoza, J.

A city connot forbid the distribution of literature within the city without the written approval of the city manager. Liberty of the press includes every sort of publication of information and opinion, here handbills. This was prior restraint. Under the Griffin, Georgia, ordinance, the approval power was not limited to offensive (obscene) matter.

Martin v. Struthers: 319 U.S. 141 (1943). Opinion: Black, J. Dissenting: Reed, Roberts, and Jackson, JJ.

A city cannot prohibit the ringing of doorbells by persons distributing literature. This violates freedom of speech and press. Struthers, Ohio, is an industrial community with numbers of persons working nights and sleeping during the day. However, this was not sufficient to justify the ordinance especially since the literature was an invitation to a religious service and thus was not commercial.

Follett v. McCormick: 321 U.S. 573 (1944). Opinion: Douglas, J. Dissenting: Roberts, Frankfurter, and Jackson, JJ.

A license tax cannot be imposed on those who make their livelihood from religious activity. Religious activities cannot be taxed. Here the tax by McCormick, South Carolina, on the sale of religious books was held void.

Tucker v. Texas: 326 U.S. 517 (1946). Opinion: Black, J. Dissenting: Stone, C.J., and Reed and Burton, JJ.

A town owned by the Federal Public Housing Authority cannot forbid the distribution of religious literature on the streets. This was an application of the *Marsh* ruling to a government-owned town. Here, as in the Griffin and McCormick cases, above, the Jehovah's Witnesses were involved.

Breard v. Alexandria: 341 U.S. 622 (1951). Opinion: Reed, J. Dissenting: Black and Douglas, JJ.

A city ordinance can prohibit door-to-door soliciting, without the prior consent of those contacted, of persons selling commercial publications as distinguished from religious publications. A "Green River ordinance" was involved here.

Lloyd Corporation, Ltd. v. Tanner: 407 U.S. 551 (1972). Opinion: Powell, J. Dissenting: Marshall, Douglas, Brennan, and Stewart, JJ.

A privately owned shopping center may prohibit the distribution of handbills on its property when the handbills are unrelated to the shopping center's operations. Here the handbills opposed the military draft and the Vietnam War. There is no such dedication of the shopping center to public use for any and all purposes however incompatible with the interests of both the stores and the shoppers. The Fifth and Fourteenth Amendment "rights of private property owners, as well as the First Amendment rights of all citizens, must be respected and protected." The shopping center property was held not to be a public forum. No religious issue was involved in this case. See *Amalgamated Food Employees Union Local* v. *Logan Valley Plaza*, p. 111, below.

NOTE:

Marsh offers a nice illustration of the "preferred position" of freedom of religion. Here even the right of private property and the rule of trespass are permitted to be infringed in order to allow a rather extreme exercise of freedom of religion. While such "discrimination" in favor of First Amendment rights, particularly religion, has been rather consistently followed by the Courts, there have been some exceptions, as witness *Breard* v. *Alexandria*, but here there was the "element of the commercial" not present in other cases. Freedom of speech and press for religious purposes means much more to the Court than such freedom for a commercial purpose. The wishes of proprietors are not controlling.

Marsh and *Smith* v. *Allwright* (321 U.S. 649, 1944) have something in common. In *Smith* the Democratic Party and in *Marsh* the town of Chickasaw were held to be engaged in functions that are basically governmental in nature and therefore bound by guarantees of the Federal Constitution.

Prince v. Massachusetts
321 U.S. 158; 64 S.Ct. 438; 88 L.Ed. 645 (1944)

(A state statute of Massachusetts forbids sales activity in a public place by a boy under twelve or a girl under eighteen. Mrs. Prince, a Jehovah's Witness, was arrested for permitting a girl nine years of age to sell religious literature in her company. This was claimed to be a restriction of religious freelom.)

Vote: 5-4

Mr. Justice Rutledge delivered the opinion of the Court:

. . . Concededly a statute or ordinance identical in terms with Section 69, except that it is applicable to adults or all persons generally, would be invalid. . . . But the mere fact a state could not wholly prohibit this form of adult activity, whether characterized locally as a "sale" or otherwise, does not mean it cannot do so for children. Such a conclusion granted would mean that a state could impose no greater limitation upon child labor than upon adult labor. . . .

The state's authority over children's activities is broader than over like actions of adults. This is peculiarly true of public activities and in matters of employment. A democratic society rests, for its continuance, upon the healthy, well-rounded growth of young people into full maturity as citizens, with all that implies. It may secure this against impeding restraints and dangers, within a broad range of selection. Among evils most appropriate for such action are the crippling effects of child employment, more especially in public places, and the possible harms arising from other activities subject to all the diverse influences of the street. . . .

It is true children have rights, in common with older people, in the primary use of highways. But even in such use streets afford dangers for them not affecting adults. And, in other uses, whether in work or in other things, this difference may be magnified. This is so not only when children are unaccompanied but certainly to some extent when they are with their parents. What may be wholly permissible for adults therefore may not be so for children, either with or without their parents' presence.

. . . We think that with reference to the public proclaiming of religion, upon the streets and in other similar public places, the power of the state to control the conduct of children reaches beyond the scope of its authority over adults, as is true in the case of other freedoms, and the rightful boundary of its power has not been crossed in this case. . . .

Mr. Justice Murphy dissented:

. . . The burden was . . . on the state of Massachusetts to prove the reasonableness and necessity of prohibiting children from engaging in religious activity of the type involved in this case.

The burden in this instance, however, is not met by vague references to the reasonableness underlying child labor legislation in general. The great interest of the state in shielding minors from the evil vicissitudes of early life does not warrant every limitation on their religious training and activities. The reasonableness that justifies the prohibition of the ordinary distribution of literature in the public streets by children is not necessarily the reasonableness that justifies such a drastic restriction when the distribution is part of their religious faith. . . . If the right of a child to practice its religion in that manner is to be forbidden by constitutional means, there must be convincing proof that such a practice constitutes a grave and immediate danger to the state or to the health, morals or welfare of the child. . . .

The state, in my opinion, has completely failed to sustain its burden of proving the existence of any grave or immediate danger to any interest which it may lawfully protect. There is no proof that Betty Simmons' mode of worship constituted a serious menace to the public. It was carried on in an orderly, lawful manner at a public street corner. . . . The sidewalk, no less than the cathedral or the evangelist's tent, is a proper place, under the Constitution, for the orderly worship of God. Such use of the streets is as necessary to the Jehovah's Witnesses, the Salvation Army and others who practice religion without benefit of conventional shelters as is the use of the streets for purposes of passage.

It is claimed, however, that such activity was likely to affect adversely the health, morals and welfare of the child. . . . The bare possibility that such harms might emanate from distribution of religious literature is not, standing alone, sufficient justification for restricting freedom of conscience and religion. . . .

Mr. Justice Jackson dissented with the concurrence of Mr. Justice Roberts and Mr. Justice Frankfurter:

. . . My own view may be shortly put: I think the limits begin to operate whenever activities begin to affect or collide with liberties of others or of the public. Religious activities which concern only members of the faith are and ought to be free—as nearly absolutey free as anything can be. But beyond these, many religious denominations or sects engage in collateral and secular activities intended to obtain means from unbelievers to sustain the worshippers and their leaders. They raise money, not merely by passing the plate to those who voluntarily attend services or by contributions by their own people, but by solicitations and drives addressed to the public by holding public dinners and entertainments, by various kinds of sales and Bingo games and lotteries. All such money-raising activities on a public scale are, I think, Caesar's affairs and may be regulated by the state so long as it does not discriminate against one because he is doing them for a religious purpose, and the regulation is not arbitrary and capricious, in violation of other provisions of the Constitution.

The court in the *Murdock* case rejected this principle of separating immune religious activities from secular ones in declaring the disabilities which the Constitution imposed on local authorities. Instead, the Court now draws a line based on age that cuts across both true exercise of religion and auxiliary secular activities. I think this is not a correct principle for defining the activities immune from regulation on grounds of religion, and *Murdock* overrules the grounds on which I think affirmance should rest. I have no alternative but to dissent from the grounds of affirmance of a judgment which I think was rightly decided, and upon right grounds, by the Supreme Judicial Court of Massachusetts.

RELATED CASES:

Reynolds v. United States: 98 U.S. 145 (1879). Opinion: Waite, C.J. No dissent.

Religious liberty does not include the performance of immoral or criminal acts even though those acts are sanctioned by religious doctrine. Here polygamy was involved as prohibited by federal legislation applying to the territory of Utah. Reynolds was a Mormon. To hold otherwise "would permit every citizen to become a law unto himself."

Davis v. Beason: 133 U.S. 333 (1890). Opinion: Field, J. No dissent.

An Idaho statute denying the right to vote or hold office to any person practicing, advocating, or belonging to any organization which practices or advocates bigamy or polygamy is an exercise of legislative power and is not open to constitutional or legal objection. It was never intended that the First Amendment prohibit legislation punishing acts inimical to the peace, good order and morals of society. Polygamy is not a "tenet of religion." Beason was a sheriff in Idaho territory and Davis a Mormon.

United States v. Ballard: 322 U.S. 78 (1944). Opinion: Douglas, J. Dissenting: Stone, C.J., and Jackson, Roberts and Frankfurter, JJ.

The truth or falsity of religious doctrine is not a proper matter for consideration by a jury.

Cleveland v. United States: 329 U.S. 14 (1946). Opinion: Douglas, J. Dissenting: Black, Murphy and Jackson, JJ.

The Mann Act applies to transportation of a woman across a state line for the purpose of entering into a plural marriage with her even though this is motivated by religious doctrine. Cleveland was a Mormon.

Sherbert v. Verner: 374 U.S. 398 (1963). Opinion: Brennan, J. Dissenting: Harlan and White, JJ.

Under South Carolina law a claimant is ineligible for unemployment compensation benefits if he will not accept suitable work when offered. However, to force a claimant to choose between not working on the Sabbath Day of the claimant's religion and forfeiting benefits, on the one hand, and to abandon religious precepts in order to accept work on the other hand is a violation of the free exercise of religion guaranteed by the First Amendment and made applicable to the states by the Fourteenth Amendment. Verner represented the South Carolina Employment Commission while Sherbert was a Seventh Day Adventist textile worker who had been discharged for refusal to work on Saturday. Here the Court held that there was no compelling state interest and the state had an available alternative, i.e., grant exemption from the statute for religious reasons. See *McGowan* v. *Maryland,* p. 14, above.

NOTE:

The *Prince* case is remarkable because it represents not only one of the very few cases in which the Jehovah's Witnesses lost a decision before the Supreme Court but also because it is a rare instance where a state criminal statute was upheld as against a claim of religious freedom. The state's power over the care of children was apparently decisive here—*parens patriae.*

Girouard v. United States
328 U.S. 61; 66 S.Ct. 826; 90 L.Ed. 1084 (1946)

(In a petition for naturalization, Girouard stated that he would not bear arms in the defense of the United States but that he would serve as a noncombatant. He claimed that his religious views (Seventh Day Adventist) would not permit him to bear arms, against the government claim that his refusal to bear arms should deny him citizenship.)

Vote: 5-3

Mr. Justice Douglas delivered the opinion of the Court:

. . . The oath required of aliens does not in terms require that they promise to bear arms. Nor has Congress expressly made any such finding a prerequisite to citizenship. To hold that it is required is to read it into the Act by implication. But we could not assume that Congress intended to make such an abrupt and radical departure from our traditions unless it spoke in unequivocal terms.

The bearing of arms, important as it is, is not the only way in which our institutions may be supported and defended, even in times of great peril. Total war in its modern form dramatizes as never before the great cooperative effort necessary for victory. The nuclear physicists who developed the atomic bomb, the worker at his lathe, the seaman on cargo vessels, construction battalions, nurses, engineers, litter bearers, doctors, chaplains—these, too, made essential contributions. And many of them made the supreme sacrifice. Mr. Justice Holmes stated in the *Schwimmer* case, 279 U.S. at page 655, 49 S.Ct. at page 451, 73 L.Ed. 889, that "the Quakers have done their share to make the country what it is." And the annals of the recent war show that many whose religious scruples prevented them from bearing arms, nevertheless were unselfish participants in the war effort. Refusal to bear arms is not necessarily a sign of disloyalty or a lack of attachment to our institutions. One may serve his country faithfully and devotedly, though his religious scruples make it impossible for him to shoulder a rifle. Devotion to one's country can be as real and as enduring among non-combatants as among combatants. One may adhere to what he deems to be his obligation to God and yet assume all military risks to secure victory. The effort of war is indivisible; and those whose religious scruples prevent them from killing are no less patriots than those whose special traits or handicaps result in their assignment to duties far behind the fighting front. Each is making the utmost contribution according to his capacity. The fact that his role may be limited by religious convictions rather than by physical characteristics has no necessary bearing on his attachment to his country or on his willingness to support and defend it to his utmost.

. . . The test oath is abhorrent to our tradition. Over the years Congress has meticulously respected that tradition and even in time of war has sought to accommodate the military requirements to the religious scruples of the individual. We do not believe that Congress intended to reverse that policy when it came to draft the naturalization oath. Such an abrupt and radical departure from our traditions should not be implied. . . . Cogent evidence would be necessary to convince us that Congress took that course.

We conclude that the *Schwimmer, Macintosh* and *Bland* cases do not state the correct rule of law.

We are met, however, with the argument that even though those cases were wrongly decided, Congress has adopted the rule which they announced. The argument runs as follows: Many efforts were made to amend the law so as to change the rule announced by those cases; but in every instance the bill died in committee. Moreover, in 1940 when the new Naturalization Act was passed, Congress reenacted the oath in its pre-existing form, though at the same time it made extensive changes in the requirements and procedure for naturalization. . . .

. . . But for us, it is enough to say that since the date of those cases Congress never acted affirmatively on this question but once and that was in 1942. At that time, as we have noted, Congress specifically granted naturalization privileges to non-combatants who like petitioner were prevented from bearing arms by their religious scruples. That was affirmative recognition that one could be attached to the principles of our government and could support and defend it even though his religious convictions prevented him from bearing arms. And, as we have said, we cannot believe that the oath was designed to exact something more from one person than from another. Thus the affirmative action taken by Congress in 1942 negatives any inference that otherwise might be drawn from its silence when it reenacted the oath in 1940.

Reversed.

Mr. Chief Justice Stone dissented:

. . . With three other Justices of the Court I dissented in the *Macintosh* and *Bland* cases, for reasons which the Court now adopts as ground for overruling them. Since this Court in three considered earlier opinions has rejected the construction of the statute for which the dissenting Justices contended, the question, which for me is decisive of the present case, is whether Congress has likewise rejected that construction by its subsequent legislative action, and has adopted and confirmed the Court's earlier construction of the statutes in question. A study of Congressional action taken with respect to proposals for amendment of the naturalization laws since the decision in the *Schwimmer* case, leads me to conclude that Congress has adopted and confirmed this Court's earlier construction of the naturalization laws. For that reason alone I think that the judgment should be affirmed.

. . . The amendments and their legislative history give no hint of any purpose of Congress to relax, at least for persons who had rendered no military service, the requirements of the oath of allegiance and proof of attachment to the Constitution as this Court had interpreted them and as the Nationality Act of 1940 plainly required them to be interpreted. It is not the function of this Court to disregard the will of Congress in the exercise of its constitutional power.

Mr. Justice Reed and Mr. Justice Frankfurter joined in this opinion.

Mr. Justice Jackson took no part in the consideration or decision of this case.

RELATED CASES:

United States v. Schwimmer: 279 U.S. 644 (1929). Opinion: Butler, J. Dissenting: Holmes, Brandeis, and Sanford, JJ.

A woman can be denied citizenship because of the refusal to bear arms. Mrs. Schwimmer, forty-nine years of age, was from Hungary. This is an example of statutory interpretation.

United States v. Macintosh: 283 U.S. 605 (1931). Opinion: Sutherland, J. Dissenting: Hughes, C.J., and Holmes, Stone, and Brandeis, JJ.

A professor of theology at Yale was denied citizenship because of refusal to swear that he would bear arms in all wars regardless of his beliefs as to the moral justification of those wars. He was from Canada where he was an army chaplain during World War I. This case is sometimes cited as *Macintosh* v. *United States*.

United States v. Bland: 283 U.S. 636 (1931). Opinion: Sutherland, J. Dissenting: Hughes, C.J., and Holmes, Stone, and Brandeis, JJ.

Deciding upon the authority of *United States* v. *Macintosh*, the Supreme Court here found that an application for citizenship was properly denied an applicant who requested that her oath of allegiance be amended so as to read that she would defend the Constitution and laws of the United States "as far as my conscience as a Christian will allow." She was a nurse from Canada.

In re Summers: 325 U.S. 561 (1945). Opinion: Reed, J. Dissenting: Black, Douglas, Murphy, and Rutledge, JJ.

A state can bar from the practice of law a person whose only disqualification is that he is a conscientious objector on religious grounds to military service. This was held not to be a violation of the Fourteenth Amendment. The Court held that a man charged with some aspect of the administration of justice could not in these circumstances in good faith take an oath to support the Constitution. The case arose in Illinois.

Sicurrela v. United States: 348 U.S. 385 (1955). Opinion: Clark, J. Dissenting: Reed, and Minton, JJ.

Conviction of a Jehovah's Witness for failure to submit to military induction is in error where the defendant is refused classification as a conscientious objector for the reason that he would use force of spiritual arms to fight at Jehovah's command. Willingness to fight in such a war does not preclude unwillingness to fight in actual military conflict.

United States v. Seeger: 380 U.S. 163 (1965). Opinion: Clark, J. No dissent.

The test of religious belief within the meaning of the exemption to military service based on conscientious objection is whether it is a sincere and meaningful belief occupying in the life of its possessor a place parallel to that filled by belief in God of those admittedly qualified for the exemption. Here there was no questioning of the *truth* of the belief, only whether it was "truly held." But this was not to be a "merely personal moral code." Again this was statutory construction and did not involve a constitutional question.

Welsh v. United States: 398 U.S. 333 (1970). Opinion: Black, J. Dissenting: White and Stewart, J.J., and Burger, C.J. Abstaining: Blackmun, J.

A conscientious objector exemption can be claimed when the opposition stems from moral, ethical, or religious beliefs about right and wrong which are sufficiently strong to be a "religious belief" even though the applicant characterizes his beliefs as "nonreligious." This decision modifies the test set down by *United States* v. *Seeger*, 380 U.S. 163 (1965).

Toussie v. United States: 397 U.S. 112 (1970). Opinion: Black, J. Dissenting: White and Harlan, JJ., and Burger, C.J.

The five-year statute of limitations runs from the eighteenth birthday of persons subject to the Selective Service Act. There is no conclusive evidence that Congress intended a violation to be a "continuing offense."

Clay v. United States: 403 U.S. 698 (1971). Per Curiam. Abstaining: Marshall, J.

Since the Selective Service Appeal Board gave no reason for its denial of conscientious objector classification, there was no way of knowing on which of the three possible grounds it relied. Since two of the three had been conceded to be untenable, under a long-established rule of law, whenever it is impossible to say on which basis a conviction was obtained, if any of the bases is invalid, the conviction could not be upheld. Here it was admitted that Clay's beliefs were religiously based and sincerely held.

NOTE:

After years of standing by an interpretation of the Naturalization Act that apparently satisfied Congress, the Court in *Girouard* did an unusual thing. Instead of assuming that the inaction of Congress meant tacit agreement with the interpretation, the court changed its interpretation. Six years later in 1952 Congress agreed with the second interpretation by passing the Immigration and Nationality Act of that year. This offers an interesting contrast to the situation involved in the Court's decisions on professional baseball. See *Federal Baseball Club of Baltimore* v. *National League of Professional Baseball Clubs,* 259 U.S. 200 (1922) and *Toolson* v. *New York Yankees, Inc.,* 346 U.S. 356 (1953). See Vol. I.

West Virginia State Board of Education v. Barnette
319 U.S. 624; 63 S.Ct. 1178; 87 L.Ed. 1628 (1943)

(The Board of Education adopted a resolution requiring a salute and pledge of allegiance to the flag. The penalty for failure to comply was expulsion from school with the parents subject to a fine. The Jehovah's Witnesses challenged the constitutionality of this regulation.)

Vote: 6-3

Mr. Justice Jackson delivered the opinion of the Court:

. . . The freedom asserted by these appellees does not bring them into collision with rights asserted by any other individual. It is such conflicts which most frequently require intervention of the State to determine where the rights of one end and those of another begin. But the refusal of these persons to participate in the ceremony does not interfere with or deny rights of others to do so. Nor is there any question in this case that their behavior is peaceable and orderly. The sole conflict is between authority and rights of the individual. The State asserts power to condition access to public education on making a prescribed sign and profession and at the same time to coerce attendance by punishing both parent and child. The latter stand on a right of self-determination in matters that touch individual opinion and personal attitude.

As the present Chief Justice said in dissent in the *Gobitis* case, the State may "require teaching by instruction and study of all in our history and in the structure and organization of our government, including the guaranties of civil liberty, which tend to inspire patriotism and love of country." Here, however, we are dealing with a compulsion of students to declare a belief. They are not merely made acquainted with the flag salute so that they may be informed as to what it is or even what it means. The issue here is whether this slow and easily neglected route to aroused loyalties constitutionally may be short-cut by substituting a compulsory salute and slogan. . . .

Whether the First Amendment to the Constitution will permit officials to order observance of ritual of this nature does not depend upon whether as a voluntary exercise we would think it to be good, bad or merely innocuous. Any credo of nationalism is likely to include what some disapprove or to omit what others think essential, and to give off different overtones as it takes on different accents or interpretations. If official power exists to coerce acceptance of any patriotic creed, what it shall contain cannot be decided by courts, but must be largely discretionary with the ordaining authority, whose power to prescribe would no doubt include power to amend. Hence validity of the asserted power to force an American citizen publicly to profess any statement of belief or to engage in any ceremony of assent to one, presents questions of power that must be considered independently of any idea we may have as to the utility of the ceremony in question. . . .

The Fourteenth Amendment, as now applied to the States, protects the citizen against the State itself and all of its creatures—Boards of Education not excepted. These have, of course, important, delicate, and highly discretionary functions, but none that they may not perform within the limits of the Bill of Rights. That they are educating the young for citizenship is reason for scrupulous protection of Constitutional freedoms of the individual, if we are not to strangle the free mind at its source and teach youth to discount important principles of our government as mere platitudes.

Such Boards are numerous and their territorial jurisdiction often small. But small and local authority may feel less sense of responsibility to the Constitution, and agencies of publicity may be less vigilant in calling it to account. The action of Congress in making flag observance voluntary and respecting the conscience of the objector in a matter so vital as raising the Army contrasts sharply with these local regulations in matters relatively trivial to the welfare of the nation. There are village tyrants as well as village Hampdens, but none who acts under color of law is beyond reach of the Constitution. [This refers to John Hampden, a British statesman, who resisted the imposition of a ship tax.]

The *Gobitis* opinion reasoned that this is a field "where courts possess no marked and certainly no controlling competence," that it is committed to the legislatures as well as the courts to guard cherished liberties and that it is constitutionally appropriate to "fight out the wise use of legislative authority in the forum of public opinion and before legislative assemblies rather than to transfer such a contest to the judicial arena," since all the "effective means of inducing political changes are left free."

The very purpose of a Bill of Rights was to withdraw certain subjects from the vicissitudes of political controversy, to place them beyond the reach of majorities and officials and to establish them as legal principles to be applied by the courts. One's rights to life, liberty, and property, to free speech, a free press, freedom of worship and assembly, and other fundamental rights may not be submitted to vote; they depend on the outcome of no elections.

In weighing arguments of the parties it is important to distinguish between the due process clause of the Fourteenth Amendment as an instrument for transmitting the principles of the First Amendment and those cases in which it is applied for its own sake. The test of legislation which collides with the Fourteenth Amendment, because it also collides with the principles of the First, is much more definite than the test when only the Fourteenth is involved. Much of the vagueness of the due process clause disappears when the specific prohibitions of the First become its standard. The right of a State to regulate, for example, a public utility may well include, so far as the due process test is concerned, power to impose all of the restrictions which a legislature may have a "rational basis" for adopting. But freedoms of speech and of press, of assembly, and of worship may not be infringed on such slender grounds. They are susceptible of restriction only to prevent grave and immediate danger to interests which the state may lawfully protect. It is important to note that while it is the Fourteenth Amendment which bears directly upon the State it is the more specific limiting principles of the First Amendment that finally govern this case. . . .

It seems trite but necessary to say that the First Amendment to our Constitution was designed to avoid those ends by avoiding these beginnings. There is no mysticism in the American concept of the State or of the nature or origin of its authority. We set up government by consent of the governed, and the Bill of Rights denies those in power any legal opportunity to coerce that consent. Authority here is to be controlled by public opinion, not public opinion by authority. . . .

If there is any fixed star in our constitutional constellation, it is that no official, high or petty, can prescribe what shall be orthodox in politics, nationalism, religion, or other matters of opinion or force citizens to confess by word or act their faith therein. If there are any circumstances which permit an exception, they do not now occur to us.

We think the action of the local authorities in compelling the flag salute and pledge transcends constitutional limitations on their power and invades the sphere of intellect and spirit which it is the purpose of the First Amendment to our Constitution to reserve from all official control.

The decision of this Court in *Minersville School District* v. *Gobitis* and the holdings of those few *per curiam* decisions which preceded and foreshadowed it are overruled, and the judgment enjoining enforcement of the West Virginia Regulation is Affirmed.

Mr. Justice Black and Mr. Justice Douglas concurred:

. . . No well-ordered society can leave to the individuals an absolute right to make final decisions, unassailable by the State, as to everything they will or will not do. The First Amendment does not go so far. Religious faiths, honestly held, do not free individuals from responsibility to conduct themselves obediently to laws which are either imperatively necessary to protect society as a whole from grave and pressingly imminent dangers or which, without any general prohibition, merely regulate time, place or manner of religious activity. Decision as to the constitutionality of particular laws which strike at the substance of religious tenets and practices must be made by this Court. The duty is a solemn one, and in meeting it we cannot say that a failure, because of religious scruples, to assume a particular physical position and to repeat the words of a patriotic formula creates a grave danger to the nation. Such a statutory exaction is a form of test oath, and the test oath has always been abhorrent in the United States. . . .

Mr. Justice Murphy concurred:

. . . A reluctance to interfere with considered state action, the fact that the end sought is a desirable one, the emotion aroused by the flag as a symbol for which we have fought and are now fighting again,—all of these are understandable. But there is before us the right of freedom to believe, freedom to worship one's Maker according to the dictates of one's conscience, a right which the Constitution specifically shelters. Reflection has convinced me that as a judge I have no loftier duty or responsibility than to uphold that spiritual freedom to its farthest reaches. . . .

. . . Official compulsion to affirm what is contrary to one's religious beliefs is the antithesis of freedom of worship which, it is well to recall, was achieved in this country only after what Jefferson characterized as the "severest contest in which I have ever been engaged." . . .

Mr. Justice Frankfurter dissented:

One who belongs to the most vilified and persecuted minority in history is not likely to be insensible to the freedoms guaranteed by our Constitution. Were my purely personal attitude relevant I should wholeheartedly associate myself with the general libertarian views in the Court's opinion, representing as they do the thought and action of a lifetime. But as judges we are neither Jew nor Gentile, neither Catholic nor agnostic. We owe equal attachment to the Constitution. . . .

. . . It can never be emphasized too much that one's own opinion about the wisdom or evil of a law should be excluded altogether when one is doing one's duty on the bench. The only opinion of our own even looking in that direction that is material is our opinion whether legislators could in reason have enacted such a law. In the light of all the circumstances, including the history of this question in this Court, it would require more daring than I possess to deny that reasonable legislators could have taken the action which is before us for review. Most unwillingly, therefore, I must differ from my brethren with regard to legislation like this. I cannot bring my mind to believe that the "liberty" secured by the Due Process Clause gives this Court authority to deny to the State of West Virginia the attainment of that which we all recognize as a legitimate legislative end, namely, the promotion of good citizenship, by employment of the means here chosen. . . .

Mr. Justice Roberts and Mr. Justice Reed dissented and adhered to *Minersville.*

RELATED CASES:

Pierce v. Society of Sisters: 268 U.S. 510 (1925). Opinion: McReynolds, J. No dissent.

The liberty of parents to educate their children and the sanctity of property of schools precludes the state from enacting legislation requiring attendance at public schools by all children between the ages of eight and sixteen. This was the Oregon Compulsory Education Act of 1922 which had been adopted by the use of the initiative. Pierce was Governor of Oregon.

Minersville School District v. Gobitis: 310 U.S. 586 (1940). Opinion: Frankfurter, J. Dissenting: Stone, J.

A flag salute of school children may be required as an aspect of national unity which is important in the area of security. The judgment of the school board must be respected. There is no such thing as judicial omniscience. The case arose in Pennsylvania. Gobitis represented the Jehovah's Witnesses.

Taylor v. Mississippi: 319 U.S. 583 (1943). Opinion: Roberts, J. No dissent.

The State of Mississippi could not prosecute under a state statute for refusal to salute the flag of the United States and of the state when there was no showing of sinister purpose and not an advocacy or incitement to subversive action against the nation or state. Here there was no clear and present danger to the government or to institutions.

Watkins v. United States: 354 U.S. 178 (1957). Opinion: Warren, C.J. Dissenting: Clark, J. Abstaining: Burton and Whittaker, JJ.

A congressional inquiry must be related to a legislative purpose. One can be held in contempt only if the question posed is within the investigative scope of the congressional committee as specified in its jurisdictional statement and commission. A congressional committee cannot infringe upon the right of privacy or abridge freedom of speech, press, religion, or assembly.

Wisconsin v. Yoder: 406 U.S. 205 (1972). Opinion: Burger, C.J. Dissenting: Douglas, J. Abstaining: Powell and Rehnquist, JJ.

A state's compulsory school attendance law must be subjected to a balancing process when it impinges on other fundamental rights and interests such as those specifically protected by the free exercise of religion clause of the First Amendment. Here the traditional way of life of the Amish is not merely a matter of personal preference but of deep religious conviction. "A way of life that is odd or even erratic but interferes with no rights or interests of others is not to be condemned because it is different."

NOTE:

The *Barnette* case involved a rather fast reversal of a prior decision. This is such a relatively rare development that it seems worthy of mention. The Court is almost always reluctant to override prior decisions. This is true even though no member of a reversing Court was a member of the Court that made the first decision. Stone's dissenting opinion in *Minersville* became essentially the majority opinion in *Barnette*, but the Court did not adopt his religious argument.

In *Barnette* the "clear and present danger" test was used to show that the legislation was not justified. Here also was set forth a concept that was to have later emphasis in *Watkins* v. *United States* (354 U.S. 178, 1957), freedom not to speak, the right to remain silent.

In a case decided the same day as *Barnette* (*Taylor* v. *Mississippi*, 319 U.S. 583, 1943) the Court set aside the lower court convictions of those who had taught pupils to refuse to salute the flag.

Cochran v. Louisiana State Board of Education
281 U.S. 370; 50 S.Ct. 335; 74 L.Ed. 913 (1930)

(The Louisiana legislature had enacted a statute providing for the use of public funds to supply books to the schoolchildren of the state regardless of school attended. Only generally used schoolbooks and not religious books were included in the subsidy. This providing of books for children in parochial schools was challenged by Louisiana taxpayers as a taking of property for private use contrary to the Fourteenth Amendment.)

Vote: 9-0

Mr. Chief Justice Hughes delivered the opinion of the Court:

. . . The contention of the appellant (the Louisiana taxpayers) under the Fourteenth Amendment is that taxation for the purchase of school books constituted a taking of private property for a private purpose. . . . The purpose is said to be to aid private, religious, sectarian, and other schools not embraced in the public educational system of the State by furnishing text-books free to the children attending such private schools. The operation and effect of the legislation were described by the Supreme Court of the State as follows (168 La., p. 1020):

"One may scan the acts in vain to ascertain where any money is appropriated for the purpose of school books for the use of any church, private, sectarian or even public school. The appropriations were made for the specific purpose of purchasing school books for the use of the school children of the state, free of cost to them. It was for their benefit and the resulting benefit to the state that the appropriations were made. True, these children attend some school, public or private, the latter, sectarian or non-sectarian, and that the books are to be furnished them for their use, free of cost, whichever they attend. The schools, however, are not the beneficiaries of these appropriations. They obtain nothing from them, nor are they relieved of a single obligation because of them. The school children and the state alone are the beneficiaries. It is also true that the sectarian schools, which some of the children attend, instruct their pupils in religion, and books are used for that purpose, but one may search diligently the acts, though without result, in an effort to find anything to the effect that it is the purpose of the state to furnish religious books for the use of such children. . . . What the statutes contemplate is that the same books that are furnished children attending public schools shall be furnished children attending private schools. This is the only practical way of interpreting and executing the statutes, and this is what the state board of education is doing. Among these books, naturally, none is to be expected, adapted to religious instruction." . . .

Viewing the statute as having the effect thus attributed to it, we can not doubt that the taxing power of the State is exerted for a public purpose. The legislation does not segregate private schools, or their pupils, as its beneficiaries or attempt to interfere with any matters of exclusively private concern. Its interest is education, broadly; its method, comprehensive. Individual interests are aided only as the common interest is safeguarded.

Judgment affirmed.

RELATED CASES:

Bradfield v. Roberts: 175 U.S. 291 (1899). Opinion: Peckham, J. No dissent.

The use of federal funds to construct a hospital ward to be open to the public but to be administered as part of a hospital under the control of an order of Catholic nuns was not contrary to the "establishment" clause of the First Amendment. This was Providence Hospital in Washington, D.C., and the hospital corporation was held to be a secular body serving all patients. Bradfield was a taxpayer and Roberts was Treasurer of the United States. As to "standing," the case was treated as directed against the District of Columbia. Resident taxpayers may sue to enjoin alleged illegal use of money by a municipal corporation.

Quick Bear v. Leupp: 210 U.S. 50 (1908). Opinion: Fuller, C.J. No dissent.

In a statement which was actually dicta, since the Court here stated that no constitutional issue was raised before it, the Supreme Court said that no violation of the nonestablishment of religion clause of the First Amendment was present where the federal government, as trustee of certain funds for an Indian tribe, contracted with a sectarian organization for the provision of schools for Indian children. The funds involved were those under a treaty, not regular public funds. The sectarian organization was the Bureau of Catholic Indian Missions. Quick Bear was a Sioux Indian and Leupp was Commissioner of Indian Affairs.

Board of Education of Central School District No. 1 v. Allen: 392 U.S. 236 (1968). Opinion: White, J. Dissenting: Black, Douglas, and Fortas, JJ.

A New York statute that requires local public school authorities to lend textbooks free of charge to students in grades 7-12 including students in private schools does not violate the "establishment" provision of the First Amendment. Parochial schools perform the task of secular education. The textbooks furnished are not instrumental in the teaching of religion. This is cooperation, not "establishment."

NOTE:

In *Cochran* the question of religion was not raised but the question was the use of public funds for a nonpublic purpose. The Court used the "child benefit theory" holding that the money was used for the welfare of the children and the state rather than for the benefit of private schools. Therefore no property of taxpayers was being used improperly in violation of the due process clause.

Committee for Public Education v. Nyquist
413 U.S. 756; 93 S.Ct. 2955; 37 L.Ed. 2d 948 (1973)

(New York state laws provided (1) funds for nonpublic schools for repairs and maintenance, including utilities, as well as (2) a program of direct payments to reimburse parents for up to 50 percent of the tuition at nonpublic schools up to a total of $50 for a pupil in grade school and $100 for a high school student. To qualify, the parents needed to have an annual taxable income of less than $5,000. (3) The law also provided for a state income tax deduction according to a set table on taxable income for each child attending a nonpublic school. This deduction was to be computed without relation to actual tuition paid, but no deduction was permitted if the gross income of the parents exceeded $25,000. Recipients were not required to spend the money on education.)

Vote: 6-3

Mr. Justice Powell delivered the opinion of the Court:

The history of the Establishment Clause has been recounted frequently and need not be repeated here. It is enough to note that it is now firmly established that a law may be one "respecting the establishment of religion" even though its consequence is not to promote a "state religion," and even though it does not aid one religion more than another but merely benefits all religions alike. It is equally well established, however, that not every law that confers an "indirect," "remote," or "incidental" benefit upon religious institutions is, for this reason alone, constitutionally invalid. What our cases require is careful examination of any law challenged on establishment grounds with a view to ascertaining whether it furthers any of the evils against which that Clause protects. Primary among those evils have been "sponsorship, financial support, and active involvement of the sovereign in religious activity."

Most of the cases coming to this Court raising Establishment Clause questions have involved the relationship between religion and education. Among these religion-education precedents, two general categories of cases may be identified: those dealing with religious activities within the public schools, and those involving public aid in varying forms to sectarian educational institutions. While the New York legislation places this case in the latter category, its resolution requires consideration not only of the several aid-to-sectarian-education cases but also of our other education precedents and of several important noneducation cases. For the now well defined three-part test that has emerged from our decisions is a product of considerations derived from the full sweep of the Establishment Clause cases. Taken together these decisions dictate that to pass muster under the Establishment Clause the law in question first must reflect a clearly secular legislative purpose, second, must have a primary effect that neither advances nor inhibits religion, and, third, must avoid excessive government entanglement with religion,

In applying these criteria to the three distinct forms of aid involved in this case, we need touch only briefly on the requirement of a "secular legislative purpose." As the recitation of legislative purposes appended to New York's law indicates, each measure is adequately supported by legitimate, nonsectarian state interests. We do not question the propriety, and fully secular content, of New York's interest in preserving a healthy and safe educational environment for all of its school children. And we do not doubt—indeed, we fully recognize—the validity of the State's interest in promoting pluralism and diversity among its public and nonpublic schools. Nor do we hesitate to acknowledge the reality of its concern for an already overburdened public school system that might suffer in the event that a significant percentage of children presently attending nonpublic schools should abandon those schools in favor of the public schools.

But the propriety of a legislature's purposes may not immunize from further scrutiny a law which either has a primary effect that advances religion, or which fosters excessive entanglements between Church and State. Accordingly, we must weigh each of the three aid provisions challenged here against three criteria of effect and entanglement.

A

The "maintenance and repair" provisions of § 1 authorize direct payments to nonpublic schools, virtually all of which are Roman Catholic schools in low income areas. The grants, totaling $30 or $40 per pupil depending on the age of the institution, are given largely without restriction on usage. So long as expenditures do not exceed 50% of comparable expenses in the public school system, it is possible for a sectarian elementary or secondary school to finance its entire "maintenance and repair" budget from state tax-raised funds. No attempt is made to restrict payments to those expenditures related to the upkeep of facilities used exclusively for secular purposes, nor do we think it possible within the context of these religion-oriented institutions to impose such restrictions. Nothing in the statute, for instance, bars a qualifying school from paying out of state funds the salary of employees who maintain the school chapel, or the cost of renovating classrooms in which religion is taught, or the cost of heating and lighting those same facilities. Absent appropriate restrictions on expenditures for these and similar purposes, it simply cannot be denied that this section has a primary effect that advances religion in that it subsidizes directly the religious activities of sectarian elementary and secondary schools.

The state officials nevertheless argue that these expenditures for "maintenance and repair" are similar to other financial expenditures approved by the Court. Primarily they rely on *Everson* v. *Board of Education, supra; Board of Education* v. *Allen, supra*; and *Tilton* v. *Richardson, supra*. In each of those cases it is true that the Court approved a form of financial assistance which conferred undeniable benefits upon private sectarian schools. But a close examination of those cases illuminates their distinguishing characteristics. In *Everson* the Court, in a five-to-four decision, approved a program of reimbursements to parents of public as well as parochial school children for bus fares paid in connection with transportation to and from school, a program which the Court characterized as approaching the "verge" of impermissible state aid. In *Allen*, decided some 20 years later, the Court upheld a New York law authorizing the provision of *secular* textbooks for all children in grades seven through 12 attending public and nonpublic schools. Finally, in *Tilton*, the Court upheld federal grants of funds for the construction of facilities to be used for clearly *secular* purposes by public and nonpublic institutions of higher learning.

These cases simply recognize that sectarian schools perform secular, educative functions as well as religious functions, and that some forms of aid may be channelled to the secular without providing direct aid to the sectarian. But the channel is a narrow one, as the above cases illustrate. Of course it is true in each case that the provision of such neutral, nonideological aid, assisting only the secular functions of sectarian schools, served indirectly and incidentally to promote the religious function by rendering it more likely that children would attend sectarian schools and by freeing the budgets of those schools for use in other nonsecular areas. But an indirect and incidental effect beneficial to religious institutions has never been thought a sufficient defect to warrant the invalidation of a state law. . . .

What we have said demonstrates that New York's maintenance and repair provisions violate the Establishment Clause because their effect, inevitably, is to subsidize and advance the religious mission of sectarian schools. We have no occasion, therefore, to consider the further question whether those provisions as presently written would also fail to survive scrutiny under the administrative entanglement aspect of the three-part test because assuring the secular use of all funds requires too intrusive and continuing a relationship between Church and State, *Lemon* v. *Kurtzman* [1971].

B

New York's tuition reimbursement program also fails the "effect" test for much the same reasons that govern its maintenance and repair grants. The state program is designed to allow direct, unrestricted grants of $50 to $100 per child (but no more than 50% of tuition actually paid) as reimbursement to parents in low-income brackets who send their children to nonpublic schools. To qualify, a parent must have earned less than $5,000 in taxable income and must present a receipted tuition bill from a nonpublic school, the bulk of which are concededly sectarian in orientation.

There can be no question that these grants could not, consistently with the Establishment Clause, be given directly to sectarian schools, since they would suffer from the same deficiency that renders invalid the grants for maintenance and repair. In the absence of an effective means of guaranteeing that the state aid derived from public funds will be used exclusively for secular, neutral, and nonideological purposes, it is clear from our cases that direct aid in whatever form is invalid.

The controlling question here, then, is whether the fact that the grants are delivered to parents rather than schools is of such significance as to compel a contrary result. The State and intervenor-appellees rely on *Everson* and *Allen* for their claim that grants to parents, unlike grants to institutions, respect the "wall of separation" required by the Constitution. It is true that in those cases the Court upheld laws that provided benefits to children attending religious schools and to their parents: As noted above, in *Everson* parents were reimbursed for bus fares paid to send children to parochial schools, and in *Allen* textbooks were loaned directly to the children. But those decisions make clear that, far from providing a *per se* immunity from examination of the substance of the State's program, the fact that aid is disbursed to parents rather than to the schools is only one among many factors to be considered.

In *Everson*, the Court found the bus fare program analogous to the provision of services such as police and fire protection, sewage disposal, highways, and sidewalks for parochial schools. Such services, provided in common to all citizens, are "so separate and so indisputably marked off from the religious function," that they may fairly be viewed as reflections of a neutral posture toward religious institutions. *Allen* is founded upon a similar principle. The Court there repeatedly emphasized that upon the record in that case there was no indication that textbooks would be provided for anything other than purely secular courses. "Of course books are different from buses. Most bus rides have no inherent religious significance, while religious books are common. However, the language of [the law under consideration] does not authorize the loan of religious books, and the State claims no right to distribute religious literature. . . . Absent evidence, we cannot assume that school authorities . . . are unable to distinguish between secular and religious books or that they will not honestly discharge their duties under the law."

The tuition grants here are subject to no such restrictions. There has been no endeavor "to guarantee the separation between secular and religious educational functions and to ensure that State financial aid supports only the former." *Lemon* v. *Kurtzman* [1971]. Indeed, it is precisely the function of New York's law to provide assistance to private schools, the great majority of which are sectarian. By reimbursing parents for a portion of their tuition bill, the State seeks to relieve their financial burdens sufficiently to assure that they continue to have the option to send their children to religion-oriented schools. And while the other purposes for that aid—to perpetuate a pluralistic educational environment and to protect the fiscal integrity of overburdened public schools—are certainly unexceptionable, the effect of the aid is unmistakably to provide desired financial support for nonpublic, sectarian institutions. . . .

C

Because we have found that the challenged sections have the impermissible effect of advancing religion, we need not consider whether such aid would result in entanglement of the State with religion in the sense of "[a] comprehensive, discriminating, and continuing state surveillance." *Lemon* v. *Kurtzman* [1971]. But the importance of the competing societal interests implicated in this case prompt us to make the further observation that apart from any specific entanglement of the State in particular religious programs, assistance of the sort here involved carries grave potential for entanglement in the broader sense of continuing political strife over aid to religion. . . .

Mr. Chief Justice Burger, joined in part by Mr. Justice White, and joined by Mr. Justice Rehnquist, concurring in part and dissenting in part.

. . . The essence of all these decisions, I suggest, is that government aid to individuals generally stands on an entirely different footing from direct aid to religious institutions. I say "generally" because it is obviously possible to conjure hypothetical statutes that constitute either a subterfuge for direct aid to religious institutions or a discriminatory enactment favoring religious over nonreligious activities. Thus, a State could not enact a statute providing for a $10 gratuity to everyone who attended religious services weekly. Such a law would plainly be governmental sponsorship of religious activities; no statutory preamble expressing purely secular legislative motives would be persuasive. But at least where the state law is genuinely directed at enhancing the freedom of individuals to exercise a recognized right, even one involving both secular and religious consequences as is true of the rights of parents to send their children to private schools, then the Establishment Clause no longer has a prohibitive effect.

This fundamental principle which I see running through our prior decisions in this difficult and sensitive field of law, and which I believe governs the present cases, is premised more on experience and history than on logic. It is admittedly difficult to articulate the reasons why a State should be permitted to reimburse parents of private-school children—partially at least—to take into account the State's enormous savings in not having to provide schools for those children, when a State is not allowed to pay the same benefit directly to sectarian schools on a per-pupil basis. In either case, the private individual makes the ultimate decision that may indirectly benefit church sponsored schools; to that extent the state involvement with religion is substantially attenuated. The answer, I believe, lies in the experienced judgment of various members of this Court over the years that the balance between the policies of free exercise and establishment of religion tips in favor of the former when the legislation moves away from direct aid to religious institutions and takes on the character of general aid to individual families. This judgment reflects the caution with which we scrutinize any effort to give official support to religion and the tolerance with which we treat general welfare legislation. But, whatever its basis, that principle is established in our cases, from the early case of *Quick Bear* to the more recent holdings in *Everson and Allen*, and it ought to be followed here.

The tuition grant and tax relief programs now before us are, in my view, indistinguishable in principle, purpose and effect from the statutes in *Everson* and *Allen*. In the instant cases as in *Everson* and *Allen* the States have merely attempted to equalize the costs incurred by parents in obtaining an education for their children. The only discernible difference between the programs in *Everson* and *Allen* and these cases is in the method of the distribution of benefit. . . .

Mr. Justice White, joined in part by The Chief Justice and Mr. Justice Rehnquist, dissenting.

. . . There is no doubt here that Pennsylvania and New York have sought in the challenged laws to keep their parochial schools system alive and capable of providing adequate secular education to substantial numbers of students. This purpose satisfies the Court, even though to rescue schools that would otherwise fail will inevitably enable those schools to continue whatever religious functions they perform. By the same token, it seems to me, preserving the secular functions of these schools is the overriding consequence of these laws and the resulting, but incidental, benefit to religion should not invalidate them.

At the very least I would not strike down these statutes on their face. The Court's opinion emphasizes a particular kind of parochial school, one restricted to students of particular religious beliefs and conditioning attendance on religious study. Concededly, there are many parochial schools that do not impose such restrictions. Where they do not, it is even more difficult for me to understand why the primary effect of these statutes is to advance religion. I do not think it is and therefore dissent from the Court's judgment invalidating the challenged New York and Pennsylvania statutes.

The Chief Justice and Mr. Justice Rehnquist join this opinion insofar at it relates to the New York and Pennsylvania tuition grant statutes and the New York tax credit statute.

RELATED CASES:

Torcasso v. Watkins: 367 U.S. 488 (1961). Opinion; Black, J. No dissent.

Maryland could not deny a notary commission because the applicant refused to declare a belief in God. This was held to be a violation of the applicant's freedom of belief and religious rights under the First Amendment as applied to the states by the Fourteenth Amendment.

Lemon v. Kurtzman and Earley v. DiCenso: 403 U.S. 602 (1971). Opinion: Burger, C.J. Marshall, J. abstaining in *Lemon*; White, J. dissenting in *Earley*.

A state's (here Pennsylvania and Rhode Island) reimbursement of nonpublic elementary and secondary schools for teacher's salaries, textbooks, and instructional materials, all in specified secular subjects, violates the Establishment Clause. Since parochial schools involve substantial religious activity and purpose, the surveillance needed to insure that teachers would remain religiously neutral would give rise to excessive entanglement between government and religion.

Tilton v. Richardson: 403 U.S. 672 (1971). Opinion: Burger, C.J. Dissenting: Douglas, Black, Marshall, and Brennan, JJ.

Federal construction grants for church-related colleges and universities for buildings and facilities used exclusively for educational purposes are valid under the Establishment Clause. There are important differences between these institutions and parochial elementary and secondary schools. The college students themselves are less susceptible to religious indoctrination, the facilities are religiously neutral, and there are no continuing financial relationships to result in excessive entanglement between church and government. However, the provision in the law (Higher Education Facilities Act) that prohibits the religious use of the federally subsidized structures for only twenty years violates the First Amendment. This makes a contribution of some value to a religious body.

Sloan v. Lemon: 413 U.S. 825 (1973). Opinion: Powell, J. Dissenting: White, J., Burger, C.J., and Rehnquist, J.

Pennsylvania provided for reimbursement of parents of a part of tuition at private schools. Under the rationale of *Nyquist* this program was held void.

NOTE:

The seemingly perrenial question of the constitutionality of government aid to nonpublic schools seems to be the No. 1 question in the field of church-state relations. Apparently the rule set down by the various cases is that any state or federal financial support to church-related educational institutions must be so arranged that any aid that will be devoted to secular functions is clearly identifiable and separable from any aid that might be given to sectarian activities.

Everson v. Board of Education of Ewing Township
330 U.S. 1; 67 S.Ct. 504; 91 L.Ed. 711 (1947)

(A statute of the state of New Jersey authorized local school districts to make rules and contracts for the transportation of children to and from schools. Here the township board of education had authorized reimbursement to parents of money expended by them for the bus transportation of their children on regular buses operated by the public transportation system. Some of these children attended Catholic parochial schools. The appellant, a district taxpayer, challenged the right of the board to reimburse the parents of parochial school children under the First and Fourteenth Amendments.)

Vote: 5-4

Mr. Justice Black delivered the opinion of the Court:

. . . The "establishment of religion" clause of the First Amendment means at least this: Neither a state nor the Federal Government can set up a church. Neither can pass laws which aid one religion, aid all religions, or prefer one religion over another. Neither can force nor influence a person to go to or to remain away from church against his will or force him to profess a belief or disbelief in any religion.

No person can be punished for entertaining or professing religious beliefs or disbeliefs, for church attendance or non-attendance. No tax in any amount, large or small, can be levied to support any religious activities or institutions, whatever they may be called, or whatever form they may adopt to teach or practice religion. Neither a state nor the Federal Government can, openly or secretly, participate in the affairs of any religious organization or groups and vice versa. In the words of Jefferson, the clause against establishment of religion by law was intended to erect "a wall of separation between Church and State." . . .

Measured by these standards, we cannot say that the First Amendment prohibits New Jersey from spending tax-raised funds to pay the bus fares of parochial school pupils as a part of a general program under which it pays the fares of pupils attending public and other schools. It is undoubtedly true that children are helped to get to church schools. There is even a possibility that some of the children might not be sent to the church schools if the parents were compelled to pay their children's bus fares out of their own pockets when transportation to a public school would have been paid for by the State. The same possibility exists where the state requires a local transit company to provide reduced fares to school children including those attending parochial schools, or where a municipally owned transportation system undertakes to carry all school children free of charge. Moreover, state-paid policemen, detailed to protect children going to and from church schools from the very real hazards of traffic, would serve much the same purpose and accomplish much the same result as state provisions intended to guarantee free transportation of a kind which the state deems to be best for the school children's welfare. And parents might refuse to risk their children to the serious danger of traffic accidents going to and from parochial schools, the approaches to which were not protected by policemen. Similarly, parents might be reluctant to permit their children to attend schools which the state had cut off from such general government services as ordinary police and fire protection, connections for sewage disposal, public highways and sidewalks. Of course, cutting off church schools from these services, so separate and so indisputably marked off from the religious function, would make it far more difficult for the schools to operate. But such is obviously not the purpose of the First Amendment. That Amendment requires the state to be a neutral in its relations with groups of religious believers and non-believers; it does not require the state to be their adversary. State power is no more to be used so as to handicap religions than it is to favor them.

This court has said that parents may, in the discharge of their duty under state compulsory education laws, send their children to a religious rather than a public school if the school meets the secular educational requirements which the state has power to impose. See *Pierce* v. *Society of Sisters,* 268 U.S. 510. It appears that these parochial schools meet New Jersey's requirements. The state contributes no money to the schools. It does not support them. Its legislation, as applied, does no more than provide a general program to help parents get their children, regardless of their religion, safely and expeditiously to and from accredited schools.

The First Amendment has erected a wall between church and state. That wall must be kept high and impregnable. We could not approve the slightest breach. New Jersey has not breached it here.

Affirmed.

Mr. Justice Jackson dissented:

It is of no importance in this situation whether the beneficiary of this expenditure of tax–raised funds is primarily the parochial school and incidentally the pupil, or whether the aid is directly bestowed on the pupil with indirect benefits to the school. The state cannot maintain a Church and it can no more tax its citizens to furnish free carriage to those who attend a Church. The prohibition against establishment of religion cannot be circumvented by a subsidy, bonus or reimbursement of expense to individuals for receiving religious instruction and indoctrination. . . .

. . . This freedom was first in the Bill of Rights because it was first in the fore-father's minds; it was set forth in absolute terms, and its strength is its rigidity. It was intended not only to keep the states' hands out of religion, but to keep religion's hands off the state, and above all, to keep bitter religious controversy out of public life by denying to every denomination any advantage from getting control of public policy or the public purse. Those great ends I cannot but think are immeasurably compromised by today's decision. . . .

But we cannot have it both ways. Religious teaching cannot be a private affair when the state seeks to impose regulations which infringe on it indirectly, and a public affair when it comes to taxing citizens of one faith to aid another, or those of no faith to aid all. If these principles seem harsh in prohibiting aid to Catholic education, it must not be forgotten that it is the same Constitution that alone assures Catholics the right to maintain these schools at all when predominant local sentiment would forbid them. *Pierce* v. *Society of Sisters,* 268 U.S. 510. Nor should I think that those who have done so well without this aid would want to see this separation between Church and State broken down. If the state may aid these religious schools, it may therefore regulate them. Many groups have sought aid from tax funds only to find that it carried political controls with it. Indeed this Court has declared that "it is hardly lack of due process for the Government to regulate that which it subsidizes." . . .

Mr. Justice Rutledge dissented, joined by Mr. Justice Frankfurter, Mr. Justice Jackson and Mr. Justice Burton:

. . . Does New Jersey's action furnish support for religion by use of the taxing power? Certainly it does, if the test remains undiluted as Jefferson and Madison made it, that money taken by taxation from one is not to be used or given to support another's religious training or belief, or indeed one's own. Today as then the furnishing of "contributions of money for the propagation of opinions which he disbelieves" is the forbidden exaction; and the prohibition is absolute for what-ever measure brings that consequence and whatever amount may be sought or given to that end.

The funds used here were raised by taxation. The Court does not dispute, nor could it, that their use does in fact give aid and encouragement to religious instruc-tion. It only concludes that this aid is not "support" in law. But Madison and Jefferson were concerned with aid and support in fact, not as a legal conclusion "entangled in precedents" . . . . Here parents pay money to send their children to parochial schools and funds raised by taxation are used to reimburse them. This not only helps the children to get to school and the parents to send them. It aids them in a particular school to secure, namely, religious training and teaching. . . .

New Jersey's action therefore exactly fits the type of exaction and the kind of evil at which Madison and Jefferson struck. Under the test they framed it cannot be said that the cost of transportation is no part of the cost of education or of the religious instruction given. That it is a substantial and a necessary element is shown most plainly by the continuing and increasing demand for the state to assume it. Nor is there pretense that it relates only to the secular instruction given in religious schools or that any attempt is or could be made toward allocating proportional shares as between the secular and the religious instruction. It is precisely because the instruction is religious and relates to a particular faith, whether one or another, that parents send their children to religious schools under the *Pierce* doctrine. And the very purpose of the state's contribution is to defray the cost of conveying the pupil to the place where he will receive not simply secular, but also and primarily religious, teaching and guidance. . . .

Finally, transportation, where it is needed, is as essential to education as any other element. Its cost is as much a part of the total expense, except at times in amount, as the cost of textbooks, of school lunches, of athletic equipment, of writing and other materials; indeed of all other items composing the total burden. Now as always the core of the educational process is the teacher-pupil relationship. Without this the richest equipment and facilities would go for naught. . . .

But we are told that the New Jersey statute is valid in its present application because the appropriation is for a public, not a private purpose, namely, the promotion of education, and the majority accept this idea in the conclusion that all we have here is "public welfare legislation." If that is true and the Amendment's force can be thus destroyed, what has been said becomes all the more pertinent. For then there could be no possible objection to more extensive support of religious education by New Jersey.

If the fact alone be determinative that religious schools are engaged in education, thus promoting the general and individual welfare, together with the legislature's decision that the payment of public moneys for their aid makes their work a public function, then I can see no possible basis, except one of dubious legislative policy, for the state's refusal to make full appropriation for support of private, religious schools, just as is done for public instruction. There could not be, on that basis, valid constitutional objection. . . .

We have here then one substantial issue, not two. To say that New Jersey's appropriation and her use of the power of taxation for raising the funds appropriated are not for public purposes but are for private ends, is to say that they are for the support of religion and religious teaching. Conversely, to say that they are for public purposes is to say that they are not for religious ones.

This is precisely for the reason that education which includes religious training and teaching, and its support, have been made matters of private right and function, not public, by the very terms of the First Amendment. That is the effect not only in its guaranty of religion's free exercise, but also in the prohibition of establishments. It was on this basis of the private character of the function of religious education that this Court held parents entitled to send their children to private, religious schools. *Pierce* v. *Society of Sisters, supra.* Now it declares in effect that the appropriation of public funds to defray part of the cost of attending those schools is for a public purpose. If so, I do not understand why the state cannot go farther or why this case approaches the verge of its power. . . .

Our constitutional policy is exactly the opposite. It does not deny the value or the necessity for religious training, teaching or observance. Rather it secures their free exercise. But to that end it does deny that the state can undertake or sustain them in any form or degree. For this reason the sphere of religious activity, as distinguished from the secular intellectual liberties, has been given the twofold protection and, as the state cannot forbid, neither can it perform or aid in performing the religious function. The dual prohibition makes that function altogether private. It cannot be made a public one by legislative act. This was the very heart of Madison's Remonstrance, as it is of the Amendment itself. . . .

No one conscious of religious values can be unsympathetic toward the burden which our constitutional separation puts on parents who desire religious instruction mixed with secular for their children. They pay taxes for others' children's education, at the same time the added cost of instruction for their own. Nor can one happily see benefits denied to children which others receive, because in conscience they or their parents for them desire a different kind of training others do not demand. . . .

. . . Hardship in fact there is which none can blink. But, for assuring to those who undergo it the greater, the most comprehensive freedom, it is one written by design and firm intent into our basic law. . . .

. . . Like St. Paul's freedom, religious liberty with a great price must be bought. And for those who exercise it most fully, by insisting upon religious education for their children mixed with secular, by the terms of our Constitution the price is greater than for others. . . .

NOTE:

While *Cantwell* was the first case to apply the "Gitlow doctrine" specifically to religious liberty, *Everson* was the first to interpret the establishment clause of the First Amendment and to apply it to the states through the due process clause of the Fourteenth Amendment. Several cases that are sometimes presumed to have treated the establishment of religion issue, did not. *Pierce* v. *Society of Sisters* (268 U.S. 510, 1925) really involved the liberty and property provisions of the Fourteenth Amendment. *Cochran* v. *Louisiana State Board of Education* used the "child benefit theory" in which the question of religion was not raised. *West Virginia State Board of Education* v. *Barnette* was really based on an invasion of "the intellect and spirit" protected by the First Amendment.

Some authorities, e.g., Corwin, have held that the establishment clause is not necessarily applied to the states by the Fourteenth Amendment. Their contention is that "establishment" is unrelated to the concept of "liberty."

Illinois ex rel. McCollum v.
Board of Education of Champaign County
333 U.S. 203; 68 S.Ct. 461; 92 L.Ed. 648 (1948)

(Representatives of the major faiths obtained permission from the Board of Education to offer classes in religious instruction to public school pupils in grades four to nine inclusive. Written consent was given by the parents for such instruction. Teachers of the religious courses were not paid by the schools but were subject to the approval and supervision of the superintendent of schools. Classes were conducted in the regular classrooms of the schools. Students who were released from secular study for the religious instruction were required to attend the religion classes, and reports of attendance were made to the regular school teachers.)

Vote: 8-1

Mr. Justice Black delivered the opinion of the Court:

Pupils compelled by law to go to school for secular education are released in part from their legal duty upon the condition that they attend the religious classes. This is beyond all question a utilization of the tax-established and tax-supported public school system to aid religious groups to spread their faith. And it falls squarely under the ban of the First Amendment (made applicable to the States by the Fourteenth) as we interpreted it in *Everson* v. *Board of Education,* 330 U.S. 1. There we said: "Neither a state nor the Federal Government can set up a church. Neither can pass laws which aid one religion, aid all religions, or prefer one religion over another. Neither can force or influence a person to go to or to remain away from church against his will or force him to profess a belief or disbelief in any religion. No person can be punished for entertaining or professing religious beliefs or disbeliefs, for church attendance or non-attendance. No tax in any amount, large or small, can be levied to support any religious activities or institutions, whatever they may be called, or whatever form they may adopt to teach or practice religion. Neither a state nor the Federal Government can, openly or secretly, participate in the affairs of any religious organizations or groups and vice versa. In the words of Jefferson, the clause against establishment of religion by law was intended to erect 'a wall of separation between Church and State.' " The majority in the Everson case, and the minority as shown by quotations from the dissenting views agreed that the First Amendment's language, properly interpreted, had erected a wall of separation between Church and State. They disagreed as to the facts shown by the record and as to the proper application of the First Amendment's language to those facts.

Recognizing that the Illinois program is barred by the First and Fourteenth Amendments if we adhere to the views expressed by both the majority and the minority in the Everson case, counsel for the respondents challenge those views as dicta and urge that we reconsider and repudiate them. They argue that historically the First Amendment was intended to forbid only government preference of one religion over another, not an impartial governmental assistance of all religions. In addition they ask that we distinguish or overrule our holding in the *Everson* Case that the Fourteenth Amendment made the "establishment of religion" clause of the First Amendment applicable as a prohibition against the States. After giving full consideration to the arguments presented we are unable to accept either of these contentions.

To hold that a state cannot consistently with the First and Fourteenth Amendments utilize its public school system to aid any or all religious faiths or sects in the dissemination of their doctrines and ideals does not, as counsel urge, manifest a governmental hostility to religion or religious teachings. A manifestation of such hostility would be at war with our national tradition as embodied in the First Amendment's guaranty of the free exercise of religion. For the First Amendment rests upon the premise that both religion and government can best work to achieve their lofty aims if each is left free from the other within its respective sphere. Or, as we said in the *Everson* Case, the First Amendment has erected a wall between Church and State which must be kept high and impregnable.

Here not only are the state's tax-supported public school buildings used for the dissemination of religious doctrines. The State also affords sectarian groups an invaluable aid in that it helps to provide pupils for their religious classes through use of the state's compulsory public school machinery. This is not separation of Church and State.

The cause is reversed and remanded to the State Supreme Court for proceedings not inconsistent with this opinion.

Mr. Justice Reed dissented:

. . . The Court's opinion quotes the gist of the Court's reasoning in *Everson.* I agree as there stated that none of our governmental entities can "set up a church." I agree that they cannot "aid" all or any religions or prefer one "over another." But "aid" must be understood as a purposeful assistance directly to the church itself or to some religious group or organization doing religious work of such a character that it may fairly be said to be performing ecclesiastical functions. "Prefer" must give an advantage to one "over another." I agree that pupils cannot "be released in part from their legal duty" of school attendance upon condition that they attend religious classes. But as Illionis has held that it is within the discretion of the School Board to permit absence from schools for religious instruction no legal duty of school attendance is violated. 396 Ill. 14, N.E.2d 161. If the sentence in the first opinion, concerning the pupils' release from legal duty, is intended to mean that the Constitution forbids a school to excuse a pupil from secular control during school hours to attend voluntarily a class in religious education, whether in or out of school buildings, I disagree. Of course, no tax can be levied to support organizations intended "to teach or practice religion." I agree too that the state cannot influence one toward religion against his will or punish him for his beliefs. Champaign's religious education course does none of these things.

It seems clear to me that the "aid" referred to by the Court in the *Everson* case could not have been those incidental advantages that religious bodies, with other groups similarly situated, obtain as a by-product of organized society. . . .

With the general statements in the opinions concerning the constitutional requirement that the nation and the states, by virtue of the First and Fourteenth Amendments, may "make no law respecting an establishment of religion," I am in agreement. But, in light of the meaning given to those words by the precedents, customs, and practices which I have detailed above, I cannot agree with the Court's decision that when pupils compelled by law to go to school for secular education are released from school so as to attend the religious classes, churches are unconstitutionally aided. Whatever may be the wisdom of the arrangement as to the use of the school buildings made with The Champaign Council of Religious Education, it is clear to me that past practice shows such cooperation between the schools and a non-ecclesiastical body is not forbidden by the First Amendment. When actual church services have always been permitted on government property, the mere use of the school buildings by a non-sectarian group for religious education ought not to be condemned as an establishment of religion. For a non-sectarian organization to give the type of instruction here offered cannot be said to violate our rule as to the establishment of religion by the state. The prohibition of enactments respecting the establishment of religion do not bar every friendly gesture between church and state. It is not an absolute prohibition against every conceivable situation where the two may work together any more than the other provisions of the First Amendment—free speech, free press—are absolutes. If abuses occur, such as the use of the instruction hour for sectarian purposes, I have no doubt, in view of the *Ring* case, that Illinois will promptly correct them. If they are of a kind that tend to the establishment of a church or interfere with the free exercise of religion, this Court is open for a review of any erroneous decision. This Court cannot be too cautious in upsetting practices embedded in our society by many years of experience. A state is entitled to have great leeway in its legislation when dealing with the important social problems of its population. A definite violation of legislative limits must be established. The Constitution should not be stretched to forbid national customs in the way courts act to reach arrangements to avoid federal taxation. Devotion to the great principle of religious liberty should not lead us into a rigid interpretation of the constitutional guarantee that conflicts with accepted habits of our people. This is an instance where, for me, the history of past practices is determinative of the meaning of a constitutional clause not a decorous introduction to the study of its text. The judgment should be affirmed.

RELATED CASES:

Ring v. Board of Education: 245 Ill. 334, 92 N.E. 251 (1910). Opinion: Dunn, J. Dissenting: Hand and Cartwright, JJ.

The reading of the Bible, singing of hymns and the repeating of the Lord's Prayer in a public school is violative of provisions of the Illinois Constitution which guarantee the free exercise and enjoyment of religious profession and worship without discrimination and prohibit the appropriation of any public fund in aid of a sectarian purpose.

Doremus v. Board of Education: 342 U.S. 429 (1952). Opinion: Jackson, J. Dissenting: Douglas, Reed, and Burton, JJ.

The Supreme Court refused jurisdiction on the basis that the plaintiff lacked standing to maintain a suit in a case in which the New Jersey state court had upheld the validity of a statute requiring the reading of five verses of the Old Testament each school day. The child had been graduated, and Doremus, parent and taxpayer, could show no loss. Incidentally, the state court had held that the Old Testament is not a "sectarian book."

NOTE:

In both *Everson* and *McCollum* the Court was unanimous on the point that there is complete separation under the First Amendment as applied to the states by the Fourteenth. The only point of disagreement was whether the specific matter under question in these cases did or did not involve state aid to religion. In *Everson* the answer of the majority was "no" and in *McCollum* the answer was "yes."

Zorach v. Clauson
343 U.S. 306; 72 S.Ct. 679; 96 L.Ed. 954 (1952)

(New York City provided a program under which public school students were released from school during the day to go to religious centers away from the school property to attend religious instruction. This was done only with the consent of the parents of the students involved. The churches sent a weekly list of absent children to the school authorities. All of the costs of the program were paid by the religious organizations.)

Vote: 6-3

Mr. Justice Douglas delivered the opinion of the Court:

. . . It takes obtuse reasoning to inject any issue of the "free exercise" of religion into the present case. No one is forced to go to the religious classroom and no religious exercise or instruction is brought to the classrooms of the public schools. A student need not take religious instruction. He is left to his own desires as to the manner or time of his religious devotions, if any.

There is a suggestion that the system involves the use of coercion to get public school students into religious classrooms. There is no evidence in the record before us that supports that conclusion. The present record indeed tells us that the school authorities are neutral in this regard and do no more than release students whose parents so request. If in fact coercion were used, if it were established that any one or more teachers were using their office to persuade or force students to take the religious instruction, a wholly different case would be presented. Hence we put aside that claim of coercion both as respects the "free exercise" of religion and "an establishment of religion" within the meaning of the First Amendment.

Moreover, apart from that claim of coercion, we do not see how New York by this type of "released time" program has made a law respecting an establishment of religion within the meaning of the First Amendment. There is much talk of the separation of Church and State in the history of the Bill of Rights and in the decisions clustering around the First Amendment. . . . There cannot be the slightest doubt that the First Amendment reflects the philosophy that Church and State should be separated. And so far as interference with the "free exercise" of religion and an "establishment" of religion are concerned, the separation must be complete and unequivocal. The First Amendment within the scope of its coverage permits no exception; the prohibition is absolute. The First Amendment, however, does not say that in every and all respects there shall be a separation of Church and State. Rather, it studiously defines the manner, the specific ways, in which there shall be no concert or union or dependency one on the other. That is the common sense of the matter. Otherwise the state and religion would be aliens to each other—hostile, suspicious, and even unfriendly, Churches could not be required to pay even property taxes. Municipalities would not be permitted to render police or fire protection to religious groups. Policemen who helped parishioners into their places of worship would violate the Constitution. Prayers in our legislative halls; the appeals to the Almighty in the messages of the Chief Executive; the proclamations making Thanksgiving Day a holiday; "so help me God" in our courtroom oaths—these and all other references to the Almighty that run through our laws, our public rituals, our ceremonies would be flouting the First Amendment. A fastidious atheist or agnostic could even object to the supplication with which the Court opens each session; "God save the United States and this Honorable Court." . . .

We are a religious people whose institutions presuppose a Supreme Being. We guarantee the freedom to worship as one chooses. We make room for as wide a variety of beliefs and creeds as the spiritual needs of man deem necessary. We sponsor an attitude on the part of government that shows no partiality to any one group and that lets each flourish according to the zeal of its adherents and the appeal of its dogma. When the state encourages religious instruction or cooperates with religious authorities by adjusting the schedule of public events to sectarian needs, it follows the best of our traditions. For it then respects the religious nature of our people and accommodates the public service to their spiritual needs. To hold that it may not would be to find in the Constitution a requirement that the government show a callous indifference to religious groups. That would be preferring those who believe in no religion over those who do believe. Government may not finance religious groups nor undertake religious instruction nor blend secular and sectarian education nor use secular institutions to force one or some religion on any person. But we find no constitutional requirement which makes it necessary for government to be hostile to religion and to throw its weight against efforts to widen the effective scope of religious influence. The government must be neutral when it comes to competition between sects. It may not thrust any sect on any person. It may not make a religious observance compulsory. It may not coerce anyone to attend church, to observe a religious holiday, or to take religious instruction. But it can close its doors or suspend its operations as to those who want to repair to their religious sanctuary for worship or instruction. No more than that is undertaken here. . . . .

In the *McCollum* case the classrooms were used for religious instruction and the force of the public school was used to promote that instruction. Here, as we have said, the public schools do no more than accommodate their schedules to a program of outside religious instruction. We follow the *McCollum* case. But we cannot expand it to cover the present released time program unless separation of Church and State means that public institutions can make no adjustments of their schedules to accommodate the religious needs of the people. We cannot read into the Bill of Rights such a philosophy of hostility to religion.

Affirmed.

Mr. Justice Jackson, dissented:

This released time program is founded upon a use of the State's power of coercion, which, for me, determines its unconstitutionality. Stripped to its essentials, the plan has two stages: first, that the State compel each student to yield a large part of his time for public·secular education; and, second, that some of it be "released" to him on condition that he devote it to sectarian religious purposes. . . .

The greater effectiveness of this system over voluntary attendance after school hours is due to the truant officer who, if the youngster fails to go to the Church school, dogs him back to the public schoolroom. Here schooling is more or less suspended during the "released time" so the nonreligious attendants will not forge ahead of the churchgoing absentees. But it serves as a temporary jail for a pupil who will not go to Church. It takes more subtlety of mind than I possess to deny that this is governmental constraint in support of religion. It is an unconstitutional, in my view, when exerted by indirection as when exercised forthrightly.

As one whose children, as a matter of free choice, have been sent to privately supported Church schools, I may challenge the Court's suggestion that opposition to this plan can only be antireligious, atheistic, or agnostic. My evangelistic brethren confuse an objection to compulsion with an objection to religion. It is possible to hold a faith with enough confidence to believe that what should be rendered to God does not need to be decided and collected by Caesar.

The day that this country ceases to be free for irreligion it will cease to be free for religion—except for the sect that can win political power. The same epithetical jurisprudence used by the Court today to beat down those who oppose pressuring children into some religion can devise as good epithets tomorrow against those who object to pressuring them into a favored religion. And, after all, if we concede to the State power and wisdom to single out "duly constituted religious" bodies as exclusive alternatives for compulsory secular instruction, it would be logical to also uphold the power and wisdom to choose the true faith among those "duly constituted." We start down a rough road when we begin to mix compulsory public education with compulsory godliness.

A number of Justices just short of a majority of the majority that promulgates today's passionate dialectics joined in answering them in *Illinois ex. rel. McCollum* v. *Board of Education*, 333 U.S. 203. . . . A reading of the Court's opinion in that case along with its opinion in this case will show such difference of overtones and undertones as to make clear that the *McCollum* case has passed like a storm in a teacup. The wall which the Court was professing to erect between Church and State has become even more warped and twisted than I expected. Today's judgment will be more interesting to students of psychology and of the judicial process than to students of constitutional law.

Mr. Justice Black, dissented:

. . . I see no significant difference between the invalid Illinois system and that of New York here sustained. Except for the use of the school buildings in Illinois, there is no difference between the systems which I consider even worthy of mention. In the New York program, as in that of Illinois, the school authorities release some of the children on the condition that they attend the religious classes, get reports on whether they attend, and hold the other children in the school building until the religious hour is over. As we attempted to make categorically clear, the *McCollum* decision would have been the same if the religious classes had not been held in the school buildings. We said:

"Here *not only* are the State's tax-supported public school buildings used for the dissemination of religious doctrines. The State also affords sectarian groups an invaluable aid in that it helps to provide pupils for their religious classes through the use of the State's compulsory school machinery. *This* is not separation of Church and State" (Emphasis supplied). *McCollum* v. *Board of Education, supra,* 333 U.S. at p. 212, 68 S.Ct. at p. 465. *McCollum* thus held that Illinois could not constitutionally manipulate the compelled classroom hours of its compulsory school machinery so as to channel children into sectarian classes. Yet that is exactly what the Court holds New York can do.

I am aware that our *McCollum* decision on separation of church and state has been subjected to a most searching examination throughout the country. Probably few opinions from this Court in recent years have attracted more attention or stirred wider debate. Our insistence on "a wall between Church and State which must be kept high and impregnable" has seemed to some a correct exposition of the philosophy and a true interpretation of the language of the First Amendment to which we should strictly adhere. With equal conviction and sincerity, others have thought the *McCollum* decision fundamentally wrong and have pledged continuous warfare against it. The opinions in the court below and the briefs here reflect these diverse viewpoints. In dissenting today, I mean to do more than give routine approval to our *McCollum* decision. I mean also to reaffirm my faith in the fundamental philosophy expressed in *McCollum* and *Everson* v. *Board of Education.* . . . That reaffirmance can be brief because of the exhaustive opinions in those recent cases.

Difficulty of decision in the hypothetical situations mentioned by the Court, but not now before us, should not confuse the issues in this case. Here the sole question is whether New York can use its compulsory education laws to help religious sects get attendants presumably too unenthusiastic to go unless moved to do so by the use of this state machinery. That this is the plan, purpose, design and consequence of the New York program cannot be denied. The state thus makes religious sects beneficiaries of its power to compel children to attend secular schools. Any use of such coercive power by the state to help or hinder some religious sects or to prefer all religious sects over nonbelievers or vice versa is just what I think the First Amendment forbids. In considering whether a state has entered this forbidden field the question is not whether it has entered too far but whether it has entered at all. New York is manipulating its compulsory education laws to help religious sects get pupils. This is not separation but combination of Church and State.

Mr. Justice Frankfurter dissented:

. . . The Court tells us that in the maintenance of its public schools, "[The State government] can close its doors or suspend its operations" so that its citizens may be free for religious devotions or instruction. If that were the issue, it would not rise to the dignity of a constitutional controversy. Of course a State may provide that the classes in its schools shall be dismissed, for any reason, or no reason, on fixed days, or for special occasions. The essence of this case is that the school system did not "close its doors" and did not "suspend its operations." There is all the difference in the world between letting the children out of school and letting some of them out of school into religious classes. If every one is free to make what use he will of time wholly unconnected from schooling required by law—those who wish sectarian instruction devoting it to that purpose, those who have ethical instruction at home, to that, those who study music, to that—then of course there is no conflict with the Fourteenth Amendment.

The pith of the case is that formalized religious instruction is substituted for other school activity which those who do not participate in the released-time program are compelled to attend. The school system is very much in operation during this kind of released time. If its doors are closed, they are closed upon those students who do not attend the religious instruction in order to keep them within the school. That is the very thing which raises the constitutional issue. It is not met by disregarding it. Failure to discuss this issue does not take it out of the case. . . .

NOTE:

This was not a reversal of *McCollum* but simply a holding that the circumstances of the case did not amount to state aid to religion. Of the six judges who voted with the majority in *Zorach,* Clark and Minton had not been on the Court for the *McCollum* decision, Douglas, Vinson, and Burton had voted against the

Illinois plan, while Reed had seen no invalidity in the plan. Reed was "for" religion in *Everson, McCollum,* and *Zorach* while Frankfurter was "opposed" in all three cases.

Just where the Court will ultimately draw the line on governmental recognition of religious activity, such as the use of chaplains in the military and "In God We Trust" on money, remains to be seen. Government cannot aid religion and is not to be hostile to religious activities, and the line of demarcation between the two notions is sometimes rather indistinct. As the Court indicated in *Zorach,* rigid separation is absurd and impossible.

Engel v. Vitale
370 U.S. 421; 82 S.Ct. 1261; 8 L.Ed. 2d 601 (1962)

(Following a recommendation of the New York State Board of Regents, the New Hyde Park Board of Education directed that the following prayer be said aloud by each class in the presence of a teacher at the beginning of each school day: "Almighty God, we acknowledge our dependence upon Thee, and we beg Thy blessings upon us, our parents, our teachers and our country." This action was challenged by the parents of ten pupils as violating the "Establishment Clause" of the First Amendment which is applied to the states by the Fourteenth Amendment under the "Gitlow doctrine.")

Vote: 6-1

Mr. Justice Black delivered the opinion of the Court:

We think that by using its public school system to encourage recitation of the Regents' prayer, the State of New York has adopted a practice wholly inconsistent with the Establishment Clause.

There can, of course, be no doubt that New York's program of daily classroom invocation of God's blessings as prescribed in the Regent's prayer is a religious activity. It is a solemn avowal of divine faith and supplication for the blessings of the Almighty. The nature of such a prayer has always been religious, none of the respondents has denied this and the trial court expressly so found:

"The religious nature of prayer was recognized by Jefferson and has been concurred in by theological writers, the United States Supreme Court and state courts and administrative officials, including New York's Commissioner of Education. A committee of the New York Legislature has agreed.

"The Board of Regents as *amicus curiae,* the respondents and intervenors all concede the religious nature of prayer, but seek to distinguish this prayer because it is based on our spiritual heritage. . . ."

The petitioners contend among other things that the state laws requiring or permitting use of the Regents' prayer must be struck down as a violation of the Establishment Clause because that prayer was composed by governmental officials as a part of a governmental program to further religious beliefs. For this reason, petitioners argue, the State's use of the Regents' prayer in its public school system breaches the constitutional wall of separation between Church and State. We agree with that contention since we think that the constitutional prohibition against laws respecting an establishment of religion must at least mean that in this country it is no part of the business of government to compose official prayers for any group of the American people to recite as a part of a religious program carried on by government.

. . . The First Amendment was added to the Constitution to stand as a guarantee that neither the power nor the prestige of the Federal Government would be used

to control, support or influence the kinds of prayer the American people can say—
that the people's religions must not be subjected to the pressures of government
for change each time a new political administration is elected to office. Under that
Amendment's prohibition against governmental establishment of religion, as rein-
forced by the provisions of the Fourteenth Amendment, government in this country,
be it state or federal, is without power to prescribe by law any particular form of
prayer which is to be used as an official prayer in carrying on any program of
governmentally sponsored religious activity.

There can be no doubt that New York's state prayer program officially establishes the religious beliefs embodied in the Regents' prayer. The respondents'
argument to the contrary, which is largely based upon the contention that the
Regents' prayer is "non-denominational" and the fact that the program, as modified
and approved by state courts, does not require all pupils to recite the prayer but
permits those who wish to do so to remain silent or be excused from the room,
ignores the essential nature of the program's constitutional defects. Neither the
fact that the prayer may be denominationally neutral, nor the fact that its observance on the part of the students is voluntary can serve to free it from the limitations of the Establishment Clause, as it might from the Free Exercise Clause, of
the First Amendment, both of which are operative against the States by virtue of
the Fourteenth Amendment. Although these two clauses may in certain instances
overlap, they forbid two quite different kinds of governmental encroachment upon
religious freedom. The Establishment Clause, unlike the Free Exercise Clause,
does not depend upon any showing of direct governmental compulsion and is
violated by the enactment of laws which establish an official religion whether those
laws operate directly to coerce nonobserving individuals or not. . . .

The judgment of the Court of Appeals of New York is reversed and the cause
remanded for further proceedings not inconsistent with this opinion.

Reversed and remanded.

Mr. Justice Frankfurter took no part in the decision of this case.

Mr. Justice White took no part in the consideration or decision of this case.

Mr. Justice Douglas concurred:

. . . Prayers of course may be so long and of such a character as to amount to
an attempt at the religious instruction that was denied the public schools by the
McCollum case. But New York's prayer is of a character that does not involve any
element of proselytizing as in the *McCollum* case.

The question presented by this case is therefore an extremely narrow one. It is
whether New York oversteps the bounds when it finances a religious exercise.

What New York does on the opening of its public schools is what we do when
we open court. Our Marshal has from the beginning announced the convening of
the Court and then added "God save the United States and this honorable court."
That utterance is a supplication, a prayer in which we, the judges, are free to
join, but which we need not recite any more than the students need recite the New
York prayer.

What New York does on the opening of its public schools is what each House
of Congress does at the opening of each day's business. Reverend Frederick B.
Harris is Chaplain of the Senate; Reverend Bernard Braskamp is Chaplain of the
House. Guest chaplains of various denominations also officiate.

In New York the teacher who leads in prayer is on the public payroll; and the
time she takes seems minuscule as compared with the salaries appropriated by
state legislatures and Congress for chaplains to conduct prayers in the legislative
halls. Only a bare fraction of the teacher's time is given to reciting this short
22-word prayer, about the same amount of time that our Marshal spends announcing the opening of our sessions and offering a prayer for this Court. Yet for me

the principle is the same, no matter how briefly the prayer is said, for in each of the instances given the person praying is a public official on the public payroll, performing a religious exercise in a governmental institution. It is said that the element of coercion is inherent in the giving of this prayer. If that is true here, it is also true of the prayer with which this Court is convened, and with those that open the Congress. Few adults, let alone children, would leave our courtroom or the Senate or the House while those prayers are being given. Every such audience is in a sense a "captive" audience.

At the same time I cannot say that to authorize this prayer is to establish a religion in the strictly historic meaning of those words. A religion is not established in the usual sense merely by letting those who chose to do so say the prayer that the public school teacher leads. Yet once government finances a religious exercise it inserts a divisive influence into our communities. The New York court said that the prayer given does not conform to all of the tenets of the Jewish, Unitarian, and Ethical Culture groups. One of petitioners is an agnostic.

"We are a religious people whose institutions presuppose a Supreme Being." *Zorach* v. *Clauson,* 343 U.S. 306, 313. . . .Under our Bill of Rights free play is given for making religion an active role in our lives. But "if a religious leaven is to be worked into the affairs of our people, it is to be done by individuals and groups, not by the government." *McGowan* v. *Maryland,* 366 U.S. 420, 563 . . . (dissenting opinion). By reason of the First Amendment government is commanded "to have no interest in theology or ritual" (id., at 564 . . .) for on those matters "government must be neutral." Ibid. The First Amendment leaves the Government in a position not of hostility to religion but of neutrality. The philosophy is that the atheist or agnostic—the non-believer—is entitled to go his own way. The philosophy is that if government interferes in matters spiritual, it will be a divisive force. The First Amendment teaches that a government neutral in the field of religion better serves all religious interests.

My problem today would be uncomplicated but for *Everson* v. *Board of Education,* 330 U.S. 1, 17 . . . which allowed taxpayers' money to be used to pay "the bus fares of parochial school pupils as a part of a general program under which" the fares of pupils attending public and other schools were also paid. The Everson case seems in retrospect to be out of line with the First Amendment. . . .

Mr. Justice Stewart dissented:

. . . With all respect, I think the Court has misapplied a great constitutional principle. I cannot see how an "official religion" is established by letting those who want to say a prayer say it. On the contrary, I think that to deny the wish of these school children to join in reciting this prayer is to deny them the opportunity of sharing in the spiritual heritage of our Nation.

The Court's historical review of the quarrels over the Book of Common Prayer in England throws no light for me on the issue before us in this case. England had then and has now an established church. Equally unenlightening, I think, is the history of the early establishment and later rejection of an official church in our own States. For we deal here not with the establishment of a state church, which would, of course, be constitutionally impermissible, but with whether school children who want to begin their day by joining in prayer must be prohibited from doing so. Moreover, I think that the Court's task, in this as in all areas of constitutional adjudication, is not responsibly aided by the uncritical invocation of metaphors like the "wall of separation," a phrase nowhere to be found in the Constitution. What is relevant to the issue here is not the history of an established church in sixteenth century England or in eighteenth century America, but the history of the religious traditions of our people, reflected in countless practices of the institutions and officials of our government.

At the opening of each day's Session of this Court we stand, while one of our officials invokes the protection of God. Since the days of John Marshall our Crier has said, "God save the United States and this Honorable Court." Both the Senate and the House of Representatives open their daily Sessions with prayer. Each of our Presidents, from George Washington to John F. Kennedy, has upon assuming his Office asked the protection and help of God.

The Court today says that the state and federal governments are without constitutional power to prescribe any particular form of words to be recited by any group of the American people on any subject touching religion. The third stanza of "The Star-Spangled Banner," made our National Anthem by Act of Congress in 1931, contains these verses:

> "Blest with victory and peace, may the heav'n rescued land
> Praise the Pow'r that hath made and preserved us a nation!
> Then conquer we must, when our cause it is just,
> And this be our motto 'In God is our Trust.' "

In 1954 Congress added a phrase to the Pledge of Allegiance to the Flag so that it now contains the words "one Nation *under God*, indivisible, with liberty and justice for all." In 1952 Congress enacted legislation calling upon the President each year to proclaim a National Day of Prayer. Since 1865 the words "IN GOD WE TRUST" have been impressed on our coins.

Countless similar examples could be listed, but there is no need to belabor the obvious. It was all summed up by this Court just ten years ago in a single sentence: "We are a religious people whose institutions presuppose a Supreme Being." *Zorach* v. *Clauson,* 343 U.S. 306, 313. . . .

I do not believe that this Court, or the Congress, or the President has by the actions and practices I have mentioned established an "official religion" in violation of the Constitution. And I do not believe the State of New York has done so in this case. What each has done has been to recognize and to follow the deeply entrenched and highly cherished spiritual traditions of our Nation—traditions which come down to us from those who almost two hundred years ago avowed their "firm reliance on the Protection of Divine Providence" when they proclaimed the freedom and independence of this brave new world.

I dissent.

NOTE:

This decision has been much misunderstood. The opinion leaves many questions unanswered, but all that is decided here is that a governmental unit—here a school board—cannot prescribe a particular form of prayer to be used as the official government-sponsored prayer. Clarification of what is meant by a "prayer" will doubtless be a task of the Court in the rather immediate future. One facet of this problem was treated by the Court in *School District of Abington Township, Pa.* v. *Schempp,* 374 U.S. 203 (1963). See also *Ring* v. *Board of Education,* p. 43, above.

In *Engel* v. *Vitale* the Court could have refused the case on the basis of lack of standing since the program involved no real added cost to education and participation was voluntary. Also it might be noted that there was no interference with the "free exercise" of religion since the prayer was denominationally neutral and, again, participation by the pupils was voluntary.

The phrase "wall of separation" has been attributed to Thomas Jefferson although James Madison had earlier used the term "separation" in this connection.

School District of Abington Township, Pennsylvania v. Schempp
374 U.S. 203; 83 S.Ct. 1560; 10 L.Ed. 2d 844 (1963)

(A Pennsylvania statute required that at least ten verses from the Bible should be read without comment at the opening of each public school on each school day. Any child was to be excused from the reading on written request of parent or guardian. The Schempp family, husband, wife, and two of their three children, Unitarians, brought suit to enjoin enforcement of the statute. They contended that their rights under the Fourteenth Amendment applying the provisions of the First Amendment to the states were being violated. A three-judge District Court for the Eastern District of Pennsylvania held the statute void because contrary to the Establishment Clause of the First Amendment.)

Vote: 8-1

Mr. Justice Clark delivered the opinion of the Court:

Once again we are called upon to consider the scope of the provision of the First Amendment to the United States Constitution which declares that "Congress shall make no law respecting an establishment of religion, or prohibiting the free exercise thereof. . . ." These companion cases present the issues in the context of state action requiring that schools begin each day with readings from the Bible. While raising the basic questions under slightly different factual situations, the cases permit of joint treatment. In light of the history of the First Amendment and of our cases interpreting and applying its requirements, we hold that the practices at issue and the laws requiring them are unconstitutional under the Establishment Clause, as applied to the States through the Fourteenth Amendment. . . .

First, this Court has decisively settled that the First Amendment's mandate that "Congress shall make no law respecting an establishment of religion, or prohibiting the free exercise thereof" has been made wholly applicable to the States by the Fourteenth Amendment. Twenty-three years ago in *Cantwell v. Connecticut,* 310 U.S. 296, 303 (1940), this Court, through Mr. Justice Roberts, said:

"The fundamental concept of liberty embodied in that [Fourteenth] Amendment embraces the liberties guaranteed by the First Amendment. The First Amendment declares that Congress shall make no law respecting an establishment of religion or prohibiting the free exercise thereof. The Fourteenth Amendment has rendered the legislatures of the states as incompetent as Congress to enact such laws. . . ."

. . . Second, this Court has rejected unequivocally the contention that the Establishment Clause forbids only governmental preference of one religion over another. Almost 20 years ago in *Everson, supra,* at 15, the Court said that "[n]either a state nor the Federal Government can set up a church. Neither can pass laws which aid one religion, aid all religions, or prefer one religion over another."

. . . As we have indicated, the Establishment Clause has been directly considered by this Court eight times in the past score of years and, with only one Justice dissenting on the point, it has consistently held that the clause withdrew all legislative power respecting religious belief or the expression thereof. The test may be stated as follows: what are the purpose and primary effect of the enactment? If either is the advancement or inhibition of religion then the enactment exceeds the scope of legislative power as circumscribed by the Constitution. That is to say that to withstand the strictures of the Establishment Clause there must be a secular legislative purpose and a primary effect that neither advances nor inhibits religion. . . .

Applying the Establishment Clause principles to the cases at bar we find that the States are requiring the selection and reading at the opening of the school day of verses from the Holy Bible and the recitation of the Lord's Prayer by the student in unison. These exercises are prescribed as part of the curricular activities of students who are required by law to attend school. They are held in the school buildings under the supervision and with the participation of teachers employed in those schools. . . .

The short answer, therefore, is that the religious character of the exercise was admitted by the State. . . .

The conclusion follows that in both cases the laws require religious exercises and such exercises are being conducted in direct violation of the rights of the appellees and petitioners. Nor are these required exercises mitigated by the fact that individual students may absent themselves upon parental request, for that fact furnishes no defense to a claim of unconstitutionality under the Establishment Clause. . . .

. . . Nothing we have said here indicates that such study of the Bible or of religion, when presented objectively as part of a secular program of education, may not be effected consistent with the First Amendment. But the exercises here do not fall into those categories. They are religious exercises, required by the States in violation of the command of the First Amendment that the Government maintain strict neutrality, neither aiding nor opposing religion.

Judgment affirmed.

Mr. Justice Douglas concurred:

. . . The vice of all such arrangements under the Establishment Clause is that the state is lending its assistance to a church's efforts to gain and keep adherents. Under the First Amendment it is strictly a matter for the individual and his church as to what church he will belong to and how much support, in the way of belief, time, activity or money, he will give to it.

. . . But the institution is an inseparable whole, a living organism, which is strengthened in proselytizing when it is strengthened in any department by contributions from other than its own members.

Such contributions may not be made by the State even in a minor degree without violating the Establishment Clause. It is not the amount of public funds expended; as this case illustrates, it is the use to which public funds are put that is controlling. For the First Amendment does not say that some forms of establishment are allowed; it says that "no law respecting an establishment of religion" shall be made. What may not be done directly may not be done indirectly lest the Establishment Clause become a mockery.

Mr. Justice Brennan concurred:

. . . The constitutional mandate expresses a deliberate and considered judgment that such matters are to be left to the conscience of the citizen, and declares as a basic postulate of the relation between the citizen and his government that "the rights of conscience are, in their nature, of peculiar delicacy, and will little bear the gentlest touch of governmental hand. . . ."*

I join fully in the opinion and the judgment of the Court. I see no escape from the conclusion that the exercises called in question in these two cases violate the constitutional mandate. The reasons we gave only last Term in *Engel* v. *Vitale,* 370 U.S. 421, for finding in the New York Regents' prayer an impermissible establishment of religion, compel the same judgment of the practices at bar. The involvement of the secular with the religious is no less intimate here; and it is constitutionally irrelevant that the State has not composed the material for the inspirational exercises presently involved. It should be unnecessary to observe that our holding does not declare that the First Amendment manifests hostility to the

* Representative Daniel Carroll of Maryland during debate upon the proposed Bill of Rights in the First Congress, August 15, 1789, I Annals of Cong. 730.

practice or teaching of religion, but only applies prohibitions incorporated in the Bill of Rights in recognition of historic needs shared by Church and State alike. While it is my view that not every involvement of religion in public life is unconstitutional, I consider the exercises at bar a form of involvement which clearly violates the Establishment Clause. . . .

In sum, the history which our prior decisions have summoned to aid interpretation of the Establishment Clause permits little doubt that its prohibition was designed comprehensively to prevent those official involvements of religion which would tend to foster or discourage religious worship or belief.

. . . It is implicit in the history and character of American public education that the public schools serve a uniquely *public* function: the training of American citizens in an atmosphere free of parochial, divisive, or separatist influences of any sort—an atmosphere in which children may assimilate a heritage common to all American groups and religions. . . .

Mr. Justice Goldberg concurred, joined by Mr. Justice Harlan:

. . . The First Amendment does not prohibit practices which by any realistic measure create none of the dangers which it is designed to prevent and which do not so directly or substantially involve the state in religious exercises or in the favoring of religion as to have meaningful and practical impact. It is of course true that great consequences can grow from small beginnings, but the measure of constitutional adjudication is the ability and willingness to distinguish between real threat and mere shadow. . . .

Mr. Justice Stewart dissented:

I think the records in the two cases before us are so fundamentally deficient as to make impossible an informed or responsible determination of the constitutional issues presented. Specifically, I cannot agree that on these records we can say that the Establishment Clause has necessarily been violated. But I think there exist serious questions under both that provision and the Free Exercise Clause—insofar as each is imbedded in the Fourteenth Amendment—which require the remand of these cases for the taking of additional evidence. . . .

The governmental neutrality which the First and Fourteenth Amendments require in the cases before us, in other words, is the extension of evenhanded treatment to all who believe, doubt, or disbelieve—a refusal on the part of the State to weight the scales of private choice. In these cases, therefore, what is involved is not state action based on impermissible categories, but rather an attempt by the State to accommodate those differences which the existence in our society of a variety of religious beliefs makes inevitable. The Constitution requires that such efforts be struck down only if they are proven to entail the use of the secular authority of government to coerce a preference among such beliefs. . . .

Viewed in this light, it seems to me clear that the records in both of the cases [See *Murray* v. *Curlett,* below, the other case to which reference is made] before us are wholly inadequate to support an informed or responsible decision. Both cases involve provisions which explicitly permit any student who wishes, to be excused from participation in the exercises. There is no evidence in either case as to whether there would exist any coercion of any kind upon a student who did not want to participate. . . .

RELATED CASES:

Murray v. Curlett: 374 U.S. 203 (1963). Opinion: Clark, J. Dissenting: Stewart, J.

The Maryland requirement that Bible passages or the Lord's Prayer be recited in public schools was held to violate the establishment clause of the First Amendment as applied to the states by the Fourteenth Amendment. This was so held even though students could be excused from the exercises on written request of parents. This case was decided with *School District of Abington Township* v. *Schempp*. Mrs. Murray claimed to be "a professed atheist."

NOTE:

Free exercise of religion is not an absolute right. Antisocial conduct cannot be indulged in under guise of religious worship. An arsonist cannot claim that he is a fire-worshipper. Under the "establishment clause" there can be no official church, no specially favored church, and no governmentally certified creed. Incidental, ceremonial, traditional connections between government and religion apparently are valid, but no public funds can be used for the support of a religious institution, and being nondiscriminatory, nonsectarian, or nonpreferential does not validate such use of public funds. Apparently, there is very real question that public funds can be granted to a school that has a close church connection. There is always the need to balance two interests—the freedom of the individual to practice religion as he sees fit, and the interest of the government in preserving the general welfare.

It is easier to satisfy the "standing" requirement in an "establishment" suit than in a "free exercise" suit since in the former no proof is needed that a particular religious freedom has been infringed.

FREEDOM OF SPEECH AND PRESS

While it is pretty generally agreed that there are no *absolute* rights that one may assert at all times against all persons and governments, those guarantees listed in the First Amendment probably come as close as any to qualifying. Justice Roberts in *Cantwell* v. *Connecticut* stated that the "establishment" provision is absolute, and Justices Black and Douglas have from time to time very strongly indicated that they regarded the rights of speech and press as virtually "absolute." One of the instances where he did this was Justice Black's concurring opinion in *Wieman* v. *Updegraff* (344 U.S. 183, 1952). Several of the justices have maintained that First Amendment rights have a "preferred position" among the constitutional guarantees. This means simply that at all times the presumption of validity is on the side of the claimed right and against the challenged statutes, whereas normally the burden of proof is on those who challenge a statute as void under some provision of the Constitution.

The "clear and present danger" test was first presented by Mr. Justice Holmes in *Schenck* and his statement therein has become a classic of its kind. However, while authorities differ, it seems that the statement was probably dictum as far as the decision in this case was concerned. In *Schenck* the basic test was "bad tendency" rather than "clear and present danger," which has sometimes been called the "rule of proximate causation." In two cases that closely followed, *Frohwerk* v. *United States* (249 U.S. 204, 1919) and *Debs* v. *United States* (249 U.S. 211, 1919), Holmes wrote the opinions for the unanimous decisions of the Court. Authorities differ as to whether Holmes used his "clear and present danger" test or the "bad tendency" test, but, if the former, it was a very mild version. In *Abrams* v. *United States* (250 U.S. 616, 1919) and *Schaefer* v. *United States,* (251 U.S. 466, 1920) Holmes, joined by Brandeis, dissented and held that the "clear and present danger" test should have been applied in these cases rather than the "bad tendency" test that the Court had applied. Actually the "clear and present danger" test was not used in a majority opinion to reverse a conviction until *Herndon* v. *Lowry* (301 U.S. 242, 1937).

It might be noted in passing that usually the guarantees of freedom of speech and press have been combined by the Court in decisions.

Schenk v. United States
249 U.S. 47; 39 S.Ct. 247; 63 L.Ed. 470 (1919)

(The Espionage Act of 1917 forbade any circulation of false statements made with intent to hinder the military effort, including attempts to cause disloyalty in the armed forces or to obstruct recruiting. Schenck, general secretary of the Socialist Party, sent out about fifteen thousand leaflets to persons who had been drafted urging them to oppose the Conscription Act. Arrested, he challenged the validity of the Espionage Act under the First Amendment guarantees of speech and press.)

Vote: No dissent

Mr. Justice Holmes delivered the opinion of the Court:

. . . We admit that in many places and in ordinary times the defendants in saying all that was said in the circular would have been within their constitutional rights. But the character of every act depends upon the circumstances in which it is done. . . . The most stringent protection of free speech would not protect a man in falsely shouting fire in a theatre and causing a panic. It does not even protect a man from an injunction against uttering words that may have all the effect of force. . . .

The question in every case is whether the words are used in such circumstances and are of such a nature as to create a clear and present danger that they will bring about the substantive evils that Congress has a right to prevent. It is a question of proximity and degree. When a nation is at war many things that might be said in time of peace are such a hindrance to its effort that their utterance will not be endured so long as men fight and that no court could regard them as protected by any constitutional right. It seems to be admitted that if an actual obstruction of the recruiting service were proved, liability for words that produced that effect might be enforced. The statute of 1917 in § 4 punishes conspiracies to obstruct as well as actual obstruction. If the act (speaking, or circulating a paper), its tendency, and the intent with which it is done are the same, we perceive no ground for saying that success alone warrants making the act a crime. . . .

Judgments affirmed.

RELATED CASES:

Frohwerk v. United States: 249 U.S. 204 (1919). Opinion: Holmes, J. No dissent.

The insertion of articles in a German language newspaper bringing into question the purposes of the war as well as the legal and practical justification of the draft is not protected by the Constitution. Here there was "clear and present danger" to the war effort—a little breath might have kindled a flame. Frohwerk was the publisher of a newspaper in Missouri. He was pro-German.

Debs v. United States: 249 U.S. 211 (1919). Opinion: Holmes, J. No dissent.

The delivery of a speech with such words and in such circumstances that the probable effect will be to prevent recruiting—and with that intent—is punishable under the Espionage Act of 1917 as amended in 1918. This case involving Eugene V. Debs arose at Canton, Ohio.

Abrams v. United States: 250 U.S. 616 (1919). Opinion: Clarke, J. Dissenting: Holmes, and Brandeis, JJ.

The publication of pamphlets opposing the sending of troops to Russia and urging a strike in the munitions industry is not protected by the Constitution. Holmes' dissent is famous. This case arose under the Sedition Act of 1918 which was repealed in 1921. Abrams had been born in Russia.

Schaefer v. United States: 251 U.S. 466 (1920). Opinion: McKenna, J. Dissenting: Brandeis, Holmes, and Clarke, JJ.

Persons conducting a newspaper who systematically took news dispatches from other papers and published them with omissions, additions and changes, with intent to promote the success of Germany and obstruct United States' enlistment and recruiting may be prosecuted under the Espionage Act.

Pierce v. United States: 252 U.S. 239 (1920). Opinion: Pitney, J. Dissenting: Brandeis and Holmes, JJ.

When a publication may "have a tendency to cause insubordination, disloyalty, and refusal of duty in the military and naval forces of the United States" those responsible may be held liable.

Hartzel v. United States: 322 U.S. 680 (1944). Opinion: Murphy, J. Dissenting: Reed, Frankfurter, Douglas, and Jackson, JJ.

The government must prove, beyond reasonable doubt, that a certain publication was distributed with the specific intent of interfering with the war effort and there must be a clear and present danger that these subversive activities will succeed.

Bond v. Floyd: 385 U.S. 116 (1966). Opinion: Warren, C.J. No dissent.

A majority of state legislators cannot test the sincerity with which another duly elected legislator can swear to uphold the Constitution. A state cannot apply to a legislator a First Amendment standard stricter than that applicable to a private citizen. Julian Bond, a Negro member of the Georgia House, had been ousted for criticism of Vietnam policy and the draft.

United States v. O'Brien: 391 U.S. 367 (1968). Opinion: Warren, C.J. Dissenting: Douglas, J. Abstaining: Marshall, J.

Federal law prohibits knowing destruction or mutilation of Selective Service registration certificates. This statute does not abridge free speech and is a proper exercise of the miltary power of Congress, the power to raise and support armies. This was the "draft card burning" case. The case arose in South Boston, Massachusetts.

Schact v. United States: 398 U.S. 58 (1970). Opinion: Black, J. No dissent.

A federal statute forbidding the wearing of the uniform or a part thereof of any of the armed forces of the United States in a theatrical production if the portrayal tends to discredit the armed forces is violative of free speech.

Cohen v. California: 403 U.S. 15 (1971). Opinion: Harlan, J. Dissenting: Blackmun, J., Burger, C.J., Black, J., and White, J.

Without a more particularized and compelling reason for actions, a state cannot, consistently with the First and Fourteenth Amendments, make the simple display of four-letter expletives a criminal offense.

NOTE:

In *Schenck* in a classic statement Justice Holmes (a Civil War veteran who had been wounded three times) first used the term "clear and present danger." It has been converted into a virtual dogma. However, it was really dictum in *Schenck* since the "bad tendency" test seems to be the basis for Holmes' decision. The first true use of "clear and present danger" (the rule of proximate causation) was in *Frohwerk*.

Following the cases that arose under the Espionage Act of 1917 the Court seemed to forget the "clear and present danger" test until 1937. Beginning then the test was revived and was given considerable application into the decade of the forties and brought about the voiding of a considerable amount of state regulatory legislation.

Gitlow v. New York
268 U.S. 652; 45 S.Ct. 625; 69 L.Ed. 1138 (1925)

(Benjamin Gitlow had been indicted for the statutory crime of criminal anarchy, that is, the advocacy that organized government should be overthrown by forceful means. He was convicted of writing and circulating publications that did just that. Gitlow challenged the validity of the statute under the Fourteenth Amendment.)

Vote: 7-2

Mr. Justice Sanford delivered the opinion of the Court:

. . . The precise question presented, and the only question which we can consider under this writ of error, then, is whether the statute, as construed and applied in this case by the state courts, deprived the defendant of his liberty of expression, in violation of the due process clause of the Fourteenth Amendment.

The statute does not penalize the utterance or publication of abstract "doctrine" or academic discussion having no quality of incitement to any concrete action. It is not aimed against mere historical or philosophical essays. It does not restrain the advocacy of changes in the form of government by constitutional and lawful means. What it prohibits is language advocating, advising, or teaching the overthrow of organized government by unlawful means. These words imply urging to action. Advocacy is defined in the Century Dictionary as: "1. The act of pleading for, supporting, or recommending; active espousal." It is not the abstract "doctrine" of overthrowing organized government by unlawful means which is denounced by the statute, but the advocacy of action for the accomplishment of that purpose. . . .

The Manifesto, plainly, is neither the statement of abstract doctrine nor, as suggested by counsel, mere prediction that industrial disturbances and revolutionary mass strikes will result spontaneously in an inevitable process of evolution in the economic system. It advocates and urges in fervent language mass action which shall progressively foment industrial disturbances, and, through political mass strikes and revolutionary mass action, overthrow and destroy organized parliamentary government. It concludes with a call to action in these words: "The proletariat revolution and the Communist reconstruction of society—*the struggle for these*—is now indispensable. . . . The Communist International calls the proletariat of the world to the final struggle!" This is not the expression of philosophical abstraction, the mere prediction of future events; it is the language of direct incitement.

The means advocated for bringing about the destruction of organized parliamentary government, namely, mass industrial revolts usurping the functions of municipal government, political mass strikes directed against the parliamentary state, and revolutionary mass action for its final destruction, necessarily imply the use of force and violence, and in their essential nature are inherently unlawful in a constitutional government of law and order. That the jury were warranted in finding that the Manifesto advocated not merely the abstract doctrine of overwhelming organized government by force, violence, and unlawful means, but action to that end, is clear.

For present purposes we may and do assume that freedom of speech and of the press—which are protected by the First Amendment from abridgement by Congress —are among the fundamental personal rights and "liberties" protected by the due process clause of the Fourteenth Amendment from impairment by the states. . . .

It is a fundamental principle, long established, that freedom of speech and of the press which is secured by the Constitution does not confer an absolute right to speak or publish, without responsibility, whatever one may choose, or an unrestricted and unbridled license that gives immunity for every possible use of language, and prevents the punishment of those who abuse this freedom. . . . Reasonably limited, it was said by Story . . . this freedom is an inestimable privilege in a free government; without such limitation, it might become the scourge of the republic.

That a state, in the exercise of its police power, may punish those who abuse this freedom by utterances inimical to the public welfare, tending to corrupt public morals, incite to crime, or disturb the public peace, is not open to question. . . . Thus it was held by this court in the *Fox* case, that a state may punish publications advocating and encouraging a breach of its criminal laws; and, in the *Gilbert* case, that a state may punish utterances teaching or advocating that its citizens should not assist the United States in prosecuting or carrying on war with its public enemies.

And, for yet more imperative reasons, a state may punish utterances endangering the foundations of organized government and threatening its overthrow by unlawful means. These imperil its own existence as a constitutional state. Freedom of speech and press, said Story . . ., does not protect disturbances of the public peace or the attempt to subvert the government. It does not protect publications or teachings which tend to subvert or imperil the government, or to impede or hinder it in the performance of its governmental duties. . . . It does not protect publications prompting the overthrow of government by force; the punishment of those who publish articles which tend to destroy organized society being essential to the security of freedom and the stability of the state. . . . And a state may penalize utterances which openly advocate the overthrow of the representative and constitutional form of government of the United States and the several states, by violence or other unlawful means. . . . In short, this freedom does not deprive a state of the primary and essential right of self-preservation, which so long as human governments endure, they cannot be denied. . . .

By enacting the present statute the state has determined, through its legislative body, that utterances advocating the overthrow of organized government by force, violence, and unlawful means, are so inimical to the general welfare, and involve such danger of substantive evil, that they may be penalized in the exercise of its police power. That determination must be given great weight. Every presumption is to be indulged in favor of the validity of the statute. . . . That utterances inciting to the overthrow of organized government by unlawful means present a sufficient danger of substantive evil to bring their punishment within the range of legislative discretion is clear. Such utterances, by their very nature, involve danger to the public peace and to the security of the state. They threaten breaches of the peace and ultimate revolution. And the immediate danger is none the less real and substantial because the effect of a given utterance cannot be accurately foreseen. The state cannot reasonably be required to measure the danger from every such utterance in the nice balance of a jeweler's scale. A single revolutionary spark may kindle a fire that, smoldering for a time, may burst into a sweeping and destructive conflagration. It cannot be said that the state is acting arbitrarily or unreasonably when, in the exercise of its judgment as to the measures necessary to protect the public peace and safety, it seeks to extinguish the spark without waiting until it has enkindled the flame or blazed into the conflagration. It cannot reasonably be required to defer the adoption of measures for its own peace and safety until the revolutionary utterances lead to actual disturbances of the public peace or imminent and immediate danger of its own destruction; but it may, in the exercise of its judgment, suppress the threatened danger of its incipiency. . . .

We cannot hold that the present statute is an arbitrary or unreasonable exercise of the police power of the state, unwarrantably infringing the freedom of speech or press; and we must and do sustain its constitutionality. . . .

Mr. Justice Holmes dissented, joined by Mr. Justice Brandeis:

Mr. Justice Brandeis and I are of opinion that this judgment should be reversed. The general principle of free speech, it seems to me, must be taken to be included in the Fourteenth Amendment, in view of the scope that has been given to the word "liberty" as there used, although perhaps it may be accepted with a somewhat larger latitude of interpretation than is allowed to Congress by the sweeping language that governs, or ought to govern, the laws of the United States. If I am right, then I think that the criterion sanctioned by the full court in *Schenck* v. *United States*, 249 U.S. 47, applies: "The question in every case is whether the words used are used in such circumstances and are of such a nature as to create a clear and present danger that they will bring about the substantive evils that [the state] has a right to prevent." It is true that in my opinion this criterion was departed from in *Abrams* v. *United States*, 250 U.S. 616, but the convictions that I express in that case are too deep for it to be possible for me as yet to believe that it and *Schaefer* v. *United States*, 251 U.S. 466, have settled the law. If what I think the correct test is applied, it is manifest that there was no present danger of an attempt to overthrow the government by force on the part of the admittedly small minority who shared the defendant's views. It is said that this Manifesto was more than a theory, that it was an incitement. Every idea is an incitement. It offers itself for belief, and if believed, it is acted on unless some other belief outweighs it, or some failure of energy stifles the movement at its birth. The only difference between the expression of an opinion and an incitement in the narrower sense is the speaker's enthusiasm for the result. Eloquence may set fire to reason. But whatever may be thought of the redundant discourse before us, it had no chance of starting a present conflagration. If, in the long run, the beliefs expressed in proletarian dictatorship are destined to be accepted by the dominant forces of the community, the only meaning of free speech is that they should be given their chance and have their way.

If the publication of this document has been laid as an attempt to induce an uprising against government at once, and not at some indefinite time in the future, it would have presented a different question. The object would have been one with which the law might deal, subject to the doubt whether there was any danger that the publication could produce any result; or, in other words, whether it was not futile and too remote from possible consequences. But the indictment alleges the publication and nothing more.

RELATED CASES:

Barron v. Baltimore: 7 Peters 243 (1833). Opinion: Marshall, C.J. No dissent.

The general provisions of the Constitution (here the Fifth Amendment) apply only to the federal government and not the states.

Prudential Insurance Company v. Cheek: 259 U.S. 530 (1922). Opinion: Pitney, J. Dissenting: Taft, C.J., VanDevanter, and McReynolds, JJ.

No part of the Constitution, including the Fourteenth Amendment, imposes on the states any restriction regarding freedom of speech.

Meyer v. Nebraska: 262 U.S. 390 (1923). Opinion: McReyonlds, J. Dissenting: Holmes and Sutherland, JJ.

"Liberty" includes the right of a person to engage in occupations of his choosing, to marry, to acquire useful knowledge, to worship God, and to enjoy those privileges long recognized as essential to the orderly pursuit of happiness by free men.

Pierce v. Society of Sisters: 268 U.S. 510 (1925). Opinion: McReynolds, J. No dissent.

A state compulsory education act which requires, in general, that children between eight and sixteen years of age be sent to the public school in the area where they reside is an unreasonable interference with the liberty of the parents and guardians to direct the upbringing of the children and in that respect violates the Fourteenth Amendment. Also the point was made that damage would be caused to the business of education and the property of the schools.

Whitney v. California: 274 U.S. 357 (1927). Opinion: Sanford, J. No dissent.

United and joint action involves greater danger to public peace and security than the isolated utterance and acts of individuals. The state may reasonably regulate such. Whitney was convicted of criminal syndicalism. Brandeis concurring opinion excellent.

Near v. Minnesota: 283 U.S. 697 (1931). Opinion: Hughes, C.J. Dissenting: Butler, VanDevanter, McReynolds, and Sutherland, JJ.

Previous restraint is invalid censorship as applied to publications. Subsequent punishment for such abuses is the proper remedy. See p. 82, below.

Powell v. Alabama: 287 U.S. 45 (1932). Opinion: Sutherland, J. Dissenting: Butler and McReynolds, JJ.

Denial of reasonable time and opportunity to secure counsel is a clear denial of due process. See p. 244, below.

DeJonge v. Oregon: 299 U.S. 353 (1937). Opinion: Hughes, C.J. No dissent. Abstaining: Stone, J.

Holding a peaceful meeting for lawful discussion, even a meeting held under the auspices of the Communist Party, cannot be held a crime. Such action is contrary to the First and Fourteenth Amendments. See p. 121, below.

Herndon v. Lowry: 301 U.S. 242 (1937). Opinion: Roberts, J. Dissenting: VanDevanter, McReynolds, Sutherland, and Butler, JJ.

Attempts to make mere membership in the Communist Party and solicitation of party membership criminal actions constitute an unwarrantable invasion of the right of free speech. Herndon, a Communist organizer in Georgia, was convicted of attempting to incite to insurrection. Lowry was the Sheriff of Fulton County. This was the first use of the "clear and present danger" test in a majority opinion to reverse a conviction.

Palko v. Connecticut: 302 U.S. 319 (1937). Opinion: Cardozo, J. Dissenting: Butler, J.

The double jeopardy provision of the Fifth Amendment does not apply to the states by virtue of the Fourteenth Amendment. Further there was no deprivation of due process in holding a second trial when there had been errors in the first trial. See p. 237, below.

United States v. Carolene Products Co.: 304 U.S. 144 (1938). Opinion: Stone, J. Dissenting: McReynolds, J. Abstaining: Reed and Cardozo, JJ.

In this context this case is noteworthy for the footnote appended by Mr. Justice Stone setting forth for probably the first time the preferred position of First Amendment freedoms. 304 U.S. 144 at 152-153; 58 S.Ct. 778 at 783-784; 82 L.Ed. 1234 at 1241-1242. However, this same idea had been expressed earlier by Mr. Justice Roberts (*Herndon* v. *Lowry*, 301 U.S. 242, 1927) and by Mr. Justice Cardozo (*Palko* v. *Connecticut*, 302 U.S. 319, 1937).

Schneider v. Irvington: 308 U.S. 147 (1939). Opinion: Roberts, J. Dissenting: McReynolds, J.

The purpose of keeping the streets clean is not sufficient to prevent persons from distributing literature on a street. This case involved the concept of "preferred position" again. Schneider was convicted of violation of a city ordinance of Irvington, New Jersey, by distributing a handbill on the war in Spain. The Court made particular note of its opinion that *commercial* activity of this sort could be regulated.

Cantwell v. Connecticut: 310 U.S. 296 (1940). Opinion: Roberts, J. No dissent.

No administrative officer can be given the discretion to determine the validity of religious causes. This is a denial of liberty and religion under the Fourteenth Amendment and First Amendment. See p. 12, above.

Thomas v. Collins: 323 U.S. 516 (1945). Opinion: Rutledge, J. Dissenting: Roberts, J., Stone, C.J., Reed and Frankfurter, JJ.

A state requirement of registration before soliciting memberships in a labor union is a violation of the guarantees of free speech and free assembly. See p. 108, below.

Wolf v. Colorado: 338 U.S. 25 (1949). Opinion: Frankfurter, J. Dissenting: Rutledge, Murphy, and Douglas, JJ.

In a prosecution in a state court for a state crime the Fourteenth Amendment does not forbid the admission of evidence obtained by unreasonable search and seizure. See p. 262, below.

Mapp v. Ohio: 367 U.S. 643 (1961). Opinion: Clark, J. Dissenting: Harlan, Frankfurter, and Whittaker, JJ.

All evidence obtained by search and seizure in violation of the Constitution is inadmissible in state courts. The Fourth Amendment's guarantee of freedom from unreasonable search and seizure is thus applied to the states completely. See p. 265, below.

Robinson v. California: 370 U.S. 660 (1962). Opinion: Stewart, J. Dissenting: Clark and White, JJ. Abstaining: Frankfurter, J.

For a state to make the status of narcotic addiction a criminal offense for which one may be prosecuted and imprisoned even though he had not possessed or used any narcotics in that state or been guilty of any antisocial behavior there is cruel and unusual punishment under the Eighth Amendment applied to the states by means of the Fourteenth Amendment.

Gideon v. Wainwright: 372 U.S. 335 (1963). Opinion: Black, J. No dissent.

The right of a person charged with either a capital or a noncaptial crime to counsel is fundamental and essential to a fair trial. Thus the "counsel provision" of the Sixth Amendment is completely applied to the states under the Fourteenth Amendment. See p. 248, below.

Brandenburg v. Ohio: 395 U.S. 444 (1969). Opinion: Per Curiam, No dissent.

An Ohio criminal syndicalism statute was ruled unconstitutional because it purported to punish advocacy and to forbid assembly merely to advocate the proscribed action. By reason thereof the statute violated the First and Fourteenth Amendments. This case overruled *Whitney* v. *California*, above.

Furman v. Georgia: 408 U.S. 238 (1972). Opinion: Per Curiam. Dissenting: Burger, C.J., Blackmun, Powell, and Rehnquist, JJ.

The imposition and carrying out of the death penalty in the three cases here under review was voided under the cruel and unusual punishment clause of the Eighth Amendment. Concurring and dissenting opinions by all nine justices seemed to hold (with the exception of Justices Brennan and Marshall) that the death penalty was not conclusively rejected and that a properly drawn and administered statute could survive a challenge in the Court. All of the opinions taken together total 242 pages in the official reports.

NOTE:

Gitlow is one of the most important and far-reaching decisions of the Court in a century. It is also surprisingly misunderstood by many persons who should know better. All that the Court does is to define the abstract term "liberty" in the Fourteenth Amendment by adopting the specifics of the First Amendment. This, then, is *liberty* and the Fourteenth Amendment says that no state can deprive any person of these things without due process. Without the "Gitlow doctrine" many, if not most, of the present-day cases voiding state laws would not be possible.

As to just where we stand now on the application to the states of the specifics of the Bill of Rights, by the simple process of elimination it can be found that the First Amendment is applied in its entirety, while the Second and Third amendments remain untouched and will probably continue so for an indefinite future for their practical inapplicability. In the Fifth Amendment, grand jury indictment has remained exclusively federal in operation, and the due process provisions of the Fifth Amendment are specifically applied to the states by the Fourteenth Amendment, so those in the Fifth need not be touched in the *Gitlow* sense. In the Sixth Amendment only the requirement that the accused be informed of the nature and cause of the accusation has not been positively applied, and this, one can confidently state, would certainly be applied if a case should arise. The Seventh Amendment remains intact as a federal "reserve." The Eighth Amendment's prohibitions of excessive bail and excessive fines have not yet been "incorporated." What will be found in the "glittering generalization" of the Ninth Amendment is an unknown quantity but the Court has already indicated that right of privacy can be found there.

Practically there remain unapplied to the states grand jury indictments, civil suit juries, and excessive bail and fines. By the cumulative process, the "absorptionists" of *Adamson* appear to have won.

Even though a specific provision of the Bill of Rights has not been declared "fundamental" this does not mean that the provision will not be applied to state operations. There is a second test which the Court applies to determine the applicability of guarantees. If under the peculiar circumstances of a case the facts show that an accused person has been denied essential justice or fairness, the Court will hold that due process requires that the accused be protected. The effective difference between the two tests is obvious. Under the definition-of-liberty test where the Court distinguishes between "formal" and "fundamental" rights, the inclusion of a specific guarantee means that henceforth that provision of the Constitution is to be as applicable in the areas of state operation as it is in regard to federal matters. In the second type of test where the Court determines that a particular procedure denies essential justice and is thus violative of due process, there is much more flexibility involved while at the same time the rights of accused persons are safeguarded. Here the particular provision is not henceforth to be applied rigidly at all times but only when under a given set of circumstances there will be lack of essential fairness.

Dennis v. United States
341 U.S. 494; 71 S.Ct. 857; 95 L.Ed. 1137 (1951)

(Congress passed the Alien Registration Act—the Smith Act—in 1940. This forbade the advocacy of force to overthrow the government or membership in an organization that advocates forceful overthrow. Eleven Communist leaders were indicted for knowingly conspiring to organize the United States Communist Party as a group teaching and advocating the violent overthrow of the government of the United States, as well as themselves teaching and advocating such overthrow. The trial was held in District Judge Harold Medina's court in New York City. It lasted eight months. The Smith Act was challenged as being contrary to free speech.)

Vote: 6-2

Mr. Chief Justice Vinson delivered the opinion of the Court:

. . . The obvious purpose of the statute is to protect existing Government, not from change by peaceable, lawful and constitutional means, but from change by violence, revolution and terrorism. That it is within the *power* of the Congress to protect the Government of the United States from armed rebellion is a proposition which requires little discussion. Whatever theoretical merit there may be to the argument that there is a "right" to rebellion against dictatorial governments is without force where the existing structure of the government provides for peaceful and orderly change. We reject any principle of governmental helplessness in the face of preparation for revolution, which principle, carried to its logical conclusion, must lead to anarchy. No one could conceive that it is not within the power of Congress to prohibit acts intended to overthrow the Government by force and violence. The question with which we are concerned here is not whether Congress has such *power*, but whether the *means* which it has employed conflict with the First and Fifth Amendments to the Constitution.

One of the bases for the contention that the means which Congress has employed are invalid takes the form of an attack on the fact of the statute on the grounds that by its terms it prohibits academic discussion of the merits of Marxism-Leninism, that it stifles ideas and is contrary to all concepts of a free speech and a free press. Although we do not agree that the language itself has that significance, we must bear in mind that it is the duty of the federal courts to interpret federal legislation in a manner not inconsistent with the demands of the Constitution. . . . This is a federal statute which we must interpret as well as judge. . . .

The very language of the Smith Act negates the interpretation which petitioners would have us impose on that Act. It is directed at advocacy, not discussion. Thus, the trial judge properly charged the jury that they could not convict if they found that petitioners did "no more than pursue peaceful studies and discussions or teaching and advocacy in the realm of ideas." He further charged that it was not unlawful "to conduct in an American college and university a course explaining the philosophical theories set forth in the books which have been placed in evidence." Such a charge is in strict accord with the statutory language, and illustrates the meaning to be placed on those words. Congress did not intend to eradicate the free discussion of political theories, to destroy the traditional rights of Americans to discuss and evaluate ideas without fear of governmental sanction. Rather Congress was concerned with the very kind of activity in which the evidence showed these petitioners engaged. . . .

We pointed out in *Douds* that the basis of the First Amendment is the hypothesis that speech can rebut speech, propaganda will answer propaganda, free debate of ideas will result in the wisest governmental policies. It is for this reason that this Court has recognized the inherent value of free discourse. An analysis of the leading cases in this Court which have involved direct limitations on speech, however, will demonstrate that both the majority of the Court and the dissenters in particular cases have recognized that this is not an unlimited, unqualified right, but that the societal value of speech must, on occasion, be subordinated to other values and considerations. . . .

. . . Speech is not an absolute, above and beyond control by the legislature when its judgment, subject to review here, is that certain kinds of speech are so undesirable as to warrant criminal sanction. Nothing is more certain in modern society than the principle that there are no absolutes, that a name, a phrase, a standard has meaning only when associated with the considerations which gave birth to the nomenclature. To those who would paralyze our Government in the face of impending threat by encasing it in a semantic straitjacket we must reply that all concepts are relative.

In this case we are squarely presented with the application of the "clear and present danger" test, and must decide what that phrase imports. We first note that many of the cases in which this Court has reversed convictions by use of this or similar tests have been based on the fact that the interest which the State was attempting to protect was itself too insubstantial to warrant restriction of speech. . . . Overthrow of the Government by force and violence is certainly a substantial enough interest for the Government to limit speech. Indeed, this is the ultimate value of any society, for if a society cannot protect its very structure from armed internal attack, it must follow that no subordinate value can be protected. If, then, this interest may be protected, the literal problem which is presented is what has been meant by the use of the phrase "clear and present danger" of the utterances bringing about the evil within the power of Congress to punish.

Obviously, the words cannot mean that before the Government may act, it must wait until the *putsch* is about to be executed, the plans have been laid and the signal is awaited. If Government is aware that a group aiming at its overthrow is attempting to indoctrinate its members and to commit them to a course whereby they will strike when the leaders feel the circumstances permit, action by the Government is required. The argument that there is no need for Governent to concern itself, for Government is strong, it possesses ample powers to put down a rebellion, it may defeat the revolution with ease needs no answer. For that is not the question. Certainly an attempt to overthrow the Government by force, even though doomed from the outset because of inadequate numbers or power of the revolutionists, is a sufficient evil for Congress to prevent. The damage which such attempts create both physically and politically to a nation makes it impossible to measure the validity in terms of the probability of success, or the immediacy of a successful attempt. In the instant case the trial judge charged the jury that they could not convict unless they found that petitioners intended to overthrow the Government "as speedily as circumstances would permit." This does not mean, and could not properly mean, that they would not strike until there was certainty of success. What was meant was that the revolutionists would strike when they thought the time was ripe. We must therefore reject the contention that success or probability of success is the criterion.

The situation with which Justices Holmes and Brandeis were concerned in *Gitlow* was a comparatively isolated event bearing little relation in their minds to any substantial threat to the safety of the community. . . . They were not confronted with any situation comparable to the instant one—the development of an apparatus designed and dedicated to the overthrow of the Government, in the context of world crisis after crisis.

Chief Judge Leonard Hand, writing for the majority below, interpreted the phrase as follows: "In each case [courts] must ask whether the gravity of the 'evil,' discounted by its improbability, justifies such invasion of free speech as is necessary to avoid the danger." We adopt this statement of the rule. As articulated by Chief Judge Hand, it is as succinct and inclusive as any other we might devise at this time. It takes into consideration those facts which we deem relevant, and relates their significances. More we cannot expect from words.

Likewise, we are in accord with the court below, which affirmed the trial court's finding that the requisite danger existed. The mere fact that from the period 1945 to 1948 petitioners' activities did not result in an attempt to overthrow the Government by force and violence is of course no answer to the fact that there was a group that was ready to make the attempt. The formation by petitioners of such a highly organized conspiracy, with rigidly disciplined members subject to call when the leaders, these petitioners, felt that the time had come for action, coupled with the inflammable nature of world conditions, similar uprisings in other countries, and the touch-and-go nature of our relations with countries with whom petitioners were in the very least ideologically attuned, convince us that their convictions were justified on this score. And this analysis disposes of the contention that a conspiracy to advocate, as distinguished from the advocacy itself, cannot be constitutionally restrained, because it comprises only the preparation. It is the existence of all conspiracy which creates the danger. . . . If the ingredients of the reaction are present, we cannot bind the Government to wait until the catalyst is added. . . .

When facts are found that establish the violation of a statute the protection against conviction afforded by the First Amendment is a matter of law. The doctrine that there must be a clear and present danger of a substantive evil that Congress has a right to prevent is a judicial rule to be applied as a matter of law by the courts. The guilt is established by proof of facts. Whether the First Amendment protects the activity which constitutes the violation of the statute must depend upon a judicial determination of the scope of the First Amendment applied to the circumstances of the case. . . .

Mr. Justice Frankfurter concurred:

. . . Free speech cases are not an exception to the principle that we are not legislators, that direct policy-making is not our province. How best to reconcile competing interests is the business of legislatures, and the balance they strike is a judgment not to be displaced by ours, but to be respected unless outside the pale of fair judgment. . . .

It is not for us to decide how we would adjust the clash of interests which this case presents were the primary responsibility for reconciling it ours. Congress has determined that the danger created by advocacy of overthrow justifies the ensuing restriction on freedom of speech. The determination was made after due deliberation, and the seriousness of the congressional purpose is attested by the volume of legislation passed to effectuate the same ends. . . .

Mr. Justice Jackson concurred:

. . . The "clear and present danger" test was an innovation by Mr. Justice Holmes in the *Schenck* case, reiterated and refined by him and Mr. Brandeis in later cases, all arising before the era of World War II revealed the subtlety and efficacy of modernized revolutionary techniques used by totalitarian parties. In those cases, they were faced with convictions under so-called criminal syndicalism statutes aimed at anarchists but which, loosely construed, had been applied to punish socialism, pacifism, and left-wing ideologies, the charges often resting on far-fetched inferences which, if true, would establish only technical or trivial violations. They proposed "clear and present danger" as a test for the sufficiency of evidence in particular cases. . . .

I think reason is lacking for applying that test to this case. . . .

The authors of the clear and present danger test never applied it to a case like this, nor would I. If applied as it is proposed here, it means that the Communist plotting is protected during its period of incubation; its preliminary stages of organization and preparation are immune from the law; the Government can move only after imminent action is manifest, when it would, of course, be too late. . . .

Mr. Justice Black dissented:

. . . At the outset I want to emphasize what the crime involved in this case is, and what it is not. These petitioners were not charged with an attempt to overthrow the Government. They were not even charged with overt acts of any kind designed to overthrow the Government. They were not even charged with saying anything or writing anything designed to overthrow the Government. The charge was that they agreed to assemble and to talk and publish certain ideas at a later date. The indictment is that they conspired to organize the Communist Party and to use speech or newspapers and other publications in the future to teach and advocate the forcible overthrow of the Government. No matter how it is worded, this is a virulent form of prior censorship of speech and press, which I believe the First Amendment forbids. I would hold § 3 of the Smith Act authorizing this prior restraint unconstitutional on its face and as applied. . . .

Public opinion being what it now is, few will protest the conviction of these Communist petitioners. There is hope, however, that in calmer times, when present pressures, passions and fears subside, this or some later Court will restore the First Amendment liberties to the high preferred place where they belong in a free society.

Mr. Justice Douglas dissented:

. . . The Act, as construed, requires the element of intent—that those who teach the creed believe in it. The crime then depends not on what is taught but on who the teacher is. That is to make freedom of speech turn not on *what is said*, but on the *intent* with which it is said. Once we start down that road we enter territory dangerous to the liberties of every citizen. . . .

NOTE:

Dennis can take its place alongside *Marbury* v. *Madison* and the *Dred Scott Case* as cases that need never have happened. The Court here could very well have interpreted the Smith Act as not applying to the actions of the defendants in this case.

The statement of Judge Learned Hand, which the Court adopted, means simply that for a grave evil there need be slight probability of the occurrence to justify restrictions on speech but for a slight evil there must be great probability of its happening before there can be justifiable limits placed on speech. This is really a reinterpretation of the Holmes-Brandeis "clear and present danger" rule. It takes the time element out of the older rule and makes it clear and *probable* danger.

This case should not be confused with the one summarized immediately below. Both involved Eugene Dennis, Executive Secretary of the Communist Party, but the matters dealt with are entirely different.

RELATED CASE:

Dennis v. United States: 339 U.S. 162 (1950). Opinion: Minton, J. Dissenting: Black and Frankfurter, J.J. Abstaining: Douglas and Clark, J.J.

The Secretary General of the Communist Party of the United States was not denied a trial "by an impartial jury" even though seven government employees served on the jury. No actual bias was shown and none was presumed merely because of government employment.

Yates v. United States
354 U.S. 298; 77 S.Ct. 1064; 1 L.Ed. 2nd 1356 (1957)

(This case—which might be called "the Second Dennis Case"—involved the convictions of fourteen Communists for violation of the Smith Act. Their conviction was for conspiring to advocate and to teach forceful overthrow of the government of the United States and for conspiring to organize the Communist Party of the United States. These were the same basic charges of the Dennis case, but the persons involved here were lesser or "second string" members of the Communist Party. The case came out of California.)

Vote: 6-1

Mr. Justice Harlan delivered the opinion of the Court:

. . . Petitioners claim that "organize" means to "establish," "found," or "bring into existence," and that in this sense the Communist Party was organized by 1945 at the latest. On this basis petitioners contend that this part of the indictment, returned in 1951, was barred by the three-year statute of limitations. . . .

We conclude, therefore, that since the Communist Party came into being in

1945, and the indictment was not returned until 1951, the three-year statute of limitations had run out on the "organizing" charge, and required the withdrawal of that part of the indictment from the jury's consideration. . . .

In failing to distinguish between advocacy of forcible overthrow as an abstract doctrine and advocacy of action to that end, the District Court appears to have been led astray by the holding in *Dennis* that advocacy of violent action to be taken at some future time was enough. It seems to have considered that, since "inciting" speech is usually thought of as calculated to induce immediate action, and since *Dennis* held advocacy of action for future overthrow sufficient, this meant that advocacy, irrespective of its tendency to generate action, is punishable, provided only that it is uttered with a specific intent to accomplish overthrow. In other words, the District Court apparently thought that *Dennis* obliterated the traditional dividing line between advocacy of abstract doctrine and advocacy of action.

This misconceives the situation confronting the Court in *Dennis* and what was held there. Although the jury's verdict, interpreted in light of the trial court's instructions, did not justify the conclusion that the defendants' advocacy was directed at, or created any danger of, immediate overthrow, it did establish that the advocacy was aimed at building up a seditious group and maintaining it in readiness for action at a propitious time. . . . The essence of the *Dennis* holding was that indoctrination of a group in preparation for future violent action, as well as exhortation to immediate action, by advocacy found to be directed to "action for the accomplishment" of forcible overthrow, to violence "as a rule or principle of action," and employing "language of incitement," is not constitutionally protected when the group is of sufficient size and cohesiveness, is sufficiently oriented towards action, and other circumstances are such as reasonably to justify apprehension that action will occur. This is quite a different thing from the view of the District Court here that mere doctrinal justification of forcible overthrow, if engaged in with the intent to accomplish overthrow, is punishable per se under the Smith Act. That sort of advocacy, even though uttered with the hope that it may ultimately lead to violent revolution, is too remote from concrete action to be regarded as the kind of indoctrination preparatory to action which was condemned in *Dennis*. As one of the concurring opinions in *Dennis* put it: "Throughout our decisions there has recurred a distinction between the statement of an idea which may prompt its hearers to take unlawful action, and advocacy that such action be taken." There is nothing in *Dennis* which makes that historic distinction obsolete. . . .

In light of the foregoing we are unable to regard the District Court's charge upon this aspect of the case as adequate. The jury was never told that the Smith Act does not denounce advocacy in the sense of preaching abstractly the forcible overthrow of the Government. We think that the trial court's statement that the proscribed advocacy must include the "urging," "necessity," and "duty" of forcible overthrow, and not merely its "desirability" and "propriety," may not be regarded as a sufficient substitute for charging that the Smith Act reaches only advocacy of action for the overthrow of government by force and violence. The essential distinction is that those to whom the advocacy is addressed must be urged to *do* something, now or in the future, rather than merely to *believe* in something. At best the expressions used by the trial court were equivocal, since in the absence of any instructions differentiating advocacy of abstract doctrine from advocacy of action, they were as consistent with the former as they were with the latter. . . .

[Of the fourteen persons involved in this proceeding, the Court ordered the acquittal of five since there was no evidence to connect them with the conspiracy except the fact of party membership. New trials were ordered for the remaining nine since the Court held that there was the possibility of their conviction by a jury since they had been active individually in a way other than party membership.]

Mr. Justice Brennan and Mr. Justice Whittaker took no part in the consideration or decision of this case.

Mr. Justice Black, with whom Mr. Justice Douglas joined, concurred in part and dissented in part:

I would reverse every one of these convictions and direct that all the defendants be acquitted. In my judgment the statutory provisions on which these prosecutions are based abridge freedom of speech, press and assembly in violation of the First Amendment to the United States Constitution. . . .

. . . I cannot agree that "justice" requires this Court to send these cases back to put these defendants in jeopardy again in violation of the spirit if not the letter of the Fifth Amendment's provision against double jeopardy. . . .

In essence, petitioners were tried upon the charge that they believe in and want to foist upon this country a different and to us a despicable form of authoritarian government in which voices criticizing the existing order are summarily silenced. I fear that the present type of prosecutions are more in line with the philosophy of authoritarian government than with that expressed by our First Amendment. . . .

Mr. Justice Clark dissented:

. . . The conspiracy charged here is the same as in *Dennis*, except that here it is geared to California conditions, and brought, for the period 1948 to 1951, under the general conspiracy statute, 18 U.S.C. § 371, rather than the old conspiracy section of the Smith Act. The indictment charges petitioners with a conspiracy to violate two sections of the Smith Act, as recodified in 18 U.S.C. § 2385 by knowingly and wilfully (1) teaching and advocating the violent overthrow of the government of the United States, and (2) organizing in California through the creation of groups, cells, schools, assemblies of persons, and the like, the Communist Party, a society which teaches or advocates the violent overthrow of the Government.

The conspiracy includes the same group of defendants as in the *Dennis* case though petitioners here occupied a lower echelon in the party hierarchy. They, nevertheless, served in the same army and engaged in the same mission. . . .

RELATED CASES:

Lightfoot v. United States: 355 U.S. 2 (1957). Per Curiam. No dissent.

In this case the Supreme Court on the authority of *Jencks* reversed *per curiam* a judgment of the Seventh Circuit Court of Appeals, affirming defendant's conviction for violation of the Smith Act. The Seventh Circuit had held constitutional the "membership clause" of the Smith Act which subjected a member of a group advocating the overthrow of the government by force or violence to a criminal penalty, provided he knew of the group's purposes.

Nowak v. United States: 356 U.S. 660 (1958). Opinion: Harlan, J. Dissenting: Burton, Clark, and Whittaker, JJ.

Naturalization can be voided only by a showing of illegal acquisition that is clear, unequivocal, and convincing. See also *Schneiderman* v. *United States*, 320 U.S. 118 (1943), p. 74, below.

Maisenberg v. United States: 356 U.S. 670 (1958). Opinion: Harlan, J. Dissenting: Burton, Clark, and Whittaker, JJ.

Appellant's citizenship (naturalized) could not be revoked because of material willful misrepresentation (membership in Communist Party within 5 years) because the government did not prove by "clear, unequivocal, and convincing evidence" that she knew the Party advocated the violent overthrow of the Government.

Communist Party v. Subversive Activities Control Board: 367 U.S. 1 (1961). Opinion: Frankfurter, J. Dissenting: Warren, C.J., and Black, Douglas, and Brennan, JJ.

Registration provisions of the Subversive Activities Control Act (Title I of the Internal Security Act of 1950, otherwise known as the McCarran Act) were held valid in this case. The Court held it would be a distortion of the First Amendment to use it to void this legislation. It was not a bill of attainder because it attaches to described activities and not to specified organizations. Further, there was adequate provision for hearings. See also *Albertson* v. *SACB,* 382 U.S. 70 (1965), p. 153, below; *Aptheker* v. *Secretary of State,* 378 U.S. 500 (1964), p. 345, below; and *United States* v. *Robel,* 389 U.S. 258 (1967), p. 74, below.

Scales v. United States: 367 U.S. 203 (1961). Opinion: Harlan, J. Dissenting: Douglas, Black, and Brennan, JJ., and Warren, C.J.

Active membership in an organization engaged in illegal advocacy by one having guilty knowledge and intent is a violation of the Smith Act. In this the Smith Act does not violate the due process guarantee of the Constitution. Involved here was *present* advocacy of *future* action. The guilt was personal, not guilt by association, and there was no punishment for membership as such.

NOTE:

Yates "clarified" *Dennis,* the Court going to great lengths to emphasize that *Dennis* had not been overruled. In *Yates,* Frankfurter and Burton changed their votes from their stand in the *Dennis* case. The other members of the majority in *Dennis* were either dead or had retired from the Court. The lone dissenter in *Yates,* Clark, did not participate in *Dennis.* Obviously the conditions set down in *Yates* make very difficult the securing of convictions under the Smith Act. The opinion made several points. Any charge of "organizing" a subversive group must be considered in connection with the statute of limitations. The trial judge's charge to the jury must distinguish between advocacy of abstract doctrine (not illegal) and advocacy directed at promoting unlawful action (illegal). The Court also set forth some rules of evidence that must be abided by in the prosecution of persons under the statute. Some measure of the difficulties posed by the decision is indicated by the fact that six months after *Yates* indictments against the remaining nine defendants were dismissed by the Department of Justice.

The question of whether the members of the Communist Party are protected by the First Amendment is fundamentally a question of fact, that is, the real objectives and means involved. Illegal advocacy involves the teaching of forceful overthrow of government accompanied by directions as to means. Mere advocacy unrelated to its tendency to produce forcible action is not regarded as criminal, but constitutional protection does not extend to the point where such advocacy involves "clear and present danger."

American Comunications Ass'n v. Douds
339 U.S. 382; 70 S.Ct. 674; 94 L.Ed. 925 (1950)

(The non-Communist affidavit provision of the Labor Management Relations Act of 1947—the Taft-Hartley Act—was brought into question here. This provision —Section 9(h)—barred any investigation by the National Labor Relations Board unless all officers of a labor organization involved in a dispute signed an affidavit certifying that they were not Communists and did not advocate the overthrow of the United States government by force or by illegal means.)

Vote: 5-1

Mr. Chief Justice Vinson delivered the opinion of the Court:

. . . The unions contend that the necessary effect of § 9(h) is to make it impossible for persons who cannot sign the oath to be officers of labor unions. They urge that such a statute violates fundamental rights guaranteed by the First Amendment: the right of union officers to hold what political views they choose and to associate with what political groups they will, and the right of unions to choose their officers without interference from government. The Board has argued, on the other hand, that § 9(h) presents no First Amendment problem because its sole sanction is the withdrawal from noncomplying unions of the "privilege" of using its facilities. . . .

Neither contention states the problem with complete accuracy. . . . The practicalities of the situation place the proscriptions of § 9(h) somewhere between those two extremes. The difficult question that emerges is whether, consistently with the First Amendment, Congress, by statute, may exert these pressures upon labor unions to deny positions of leadership to certain persons who are identified by particular beliefs and political affiliations.

There can be no doubt that Congress may, under its constitutional power to regulate commerce among the several States, attempt to prevent political strikes and other kinds of direct action designed to burden and interrupt the free flow of commerce. We think it is clear, in addition, that the remedy provided by § 9(h) bears reasonable relation to the evil which the statute was designed to reach. Congress could rationally find that the Communist Party is not like other political parties in its utilization of positions of union leadership as means by which to bring about strikes and other obstructions of commerce for purposes of political advantage, and that many persons who believe in overthrow of the Government by force and violence are also likely to resort to such tactics when, as officers, they formulate union policy.

The fact that the statute identifies persons by their political affiliations and beliefs, which are circumstances ordinarily irrelevant to permissible subjects of government action, does not lead to the conclusion that such circumstances are never relevant. . . . If accidents of birth and ancestry under some circumstances justify an inference concerning future conduct, it can hardly be doubted that voluntary affiliations and beliefs justify a similar inference when drawn by the legislature on the basis of its investigations.

. . . Government's interest here is not in preventing the dissemination of Communist doctrine or the holding of particular beliefs because it is feared that unlawful action will result therefrom if free speech is practiced. Its interest is in protecting the free flow of commerce from what Congress considers to be substantial evils of conduct that are not the products of speech at all. Section 9(h), in other words, does not interfere with speech because Congress fears the consequences of speech; it regulates harmful conduct which Congress has determined is carried on by persons who may be identified by their political affiliations and beliefs. The Board does not contend that political strikes, the substantive evil at which § 9(h) is aimed, are the present or impending products of advocacy of the doctrines of Communism or the expression of belief in overthrow of the Government by force. On the contrary, it points out that such strikes are called by persons who, so Congress has found, have the will and power to do so *without* advocacy or persuasion that seeks acceptance in the competition of the market. Speech may be fought with speech. Falsehoods and fallacies must be exposed, not suppressed, unless there is not sufficient time to avert the evil consequences of noxious doctrine by argument and education. That is the command of the First Amendment. But force may and must be met with force. Section 9(h) is designed to protect the public not against what Communists and others identified therein advocate or believe, but against what Congress has concluded they have done and are likely to do again. . . .

On the other hand, legitimate attempts to protect the public, not from the remote possible effects of noxious ideologies, but from present excesses of direct, active conduct, are not presumptively bad because they interfere with and, in some of its manifestations, restrain the exercise of First Amendment rights.

. . . In essence, the problem is one of weighing the probable effects of the statute upon the free exercise of the right of speech and assembly against the congressional determination that political strikes are evils of conduct which cause substantial harm to interstate commerce and that Communists and others identified by § 9(h) pose continuing threats to that public interest when in positions of union leadership. . . .

. . . Those who, so Congress has found, would subvert the public interest cannot escape all regulation because, at the same time, they carry on legitimate political activities. . . . To encourage unions to displace them from positions of great power over the national economy, while at the same time leaving free the outlets by which they may pursue legitimate political activities of persuasion and advocacy, does not seem to us to contravene the purposes of the First Amendment. That Amendment requires that one be permitted to believe what he will. It requires that one be permitted to advocate what he will unless there is a clear and present danger that a substantial public evil will result therefrom. It does not require that he be permitted to be the keeper of the arsenal. . . .

Section 9(h) is designed to protect the public not against what Communists and others identified therein advocate or believe but against what Congress has concluded they have done and are likely to do again.

[The Court found no merit in the contention that this was a bill of attainder or *ex post facto* legislation or unconstitutionally vague.]

We conclude that § 9(h) of the Labor Management Relations Act, as herein construed, is compatible with the Federal Constitution and may stand. The judgments of the courts below are therefore

Affirmed.

Mr. Justice Douglas, Mr. Justice Clark, and Mr. Justice Minton took no part in the consideration or decision of these cases.

Mr. Justice Jackson, concurred in part and dissented in part:

If the statute before us required labor union officers to forswear membership in the Republican Party, the Democratic Party or the Socialist Party, I suppose I agree that it would be unconstitutional. But why, if it is valid as to the Communist Party?

The answer, for me, is in the decisive differences between the Communist Party and every other party of any importance in the long experience of the United States with party government. In order that today's decision may not be useful as a precedent for suppression of any political opposition compatible with our free institutions, I limit concurrence to grounds and distinctions explicitly set forth herein, without which I should regard this Act as unconstitutional. . . .

1. *The goal of the Communist Party is to seize powers of government by and for a minority rather than to acquire power through the vote of a free electorate.* It seeks not merely a change of administration, or of Congress, or reform legislation within the constitutional framework. Its program is not merely to socialize property more rapidly and extensively than the other parties are doing. While the difference between other parties in these matters is largely as to pace, the Communist Party's difference is one of direction. . . .

2. *The Communist Party alone among American parties past or present is*

dominated and controlled by a foreign government. It is a satrap party which, to the threat of civil disorder, adds the threat of betrayal into alien hands. . . .

3. *Violent and undemocratic means are the calculated and indispensable methods to attain the Communist Party's goal.* It would be incredible naïveté to expect the American branch of this movement to forego the only methods by which a Communist Party has anywhere come into power. In not one of the countries it now dominates was the Communist Party chosen by a free or contestable election; in not one can it be evicted by any election. . . .

4. *The Communist Party has sought to gain this leverage and hold on the American population by acquiring control of the labor movement.* All political parties have wooed labor and its leaders. But what other parties seek is principally the vote of labor. The Communist Party, on the other hand, is not primarily interested in labor's vote, for it does not expect to win by votes. It strives for control of labor's coercive power—the strike, the sit-down, the slow-down, sabotage, or other means of producing industrial paralysis. . . .

5. *Every member of the Communist Party is an agent to execute the Communist program.* What constitutes a party? Major political parties in the United States have never been closely knit or secret organizations. Anyone who usually votes the party ticket is reckoned a member, although he has not applied for or been admitted to membership, pays no dues, has taken no pledge, and is free to vote, speak and act as he wills. Followers are held together by rather casual acceptance of general principles, the influence of leaders, and sometimes by the cohesive power of patronage. Membership in the party carries with it little assurance that the member understands or believes in its principles and none at all that he will take orders from its leaders. One may quarrel with the party and bolt its candidates and return again as much a member as those who were regular. And it is often a source of grief to those who have labored long in the vineyard that late arrivals are taken into the party councils from other parties without scrutiny. Of course, when party organization is of this character, there is little ground for inference that all members are committed to party plans or that they are agents for their execution.

Membership in the Communist Party is totally different. The Party is a secret conclave. Members are admitted only upon acceptance as reliable and after indoctrination in its policies, to which the member is fully committed. They are provided with cards or credentials, usually issued under false names so that the identification can only be made by officers of the Party who hold the code. Moreover, each pledges unconditional obedience to party authority. Adherents are known by secret or code names. They constitute "cells" in the factory, the office, the political society, or the labor union. For any deviation from the party line they are purged and excluded. . . .

Congress has, however, required an additional disclaimer, which in my view does encounter serious constitutional objections. A union officer must also swear that "he does not believe in . . . the overthrow of the United States Government by force or by any illegal or unconstitutional methods." . . .

The men who led the struggle forcibly to overthrow lawfully constituted British authority found moral support by asserting a natural law under which their revolution was justified, and they broadly proclaimed these beliefs in the document basic to our freedom. Such sentiments have also been given ardent and rather extravagant expression by Americans of undoubted patriotism. Most of these utterances were directed against a tyranny which left no way to change by suffrage. It seems to me a perversion of their meaning to quote them, as the Communists often do, to sanction violent attacks upon a representative government which does afford such means. But while I think Congress may make it a crime to take one overt step to use or to incite violence or force against our Government, I do not see how in the light of our history, a mere belief that one has a natural right under some circumstances to do so can subject an American citizen to prejudice any more than possession of any other erroneous belief. Can we say that men of our time must not even think about the propositions on which our own Revolution was justified? . . .

Mr. Justice Frankfurter concurred except as to Part VII involving chiefly the vagueness of the legislation.

Mr. Justice Black dissented:

. . . Under such circumstances, restrictions imposed on proscribed groups are seldom static, even though the rate of expansion may not move in geometric progression from discrimination to arm-band to ghetto and worse. Thus I cannot regard the Court's holding as one which merely bars Communists from holding union office and nothing more. For its reasoning would apply just as forcibly to statutes barring Communists and their suspected sympathizers from election to political office, mere membership in unions, and in fact from getting or holding any jobs whereby they could earn a living. . . .

RELATED CASES:

Schneiderman v. United States: 320 U.S. 118 (1943). Opinion: Murphy, J. Dissenting: Stone, C.J., and Roberts and Frankfurter, JJ.

The government did not prove its case in the denaturalization proceeding beyond reasonable doubt. Fraud was alleged since the government claimed that Schneiderman, a Communist, could not have been attached to the principles of the Constitution.

Bridges v. Wixon: 326 U.S. 135 (1945). Opinion: Douglas, J. Dissenting: Stone, C.J., and Roberts and Frankfurter, JJ.

Certain activities of the Communist Party may be wholly legal, so membership is not necessarily incriminating. This was a deportation proceeding against Harry Bridges.

Barenblatt v. United States: 360 U.S. 109 (1959). Opinion: Harlan, J. Dissenting: Black, Brennan, and Douglas. JJ. and Warren, C.J.

In an investigation related to a valid legislative purpose and with the House Committee's authority sufficiently specific, there may be a proper investigation into the field of education and Communist Party influence. See Vol. I.

United States v. Robel: 389 U.S. 258 (1967). Opinion: Warren, C.J. Dissenting: White and Harlan, JJ. Abstaining: Marshall, J.

Under the Subversive Activities Control Act no member of the Communist-action organization could be employed in any defense facility. The Court held that the First Amendment forbids use of guilt by association alone as a basis for such action without regard to the quality and degree of membership in an organization. Robel was a shipyard employee. This was an overbroad use of the war power.

Schneider v. Smith: 390 U.S. 17 (1968). Opinion: Douglas, J. No dissent. Abstaining: Marshall, J.

Congress can enact legislation to safeguard American shipping from subversive activity but here the action of the Coast Guard in refusing to process Schneider's merchant mariner's document was not justified. It was based on ideas or beliefs and not actions. Smith, Coast Guard Commandant, had exceeded his authority under regulations promulgated by the President under the Magnuson Act of 1950.

NOTE:

In *Douds* the Court avoided the real constitutional difficulty involved by holding that the oath requirement was a regulation of commerce rather than a regulation of freedom of speech.

The "Non-Communist Oath" requirement of Taft-Hartley was repealed by the Landrum-Griffin Act of 1959—The Labor-Management Reporting and Disclosure Act—but the provision that union officers cannot be members of the Communist Party was held void in *United States* v. *Brown*, 381 U.S. 437 (1965) as a bill of attainder. See p. 8, above. *Brown,* in effect, overruled *Douds.*

Douds involved governmental action affecting private employment. The Court noted that congressional judgment is that beliefs and loyalties will be transformed into *future* conduct. Both *Dennis* (1951) and *Douds* (1950) put the clear and present danger rule on the defensive in federal legislation. In *Douds* the Court used what might be called a "balance standard."

Adler v. Board of Education
342 U.S. 485; 72 S.Ct. 380; 96 L.Ed. 517 (1952)

(New York State's Feinberg Law specifically makes ineligible for employment in the public schools of the state any person who is a member of an organization advocating the unlawful overthrow of the government of the United States. Under the law, the Board of Regents is to compile a list, after full notice and hearing, of such subversive organizations. Any person who is disqualified for employment under the terms of this law is entitled to a full hearing with the privilege of representation by counsel and the right of judicial review.)

Vote: 6-3

Mr. Justice Minton delivered the opinion of the Court:

. . . A teacher works in a sensitive area in a schoolroom. There he shapes the attitude of young minds towards the society in which they live. In this, the state has a vital concern. It must preserve the integrity of the schools. That the school authorities have the right and the duty to screen the officials, teachers, and employees as to their fitness to maintain the integrity of the schools as a part of ordered society, cannot be doubted. One's associates, past and present, as well as one's conduct, may properly be considered in determining fitness and loyalty. From time immemorial, one's reputation has been determined in part by the company he keeps. In the employment of officials and teachers of the school system, the state may very properly inquire into the company they keep, and we know of no rule, constitutional or otherwise, that prevents the state, when determining the fitness and loyalty of such persons, from considering the organizations and persons with whom they associate.

If, under the procedure set up in the New York law, a person is found to be unfit and is disqualified from employment in the public school system because of membership in a listed organization, he is not thereby denied the right of free speech and assembly. His freedom of choice between membership in the organization and employment in the school system might be limited, but not his freedom of speech or assembly, except in the remote sense that limitation is inherent in every choice. Certainly such limitation is not one the state may not make in the exercise of its police power to protect the schools from pollution and thereby to defend its own existence. . . .

Membership in a listed organization found to be within the statute and known by the member to be within the statute is a legislative finding that the member by his membership supports the thing the organization stands for, namely, the overthrow of government by unlawful means. We cannot say that such a finding is contrary to fact or that "generality of experience" points to a different conclusion. Disqualification follows therefore as a reasonable presumption from such membership and support. Nor is there here a problem of procedural due process. The presumption is not conclusive but arises only in a hearing where the person against whom it may arise has full opportunity to rebut it. . . .

Where, as here, the relation between the fact found and the presumption is clear and direct and is not conclusive, the requirements of due process are satisfied. . . .

We find no constitutional infirmity in § 12(a) of the Civil Service Law of New York or in the Feinberg Law which implemented it, and the judgment is affirmed.

Mr. Justice Frankfurter dissented, holding that the Court should have declined jurisdiction.

Mr. Justice Black dissented:

. . . This policy of freedom is in my judgment embodied in the First Amendment and made applicable to the states by the Fourteenth. Because of this policy public officials cannot be constitutionally vested with powers to select the ideas people can think about, censor the public views they can express, or choose the persons or groups people can associate with. Public officials with such power are not public servants; they are public masters.

I dissent from the Court's judgment sustaining this law which effectively penalizes school teachers for their thoughts and their associates.

Mr. Justice Douglas dissented, with the concurrence of Mr. Justice Black:

. . . The present law proceeds on a principle repugnant to our society—guilt by association. A teacher is disqualified because of her membership in an organization found to be "subversive." . . . The mere fact of membership in the organization raises a *prima facie* case of her own guilt. She may, it is said, show her innocence. But innocence in this case turns on knowledge; and when the witch hunt is on, one who must rely on ignorance leans on a feeble reed.

The very threat of such a procedure is certain to raise havoc with academic freedom. Youthful indiscretions, mistaken causes, misguided enthusiasms—all long forgotten—become the ghosts of a harrowing present. Any organization committed to a liberal cause, any group organized to revolt against an hysterical trend, any committee launched to sponsor an unpopular program becomes suspect. These are the organizations into which Communists often infiltrate. Their presence infects the whole, even though the project was not conceived in sin. A teacher caught in that mesh is almost certain to stand condemned. Fearing condemnation, she will tend to shrink from any association that stirs controversy. In that manner freedom of expression will be stifled. . . .

RELATED CASES:

Cramp v. Board of Public Instruction of Orange County: 368 U.S. 278 (1961). Opinion: Stewart, J. No dissent.

A state cannot consistently with the due process clause of the Fourteenth Amendment force an employee either to take a loyalty oath that is vague and uncertain at the risk of subsequent prosecution for perjury or face immediate dismissal from public service. Cramp, a teacher, was supposed to swear that he had never given "aid," "counsel," "influence," "advice," or "support" to the Communist Party. The case arose in Florida.

Baggett v. Bullitt: 377 U.S. 360 (1964). Opinion: White, J. Dissenting: Clark and Harlan, JJ.

Here a Washington state loyalty oath statute was declared void because of vagueness. The requirement was held not open to one or a few interpretations but to an indefinite number. This decision overruled *Gerende* v. *Board of Supervisors of Elections*, 341 U.S. 56 (1951). See p. 278, below. *Baggett* v. *Bullitt* came out of the University of Washington.

Cole v. Richardson: 405 U.S. 676 (1972). Opinion: Burger, C.J. Dissenting: Douglas, Marshall, and Brennan, JJ. Abstaining: Powell and Rehnquist, JJ.

The requirement that all public employees in a state take an oath to oppose the overthrow of either state or federal governments by force, violence, or any illegal or unconstitutional method can be enforced. While no government can condition employment on taking oaths which impinge rights guaranteed by the Constitution, there is no such infringement here since there is no constitutionally protected right to overthrow a government by force, violence, or illegal or unconstitutional means. Cole was Superintendent at Boston State Hospital and Richardson was a research biologist there.

NOTE:

The statute in question in *Adler*, in spite of its adherence to "guilt by association," had no retroactive effect, and provided for a defense on the part of the teachers that their membership was innocent, and organizations were to be labeled as subversive only after notice and hearing. These points must have influenced the Court. This case is a reiteration of the maxim that public employment is not a personal right. But see *Keyishian*, immediately following.

Keyishian v. Board of Regents of the University of the State of New York
385 U.S. 589; 87 S.Ct. 675; 17 L.Ed. 2d 629 (1967)

(Appellants, faculty members of the State University of New York and a non-faculty employee, brought this action for declaratory and injunctive relief, claiming that New York's teacher loyalty laws and regulations were unconstitutional. Their continued employment had been terminated or was threatened when each appellant faculty member refused to comply with a requirement of the university trustees that he certify that he was not a Communist and that if he had ever been one he had so advised the university president; and the nonfaculty employee refused to state under oath whether he had advocated or been a member of a group which advocated forceful overthrow of the government. Under § 3021 of New York's Education Law "treasonable or seditious" utterances or acts are grounds for dismissal from the public school system: Section 3022 (the Feinberg Law) of the Education Law requires the State Board of Regents to issue regulations for the disqualification or removal on loyalty grounds of faculty or other personnel in the state educational system, to make a list of "subversive" organizations, and to provide that membership therein constitutes *prima facie* evidence of disqualification for employment. The Board listed the National and State Communist Parties as "subversive organizations" under the law, but shortly before the trial of this case the university trustees' certificate requirement was rescinded and it was announced that no person would be ineligible for employment "solely" because he refused to sign the certificate.)

Vote: 5-4

Mr. Justice Brennan delivered the opinion of the Court:

. . . We emphasize once again that ". . . precision of regulation must be the touchstone in an area so closely touching our most precious freedoms," *NAACP* v. *Button*, 371 U.S. 415, 438; ". . . for standards of permissible statutory vagueness are strict in the area of free expression. . . . Because First Amendment freedoms need breathing space to survive, government may regulate in the area only with narrow specificity." *Id.*, at 432-433. New York's complicated and intricate scheme plainly violates that standard. When one must guess what conduct or utterance may lose him his position, one necessarily will "steer far wider of the unlawful zone . . ." *Speiser* v. *Randall*, 357 U.S. 513, 526.

. . . Vagueness of wording is aggravated by prolixity and profusion of statutes, regulations, and administrative machinery, and by manifold cross-references to inter-related enactments and rules.

We therefore hold that § 3021 of the Education Law and subdivisions 1(a), 1(b) and 3 of § 105 of the Civil Service Law as implemented by the machinery created pursuant to § 3022 of the Education Law are unconstitutional.

. . . Subdivision 2 of the Feinberg Law was, however, before the Court in *Adler* and its constitutionality was sustained. But constitutional doctrine which has emerged since that decision has rejected its major premise. That premise was that public employment, including academic employment, may be conditioned upon the surrender of constitutional rights which could not be abridged by direct government action. Teachers, the Court said in *Adler*, "may work for the school system upon the reasonable terms laid down by the proper authorities of New York. If they do not choose to work on such terms, they are at liberty to retain their beliefs and associations and go elsewhere." 342 U.S., at 492.

. . . We proceed then to the question of the validity of the provisions of sub-division 1(c) of § 105 and subdivision 2 of § 3022, barring employment to members of listed organizations. Here again constitutional doctrine has developed since *Adler*. Mere knowing membership without a specific intent to further the unlawful aims of an organization is not a constitutionally adequate basis for exclusion from such positions as those held by appellants.

. . . Measured against this standard, both Civil Service Law § 105, subd. 1(c), and Education Law § 3022, subd. 2, sweep overbroadly into association which may not be proscribed. . . . Where statutes have an overbroad sweep, just as where they are vague, "the hazard of loss or substantial impairment of those precious rights may be critical," *Dombrowski* v. *Pfister, supra*, at 486, since those covered by the statute are bound to limit their behavior to that which is unquestionably safe. . . .

We therefore hold that Civil Service Law § 105, subd. 1(c), and Education Law § 3022, subd. 2, are invalid insofar as they proscribe mere knowing membership without any showing of specific intent to further the unlawful aims of the Communist Party of the United States or of the State of New York.

The judgment of the District Court is reversed and the case is remanded for further proceedings consistent with this opinion.

Reversed and remanded.

Mr. Justice Clark dissented, joined by Mr. Justice Harlan, Mr. Justice Stewart, and Mr. Justice White:

. . . It is clear that the Feinberg Law, in which this court found "no constitutional infirmity" in 1952, has been given its death blow today. Just as the majority here finds that there "can be no doubt of the legitimacy of New York's interest in protecting its education system from subversion" there can also be no doubt that "the be-all and end-all" of New York's effort is here. And, regardless of its correctness, neither New York nor the several States that have followed the teaching of *Adler* v. *Board of Education*, 342 U.S. 485, for some 15 years, can ever put the pieces together again. No court has ever reached out so far to destroy so much with so little. . . .

In view of this long list of decisions covering over 15 years of this Court's history, in which no opinion of this Court even questioned the validity of the *Adler* line of cases, it is strange to me that the Court now finds that the "constitutional doctrine which has emerged since . . . has rejected [*Adler*'s] major premise." With due respect, as I read them, our cases have done no such thing. . . .

The majority says that the Feinberg Law is bad because it has an "overbroad sweep." I regret to say—and I do so with deference—that the majority has by its broadside swept away one of our most precious rights, namely, the right of self-preservation. Our public educational system is the genius of our democracy. The minds of our youth are developed there and the character of that development will determine the future of our land. Indeed, our very existence depends upon it. The issue here is a very narrow one. It is not freedom of speech, freedom of thought, freedom of press, freedom of assembly, or of association, even in the Communist Party. It is simply this: May the State provide that one who, after a hearing with full judicial review, is found to have wilfully and deliberately advocated, advised, or taught that our Government should be overthrown by force or violence or other unlawful means; or to have wilfully and deliberately printed, published, etc., any book or paper that so advocated *and to have personally* advocated such doctrine himself; or to have wilfully and deliberately become a member of an organization that advocates such doctrine, is *prima facie* disqualified from teaching in its university? My answer, in keeping with all of our cases up until today, is "Yes"!

I dissent.

RELATED CASES:

NAACP v. Button: 371 U.S. 415 (1963). Opinion: Brennan, J. Dissenting: Harlan, Clark, Stewart, and White, JJ.

The Court ruled a Virginia statute unconstitutional as it applied to the National Association for the Advancement of Colored People because the act infringed on First Amendment rights of association and expression (of the NAACP, its affiliates, and legal staff) as incorporated into the Fourteenth Amendment. The statute was passed by the legislature to regulate the legal profession and the practice of law. However, it would have seriously hampered the activities of the NAACP in its financing and furnishing of legal services in racial desegregation suits.

Dombrowski v. Pfister: 380 U.S. 479 (1965). Opinion: Brennan, J. Abstaining: Black and Stewart, JJ. Dissenting: Harlan and Clark, JJ.

The Court enjoined prosecution of civil rights leaders and organizations under a state subversive activities statute overbroad on its face where there was evidence of harassment and continued litigation without final resolution so as to protect the First Amendment rights of expression.

Pickering v. Board of Education of Township High School District 205, Will County, Illinois: 391 U.S. 563 (1968). Opinion: Marshall, J. Dissenting: White, J.

Absent proof of false statements knowingly or recklessly made by a teacher (here a letter to a local newspaper), the exercise of his right to speak on issues of public importance may not furnish the basis for dismissal from public employment.

Tinker v. Des Moines Independent Community School District: 393 U.S. 503 (1969). Opinion: Fortas, J. Dissenting: Black and Harlan, JJ.

Where there was neither interruption of school activities nor intrusion in the school affairs or lives of others, students could not be prevented by school authorities from wearing on their sleeves black arm bands as an expression of opposition to the hostilities in Viet Nam. Such a mode of expression is guaranteed by the First Amendment.

Bridges v. California, and
Times-Mirror Co. v. Superior Court of California
314 U.S. 252; 62 S.Ct. 190; 86 L.Ed. 192 (1941)

(At the time that a motion for a new trial was pending in a case involving a dispute between an AFL union and a CIO union of which Harry Bridges was an officer, he sent to the Secretary of Labor a telegram, which he released also to the press. This telegram termed the judge's decision "outrageous" and threatened that attempted enforcement of the decision would tie up the port of Los Angeles and would involve the entire Pacific Coast. The action against the newspaper, the *Los Angeles Times*, was based on the publication of three editorials. Two members of a labor union in Los Angeles had been found guilty of assaulting nonunion truck drivers and the date for sentence had been set by the court. The editorial said the judge, A. A. Scott, would make a serious mistake if he granted probation.

Both Bridges and the *Times-Mirror* were cited for contempt and convicted, and these convictions were challenged as violating freedom of speech and press.)

Vote: 5-4

Mr. Justice Black delivered the opinion of the Court:

. . . What finally emerges from the "clear and present danger" cases is a working principle that the substantive evil must be extremely serious and the degree of imminence extremely high before utterances can be punished. Those cases do not purport to mark the furthermost constitutional boundaries of protected expression, nor do we here. They do no more than recognize a minimum compulsion of the Bill of Rights. For the First Amendment does not speak equivocally. It prohibits any law "abridging the freedom of speech or of the press." It must be taken as a command of the broadest scope that explicit language, read in the context of a liberty-loving society, will allow. . . .

. . . We must therefore turn to the particular utterances here in question and the circumstances of their publication to determine to what extent the substantive evil of unfair administration of justice was a likely consequence, and whether the degree of likelihood was sufficient to justify summary punishment. . . .

This editorial, given the most intimidating construction it will bear, did no more than threaten future adverse criticism which was reasonably to be expected anyway in the event of a lenient disposition of the pending case. To regard it, therefore, as in itself of substantial influence upon the course of justice would be to impute to judges a lack of firmness, wisdom, or honor, which we cannot accept as a major premise.

Let us assume that the telegram could be construed as an announcement of Bridges' intention to call a strike, something which, it is admitted, neither the general law of California nor the court's decree prohibited. With an eye on the realities of the situation, we cannot assume that Judge Schmidt [in the Bridges case] was unaware of the possibility of a strike as a consequence of his decision. If he was not intimidated by the facts themselves, we do not believe that the most explicit statement of them could have sidetracked the course of justice. Again, we find exaggeration in the conclusion that the utterance even "tended" to interfere with justice. If there was electricity in the atmosphere, it was generated by the facts; the charge added by the Bridges telegram can be dismissed as negligible. . . .

Mr. Justice Frankfurter dissented, joined by Mr. Chief Justice Stone and Mr. Justice Roberts and Mr. Justice Byrnes:

. . . Our duty is not ended with the recitation of phrases that are the short-hand of a complicated historic process. . . . The fact that the communication to the Secretary of Labor may have been privileged does not constitutionally protect whatever extraneous use may have been made of the communication. It is said that the possibility of a strike, in case of an adverse ruling, must in any event have suggested itself to the private thoughts of a sophisticated judge. Therefore the publication of the Bridges telegram, we are told, merely gave that possibility public expression. To afford constitutional shelter for a definite attempt at coercing a court into a favorable decision because of the contingencies of frustration to which all judicial action is subject, is to hold, in effect, that the Constitution subordinates the judicial settlement of conflicts to the unfettered indulgence of violent speech. The mere fact that after an unfavorable decision men may, upon full consideration of their responsibilities as well as their rights, engage in a strike or a lockout, is a poor reason for denying a state the power to protect its courts from being bludgeoned by serious threats while a decision is hanging in the judicial balance. A vague, undetermined possibility that a decision of a court may lead to a serious manifestation of protest is one thing. The impact of a definite threat of action to prevent a decision is a wholly different matter. To deny such realities is to stultify law. Rights must be judged in their context and not *in vacuo*.

RELATED CASES:

Toledo Newspaper Co. v. United States: 247 U.S. 402 (1918). Opinion: White, C.J. Dissenting: Holmes and Brandeis, JJ. Abstaining: Day and Clark, JJ.

A newspaper's publication of comment on a pending case in a federal court and on the conduct of the judge in the case was held to have a reasonable tendency to obstruct the administration of justice. This was an interpretation of a federal statute of 1831 limiting contempt citations.

Craig v. Hecht: 263 U.S. 255 (1923). Opinion: McReynolds, J. Dissenting: Holmes and Brandeis, JJ. Abstaining: Sutherland, J.

Review of a conviction for contempt handed down by a United States District Court can be made only by a federal Circuit Court of Appeals. It is improper for a convicted party to seek review of his conviction by a proceeding in habeas corpus in the District Court. Hecht was a United States Marshall in New York.

Nye v. United States: 313 U.S. 33 (1941). Opinion: Douglas, J. Dissenting: Stone and Roberts, JJ., and Hughes, C.J.

Overruled the *Toledo* decision by holding invalid citation for contempt for actions that took place more than one hundred miles from the court, specifically influencing a plaintiff to withdraw a suit. There needs to be physical proximity. The Court emphasized that this was statutory construction and not a constitutional issue.

Pennekamp v. Florida: 328 U.S. 33 (1946). Opinion: Reed, J. Abstaining: Jackson, J.

The publication of editorials in the *Miami Herald* concerning the attitude of a judge toward persons charged with crime has too remote an effect on juries to be a clear and present danger to justice. See also *Maryland* v. *Baltimore Radio Show*, below.

Craig v. Harney: 331 U.S. 367 (1947). Opinion: Douglas, J. Dissenting: Frankfurter, J., Vinson, C.J., and Jackson, J.

An inaccurate news story on a trial and an editorial written in intemperate language do not constitute a real danger to the administration of justice. See also statement by Mr. Justice Frankfurter and Mr. Justice Jackson concurring in the result in *Shepherd* v. *Florida*, below.

Fisher v. Pace: 336 U.S. 132 (1949). Opinion: Reed, J. Dissenting: Douglas, Black, and Rutledge, JJ.

Citation for contempt of a lawyer who refused to stop talking on orders from the judge is not a denial of free speech in the courtroom.

Maryland v. Baltimore Radio Show: 338 U.S. 912 (1950). Opinion: Frankfurter, J. No dissent.

The Supreme Court refused *certiorari* in a case where the lower court had reversed the conviction of a broadcasting company for contempt for permitting the broadcast of prejudicial matter concerning a pending murder trial. Mr. Justice Frankfurter's opinion is notable for its explanation of why the Court denies petitions certiorari.

Shepherd v. Florida: 341 U.S. 50 (1951). Per curiam. No dissent.

In a *per curiam* opinion the Court here reversed a Florida conviction of a Negro for rape. The Court cited *Cassell* v. *Texas,* 339 U.S. 282 (see p. 239, below) as its authority. In the only opinion, a concurring opinion by Mr. Justice Jackson and Mr. Justice Frankfurter, it was stated that the Fourteenth Amendment right to fair trial is violated by a trial in an atmosphere of violent prejudice against the defendant. In this case discrimination was charged in the selection of the jury.

Sacher v. United States: 343 U.S. 1 (1952). Opinion: Jackson, J. Dissenting: Black, Frankfurter, and Douglas, JJ. Abstaining: Clark, J.

A federal judge may summarily dispose of a contempt charge if he certifies that he saw or heard the conduct constituting the contempt and that it was committed in the actual presence of the court. Here were involved the lawyers for the eleven Communist Party leaders tried before Judge Medina in 1951 under the Smith Act.

NOTE:

Bridges was another "clear and present danger" case but here in the sense that the Court felt that there was no such danger. The case also is an example of preferential treatment being accorded First Amendment rights. This treatment is also exemplified by *Murdock* v. *Pennsylvania, United States* v. *Carolene Products Co., Schneider* v. *Irvington, Thomas* v. *Collins,* and *West Virginia State Board of Education* v. *Barnette.* See pp. 15, 26, 61, and 108.

In *Bridges* there was no jury; the judge alone was the one to be influenced. In such influence there must be a causal relationship between the utterance and the evil result.

Near v. Minnesota
283 U.S. 697; 51 S.Ct. 625; 75 L.Ed. 1357 (1931)

(A statute of the State of Minnesota provided for the abatement, as a public nuisance, of a "malicious, scandalous and defamatory newspaper, magazine or other periodical." *The Saturday Press,* published by the defendants, in Minneapolis, was charged by the county attorney of Hennepin County with being such a publication and he brought suit to enjoin publication. The periodical had accused certain public officials of gross negligence and misconduct in office.)

Vote: 5-4

Mr. Chief Justice Hughes delivered the opinion of the Court:

. . . This statute, for the suppression as a public nuisance of a newspaper or periodical, is unusual, if not unique, and raises questions of grave importance transcending the local interests involved in the particular action. It is no longer open to doubt that the liberty of the press, and of speech, is within the liberty safeguarded by the due process clause of the Fourteenth Amendment from invasion by state action. . . . In maintaining this guaranty, the authority of the State to enact laws to promote the health, safety, morals and general welfare of its people is necessarily admitted. The limits of this sovereign power must always be determined with appropriate regard to the particular subject of its exercise . . . Liberty of speech and of the press is also not an absolute right, and the state may punish its abuse . . . Liberty, in each of its phases, has its history and connotation and, in the present instance, the inquiry is as to the historic conception of the liberty of the press and whether the statute under review violates the essential attributes of that liberty. . . .

If we cut through mere details of procedure, the operation and effect of the statute in substance is that public authorities may bring the owner or publisher of a newspaper or periodical before a judge upon a charge of conducting a business of publishing scandalous and defamatory matter—in particular that the matter consists of charges against public officers of official dereliction—and unless the owner or publisher is able and disposed to bring competent evidence to satisfy the judge that the charges are true and are published with good motives and for justifiable ends, his newspaper or periodical is suppressed and further publication is made punishable as a contempt. This is of the essence of censorship.

The question is whether a statute authorizing such proceedings in restraint of publication is consistent with the conception of the liberty of the press as historically conceived and guaranteed. . . .

The exceptional nature of its limitations places in a strong light the general conception that liberty of the press, historically considered and taken up by the Federal Constitution, has meant, principally although not exclusively, immunity from previous restraints or censorship. The conception of the liberty of the press in this country had broadened with the exigencies of the colonial period and with the efforts to secure freedom from oppressive administration. That liberty was especially cherished for the immunity it afforded from previous restraint of the publication of censure of public officers and charges of official misconduct. . . .

The importance of this immunity has not lessened. While reckless assaults upon public men, and efforts to bring obloquy upon those who are endeavoring faithfully to discharge official duties, exert a baleful influence and deserve the severest condemnation in public opinion, it cannot be said that this abuse is greater, and it is believed to be less, than that which characterized the period in which our institutions took shape. Meanwhile, the administration of government has become more complex, the opportunities for malfeasance and corruption have multiplied, crime has grown to most serious proportions, and the danger of its protection by unfaithful officials and of the impairment of the fundamental security of life and property by criminal alliances and official neglect, emphasizes the primary need of a vigilant and courageous press, especially in great cities. The fact that the liberty of the press may be abused by miscreant purveyors of scandal does not make any the less necessary the immunity of the press from previous restraint in dealing with official misconduct. Subsequent punishment for such abuses as may exist is the appropriate remedy, consistent with constitutional privilege. . . .

Equally unavailing is the insistence that the statute is designed to prevent the circulation of scandal which tends to disturb the public peace and to provoke assaults and the commission of crime. Charges of reprehensible conduct, and in particular of official malfeasance, unquestionably create a public scandal, but the theory of the constitutional guaranty is that even a more serious public evil would be caused by authority to prevent publication. . . . There is nothing new in the fact that charges of reprehensible conduct may create resentment and the disposition to resort to violent means of redress, but this well-understood tendency did not alter the determination to protect the press against censorship and restraint upon publication. . . . The danger of violent reactions becomes greater with effective organization of defiant groups resenting exposure, and if this consideration warranted legislative interference with the initial freedom of publication, the constitutional protection would be reduced to a mere form of words.

For these reasons we hold the statute, so far as it authorized the proceedings in this action under clause (b) of section one, to be an infringement of the liberty of the press guaranteed by the Fourteenth Amendment. We should add that this decision rests upon the operation and effect of the statute, without regard to the question of the truth of the charges contained in the particular periodical. The fact that the public officers named in this case, and those associated with the charges of official dereliction, may be deemed to be impeccable, cannot affect the conclusion that the statute imposes an unconstitutional restraint upon publication.

Judgment reversed.

Mr. Justice Butler dissented, joined by Mr. Justice VanDevanter, Mr. Justice McReynolds and Mr. Justice Sutherland:

Defendant concedes that the editions of the newspapers complained of are "defamatory *per se.*" And he says: "It has been asserted that the constitution was never intended to be a shield for malice, scandal, and defamation when untrue, or published with bad motives, or for unjustifiable ends. . . . The contrary is true; every person *does* have a constitutional right to publish malicious, scandalous, and defamatory matter though untrue, and with bad motives, and for unjustifiable ends, *in the first instance*, though he is subject to responsibility therefor *afterwards.*" The record, when the substance of the article is regarded, require that concession here. And this Court is required to pass on the validity of the state law on that basis. . . .

The Minnesota statute does not operate as a *previous* restraint on publication within the proper meaning of that phrase. It does not authorize administrative control in advance such as was formerly exercised by the licensers and censors, but prescribes a remedy to be enforced by a suit in equity. In this case there was previous publication made in the course of the business of regularly producing malicious, scandalous, and defamatory periodicals. The business and publications unquestionably constitute an abuse of the right of free press. The statute denounces the things done as a nuisance on the ground, as stated by the state supreme court, that they threaten morals, peace, and good order. There is no question of the power of the State to denounce such transgressions. The restraint authorized is only in respect of continuing to do what has been duly adjudged to constitute a nuisance. . . . There is nothing in the statute purporting to prohibit publications that have not been adjudged to constitute a nuisance. It is fanciful to suggest similarity between the granting of enforcement of the decree authorized by this statute to prevent *further* publication of malicious, scandalous, and defamatory articles and the *previous restraint* upon the press by licensers as referred to by Blackstone and described in the history of the times to which he alludes. . . .

The judgment should be affirmed.

RELATED CASES:

United States v. Paramount Pictures: 334 U.S. 131 (1948). Opinion: Douglas, J. Dissenting: Frankfurter, J. Abstaining: Jackson, J.

Held that "moving pictures, like newspapers and radio, are included in the press whose freedom is guaranteed by the First Amendment." This was an antitrust case so this statement is dictum here.

Beaurharnais v. Illinois: 343 U.S. 250 (1952). Opinion: Frankfurter, J. Dissenting: Black, Douglas, Reed, and Jackson, JJ.

A state may prohibit speech or publications aimed at defamation of a group with which individuals are "inextricably involved" when such speech or publication would be libel if directed to an individual. Libelous utterances are not constitutionally protected. These were anti-Negro pamphlets so group libel law was involved. This case represents a seeming retreat from the preferred position of the First Amendment.

Butler v. Michigan: 352 U.S. 380 (1957). Opinion: Frankfurter, J. No dissent.

A state cannot prohibit the distribution of any literature tending to the corruption of the morals of youth. Otherwise adults would be reduced to reading only what is fit for children. The opinion noted, "Surely, this is to burn the house to roast the pig."

Kingsley Books v. Brown: 354 U.S. 436 (1957). Opinion: Frankfurter, J. Dissenting: Warren, C.J.

A state (here New York) may provide for restraint of circulation of material already published if a judicial hearing determines that the material is obscene. Procedural due process here was adequate.

Roth v. United States (Alberts v. California): 354 U.S. 476 (1957). Opinion: Brennan, J. Dissenting: Harlan, Douglas, and Black, JJ.

The First Amendment was not designed to protect obscenity. Therefore, the publication or the mailing of obscene matter can validly be prohibited. See p. 87, below.

Smith v. California: 361 U.S. 147 (1959). Opinion: Brennan, J. Dissenting: Harlan, J.

A city ordinance construed as making a bookstore proprietor absolutely liable criminally for the mere possession in his store of a book later judicially determined to be obscene, even if he had no knowledge as to the contents of the book, violates freedom of the press.

Talley v. California: 362 U.S. 60 (1960). Opinion: Black, J. Dissenting: Clark, Frankfurter, and Whittaker, JJ.

An ordinance is declared void on its face that forbids distribution, in any place under any circumstances, of a handbill which did not have printed thereon the name and address of the person who prepared, distributed, or sponsored it. There is a right to privacy, to anonymity.

Bantam Books, Inc. v. Sullivan: 372 U.S. 58 (1963). Opinion: Brennan, J. Dissenting: Harlan, J.

To subject the distribution of publications to a system of prior administrative restraints by a commission that does not even have the saving feature of judicial superintendence is void. This case arose in Rhode Island.

New York Times Company v. Sullivan: 376 U.S. 254 (1964). Opinion: Brennan, J. No dissent.

A state cannot, under the First and Fourteenth Amendments, award damages to a public official for defamatory falsehood regarding his official conduct unless the officer can prove "actual malice." Sullivan was Commissioner of Montgomery, Alabama.

Garrison v. Louisiana: 379 U.S. 64 (1964). Opinion: Brennan, J. No dissent.

Where criticism is of public officials and their conduct of public business, the interest in private reputation is overborne by the larger public interest. Only false statements made with a high degree of awareness of their probable falsity may be the subject of either civil or criminal sanctions. Garrison was a district attorney.

Ginzburg v. United States: 383 U.S. 463 (1966). Opinion: Brennan, J. Dissenting: Douglas, Black, Harlan, and Stewart, JJ.

Because of the fact that each of the publications was created, advertised, or exploited entirely on the basis of its appeal to prurient interests strengthens the conclusion that the transactions here were sales of illicit merchandise and not sales of constitutionally protected matter. Thus pandering was involved and the "*Roth* test" was correctly applied. If something is not obscene in itself but pandering is added, the net result is obscenity.

Mishkin v. New York: 383 U.S. 502 (1966). Opinion: Brennan, J. Dissenting: Black and Stewart, JJ.

Where published material is designed for and primarily disseminated to a clearly defined deviant sexual group rather than to the public at large, the prurient-appeal requirement of the "*Roth* test" is satisfied if the dominant theme of the material taken as a whole appeals to the prurient interest in sex of the members of that group. The context, the primary audience, was important here.

Time, Inc. v. Hill: 385 U.S. 374 (1967). Opinion: Brennan, J. Dissenting: Fortas, Clark, and Harlan, JJ., and Warren, C.J.

A New York statute providing a cause of action to a person whose name or picture is used by another without consent for purposes of trade or advertising is prevented by free speech and press guarantees from being applied unless there is proof that the publisher knew the reports to be false or that he acted in reckless disregard of the truth. Truth is a complete defense in actions under the statute based on reports of newsworthy people or events. The test is knowing material and substantial falsification. *Life* magazine was involved.

Curtis Publishing Co. v. Butts: 388 U.S. 130 (1967). Opinion: Harlan, J. Dissenting: Black, Brennan, Douglas, and White, JJ.

A "public figure" who is not a public official may recover damages for a defamatory falsehood whose substance makes substantial danger to reputation apparent, on a showing of highly unreasonable conduct constituting an extreme departure from the standards of investigation and reporting normally adhered to by responsible publishers. The *Saturday Evening Post* in publishing an article in which Butts, then athletic director at the University of Georgia, was accused of "fixing" a football game between Georgia and the University of Alabama had ignored "elementary precautions."

St. Amant v. Thompson: 390 U.S. 727 (1968). Opinion: White, J. Dissenting: Fortas, J.

For a court to hold that a defendant acted in "reckless disregard" of whether a defamatory statement made about a public official was false or not there must be sufficient evidence to permit the conclusion that the defendant had serious doubts as to the truth of his statement. A televised speech in Baton Rouge, Louisiana, was involved.

Stanley v. Georgia: 349 U.S. 557 (1969). Opinion: Marshall, J. No dissent.

Under the First and Fourteenth Amendments a state cannot make mere private possession in one's own home of obscene materials a crime. Here while officers were searching under a warrant for evidence of bookmaking, the films were found.

Greenbelt Cooperative Publishing Association v. Bresler: 398 U.S. 6 (1970). Opinion: Stewart, J. No dissent.

A real estate developer and member of the state legislature is a "public figure" of the sort that cannot bring suit for libel unless it is established that there was "knowing or reckless falsehood."

Rosenbloom v. Metromedia: 403 U.S. 29 (1971). Opinion: Brennan, J. Dissenting: Harlan, Marshall, and Stewart, JJ. Abstaining: Douglas, J.

Civil libel action by a private person against a medium of public information (here a Philadelphia radio station) requires proof that a defamatory falsehood was uttered with knowledge that it was false or with reckless disregard of whether it was false or not. Since here such proof was lacking, there was no basis for suit. A distinction between "public" and "private" figures makes no sense in terms of the First Amendment guarantees of free speech and press. Here the news report had dealt with Rosenbloom's arrest for possession of obscene literature.

New York Times Company v. United States; United States v. The Washington Post Company: 403 U.S. 713 (1971). Opinion: Per curiam.

Regarding prohibition of publication of the "Pentagon Papers," any prior restraint of expression bears a heavy presumption against its constitutionality and here the Court held that the Government had not met the burden of showing justification for the imposition of such restraint, here a court injunction.

Branzburg v. Hayes: 408 U.S. 665 (1972). Opinion: White, J. Dissenting: Douglas, Stewart, Brennan, and Marshall, JJ.

The great weight of judicial authority is that newsmen are not exempt from the normal duty of appearing before a grand jury and answering questions relevant to a criminal investigation. The First Amendment interest asserted by newsmen that the identification of their sources of information would measurably deter these sources from furnshing publishable information is "outweighed by the general obligation of a citizen to appear before a grand jury or at a trial, pursuant to a subpeona, and give what information he possesses." This case involved an article on dope peddling in the *Louisville Courier-Journal*.

Miller v. California: 413 U.S. 15 (1973). Opinion: Burger, C.J. Dissenting: Douglas, Brennan, Stewart, and Marshall, JJ.

Miller sent mass mailings of a brochure advertising sexually explicit books and a movie. California attempted to apply its criminal obscenity statute and the Court upheld the state's action. The Court set new guidelines for states in framing obscenity statutes. These are (1) whether the average person, applying contemporary community standards, would find the work as a whole appealing to prurient interest; (2) whether the work depicts or describes in a patently offensive way sexual conduct specifically defined by the applicable state law; and (3) whether the work as a whole lacks serious literary, artistic, political, or scientific value. These changed previous guidelines (particularly the "*Roth* rule") in at least two particulars. (a) The "utterly without redeeming social value test" was rejected. (b) The community standards to be used were changed from a national standard to local standards.

Cantrell v. Forest City Publishing Co.: 419 U.S. 245 (1974). Opinion: Stewart, J. Dissenting: Douglas, J.

Mrs. Cantrell brought suit for invasion of privacy alleging that an article in the Cleveland *Plain Dealer* placed her family in a false light through the article's many inaccuracies and untruths. The Court ruled that there was sufficient evidence to support the finding of the jury that the newspaper had published knowing or reckless falsehoods.

Cox Broadcasting Corporation v. Cohn: 420 U.S. 469 (1975). Opinion: White, J. Dissenting: Rehnquist, J.

The name of the victim of rape was revealed in a television broadcast and her father brought suit claiming invasion of privacy. The reporter had secured the name as the result of the examination of the indictments as public records. The Court held that "the interests in privacy fade when the information involved already appears on the public record."

Roth v. United States; Alberts v. California
354 U.S. 476; 77 S.Ct. 1304; 1 L.Ed. 2d 1498 (1957)

(Samuel Roth conducted a business in New York in the publication and sale of books, photographs, and magazines. He used circulars and advertising matter to solicit sales. He was convicted by a jury in the District Court for the Southern District of New York upon 4 counts of a 26-count indictment charging him with mailing obscene circulars and advertising, and an obscene book, in violation of the federal obscenity statute. Combined with this case was *Alberts* v. *California* in which David Alberts had been convicted of publishing obscene matter in violation of the California Penal Code.)

Vote: 6-3 in *Roth*; 7-2 in *Alberts*

Mr. Justice Brennan delivered the opinion of the Court:

. . . The dispositive question is whether obscenity is utterance within the area of protected speech and press. Although this is the first time the question has been squarely presented to this Court, either under the First Amendment or under the Fourteenth Amendment, expressions found in numerous opinions indicate that this Court has always assumed that obscenity is not protected by the freedoms of speech and press. . . .

All ideas having even the slightest redeeming social importance—unorthodox ideas, controversial ideas, even ideas hateful to the prevailing climate of opinion— have the full protection of the guaranties, unless excludable because they encroach upon the limited area of more important interests. But implicit in the history of the First Amendment is the rejection of obscenity as utterly without redeeming social importance. . . . We hold that obscenity is not within the area of constitutionally protected speech or press. . . .

In summary, then, we hold that these statutes, applied according to the proper standard for judging obscenity, do not offend constitutional safeguards against convictions based upon protected material, or fail to give men in acting adequate notice of what is prohibited.

Roth's argument that the federal obscenity statute unconstitutionally encroaches upon the powers reserved by the Ninth and Tenth Amendments to the States and to the people to punish speech and press where offensive to decency and morality is hinged upon his contention that obscenity is expression not excepted from the sweep of the provision of the First Amendment that *"Congress shall make no law . . . abridging the freedom of speech, or of the press . . . ."* (Emphasis added.) That argument falls in light of our holding that obscenity is not expression protected by the First Amendment. We therefore hold that the federal obscenity statute punishing the use of the mails for obscene material is a proper exercise of the postal power delegated to Congress by Art. 1, § 8, cl. 7. . . .

Alberts argues that because his was a mail-order business, the California statute is repugnant to Art. 1, § 8, cl. 7, under which the Congress allegedly preempted the regulatory field by enacting the federal obscenity statute punishing the mailing or advertising by mail of obscene material. The federal statute deals only with actual mailing; it does not eliminate the power of the state to punish "keeping for sale" or "advertising" obscene material. The state statute in no way imposes a burden or interferes with the federal postal functions. . . .

Mr. Justice Harlan dissented in *Roth*:

. . . It is no answer to say, as the Court does, that obscenity is not protected speech. The point is that this statute, as here construed, defines obscenity so widely that it encompasses matters which might very well be protected speech. I do not think that the federal statute can be constitutionally construed to reach other than what the Government has termed as "hard-core" pornography. Nor do I think the statute can fairly be read as directed only at *persons* who are engaged in the business of catering to the prurient minded, even though their wares fall short of hard-core pornography. Such a statute would raise constitutional questions of a different order. That being so, and since in my opinion the material here involved cannot be said to be hard-core pornography, I would reverse this case with instructions to dismiss the indictment.

Mr. Justice Douglas, with whom Mr. Justice Black concurred, dissented.

When we sustain these convictions, we make the legality of a publication turn on the purity of thought which a book or tract instills in the mind of the reader. I do not think we can approve that standard and be faithful to the command of the First Amendment which by its terms is a restraint on Congress and which by the Fourteenth is a restraint on the States. . . .

I assume there is nothing in the Constitution which forbids Congress from using its power over the mails to proscribe *conduct* on the grounds of good morals. No one would suggest that the First Amendment permits nudity in public places, adultery, and other phases of sexual misconduct.

I can understand (and at times even sympathize) with programs of civic groups and church groups to protect and defend the existing moral standards of the community. I can understand the motives of the Anthony Comstocks who would impose Victorian standards on the community. When speech alone is involved, I do not think that government, consistently with the First Amendment, can become the sponsor of any of these movements. I do not think that government, consistently with the First Amendment, can throw its weight behind one school or another. . . .

I would give the broad sweep of the First Amendment full support. I have the same confidence in the ability of our people to reject noxious literature as I have in their capacity to sort out the true from the false in theology, economics, politics, or any other field.

NOTE:

In *Near* the Court applied the "Gitlow doctrine" to freedom of press and held a statute void on that basis for the first time. Prior censorship was particularly condemned. Here the attempt had been made to stop future publication on the basis of past activities.

Obscenity is a "constitutional outlaw" and in *Roth* v. *United States* the Court attempted to define obscenity by setting up what has come to be known as the "*Roth*" test. This attempts to determine whether to the average person, applying contemporary community standards, the dominant theme of the material taken as a whole appeals to prurient interest. See *Burstyn, Kingsley*, and cases noted there.

Burstyn v. Wilson
343 U.S. 495; 72 S.Ct. 777; 96 L.Ed. 1098 (1952)

(A statute of the state of New York permitted the banning by the state Board of Regents of motion picture films on the ground that they were "sacrilegious." The highly controversial Italian film, *The Miracle*, had been so judged by the Board, and this decision under power granted by the statute was challenged in the courts as being in conflict with the First and Fourteenth Amendments. Joseph Burstyn was a motion picture distributor and Lewis A. Wilson was New York State Commissioner of Education.)

Vote: No dissent

Mr. Justice Clark delivered the opinion of the Court:

. . . It cannot be doubted that motion pictures are a significant medium for the communication of ideas. They may affect public attitudes and behavior in a variety of ways, ranging from direct espousal of a political or social doctrine to the subtle shaping of thought which characterizes all artistic expression. The importance of motion pictures as an organ of public opinion is not lessened by the fact that they are designed to entertain as well as to inform. . . .

It is urged that motion pictures do not fall within the First Amendment's aegis because their production, distribution, and exhibition is a large-scale business conducted for private profit. We cannot agree. That books, newspapers, and magazines are published and sold for profit does not prevent them from being a form of expression whose liberty is safeguarded by the First Amendment. We fail to see why operation for profit should have any different effect in the case of motion pictures.

It is further urged that motion pictures possess a greater capacity for evil, particularly among the youth of a community, than other modes of expression. Even if one were to accept this hypothesis, it does not follow that motion pictures should be disqualified from First Amendment protection. If there be capacity for evil it may be relevant in determining the permissible scope of community control, but it does not authorize substantially unbridled censorship such as we have here.

For the foregoing reasons, we conclude that expression by means of motion pictures is included within the free speech and free press guaranty of the First and Fourteenth Amendments. To the extent that language in the opinion in *Mutual*

Film Corp. v. *Industrial Commission, supra*, is out of harmony with the views here set forth, we no longer adhere to it.

To hold that liberty of expression by means of motion pictures is guaranteed by the First and Fourteenth Amendments, however, is not the end of our problem. It does not follow that the Constitution requires absolute freedom to exhibit every motion picture of every kind at all times and all places. That much is evident from the series of decisions of this Court with respect to other media of communication of ideas. Nor does it follow that motion pictures are necessarily subject to the precise rules governing any other particular method of expression. Each method tends to present its own peculiar problems. But the basic principles of freedom of speech and the press, like the First Amendment's command, do not vary. Those principles, as they have frequently been enunciated by this Court, make freedom of expression the rule. There is no justification in this case for making an exception to that rule. . . .

New York's highest court says there is "nothing mysterious" about the statutory provision applied in this case: "It is simply this: that no religion, as that word is understood by the ordinary, reasonable person, shall be treated with contempt, mockery, scorn and ridicule. . . ." This is far from the kind of narrow exception to freedom of expression which a state may carve out to satisfy the adverse demands of other interests of society. In seeking to apply the broad and all-inclusive definition of "sacrilegious" given by the New York courts, the censor is set adrift upon a boundless sea amid a myriad of conflicting currents of religious views, with no charts but those provided by the most vocal and powerful orthodoxies. New York cannot vest such unlimited restraining control over motion pictures in a censor. . . . Under such a standard the most careful and tolerant censor would find it virtually impossible to avoid favoring one religion over another, and he would be subject to an inevitable tendency to ban the expression of unpopular sentiments sacred to a religious minority. Application of the "sacrilegious" test, in these or other respects, might raise substantial questions under the First Amendment's guaranty of separate church and state with freedom of worship for all. However, from the standpoint of freedom of speech and the press, it is enough to point out that the state has no legitimate interest in protecting any or all religions from views distasteful to them which is sufficient to justify prior restraints upon the expression of those views. It is not the business of government in our nation to suppress real or imagined attacks upon a particular religious doctrine, whether they appear in publications, speeches, or motion pictures.

Since the term "sacrilegious" is the sole standard under attack here, it is not necessary for us to decide, for example, whether a state may censor motion pictures under a clearly-drawn statute designed and applied to prevent the showing of obscene films. That is a very different question from the one now before us. We hold only that under the First and Fourteenth Amendments a state may not ban a film on the basis of a censor's conclusion that it is "sacrilegious."

Reversed.

Mr. Justice Frankfurter, whom Mr. Justice Jackson joined, concurred. Mr. Justice Burton, having concurred in the opinion of the court, also joined this opinion:

. . . In *Cantwell* v. *Connecticut*, 310 U.S. 296, 310, Mr. Justice Roberts, speaking for the whole Court, said: "In the realm of religious faith, and in that of political belief, sharp differences arise. In both fields the tenets of one man may seem the rankest error to his neighbor." Conduct and beliefs dear to one may seem the rankest "sacrilege" to another. A few examples suffice to show the difficulties facing a conscientious censor or motion picture producer or distributor in determining what the New York statute condemns as sacrilegious. A motion picture portraying Christ as divine—for example, a movie showing medieval Church art —would offend the religous opinions of the members of several Protestant denominations who do not believe in the Trinity, as well as those of a non-Christian faith. Conversely, one showing Christ as merely an ethical teacher could not but offend millions of Christians of many denominations. Which is "sacrilegious"? The doctrine of transubstantiation, and the veneration of relics or particular stone and wood embodiments of saints or divinity, both sacred to Catholics, are offensive to a great many Protestants, and therefore for them sacrilegious in the view of the New York court. Is a picture treating either subject, whether sympathetically, unsympathetically, or neutrally, "sacrilegious"? It is not a sufficient answer to say that "sacrilegious" is definite, because all subjects that in any way might be interpreted as offending the religious beliefs of any one of the 300 sects of the United States are banned in New York. To allow such vague, undefinable powers of censorship to be exercised is bound to have stultifying consequences on the creative process of literature and art—for the films are derived largely from literature. History does not encourage reliance on the wisdom and moderation of the censor as a safeguard in the exercise of such drastic power over the minds of men. We not only do not know but cannot know what is condemnable by "sacrilegious." And if we cannot tell, how are those to be governed by the statute to tell?

It is this impossibility of knowing how far the form of words by which the New York Court of Appeals explained "sacrilegious" carries the proscription of religious subjects that makes the term unconstitutionally vague. . . .

. . . Prohibition through words that fail to convey what is permitted and what is prohibited for want of appropriate objective standards, offends Due Process in two ways. First, it does not sufficiently apprise those bent on obedience of law of what may reasonably be foreseen to be found illicit by the law-enforcing authority, whether court or jury or administrative agency. Secondly, where licensing is rested, in the first instance, in an administrative agency, the available judicial review is in effect rendered inoperative. On the basis of such a portmanteau word as "sacrilegious," the judiciary has no standards with which to judge the validity of administrative action which necessarily involves, at least in large measure, subjective determinations. Thus, the administrative first step becomes the last step. . . .

RELATED CASES:

Mutual Film Corp. v. Industrial Commission of Ohio: 236 U.S. 230 (1915). Opinion: McKenna, J. No dissent.

The moving picture censorship act of Ohio of 1913 is not unconstitutional either as depriving the owners of moving pictures of their property without due process of law, as a burden on interstate commerce, or as abridging freedom and liberty of speech and opinion. Motion pictures do not come under the Constitutional guarantee of freedom of the press. This case antedated the Court's vital concern with civil rights and liberties problems. Here movies were held not to be a part of the press but a commercial enterprise. This case was overruled by *Burstyn* v. *Wilson*.

Interstate Circuit, Inc. v. Dallas: 390 U.S. 676 (1968). Opinion: Marshall, J. Dissenting: Harlan, J.

The vice of vagueness is present when standards do not sufficiently guide the censor. The absence of narrowly drawn, reasonable, and definite standards for officials to follow is fatal.

NOTE:

In *Burstyn* the Court made "official" the dictum of *United States* v. *Paramount Pictures, Inc.* (334 U.S. 131, 1948) (see p. 84, above), which had declared movies to be a part of the "press" of the country in the sense in which that term is used in the First Amendment. Movies were simply recognized as a significant means of communication. Prior censorship was condemned here also and there was as well the "vice of vagueness" in the lack of adequate standards. Public interest in the matter—the protection of religious sensibilities—was held not sufficient to justify the sort of restriction involved here.

Kingsley International Pictures Corporation v. Regents
360 U.S. 684; 79 S.Ct. 1362; 3 L.Ed. 2nd 1512 (1959)

(The Kingsley Corporation was the distributor for a motion picture entitled *Lady Chatterley's Lover*, and, in accordance with the provisions of the New York Education Law, requested a license to exhibit the movie. This was refused because the film presented adultery "as being right and desirable for certain people under certain circumstances." This denial was upheld by the New York Court of Appeals against the contention that the proceeding violated the First Amendment guarantees of free speech and press as applied to the states by means of the Fourteenth Amendment.)

Vote: 9-0

Mr. Justice Stewart delivered the opinion of the Court:

. . . What New York has done . . . is to prevent the exhibition of a motion picture because that picture advocates an idea—that adultery under certain circumstances may be proper behavior. Yet the First Amendment's basic guarantee is of freedom to advocate ideas. The State, quite simply, has thus struck at the very heart of constitutionally protected liberty.

It is contended that the State's action was justified because the motion picture attractively portrays a relationship which is contrary to the moral standards, the religious precepts, and the legal code of its citizenry. This argument misconceives what it is that the Constitution protects. Its guarantee is not confined to the expression of ideas that are conventional or shared by a majority. It protects advocacy of the opinion that adultery may sometimes be proper, no less than advocacy of socialism or the single tax. And in the realm of ideas it protects expression which is eloquent no less than that which is unconvincing.

Advocacy of conduct proscribed by law is not, as Mr. Justice Brandeis long ago pointed out, "a justification for denying free speech where the advocacy falls short of incitement and there is nothing to indicate that the advocacy would be immediately acted on." *Whitney* v. *California*, 274 U.S. 357, at 376 (concurring opinion). "Among free men, the deterrents ordinarily to be applied to prevent crime are education and punishment for violations of the law, not abridgment of the rights of free speech. . . ." *Id.*, at 378.

The inflexible command which the New York Court of Appeals has attributed to the State Legislature thus cuts so close to the core of constitutional freedom as to make it quite needless in this case to examine the periphery. Specifically, there is not occasion to consider the appellant's contention that the State is entirely without power to require films of any kind to be licensed prior to their exhibition. Nor need we here determine whether despite problems peculiar to motion pictures, the controls which a State may impose upon this medium of expression are precisely coextensive with those allowable for newspapers, books, or individual speech. It

is enough for the present case to reaffirm that motion pictures are within the First and Fourteenth Amendments' basic protection. . . .
Reversed.

RELATED CASES:

In a series of *per curiam* decisions chiefly following the *Burstyn* case, and citing that case, the Court held invalid attempts by various states and cities to censor movies. There was no dissent.

United Artists Corp. v. Board of Censors: 339 U.S. 952 (1950).
Memphis. The movie was *Curley*.

RD-DR Corp. v. Smith: 340 U.S. 853 (1950).
Atlanta. The movie was *Lost Boundaries*.

Gelling v. Texas: 343 U.S. 960 (1952).
Marshall, Texas. The movie was *Pinky*.

Superior Films v. Ohio Department of Education: 346 U.S. 587 (1954).
The movie was *M*.

Commercial Pictures Corp. v. Regents: 346 U.S. 587 (1954).
New York. The movie was *La Ronde*.

Holmby Productions, Inc. v. Vaughn: 350 U.S. 870 (1955).
Kansas. The movie was *The Moon Is Blue*.

Adams Newark Theater Co. v. Newark: 354 U.S. 931 (1957). Opinion: Per curiam. Dissenting: Black and Douglas, JJ. Abstaining: Brennan, J.
The Court here in a *per curiam* opinion affirmed a judgment of the Supreme Court of New Jersey which declared that ordinances specifically placing certain types of conduct within the general terms of previous ordinances condemning lewdness, obscenity, or indecency are not unconstitutional violations of the right of free speech since some of the behavior prohibited is so violently contrary to good morals and decency as to be condemnable even though some behavior is not subject to censorship because of free speech.

Times Film Corp. v. City of Chicago: 365 U.S. 43 (1961). Opinion: Clark, J. Dissenting: Warren, C.J., and Black, Douglas, and Brennan, JJ.
Chicago's municipal code provision that all motion pictures be submitted for examination before a license for their public exhibition will be granted was challenged. The film was *Don Juan*, a movie version of Mozart's *Don Giovanni*. The Court upheld the ordinance and noted that there is no complete and absolute freedom to exhibit, at least once, any and every kind of motion picture. Freedom from prior restraint is not an absolute privilege under the First Amendment. Cities have some power. They can prevent the showing of obscene pictures. The Court's concern here was for standards and procedures.

Jacobellis v. State of Ohio: 378 U.S. 184 (1964). Opinion: Brennan, J. Dissenting: Warren, C.J., and Harlan and Clark, JJ.
Obscenity in movies is not subject to constitutional protection and the Court must in such cases make an independent constitutional judgment on the facts of the case as to whether the material involved is constitutionally protected. The opinion reaffirmed the "*Roth* test" but noted that the "community standards" involved were national, not local, standards.

Freedman v. Maryland: 380 U.S. 51 (1965). Opinion: Brennan, J. No dissent.
A noncriminal process which requires the prior submission of a movie film to a censor avoids constitutional infirmity only if it takes place under procedural safeguards designed to obviate the dangers of a censorship system. Among other things this must

include assurance of a prompt final judicial determination of obscenity. The opinion noted that the burden of proof is on the censor. The case arose in Baltimore.

Ginsberg v. New York: 390 U.S. 629 (1968). Opinion: Brennan, J. Dissenting: Douglas, Black, and Fortas, JJ.

Obscenity is not within the area of protected speech and press. New York's regulation in defining obscenity on the basis of appeal to minors under seventeen is valid. Sales to minors were prohibited. The rule of this case should be distinguished from that of *Butler* v. *Michigan,* p. 85, above.

Southeastern Promotions, Ltd. v. Conrad: 420 U.S. 546 (1975). Opinion: Blackmun, J. Dissenting: Douglas, White, and Rehnquist, JJ., and Burger, C.J.

The management of the Chattanooga Municipal Auditorium, a municipal theater, could not deny the use of the facility for the controversial musical *Hair* unless there were appropriate procedural safeguards. Otherwise it would be prior restraint.

NOTE:

The basic point in *Kingsley* is that there may be no official prior restraint on the expression and advocacy of opinions or ideas no matter how unconventional they may be. Because there was no need to determine the matter in reaching the decision, the Court did not pass on whether a state may provide for the licensing of movies.

By way of summation, from the Court's decisions it appears that states may ban motion pictures under certain circumstances. Just what these circumstances are is not entirely clear. The burden appears to be on the state to show that the instances of attempted censorship are exceptional. Apparently, within limits, decency and morals may be protected by prior restraint under properly established standards, Vagueness has voided a number of statutes. Also, since little discretion can be given to a censor, in practice there is virtually a requirement that the act of censorship be almost ministerial in its operation. Still another requirement for censorship is that there must be what might be called a "clear and present danger" of substantial evil to the community. There must, presumably, be a real and actual danger that the exhibition of the film will abnormally affect the *average* person as opposed to the unusual person, and it would need to appeal *solely* to one's prurient interest, "the prurient interest test."

Applicable here also is the "dominant effect test" according to which the dominant note of a movie would be the presentation of erotic allurement tending to excite lustful and lecherous desire, or "dirt for dirt's sake" only. Also, it should be borne in mind that the Court has noted that obscenity is a constitutional outlaw and not within the protection of free speech and press.

If censorship is ever upheld apart from national security it will need to be almost ministerial in its operation eliminating any real element of discretion. Further it will operate only where there is clear and present danger of substantial evil to the community and the statute itself cannot be vague.

Miller v. California
413 U.S. 15; 93 S.Ct. 2067; 37 L.Ed. 2d 419 (1973)

(Marvin Miller conducted a mass mailing campaign to advertise the sale of illustrated books, euphemistically called "adult" material. After a jury trial, he was convicted of violating California Penal Code § 311.2(a), a misdemeanor, by knowingly distributing obscene matter, and the Appellate Department, Superior Court of California, County of Orange, summarily affirmed the judgment without opinion.

Appellant's conviction was specifically based on his conduct in causing five unsolicited advertising brochures to be sent through the mail in an envelope addressed to a restaurant in Newport Beach, California. The envelope was opened by the manager of the restaurant and his mother. They had not requested the brochures; they complained to the police.)

Vote: 5-4

Mr. Chief Justice Burger delivered the opinion of the Court:

. . . This much has been categorically settled by the Court, that obscene material is unprotected by the First Amendment. . . .

We acknowledge, however, the inherent dangers of undertaking to regulate any form of expression. State statutes designed to regulate obscene materials must be carefully limited. . . .

. . . As a result, we now confine the permissible scope of such regulation to works which depict or describe sexual conduct. That conduct must be specifically defined by the applicable state law, as written or authoritatively construed. A state offense must also be limited to works which, taken as a whole, appeal to the prurient interest in sex, which portray sexual conduct in a patently offensive way, and which, taken as a whole, do not have serious literary, artistic, political, or scientific value.

The basic guidelines for the trier of fact must be: (a) whether "the average person, applying contemporary community standards" would find that the work, taken as a whole, appeals to the prurient interest, . . . (b) whether the work depicts or describes, in a patently offensive way, sexual conduct specifically defined by the applicable state law, and (c) whether the work, taken as a whole, lacks serious literary, artistic, political, or scientific value. We do not adopt as a constitutional standard the *"utterly* without redeeming social value" test of *Memoirs* v. *Massachusetts, supra,* 383 U.S. at 419, 86 S.Ct., at 977 (1966); that concept has never commanded the adherence of more than three Justices at one time. If a state law that regulates obscene material is thus limited, as written or construed, the First Amendment values applicable to the States through the Fourteenth Amendment are adequately protected by the ultimate power of appellate courts to conduct an independent review of constitutional claims when necessary. . . .

. . . Under the holdings announced today, no one will be subject to prosecution for the sale or exposure of obscene materials unless these materials depict or describe patently offensive "hard core" sexual conduct specifically defined by the regulating state law, as written or construed. We are satisfied that these specific prerequisites will provide fair notice to a dealer in such materials that his public and commercial activities may bring prosecution. . . .

Under a national Constitution, fundamental First Amendment limitations on the powers of the States do not vary from community to community, but this does not mean that there are, or should or can be, fixed, uniform national standards of precisely what appeals to the "prurient interest" or is "patently offensive." These are essentially questions of fact, and our nation is simply too big and too diverse for this Court to reasonably expect that such standards could be articulated for all 50 States in a single formulation, even assuming the prerequisite consensus exists. When triers of fact are asked to decide whether "the average person, applying contemporary community standards" would consider certain materials "prurient" it would be unrealistic to require that the answer be based on some abstract formulation. The adversary system, with lay jurors as the usual ultimate fact-finders in criminal prosecutions, has historically permitted triers-of-fact to draw on the standards of their community guided always by limiting instructions on the law. To require a State to structure obscenity proceedings around evidence of a *national* "community standard" would be an exercise in futility. . . . The First Amendment protects works which, taken as a whole, have serious literary, artistic, political or scientific value, regardless of whether the government or a majority of the people approve of the ideas these works represent. "The protection given speech and press was fashioned to assure unfettered interchange of *ideas* for the bringing about of political changes desired by the people." . . . But the public portrayal of hard core sexual conduct for its own sake, and for the ensuing commercial gain, is a different matter. . . .

In sum we (a) reaffirm the *Roth* holding that obscene material is not protected by the First Amendment, (b) hold that such material can be regulated by the States, subject to the specific safeguards enunciated above, without a showing that the material is "*utterly* without redeeming social value," and (c) hold that obscenity is to be determined by applying "contemporary community standards," . . . not "national standards."

Vacated and remanded for further proceedings.

Mr. Justice Douglas dissented.

. . . We deal with highly emotional, not rational, questions. To many the Song of Solomon is obscene. I do not think we, the judges, were ever given the constitutional power to make definitions of obsenity. If it is to be defined, let the people debate and decide by a constitutional amendment what they want to ban as obscene and what standards they want the legislatures and the courts to apply. Perhaps the people will decide that the path towards a mature, integrated society requires that all ideas competing for acceptance must have no censor. Perhaps they will decide otherwise. Whatever the choice, the courts will have some guidelines. Now we have none except our own predilections.

Mr. Justice Brennan, with whom Mr. Justice Stewart and Mr. Justice Marshall join, dissented:

. . . I need not now decide whether a statute might be drawn to impose, within the requirements of the First Amendment, criminal penalties for the precise conduct at issue here. For it is clear that under my dissent in *Slaton*, the statute under which the prosecution was brought is unconstitutionally overbroad, and therefore invalid on its face.

RELATED CASES:

Memoirs v. Massachusetts: 383 U.S. 413 (1966). Opinion: Brennan, J. Dissenting: Clark, Harlan, and White, JJ.

In this case a book commonly known as *Fanny Hill* had been adjudged obscene in a proceeding that put the book itself on trial and not its publisher or distributor. Here the Court reversed the lower court's obscenity ruling, noting that "a book cannot be proscribed unless it is found to be *utterly* without redeeming social value. This is so even though the book is found to possess the requisite prurient appeal and to be patently offensive. Each of the three federal constitutional criteria is to be applied independently; the social value of the book can neither be weighed against nor canceled by its prurient appeal or patent offensiveness."

Paris Adult Theater I v. Slaton: 413 U.S. 49 (1973). Opinion: Burger, C.J. Dissenting: Douglas, Brennan, Stewart, and Marshall, JJ.

There are legitimate state interests at stake in stemming the tide of commercialized obscenity. The state's interest extends to regulating the exhibition of obscene material in places of public accommodation including so-called "adult theaters" from which minors are excluded. State action in such instances is valid as long as the First Amendment standards set forth in *Miller* v. *California* are met.

Kaplan v. California: 413 U.S. 115 (1973). Opinion: Burger, C.J. Dissenting: Douglas, Brennan, Stewart and Marshall, JJ.

Here a book was declared obscene on the basis of the *Miller* standards. Contemporary community standards were applied.

United States v. 12 200-ft. Reels of Super 8 mm. Film: 413 U.S. 123 (1972). Opinion: Burger, C.J. Dissenting: Douglas, Brennan, Stewart, and Marshall, JJ.

Congress may prohibit the importation of obscene materials (here films, slides, and photographs) under the standards of *Miller.* This is true even though the material is for private, personal use and possession only.

United States v. Orito: 413 U.S. 139 (1973). Opinion: Burger, C.J. Dissenting: Douglas, Brennan, Stewart, and Marshall, JJ.

Congress may prohibit the transportation in interstate commerce of obscene material as determined by the standards of *Miller.* Here films were involved.

New York Times Company v. United States
403 U.S. 713; 91 S.Ct. 2140; 29 L.Ed. 2d 820 (1971)

(The *New York Times* was enjoined by a federal District Court injunction from publication of the "Pentagon Papers." Later the injunction was dissolved. These papers had been turned over to the *Times* and the *Washington Post* by Daniel Ellsberg, a Pentagon employee. The study was entitled "History of U.S. Decision-Making Process on Viet Nam Policy.")

Per curiam.

. . . "Any system of prior restraints of expression comes to this Court bearing a heavy presumption against its constitutional validity." *Bantam Books, Inc.* v. *Sullivan,* 372 U.S. 58, 70, 83 S.Ct. 631, 639, 9 L.Ed. 2d 584 (1963); see also *Near* v. *Minnesota ex rel. Olson,* 283 U.S. 697, 51 S.Ct. 625, 75 L. Ed. 1357 (1931). The Government "thus carries a heavy burden of showing justification for the imposition of such a restraint." *Organization for a Better Austin* v. *Keefe,* 401 U.S. —, 91 S.Ct. 1575, 28 L.Ed. 2d — (1971). The District Court for the Southern District of New York in the *New York Times* case, — F.Supp. — and the District Court for the District of Columbia and the Court of Appeals for the District of Columbia Circuit — F.2d — in the *Washington Post* case held that the Government had not met that burden. We agree.

The judgment of the Court of Appeals for the District of Columbia Circuit is therefore affirmed. The order of the Court of Appeals for the Second Circuit is reversed, — F.2d — and the case is remanded with directions to enter a judgment affirming the judgment of the District Court for the Southern District of New York. The stays entered June 25, 1971, by the Court are vacated. The judgments shall issue forthwith.

Mr. Justice Brennan concurred:

. . . The error which has pervaded these cases from the outset was the granting of any injunctive relief whatsoever, interim or otherwise. The entire thrust of the Government's claim throughout these cases has been that publication of the material sought to be enjoined "could," or "might," or "may" prejudice the national interest in various ways. But the First Amendment tolerates absolutely no prior judicial restraints of the press predicated upon surmise or conjecture that untoward consequences may result. . . .

Mr. Justice Stewart, with whom Mr. Justice White joined, concurred:

. . . Yet it is elementary that the successful conduct of international diplomacy and the maintenance of an effective national defense require both confidentiality and secrecy. Other nations can hardly deal with this Nation in an atmosphere of mutual trust unless they can be assured that their confidences will be kept. . . .

Undoubtedly Congress has the power to enact specific and appropriate criminal laws to protect government property and preserve government secrets. Congress has passed such laws, and several of them are of very colorable relevance to the apparent circumstances of these cases. . . .

I am convinced that the Executive is correct with respect to some of the documents involved. But I cannot say that disclosure of any of them will surely result in direct, immediate, and irreparable damage to our Nation or its people. That being so, there can under the First Amendment be but one judicial resolution of the issues before us. I join the judgments of the Court.

Mr. Justice White, with whom Mr. Justice Stewart joins, concurred:

I concur in today's judgments, but only because of the concededly extraordinary protection against prior restraints enjoyed by the press under our constitutional system. I do not say that in no circumstances would the First Amendment permit an injunction against publishing information about government plans or operations. Nor, after examining the materials the Government characterizes as the most sensitive and destructive, can I deny that revelation of these documents will do substantial damage to public interests. Indeed, I am confident that their disclosure will have that result. But I nevertheless agree that the United States has not satisfied the very heavy burden which it must meet to warrant an injunction against publication in these cases, at least in the absence of express and appropriately limited congressional authorization for prior restraints in circumstances such as these. . . .

Mr. Justice Marshall concurred:

The Government contends that the only issue in this case is whether in a suit by the United States, "the First Amendment bars a court from prohibiting a newspaper from publishing material whose disclosure would pose a grave and immediate danger to the security of the United States." Brief of the Government, at 6. With all due respect, I believe the ultimate issue in this case is even more basic than the one posed by the Solicitor General. The issue is whether this Court or the Congress has the power to make law. . . .

The problem here is whether in this particular case the Executive Branch has authority to invoke the equity jurisdiction of the courts to protect what it believes to be the national interest. . . .

Mr. Chief Justice Burger dissented:

. . . I suggest we are in this posture because these cases have been conducted in unseemly haste. Mr. Justice Harlan covers the chronology of events demonstrating the hectic pressures under which these cases have been processed and I need not restate them. The prompt settling of these cases reflects our universal abhorrence of prior restraint. But prompt judicial action does not mean unjudicial haste. . . .

The newspapers make a derivative claim under the First Amendment; they denominate this right as the public right-to-know; by implication, the *Times* asserts a sole trusteeship of that right by virtue of its journalist "scoop." The right is asserted as an absolute. Of course, the First Amendment right itself is not an absolute, as Justice Holmes so long ago pointed out in his aphorism concerning the right to shout of fire in a crowded theater. There are other exceptions, some of which Chief Justice Hughes mentioned by way of example in *Near* v. *Minnesota ex rel. Olson.* There are no doubt other exceptions no one has had occasion to describe or discuss. Conceivably such exceptions may be lurking in these cases and would have been flushed had they been properly considered in the trial courts, free from unwarranted deadlines and frenetic pressures. A great issue of this kind should be tried in a judicial atmosphere conducive to thoughtful, reflective deliberation, especially when haste, in terms of hours, is unwarranted in light of the long period the *Times*, by its own choice, deferred publication.

It is not disputed that the *Times* has had unauthorized possession of the documents for three to four months, during which it has had its expert analysts studying them, presumably digesting them and preparing the material for publication. During all of this time, the *Times* presumably in its capacity as trustee of the public's "right to know," has held up publication for purposes it considered proper and thus public knowledge was delayed. No doubt this was for a good reason; the analysis of 7,000 pages of complex material drawn from a vastly greater volume of material would inevitably take time and the writing of good news stories takes time. But why should the United States Government, from whom this information was illegally acquired by someone, along with all the counsel, trial judges, and appellate judges be placed under needless pressure? After these months of deferral, the alleged right-to-know has somehow and suddenly become a right that must be vindicated instanter.

. . . To me it is hardly believable that a newspaper long regarded as a great institution in American life would fail to perform one of the basic and simple duties of every citizen with respect to the discovery or possession of stolen property or secret government documents. That duty, I had thought—perhaps naively—was to report forthwith, to responsible public officers. This duty rests on taxi drivers, Justices and the New York *Times*. The course followed by the *Times*, whether so calculated or not, removed any possibility of orderly litigation of the issues. If the action of the judges up to now has been correct, that result is sheer happenstance.

Our grant of the writ before final judgment in the *Times* case aborted the trial in the District Court before it had made a complete record pursuant to the mandate of the Court of Appeals, Second Circuit.

The consequence of all this melancholy series of events is that we literally do not know what we are acting on. . . .

Mr. Justice Harlan, with whom the Chief Justice and Mr. Justice Blackmun joined, dissented:

. . . Pending further hearings in each case conducted under the appropriate ground rules, I would continue the restraints on publication. I cannot believe that the doctrine prohibiting prior restraints reaches to the point of preventing courts from maintaining the *status quo* long enough to act responsibly in matters of such national importance as those involved here.

Mr. Justice Blackmun dissented:

The First Amendment, after all, is only one part of an entire Constitution. Article II of the great document vests in the Executive Branch primary power over the conduct of foreign affairs and places in that branch the responsibility for the Nation's safety. Each provision of the Constitution is important, and I cannot subscribe to a doctrine of unlimited absolutism for the First Amendment at the cost of downgrading other provisions. First Amendment absolutism has never commanded a majority of this Court. . . .

I know from past personal experience the agony of time pressure in the preparation of litigation. But these cases and the issues involved and the courts, including this one, deserve better than has been produced thus far. . . .

RELATED CASES:

Miami Herald Publishing Co. v. Tornillo: 418 U.S. 241 (1974). Opinion: Burger, C.J. No dissent.

Under Florida's "right of reply" statute a political candidate had the right to equal space to answer criticism and attacks made by a newspaper. The *Miami Herald* had repeatedly published editorials critical of Pat Tornillo, a candidate for the Florida House of Representatives, but had refused to allow him to reply according to the terms of the statute. The Court noted that compulsion of the press to publish that which " 'reason' tells them should not be published" is violative of the First Amendment. There is an infringement on "the exercise of editorial control and judgment."

Gertz v. Robert Welch, Inc.: 418 U.S. 323 (1974). Opinion: Powell, J. Dissenting: Burger, C.J., and Douglas, Brennan, and White, JJ.

After a Chicago police officer was convicted of murder the victim's family retained Elmer Gertz as counsel in civil litigation against the officer. A magazine published by Welch published an article charging that Gertz was part of a Communist campaign against the police. The Court held that the rule set down in *New York Times* v. *Sullivan* (see p. 85, above) under which knowledge of falsity or reckless disregard for the truth is to be proved did not apply here because Gertz was neither a public official nor a public figure. The state has a legitimate interest in providing a legal remedy for defamatory falsehoods which are injurious to the reputation of a private individual. Also see *Cantrell* v. *Forest City Publishing Co.,* p. 87, above.

Feiner v. New York
340 U.S. 315; 71 S.Ct. 303; 95 L.Ed. 295 (1951)

(The petitioner, Irving Feiner, a university student, addressed an open-air meeting in a Negro neighborhood in Syracuse, N.Y. His speech appeared to police officers to be arousing the crowd of 75-80 people, and, after repeated requests by the police that he stop speaking, he was arrested for disorderly conduct. This was challenged as violating Feiner's right of free speech under the Fourteenth Amendment.)

Vote: 6-3

Mr. Chief Justice Vinson delivered the opinion of the Court:

The language of *Cantwell* v. *Connecticut*, 310 U.S. 296 (1940) is appropriate here. "The offense known as breach of the peace embraces a great variety of conduct destroying or menacing public order and tranquility. It includes not only violent acts but acts and words likely to produce violence in others. No one would have the hardihood to suggest that the principle of freedom of speech sanctions incitement to riot or that religious liberty connotes the privilege to exhort others to physical attack upon those belonging to another sect. When clear and present danger of riot, disorder, interference with traffic upon the public streets, or other immediate threat to public safety, peace, or order, appears, the power of the State to prevent or punish is obvious." The findings of the New York courts as to the condition of the crowd and the refusal of petitioner to obey the police requests, supported as they are by the record of this case, are persuasive that the conviction of petitioner for violation of public peace, order and authority does not exceed the bounds of proper state action. This Court respects, as it must, the interest of the community in maintaining peace and order on its streets. . . . We cannot say that the preservation of that interest here encroaches on the constitutional rights of this petitioner.

We are well aware that the ordinary murmurings and objections of a hostile audience cannot be allowed to silence a speaker, and are also mindful of the possible danger of giving overzealous police officials complete discretion to break up otherwise lawful public meetings. "A state may not unduly suppress free communication of views, religious or other, under the guise of conserving desirable conditions."

But we are not faced here with such a situation. It is one thing to say that the police cannot be used as an instrument for the suppression of unpopular views, and another to say that, when as here the speaker passes the bounds of argument or persuasion and undertakes incitement to riot, they are powerless to prevent a breach of the peace. Nor in this case can we condemn the considered judgment of three New York courts approving the means which the police, faced with a crisis, used in the exercise of their power and duty to preserve peace and order. The findings of the state courts as to the existing situation and the imminence of greater disorder coupled with petitioner's deliberate defiance of the police officers convince us that we should not reverse this conviction in the name of free speech.

Affirmed.

Mr. Justice Black dissented:

. . . Moreover, assuming that the "facts" did indicate a critical situation, I reject the implication of the Court's opinion that the police had no obligation to protect petitioner's constitutional right to talk. The police of course have power to prevent breaches of the peace. But if, in the name of preserving order, they ever can interfere with a lawful public speaker, they first must make all reasonable efforts to protect him. Here the policemen did not even pretend to try to protect petitioner. According to the officers' testimony, the crowd was restless but there is no showing of any attempt to quiet it; pedestrians were forced to walk into the street, but there was no effort to clear a path on the sidewalk; one person threatened to assault petitioner but the officers did nothing to discourage this when even a word might have sufficed. Their duty was to protect petitioner's right to talk, even to the extent of arresting the man who threatened to interfere. Instead, they shirked that duty and acted only to suppress the right to speak. . . .

Mr. Justice Douglas dissented, with the concurrence of Mr. Justice Minton:

. . . A speaker may not, of course, incite a riot any more than he may incite a breach of the peace by the use of "fighting words." . . . But this record shows no such extremes. It shows an unsympathetic audience and the threat of one man to haul the speaker from the stage. It is against that kind of threat that speakers need police protection. If they do not receive it and instead the police throw their weight on the side of those who would break up the meetings, the police become the new censors of speech. Police censorship has all the vices of censorship from city halls which we have repeatedly struck down. . . .

RELATED CASES:

Davis v. Massachusetts: 167 U.S. 43 (1897). Opinion: White, J. No dissent.
A city ordinance which provides that no person shall make a public address in or upon any of the city's public ground, except in accordance with a permit from the Mayor, is not in conflict with the Constitution of the United States, and particularly the Fourteenth Amendment. This is not a grant to the Mayor of arbitrary power. The Fourteenth Amendment does not destroy state police power. This is a pioneer case in this field.

DeJonge v. Oregon: 299 U.S. 353 (1937). Opinion: Hughes, C.J. No dissent. Abstaining: Stone, J.
Holding a peaceful public meeting for lawful discussion, carried on in a lawful manner, without incitement to violence or crime, cannot be made a crime under the due process clause of the Fourteenth Amendment. See p. 121, below.

Terminiello v. Chicago: 337 U.S. 1 (1949). Opinion: Douglas, J. Dissenting: Vinson, C.J., and Frankfurter, Jackson, and Burton, JJ.
The city ordinance as construed by the trial court "permitted conviction of petitioner if his speech stirred people to anger, invited public dispute, or brought about a condition of unrest. A conviction resting on any of those grounds may not stand." This case and *DeJonge* have some similarity. The dissenting opinions of both Justice Frankfurter and Justice Jackson here are worthy of attention.

Gregory v. Chicago: 394 U.S. 111 (1969). Opinion: Warren, C.J. No dissent.
In the case of a peaceful march from Chicago's City Hall to the residence of Mayor Daley to press claims for desegregation of public schools police feared civil disorder.

Therefore, they demanded that the demonstrators, including Dick Gregory, civil liberties activist, disperse. When this demand was not obeyed the marchers were arrested for disorderly conduct. The Court held that there was denial of due process because of lack of evidence to support the charge that there was disorderly conduct. The acts here were clearly entitled to First Amendment protection.

Cohen v. California: 403 U.S. 15 (1971). Opinion: Harlan, J. Dissenting: Blackmun, J., Burger, C.J., and Black and White, JJ.

The state could not prosecute for disturbing the peace by wearing an emblazoned tee-shirt, which expressed displeasure with the draft, in the courthouse corridor. Without a showing of a more particularized and compelling reason, the statute as applied violated the First and Fourteenth Amendment rights of expression.

NOTE:

There is a certain parallel between *Feiner* and *Terminiello* although in the latter case the Court reversed the conviction, and in *Feiner* there was a public street and in *Terminiello* a private hall. In both cases the public disturbance was brought about by persons who objected to what was being said. The speaker was thus "inciting to riot." *Feiner* represents a departure from previous views of the Court that free speech was almost an absolute right.

Kunz v. New York
340 U.S. 290; 71 S.Ct. 312; 95 L.Ed. 280 (1951)

(The appellant, Carl Jacob Kunz, a Baptist minister, was convicted of holding a religious meeting in Columbus Circle without a permit from the city police commissioner as required by city ordinance.)

Vote: 8-1

Mr. Chief Justice Vinson delivered the opinion of the Court:

. . . Appellant's conviction was thus based upon his failure to possess a permit for 1948. We are here concerned only with the propriety of the action of the police commissioner in refusing to issue that permit. Disapproval of the 1948 permit application by the police commissioner was justified by the New York courts on the ground that a permit had previously been revoked "for good reasons." It is noteworthy that there is no mention in the ordinance of reasons for which such a permit application can be refused. This interpretation allows the police commissioner, an administrative official, to exercise discretion in denying subsequent permit applications on the basis of his interpretation, at that time, of what is deemed to be conduct condemned by the ordinance. We have here, then, an ordinance which gives an administrative official discretionary power to control in advance the right of citizens to speak on religious matters on the streets of New York. As such, the ordinance is clearly invalid as a prior restraint on the exercise of First Amendment rights.

In considering the right of a municipality to control the use of public streets for the expression of religious views, we start with the words of Mr. Justice Roberts that "Wherever the title of streets and parks may rest, they have immemorially been held in trust for the use of the public and, time out of mind, have been used for purposes of assembly, communicating thoughts between citizens, and discussing public questions." *Hague* v. *CIO*, 307 U.S. 496 (1939). Although this Court has recognized that a statute may be enacted which prevents serious interference with normal usage of streets and parks, *Cox* v. *New Hampshire*, 312 U.S. 569 (1941), we have consistently condemned licensing systems which vest in an administrative official discretion to grant or withhold a permit upon broad criteria unrelated to proper regulation of public places. In *Cantwell* v. *Connecticut*, 310 U.S. 296 (1940), this Court held invalid an ordinance which required a license for soliciting money for religious causes. Speaking for a unanimous Court, Mr. Justice Roberts said: "But to condition the solicitation of aid for the perpetuation of religious views or systems upon a license, the grant of which rests in the exercise of a determination by state authority as to what is a religious cause, is to lay a forbidden burden upon the exercise of liberty protected by the Constitution." . . . In *Saia* v. *New York*, 334 U.S. 558 (1948), we reaffirmed the invalidity of such prior restraints upon the right to speak: "We hold that § 3 of this ordinance is unconstitutional on its face, for it establishes a previous restraint on the right of free speech in violation of the First Amendment which is protected by the Fourteenth Amendment against State action. To use a loud-speaker or amplifier one has to get a permit from the Chief of Police. There are no standards prescribed for the exercise of his discretion."

The court below has mistakenly derived support for its conclusion from the evidence produced at the trial that appellant's religious meetings had, in the past, caused some disorder. There are appropriate public remedies to protect the peace and order of the community if appellant's speeches should result in disorder or violence. "In the present case, we have no occasion to inquire as to permissible scope of subsequent punishment." *Near* v. *Minnesota*, 283 U.S. 697 (1931). We do not express any opinion on the propriety of punitive remedies which the New York authorities may utilize. We are here concerned with suppression—not punishment. It is sufficient to say that New York cannot vest restraining control over the right to speak on religious subjects in an administrative official where there are no appropriate standards to guide his action.

Reversed.

Mr. Justice Jackson dissented:

. . .If any two subjects are intrinsically incendiary and divisive, they are race and religion. Racial fears and hatreds have been at the root of the most terrible riots that have disgraced American civilization. They are ugly possibilities that overhang every great American city. The "consecrated hatreds of sect" account for more than a few of the world's bloody disorders. These are the explosives which the Court says Kunz may play with in the public streets, and the community must not only tolerate but aid him. I find no such doctrine in the Constitution.

In this case there is no evidence of a purpose to suppress speech, except to keep it in bounds that will not upset good order. If there are abuses of censorship or discrimination in administering the ordinance, as well there may be, they are not proved in this case. This Court should be particularly sure of its ground before it strikes down, in a time like this, the going, practical system by which New York has sought to control its street-meeting problem.

Addressing himself to the subject, "Authority and the individual," one of the keenest philosophers of our time observes: "The problem, like all those with which we are concerned, is one of balance; too little liberty brings stagnation, and too much brings chaos." Perhaps it is the fever of our times that inclines the Court today to favor chaos. My hope is that few will take advantage of the license granted by today's decision. But life teaches one to distinguish between hope and faith.

RELATED CASES:

Cox v. New Hampshire: 312 U.S. 569 (1941). Opinion: Hughes, C.J. No dissent.

A city may properly require a permit for a parade or procession as a part of the task of government in safeguarding liberties and affording an opportunity for proper policing, here traffic regulation. See p. 17, above.

Jamison v. Texas: 318 U.S. 413 (1943). Opinion: Black, J. Abstaining: Rutledge, J. No dissent.

The right to distribute handbills on religious subjects on the public streets cannot be prohibited at all times, at all places, and under all circumstances. This was not a commercial venture. The case arose in Dallas, and is important chiefly as illustrating the evolution of thought of the Supreme Court.

Niemotko v. State of Maryland: 340 U.S. 268 (1951). Opinion: Vinson, C.J. No dissent.

Local officials cannot be empowered to determine the use of public places unless narrowly drawn, reasonable, and definite standards are established. Here there was a denial of freedom of speech and of equal protection. The case arose in Havre de Grace.

Poulos v. New Hampshire: 345 U.S. 395 (1953). Opinion: Reed, J. Dissenting: Black, and Douglas, JJ.

A license to speak in a public park is a proper requirement but there must be uniformity and impartiality of treatment of those who apply for such license.

NOTE:

Kunz is a case of freedom of religion and speech coming into conflict with the rights of other persons, and, more particularly, with a city ordinance that attempted to protect those other rights of citizens. As in censorship, the Court seems to regard the individual's right to speak as superior to the power of the state to take action to protect others from possible evil results. At the very least there must be a balancing of the individual's rights against the needs of the state, but even with such a doctrine there is room for judicial discretion. Here in *Kunz* there was no adequate standard for action by the police commissioner. This case was decided the same day as *Feiner*. Incidentally, as a matter of interest, all of the Related Cases here involved Jehovah's Witnesses.

Kovacs v. Cooper
336 U.S. 77; 69 S.Ct. 448; 93 L.Ed. 513 (1949)

(An ordinance of Trenton, New Jersey, prohibited the playing, use, or operation for advertising or any other purpose on the public streets of sound trucks or any instrument which emitted "loud and raucous noises." This was challenged as violating freedom of speech. Here the use was for commenting on a local labor dispute.)

Vote: 5-4

Mr. Justice Reed delivered the opinion of the Court:

. . . City streets are recognized as a normal place for the exchange of ideas by speech or paper. But this does not mean the freedom is beyond all control. We think it is a permissible exercise of legislative discretion to bar sound trucks with broadcasts of public interest, amplified to a loud and raucous volume, from the public ways of municipalities. On the business streets of cities like Trenton, with its more than 125,000 people, such distractions would be dangerous to traffic at all hours useful for the dissemination of information, and in the residential thoroughfares the quiet and tranquility so desirable for city dwellers would likewise be at the mercy of advocates of particular religious, social or political persuasions. We cannot believe that rights of free speech compel a municipality to allow such mechanical voice amplification on any of its streets.

The right of free speech is guaranteed every citizen that he may reach the minds of willing listeners and to do so there must be opportunity to win their attention. This is the phase of freedom of speech that is involved here. We do not think the Trenton ordinance abridges that freedom. It is an extravagant extension of due process to say that because of it a city cannot forbid talking on the streets through a loud speaker in a loud and raucous tone. Surely such an ordinance does not violate our people's "concept of ordered liberty" so as to require federal intervention to protect a citizen from the action of his own local government. . . . Opportunity to gain the public's ears by objectionably amplified sound on the streets is no more assured by the right of free speech than is the unlimited opportunity to address gatherings on the streets. The preferred position of freedom of speech in a society that cherishes liberty for all does not require legislators to be insensible to claims by citizens to comfort and convenience. To enforce freedom of speech in disregard of the rights of others would be harsh and arbitrary in itself. That more people may be more easily and cheaply reached by sound trucks, perhaps borrowed without cost from some zealous supporter, is not enough to call forth constitutional protection for what those charged with public welfare reasonably think is a nuisance when easy means of publicity are open. Section 4 of the ordinance bars sound trucks from broadcasting in a loud and raucous manner on the streets. There is no restriction upon the communication of ideas or discussion of issues by the human voice, by newspapers, by pamphlets, by dodgers. We think that the need for reasonable protection in the homes or business houses from the distracting noises of vehicles equipped with such sound amplifying devices justifies the ordinance.

Affirmed.

Mr. Justice Frankfurter concurred:

. . . Only a disregard of vital differences between natural speech, even of the loudest spellbinder, and the noise of sound trucks would give sound trucks the constitutional rights accorded to the unaided human voice. Nor is it for this Court to devise the terms on which sound trucks should be allowed to operate, if at all. These are matters for the legislative judgment controlled by public opinion. So long as a legislature does not prescribe what ideas may be noisily expressed and what may not be, nor discriminate among those who would make inroads upon the public peace, it is not for us to supervise the limits the legislature may impose in safeguarding the steadily narrowing opportunities for serenity and reflection. Without such opportunities freedom of thought becomes a mocking phrase, and without freedom of thought there can be no free society.

Mr. Justice Jackson concurred:

I join the judgment sustaining the Trenton ordinance because I believe that operation of mechanical sound-amplifying devices conflicts with quiet enjoyment of home and park and with safe and legitimate use of street and market place, and that it is constitutionally subject to regulation or prohibition by the state or municipal authority. No violation of the Due Process Clause of the Fourteenth Amendment by reason of infringement of free speech arises unless such regulation or prohibition undertakes to censor the contents of the broadcasting. Freedom of speech for Kovacs does not, in my view, include freedom to use sound amplifiers to drown out the natural speech of others. . . .

Mr. Justice Black dissented, joined by Mr. Justice Douglas and Mr. Justice Rutledge:

... In *Saia* v. *New York*, 334 U.S. 558, we . . . placed use of loud speakers in public streets and parks on the same constitutional level as freedom to speak on streets without such devices, freedom to speak over radio, and freedom to distribute literature.

In this case the Court denies speech amplifiers the constitutional shelter recognized by our decision and holding in the *Saia* case. This is true because the Trenton, New Jersey ordinance here sustained goes beyond a mere prior censorship of all loud speakers with authority in the censor to prohibit some of them. This Trenton ordinance wholly bars the use of all loud speakers mounted upon any vehicle in any of the city's public streets.

In my view this repudiation of the prior *Saia* opinion makes a dangerous and unjustifiable breach in the constitutional barriers designed to insure freedom of expression. Ideas and beliefs are today chiefly disseminated to the masses of people through the press, radio, moving pictures, and public address systems. To some extent at least there is competition of ideas between and within these groups. The basic premise for the First Amendment is that all present instruments of communication, as well as others that inventive genius may bring into being, shall be free from governmental censorship or prohibition. Laws which hamper the free use of some instruments of communication thereby favor competing channels. Thus, unless constitutionally prohibited, laws like this Trenton ordinance can give an overpowering influence to views of owners of legally favored instruments of communication. . . . And it is an obvious fact that public speaking today without sound amplifiers is a wholly inadequate way to reach the people on a large scale. . . . A city ordinance that reasonably restricts the volume of sound, or the hours during which an amplifier may be used does not, in my mind, infringe the constitutionally protected area of free speech. It is because this ordinance does none of these things, but is instead an absolute prohibition of all uses of an amplifier on any of the streets of Trenton at any time that I must dissent. . . .

Mr. Justice Murphy dissented without written opinion.

RELATED CASES:

Lovell v. Griffin: 303 U.S. 444 (1938). Opinion: Hughes, C.J. No dissent. Abstaining: Cardozo, J.
An ordinance that requires permission from the city manager to distribute "literature of any kind" is "invalid on its face." Freedom of the press includes various types of publications and covers distribution and selling of publications. Municipal ordinances are "state action." The city here was Griffin, Georgia.

Schneider v. Irvington: 308 U.S. 147 (1939). Opinion: Roberts, J. No dissent. Abstaining: McReynolds, J.
A city cannot prohibit "a person rightfully on a public street from handing literature to one willing to receive it." However, commercial soliciting can be regulated. Here the literature concerned the war in Spain. This was the town of Irvington in New Jersey.

Largent v. Texas: 318 U.S. 418 (1943). Opinion: Reed, J. No dissent. Abstaining: Rutledge, J.
A city ordinance was void which empowered the mayor to grant or withhold a license for the sale of books as he deemed it "proper and advisable." This was held to be administrative censorship.

Thomas v. Collins: 323 U.S. 516 (1945). Opinion: Rutledge, J. Dissenting: Roberts, J., Stone, C.J., and Reed and Frankfurter, JJ.
See p. 108, below.

Saia v. New York: 334 U.S. 558 (1948). Opinion: Douglas, J. Dissenting: Frankfurter, Reed, Burton, and Jackson, JJ.

A city cannot vest in the Chief of Police the power to forbid the use of a sound truck on a street. No standards were prescribed for the exercise of the officer's discretion. *Kovacs* reversed this case.

Coates v. City of Cincinnati: 402 U.S. 611 (1971). Opinion: Stewart, J. Dissenting: Black, White, and Blackmun, JJ., and Burger, C.J.

Cincinnati had an ordinance which made it a criminal offense for three or more persons to assemble on a sidewalk and there conduct themselves in a manner annoying to persons passing by. The Court held the ordinance void for vagueness since no standard of conduct was specified. The Court thought there was also an obvious invitation to discriminatory enforcement against those whose association is "annoying" because "their ideas, their lifestyle, or their physical appearance is resented by the majority of their fellow citizens."

NOTE:

In *Kovacs,* Mr. Chief Justice Vinson changed from his position in *Saia* v. *New York,* thus changing the result. He was the only justice voting with the majority in both cases. As in *Kunz, Kovacs* involved a conflict of "interests" with, here, the "general welfare" winning over individual freedom of speech. Too, the Court was satisfied with the sufficiency of the ordinance as framed so that it did not suffer from the "vice of vagueness." Also, here there was no prior restraint as in *Saia.* In *Kovacs* there was merely the prevention of "loud and raucous noises." A city may regulate the place, time, and volume of sound trucks but may not ban them.

In his concurring opinion in *Kovacs,* Mr. Justice Frankfurter included a catalog of instances where the Court used the preferred freedoms approach prior to 1945. See 366 U.S. at 90–94.

Staub v. City of Baxley
355 U.S. 313; 78 S.Ct. 277; 2 L.Ed. 2nd 302 (1958)

(Rose Staub was convicted of violation of a city ordinance which made it an offense to solicit citizens of the city of Baxley, Georgia, to become members of any organization which required fees from members, without first securing a permit from the Mayor and Council. No standards were established in the ordinance. The lower courts held that the issue of constitutionality of the ordinance had not been properly raised under Georgia procedure practice.)

Vote: 7-2

Mr. Justice Whittaker delivered the opinion of the Court:

. . . It is undeniable that the ordinance authorized the Mayor and Council of the City of Baxley to grant "or refuse to grant" the required permit in their uncontrolled discretion. It thus makes enjoyment of speech contingent upon the will of the Mayor and Council of the City, although that fundamental right is made free from congressional abridgment by the First Amendment and is protected by the Fourteenth from invasion by state action. For these reasons, the ordinance, on its face, imposes an unconstitutional prior restraint upon the enjoyment of First Amendment freedoms and lays "a forbidden burden upon the exercise of liberty protected by the Constitution." *Cantwell* v. *State of Connecticut, supra,* 310 U.S. at page 307, 60 S.Ct. at page 905. Therefore, the judgment of conviction must fall.

Reversed.

Mr. Justice Frankfurter, whom Mr. Justice Clark joined, dissented:

This is one of those small cases that carries a large issue, for it concerns the essence of our federalism—due regard for the constitutional distribution of power as between the Nation and the States, and more particularly the distribution of judicial power as between this Court and the judiciaries of the States. . . .

The record before us presents not the remotest basis for attributing to the Georgie court any desire to limit the appellant in the fullest opportunity to raise claims of federal right or to prevent an adverse decision on such claims in the Georgia court from review by this Court. Consequently, this Court is left with no proper choice but to give effect to the rule of procedure on the basis of which this case was disposed of below. "Without any doubt it rests with each state to prescribe the jurisdiction of its appellate courts, the mode and time of invoking that jurisdiction, and the rules of practice to be applied in its exercise; and the state law and practice in this regard are no less applicable when Federal rights are in controversy than when the case turns entirely upon questions of local or general law. . . ."

NOTE:

Staub was another case in the long line that holds that there can be no unlimited discretion vested in officials to give or to refuse a permit to do something that basically involves an exercise of freedom of speech. This case is a good example of the Supreme Court of the United States reversing a state decision on the basis of a matter that was not the basis of the lower court's decision and was not really in issue in the lower court.

Thomas v. Collins
323 U.S. 516; 65 S.Ct. 315; 89 L.Ed. 430 (1945)

(A statute of the state of Texas required all persons soliciting members for a labor organization to secure an organizer's card from the Secretary of State prior to such activity. This officer had no discretion to refuse to issue the card. Thomas openly violated the law in Houston, was arrested and convicted. He challenged the statute as violating the First and Fourteenth Amendments by imposing a prior restraint on freedom of speech and assembly.)

Vote: 5-4

Mr. Justice Rutledge delivered the opinion of the Court:

. . . The case confronts us again with the duty our system places on this Court to say where the individual's freedom ends and the State's power begins. Choice on that border, now as always delicate, is perhaps more so where the usual presumption supporting legislation is balanced by the preferred place given in our scheme to the great, the indispensable democratic freedoms secured by the First Amendment. . . . That priority gives these liberties a sanctity and a sanction not permitting dubious intrusion. And it is the character of the right, not of the limitation, which determines what standard governs the choice. . . .

. . . That the State has power to regulate labor unions with a view to protecting the public interest is, as the Texas court said, hardly to be doubted. They cannot claim special immunity from regulation. Such regulation however, whether aimed at fraud or other abuses, must not trespass upon the domain set apart for free speech and free assembly. . . .

That there was restriction upon Thomas' right to speak and the rights of the workers to hear what he had to say, there can be no doubt. The threat of the restraining order, backed by the power of contempt, and of arrest for crime, hung over every word. A speaker in such circumstances could avoid the words "solicit," "invite," "join." It would be impossible to avoid the idea. The statute requires no specific formula. It is not contended that only the use of the word "solicit" would violate the prohibition. Without such a limitation, the statute forbids any language which conveys, or reasonably could be found to convey, the meaning of invitation. That Thomas chose to meet the issue squarely, not to hide in ambiguous phrasing does not counteract this fact. General words create different and often particular impressions on different minds. No speaker, however careful, can convey exactly his meaning, or the same meaning, to the different members of an audience. How one might "laud unionism," as the State and the State Supreme Court concede Thomas was free to do, yet in these circumstances not imply an invitation, is hard to conceive. This is the nub of the case, which the State fails to meet because it cannot do so. . . .

As a matter of principle a requirement of registration in order to make a public speech would seem generally incompatible with an exercise of the rights of free speech and free assembly. . . .

We think the controlling principle is stated in *De Jonge* v. *Oregon*, 299 U.S. 353, 365. . . .

If the exercise of the rights of free speech and free assembly cannot be made a crime, we do not think this can be accomplished by the device of requiring previous registration as a condition for exercising them and making such a condition the foundation for restraining in advance their exercise and for imposing a penalty for violating such a restraining order. So long as no more is involved than exercise of the rights of free speech and free assembly, it is immune to such a restriction. If one who solicits support for the cause of labor may be required to register as a condition to the exercise of his right to make a public speech, so may he who seeks to rally support for any social, business, religious or political cause. We think a requirement that one must register before he undertakes to make a public speech to enlist support for a lawful movement is quite incompatible with the requirements of the First Amendment.

Once the speaker goes further, however, and engages in conduct which amounts to more than the right of free discussion comprehends, as when he undertakes the collection of funds or securing subscriptions, he enters a realm where a reasonable registration or identification requirement may be imposed. In that context such solicitation would be quite different from the solicitation involved here. . . .

Mr. Justice Roberts dissented, and was joined by Mr. Chief Justice Stone, Mr. Justice Reed, and Mr. Justice Frankfurter:

. . . Stripped to its bare bones, this argument is that labor organizations are beneficial and lawful; that solicitation of members by and for them is a liberty of speech protected against state action by the Fourteenth Amendment . . . , and hence Texas cannot require a paid solicitor to identify himself. I think this is the issue and the only issue presented to the courts below and decided by them, and the only one raised here. The opinion of the court imports into the case elements on which counsel for appellant did not rely; elements which in fact counsel strove to eliminate in order to come at the fundamental challenge to any requirement of identification of a labor organizer.

The position taken in the court's opinion that in some way the statute interferes with the right to address a meeting, to speak in favor of a labor union, to persuade one's fellows to join a union, or that at least its application in this case does, or may, accomplish that end is, in my judgment, without support in the record. . . .

We should face a very different question if the statute attempted to define the necessary qualifications of an organizer; purported to regulate what organizers might say; limited their movements or activities; essayed to regulate time, place or purpose of meetings; or restricted speakers in the expression of views. But it does none of these things. . . .

We may deem the statutory provision under review unnecessary or unwise, but it is not our function as judges to read our views of policy into a Constitutional guarantee, in order to overthrow a state policy we do not personally approve, by denominating that policy a violation of the liberty of speech. The judgment should be affirmed.

NOTE:

Thomas v. *Collins* probably set forth the strongest case for the "preferred position status for First Amendment rights. The opinion also reiterated the "clear and present danger" doctrine in holding that the licensing of public meetings could be justified only when such danger was present. Otherwise individual rights of free speech prevailed against state power. Public solicitation is free speech, and licensing cannot interfere with free speech. However, individual contacts for dues or subscriptions can be reasonably regulated. Here the statute was too broad. It made possible the punishment of legitimate speech.

Thornhill v. Alabama
310 U.S. 88; 60 S.Ct. 736; 84 L.Ed. 1093 (1940)

(Thornhill was convicted of violation of Section 3448 of the Alabama State Code that prohibited loitering or picketing about a place of business for the purpose of influencing or inducing other persons not to trade with or work for the place of business, here the Brown Wood Preserving Co., Tuscaloosa.)

Vote: 8-1

Mr. Justice Murphy delivered the opinion of the Court:

. . . We think that § 3448 is invalid on its face.

The freedom of speech and of the press guaranteed by the Constitution embraces at the least the liberty to discuss publicly and truthfully all matters of public concern without previous restraint or fear of subsequent punishment. . . .

In the circumstances of our times the dissemination of information concerning the facts of a labor dispute must be regarded as within that area of free discussion that is guaranteed by the Constitution. . . . It is recognized now that satisfactory hours and wages and working conditions in industry and a bargaining position which makes these possible have an importance which is not less than the interests of those in the business or industry directly concerned. The health of the present generation and of those as yet unborn may depend on these matters, and the practices in a single factory may have economic repercussions upon a whole region and affect widespread systems of marketing. The merest glance at State and Federal legislation on the subject demonstrates the force of the argument that labor relations are not matters of mere local or private concern. Free discussion concerning the conditions in industry and the causes of labor disputes appears to us indispensable to the effective and intelligent use of the processes of popular government to shape the destiny of modern industrial society. The issues raised by regulations, such as are challenged here, infringing upon the right of employees effectively to inform the public of the facts of a labor dispute are part of this larger problem. . . .

It is not enough to say that § 3448 is limited or restricted in its application to such activity as takes place at the scene of the labor dispute. "[The] streets are natural and proper places for the dissemination of information and opinion; and one is not to have the exercise of his liberty of expression in appropriate places abridged on the plea that it may be exercised in some other place." *Schneider* v. *State*, 308 U.S. 147. . . . The danger of breach of the peace or serious invasion of rights of property or privacy at the scene of a labor dispute is not sufficiently imminent in all cases to warrent the legislature in determining that such place is not appropriate for the range of activities outlawed by § 3448.

Reversed.

Mr. Justice McReynolds dissented without written opinion.

RELATED CASES:

Senn v. Tile Layers' Protective Union: 301 U.S. 468 (1937). Opinion: Brandeis, J. Dissenting: Butler, VanDevanter, McReynolds, and Sutherland, JJ.

The rights under the Fourteenth Amendment of a building contractor running nearly a one-man business are not infringed upon by a state statute which authorizes picketing publicizing a labor dispute between the contractor and a union. This case arose in Wisconsin.

Milk Wagon Drivers' Union v. Meadowmoor Dairies: 312 U.S. 287 (1941). Opinion: Frankfurter, J. Dissenting: Black, Douglas, and Reed, JJ.

Even though pickets engage in no violence, if there is "a context of violence," and there is a threat that a continuation of the picketing will cause further violence, the picketing may be enjoined without violation of the Fourteenth Amendment. This case came out of Chicago.

Carpenters and Joiners Union v. Ritter's Cafe: 315 U.S. 722 (1942). Opinion: Frankfurter, J. Dissenting: Black, Douglas, Murphy, and Reed, JJ.

Where there is no connection between "the dispute or the industry in which it arose" and the specific picketing activities, picketing may be forbidden. Here Ritter had engaged a contractor to build an unrelated building and he in turn had hired nonunion labor. The union then proceeded to picket Ritter's restaurant. The Court enjoined the picketing. The Court refused to identify picketing with free speech. Here was applied the "unity of interest" test. The case arose in Texas.

International Brotherhood v. Vogt: 354 U.S. 284 (1957). Opinion: Frankfurter, J. Abstaining: Whittaker, J. Dssenting: Douglas, J., Warren, C.J., and Black, J.

A state may prohibit peaceful picketing in a labor dispute where the purpose of the picketing is contrary to a state purpose or public policy, in this case to coerce an employer to force his employees to join a union.

Amalgamated Food Employees Union Local 590 v. Logan Valley Plaza: 391 U.S. 308 (1968). Opinion: Marshall, J. Dissenting: Black, Harlan, and White, JJ.

As to picketing a business located within a shopping center (here near Altoona, Pennsylvania) the Court noted that prior cases had well established the rule that peaceful picketing carried on in a location open generally to the public is, with possible exceptions, protected by the First Amendment. A shopping center is the functional equivalent of a downtown "business block" and for First Amendment purposes must be treated in substantially the same manner. See *Lloyd Corporation, Ltd.* v. *Tanner,* p. 20, above.

NOTE:

Thornhill did not consider the question of whether a state can regulate picketing when other guarantees are endangered. The concept of "speech plus" was first developed by the Court in its picketing decisions. Obviously, picketing may be for economic coercion rather than communication. Incidentally, the presence of a single picket is called "signal picketing."

Picketing obviously involves a matter of a possible clash with the public interest.

Cases decided since *Thornhill* have narrowed its application. If the general welfare—public interest—demands it, picketing may be restricted, but there can be no blanket prohibition of picketing. The "clear and present danger" test is almost never used now in connection with picketing cases.

Generally speaking, there must be some fairly direct economic connection between those picketing and those picketed. This need not involve an immediate employer-employee relationship but may be as indirect as to involve those in the same industry. This is simply common law policy.

State police power cannot be nullified by the exercise of picketing. The purpose of the picketing must be taken into account and the interests of the state must be balanced against this purpose. If picketing will aid and abet violence, the picketing can be prohibited.

See *International Brotherhood* v. *Vogt*, 354 U.S. 284 (1957) for a good listing of the cases on picketing.

Giboney v. Empire Storage and Ice Co.
336 U.S. 490; 69 S.Ct. 684; 93 L.Ed. 834 (1949)

(The ice peddlers union of Kansas City, Missouri, in an effort to unionize all ice peddlers in that city, attempted to make agreements with ice wholesalers to refuse to sell ice to nonunion peddlers. Only the Empire Company refused to agree. Its place of business was thereupon picketed by union members as a means of compelling the company to stop selling ice to nonunion peddlers. A Missouri statute prohibited any agreement in restraint of trade or competition.)

Vote: No dissent

Mr. Justice Black delivered the opinion of the Court:

. . . We are without constitutional authority to modify or upset Missouri's determination that it is in the public interest to make combinations of workers subject to laws designed to keep the channels of trade wholly free and open. To exalt all labor union conduct in restraint of trade above all state control would greatly reduce the traditional powers of states over their domestic economy and might conceivably make it impossible for them to enforce their antitrade restraint laws. . . . More than that, if for the reasons here contended, states cannot subject union members to such antitrade restraint laws as Missouri's, neither can Congress. The Constitution has not so greatly impaired the states' or nation's power to govern. . . .

It rarely has been suggested that the constitutional freedom for speech and press extends its immunity to speech or writing as an integral part of conduct in violation of a valid criminal statute. We reject the contention now.

Nothing that was said or decided in any of the cases relied on by appellants calls for a different holding. . . .

"The conditions developed in industry may be such that those engaged in it cannot continue their struggle without danger to the community. But it is not for judges to determine whether such conditions exist, nor is it their function to set the limits of permissible contest and to declare the duties which the new situation demands. This is the function of the legislature which, while limiting individual and group rights of aggression and defense, may substitute processes of justice for the more primitive method of trial by combat." . . .

. . . States cannot consistently with our Constitution abridge those freedoms [of speech and press] to obviate slight inconveniences or annoyances. . . . But placards used as an essential and inseparable part of a grave offense against an important public law cannot immunize that unlawful conduct from state control. . . . Nor can we say that the publication here should not have been restrained because of the possibility of separating the picketing conduct into illegal and legal parts. . . . For the placards were to effectuate the purposes of an unlawful combination, and their sole unlawful immediate objective was to induce Empire to violate the Missouri law by acquiescing in unlawful demands to agree not to sell ice to non-union peddlers. It is true that the agreements and course of conduct here were as in most instances brought about through speaking or writing. But it has never been deemed an abridgment of freedom of speech or press to make a course of conduct illegal merely because the conduct was in part initiated, evidenced, or carried out by means of language, either spoken, written, or printed. . . . Such an expansive interpretation of the constitutional guaranties of speech and press would make it practically impossible ever to enforce laws against agreements in restraint of trade as well as many other agreements and conspiracies deemed injurious to society.

The interest of Missouri in enforcement of its antitrust laws cannot be classified as an effort to outlaw only a slight public inconvenience or annoyance. The Missouri policy against restraints of trade is of long standing and is in most respects the same as that which the Federal Government has followed for more than half a century. It is clearly drawn in an attempt to afford all persons an equal opportunity to buy goods. There was clear danger, imminent and immediate, that unless restrained, appellants would succeed in making that policy a dead letter insofar as purchases by non-union men were concerned. Appellants' power with that of their allies was irresistible. And it is clear that appellants were doing more than exercising a right of free speech or press. . . . They were exercising their economic power together with that of their allies to compel Empire to abide by union rather than by state regulation of trade.

What we have said emphasizes that this is not a case in which it can be assumed that injury from appellants' conduct would be limited to this single appellee. . . . Missouri, acting within its power, has decided that such restraints of trade as petitioners sought are against the interests of the whole public. This decision is in accord with the general ideas underlying all antitrade restraint laws. It is not for us to overrule this clearly adopted state policy.

While the State of Missouri is not a party in this case it is plain that the basic issue is whether Missouri or a labor union has paramount constitutional power to regulate and govern the manner in which certain trade practices shall be carried on in Kansas City, Missouri. Missouri has by statute regulated trade one way. The appellant union members have adopted a program to regulate it another way. The state has provided for enforcement of its statutory rule by imposing civil and criminal sanctions. The union has provided for enforcement of its rule by sanctions against union members who cross picket lines. . . . We hold that the state's power to govern in this field is paramount, and that nothing in the constitutional guaranties of speech or press compels a state to apply or not to apply its antitrade restraint law to groups of workers, businessmen or others. Of course, this Court does not pass on the wisdom of the Missouri statute. We hold only that as here construed and applied it does not violate the Federal Constitution.

Affirmed.

RELATED CASES:

American Federation of Labor v. Swing: 312 U.S. 321 (1941). Opinion: Frankfurter, J. Dissenting: Roberts, J., and Hughes, C.J.

Picketing may not be enjoined in the absence of an immediate dispute between employer and employee.

Hughes v. Superior Court of California: 339 U.S. 460 (1950). Opinion: Frankfurter, J. No dissent. Abstaining: Douglas, J.

If picketing is for a purpose contrary to basic state policy, it can be enjoined. Picketing is not the legal equivalency of speech. The purpose of the picketing was to secure compliance with a demand that the employees of the business be in proportion to the racial origin of its then customers. This was contrary to the state's antidiscrimination law. This case is an extension of *Giboney*.

Local Union No. 10 v. Graham: 345 U.S. 192 (1953). Opinion: Burton, J. Dissenting: Black and Douglas, JJ.

State statutes are valid that prohibit placing the right to work on the basis of membership or nonmembership in a union. Picketing to force agreements making union membership a condition of continued employment can be enjoined. This action was in conflict with policy set down by the Virginia state legislature. See *Lincoln Federal Labor Union* v. *Northwestern Iron and Metal Company*, p. 213, below.

NOTE:

Giboney offers one example of a situation where a state can properly prohibit picketing. Here the public interest involved a state criminal statute, violation of which the picketing was to encourage. Picketing carried on for an illegal purpose can be regulated or even prohibited.

Youngdahl v. Rainfair
355 U.S. 131; 78 S.Ct. 206; 2 L.Ed. 2nd 151 (1957)

(A strike was called against Rainfair, Inc., at Wynne, Arkansas, in an effort to compel the employer to recognize the union as the bargaining agent of the employees. The picketing was accompanied by massed name-calling, threats, and other conduct calculated to intimidate the officers and nonstriking employees of the company. The validity of the state court's enjoining the picketing was questioned.)

Vote: 6-3

Mr. Justice Burton delivered the opinion of the Court:

. . . The issue here is whether or not the conduct and language of the strikers were likely to cause physical violence. Petitioners urge that all of this abusive language was protected and that they could not, therefore, be enjoined from using it. We cannot agree. Words can readily be so coupled with conduct as to provoke violence. . . . Petitioners contend that the words used, principally "scab" and variations thereof, are within a protected terminology. But if a sufficient number yell any word sufficiently loudly showing an intent to ridicule, insult or annoy, no matter how innocuous the dictionary definition of that word, the effect may cease to be persuasion and become intimidation and incitement to violence. Wynne is not an industrial metropolis. When, in a small community, more than 30 people get together and act as they did here, and heap abuse on their neighbors and former friends, a court is justified in finding that violence is imminent. Recognizing that the trial court was in a better position that we can be to assess the local situation, we think the evidence supports its conclusion, affirmed by the State Supreme Court, that the conduct and massed name-calling by petitioners were calculated to provoke violence and were likely to do so unless promptly restrained.

Though the state court was within its discretionary power in enjoining future acts of violence, intimidation and threats of violence by the strikers and the union, yet it is equally clear that such court entered the pre-empted domain of the

National Labor Relations Board insofar as it enjoined peaceful picketing by petitioners. The picketing proper, as contrasted with the activities around the head-quarters, was peaceful. There was little, if any, conduct designed to exclude those who desired to return to work. Nor can we say that a pattern of violence was established which would inevitably reappear in the event picketing were later resumed. . . . What violence there was was scattered in time and much of it was unconnected with the picketing. There is nothing in the record to indicate that an injunction against such conduct would be ineffective if picketing were resumed.

Accordingly, insofar as the injunction before us prohibits petitioners and others cooperating with them from threatening violence against, or provoking violence on the part of any of the officers, agents or employees of respondent and prohibits them from obstructing or attempting to obstruct the free use of the streets adjacent to respondent's place of business, and the free ingress and egress to and from that property, it is affirmed. On the other hand, to the extent the injunction prohibits all other picketing and patrolling of respondent's premises and in particular prohibits peaceful picketing, it is set aside. The judgment of the Supreme Court of Arkansas is vacated and the case is remanded to it for further proceedings not inconsistent with this opinion.

It is so ordered.

Judgment of Supreme Court of Arkansas vacated and case remanded with directions.

The Chief Justice [Warren], Mr. Justice Black, and Mr. Justice Douglas, being of the opinion that Congress has given the National Labor Relations Board exclusive jurisdiction of this controversy, would reverse the judgment in its entirety and remand the cause to the state court for dismissal of the injunction.

NOTE:

Intimidation and coercion of nonstriking workers and others can be enjoined by a state court but the regulation of truly peaceful picketing in labor disputes has been preempted by the power vested in the National Labor Relations Board.

United Public Workers of America v. Mitchell
330 U.S. 75; 67 S.Ct. 556; 91 L.Ed. 754 (1947)

(The Hatch Act of 1940 prohibits federal employees engaging in certain specified political activities. The appellants sought an injunction to prohibit the enforcement against them of the Hatch Act as violative of political rights reserved to the people under the Ninth and Tenth Amendments. Only one of this group, George P. Poole, a skilled laborer, a roller, in the Philadelphia mint, had violated the provisions of the Act. He had been active as a worker at the polls. Except for his offense, the Court refused to take jurisdiction.)

Vote: 4-3

Mr. Justice Reed delivered the opinion of the Court:

. . . As pointed out hereinbefore in this opinion, the practice of excluding classi-fied employees from party offices and personal political activity at the polls has been in effect for several decades. Some incidents similar to those that are under examination here have been before this Court and the prohibition against certain types of political activity by office holders has been upheld. The leading case was decided in 1882. *Ex parte Curtis,* 106 U.S. 371. There a subordinate United States employee was indicted for violation of an act that forbade employees who were not appointed by the President and confirmed by the Senate from giving or receiving money for political purposes from or to other employees of the government on penalty of discharge and criminal punishment. Curtis urged that the statute was unconstitutional. This Court upheld the right of Congress to punish the infraction of this law. The decisive principle was the power of Congress, within reasonable limits to regulate, so far as it might deem necessary, the political conduct of its employees. A list of prohibitions against acts by public officials that are permitted to other citizens was given. This Court said:

"The evident purpose of Congress in all this class of enactments has been to promote efficiency and integrity in the discharge of official duties, and to maintain proper discipline in the public service. Clearly such a purpose is within the just scope of legislative power, and it is not easy to see why the act now under consideration does not come fairly within the legitimate means to such an end."

The right to contribute money through fellow employees to advance the contributor's political theories was held not to be protected by any constitutional provision. It was held subject to regulation. A dissent by Mr. Justice Bradley emphasized the broad basis of the Court's opinion. He contended that a citizen's right to promote his political views could not be so restricted merely because he was an official of government.

No other member of the Court joined in this dissent. The conclusion of the Court, that there was no constitutional bar to regulation of such financial contributions of public servants as distinguished from the exercise of political privileges such as the ballot, has found acceptance in the subsequent practice of Congress and the growth of the principle of required political neutrality for classified public servants as a sound element for efficiency. The conviction that an actively partisan governmental personnel threatens good administration has deepened since *Ex parte Curtis.* Congress recognized danger to the service in that political rather than official effort may earn advancement and to the public in that governmental favor may be channeled through political connections.

In *United States* v. *Wurzbach,* 280 U.S. 396, the doctrine of legislative power over actions of governmental officials was held valid when extended to members of Congress. The members of Congress were prohibited from receiving contributions for "any political purpose whatever" from any other federal employees. Private citizens were not affected. The argument of unconstitutionality because of interference with the political rights of a citizen by that time was dismissed in a sentence. . . .

The provisions of § 9 of the Hatch Act and the Civil Service Rule 1 are not dissimilar in purpose from the statutes against political contributions of money. The prohibitions now under discussion are directed at political contributions of energy by Government employees. These contributions, too, have a long background of disapproval. Congress and the President are responsible for an efficient public service. If, in their judgment, efficiency may be best obtained by prohibiting active participation by classified employees in politics as party officers or workers, we see no constitutional objection.

Another Congress may determine that on the whole, limitations on active political management by federal personnel are unwise. The teaching of experience has evidently led Congress to enact the Hatch Act provisions. To declare that the present supposed evils of political activity are beyond the power of Congress to redress would leave the nation impotent to deal with what many sincere men believe is a material threat to the democratic system. Congress is not politically naive or regardless of public welfare or that of the employees. It leaves untouched full participation by employees in political decisions at the ballot box and forbids only the partisan activity of federal personnel deemed offensive to efficiency. With that limitation only, employees may make their contributions to public affairs or protect their own interests, as before the passage of the act.

. . . There are hundreds of thousands of United States employees with positions no more influential upon policy determination than that of Mr. Poole. Evidently what Congress feared was the cumulative effect on employee morale of political activity by all employees who could be induced to participate actively. It does not seem to us an unconstitutional basis for legislation. . . .

We have said that Congress may regulate the political conduct of Government employees "within reasonable limits," even though the regulation trenches to some extent upon unfettered political action. The determination of the extent to which political activities of governmental employees shall be regulated lies primarily with Congress. Courts will interfere only when such interference passes beyond the general existing conception of governmental power. That conception develops from practice, history, and changing educational, social and economic conditions. The regulation of such activities as Poole carried on has the approval of long practice by the Commission, court decisions upon similar problems and a large body of informed public service. When actions of civil servants in the judgment of Congress menaced the integrity and the competency of the service, legislation to forestall such danger and adequate to maintain its usefulness is required. The Hatch Act is the answer of Congress to this need. We cannot say with such a background that these restrictions are unconstitutional. . . .

The judgment of the District Court is accordingly affirmed.

Mr. Justice Black dissented, with the concurrence of Mr. Justice Rutledge:

. . . There is nothing about federal and state employees as a class which justifies depriving them or society of the benefits of their participation in public affairs. They, like other citizens, pay taxes and serve their country in peace and in war. The taxes they pay and the wars in which they fight are determined by the elected spokesmen of all the people. They come from the same homes, communities, schools, churches, and colleges as do the other citizens. I think the Constitution guarantees to them the same right that other groups of good citizens have to engage in activities which decide who their elected representatives shall be . . . .

The section of the Act here held valid reduces the constitutionally protected liberty of several million citizens to less than a shadow of its substance. It relegates millions of federal, state, and municipal employees to the role of mere spectators of events upon which hinge the safety and welfare of all the people, including public employees. It removes a sizable proportion of our electorate from full participation in affairs destined to mould the fortunes of the Nation. It makes honest participation in essential political activities an offense punishable by proscription from public employment. It endows a governmental board with the awesome power to censor the thoughts, expressions, and activities of law-abiding citizens in the field of free expression from which no person should be barred by a government which boasts that it is a government of, for, and by the people—all the people. Laudable as its purpose may be, it seems to me to hack at the roots of a Government by the people themselves; and consequently I cannot agree to sustain its validity.

Mr. Justice Douglas dissented:

. . . The philosophy is to develop a civil service which can and will serve loyally and equally well any political party which comes into power.

Those considerations might well apply to the entire group of civil servants in the administrative category—whether they are those in the so-called expert classification or are clerks, stenographers and the like. They are the ones who have access to the files, who meet the public, who arrange appointments, who prepare the basic data on which policy decisions are made. Each may be a tributary, though perhaps a small one, to the main stream which we call policy making or administrative action. If the element of partisanship enters into the official activities of any member of the group it may have its repercussions or effect throughout the administrative process. Thus in that type of case there would be much to support the view of the Court that Congress need not undertake to draw the line to include only the more important offices but can take the precaution of protecting the whole by insulating even the lowest echelon from partisan activities.

So, I think that if the issues tendered by Poole were tendered by an administrative employee, we would have quite a different case. For Poole claims the right to work as a ward executive committeeman, i.e., as an office holder in a political party.

But Poole, being an industrial worker, is as remote from contact with the public or from policy making or from the functioning of the administrative process as a charwoman. The fact that he is in the classified civil service is not, I think, relevant to the question of the degree to which his political activities may be curtailed. He is in a position not essentially different from one who works in the machine shop of a railroad or steamship which the Government runs, or who rolls aluminum in a manufacturing plant which the Government owns and operates. Can all of those categories of industrial employees constitutionally be insulated from American political life? If at some future time it should come to pass in this country, as it has in England, that a broad policy of state ownership of basic industries is inaugurated, does this decision mean that all of the hundreds of thousands of industrial workers affected could be debarred from the normal political activity which is one of our valued traditions?

. . . If those rights are to be qualified by the larger requirements of modern democratic government, the restrictions should be narrowly and selectively drawn to define and punish the specific conduct which constitutes a clear and present danger to the operations of government. It seems plain to me that that evil has its roots in the coercive activity of those in the hierarchy who have the power to regiment the industrial group or who undertake to do so. To sacrifice the political rights of the industrial workers goes far beyond any demonstrated or demonstrable need. Those rights are too basic and fundamental in our democratic political society to be sacrificed or qualified for anything short of a clear and present danger to the civil service system. No such showing has been made in the case of these industrial workers, which justifies their political sterilization as distinguished from selective measures aimed at the coercive practices on which the spoils system feeds.

Mr. Justice Murphy and Mr. Justice Jackson abstained.

RELATED CASES:

Ex parte Curtis: 106 U.S. 371 (1882). Opinion: Waite, C.J. Dissenting: Bradley, J.

Congress has the power to regulate reasonably, within the bounds of necessity, the political conduct of federal employees. The promotion of efficiency and integrity and the maintenance of proper discipline in the public service are purposes within the just scope of legislative power—the establishment of "political neutrality."

United States v. Wurzbach: 280 U.S. 396 (1930). Opinion: Holmes, J. No dissent.

Congress has the power to protect federal officers and employees from being subjected to various types of political pressure. Here federal employees were prohibited from contributing to congressional campaigns.

United States v. Harriss: 347 U.S. 612 (1954). Opinion: Warren, C.J. Dissenting: Douglas, Jackson, and Black, JJ.

The Federal Regulation of Lobbying Act was declared valid as applying to lobbying in its generally accepted sense, that is, direct communication with members of Congress on pending or proposed federal legislation. This was held not to be a violation of the First Amendment's guarantee of the right of petition. The Court did indulge in extensive "rewriting" of the act.

United States Civil Service Commission v. National Association of Letter Carriers, AFL-CIO: 413 U.S. 548 (1973). Opinion: White, J. Dissenting: Douglas, Brennan, and Marshall, JJ.

The Court upheld the Hatch Act against the charge of its being unconstitutionally vague and overbroad. The intent of Congress was that the regulations of the Civil Service Commission, the agency charged with the interpretation and enforcement of the statute, should make specific the general provisions of the statute. These regulations, the Court held, are set forth in terms that the ordinary person exercising ordinary common sense can sufficiently understand and observe and are not impermissibly vague.

NOTE:

In *Mitchell* the Court followed the policy judgment of Congress that there is danger in government employees engaging in partisan political activity. The Court held this to be true even in the case of industrial workers as well as policy-making employees.

Grosjean v. American Press Co.
297 U.S. 233; 56 S.Ct. 444; 80 L.Ed. 660 (1936)

(A group of newspapers in Louisiana brought this suit to prevent the enforcement of a statute which levied a 2 percent gross receipts tax on newspapers. Only those newspapers having a circulation of 20,000 copies per week or more were included, which made the tax applicable to only thirteen newspapers. All but one of these had been openly opposed to Senator Huey P. Long, under whose influence the law had been passed. The statute was challenged as abridging the freedom of the press contrary to the due process clause and the equal protection guarantees of the Fourteenth Amendment.)

Vote: 9-0

Mr. Justice Sutherland delivered the opinion of the Court:

. . . Judge Cooley has laid down the test to be applied—"The evils to be prevented were not the consorship of the press merely, but any action of the government by means of which it might prevent such free and general discussion of public matters as seems absolutely essential to prepare the people for an intelligent exercise of their rights as citizens." 2 Cooley's Constitutional Limitations, 8th Ed., p. 886.

It is not intended by anything we have said to suggest that the owners of newspapers are immune from any of the ordinary forms of taxation for support of the government. But this is not an ordinary form of tax, but one single in kind, with a long history of hostile misuse against the freedom of the press.

The predominant purpose of the grant of immunity here invoked was to preserve an untrammeled press as a vital source of public information. The newspapers, magazines and other journals of the country, it is safe to say, have shed and continue to shed, more light on the public and business affairs of the nation than any other instrumentality of publicity; and since informed public opinion is the most potent of all restraints upon misgovernment, the suppression or abridgement of the publicity afforded by a free press cannot be regarded otherwise than with grave concern. The tax here involved is bad not because it takes money from the pockets of the appellees. If that were all, a wholly different question would be presented. It is bad because, in the light of its history and of its present setting, it is seen to be a deliberate and calculated device in the guise of a tax to limit the circulation of information to which the public is entitled in virtue of the constitutional guarantees. A free press stands as one of the great interpreters between the government and the people. To allow it to be fettered is to fetter ourselves.

In view of the persistent search for new subjects of taxation, it is not without significance that, with the single exception of the Louisiana statute, so far as we can discover, no state during the one hundred fifty years of our national existence has undertaken to impose a tax like that now in question.

The form in which the tax is imposed is in itself suspicious. It is not measured or limited by the volume of advertisements. It is measured alone by the extent of the circulation of the publication in which the advertisements are carried, with the plain purpose of penalizing the publishers and curtailing the circulation of a selected group of newspapers.

2. Having reached the conclusion that the act imposing the tax in question is unconstitutional under the due process of law clause because it abridges the freedom of the press, we deem it unnecessary to consider the further ground assigned that it also constitutes a denial of the equal protection of the laws.

Decree affirmed.

RELATED CASES:

Associated Press v. NLRB: 301 U.S. 103 (1937). Opinion: Roberts, J. Dissenting: Sutherland, VanDevanter, McReynolds, and Butler, JJ.

The Associated Press was held to be engaged in interstate commerce. Its operations involved the constant use of the means of interstate and foreign communication. "Interstate communication of a business nature, whatever the means of such communication, is interstate commerce regulable by Congress under the Constitution." Further such regulation is not violative of freedom of the press. Here the AP had fired Watson, a copy editor, for union activity with the American Newspaper Guild.

Associated Press v. United States: 326 U.S. 1 (1945). Opinion: Black, J. Dissenting: Stone, C.J., and Roberts and Murphy, JJ.

The Court held the AP in violation of the Sherman Act in that its by-laws were in restraint of trade. Freedom of the press does not include the right to combine to restrain trade in news.

Oklahoma Press Publishing Co. v. Walling: 327 U.S. 186 (1946). Opinion: Rutledge, J. Dissenting: Murphy, J.

Congress may subject newspapers to the wage and hour provisions of the Fair Labor Standards Act. There is no denial of freedom of the press, there is no restraint upon expression, and publishers of newspapers have been placed on the same plane with other businesses.

NOTE:

The *Grosjean* opinion includes a good account of attempts that have been made over the years to restrict the free press by taxation. Here the taxing power rather than the police power was used, but the Court looked beyond the face of the statute to discover the true purpose of the legislation. Special taxes are not void unless they are discriminatory.

THE RIGHT OF ASSEMBLY AND PETITION

"The right of the people peaceably to assemble, and to petition the government for a redress of grievances" is the last of the First Amendment guarantees. Over the years very few cases have arisen involving this provision, probably because of its very close relation with freedom of speech. As a result of *DeJonge* v. *Oregon* the guarantee of assembly and petition was brought within the scope of the "Gitlow doctrine," that is, applied to the states by means of the Fourteenth Amendment.

DeJonge v. Oregon
299 U.S. 353; 57 S.Ct. 255; 81 L.Ed. 278 (1937)

(DeJonge, a member of the Communist Party, spoke at a meeting held under the auspices of that party. He was indicted and convicted in Multnomah County, Oregon, of violation of the Criminal Syndicalism Law of Oregon. This statute made criminal advocacy of crime, physical violence, sabotage, or any unlawful acts as methods of accomplishing industrial change. The statute was assailed as denying due process.)

Vote: 8-0

Mr. Chief Justice Hughes delivered the opinion of the Court:

. . . Freedom of speech and the press are fundamental rights which are safeguarded by the due process clause of the Fourteenth Amendment of the Federal Constitution. . . . The right of peaceable assembly is a right cognate to those of free speech and free press and is equally fundamental. As this court said in *United States* v. *Cruikshank*, 92 U.S. 542: "The very idea of a government, republican in form, implies a right on the part of its citizens to meet peaceably for consultation in respect to public affairs and to petition for a redress of grievances." The First Amendment of the Federal Constitution expressly guarantees that right against abridgement by Congress. But explicit mention there does not argue exclusion elsewhere. For the right is one that cannot be denied without violating those fundamental principles of liberty and justice which lie at the base of all civil and political institutions,—principles which the Fourteenth Amendment embodies in the general terms of its due process clause. . . .

These rights may be abused by using speech or press or assembly in order to incite to violence and crime. The people through their legislatures may protect themselves against that abuse. But the legislative intervention can find constitutional justification only by dealing with the abuse. The rights themselves must not be curtailed. The greater the importance of safeguarding the community from incitements to the overthrow of our institutions by force and violence, the more imperative is the need to preserve inviolate the constitutional rights of free speech, free press and free assembly in order to maintain the opportunity for free political discussion, to the end that government may be responsive to the will of the people and that changes, if desired, may be obtained by peaceful means. Therein lies the security of the Republic, the very foundation of constitutional government.

It follows from these considerations that, consistently with the Federal Constitution, peaceable assembly for lawful discussion cannot be made a crime. The holding of meetings for peaceable political action cannot be proscribed. Those who assist in the conduct of such meetings cannot be branded as criminals on that score. The question, if the rights of free speech and peaceable assembly are to be preserved, is not as to the auspices under which the meeting is held but as to its purpose; not as to the relations of the speakers, but whether their utterances transcend the bounds of the freedom of speech which the Constitution protects. If the persons assembling have committed crimes elsewhere, if they have formed or are engaged in a conspiracy against the public peace and order, they may be prosecuted for their conspiracy or other violation of valid laws. But it is a different matter when this State, instead of prosecuting them for such offenses, seizes upon mere participation in a peaceable assembly and a lawful public discussion as the basis for a criminal charge.

We are not called upon to review the findings of the state court as to the objectives of the Communist Party. Notwithstanding those objectives, the defendant still enjoyed his personal right of free speech and to take part in a peaceable assembly having a lawful purpose, although called by that Party. The defendant was none the less entitled to discuss the public issues of the day and thus in a lawful manner, without incitement to violence or crime, to seek redress of alleged grievances. That was of the essence of his guaranteed personal liberty.

We hold that the Oregon statute as applied to the particular charge as defined by the state court is repugnant to the due process clause of the Fourteenth Amendment. The judgment of conviction is reversed and the cause is remanded for further proceedings not inconsistent with this opinion.

Reversed.

Mr. Justice Stone took no part in the consideration or the decision of this case.

RELATED CASES:

United States v. Cruikshank: 92 U.S. 542 (1876). Opinion: Waite, C.J. Dissenting: Clifford, J.

No state can impose any restrictions on the right of the people to assemble peaceably and petition Congress or "for consultation in respect to public affairs." The Court also indicated that there is no guarantee to individuals under the Second Amendment of the right to bear arms.

Whitney v. California: 274 U.S. 357 (1927). Opinion: Sanford, J. No dissent.

A state may make criminal the teaching of subversive activity when groups are involved because "united and joint action involves even greater danger to public peace and security than the isolated utterances and acts of individuals."

This case is possibly the single exception to the condemnation by the Court of guilt by association. Contained herein also is one of Brandeis' and Holmes' better statements on "clear and present danger" in their concurring opinion. Miss Whitney, a niece of Justice Stephen Field, had participated in the convention that set up the Communist Labor Party in California. This case was overruled by *Brandenburg* v. *Ohio* (see p. 122, above) which held that a state can only forbid advocacy directed to producing imminent lawless action and likely to produce such action.

Herndon v. Lowry: 301 U.S. 242 (1937). Opinion: Roberts, J. Dissenting: Van-Devanter, McReynolds, Sutherland, and Butler, JJ.

Conviction for subversive activity must be on the basis of personal guilt and not on guilt by association with others. See p. 122, above.

Hague v. CIO: 307 U.S. 496 (1939). Opinion: Roberts, J. Dissenting: McReynolds, and Butler, JJ. Abstaining: Frankfurter and Douglas, JJ.

A city cannot prohibit assemblies "in or upon the public streets, highways, public parks or public buildings" without securing a permit from the Director of Public Safety. This case arose in Jersey City.

National Association for the Advancement of Colored People v. Alabama: 357 U.S. 449 (1958). Opinion: Harlan, J. No dissent.

A state cannot require an organization to disclose its membership. This is a violation of the freedom of association which is "an inseparable aspect of the 'liberty' assured by the due process clause of the Fourteenth Amendment." The right of privacy was involved also.

Bates v. City of Little Rock: 361 U.S. 516 (1960). Opinion: Stewart, J. No dissent.

A city cannot compel disclosure of membership lists of members of the National Association for the Advancement of Colored People as a means of determining compliance with a license tax. This would work a significant interference with the freedom of association of these members. There is no relevant correlation between the enforcement of the tax and the disclosure of the membership lists. Here again there was a balancing of the interests of the government and of individuals. Bates was custodian of NAACP records.

Gibson v. Florida Legislative Investigation Committee: 372 U.S. 539 (1963). Opinion: Goldberg, J. Dissenting: Harlan, Clark, Stewart, and White, JJ.

Groups which themselves are neither engaged in subversive or other illegal or improper activities nor demonstrated to have any substantial connections with such activities are to be protected in their right of free and private association under the First and Fourteenth Amendments. Here the Court held that the membership list of the NAACP need not be produced.

NAACP v. Alabama ex rel. Flowers: 377 U.S. 288 (1964). Opinion: Harlan, J. No dissent.

Alabama could not oust the NAACP from the state since there was directly involved here the freedom of individuals to associate for the collective advocacy of ideas.

Elfbrandt v. Russell: 384 U.S. 11   (1966). Opinion: Douglas, J. Dissenting: White, Clark, Harlan, and Stewart, JJ.

The freedom of association guaranteed by the First Amendment protects those who join an organization but do not share its unlawful purposes and who do not participate in its unlawful activities. Elfbrandt was a teacher in Arizona. This case is regarded by some persons as an apparent reversal of *Garner* v. *Board of Public Works*. (See p. 280, below.) It was certainly prophetic of *Keyishian* v. *Board of Regents*. (See p. 77, above.)

Healy v. James: 408 U.S. 169 (1972). Opinion: Powell, J. No dissent.

Students at a state-supported college may form an organization even though the administrative officers of the college may disagree with the aims and purposes of the organization. Freedom of association has long been held to be implicit in the First Amendment freedoms of speech, assembly, and petition. College administrators may require an organization to affirm in advance its willingness to adhere to reasonable campus rules and laws. The organization here was Students for a Democratic Society (SDS) at Central Connecticut State College.

NOTE:

In *DeJonge* the "Gitlow doctrine" was applied to freedom of assembly. Guilt by association was condemned and the objectives of an organization with which a person is associated were held to be irrelevant as far as his personal guilt was concerned. Also it should be noted that an accused person cannot be convicted on the basis of a charge not contained in the indictment. This statement by the Court resulted from confusion in *DeJonge* as to the meaning of the indictment.

In recent years the chief use of the assembly and petition guarantee has been in connection with activities of the National Association for the Advancement of Colored People and the regulation of lobbying activities. See *United States* v. *Rumely*, 345 U.S. 41 (1953) (see Vol. I.) and *United States* v. *Harriss*, 347 U.S. 612 (1954) (see p. 118, above).

CHAPTER V

OTHER BILL OF RIGHTS GUARANTEES

The First Amendment is so basic in our conception of the relation of man to government that sometimes it seems that the remaining guarantees of the Bill of Rights are placed in the category of "second class rights." Nevertheless, some of the most important of the safeguards of human freedom and justice are to be found in Amendments Two to Eight inclusive.

UNREASONABLE SEARCH AND SEIZURE

It is entirely obvious from a mere reading of the Fourth Amendment that what is forbidden is *unreasonable* search and seizure of "persons, houses, papers, and effects" but the likewise obvious difficulty that the Court has encountered over the years (and is still encountering) is the matter of determining just what is "unreasonable." Basically the amendment implies that a warrant of arrest or of search is to be used. This is underlined by the emphasis that the wording of the amendment places on the details of process involved in securing a warrant—probable cause, oath or affirmation, particular description of the persons, places, or things to be searched or seized. This guarantee has its origin in English experience and in the experience of the Colonies with the "writs of assistance." The bulk of the case law dealing with this particular provision is a matter of "spelling out" when a search is "reasonable" without the use of a warrant, as well as determining usage even with a warrant, either arrest or search. This is well exemplified by *Harris*.

Harris v. United States
331 U.S. 145; 67 S.Ct. 1098; 91 L.Ed. 1399 (1947)

(George Harris was arrested for using the mails to defraud by the use of forged checks and for violating the National Stolen Property Act. Using two arrest warrants, FBI agents arrested Harris in his apartment. After the arrest the agents searched the entire apartment over a five-hour period. In the course of this search a sealed envelope marked "George Harris, personal papers" was found. This contained Selective Service Notice of Classification cards and Registration Certificates. On this evidence, Harris was convicted of unlawful possession, concealment, and alteration of these cards. Harris challenged his conviction on the basis of unreasonable search and seizure and self-incrimination.)

Vote: 5-4

Mr. Chief Justice Vinson delivered the opinion of the Court:

. . . Nor is it a significant consideration that the draft cards which were seized were not related to the crimes for which petitioner was arrested. Here during the course of a valid search the agents came upon property of the United States in

124

the illegal custody of the petitioner. It was property to which the Government was entitled to possession. In keeping the draft cards in his custody petitioner was guilty of a serious and continuing offense against the laws of the United States. A crime was thus being committed in the very presence of the agents conducting the search. Nothing in the decisions of this Court gives support to the suggestion that under such circumstances the law-enforcement officials must impotently stand aside and refrain from seizing such contraband material. If entry upon the premises be authorized and the search which follows be valid, there is nothing in the Fourth Amendment which inhibits the seizure by law-enforcement agents of government property the possession of which is a crime, even though the officers are not aware that such property is on the premises when the search is initiated.

The dangers to fundamental personal rights and interests resulting from excesses of law-enforcement officials committed during the course of criminal investigations are not illusory. This Court has always been alert to protect against such abuse. But we should not permit our knowledge that abuses sometimes occur to give sinister coloration to procedures which are basically reasonable. We conclude that in this case the evidence which formed the basis of petitioner's conviction was obtained without violation of petitioner's rights under the Constitution.

Affirmed.

Mr. Justice Frankfurter dissented, and was joined by Mr. Justice Murphy and Mr. Justice Rutledge:

. . . If the search is illegal when begun, as it clearly was in this case if past decisions mean anything, it cannot retrospectively gain legality. If the search was illegal, the resulting seizure in the course of the search is illegal. It is no answer to say that possession of a document may itself be a crime. There is no suggestion here that the search was based on even a suspicion that Harris was in possession of illicit documents. The search was justified and is justified only in connection with the offense for which there was a warrant of arrest. . . .

Mr. Justice Murphy dissented, joined by Mr. Justice Frankfurter and Mr. Justice Rutledge.

. . . The key fact of this case is that the search was lawless. A lawless search cannot give rise to a lawful seizure, even of contraband goods. And "good faith" on the part of the arresting officers cannot justify a lawless search, nor support a lawless seizure. In forbidding unreasonable searches and seizures, the Constitution made certain procedural requirements indispensable for lawful searches and seizures. It did not mean, however, to substitute the good intentions of the police for judicial authorization except in narrowly confined situations. History, both before and after the adoption of the Fourth Amendment has shown good police intentions to be inadequate safeguards for the precious rights of man. But the Court now turns its back on that history and leaves the reasonableness of searches and seizures without warrants to the unreliable judgment of the arresting officers. As a result, the rights of those placed under arrest to be free from unreasonable searches and seizures are precarious to the extreme. . . .

Mr. Justice Jackson dissented:

. . . I cannot escape the conclusion that a search, for which we can assign no practicable limits, on premises and for things which no one describes in advance, is such a search as the Constitution considered "unreasonable" and intended to prohibit.

In view of the long history of abuse of search and seizure which led to the Fourth Amendment, I do not think it was intended to leave open an easy way to circumvent the protection it extended to the privacy of individual life. In view of the readiness of zealots to ride roughshod over claims of privacy for any ends that impress them as socially desirable, we should not make inroads on the rights protected by this Amendment. The fair implication of the Constitution is that no search of premises, as such, is reasonable except the cause for it to be approved and the limits of it fixed and the scope of it particularly defined by a disinterested magistrate. If these conditions are necessary limitations on a court's power expressly to authorize a search, it would not seem that they should be entirely dispensed with because a magistrate has issued a warrant which contains no express authorization to search at all.

Of course, this, like each of our constitutional guaranties, often may afford a shelter for criminals. But the forefathers thought this was not too great a price to pay for that decent privacy of home, papers and effects which is indispensable to individual dignity and self-respect. They may have overvalued privacy, but I am not disposed to set their command at naught.

RELATED CASES:

Boyd v. United States: 116 U.S. 616 (1886). Opinion: Bradley, J. No dissent.

Compulsory production of private books and papers of the owner of goods sought to be forfeited in such a suit is compelling him to be a witness against himself, within the meaning of the Fifth Amendment to the Constitution, and is the equivalent of a search and seizure, and an unreasonable search and seizure, within the meaning of the Fourth Amendment. The two provisions "run almost into each other" and offer protection against all governmental intrusion into privacy.

Hale v. Henkel: 201 U.S. 43 (1906). Opinion: Brown, J. Dissenting: Brewer, J., and Fuller, C.J.

There is a clear distinction between an individual and a corporation. A corporation being a creature of the state has not the constitutional right to refuse to submit its books and papers for an examination at the suit of the state. Corporations have no immunity from self-incrimination.

However, a corporation is entitled to protection from *unreasonable* searches and seizures. Thus, where an examination of its books is not authorized by an act of Congress a subpoena *duces tecum* requiring the production of practically all of its books and papers is as indefensible as a search warrant would be if couched in similar terms. It required the production of too much material.

A corporate officer cannot refuse to produce corporate records. See *Wilson* v. *United States,* p. 155, below, and *Bellis* v. *United States,* below.

Federal Trade Commission v. American Tobacco Co.: 264 U.S. 298 (1924). Opinion: Holmes, J. No dissent.

Access to the Federal Trade Commission to corporate documents under the Federal Trade Commission Act is confined to such documents as are relevant as evidence to an inquiry or complaint before the FTC and their disclosure cannot be compelled without some evidence of their relevancy and upon a reasonable demand. There are to be no "fishing" expeditions.

Hester v. United States: 265 U.S. 57 (1924). Opinion: Holmes, J. No dissent.

It is not considered illegal for federal revenue officers to seize and examine goods abandoned by alleged violators.

The special protection accorded by the Fourth Amendment to the people in their "persons, houses, and effects," is not extended to open fields (where the whiskey in this case was seized). The distinction between the latter and the house is as old as common law.

United States v. Morton Salt: 338 U.S. 632 (1950). Opinion: Jackson, J. Abstaining: Douglas and Minton, JJ.

A Federal Trade Commission order that certain corporations file special reports showing continuing compliance with a previous FTC order to cease and desist from certain unfair trade practices is not a violation of the prohibition against unreasonable searches and seizures as long as the inquiry is within the authority of the agency, the demand is not too indefinite, and the information sought is reasonably relevant.

Miller v. United States: 357 U.S. 301 (1958). Opinion: Brennan, J. Dissenting: Clark and Burton, JJ.

An individual cannot be arrested in his house by officers breaking in without first giving notice of their authority and purpose. This is true even with a warrant.

Jones v. United States: 357 U.S. 493 (1958). Opinion: Harlan, J. Dissenting: Clark and Burton, JJ.

Probable cause for belief that certain articles subject to seizure are in a home cannot of itself justify a search without a warrant. Here there had been protracted observation of mash flowing from a house.

Frank v. Maryland: 359 U.S. 360 (1959). Opinion: Frankfurter, J. Dissenting: Douglas, Black, and Brennan, JJ., and Warren, C.J.

A city health inspector may demand entry into a house without a warrant for the purpose of determining the existence of a nuisance. This does not violate the due process clause of the Fourteenth Amendment. This is administrative inspection. The interests of the community ·override the right to privacy.

Camara v. Municipal Court of City and County of San Francisco: 378 U.S. 523 (1967). Opinion: White, J. Dissenting: Clark, Harlan, and Stewart, JJ.

Administrative searches (here by a representative of the Department of Public Health) are significant intrusions upon the interest protected by the Fourth Amendment. Such searches without proper consent are "unreasonable" unless authorized by a valid search warrant. This case overruled *Frank* v. *Maryland*, above.

Chimel v. California: 395 U.S. 752 (1969). Opinion: Stewart, J. Dissenting: White and Black, JJ.

There is no constitutional justification, in the absence of a search warrant, for extending a search beyond the area of the arrestee's "immediate control;" that is, where he might gain possession of a weapon or destructible evidence. This case reversed *Harris* and *Rabinowitz*. See p. 141, below.

Von Cleef v. New Jersey: 395 U.S. 814 (1969). Opinion: Per Curiam. Dissenting: Black and White, JJ.

A search of a sixteen-room house without a warrant with a resulting seizure was unreasonable even though in conjunction with a lawful arrest of an individual on the third floor.

Shipley v. California: 395 U.S. 818 (1969). Opinion: Per Curiam. Dissenting: Black and White, JJ.

Search of a home was unreasonable and the resulting seizure unlawful, when the arrest was made fifteen to twenty feet outside of the home without a warrant and when no emergency existed.

Wyman v. James: 400 U.S. 309 (1970). Opinion: Blackmun, J. Dissenting: Douglas, Marshall, and Brennan, JJ.

A state (here New York) may require home visits by caseworkers as a condition for welfare assistance. It is not unreasonable that the taxpaying public know how its charitable funds are utilized and put to work.

United States v. Mara: 410 U.S. 19 (1973). Opinion: Stewart, J. Dissenting: Brennan, Douglas, and Marshall, JJ.

A grand jury directed Mara to produce handwriting and printing exemplars in the course of an investigation of thefts of interstate shipments. The Court held that this did not violate the Fourth Amendment since handwriting, like speech, is frequently shown to the public and so has no expectation of privacy.

Bellis v. United States: 417 U.S. 85 (1974). Opinion: Marshall, J. Dissenting: Douglas, J.

The Fifth Amendment's provision against self-incrimination is limited to natural individuals concerning their testimony and records. It is not available to a person who was a former partner in a dissolved legal partnership who is directed to produce partnership records. The partnership is deemed to be a separate legal entity.

NOTE:

Harris marks the "high water mark" in the liberalization of "possession" and "control" in search and seizure. Over the years the interpretation has varied from the articles found on a person to those under his immediate control, in plain sight, such as on a desk, to, in *Harris*, a four-room apartment. (This case has a fine chart in the appendix.) A year later, in *Trupiano* v. *United States*, 334 U.S. 699 (1948), (see p. 129, below) the Court held that a search warrant had to be secured whenever this was reasonably practical even though the evidence was certainly "in plain sight." In another two years the pendulum swung back from this extreme position and in *Rabinowitz* (see p. 141, below) the Court upheld the search of the office in which the arrest was made. Thus the rule today appears to be that a reasonable amount of "exploring" can be done, but there are limits to this, as the Court noted in *Kremen* v. *United States,* 353 U.S. 346 (1957). (See p. 144, below.) The decision in *Chimel* indicates that this can be done only in an area from within which the arrestee might gain possession of a weapon or destructible evidence. (See p. 144, below.)

Agnello v. United States
269 U.S. 20; 46 S.Ct. 4; 70 L.Ed. 145 (1925)

(Two federal revenue agents went to the home of a person named Alba to purchase narcotics. They were given samples and arranged for a return visit. They returned with more agents and the police. This time Alba had an accomplice named Agnello bring the narcotics from Agnello's home. After the transaction of sale, the participants were arrested for conspiracy to violate the Harrison Act. The police then instituted a search of Agnello's home where more drugs were discovered. This was done without a warrant, and the action was challenged as violating the Fourth and Fifth Amendments.)

Vote: 9-0

Mr. Justice Butler delivered the opinion of the Court:

. . . The right without a search warrant contemporaneously to search persons lawfully arrested while committing crime and to search the place where the arrest is made in order to find and seize things connected with the crime as its fruits or as the means by which it was committed, as well as weapons and other things to effect an escape from custody, is not to be doubted. . . . The legality of the arrests or of the searches and seizures made at the home of Alba is not questioned. Such searches and seizures naturally and usually appertain to and attend such arrests. But the right does not extend to other places. . . . That search cannot be sustained as an incident of the arrests. . . .

While the question has never been directly decided by this Court, it has always been assumed that one's house cannot lawfully be searched without a search warrant, except as incident to a lawful arrest therein. . . . The protection of the Fourth Amendment extends to all equally—to those justly suspected or accused, as well as to the innocent. The search of a private dwelling without a warrant is in itself unreasonable and abhorrent to our laws. . . . Save in certain cases as incident to arrest, there is no sanction in the decisions of the courts, federal or state, for the search of a private dwelling house without a warrant. Absence of any judicial approval is persuasive authority that it is unlawful. . . . Belief, however well founded, that an article sought is concealed in a dwelling house furnishes no justification for a search of that place without a warrant. And such searches are held unlawful notwithstanding facts unquestionably showing probable cause. . . .

It is well settled that, when properly invoked, the Fifth Amendment protects every person from incrimination by the use of evidence obtained through search or seizure made in violation of his rights under the Fourth Amendment. . . .

Judgment against Frank Agnello reversed; judgment against other defendants affirmed.

RELATED CASES:

Johnson v. United States: 333 U.S. 10 (1948)). Opinion: Jackson, J. Dissenting: Vinson, C.J., and Black, Reed, and Burton, JJ.

The protection of the Fourth Amendment consists in requiring that the usual inferences which reasonable men draw from evidence be drawn by a neutral and detached magistrate instead of being judged by the officer engaged in the often competitive enterprise of ferreting out crime. An officer gaining access to private living quarters under color of his office and of the law which he personifies must then have valid basis in law for the intrusion at the time of the intrusion. Here the smell of burning opium was insufficient.

Trupiano v. United States: 334 U.S. 699 (1948). Opinion: Murphy, J. Dissenting: Vinson, C.J., and Black, Reed, and Burton, JJ.

"The mere fact that there is a valid arrest does not *ipso facto* legalize a search or seizure without a warrant . . . there must be some other factor in the situation that would make it unreasonable or impracticable to require the arresting officer to equip himself with a search warrant." Here the officer had observed the construction of a still on a New Jersey farm and thus had plenty of time to get a warrant.

McDonald v. United States: 335 U.S. 451 (1948). Opinion: Douglas, J. Dissenting: Burton, J., and Vinson, C.J., and Reed, J.

Where officers are not responding to an emergency, there must be compelling reasons to justify the absence of a search warrant. A search without warrant demands exceptional circumstances. The exigencies of the situation must make that course imperative. Here lottery paraphernalia was involved.

United States v. Rabinowitz: 339 U.S. 56 (1950). Opinion: Minton, J. Dissenting: Frankfurter, Jackson, and Black, JJ. Abstaining: Douglas, J.

Searches, as an incident to lawful arrests, turn upon the reasonableness under all the circumstances and not upon the practicality of procuring a search warrant. "The relevant test is not whether it is reasonable to procure a search warrant, but whether the search was reasonable." Search without a warrant incident to arrest may extend to the immediate area where the arrest was made, here a one-room office. See p. 141, below. This case overruled *Trupiano* v. *United States,* above.

Draper v. United States: 358 U.S. 307 (1959). Opinion: Whittaker, J. Dissenting: Douglas, J. Abstaining: Warren, C.J., and Frankfurter, J.

Arrest without warrant on the basis of "hearsay" information from a reliable source is lawful, and search and seizure made incident to the lawful arrest is also valid. There can easily be confusion and disregard for the difference between what is required to prove *guilt* in a criminal case and what is required to show *probable cause* for arrest or search. Here a paid informer had advised that Draper would be carrying narcotics.

NOTE:

Agnello points up the second of the two great exceptions to the general rule that a warrant is necessary in order for a search to qualify as "reasonable." In *Harris* the point was made that evidence that results from a search (possibly of some extent although recent decisions are much more restrictive) in connection with a lawful arrest may well be seized. In *Agnello* the Court emphasized that search without warrant may not be conducted unless there is "probable cause" for such action. This, in a sense, begs the question because then each instance must be examined to determine the presence of such probable cause. Certainly where there is visible evidence of the commission of a crime a search may be made, but this does not justify the search of property, even of participants in the crime, apart from the scene of the crime. Moreover, the "probable cause" must exist prior to such search. This involves the factual and practical considerations on which reasonable and prudent persons act, not technicalities. An element of subjectivity does enter, of course. The results of a search cannot be made to justify retroactively the search. This matter will probably become clearer after a discussion of some of the cases that follow.

Olmstead v. United States
277 U.S. 438; 48 S.Ct. 564; 72 L.Ed. 944 (1928)

(Olmstead was the leading member of a group conspiring to violate the National Prohibition Act by unlawfully possessing, transporting, importing, and selling intoxicating liquors and maintaining nuisances. One of the conspirators was always on duty to receive orders by telephone and see to the filling of these orders by employees. The information which led to the discovery of the conspiracy and its nature and intent was largely obtained by the tapping of telephones by federal officers. The tapping was done outside of the home of Olmstead and in the basement of the buildings housing the offices. The conversations were recorded and were used in court against the conspirators.)

Vote: 5-4

Mr. Chief Justice Taft delivered the opinion of the Court:

. . . The well known historical purpose of the Fourth Amendment, directed against general warrants and writs of assistance, was to prevent the use of governmental force to search a man's house, his person, his papers, and his effects, and to prevent their seizure against his will. . . .

The Amendment itself shows that the search is to be of material things—the person, the house, his papers or his effects. The description of the warrant necessary to make the proceeding lawful is that it must specify the place to be searched and the person or *things* to be seized.

It is urged that the language of Mr. Justice Field in *Ex parte Jackson* . . . offers an analogy to the interpretation of the Fourth Amendment in respect of wire tapping. But the analogy fails. The Fourth Amendment may have proper application to a sealed letter in the mail because of the constitutional provision for the Post Office Department and the relations between the government and those who pay to secure protection of their sealed letters. See Revised Statutes, § § 3978 to 3988, . . . whereby Congress monopolizes the carriage of letters and excludes from that business everyone else, and § 3929, . . . which forbids any postmaster or other person to open any letter not addressed to himself. It is plainly within the words of the Amendment to say that the unlawful rifling by a government agent of a sealed letter is a search and seizure of the sender's papers or effects. The letter is a paper, an effect, and in the custody of a Government that forbids carriage except under its protection.

The United States takes no such care of telegraph or telephone messages as of mailed sealed letters. The Amendment does not forbid what was done here. There was no searching. There was no seizure. The evidence was secured by the use of the sense of hearing and that only. There was no entry of the houses or offices of the defendants.

By the invention of the telephone fifty years ago, and its application for the purpose of extending communications, one can talk with another at a far distant place.

The language of the Amendment can not be extended and expanded to include telephone wires reaching to the whole world from the defendant's house or office. The intervening wires are not part of his house or office, any more than are the public highways along which they are stretched. . . .

Congress may, of course, protect the secrecy of telephone messages by making them, when intercepted, inadmissible in evidence in Federal criminal trials, by direct legislation, and thus adopt such a policy by attributing an enlarged and unusual meaning to the Fourth Amendment. The reasonable view is that one who installs in his house a telephone instrument with connecting wires intends to project his voice to those quite outside, and that the wires beyond his house and messages while passing over them are not within the protection of the Fourth Amendment. Here those who intercepted the projected voices were not in the house of either party to the conversation.

Neither the cases we have cited nor any of the many Federal decisions brought to our attention hold the Fourth Amendment to have been violated as against a defendant unless there has been an official search and seizure of his person or such a seizure of his papers or his tangible material effects or an actual physical invasion of his house "or curtilage" for the purpose of making a seizure.

We think, therefore, that the wire tapping here disclosed did not amount to a search or seizure within the meaning of the Fourth Amendment. . . .

Mr. Justice Holmes dissented:

. . . We have to choose, and for my part I think it a less evil that some criminals should escape than that the government should play an ignoble part.

For those who agree with me, no distinction can be taken between the government as prosecutor and the government as judge. If the existing code does not permit district attorneys to have a hand in such dirty business, it does not permit the judge to allow such iniquities to succeed. . . . And if all that I have said so far be accepted, it makes no difference that in this case wire tapping is made a crime by the law of the state, not by the law of the United States. It is true that a state cannot make rules of evidence for courts of the United States, but the state has authority over the conduct in question, and I hardly think that the United States would appear to greater advantage when paying for an odious crime against state law than when inciting to the disregard of its own. . . . I have said that we are free to choose between two principles of policy. But if we are to confine ourselves to precedent and logic, the reason for excluding evidence obtained by violating the Constitution seems to me logically to lead to excluding evidence obtained by a crime of the officers of the law.

Mr. Justice Brandeis dissented:

. . . The progress of science in furnishing the government with means of espionage is not likely to stop with wire-tapping. Ways may some day be developed by which the government, without removing papers from secret drawers, can reproduce them in court, and by which it will be enabled to expose to a jury the most intimate occurrences of the home. Advances in the psychic and related sciences may bring means of exploring unexpressed beliefs, thoughts and emotions. . . . Can it be that the Constitution affords no protection against such invasions of individual security? . . .

Decency, security, and liberty alike demand that government officials shall be subjected to the same rules of conduct that are commands to the citizen. In a government of laws, existence of the government will be imperiled if it fails to observe the law scrupulously. Our government is the potent, the omnipresent, teacher. For good or for ill, it teaches the whole people by its example. Crime is contagious. If the government becomes a law-breaker, it breeds contempt for law; it invites every man to become a law unto himself; it invites anarchy. To declare that in the administration of the criminal law the end justifies the means—to declare that the government may commit crimes in order to secure the conviction of a private criminal—would bring terrible retribution. Against that pernicious doctrine this Court should resolutely set its face.

Mr. Justice Stone concurred in these dissents.

Mr. Justice Butler dissented:

. . . The Fifth Amendment prevents the use of evidence obtained through searches and seizures in violation of the rights of the accused protected by the Fourth Amendment.

The single question for consideration is this: May the Government, consistently with that clause, have its officers whenever they see fit, tap wires, listen to, take down and report, the private messages and conversations transmitted by telephones? . . .

The question at issue depends upon a just appreciation of the facts. . . .

This Court has always construed the Constitution in the light of the principles upon which it was founded. The direct operation or literal meaning of the words used do not measure the purpose or scope of its provisions. Under the principles established and applied by this Court, the Fourth Amendment safeguards against all evils that are like and equivalent to those embraced within the ordinary meaning of its words. . . .

When the facts in these cases are truly estimated, a fair application of that principle decides the constitutional question in favor of the petitioners. With great deference, I think they should be given a new trial.

RELATED CASES:

Ex parte Jackson: 96 U.S. 727 (1878). Opinion: Field, J. No dissent.

In this case the Supreme Court declared that Congress constitutionally could prohibit the transport in the mails of circulars concerning lotteries. Despite its statement that this was the only issue before it, the Court said that sealed letters and packages in the mails could be opened and examined only under a warrant. It held that the constitutional right to be secure in one's papers against unreasonable searches and seizures extends to papers closed against inspection wherever they may be. The postal power includes a police power under which Congress can exclude things. The guarantee does not extend to printed matter, not sealed.

Nardone v. United States: 302 U.S. 379 (1937). Opinion: Roberts, J. Dissenting: Sutherland and McReynolds, JJ.

The Communications Act of 1934 forbidding wire tapping was held to prevent the use in federal courts of evidence secured by wire tapping of interstate communications. In *Nardone* v. *United States*, 308 U.S. 338 (1939), this prohibition was extended to the use of evidence discovered as a result of wire tapping tips, that is, the indirect or derivative use of evidence secured by wire tapping, the "fruit of the poisonous tree." But it can be used to impeach a defendant's credibility. Nardone was accused of smuggling liquor.

Weiss v. United States: 308 U.S. 321 (1939). Opinion: Roberts, J. No dissent.

Evidence secured by the tapping of wires in intrastate communications is inadmissible in federal courts as contrary to the 1934 Communications Act. This was an exercise of the interstate commerce power.

Goldstein v. United States: 316 U.S. 114 (1942). Opinion: Roberts, J. Dissenting: Murphy, J., Stone, C.J., and Frankfurter, J. Abstaining: Jackson, J.

Section 605 of the Federal Communications Act does not render inadmissible in a criminal trial in a federal court, testimony (otherwise admissible) of witnesses who were induced to testify by the use, in advance of trial, of communications intercepted in violation of the Act, but to which communications the defendants were not parties. Goldstein was charged with mail fraud. See also page 140, below.

Goldman v. United States: 316 U.S. 129 (1942). Opinion: Roberts, J. Dissenting: Stone, C.J., and Frankfurter and Murphy, JJ. Abstaining: Jackson, J.

The use of a detectaphone—a device that picks up sounds in an adjoining room when attached to a wall—for the securing of evidence is legal as long as there is no trespassing. This decision was reversed by *Katz* v. *United States,* p. 135, below.

On Lee v. United States: 343 U.S. 747 (1952). Opinion: Jackson, J. Dissenting: Black, Frankfurter, Douglas, and Burton, JJ.

The use of evidence secured by means of "walkie-talkie" communication is valid, as long as the operator of the concealed transmitter is not trespassing.

Silverman v. United States: 365 U.S. 505 (1961). Opinion: Stewart, J. No dissent.

Eavesdropping by police officers achieved through the use of an electronic listening device pushed through the party wall of the house adjoining the defendant's violated the defendant's rights under the Fourth Amendment and testimony by the officers to conversations obtained in this manner is inadmissible as evidence in a federal court. This case involved a "spike mike." It arose in Washington, D.C.

Osborn v. United States: 385 U.S. 323 (1966). Opinion: Stewart, J. Dissenting: Douglas, J. Abstaining: White, J.

The primary evidence of an attempt to bribe a member of a jury panel in a prospective federal criminal trial was a tape recording of a conversation. The federal judges in the case had authorized the recording. The Court noted that the electronic device was used under the most precise and discriminate circumstances, so the recording itself was properly admissible as evidence. This case came out of Nashville, Tennessee. Osborn was James Hoffa's attorney there.

Berger v. New York: 388 U.S. 41 (1967). Opinion: Clark, J. Dissenting: Black, Harlan, and White, JJ.

A court eavesdrop order under New York statutes was obtained to install a recording device in a suspected attorney's office. The Court held that the statute authorized the indiscriminate use of electronic devices and permitted a trespassory invasion contrary to the command of the Fourth Amendment. There was overbreadth and vagueness about the statute. There is a good short review of wiretapping in this opinion.

NOTE:

Berger illustrates the fact that search and seizure of speech is included in the Fourth Amendment guarantee. Indeed the case illustrates also, as does *Boyd* v. *United States,* 116 U.S. 616 (1886), the "back to back" character of the "seizure" of speech under the Fourth Amendment and self-incrimination under the Fifth Amendment. In *Olmstead,* however, the Court determined that what had been done by the officers was not illegal. Legislation by Congress after *Olmstead* outlawed wire tapping and *Olmstead* itself has since been overruled by *Katz* v. *United States,* p. 135.

Benanti v. United States
355 U.S. 96; 78 S.Ct. 155; 2 L.Ed. 2nd 126 (1957)

(New York police, suspicious that Benanti was dealing in narcotics in violation of state law, obtained a warrant in accordance with state law authorizing them to tap the lines of a bar which Benanti was known to frequent. Acting on information secured through the wire tapping, the police followed and stopped a car driven by petitioner's brother. No narcotics were found but hidden in the car was a quantity of alcohol without federal tax stamps. The brother and the alcohol were turned over to the federal authorities and this prosecution followed. The resulting conviction was challenged as violating federal statutes as well as the Fourth Amendment, because of the use of evidence obtained as a result of wire tapping.)

Vote: No dissent

Mr. Chief Justice Warren delivered the opinion of the Court:

. . . We do not reach the constitutional questions as this case can be determined under the statute. .

Section 605 states in pertinent part: ". . . no person not being authorized by the sender shall intercept any communication and divulge or publish the existence, contents, substance, purport, effect, or meaning of such intercepted communication to any person. . . ."

The Federal Communications Act is a comprehensive scheme for the regulation of interstate communication. In order to safeguard those interests protected under Section 605, that portion of the statute pertinent to this case applies both to intrastate and to interstate communications. . . . The natural result of respondent's argument is that both interstate and intrastate communication would be removed from the statute's protection because, as this Court noted in *Weiss*, the interceptor cannot discern between the two and will listen to both. Congress did not intend to place the protections so plainly guaranteed in Section 605 in such a vulnerable position. Respondent points to portions of the Act which place some limited authority in the States over the field of interstate communication. The character of these matters, dealing with aspects of the regulation of utility service to the public, are technical in nature in contrast to the broader policy considerations motivating Section 605. Moreover, the very existence of these grants of authority to the States underscores the conclusion that had Congress intended to allow the States to make exceptions to Section 605, it would have said so. In light of the above considerations, and keeping in mind this comprehensive scheme of interstate regulation and the public policy underlying Section 605 as part of that scheme, we find that Congress, setting out a prohibition in plain terms, did not mean to allow state legislation which would contradict that section and that policy. . . .

Reversed.

RELATED CASES:

Ex parte Siebold: 100 U.S. 371 (1880). Opinion: Bradley, J. Dissenting: Clifford and Field, JJ.

Congress has the authority to make interference with United States marshals charged with supervising a federal election a federal offense. The state and national sovereignties can cooperate in the matter of election of representatives.

Rathbun v. United States: 355 U.S. 107 (1957). Opinion: Warren, C.J. Dissenting: Frankfurter and Douglas, JJ.

Contents of a communication overheard by police officers on a regularly used telephone extension, with the consent of the person who is both the subscriber to the extension and a party to the conversation, are admissible in a criminal trial in a federal court because such use of a regularly used telephone extension does not involve any "interception of a telephone message" as Congress intended that word to be used in Section 605 of the Federal Communications Act.

Monroe v. Pape: 365 U.S. 167 (1961). Opinion: Douglas, J. Dissenting: Frankfurter, J.

Congress has the authority to make an unlawful search and arrest a federal cause of action supplementary to the relief provided by state law.

NOTE:

In *Benanti* the basic opinion of the Court was that wire tapping by state officers violated the Federal Communications Act and, presumably, that such evidence could not be admitted in federal courts even though the wire tapping had been done by state officers. *Benanti* basically involved the interpretation of a statute and was not concerned with the scope of the Fourth Amendment. This is an example of the application of federal statutes to state officials as well as to federal. Other examples are *Ex parte Siebold* and *Monroe* v. *Pape*, above, as well as *Screws* v. *United States,* 325 U.S. 91, 1945 (see p. 313, below) and *United States* v. *Classic,* 313 U.S. 299, 1941 (see p. 325, below). In 1961 in *Mapp* v. *Ohio,* (see p. 265, below) the Court outlawed the use of illegally obtained evidence in state courts.

Katz v. United States
389 U.S. 347; 88 S.Ct. 507; 19 L.Ed. 2d 576 (1967)

(Katz was convicted under an indictment charging him with transmitting wagering information by telephone across state lines in violation of federal statute. Evidence of Katz's end of the conversations, overheard by FBI agents who had attached an electronic listening and recording device to the outside of the telephone booth from which the calls were made, was introduced at the trial. There was no physical entrance by officers into the area occupied by Katz.)

Vote: 7-1

Mr. Justice Stewart delivered the opinion of the Court:

. . . Because of the misleading way the issues have been formulated, the parties have attached great significance to the characterization of the telephone booth from which the petitioner placed his calls. The petitioner has strenuously argued that the booth was a "constitutionally protected area." The Government has maintained with equal vigor that it was not. But this effort to decide whether or not a given "area," viewed in the abstract, is "constitutionally protected" deflects attention from the problem presented by this case. For the Fourth Amendment protects people, not places. What a person knowingly exposes to the public, even in his own home or office, is not a subject of Fourth Amendment protection. See *Lewis* v. *United States*, 385 U.S. 206, 210; *United States* v. *Lee*, 274 U.S. 559, 563. But what he seeks to preserve as private, even in an area accessible to the public, may be constitutionally protected. See *Rios* v. *United States*, 364 U.S. 253; *Ex parte Jackson*, 96 U.S. 727, 733.

The Government stresses the fact that the telephone booth from which the petitioner made his calls was constructed partly of glass, so that he was as visible after he entered it as he would have been if he had remained outside. But what he sought to exclude when he entered the booth was not the intruding eye—it was the uninvited ear. He did not shed his right to do so simply because he made his calls from a place where he might be seen. No less than an individual in a business office, in a friend's apartment, or in a taxicab, a person in a telephone booth may rely upon the protection of the Fourth Amendment. One who occupies it, shuts the door behind him, and pays the toll that permits him to place a call is surely entitled to assume that the words he utters into the mouthpiece will not be broadcast to the world. To read the Constitution more narrowly is to ignore the vital role that the public telephone has come to play in private communication. . . .

. . . Thus, although a closely divided Court supposed in *Olmstead* that surveillance without any trespass and without the seizure of any material object fell outside the ambit of the Constitution, we have since departed from the narrow view on which that decision rested. Indeed, we have expressly held that the Fourth Amendment governs not only the seizure of tangible items, but extends as well to the recording of oral statements, overheard without any "technical trespass under . . . local property law." *Silverman* v. *United States*, 365 U.S. 505, 511. Once this much is acknowledged, and once it is recognized that the Fourth Amendment protects people—and not simply "areas"—against unreasonable searches and seizures, it becomes clear that the reach of that Amendment cannot turn upon the presence or absence of a physical intrusion into any given enclosure.

We conclude that the underpinnings of *Olmstead* and *Goldman* have been so eroded by our subsequent decisions that the "trespass" doctrine there enunciated can no longer be regarded as controlling. The Government's activities in electronically listening to and recording the petitioner's words violated the privacy upon which he justifiably relied while using the telephone booth and thus constituted a "search and seizure" within the meaning of the Fourth Amendment. The fact that the electronic device employed to achieve that end did not happen to penetrate the wall of the booth can have no constitutional significance. [This could be interpreted to include all wire tapping and "bugging".]

The question remaining for decision, then, is whether the search and seizure conducted in this case complied with constitutional standards. In that regard, the Government's position is that its agents acted in an entirely defensible manner: They did not begin their electronic surveillance until investigation of the petitioner's activities had established a strong probability that he was using the telephone in question to transmit gambling information to persons in other States, in violation of federal law. Moreover, the surveillance was limited, both in scope and in duration, to the specific purpose of establishing the contents of the petitioner's unlawful telephonic communications. The agents confined their surveillance to the brief periods during which he used the telephone booth, and they took great care to overhear only the conversations of the petitioner himself.

Accepting this account of the Government's actions as accurate, it is clear that this surveillance was so narrowly circumscribed that a duly authorized magistrate, properly notified of the need for such investigation, specifically informed of the basis on which it was to proceed, and clearly apprised of the precise intrusion it would entail, could constitutionally have authorized, with appropriate safeguards, the very limited search and seizure that the Government asserts in fact took place. . . .

These considerations do not vanish when the search in question is transferred from the setting of a home, an office, or a hotel room to that of a telephone booth. Wherever a man may be, he is entitled to know that he will remain free from unreasonable searches and seizures. The government agents here ignored "the procedure of antecedent justification . . . that is central to the Fourth Amendment," a procedure that we hold to be a constitutional precondition of the kind of electronic surveillance involved in this case. Because the surveillance here failed to meet that condition, and because it led to the petitioner's conviction, the judgment must be reversed.

It is so ordered.

Mr. Justice Marshall took no part in the consideration or decision of this case.

Mr. Justice Black dissented:

. . . My basic objection is twofold: (1) I do not believe that the words of the Amendment will bear the meaning given them by today's decision, and (2) I do not believe that it is the proper role of this Court to rewrite the Amendment in order "to bring it into harmony with the times" and thus reach a result that many people believe to be desirable.

. . . Thus the clear holding of the *Olmstead* and *Goldman* cases, undiluted by any question of trespass, is that eavesdropping, in both its original and modern forms, is not violative of the Fourth Amendment.

While my reading of the *Olmstead* and *Goldman* cases convinces me that they were decided on the basis of the inapplicability of the wording of the Fourth Amendment to eavesdropping, and not on any trespass basis, this is not to say that unauthorized intrusion has not played an important role in search and seizure cases. This Court had adopted an exclusionary rule to bar evidence obtained by means of such intrusions. . . .

The Fourth Amendment protects privacy only to the extent that it prohibits unreasonable searches and seizures of "persons, houses, papers, and effects." No general right is created by the Amendment so as to give this Court the unlimited power to hold unconstitutional everything which affects privacy. Certainly the Framers, well acquainted as they were with the excesses of governmental power, did not intend to grant this Court such omnipotent lawmaking authority as that. The history of governments proves that it is dangerous to freedom to repose such powers in courts.

For these reasons I respectfully dissent.

RELATED CASES:

United States v. Lee: 274 U.S. 559 (1927). Opinion: Brandeis, J. No dissent.

A search by searchlight of a boat suspected of violating revenue laws beyond the twelve-mile limit in connection with a lawful arrest does not violate the Constitution. The subsequent trepass to seize legal evidence did not render the evidence inadmissible.

Rios v. United States: 364 U.S. 253 (1960). Opinion: Stewart, J. Dissenting: Frankfurter, Clark, Harlan, and Whittaker, JJ.

Evidence seized in an unreasonable search by state officers must be excluded from a federal criminal trial upon the timely objection of a defendant.

Carroll v. United States
267 U.S. 132; 45 S.Ct. 280; 69 L.Ed. 543 (1925)

(Carroll and two other persons had agreed to procure three cases of whisky for a federal agent posing as a customer. However, the three men failed to return with the whisky. Later, the federal agents were patrolling the highway between Detroit and Grand Rapids. At that point Carroll drove past the agents in a car they recognized as his. Sixteen miles east of Grand Rapids they stopped and searched the automobile. They found sixty-eight bottles of whisky and gin. The agents were not anticipating that the violators would be coming through on the highway at that particular time, but when they spotted them they believed that they were carrying whisky or gin. The search was challenged as violating the Fourth Amendment.)

Vote: 7-2

Mr. Chief Justice Taft delivered the opinion of the Court:

. . . The Fourth Amendment does not denounce all searches or seizures, but only such as are unreasonable. . . .

On reason and authority the true rule is that if the search and seizure without a warrant are made upon probable cause, that is, upon a belief, reasonably arising out of circumstances known to the seizing officer, that an automobile or other vehicle contains that which by law is subject to seizure and destruction, the search and seizure are valid. The Fourth Amendment is to be construed in the light of what was deemed an unreasonable search and seizure when it was adopted, and in a manner which will conserve public interests as well as the interests and rights of individual citizens. . . .

. . . In cases where the securing of a warrant is reasonably practicable, it must be used, and when properly supported by affidavit and issued after judicial approval protects the seizing officer against a suit for damages. In cases where seizure is impossible except without warrant, the seizing officer acts unlawfully and at his peril unless he can show the court probable cause. . . .

. . . It is clear the officers here had justification for the search and seizure . . . the facts and circumstances within their knowledge and of which they had reasonably trustworthy information were sufficient in themselves to warrant a man of reasonable caution in the belief that intoxicating liquor was being transported in the automobile which they stopped and searched.

The judgment is affirmed.

Mr. Justice McKenna concurred.

Mr. Justice McKeynolds dissented, with the concurrence of Mr. Justice Sutherland:

. . . If an officer, upon mere suspicion of a misdemeanor, may stop one on a public highway, take articles away from him and thereafter use them as evidence to convict him of crime, what becomes of the Fourth and Fifth Amendments?

. . . The facts known when the arrest occurred were wholly insufficient to engender reasonable belief that plaintiffs in error were committing a misdemeanor, and the legality of the arrest cannot be supported by facts ascertained through the search which followed. . . .

RELATED CASES:

Henry v. United States: 361 U.S. 98 (1959). Opinion: Douglas, J. Dissenting: Clark, J., and Warren, C.J.

Federal officers, investigating a theft from an interstate shipment of whisky, who had twice observed cartons being placed in an automobile in a residential district and who followed and stopped the car, arrested two men in the car, searched the car and found and seized cartons containing radios stolen from an interstate shipment, did not have probable cause for the arrest when they stopped the car. The search was illegal, the articles seized were not admissible in evidence and the conviction was reversed. Probable cause must be had *before* a car is stopped.

Chambers v. Maroney: 399 U.S. 42 (1970). Opinion: White, J. Dissenting: Harlan, J. Abstaining: Blackmun, J.

Search by police without a warrant of a car at the police station when the car might have been searched at the time of arrest is valid since there was probable cause to search the car apart from the arrest.

NOTE:

The elusive meaning of "reasonable" is here given some concreteness when the Court held that the mobility of a car can be held to justify police action without a warrant. *Henry* v. *United States* is further illustration of the complexities of the situation. In *Henry* the Court held that officers who stop a car must have probable cause for arrest. Mere suspicion is not enough. Further, it cannot be too much emphasized that the "probable cause" that is a prerequisite to search by officers without a warrant if it is to be regarded as "reasonable" must be present at the time of the arrest or the search and is not to be justified by the results of the search.

Weeks v. United States
232 U.S. 383; 34 S.Ct. 341; 58 L.Ed. 652 (1914)

(The defendant, Weeks, was convicted in federal court of the charge of using the mails to transmit lottery material in violation of a federal statute. Both state police and a federal marshall entered Weeks' room and searched it without benefit of a warrant. Certain private papers belonging to Weeks were seized. These papers concerned his connection with the lottery project. Before the trial and again after the jury was sworn, the defendant moved in the district court for the return of these papers, but both applications were denied. The admission of these papers in evidence was then challenged as contrary to the Fourth and Fifth Amendments.)

Vote: No dissent

Mr. Justice Day delivered the opinion of the Court:

. . . The case in the aspect in which we are dealing with it involves the right of the court in a criminal prosecution to retain for the purposes of evidence the letters and correspondence of the accused, seized in his house in his absence and without his authority, by a United States marshal holding no warrant for his arrest and none for the search of his premises. The accused, without awaiting his trial, made timely application to the court for an order for the return of these letters, as well as other property. This application was denied, the letters retained and put in evidence, after a further application at the beginning of the trial, both applications asserting the rights of the accused under the Fourth and Fifth Amendments to the Constitution. If letters and private documents can thus be seized and held and used in evidence against a citizen accused of an offense, the protection of the Fourth Amendment, declaring his right to be secure against such searches and seizures is of no value, and, so far as those thus placed are concerned, might as well be stricken from the Constitution. The efforts of the courts and their officials to bring the guilty to punishment, praiseworthy as they are, are not to be aided by the sacrifice of those great principles established by years of endeavor and suffering which have resulted in their embodiment in the fundamental law of the land. The United States marshal could only have invaded the house of the accused when armed with a warrant issued as required by the Constitution, upon sworn information, and describing with reasonable particularity the thing for which the search was to be made. Instead, he acted without sanction of law, doubtless prompted by the desire to bring further proof to the aid of the government, and under color of his office undertook to make a seizure of private papers in direct violation of the constitutional prohibition against such action. Under such circumstances, without sworn information and particular description, not even an order of court would have justified such procedure; much less was it within the authority of the United States marshal to thus invade the house and privacy of the accused. In *Adams* v. *New York*, 192 U.S. 585 . . . this Court said that the Fourth Amendment was intended to secure the citizen in person and property against unlawful invasion of the sanctity of his home by officers of the law, acting under it. . . . To sanction such proceedings would be to affirm by judicial decision a manifest neglect, if not an open defiance, of the prohibitions of the Constitution, intended for the protection of the people against such unauthorized action.

Judgment reversed.

RELATED CASES:

Adams v. New York: 192 U.S. 585 (1904). Opinion: Day, J. No dissent.

A court will not in trying a criminal case permit a collateral issue to be raised as to the source of competent testimony, that is, the illegality of the means used to obtain evidence.

Silverthorne Lumber Co. v. United States: 251 U.S. 385 (1920). Opinion: Holmes, J. Dissenting: White, C.J., and Pitney, J.

The prohibition of the acquisition of evidence in a certain manner prohibits the use of that evidence in any way by the prosecution.

Burdeau v. McDowell: 256 U.S. 465 (1921). Opinion: Day, J. Dissenting: Brandeis and Holmes, JJ.

Evidence improperly seized by private persons and then turned over to federal officers can be used as evidence in a trial since the Fourth Amendment is a prohibition only against official federal action. Here there was no complicity of federal officers. See p. 151, below.

Goldstein v. United States: 316 U.S. 114 (1942). Opinion: Roberts, J. Dissenting: Murphy, J., Stone, C.J., and Frankfurter, J. Abstaining: Jackson, J.

Evidence secured by federal officers using an illegal telephone tap can be used against a person who has not been the victim of the illegal action. See p. 133, above.

Wolf v. Colorado: 338 U.S. 25 (1949). Opinion: Frankfurter, J. Dissenting: Douglas, Murphy, and Rutledge, JJ.

In a prosecution in a state court for a state crime, the Fourteenth Amendment of the Federal Constitution does not forbid the admission of relevant evidence even though obtained by an unreasonable search and seizure. See p. 262, below.

United States v. Jeffers: 342 U.S. 48 (1951). Opinion: Clark, J. Dissenting: Vinson, C.J., and Reed, J. Abstaining: Minton, J.

Articles of contraband, illegally seized, cannot be used against their owner, but the owner has no right to the return of the contraband goods.

Walder v. United States: 347 U.S. 62 (1954). Opinion: Frankfurter, J. Dissenting: Black and Douglas, JJ.

Evidence obtained through unlawful search and seizure can be used to attack the *credibility* of an accused person's testimony.

Rea v. United States: 350 U.S. 214 (1956). Opinion: Douglas, J. Dissenting: Harlan, Reed, Burton, and Minton, JJ.

Evidence illegally secured by a federal officer cannot be transferred to state authorities for use in prosecution in state courts. This would be contrary to proper standards of federal procedure and evidence which must be adhered to by federal agents. The basis of the decision was the Court's supervisory power over law-enforcement agencies.

Elkins v. United States: 364 U.S. 206 (1960). Opinion: Stewart, J. Dissenting: Frankfurter, Clark, Harlan, and Whittaker, JJ.

Evidence secured by state officers by illegal means, here by wire tapping, cannot be handed over to federal officers, even though they had not been at all involved in the search, and subsequently used in a prosecution in a federal court. The Court held that considerations of reason, of experience, and of judicial integrity required this decision. Thus was the "silver platter" doctrine rescinded. The "silver platter" doctrine had not applied to wire tapping because of a statutory ban. This opinion has a valuable historical appendix.

Harris v. New York: 401 U.S. 222 (1971). Opinion: Burger, C.J. Dissenting: Black, Brennan, Douglas, and Marshall, JJ.

After his arrest and before being advised of his right to counsel, Harris made statements that were later used to impeach the credibility of his testimony. The Court held that the defendant does not have the right to commit perjury. Since he voluntarily took the stand, he had obligation to speak truthfully and prosecution could impeach his credibility.

NOTE:

The common law rule on the admission of evidence to which about two-thirds of the states adhere is that the illegality of the method of securing of evidence is no bar to the admission of such evidence at the trial. The *"Weeks* rule" is a rule of exclusion of evidence in federal courts when this has been obtained illegally by federal officers. Since *Mapp* v. *Ohio* (see p. 265, below) this is a constitutional mandate. Under *Weeks*, evidence illegally secured by state officers could be turned over to federal officers—the "silver platter" rule—and used in the federal courts. The Court began to change this rule in *Benanti*, there specifically regarding wire tapping, and the change was completed in *Elkins* v. *United States*. (See p. 140, above.) The logical conclusion was reached in applying the *Weeks* rule to state officers in *Mapp* v. *Ohio*, 367 U.S. 643, 1961. As a result of *Mapp*, the "Gitlow doctrine" has been extended to the Fourth Amendment.

United States v. Rabinowitz
339 U.S. 56; 70 S.Ct. 430; 94 L.Ed. 653 (1950)

(Albert J. Rabinowitz was convicted of selling and possessing postage stamps bearing a forged overprint. An arrest warrant had been issued, but the police then proceeded, without a search warrant, to search the one-room office including a desk, file cabinets, and a safe. The altered stamps were found, and Rabinowitz was convicted on the basis of this evidence. He objected that the evidence had been secured by unreasonable search and seizure.)

Vote: 5-3

Mr. Justice Minton delivered the opinion of the Court:

. . . The question presented here is the reasonableness of a search without a search warrant of a place of business consisting of a one-room office, incident to a valid arrest. . . .

Respondent made timely motions for suppression and to strike the evidence pertaining to the 573 stamps, all of which were eventually denied. Respondent was convicted on both counts after trial before a jury in which he offered no evidence. Relying on *Trupiano* v. *United States*, 334 U.S. 699, the Court of Appeals, one judge dissenting, reversed on the ground that since the officers had had time in which to procure a search warrant and had failed to do so the search was illegal, and the evidence therefore should have been excluded. We granted certiorari to determine the validity of the search because of the question's importance in the administration of the law of search and seizure. . . .

What is a reasonable search is not to be determined by any fixed formula. The Constitution does not define what are "unreasonable" searches and, regrettably, in our discipline we have no ready litmuspaper test. The recurring questions of the reasonableness of searches must find resolution in the facts and circumstances of each case. . . . Reasonableness is in the first instance for the District Court to determine. We think the District Court's conclusion that here the search and seizure were reasonable should be sustained because: (1) the search and seizure were incident to a valid arrest; (2) the place of the search was a business room to which the public, including the officers, was invited; (3) the room was small and under the immediate and complete control of respondent; (4) the search did not extend beyond the room used for unlawful purposes; (5) the possession of the forged and altered stamps was a crime, just as it is a crime to possess burglars' tools, lottery tickets or counterfeit money.

Assuming that the officers had time to procure a search warrant, were they bound to do so? We think not, because the search was otherwise reasonable, as previously concluded. In a recent opinion, *Trupiano* v. *United States*, . . . this Court first enunciated the requirement that search warrants must be procured when "practicable" in case of search incident to arrest. . . .

A rule of thumb requiring that a search warrant always be procured whenever practicable may be appealing from the vantage point of easy administration. But we cannot agree that this requirement should be crystallized into a *sine qua non* to the reasonableness of a search. It is fallacious to judge events retrospectively and thus to determine, considering the time element alone, that there was time to procure a search warrant. Whether there was time may well be dependent upon considerations other than the ticking off of minutes or hours. The judgment of the officers as to when to close the trap on a criminal committing a crime in their presence or who they have reasonable cause to believe is committing a felony is not determined solely upon whether there was time to procure a search warrant. Some flexibility will be accorded law officers engaged in daily battle with criminals for whose restraint criminal laws are essential.

It is appropriate to note that the Constitution does not say that the right of the people to be secure in their persons should not be violated without a search warrant if it is practicable for the officers to procure one. The mandate of the Fourth Amendment is that the people shall be secure against *unreasonable* searches. It is not disputed that there may be reasonable searches, incident to an arrest, without a search warrant. Upon acceptance of this established rule that some authority to search follows from lawfully taking the person into custody, it becomes apparent that such searches turn upon the reasonableness under all the circumstances and not upon the practicability of procuring a search warrant, for the warrant is not required. To the extent that *Trupiano* v. *United States*, . . . requires a search warrant solely upon the basis of the practicability of procuring it rather than upon the reasonableness of the search after a lawful arrest, that case is overruled. The relevant test is not whether it is reasonable to procure a search warrant, but whether the search was reasonable. That criterion in turn depends upon the facts and circumstances—the total atmosphere of the case. It is a sufficient precaution that law officers must justify their conduct before courts which have always been, and must be, jealous of the individual's right of privacy within the broad sweep of the Fourth Amendment. . . .

The motion to suppress the evidence was properly denied by the District Court. The judgment of the Court of Appeals is

Reversed.

Mr. Justice Douglas took no part in the consideration or decision of this case.

Mr. Justice Frankfurter, whom Mr. Justice Jackson joined, dissented:

The clear-cut issue before us is this: in making a lawful arrest, may arresting officers search without a search warrant not merely the person under arrest or things under his immediate physical control, but the premises where the arrest is made, although there was ample time to secure such a warrant and no danger that the "papers and effects" for which a search warrant could be issued would be despoiled or destroyed? . . .

The short of it is that the right to search the place of arrest is an innovation based on confusion, without historic foundation, and made in the teeth of a historic protection against it.

. . . What is the test of reason which makes a search reasonable? The test is the reason underlying and expressed by the Fourth Amendment: the history and the experience which it embodies and the safeguards afforded by it against the evils to which it was a response. There must be a warrant to permit search, barring only inherent limitations upon that requirement when there is a good excuse for not getting a search warrant, i.e., the justifications that dispense with search warrants when searching the person in his extension, which is his body and that which his body can immediately control, and moving vehicles. It is for this Court to lay down criteria that the district judges can apply. It is no criterion of reason to say that the district court must find it reasonable. . . .

In the case before us there is not the slightest suggestion that the arresting officers had not the time to secure a search warrant. The arrest and search were made on February 16, 1943. On February 1, there was strong evidence that respondent had in his possession large numbers of stamps bearing forged over-prints, in violation of 18 U.S.C. § 265 [1948 Revised Criminal Code, 18 U.S.C.A. § 472]. On February 6, a postal employee purchased from respondent four stamps bearing overprints and, on February 9, reports were received showing the over-prints to be forgeries. Thus, the Government had at least seven, and more accurately fifteen, days in which to procure a search warrant. Nor was this a case in which the need for a search became apparent at the time of arrest. The arresting officers were accompanied by two stamp experts, whose sole function was to examine the fruits of the search which they knew would be made. This is hardly a natural description of a "search incidental to an arrest."

It is most relevant that the officers had "no excuse for not getting a search warrant," 2 Cir., 176 F.2d 732, 735, for that is precisely what the Fourth Amendment was directed against—that some magistrate and not the police officer should determine, if such determination is not precluded by necessity, who shall be rummaging around in my room, whether it be a small room or a very large room, whether it be one room, or two rooms, or three rooms, or four rooms. . . .

Mr. Justice Black dissented:

. . . Whether this Court should adhere to the *Trupiano* principle making evidence so obtained inadmissible in federal courts now presents no more than a question of what is wise judicial policy. Although the rule does not in all respects conform to my own ideas, I think that the reasons for changing it are outweighed by reasons against its change.

In recent years, the scope of the rule has been a subject of almost constant judicial controversy both in trial and appellate courts. In no other field has the law's uncertainty been more clearly manifested. To some extent that uncertainty may be unavoidable. The *Trupiano* case itself added new confusions "in a field already replete with complexities." . . . But overruling that decision merely aggravates existing uncertainty. For as Mr. Justice Frankfurter points out, today's holding casts doubt on other cases recently decided. And I do not understand how trial judges can be expected to foresee what further shifts may occur. In my judgment it would be wiser judicial policy to adhere to the *Trupiano* rule of evidence, at least long enough to see how it works. . . .

RELATED CASES:

Harris v. United States: 331 U.S. 145 (1947). Opinion: Vinson, C.J. Dissenting: Frank-furter, Murphy, Rutledge, and Jackson, JJ.

Police in possession of an arrest warrant could search the four-room apartment where the accused was arrested. This area was under his possession and control. Here the possession of Selective Service draft cards was a crime being committed in the presence of the officers. There is a good chart in the appendix of this case.

United States v. Di Re: 332 U.S. 581 (1948). Opinion: Jackson, J. Dissenting: Vinson, C.J., and Black, J.

Where an arrest is made without probable cause the search is also illegal. Here one of two men was identified as a criminal by an informer. Without more, the other man was also arrested, and searched, and incriminating evidence was found. Both arrest and search were held void.

Kremen v. United States: 353 U.S. 346 (1957). Opinion: Per curiam. Dissenting: Burton and Clark, JJ. Abstaining: Whittaker, J.

An illegal search and seizure occurs where federal officers arrest three persons in a cabin, only one of whom they have an arrest warrant for, and where without search warrants they search the cabin and remove the entire contents of it. Kremen was charged with harboring a fugitive. The incident occurred near Twain Harte, California, about two hundred miles from San Francisco. The Court held that this goes "beyond the sanction of any of our cases" that it was an "evidence hunt." About ten pages of FBI inventory are in the Appendix of the case.

NOTE:

Rabinowitz presents one aspect of the current rule on search in connection with a valid arrest. This rule appears to be that officers may do a *reasonable* amount of seeking and exploring. "Reasonableness" depends on the circumstances in a case but since *Chimel* v. *California*, 395 U.S. 752 (1969) valid search cannot go beyond the area of the arrestee's "immediate control."

Chimel v. California
395 C.S. 752; 89 S.Ct. 2034; 23 L.Ed. 2d 685 (1969)

(The relevant facts are essentially undisputed. Late in the afternoon of September 13, 1965, three police officers arrived at the Santa Ana, California, home of the petitioner with a warrant authorizing his arrest for the burglary of a coin shop. The officers knocked on the door, identified themselves to the petitioner's wife, and asked if they might come inside. She ushered them into the house, where they waited 10 or 15 minutes until the petitioner returned home from work. When the petitioner entered the house, one of the officers handed him the arrest warrant and asked for permission to "look around." The petitioner objected, but was advised that "on the basis of the lawful arrest," the officers would nonetheless conduct a search. No search warrant had been issued.

Accompanied by the petitioner's wife, the officers then looked through the entire three-bedroom house, including the attic, the garage, and a small workshop. In some rooms the search was relatively cursory. In the master bedroom and sewing room, however, the officers directed the petitioner's wife to open drawers and "to physically move contents of the drawers from side to side so that [they] might view any items that would have come from [the] burglary." After completing the search, they seized numerous items—primarily coins, but also several medals, tokens, and a few other objects. The entire search took between 45 minutes and an hour.

At the petitioner's subsequent state trial on two charges of burglary, the items taken from his house were admitted into evidence against him, over his objection that they had been unconstitutionally seized. He was convicted, and the judgments of conviction were affirmed.)

Vote: 7-2

Mr. Justice Stewart delivered the opinion of the Court.

This case raises basic questions concerning the permissible scope under the Fourth Amendment of a search incident to a lawful arrest. . . .

. . . When an arrest is made, it is reasonable for the arresting officer to search the person arrested in order to remove any weapons that the latter might seek to use in order to resist arrest or effect his escape. Otherwise, the officer's safety might well be endangered, and the arrest itself frustrated. In addition, it is entirely reasonable for the arresting officer to search for and seize any evidence on the arrestee's person in order to prevent its concealment or destruction. And the area into which an arrestee might reach in order to grab a weapon or evidentiary items must, of course, be governed by a like rule. A gun on a table or in a drawer in front of one who is arrested can be as dangerous to the arresting officer as one concealed in the clothing of the person arrested. There is ample justification, therefore, for a search of the arrestee's person and the area "within his immediate control"— construing that phrase to mean the area from within which he might gain possession of a weapon or destructible evidence.

There is no comparable justification, however, for routinely searching rooms other than that in which an arrest occurs—or, for that matter, for searching through all the desk drawers or other closed or concealed areas in that room itself. Such searches, in the absence of well-recognized exceptions, may be made only under the authority of a search warrant. The "adherence to judicial processes" mandated by the Fourth Amendment requires no less.

Rabinowitz and *Harris* have been the subject of critical commentary for many years and have been relied upon less and less in our own decisions. It is time, for the reasons we have stated, to hold that on their own facts, and insofar as the principles they stand for are inconsistent with those that we have endorsed today, they are no longer to be followed.

Application of sound Fourth Amendment principles to the facts of this case produces a clear result. The search here went far beyond the petitioner's person and the area from within which he might have obtained either a weapon or something that could have been used as evidence against him. There was no constitutional justification, in the absence of a search warrant, for extending the search beyond that area. The scope of the search was, therefore, "unreasonable" under the Fourth and Fourteenth Amendments and the petitioner's conviction cannot stand.

Reversed.

Mr. Justice Harlan, concurring.

I join the Court's opinion with these remarks concerning a factor to which the Court has not alluded.

The only thing that has given me pause in voting to overrule *Harris* and *Rabinowitz* is that as a result of *Mapp* v. *Ohio* . . . and *Ker* v. *California*, . . . every change in Fourth Amendment law must now be obeyed by state officials facing widely different problems of local law enforcement. We simply do not know the extent to which cities and towns across the Nation are prepared to administer the greatly expanded warrant system which will be required by today's decision: nor can we say with assurance that in each and every local situation, the warrant requirement plays an essential role in the protection of those fundamental liberties protected against state infringement by the Fourteenth Amendment.

Mr. Justice White, with whom Mr. Justice Black joined, dissented:

An arrested man, by definition conscious of the police interest in him, and provided almost immediately with a lawyer and a judge, is in an excellent position to dispute the reasonableness of his arrest and contemporaneous search in a full adversary proceeding. I would uphold the constitutionality of this search contemporaneous with an arrest since there was probable cause both for the search and for the arrest, exigent circumstances involving the removal or destruction of evidence, and a satisfactory opportunity to dispute the issues of probable cause shortly thereafter. In this case, the search was reasonable.

THE GUARANTEE AGAINST COMPULSORY SELF-INCRIMINATION

As already noted, a corollary guarantee to the Fourth Amendment's prohibition against unreasonable searches and seizures is the provision of the Fifth Amendment that no person is to be "compelled in any criminal case to be a witness against himself." This guarantee developed in England and was part of the heritage of the colonists. The primary judicial interpretation of the amendment has been in connection with statutes that have presumed to extend immunity from prosecution to witnesses in hearings before courts as well as before congressional committees.

The Court has held repeatedly that the Fifth Amendment is a guarantee solely against a person being placed at a disadvantage in a criminal prosecution as a result of his forced testimony and does not at all apply to something that might simply "disgrace him or bring him into disrepute." Within the limits thus set the Court has been engaged in attempting to determine when by statute he has been given an equivalent guarantee and thus may be compelled to testify.

Ullmann v. United States
350 U.S. 422; 76 S.Ct. 497; 100 L.Ed. 511 (1956)

(The Immunity Act of 1954 provided that where "in the judgment of a United States attorney the testimony of any witness, or the production of books, papers, or other evidence by any witness, in any case or proceeding before any grand jury or court of the United States involving any interference with or endangering of, or any plans or attempts to interfere with or endanger the national security or defense of the United States . . . is necessary to the public interest," the United States attorney upon the approval of the Attorney General shall make application to the court for an order to the witness to testify. But the testimony thus secured is not to be used against the witness in any court. In this case, William L. Ullmann refused to answer even after the provisions of the Immunity Act had been invoked in an espionage inquiry before a federal grand jury. Ullmann was convicted of contempt.)

Vote: 7-2

Mr. Justice Frankfurter delivered the opinion of the Court:

. . . Four major questions are raised by this appeal: Is the immunity provided by the Act sufficiently broad to displace the protection afforded by the privilege against self-incrimination? Assuming that the statutory requirements are met, does the Act give the district judge discretion to deny an application for an order requiring a witness to answer relevant questions put by the grand jury, and, if so, is the court thereby required to exercise a function that is not an exercise of "judicial Power"? Did Congress provide immunity from state prosecution for crime, and, if so, is it empowered to do so? Does the Fifth Amendment prohibit compulsion of what would otherwise be self-incriminating testimony no matter what the scope of the immunity statute?

It is relevant to define explicity the spirit in which the Fifth Amendment's privilege against self-incrimination should be approached. This command of the Fifth Amendment ("nor shall any person . . . be compelled in any criminal case to be a witness against himself . . .") registers an important advance in the development of our liberty—"one of the great landmarks in man's struggle to make himself civilized." Time has not shown that protection from the evils against which this safeguard was directed is needless or unwarranted. This constitutional protection must not be interpreted in a hostile or niggardly spirit. Too many, even those who should be better advised, view this privilege as a shelter for wrongdoers. They too readily assume that those who invoke it are either guilty of crime or commit perjury in claiming the privilege. Such a view does scant honor to the patriots who sponsored the Bill of Rights as a condition to acceptance of the Constitution by the ratifying States. The Founders of the Nation were not naive or disregardful of the interests of justice. . . .

No doubt the constitutional privilege may, on occasion, save a guilty man from his just deserts. It was aimed at a more far-reaching evil—a recurrence of the Inquisition and the Star Chamber, even if not in their stark brutality. Prevention of the greater evil was deemed of more important than occurrence of the lesser evil. Having had much experience with a tendency in human nature to abuse power, the Founders sought to close the doors against like future abuses by law-enforcing agencies.

As no constitutional guarantee enjoys preference, so none should suffer subordination or deletion. . . . To view a particular provision of the Bill of Rights with disfavor inevitably results in a constricted application of it. This is to disrespect the Constitution. . . .

Petitioner further argues that the immunity is not constitutionally sufficient so long as a witness is subject to the very real possibility of state prosecution. He urges that the statute does not, and constitutionally could not, grant such immunity. The immunity portion of the statute contains two parts. The first prohibits prosecutions and is worded virtually in the terms of the 1893 Act. The second makes explicit that the compelled testimony shall not be used against the witness in any proceeding in any court. Such a clause was construed in *Adams* v. *Maryland*, 347 U.S. 179, to apply to state courts. . . .

. . . We cannot say that Congress' paramount authority in safeguarding national security does not justify the restriction it has placed on the exercise of state power for the more effective exercise of conceded federal power. . . .

We are not dealing here with one of the vague, undefinable, admonitory provisions of the Constitution whose scope is inevitably addressed to changing circumstances. The privilege against self-incrimination is a specific provision of which it is peculiarly true that "a page of history is worth a volume of logic." *New York Trust Co.* v. *Eisner*, 256 U.S. 345. For the history of the privilege established not only that it is not to be interpreted literally, but also that its sole concern is, as its name indicates, with the danger to a witness forced to give testimony leading to the infliction of "penalties affixed to the criminal acts. . . ." *Boyd* v. *United States*, 116 U.S. 616. We leave *Boyd* v. *United States* unqualified, as it was left unqualified in *Brown* v. *Walker*. Immunity displaces the danger. Once the reason for the privilege ceases, the privilege ceases. We reaffirm *Brown* v. *Walker,* and in so doing we need not repeat the answers given by that case to the other points raised by petitioner.

The judgment of the Court of Appeals is
Affirmed.

Mr. Justice Douglas, with whom Mr. Justice Black concurred, dissented:

I would reverse the judgment of conviction. I would base the reversal on *Boyd* v. *United States*, 116 U.S. 616, or, in the alternative, I would overrule the five-to-four decision of *Brown* v.*Walker*, 161 U.S. 591, and adopt the view of the minority in that case that the right of silence created by the Fifth Amendment is beyond the reach of Congress.

First, as to the *Boyd* case. There are numerous disabilities created by federal law that attach to a person who is a Communist. These disabilities include ineligibility for employment in the Federal Government and in defense facilities, disqualification for a passport, the risk of internment, the risk of loss of employment as a long-shoreman—to mention only a few. These disabilities imposed by federal law are forfeitures within the meaning of our cases and as much protected by the Fifth Amendment as criminal prosecution itself. But there is no indication that the Immunity Act, 68 Stat. 745, 18 U.S.C. (Supp. II) § 3486, grants protection against those disabilities. The majority will not say that it does. I think, indeed, that it must be read as granting only partial, not complete, immunity for the matter disclosed under compulsion. Yet, as the Court held in *Counselman* v. *Hitchcock*, 142 U.S. 547, 586, an immunity statute to be valid must "supply a complete protection from all the perils against which the constitutional prohibition was designed to guard. . . ."

Boyd v. *United States, supra,* involved a proceeding to establish a forfeiture of goods alleged to have been fraudulently imported without payment of duties. The claimants resisted an order requiring the production of an invoice to be used against them in the forfeiture proceedings. The Court in an opinion by Mr. Justice Bradley sustained the defense of the Fifth Amendment. The Court said, "A witness, as well as a party, is protected by the law from being compelled to give evidence that tends to criminate him, or to subject his property to forfeiture." 116 U.S., at page 638. . . .

The Court may mean that if disqualification for government employment or ineligibility for a passport is a forfeiture within the meaning of the *Boyd* case, Congress has lifted these disabilities in exchange for the witness' testimony. Congress, I think, will be surprised to hear this. There is nothing in the legislative history that would suggest that Congress was willing to pay any such price for the testimony. If the disabilities which attack under existing law are forfeitures, the Court should strike down the Act. If Congress chooses to enact a new Immunity Act broad enough to protect against all forfeitures, it is free to do so. The Court seems to commit Congress to a policy that there is no indication Congress favors.

We should apply the principle of the *Boyd* case to the present one and hold that since there is no protection in the Immunity Act against loss of rights of citizenship, the immunity granted is less than the protection afforded by the Constitution. Certainly personal freedom has at least as much constitutional dignity as property. . . .

It is no answer to say that a witness who exercises his Fifth Amendment right of silence and stands mute may bring himself into disrepute. If so, that is the price he pays for exercising the right of silence granted by the Fifth Amendment. The critical point is that the Constitution places the right of silence *beyond the reach of government*. The Fifth Amendment stands between the citizen and his government. When public opinion casts a person into the outer darkness, as happens today when a person is exposed as a Communist, the government brings infamy on the head of the witness when it compels disclosure. That is precisely what the Fifth Amendment prohibits. . . .

RELATED CASES:

Counselman v. Hitchcock: 142 U.S. 547 (1892). Opinion: Blatchford, J. No dissent.

An immunity statute must provide complete immunity even against the indirect use of his testimony such as a lead or a means to the discovery of other evidence.

Brown v. Walker: 161 U.S. 591 (1896). Opinion: Brown, J. Dissenting: Shiras, Gray, White, and Field, JJ.

When a witness is secured against criminal prosecution which might be aided directly or indirectly by his disclosure, there is no violation of the Fifth Amendment. There is no protection against public opinion.

United States v. Bryan: 339 U.S. 323 (1950). Opinion: Vinson, C.J. Dissenting: Black and Frankfurter, JJ.

The government is not required to prove that a quorum was present when a witness refused to produce papers required by a previously issued subpoena, nor was the matter of lack of a quorum a valid defense on the part of the accused.

Adams v. Maryland: 347 U.S. 179 (1954). Opinion: Black, J. No dissent.

A federal statute may, under the supremacy doctrine, forbid the use in state courts of testimony given before a congressional committee.

Quinn v. United States: 349 U.S. 155 (1955). Opinion: Warren, C.J. Dissenting: Reed, and Minton, JJ.

An individual who is asked, while testifying before a congressional committee, whether he was or had been a member of the Communist Party sufficiently invokes the privilege against self-incrimination when he bases his refusal to answer on the "First and Fifth Amendments," as well as "the First Amendment to the Constitution supplemented by the Fifth Amendment."

Emspak v. United States: 349 U.S. 190 (1955). Opinion: Warren, C.J. Dissenting: Harlan, Reed, and Minton, JJ.

A labor union official, called before a congressional committee investigating Communist infiltration of labor unions, may invoke the privilege against self-incrimination when confronted with questions concerning his alleged membership and activities in the Communist Party, his alleged membership in Communist front organizations and whether he knew certain individuals who had been charged with having Communist affiliations and whether they had held positions in the union.

Kastigar v. United States: 406 U.S. 441 (1972). Opinion: Powell, J. Dissenting: Douglas and Marshall, JJ. Abstaining: Brennan and Rehnquist, JJ.

The protection of an immunity statute must be coextensive with the Fifth Amendment privilege, which is protection from the use of the compelled testimony and evidence derived therefrom. There is no necessity to grant immunity also from prosecution for offenses to which the compelled testimony relates ("transactional" immunity) but the prosecution has the affirmative duty of proving that the evidence it proposes to use is derived from a legitimate source wholly independent from the compelled testimony.

NOTE:

Ullmann represents additional determination by the Court on the matter of immunity to witnesses. The Court had decided earlier that witnesses need not be given protection by a federal immunity statute against state prosecution (*United States* v. *Murdock*, 284 U.S. 141, 1931) and that a state immunity statute does not protect against federal prosecution (*Knapp* v. *Schweitzer*, 357 U.S. 371, 1958). However, Congress could, if it wished, provide that federal immunity was to be observed by state courts. (*Adams* v. *Maryland*, 347 U.S. 179, 1954). The Immunity Act of 1954 contains the "in any court" phraseology used in the statute ruled on in *Adams*, and this was also upheld in *Ullmann*. See also *Reina* v. *United States*, 364 U.S. 507, 1960. This situation was changed completely by the Court's decisions in *Malloy* v. *Hogan* and *Murphy* v. *Waterfront Commission*. (See pp. 151 and 153, below.)

United States v. Murdock
284 U.S. 141; 52 S.Ct. 63; 76 L.Ed. 210 (1931)

(Murdock filed his individual federal income tax returns for 1927-1928, and in each year deducted $12,000 which he claimed to have paid others. An authorized revenue agent summoned Murdock to appear before him and disclose the recipients. He appeared but refused to give the information on the ground that to do so might incriminate him and degrade him. The United States demurred to the plea on the grounds that it failed to show that the information demanded would have incriminated him or subjected him to prosecution under federal laws, and that the defendant had waived his privileges under the Fifth Amendment. The trial court overruled the demurrer and entered judgment discharging the defendant.)

Vote: 9-0

Mr. Justice Butler delivered the opinion of the Court:

. . . Immediately in advance of the examination, appellee's counsel discussed with counsel for the Internal Revenue Bureau the matter of appellee's privilege against self-incrimination and stated that he had particularly in mind incrimination under state law. And at the hearing appellee repeatedly stated that, in answering, "I might incriminate or degrade myself"; he had in mind "the violation of a state law and not the violation of a federal law." The transcript included in the plea plainly shows that appellee did not rest his refusal upon apprehension of, or a claim for protection against federal prosecution. The validity of his justification depends, not upon claims that would have been warranted by the facts shown, but upon the claim that actually was made. The privilege of silence is solely for the benefit of the witness and is deemed waived unless invoked. . . .

. . . Investigations for federal purposes may not be prevented by matters depending upon state law. Constitution, art. 6, cl. 2. The English rule of evidence against compulsory self-incrimination, on which historically that contained in the Fifth Amendment rests, does not protect witnesses against disclosing offenses in violation of the laws of another country. . . . This court has held that immunity against state prosecution is not essential to the validity of federal statutes declaring that a witness shall not be excused from giving evidence on the ground that it will incriminate him, and also that the lack of state power to give witnesses protection against federal prosecution does not defeat a state immunity statute. The principle established is that full and complete immunity against prosecution by the government compelling the witness to answer is equivalent to the protection furnished by the rule against compulsory self-incrimination. . . . As appellee at the hearing did not invoke protection against federal prosecution, his plea is without merit and the government's demurrer should have been sustained.

Judgment reversed.

RELATED CASES:

Twining v. New Jersey: 211 U.S. 78 (1908). Opinion: Moody, J. Dissenting: Harlan, J.

Immunity from self-incrimination is not an essential element in the concept of due process of law on the basis of the history of its development. Further, "exemption from compulsory self-incrimination is not a privilege or immunity of national citizenship guaranteed by this clause of the Fourteenth Amendment against abridgement by the states." The exemption from self-incrimination is not one of the privileges and immunities protected by the Fourteenth Amendment; they are only such as arise out of the nature and essential character of the national government or that are specifically granted or secured by the Constitution. This decision was reversed by *Griffin* v. *California*. See below.

Burdeau v. McDowell: 256 U.S. 465 (1921). Opinion: Day, J. Dissenting: Brandeis, and Holmes, JJ.

The United States may retain for use as evidence in the criminal prosecution of their owner incriminating documents which are turned over to it by private individuals who procured them, without the participation or knowledge of any government official, through a wrongful search of the owner's private desk and papers in an office. Such production would require no unreasonable search or seizure nor would it amount to compelling the accused to testify against himself. The Fourth Amendment prohibition against unreasonable searches and seizures refers to governmental action.

Feldman v. United States: 322 U.S. 487 (1944). Opinion: Frankfurter, J. Dissenting: Black, Douglas, and Rutledge, JJ. Abstaining: Murphy and Jackson, JJ.

A state immunity statute is no bar to the use in prosecuting for a federal offense in a federal court of evidence extracted under the state immunity statute. However, there is to be no "complicity" of federal officers in the state proceedings. There can be no state interference with the operations of the federal government within its sphere.

Knapp v. Schweitzer: 357 U.S. 371 (1958). Opinion: Frankfurter, J. Dissenting: Warren, C.J., and Black and Douglas, JJ.

Under our federal system a person who has been granted under a state statute immunity from state prosecution cannot refuse to answer questions in a state court on the ground that to answer might expose him to federal prosecution for violation of a federal statute. The Fifth Amendment limits only the powers of the federal government and not those of the states.

Griffin v. California: 380 U.S. 609 (1965). Opinion: Douglas, J. Dissenting: Stewart, and White, JJ. Abstaining: Warren, C.J.

The guarantee against self-incrimination includes prohibition against either comment by the prosecution on the accused's silence or instructions by the court that such silence is evidence of guilt. This decision reversed *Twining* v. *New Jersey*, 211 U.S. 78 (1908) (see above) and *Adamson* v. *California*, 332 U.S. 46 (1947) (see p. 259, below). In *Griffin* the charge was murder.

Tehan v. United States ex rel. Shott: 328 U.S. 406 (1966). Opinion: Stewart, J. Dissenting: Black and Douglas, JJ.

To require all of those states now to void the conviction of every person who did not testify at his trial and in respect to which there was adverse comment by a prosecutor or trial judge would have an impact upon the administration of their criminal law so devastating as to need no elaboration. Retroactive application of a new rule is not a general proposition.

NOTE:

The rule of *Murdock* that a federal immunity statute loses none of its validity because it does not protect against possible state prosecution was later expanded to note that Congress *may* provide in federal immunity statutes for immunity against state prosecution. Still later decisions have completely changed the rule. See *Murphy* v. *Waterfront Commission,* p. 153, below, and *Adams* v. *Maryland,* p. 149, above.

Malloy v. Hogan
378 U.S. 1; 84 S.Ct. 1489; 12 L.Ed. 2d 653 (1964)

(William Malloy was on probation after pleading guilty to a gambling misdemeanor in Connecticut. He was ordered to testify before a referee appointed by a state court to investigate gambling and other criminal activities. He refused to answer questions about the circumstances of his arrest and conviction on the

State
Own

ground that the answers might incriminate him and he invoked his alleged privileges under the Fifth Amendment. He was held in contempt and made application for a writ of habeas corpus which the highest state court in Connecticut denied.)

Vote: 5-4

Mr. Justice Brennan delivered the opinion of the Court:

In this case we are asked to reconsider prior decisions holding that the privilege against self-incrimination is not safeguarded against state action by the Fourteenth Amendment. . . .

We hold today that the Fifth Amendment's exception from compulsory self-incrimination is also protected by the Fourteenth Amendment against abridgment by the States. Decisions of the Court since *Twining* and *Adamson* have departed from the contrary view expressed in those cases. We discuss first the decisions which forbid the use of coerced confessions in state criminal prosecutions.

The conclusions of the Court of Errors, tested by the federal standard, fail to take sufficient account of the setting in which the questions were asked. The interrogation was part of a wide-ranging inquiry into crime, including gambling, in Hartford. It was admitted on behalf of the State at oral argument—and indeed it is obvious from the questions themselves—that the State desired to elicit from the petitioner the identity of the person who ran the pool-selling operation in connection with which he had been arrested in 1959. It was apparent that petitioner might apprehend that if this person were still engaged in unlawful activity, disclosure of his name might furnish a link in a chain of evidence sufficient to connect the petitioner with a more recent crime for which he might still be prosecuted.

Mr. Justice Harlan dissented, joined by Mr. Justice Clark:

. . . Believing that the reasoning behind the Court's decision carries extremely mischievous, if not dangerous consequences for our federal system in the realm of criminal law enforcement, I must dissent. The importance of the issue presented and the serious incursion which the Court makes on time-honored, basic constitutional principles justifies a full exposition of my reasons.

I can only read the Court's opinion as accepting in fact what it rejects in theory: the application to the States, via the Fourteenth Amendment, of the forms of federal criminal procedure embodied within the first eight Amendments to the Constitution. While it is true that the Court deals today with only one aspect of state criminal procedure, and rejects the wholesale "incorporation" of such federal constitutional requirements, the logical gap between the Court's premises and its novel constitutional conclusion can, I submit, be bridged only by the additional premises that the Due Process Clause of the Fourteenth Amendment is a shorthand directive to this Court to pick and choose among the provisions of the first eight Amendments and apply those chosen, freighted with their entire accompanying body of federal doctrine, to law enforcement in the States.

I accept and agree with the proposition that continuing re-examination of the constitutional conception of Fourteenth Amendment "due process" of law is required, and that development of the community's sense of justice may in time lead to expansion of the protection which due process affords. In particular in this case, I agree that principles of justice to which due process gives expression, as reflected in decisions of this Court, prohibit a State, as the Fifth Amendment prohibits the Federal Government, from imprisoning a person *solely* because he refuses to give evidence which may incriminate him under the laws of the State. . . .

Rather than insisting, almost by rote, that the Connecticut court, in considering the petitioner's claim of privilege, was required to apply the "federal standard," the Court should have fulfilled its responsibility under the Due Process Clause by inquiring whether the proceedings below met the demands of fundamental fairness which due process embodies. Such an approach may not satisfy those who see in the Fourteenth Amendment a set of easily applied "absolutes" which can afford a haven from unsettling doubt. It is, however, truer to the spirit which requires this Court constantly to re-examine fundamental principles and at the same time enjoins if from reading its own preferences into the Constitution. . . .

Mr. Justice White dissented, joined by Mr. Justice Stewart:

The Fifth Amendment safeguards an important complex of values, but it is difficult for me to perceive how these values are served by the Court's holding that the privilege was properly invoked in this case. While purporting to apply the prevailing federal standard of incrimination—the same standard of incrimination that the Connecticut courts applied—the Court has all but stated that a witness' invocation of the privilege to any question is to be automatically, and without more, accepted. With deference, I prefer the rule permitting the judge rather than the witness to determine when an answer sought is incriminating. . . .

RELATED CASES:

Murphy v. Waterfront Commission of New York Harbor: 378 U.S. 52 (1964). Opinion: Goldberg, J. No dissent.

The constitutional privilege against self-incrimination protects a state witness against incrimination under federal as well as state law and a federal witness against incrimination under state as well as federal law.

Albertson v. Subversive Activities Control Board: 382 U.S. 70 (1965). Opinion: Clark, J. No dissent.

The registration forms required to be completed by the Communist Party were inconsistent with the protection of the self-incrimination clause of the Constitution. The immunity provision was not adequate since it did not preclude use of the information either as evidence or as an investigatory lead.

NOTE:

As a result of *Malloy* and *Murphy* there is now mutual immunity extended to witnesses in federal and state courts based on the Fifth Amendment's guarantee. This does not include an individual testifying voluntarily at his own trial.

United States v. Kahriger
345 U.S. 22; 73 S.Ct. 510; 97 L.Ed. 754 (1953)

(Kahriger had violated the provisions of the federal Gamblers' Occupational Tax Act by failing to register as a gambler and to pay the tax imposed by the act.)

Vote: 6-3

Mr. Justice Reed delivered the opinion of the Court:

The issue raised by this appeal is the constitutionality of the occupational tax provisions of the Revenue Act of 1951, which levy a tax on persons engaged in the business of accepting wagers, and require such persons to register with the Collector of Internal Revenue. The unconstitutionality of the tax is asserted on two grounds. First, it is said that Congress, under the pretense of exercising its power to tax has attempted to penalize illegal intrastate gambling through the regulatory features of the Act, 26 U.S.C. (Supp. V) § 3291, 26 U.S.C.A. § 3291, and has thus infringed the police power which is reserved to the states. Secondly, it is urged that the registration provisions of the tax violate the privilege against self-incrimination and are arbitrary and vague, contrary to the guarantees of the Fifth Amendment. . . .

It is conceded that a federal excise tax does not cease to be valid merely because it discourages or deters the activities taxed. Nor is the tax invalid because the revenue obtained is negligible. Appellee, however, argues that the sole purpose of the statute is to penalize only illegal gambling in the states through the guise of a tax measure. As with the above excise taxes which we have held to be valid [on paper money issued by State banks, on colored oleomargarine, on narcotics, on firearms, and on marihuana] the instant tax has a regulatory effect. But regardless of its regulatory effect, the wagering tax produces revenue. As such it surpasses both the narcotics and firearms taxes which we have found valid. . . .

Nor do we find the registration requirements of the wagering tax offensive. All that is required is the filing of names, addresses, and places of business. This is quite general in tax returns. Such data are directly and intimately related to the collection of the tax and are "obviously supportable as in aid of a revenue purpose." *Sonzinsky* v. *United States*, 300 U.S. 506, at page 513. . . . The registration provisions make the tax simpler to collect.

Appellee's second assertion is that the wagering tax is unconstitutional because it is a denial of the privilege against self-incrimination as guaranteed by the Fifth Amendment.

Since appellee failed to register for the wagering tax, it is difficult to see how he can now claim the privilege even assuming that the disclosure of violations of law are called for. . . .

Assuming that respondent can raise the self-incrimination issue, that privilege has relation only to past acts, not to future acts that may or may not be committed. 8 Wigmore (3rd ed., 1940) § 2259(c). If respondent wished to take wagers subject to excise taxes under § 3285, *supra*, he must pay an occupational tax and register. Under the registration provisions of the wagering tax, appellee is not compelled to confess to acts already committed, he is merely informed by the statute that in order to engage in the business of wagering in the future he must fulfill certain conditions.

Reversed.

Mr. Justice Frankfurter dissented:

. . . A nominal taxing measure must be found an inadmissible intrusion into a domain of legislation reserved for the States not merely when Congress requires that such a measure is to be enforced through a detailed scheme of administration beyond the obvious fiscal needs, as in the Child Labor Tax Case, *supra*. That is one ground for holding that Congress was constitutionally disrespectful of what is reserved to the States. Another basis for deeming such a formal revenue measure inadmissible is presented by this case. In addition to the fact that Congress was concerned with activity beyond the authority of the Federal Government, the enforcing provision of this enactment is designed for the systematic confession of crimes with a view to prosecution for such crimes under State law.

It is one thing to hold that the exception, which the Fifth Amendment makes to the duty of a witness to give his testimony when relevant to a proceeding in a federal court, does not include the potential danger to that witness of possible prosecution in a State court, *Brown* v. *Walker*, 161 U.S. 591, 606 . . . and, conversely, that the Fifth Amendment does not enable States to give immunity from use in federal courts of testimony given in a state court. *Feldman* v. *United States*, 322 U.S. 487. . . It is a wholly different thing to hold that Congress, which cannot constitutionally grapple directly with gambling in the States, may compel self-incriminating disclosures for the enforcement of State gambling laws, merely because it does so under the guise of a revenue measure obviously passed not for revenue purposes. The motive of congressional legislation is not for our scrutiny, provided only that the ulterior purpose is not expressed in ways which negative what the revenue words on their face express and, as in this case, which do not seek enforcement of the formal revenue purpose through means that offend those standards of decency in our civilization against which due process is a barrier.

I would affirm this judgment.

Mr. Justice Black dissented, joined by Mr. Justice Douglas:

The Fifth Amendment declares that no person "shall be compelled in any criminal case to be a witness against himself." The Court nevertheless here sustains an Act which requires a man to register and confess that he is engaged in the business of gambling. I think this confession can provide a basis to convict him of a federal crime for having gambled before registration without paying a federal tax. . . . Whether or not the Act has this effect, I am sure that it creates a squeezing device contrived to put a man in federal prison if he refuses to confess himself into a state prison as a violator of state gambling laws. The coercion of confessions is a common but justly criticized practice of many countries that do not have or live up to a Bill of Rights. But we have a Bill of Rights that condemns coerced confessions, however refined or legalistic may be the technique of extortion. I would hold that this Act violates the Fifth Amendment. See my dissent in *Feldman* v. *United States*, 322 U.S. 487, 494-503.

RELATED CASES:

Wilson v. United States: 221 U.S. 361 (1911). Opinion: Hughes, J. Dissenting: McKenna, J.

Officers of a corporation cannot refuse to produce records of the corporation on the grounds of possible self-incrimination. These records are "held subject to examination by the demanding authority." The corporation officer assumes "a duty which overrides his claim of privilege."

Powers v. United States: 223 U.S. 303 (1912). Opinion: Day, J. No dissent.

Testimony voluntarily given may be subsequently used against a person even though he was not warned of this possibility. The voluntary character of the action serves as a waiver and the individual may then be cross-examined. But see *Escobedo* v. *Illinois*, p. 249, below.

Heike v. United States: 227 U.S. 131 (1913). Opinion: Holmes, J. No dissent.

There is a clear distinction between an amnesty for crime committed and the constitutional protection under the Fifth Amendment from being compelled to be a witness against oneself. An amnesty blots out the offense. There can be no prosecution. Here a federal grand jury under the Sherman Anti-Trust Act was involved.

Mason v. United States: 244 U.S. 362 (1917). Opinion: McReynolds, J. No dissent.

The Fifth Amendment does not relieve a witness from answering merely on his own declaration or judgment that an answer might incriminate him; whether he must answer is determinable by the trial court in the exercise of its sound discretion; and unless there is reasonable ground, as distinct from a remote or speculative possibility, to apprehend that a direct answer may prove dangerous to the witness, his answer should be compelled.

Essgee Co. v. United States: 262 U.S. 151 (1923). Opinion: Taft, C.J. No dissent.

A corporation is not protected by the Fourth and Fifth Amendments from producing its books and records before a federal grand jury engaged in investigating its conduct in relation to the federal criminal laws.

United States v. White: 322 U.S. 694 (1944). Opinion: Murphy, J. No dissent.

An officer of an unincorporated labor union has no right, under the Fourth and Fifth Amendments, to refuse to produce books and records of the union—which are in his possession and which a federal court by subpoena *duces tecum* required to be produced—on the ground that they might tend to incriminate the union or himself as an officer thereof and individually. These books were kept in a representative rather than a personal capacity. The right is limited to natural persons.

Shapiro v. United States: 335 U.S. 1 (1948). Opinion: Vinson, C.J. Dissenting: Frankfurter, Jackson, Murphy, and Rutledge, JJ.

Any records required by law to be kept may be inspected and used as evidence or leads to other evidence to incriminate an accused. The privilege against self-incrimination does not apply to such records since they are, in effect, quasi-public documents. The conviction was for violation of the Price Control Act of 1942.

Blau v. United States: 340 U.S. 159 (1950). Opinion: Black, J. No dissent. Abstaining: Clark, J.

Where answers to questions asked by the grand jury would have furnished a link in the chain of evidence needed in a prosecution for violation of a federal statute, the accused need not answer. The Smith Act was involved here. Blau had been Treasurer of the Communist Party in Denver.

Rogers v. United States: 340 U.S. 367 (1951). Opinion: Vinson, C.J. Dissenting: Black, Frankfurter, and Douglas, JJ. Abstaining: Clark, J.

After a witness has voluntarily answered some questions, he cannot refuse to answer related questions on the grounds of self-incrimination. The privilege of self-incrimination is deemed waived unless invoked, and it is the function of the court to determine whether an answer would subject the witness to real danger of further crimination. This is a personal privilege and cannot be claimed for third parties.

Hoffman v. United States: 341 U.S. 479 (1951). Opinion: Clark, J. Dissenting: Reed, J.

To sustain the privilege against self-incrimination, it need only be evident from the implications of the question, in the setting in which it is asked, that a responsive answer to the question or an explanation of why it cannot be answered might be dangerous because injurious disclosure could result. The judge in the case decides.

Curcio v. United States: 354 U.S. 118 (1957). Opinion: Burton, J. No dissent.

The custodian ·of a union's books and records, who had failed to produce them before a federal grand jury pursuant to subpoena, could, on the ground of his privilege against self-incrimination, lawfully refuse to answer questions asked by the grand jury as to the whereabouts of such books and records. Oral testimony is to be distinguished from records. The former would require him "to disclose the contents of his own mind."

Brown v. United States: 356 U.S. 148 (1958). Opinion: Frankfurter, J. Dissenting: Black, J., Warren, C.J., Douglas and Brennan, JJ.

When a party to a suit takes the stand and testifies in his own behalf, he has waived the right to invoke on cross-examination the privilege against self-incrimination regarding matters made relevant by his direct examination. Otherwise, he could set forth all the facts which tend in his favor, and set a bar to their further examination.

NOTE:

Kahriger indicates that the rule set down in *Bailey* v. *Drexel Furniture Co.* (259 U.S. 20, 1922) still has some validity. All that has changed is that the Supreme Court may seem easier to convince that a tax is a revenue measure rather than primarily a regulatory measure. Too, past decisions liberalizing the substantive powers of Congress have widened the field to which frankly regulative taxes can be applied. These two points in combination offer great potential for the expansion of federal powers.

More important at this point is the interesting ruling by the Court on the question of self-incrimination that since the tax did not apply to past actions whatever was done by the individual after the payment of the tax was purely voluntary on his part. *Marchetti* v. *United States*, immediately following, reversed *Kahriger* on the point of self-incrimination.

By way of summation the following points can be noted that are still controlling even after *Marchetti*.

(1) When a person has waived the guarantee then he can be forced to testify, as when an accused person agrees to take the witness stand by way of defense.

(2) Where further prosecution is barred by a statute of limitations there can be no claim to the self-incrimination guarantee.

(3) When a person has been given a full pardon and stands in no danger of further prosecution on that charge he cannot invoke the guarantee.

(4) Where an adequate immunity statute has been passed that protects a person against both direct and indirect use of his testimony the guarantee does not apply to him. As the Court noted, "Immunity displaces the danger."

Marchetti v. United States
390 U.S. 39; 88 S.Ct. 697; 19 L.Ed. 2d 889 (1968)

(Marchetti was convicted for conspiring to evade payment of the occupational tax relating to wagers imposed by 26 U.S.C. § 4411, for evading such payment, and for failing to comply with § 4412, which requires those liable for the occupational tax to register annually with the Internal Revenue Service and to supply detailed information for which a special form is prescribed. Under other provisions of the interrelated statutory system for taxing wagers, registrants must "conspicuously" post at their business places or keep on their persons stamps showing payment of the tax, maintain daily wagering records, and keep their books open for inspection. Payment of the occupational taxes is declared not to exempt persons from federal or state laws which broadly proscribe wagering, and federal tax authorities are required by § 6107 to furnish prosecuting officers lists of those who have paid the occupational tax. The contention was that this violated the privilege against self-incrimination.)

Vote: 7-1

Mr. Justice Harlan delivered the opinion of the Court:

. . . We see no reason to suppose that the force of the constitutional prohibition is diminished merely because confession of a guilty purpose precedes the act which it is subsequently employed to evidence. Yet, if the factual situations in which the privilege may be claimed were inflexibly defined by a chronological formula, the policies which the constitutional privilege is intended to serve could easily be evaded. Moreover, although prospective acts will doubtless ordinarily involve only speculative and insubstantial risks of incrimination, this will scarcely always prove true. As we shall show, it is not true here. We conclude that it is not mere time to which the law must look, but the substantiality of the risks of incrimination.

The hazards of incrimination created by § § 4411 and 4412 as to future acts are not trifling or imaginary. Prospective registrants can reasonably expect that registration and payment of the occupational tax will significantly enhance the likelihood of their prosecution for future acts, and that it will readily provide evidence which will facilitate their convictions. . . .

We conclude that nothing in the Court's opinions in *Kahriger* and *Lewis* now suffices to preclude petitioner's assertion of the constitutional privilege as a defense to the indictments under which he was convicted. To this extent *Kahriger* and *Lewis* are overruled. . . .

Nonetheless, we can only conclude, under the wagering tax system as presently written, that petitioner properly asserted the privilege against self-incrimination, and that his assertion should have provided a complete defense to this prosecution. . . .

The judgment of the Court of Appeals is

Reversed.

Mr. Chief Justice Warren dissented:

. . . Certainly no Fifth Amendment issue arises from the fact of registration until an effort is made to use the registration procedure in aid of criminal prosecution. To the extent that the disclosure requirements of § 6107 would raise a Fifth Amendment problem because some of the names on the public list have admitted unlawful activities, that statutory provision is severable for purposes of constitutional adjudication. In fact, in the Internal Revenue Code itself, Congress has specifically enacted a severability clause. . . .

See also *Grosso* v. *United States*, 390 U.S. 62 (1968), decided with *Marchetti*, where the Court held that the privilege against self-incrimination applied also to the required monthly reports by those paying the gambling stamp tax.

RELATED CASES:

New York Trust Co. v. Eisner: 256 U.S. 345 (1921). Opinion: Holmes, J. No dissent.

A graduated estate tax may be imposed by the United States and is not an unconstitutional interference with the rights of the States to regulate descent and distribution. The tax is deemed indirect, and, therefore, need not be apportioned.

Sonzinsky v. United States: 300 U.S. 506 (1937). Opinion: Stone, J. No dissent.

Congress can impose a tax on dealers in firearms by the National Firearms Act of 1934 which may have regulatory effects. The Court will not examine the motives of Congress in its imposition of a tax.

Lewis v. United States: 348 U.S. 419 (1955). Opinion: Minton, J. Dissenting: Black, Douglas, and Frankfurter, JJ.

Congress can make it an offense to engage in the business of accepting wagers without paying an occupational tax in Washington, D.C. This was held to be a valid exercise of the taxing power and not violative of the privilege against self-discrimination of the Fifth Amendment.

Haynes v. United States: 390 U.S. 85 (1968). Opinion: Harlan, J. Dissenting: Warren, C.J.

The hazards of incrimination created by the registration requirements of the National Firearms Act are "real and appreciable." This decision casts doubt on the continuing validity of *Zonzinski* v. *United States*, 300 U.S. 506 (1937).

DOUBLE JEOPARDY

Another guarantee of the Fifth Amendment is that a person is not to be "subject for the same offense to be twice put in jeopardy of life or limb." This immediately raises the question of just when an accused person is placed in jeopardy once. The general rule on this is that one has been placed in jeopardy when a jury has been impaneled, the judge is on the bench, and the accused is in court. Unless the accused waives the guarantee he cannot later be tried again for that offense. An exception to this would be a hung jury or a mistrial of some sort. A further exception is exemplified by *United States* v. *Lanza*, where there was a corollary charge.

United States v. Lanza
260 U.S. 377; 43 S.Ct. 141; 67 L.Ed. 314 (1922)

(In 1922 both the United States and the State of Washington had statutes prohibiting traffic in alcoholic beverages. Lanza had been convicted for violation of the Washington statute, and was subsequently arrested for violation of the federal law on the basis of the same action already involved in the state conviction. Lanza challenged the federal action on the basis of double jeopardy.)

Vote: No dissent

Mr. Chief Justice Taft delivered the opinion of the Court:

. . . The defendants insist that two punishments for the same act, one under the National Prohibition Act and the other under a state law, constitute double jeopardy under the Fifth Amendment; and in support of this position it is argued that both laws derive their force from the same authority,—the second section of the Amendment,—and therefore that, in principle, it is as if both punishments were in prosecutions by the United States in its courts. . . .

To regard the Amendment as the source of the power of the states to adopt and enforce prohibition measures is to take a partial and erroneous view of the matter. Save for some restrictions arising out of the Federal Constitution, chiefly the commerce clause, each state possessed that power in full measure prior to the Amendment, and the probable purpose of declaring a concurrent power to be in the states was to negative any possible inference that, in vesting the national government with the power of country-wide prohibition, state power would be excluded. In effect the second section of the Eighteenth Amendment put an end to restrictions upon the state's power arising out of the Federal Constitution, and left her free to enact prohibition laws applying to all transactions within her limits. To be sure, the first section of the Amendment took from the states all power to authorize acts falling within its prohibition, but it did not cut down or displace prior state laws not inconsistent with it. Such laws derive their force, as do all new ones consistent with it, not from this Amendment, but from power originally belonging to the states, preserved to them by the Tenth Amendment, and now relieved from the restriction heretofore arising out of the Federal Constitution. . . .

We have here two sovereignties, deriving power from different sources, capable of dealing with the same subject-matter within the same territory. Each may, without interference by the other, enact laws to secure prohibition, with the limitation that no legislation can give validity to acts prohibited by the Amendment. Each government, in determining what shall be an offense against its peace and dignity, is exercising its own sovereignty, not that of the other.

It follows that an act denounced as a crime by both national and state sovereignties is an offense against the peace and dignity of both, and may be punished by each. The Fifth Amendment, like all the other guaranties in the first eight amendments, applies only to proceedings by the Federal Government, *Barron* v. *Baltimore*, 7 Pet. 243, and the double jeopardy therein forbidden is a second prosecution under authority of the Federal Government after a first trial for the same offense under the same authority. Here the same act was an offense against the State of Washington, because a violation of its law, and also an offense against the United States under the National Prohibition Act. The defendants thus committed two different offenses by the same act, and a conviction by the court of Washington of the offense against that State is not a conviction of the different offense against the United States, and so is not double jeopardy. . . .

RELATED CASES:

United States v. Perez: 9 Wheat. 579 (1824). Opinion: Story, J. No dissent.

Retrial after a "hung" jury is not double jeopardy. "The prisoner has not been convicted or acquitted, and may again be put upon his defense." There is simply a continuation of the trial.

United States v. Sanges: 144 U.S. 310 (1892). Opinion: Gray, J. No dissent.

There is no indication in the Judiciary Act of 1891 of an intention to confer upon the United States the right to bring up a criminal case of any grade after the judgment below has been declared in favor of the defendant. The appellant jurisdiction of the Supreme Court rests wholly on the acts of Congress.

Trono v. United States: 199 U.S. 521 (1905). Opinion: Peckham, J. Dissenting: Harlan, McKenna, and White, JJ., and Fuller, C.J.

The appeal of the accused in such case amounts to a waiver to the plea of second jeopardy by asking that he be again tried for the offense for which he has once been convicted and if that request be granted he must take the burden with the benefit and go back for the new trial upon the whole case.

Morgan v. Devine: 237 U.S. 632 (1915). Opinion: Day, J. No dissent. Abstaining: McReynolds, J.

In this case it was held that a person who broke into a post office and also committed larceny therein, and who was convicted under separate counts of the same indictment for violations of sections 190 and 192 of the Penal Code, and sentenced separately under each, was not, after having served the sentence under one count, entitled to be released on the ground of double jeopardy, because the several things charged were done at the same time and as a part of one transaction.

Brock v. North Carolina: 344 U.S. 424 (1953). Opinion: Minton, J. Dissenting: Vinson, C.J., and Douglas. Abstaining: Black, J.

Here the judge in the case withdrew a juror and declared a mistrial, when two key witnesses claimed possible self-incrimination. This was a practice long in use in North Carolina. Later, after the grounds for self-incrimination had been removed, the accused was again placed on trial for the same offense and convicted. Held not to violate due process since justice to either side might indicate to the trial judge the wisdom of such procedure.

Green v. United States: 355 U.S. 184 (1957). Opinion: Black, J. Dissenting: Frankfurter, Burton, Clark, and Harlan, JJ.

An accused person who was indicted and tried for first degree murder in a federal court and found guilty by a jury of second degree murder cannot, after appeal and remanding of the case for new trial, be tried again for first degree murder under the original indictment. His appeal did not waive his constitutional defense of former jeopardy. He had, in effect, been acquitted of first degree murder. The defendant cannot be subjected to the risk of being convicted of a more serious *charge* than the first conviction, but may be subject to a heavier *penalty*.

Gore v. United States: 357 U.S. 386 (1958). Opinion: Frankfurter, J. Dissenting: Warren, C.J., and Douglas, Black, and Brennan, JJ.

When single action violates several sections of a federal statute, the statutory provision for separate punishment for the violation of each section does not offend double jeopardy. The question of policy involved is a matter for Congress to decide. Here there had been sale of narcotics, the official form had not been used, the drugs were not in a stamped pack, and fraudulent information had been given.

North Carolina v. Pearce: 395 U.S. 711 (1969). Opinion: Stewart, J. Dissenting: Black, and Harlan, JJ.

Neither the double jeopardy provision nor the equal protection clause imposes an absolute bar to a more severe sentence upon reconviction. However, whenever a judge imposes a more severe sentence upon a defendant after a new trial, the reasons for his doing so must affirmatively appear. Those reasons must be based on objective information concerning identifiable conduct on the part of the defendant occurring after the time of the original sentencing proceeding.

Price v. Georgia: 398 U.S. 323 (1970). Opinion: Burger, C.J. Abstaining: Blackmun, J.

Under an indictment for murder and voluntary manslaughter, conviction of the latter charge is an "implicit acquittal" of the murder charge. Further proceeding on that charge would be double jeopardy.

United States v. Jorn: 400 U.S. 470 (1971). Opinion: Harlan, J. Dissenting: Stewart, White, and Blackmun, JJ.

Where the trial judge has declared a mistrial so that witnesses can consult with attorneys so as to guard against self-incrimination, retrial would be double jeopardy. The defendant had the right to have his trial completed by a particular tribunal, here the original jury. Thus there was an abuse of discretion on the part of the trial judge.

NOTE:

The rule of *Lanza* is still good law. It has recently been reiterated in *Abbate* v. *United States,* 359 U.S. 187, 1959. See p. 164, below.

Bartkus v. Illinios
359 U.S. 121; 79 S.Ct. 676; 3 L.Ed. 2nd 684 (1959)

(Bartkus was tried and acquitted in the Federal District Court for the Northern District of Illinois for robbery of a federally insured savings and loan association. Later he was tried under Illinois statutes covering the same action and convicted. This was challenged as violating the due process clause of the Fourteenth Amendment.)

Vote: 5-4

Mr. Justice Frankfurter delivered the opinion of the Court:

. . . Prior cases in this Court relating to successive state and federal prosecutions have been concerned with the Fifth Amendment, and the scope of its proscription of second prosecutions by the Federal Government, not with the Fourteenth Amendment's effect on state action. We are now called upon the draw on the considerations which have guided the Court in applying the limitations of the Fourteenth Amendment on state powers. We have held from the beginning and uniformly that the Due Process Clause of the Fourteenth Amendment does not apply to the States any of the provisions of the first eight amendments as such. The relevant historical materials have been canvased by this Court and by legal scholars. These materials demonstrate conclusively that Congress and the members of the legislatures of the ratifying States did not contemplate that the Fourteenth Amendment was a shorthand incorporation of the first eight amendments making them applicable as explicit restrictions upon the States. . . .

Similarly imposing evidence of the understanding of the Due Process Clause is supplied by the history of the admission of the twelve States entering the Union after the ratification of the Fourteenth Amendment. In the case of each, Congress required that the State's constitution be "not repugnant" to the Constitution of the United States. Not one of the constitutions of the twelve States contains all three of the procedures relating to grand jury, criminal jury, and civil jury. In fact all twelve have provisions obviously different from the requirements of the Fifth, Sixth, or Seventh Amendments. And yet, in the case of each admission, either the President of the United States, or Congress, or both have found that the constitution was in conformity with the Enabling Act and the Constitution of the United States. Nor is there warrant to believe that the States in adopting constitutions with the specific purpose of complying with the requisites of admission were in fact evading the demands of the Constitution of the United States.

Surely this compels the conclusion that Congress and the States have always believed that the Due Process Clause brought into play a basis of restrictions upon the States other than the undisclosed incorporation of the original eight amendments. . . .

Constitutional challenge to successive state and federal prosecutions based upon the same transaction or conduct is not a new question before the Court though it has now been presented with conspicuous ability. The Fifth Amendment's proscription of double jeopardy has been invoked and rejected in over twenty cases of real or hypothetical successive state and federal prosecution cases before this Court. While *United States* v. *Lanza*, 260 U.S. 377 . . . was the first case in which we squarely held valid a federal prosecution arising out of the same facts which had been the basis of a state conviction, the validity of such a prosecution by the Federal Government has not been questioned by this Court since the opinion in *Fox* v. *State of Ohio*, 5 How. 4J0, more than one hundred years ago. . . .

Precedent, experience, and reason all support the conclusion that Alfonse Bartkus has not been deprived of due process of law by the State of Illinois.

Affirmed.

(The Appendix of this case contains the provisions of state constitutions which correspond to the federal guarantees of the Fifth, Sixth, and Seventh Amendments.)

Mr. Justice Black dissented, with Mr. Chief Justice Warren and Mr. Justice Douglas concurring:

. . . The Court's holding further limits our already weakened constitutional guarantees against double prosecutions. *United States* v. *Lanza*, 260 U.S. 377, decided in 1922, allowed federal conviction and punishment of a man who had been previously convicted and punished for the identical acts by one of our States. Today, for the first time in its history, this Court upholds the state conviction of a defendant who had been *acquitted* of the same offense in the federal courts. I would hold that a federal trial following either state acquittal or conviction is barred by the Double Jeopardy Clause of the Fifth Amendment. *Abbate* v. *United States*, 359 U.S. 187 (dissenting opinion). And, quite apart from whether that clause is as fully binding on the States as it is on the Federal Government, see *Adamson* v. *People of State of California*, 332 U.S. 46, 68 (dissenting opinion), I would hold that Bartkus' conviction cannot stand. For I think double prosecutions for the same offense are so contrary to the spirit of our free country that they violate even the prevailing view of the Fourteenth Amendment, expressed in *Palko* v. *Connecticut*, 302 U.S. 319. . . .

The Court, without denying the almost universal abhorrence of such double prosecutions, nevertheless justifies the practice here in the name of "federalism." This, it seems to me, is a misuse and desecration of the concept. Our Federal Union was conceived and created "to establish Justice" and to "secure the Blessings of Liberty," not to destroy any of the bulwarks on which both freedom and justice depend. We should, therefore, be suspicious of any supposed "requirements" of "federalism" which result in obliterating ancient safeguards. I have been shown nothing in the history of our Union, in the writings of its Founders, or elsewhere, to indicate that individual rights deemed essential by both State and Nation were to be lost through the combined operations of the two governments. Nor has the Court given any sound reason for thinking that the successful operation of our dual system of government depends in the slightest on the power to try people twice for the same act. . . .

Ultimately the Court's reliance on federalism amounts to no more than the notion that, somehow, one act becomes two because two jurisdictions are involved. Hawkins, in his Pleas of the Crown, long ago disposed of a similar contention made to justify two trials for the same offense by different counties as "a mere Fiction or Construction of Law, which shall hardly take Place against a Maxim made in Favour of Life." It was discarded as a dangerous fiction then, it should be discarded as a dangerous fiction now. . . .

Mr. Justice Brennan dissented, with the concurrence of Mr. Chief Justice Warren and Mr. Justice Douglas:

. . . I think that the record before us shows that the extent of participation of the federal authorities here constituted this state prosecution actually a second federal prosecution of Bartkus. . . .

. . . Cooperation in order to permit the Federal Government to harass the accused so as to deny him his protection under the Fifth Amendment is not to be tolerated as a legitimate requirement of federalism. The lesson of the history which wrought the Fifth Amendment's protection has taught us little if that shield may be shattered by reliance upon the requirements of federalism and state sovereignty to sustain this transparent attempt of the Federal Government to have two tries at convicting Bartkus for the same alleged crime. What happened here was simply that the federal effort which failed in the federal courthouse was renewed a second time in the state courthouse across the street. Not content with the federal jury's resolution of conflicting testimony in Bartkus' favor, the federal officers engineered this second prosecution and on the second try obtained the desired conviction. It is exactly this kind of successive prosecution by federal officers that the Fifth Amendment was intended to prohibit. This Court has declared principles in clearly analogous situations which I think should control here. In *Rea* v. *United States*, 350 U.S. 214, the Court held that an injunction should issue against a federal agent's transference of illegally obtained evidence to state authorities for use as the basis of a state charge. If the federal courts have power to defeat a state prosecution by force of their supervision of federal officers, surely the federal courts have power to defeat a state prosecution transparently employed by federal authorities in violation of the Fifth Amendment. In *Knapp* v. *Schweitzer*, 357 U.S. 371, 380, we declared: "Of course the Federal Government may not take advantage of . . . the States' autonomy in order to evade the Bill of Rights." . . . These principles require, I think, that we set aside the state conviction.

RELATED CASES:

Thompson v. United States: 155 U.S. 271 (1894). Opinion: Shiras, J. No dissent.

A court of law has authority to discharge a jury from the duty of rendering a verdict whenever in its opinion there is manifest necessity for the discharge, or the ends of public justice would otherwise be defeated. The court may order trial by another jury without placing the defendant twice in jeopardy within the meaning of the Fifth Amendment. Here a juror was disqualified.

In re Chapman: 166 U.S. 661 (1897). Opinion: Fuller, C.J. No dissent.

Congress possesses the constitutional power to enact a statute to enforce the attendance of witnesses and to compel them to make disclosure of evidence to enable the respective bodies to discharge their legislative functions. There is nothing to prohibit Congress from providing that contumacy in a witness called to testify and deliberate refusal to answer pertinent questions shall be a misdemeanor against the United States.

Wade v. Hunter: 336 U.S. 684 (1949). Opinion: Black, J. Dissenting: Murphy, Douglas, and Rutledge, JJ.

Where a trial by court-martial is forced to be discontinued because of combat circumstances, the double-jeopardy provision of the Fifth Amendment is no bar to a subsequent trial before a second court-martial. This is analogous to an emergency in a civil court. The double jeopardy applies to court-martial.

Ladner v. United States: 358 U.S. 169 (1958). Opinion: Brennan, J. Dissenting: Clark, J.

The intention of Congress in enacting the statute determines whether an assault which injured two federal officers was a single or double offense. Here the single discharge of the gun involved only one violation even though two officers were wounded.

Williams v. Oklahoma: 358 U.S. 576 (1959). Opinion: Whittaker, J. Dissenting: Douglas, J.

When a kidnapped person has been killed, the accused may be tried separately for the kidnapping and for the murder without violation of due process. The first sentence was life for the murder, the second was death for the kidnapping. Held valid.

Abbate v. United States: 359 U.S. 187 (1959). Opinion: Brennan, J. Dissenting: Black and Douglas, JJ., and Warren, C.J.

Conviction in a state court is no bar to subsequent trial in a federal court for violation of a federal statute by the same action. Involved here was a conspiracy to destroy communications facilities.

Benton v. Maryland: 395 U.S. 784 (1969). Opinion: Marshall, J. Dissenting: Harlan and Stewart, JJ.

The Court held that "the double jeopardy prohibition of the Fifth Amendment represents a fundamental ideal in our constitutional heritage, and that it should apply to the States through the Fourteenth Amendment. Insofar as it is inconsistent with this holding, *Palko* v. *Connecticut* is overruled." Here in the first trial the defendant was found not guilty of larceny but was convicted of burglary. When appeal for second trial was granted, he could not be tried for larceny.

NOTE:

Bartkus adds a note of completion to the "double-prosecution-is-not-double-jeopardy" picture. Here the point is made clear that neither prior acquittal nor prior conviction in a federal or state court is a bar to prosecution in the courts of the other jurisdiction if the offenses should be a crime in both. There is also the possibility that an accused person may have committed two or more state offenses or two or more federal offenses by one act and thus might be tried successively for each. The important point to be noted in this connection is that the same evidence may not be used in such a corollary charge in the same jurisdiction. Identity of evidence equals identity of offense and such a trial would amount to double jeopardy.

FORMAL PLACEMENT OF CHARGES

Under the terms of the Fifth Amendment a person is not to be brought to trial "for a capital, or otherwise infamous crime, unless on a presentment or indictment of a grand jury." The term "infamous crime" has never been concisely defined by the courts but the judiciary has generally adopted the point that the punishment set for a crime indicates the character of the crime. Specific cases have placed certain crimes in the "infamous" category.

In more recent times the device of the "information" has been developed as another means of formally placing charges against an accused person. Since this provision of the Fifth Amendment has not yet been included in the litany of those applied to the states by the Fourteenth Amendment, the states are free to use the information for any type of offense. However, in federal courts this device can be used only in cases that do not involve crimes that are "capital" or "infamous."

Ex parte Wilson
114 U.S. 417; 5 S.Ct. 935; 29 L.Ed. 89 (1885)

(Wilson had been convicted of counterfeiting the securities of the United States. He had been brought to trial by means of an information and subsequently tried by a jury. The lack of grand jury procedure and subsequent imprisonment upon conviction were challenged.)

Vote: 9-0

Mr. Justice Gray delivered the opinion of the Court:

. . . But if the crime of which the petitioner was accused was an infamous crime, within the meaning of the Fifth Amendment of the Constitution, no court of the United States had jurisdiction to try or punish him, except upon presentment or indictment by a grand jury. . . .

Whether a convict shall be permitted to testify is not governed by a regard to his rights or to his protection, but by the consideration whether the law deems his testimony worthy of credit upon the trial of the rights of others. But whether a man shall be put upon his trial for crime without a presentment or indictment by a grand jury of his fellow citizens depends upon the consequences to himself if he shall be found guilty. . . .

The question is whether the crime is one for which the statutes authorize the court to award an infamous punishment, not whether the punishment ultimately awarded is an infamous one. When the accused is in danger of being subjected to an infamous punishment if convicted, he has the right to insist that he shall not be put upon his trial, except on the accusation of a grand jury. . . .

For more than a century, imprisonment at hard labor in the State prison or penitentiary or similar institution has been considered an infamous punishment in England and America. . . .

Deciding nothing beyond what is required by the facts of the case before us, our judgment is that a crime punishable by imprisonment for a term of years at hard labor is an infamous crime, within the meaning of the Fifth Amendment of the Constitution; and that the District Court, in holding the petitioner to answer for such a crime, sentencing him to such imprisonment, without indictment or presentment by a grand jury, exceeded its jurisdiction, and he is therefore entitled to be discharged.

RELATED CASES:

Mackin v. United States: 117 U.S. 348 (1886). Opinion: Gray, J. No dissent.

A crime punishable by imprisonment in a state prison or penitentiary, with or without hard labor, is an infamous crime, within the provision of the Fifth Amendment, that "No person shall be held to answer for a capital, or otherwise infamous crime, unless on a presentment or indictment of a grand jury." The provision applies to punishment that *can* be inflicted, not only to that which actually was inflicted.

United States v. Ball: 163 U.S. 662 (1896). Opinion: Gray, J. No dissent.

Where a defendant is brought to trial by a defective indictment and pleads guilty to this charge, and where no objection to the sufficiency of the indictment is raised before the verdict, the prosecution will be precluded both from appealing a judgment for the defendant on the ground of insufficiency of indictment and from subsequently indicting him for the same offense.

Ruthenberg v. United States: 245 U.S. 480 (1918). Opinion: White, C.J. No dissent.

No infraction of constitutional or statutory right is predictable of the fact that the indictment and conviction of a Socialist for failure to register for the draft are returned by grand and petit juries composed exclusively of members of other political parties, and property owners.

Upon a criminal trial of defendants who are Socialists it is not error for the District Court to refuse them permission to ask the jurors whether they distinguish between Socialists and Anarchists.

Costello v. United States: 350 U.S. 359 (1956). Opinion: Black, J. No dissent. Abstaining: Clark and Harlan, JJ.

An indictment based solely on hearsay evidence does not violate the provision of the Fifth Amendment that "No person shall be held to answer for a capital, or otherwise infamous crime, unless on a presentment or indictment of a Grand Jury. . . ." The Court refused to establish a rule permitting defendants in criminal cases to challenge indictments on the ground that they are not supported by adequate or competent evidence. Only bias and the irregular impaneling of a grand jury are open to review.

NOTE:

Since, as noted, the Court has held that the punishment determines whether a crime is "infamous" or not, it should be added that the notion as to what is "infamous punishment" has varied from generation to generation.

Trial By Jury

In the Sixth and Seventh Amendments are the guarantees to jury trial in both criminal and civil cases. This, again, is a personal privilege and in all jurisdictions and for almost all offenses the guarantee can be waived. These particular guarantees apply only in federal courts, which means that the states are pretty much free to do as they wish as to size and vote on a verdict just so long as there has been no discrimination in the selection of the jury. In federal courts, however, the jury guarantee has been construed to mean a jury as it was known to common law at the time of the adoption of the amendment, that is, twelve persons before a judge and with a unanimous verdict.

Patton v. United States
281 U.S. 276; 50 S.Ct. 253; 74 L.Ed. 854 (1930)

(Patton and others were indicted in a federal district court charged with conspiring to bribe a federal prohibition agent. After the trial before a jury had continued for a week, one of the jurors, because of severe illness, became unable to serve further as a juror. Both prosecution and defense in open court waived all objections to the loss of that juror. A verdict of guilty was rendered by the jury of eleven persons. Appeal was taken on the question of the validity of the agreement under the circumstances for the trial before a jury of eleven persons.)

Vote: 8-0

Mr. Justice Sutherland delivered the opinion of the Court:

. . . Passing for later consideration the question whether these provisions, although varying in language, should receive the same interpretation, and whether taken together or separately the effect is to guarantee a right or establish a tribunal as an indispensable part of the government structure, we first inquire what is embraced by the phrase "trial by jury." That it means a trial by jury as understood and applied at common law, and includes all the essential elements as they were recognized in this country and England when the Constitution was adopted, is not open to question. Those elements were: (1) That the jury should consist of twelve men, neither more nor less; (2) that the trial should be in the presence and under the superintendence of a judge having power to instruct them as to the law and advise them in respect of the facts; and (3) that the verdict should be unanimous. . . .

A constitutional jury means twelve men as though that number had been specifically named; and it follows that, when reduced to eleven, it ceases to be such a jury quite as effectively as though the number had been reduced to a single person. . . . To uphold the voluntary reduction of a jury from twelve to eleven upon the ground that the reduction—though it destroys the jury of the Constitution—is only a slight reduction, is not to interpret that instrument but to disregard it. It is not our province to measure the extent to which the Constitution has been contravened and ignore the violation, if in our opinion, it is not, relatively, as bad as it might have been.

We come, then, to the crucial inquiry: Is the effect of the constitutional provisions in respect of trial by jury to establish a tribunal as a part of the frame of government, or only to guarantee to the accused the right to such a trial? If the former, the question certified by the lower court must, without more, be answered in the negative. . . .

In the light of the foregoing it is reasonable to conclude that the framers of the Constitution simply were intent upon preserving the right of trial by jury primarily for the protection of the accused. . . . That this was the purpose of the third article is rendered highly probable by a consideration of the form of expression used in the Sixth Amendment.

"In all criminal prosecutions, the accused shall enjoy the right to a speedy and public trial, by an impartial jury. . . ."

This provision, which deals with trial by jury clearly in terms of privilege, although occurring later than that in respect of jury trials contained in the original Constitution, is not to be regarded as modifying or altering the earlier provision; and there is no reason for thinking such was within its purpose. The first ten amendments and the original Constitution were substantially contemporaneous and should be construed *in pari materia*. . . .

Upon this view of the constitutional provisions we conclude that Article Three, §2, is not jurisdictional, but was meant to confer a right upon the accused which he may forego at his election. To deny his power to do so is to convert a privilege into an imperative requirement. . . .

The truth is that the theory of public policy embodies a doctrine of vague and variable quality, and, unless deducible in the given circumstances from constitutional or statutory provisions, should be accepted as the basis of a judicial determination, if at all, only with the utmost circumspection. The public policy of one generation may not, under changed conditions, be the public policy of another. . . .

The view that power to waive a trial by jury in criminal cases should be denied on grounds of public policy must be rejected as unsound. . . .

The question submitted must be answered in the affirmative.

It is so ordered.

Mr. Justice Holmes, Mr. Justice Brandeis, and Mr. Justice Stone concurred in the result.

Mr. Chief Justice Hughes took no part in this case.

Mr. Justice Sanford participated in the consideration and agreed to a disposition of the case in accordance with this opinion.

RELATED CASES:

Crawford v. United States: 212 U.S. 183 (1909). Opinion: Peckham, J. No dissent. Abstaining: Moody, J.

Because of the need for impartiality and freedom from bias on the part of jurors under the common law, government employees in the District of Columbia were held to be ineligible for jury duty.

United States v. Wood: 299 U.S. 123 (1936). Opinion: Hughes, C.J. Dissenting: Mc-Reynolds, Sutherland, and Butler, JJ. Abstaining: Stone, J.

An act of August 22, 1935, in qualifying governmental employees and pensioners for service as jurors to try criminal cases in Washington, D.C., subject to challenge for actual bias, is consistent with the Sixth Amendment and the due process clause of the Fifth Amendment.

Frazier v. United States: 335 U.S. 497 (1948). Opinion: Rutledge, J. Dissenting: Jackson, Frankfurter, Douglas, and Murphy, JJ.

Trial by a jury composed entirely of government employees in the District of Columbia was deemed not to deny trial "by an impartial jury" as guaranteed by the Fifth Amendment. Two jurors from the government department which enforced the Harrison Narcotics Act were involved but bias cannot be implied from government employment.

Dennis v. United States: 339 U.S. 162 (1950). Opinion: Minton, J. Abstaining: Douglas and Clark, JJ. Dissenting: Black and Frankfurter, JJ.

The Secretary General of the Communist Party of the United States was not denied a trial "by an impartial jury" even though seven government employees served on the jury. No actual bias was shown and none was presumed merely because of government employment.

Morford v. United States: 339 U.S. 258 (1950). Per Curiam. Abstaining: Clark, J.

Failure of the trial court to permit counsel for the defense to question prospective government employee jurors with specific reference to the possible influence of an executive order dealing with loyalty on their ability to render a just and impartial verdict was a denial of the opportunity to prove actual bias as a part of the defendant's right to an impartial jury.

Offutt v. United States: 348 U.S. 11 (1954). Opinion: Frankfurter, J. Dissenting: Reed, Burton, and Minton, JJ.

The Supreme Court, in the exercise of its supervisory authority over the administration of criminal justice in the federal courts, set aside the summary conviction of defense counsel with whom the judge became personally embroiled during the trial and directed that the contempt charges be retried before a different judge.

Parker v. Gladden: 385 U.S. 363 (1966). Opinion: Per Curiam. Dissenting: Harlan, J.

The Fourteenth Amendment applies to the states the provision of the Sixth Amendment guaranteeing that an accused shall enjoy the right to a trial by an impartial jury. Here the conviction was for second degree murder. A court bailiff had made prejudicial remarks about the defendant to the jurors.

United States v. Jackson: 390 U.S. 570 (1968). Opinion: Stewart, J. Dissenting: White and Black, JJ. Abstaining: Marshall, J.

The Federal Kidnapping Act provides for the death penalty if the jury so recommends. Without a jury no death penalty is possible under the act. The Court held that Congress cannot impose such a penalty in a manner that needlessly penalizes the assertion of a constitutional right.

Duncan v. Louisiana: 391 U.S. 145 (1968). Opinion: White, J. Dissenting: Harlan and Stewart, JJ.

The Fourteenth Amendment guarantees a right of jury trial in all state criminal cases which, were they to be tried in a federal court, would come within the Sixth Amendment's guarantee. The penalty set for a particular crime is of major relevance in determining whether it is serious or not and may, in itself, if severe enough, subject the trial to the mandates of the Sixth Amendment. Here there was simple battery and misdemeanor in Louisiana, but the penalty was two years in prison, so jury trial was required.

Bloom v. Illinois: 391 U.S. 194 (1968). Opinion: White, J. Dissenting: Harlan, and Stewart, JJ.

Criminal contempt with a severe punishment attached is a serious crime and must be treated like other serious crimes in determining whether a jury trial is guaranteed or not. In the absence of legislative determination of a penalty, the penalty actually imposed is the best evidence of the seriousness of the offense. In *DeStefano* v. *Woods*, 392 U.S. 631 (1968) the Court held that the determinations in *Duncan* and *Bloom* were to receive only prospective application.

Witherspoon v. Illinois: 391 U.S. 510 (1968). Opinion: Stewart, J. Dissenting: Black, Harlan, and White, JJ.

A sentence of death cannot be carried out if the jury that imposed or recommended it was chosen by excluding veniremen for cause simply because they voiced general objections to the death penalty or expressed conscientious or religious scruples against its infliction. Such a jury violates due process. It stacks the deck against the defendant.

Carter v. Jury Commission of Greene County: 396 U.S. 320 (1970). Opinion: Stewart, J. Dissenting: Douglas, J.

Where there is no *prima facie* showing of discriminatory exclusion of Negroes from the Jury Commission the procedure of choice is valid. There is no right of proportional representation by race.

Williams v. Florida: 399 U.S. 78 (1970). Opinion: White, J. Dissenting: Harlan and Stewart, JJ.

The constitutional requirement of a trial by jury does not require that the jury consist of twelve people. A six-person jury authorized by Florida in noncapital cases was valid.

Johnson v. Louisiana: 406 U.S. 356 (1972). Opinion: White, J. Dissenting: Stewart, Marshall, Brennan, and Douglas, JJ.

Under Louisiana law conviction of armed robbery was reached by a nine-to-three vote of a jury. The Court held that unanimity is not a requisite of due process of law. The state satisfied its burden of proving guilt beyond a reasonable doubt. The Court also upheld the provisions of Louisiana law requiring unanimous verdicts in capital cases. There is nothing unconstitutional or invidiously discriminatory in a state's insisting that its burden of proof be carried with more jurors where more serious crimes or more severe punishments are at issue.

NOTE:

Patton reiterates the definition of a jury under the Constitution as the common law jury of twelve persons. Too, the case underlines the right of an accused to waive a jury. This can be done even without benefit of counsel.

Thiel v. Southern Pacific Company
328 U.S. 217; 66 S.Ct. 984; 90 L.Ed. 1181 (1946)

(Thiel, a passenger, jumped out of the window of a moving train operated by the Southern Pacific Company. He sued for damages alleging that the agents of the railroad knew that he was "out of his normal mind," and that he should either not have been accepted as a passenger or guarded. He demanded a jury trial and then later challenged the composition of the jury on the ground that the panel contained mostly business executives or those having the employer's viewpoint.

Later he further challenged the jury on the ground that six of the twelve members were closely affiliated and connected with the company.)

Vote: 6-2

Mr. Justice Murphy delivered the opinion of the Court:

. . . The American tradition of trial by jury, considered in connection with either criminal or civil proceedings, necessarily contemplates an impartial jury drawn from a cross-section of the community. . . . This does not mean, of course, that every jury must contain representatives of all the economic, social, religious, racial, political and geographical groups of the community; frequently such complete representation would be impossible. But it does mean that prospective jurors shall be selected by court officials without systematic and intentional exclusion of any of these groups. Recognition must be given to the fact that those eligible for jury service are to be found in every stratum of society. Jury competence is an individual rather than a group or class matter. That fact lies at the very heart of the jury system. To disregard it is to open the door to class distinctions and discriminations which are abhorrent to the democratic ideals of trial by jury.

The choice of the means by which unlawful distinctions and discriminations are to be avoided rests largely in the sound discretion of the trial courts and their officers. This discretion, of course, must be guided by pertinent statutory provisions. So far as federal jurors are concerned, they must be chosen "without reference to party affiliations," and citizens cannot be disqualified "on account of race, color, or previous condition of servitude." In addition, jurors must be returned from such parts of the district as the court may direct "so as to be most favorable to an impartial trial, and so as not to incur an unnecessary expense, or unduly burden the citizens of any part of the district with such service." For the most part, of course, the qualifications and exemptions in regard to federal jurors are to be determined by the laws of the state where the federal court is located. . . . A state law creating an unlawful qualification, however, is not binding and should not be utilized in selecting federal jurors. . . .

The undisputed evidence in this case demonstrates a failure to abide by the proper rules and principles of jury selection. Both the clerk of the court and the jury commissioner testified that they deliberately and intentionally excluded from the jury lists all persons who work for a daily wage. They generally used the city directory as the source of names of prospective jurors. In the words of the clerk, "If I see in the directory the name of John Jones and it says he is a longshoreman, I do not put his name in, because I have found by experience that that man will not serve as a juror, and I will not get people who will qualify. The minute that a juror is called into court on a venire and says he is working for $10 a day and cannot afford to work for four, the Judge has never made one of those men serve, and so in order to avoid putting names of people in who I know won't become jurors in the court, won't qualify as jurors in this court, I do leave them out. . . . Where I thought the designation indicated that they were day laborers, I mean they were people who were compensated solely when they were working by the day, I leave them out." The jury commissioner corroborated this testimony, adding that he purposely excluded "all the iron craft, bricklayers, carpenters, and machinists" because in the past "those men came into court and offered that [financial hardship] as an excuse, and the judge usually let them go." The evidence indicated, however, that laborers who were paid weekly or monthly wages were placed on the jury lists, as well as the wives of daily wage earners.

It was further admitted that business men and their wives constituted at least 50% of the jury lists, although both the clerk and the commissioner denied that they consciously chose according to wealth or occupation. Thus the admitted discrimination was limited to those who worked for a daily wage, many of whom might suffer financial loss by serving on juries at the rate of $4 a day and would be excused for that reason.

This exclusion of all those who earn a daily wage cannot be justified by federal or state law. . . .

. . . Jury service is a duty as well as a privilege of citizenship; it is a duty that cannot be shirked on a plea of inconvenience or decreased earning power. Only when the financial embarrassment is such as to impose a real burden and hardship does a valid excuse of this nature appear. Thus a blanket exclusion of all daily wage earners, however well-intentioned and however justified by prior actions of trial judges, must be counted among those tendencies which undermine and weaken the institution of jury trial. "That the motives influencing such tendencies may be of the best must not blind us to the dangers of allowing any encroachment whatsoever on this essential right. Steps innocently taken may one by one, lead to the irretrievable impairment of substantial liberties." . . .

It follows that we cannot sanction the method by which the jury panel was formed in this case. . . . The evil lies in the admitted wholesale exclusion of a large class of wage earners in disregard of the high standards of jury selection. To reassert those standards, to guard against the subtle undermining of the jury system, requires a new trial by a jury drawn from a panel properly and fairly chosen.

Reversed.

Mr. Justice Frankfurter dissented, with the concurrence of Mr. Justice Reed:

. . . No constitutional issue is at stake. The problem is one of judicial administration. The sole question over which the Court divides is whether the established practice in the Northern District of California not to call for jury duty those otherwise qualified but dependent on a daily wage for their livelihood requires reversal of a judgment which is inherently without flaw. . . .

The Court now deals by adjudication with one phase of an organic problem and does so by nullifying a judgment which, on the record, was wholly unaffected by difficulties inherent in a situation that calls for comprehensive treatment, both legislative and administrative. If it be suggested that until there is legislation this decision will be the means of encouraging the district judges to uncover a better answer than they have thus far given to a lively problem, an appropriate admonition from the Court would accomplish the same result, or common action regarding the practice now under review may be secured from the Conference of Senior Circuit Judges. To reverse a judgment free from intrinsic infirmity and perhaps to put in question other judgments based on verdicts that resulted from the same method of selecting juries, reminds too much of burning the barn in order to roast the pig.

I would affirm the judgment.

Mr. Justice Jackson took no part in the consideration or decision of this case.

RELATED CASES:

Norris v. Alabama: 294 U.S. 587 (1935). Opinion: Hughes, C.J. Abstaining: McReynolds, J.

The exclusion of all Negroes from a grand jury and a petit jury involving a Negro defendant resulting from systematic and arbitrary exclusion of Negroes from the jury lists solely because of race or color is a denial of equal protection of the laws under the Fourteenth Amendment.

Glasser v. United States: 315 U.S. 60 (1942). Opinion: Murphy, J. Abstaining: Jackson, J.

If a jury panel is composed entirely of persons who have attended special "jury classes," a new trial must be granted. A jury panel must represent "a cross-section of the community."

Ballard v. United States: 329 U.S. 187 (1946). Opinion: Douglas, J. Dissenting: Burton, Jackson, and Frankfurter, JJ., and Vinson, C.J.

If women are excluded from a jury panel, the proceeding is invalid.

Fay v. New York: 332 U.S. 261 (1947). Opinion: Jackson, J. Dissenting: Murphy, Black, Douglas, and Rutledge, JJ.

A "blue ribbon" jury (one composed of persons selected for their particular knowledge) does not deny either due process or equal protection of the laws. In this case the Court also held that there had been no deliberate discrimination in the administration of the jury statute.

Colgrove v. Battin: 413 U.S. 149 (1973). Opinion: Brennan, J. Dissenting: Douglas, Powell, Marshall, and Stewart, JJ.

Some fifty-five federal District Courts have adopted a local rule applying to at least some civil cases that a jury for such cases shall consist of six persons. The Court upheld this arrangement noting that the framers of the Seventh Amendment were concerned with preserving the *right* of trial by jury in civil cases where it existed at common law rather than the various incidents of trial by jury. It cannot be said that twelve members is a substantive aspect of the right to trial by jury.

NOTE:

Thiel is an unusual example of the reversal of a jury verdict even though this was in a personal injury suit. The case notes that groups of citizens such as laborers, women, members of certain organizations, and others cannot be made the victims of blanket exclusion from jury duty.

Jurors in federal courts are qualified according to the law of the state in which the court is sitting.

Special juries, such as "blue ribbon" juries, have been sanctioned by both history and precedent. Either party to a suit may ask for a special jury if it is felt that the nature of the case, such as its technical intricacy, demands this. It must be noted that the Court in recent years has shown some inclination to reconsider the validity of "blue ribbon" juries. They were abolished in New York in 1965.

". . . To Be Confronted with the Witnesses Against Him."

In the Sixth Amendment there is a guarantee that a criminally accused person has the right to be confronted with the witnesses against him. One of the most controversial cases to be decided by the Court in recent years really involved this concept although technically the decision was not based on constitutional grounds but was an exercise of the authority of the Supreme Court over the lower federal courts. This was the case of *Jencks* v. *United States.*

Jencks v. United States
353 U.S. 657; 77 S.Ct. 1007; 1 L.Ed. 2nd 1103 (1957)

(Clinton E. Jencks, the president of a labor union, was convicted of swearing falsely that he was not a member of the Communist Party. Two Communist Party members, Harvey F. Matusow and John W. Ford, in the employ of the Federal Bureau of Investigation, had been the Government's principal witnesses. Jencks had demanded that the reports that these men had made to the F.B.I. be produced in court for inspection with a view to their possible use by defense counsel in impeaching the testimony. The denial of this motion was challenged.)

Vote: 7-1

Mr. Justice Brennan delivered the opinion of the Court:

. . . The crucial nature of the testimony of Ford and Matusow to the Government's case is conspicuously apparent. The impeachment of that testimony was singularly important to the petitioner. The value of the reports for impeachment purposes was highlighted by the admissions of both witnesses that they could not remember what reports were oral and what written, and by Matusow's admission: "I don't recall what I put in my reports two or three years ago, written or oral, I don't know what they were."

Every experienced trial judge and trial lawyer knows the value for impeaching purposes of statements of the witness recording the events before time dulls treacherous memory. Flat contradiction between the witness' testimony and the version of the events given in his reports is not the only test of inconsistency. The omission from the reports of facts related at the trial, or a contrast in emphasis upon the same facts, even a different order of treatment, are also relevant to the cross-examining process of testing the credibility of a witness' trial testimony.

Requiring the accused first to show conflict between the reports and the testimony is actually to deny the accused evidence relevant and material to his defense. The occasion for determining a conflict cannot arise until after the witness has testified, and unless he admits conflict, as in *Gordon*, the accused is helpless to know or discover conflict without inspecting the reports. A requirement of a showing of conflict would be clearly incompatible with our standards for the administration of criminal justice in the federal courts and must therefore be rejected. For the interest of the United States in a criminal prosecution ". . . is not that it shall win a case, but that justice shall be done. . . ." *Berger* v. *United States*, 295 U.S. 78, 88. . . .

This Court held in *Goldman* v. *United States*, 316 U.S. 129, 132, that the trial judge had discretion to deny inspection when the witness ". . . does not use his notes or memoranda [relating to his testimony] in court. . . ." We now hold that the petitioner was entitled to an order directing the Government to produce for inspection all reports of Matusow and Ford in its possession, written and, when orally made, as recorded by the F.B.I., touching the events and activities as to which they testified at the trial. We hold, further, that the petitioner is entitled to inspect the reports to decide whether to use them in his defense. Because only the defense is adequately equipped to determine the effective use for purpose of discrediting the Government's witness and thereby furthering the accused's defense, the defense must initially be entitled to see them to determine what uses may be made of them. Justice requires no less.

The practice of producing government documents to the trial judge for his determination of relevancy and materiality, without hearing the accused, is disapproved. Relevancy and materiality for the purpose of production and inspection, with a view to use on cross-examination, are established when the reports are shown to relate to the testimony of the witness. Only after inspection of the reports by the accused, must the trial judge determine admissibility—e.g., evidentiary questions of inconsistency, materiality and relevancy—of the contents and the method to be employed for the elimination of parts immaterial or irrelevant. . . .

Mr. Justice Whittaker took no part in the consideration or decision of this case.

Mr. Justice Clark dissented:

The Court holds "that the criminal action must be dismissed when the Government, on the grounds of privilege, elects not to comply with an order to produce, for the accused's inspection and for admission in evidence, relevant statements or reports in its possession of government witnesses touching the subject matter of their testimony at the trial." This fashions a new rule of evidence which is foreign to our federal jurisprudence. The rule has always been to the contrary. It seems to me that proper judicial administration would require that the Court expressly overrule *Goldman* v. *United States*, 1942, 316 U.S. 129, 132, which is *contra* to the rule announced today. But that is not done. That case is left on the books to haunt lawyers and trial courts in their search for the proper rule. In *Goldman* the Court was unanimous on the issue of disclosure of documents and refused to order produced "notes and memoranda made by the [federal] agents during the investigation." The rule announced today has no support in any of our cases. Every federal judge and every lawyer of federal experience knows that it is not the present rule. Even the defense attorneys did not have the temerity to ask for such a sweeping decision. They only asked that the documents be delivered to the judge for his determination of whether the defendant should be permitted to examine them. This is the procedure followed in some of our circuits. . . .

Unless the Congress changes the rule announced by the Court today, those intelligence agencies of our Government engaged in law enforcement may as well close up shop for the Court has opened their files to the criminal and thus afforded him a Roman holiday for rummaging through confidential information as well as vital national secrets. This may well be a reasonable rule in state prosecutions where none of the problems of foreign relations, espionage, sabotage, subversive activities, counterfeiting, internal security, national defense, and the like exist, but any person conversant with federal government activities and problems will quickly recognize that it opens up a veritable Pandora's box of troubles. And all in the name of justice. For over eight score years now our federal judicial administration has gotten along without it and today that administration enjoys the highest rank in the world. . . .

RELATED CASES:

Berger v. United States: 295 U.S. 78 (1935). Opinion: Sutherland, J. No dissent.
An error in a criminal trial must actually be substantially prejudicial to justify reversal of a criminal conviction. The record must reflect substantial prejudice of appellant's rights or else it must be regarded as harmless.

United States v. Reynolds: 345 U.S. 1 (1953). Opinion: Vinson, C.J. Dissenting: Black, Frankfurter, and Jackson, JJ.
When circumstances indicate a reasonable possibility that military secrets are involved, there is sufficient showing of privilege to cut off further demand for the production of a document, here an Air Force official accident investigation report. This suit was brought under the Federal Tort Claims Act.

Roviaro v. United States: 353 U.S. 53 (1957). Opinion: Burton, J. Dissenting: Clark, J. Abstaining: Black and Whittaker, JJ.
When an undercover informer has had a material part in bringing about petitioner's conviction, disclosure of his identity may be required. There is no fixed rule. Circumstances must govern each case. The public interest in protecting the flow of information must be balanced against the individual's right to prepare his defense.

NOTE:

As a result of the decision in *Jencks*, Congress enacted the "Jencks law" which regulated the procedure for securing information in government files. Henceforth this was to be done through the judge rather than solely by request of the defense. This restored the previous practice in the lower federal courts.

THE ASSISTANCE OF COUNSEL

The Sixth Amendment guarantees that accused persons shall have the benefit of counsel, his own if he can afford it, court-appointed counsel at government expense if the accused is unable to furnish his own attorney. Until very recent times this provision has applied in its entirety only to cases in federal courts, but, as will be noted later, recent decisions have extended it completely to state courts as well. This is a personal guarantee and can be waived but such waiver must be made by the accused in clear understanding of what he is doing.

Johnson v. Zerbst, Warden
304 U.S. 458; 58 S.Ct. 1019; 82 L.Ed. 1461 (1938)

(Johnson and Bridwell were indicted on the charge of possessing and passing counterfeit Federal Reserve Notes. Upon arraignment, both pleaded not guilty, said that they had no lawyers, and, in response to an inquiry of the court, stated that they were ready for trial. They were tried, convicted, and sentenced without assistance of counsel in one afternoon.)

Vote: 6-2

Mr. Justice Black delivered the opinion of the Court:

. . . It [the Sixth Amendment] embodies a realistic recognition of the obvious truth that the average defendant does not have the professional legal skill to protect himself when brought before a tribunal with the power to take his life or liberty, wherein the prosecution is presented by experienced and learned counsel. . . .

. . . The Sixth Amendment withholds from federal courts, in all criminal proceedings, the power and authority to deprive an accused of his life or liberty unless he has or waives the assistance of counsel.

. . . A waiver is ordinarily an intentional relinquishment or abandonment of a known right or privilege. The determination of whether there has been an intelligent waiver of the right to counsel must depend, in each case, upon the particular facts and circumstances surrounding that case, including the background, experience, and conduct of the accused. . . .

The constitutional right of an accused to be represented by counsel invokes, of itself, the protection of a trial court, in which the accused—whose life or liberty is at stake—is without counsel. This protecting duty imposes the serious and weighty responsibility upon the trial judge of determining whether there is an intelligent and competent waiver by the accused. While an accused may waive the right to counsel, whether there is a proper waiver should be clearly determined by the trial court, and it would be fitting and appropriate for that determination to appear upon the record. . . .

The purpose of the constitutional guaranty of a right to counsel is to protect an accused from conviction resulting from his own ignorance of his legal and constitutional rights, and the guaranty would be nullified by a determination that an accused's ignorant failure to claim his rights removes the protection of the Constitution. . . . The scope of inquiry in *habeas corpus* proceedings has been broadened —not narrowed—since the adoption of the Sixth Amendment. . . .

. . . Where a defendant, without counsel, acquiesces in a trial resulting in his conviction and later seeks release by the extraordinary remedy of *habeas corpus*, the burden of the proof rests upon him to establish that he did not completely and intelligently waive his constitutional right to assistance of counsel. If in a *habeas corpus* hearing, he does meet this burden and convinces the court by a preponderance of evidence that he neither had counsel nor properly waived his constitutional right to counsel, it is the duty of the court to grant the writ.

. . . If petitioner fails to sustain this burden, he is not entitled to the writ.

Reversed.

Justice Reed concurred in the reversal.

Justice McReynolds was of the opinion that the judgment of the court below should be affirmed.

Justice Butler was of the opinion that the record showed that the petitioner waived the right to have counsel, that the trial court had jurisdiction, and that the judgment of the Circuit Court of Appeals should be affirmed.

Justice Cardozo took no part in the consideration or decision of the case.

RELATED CASES:

DeMeerleer v. Michigan: 329 U.S. 663 (1947). Opinion: Per Curiam. No dissent.

A seventeen-year-old boy accused of first-degree murder was arraigned, tried, convicted (after his plea of guilty), and sentenced to life imprisonment all on the same day. The accused did not have counsel nor was he advised of his right to counsel. This was a denial of rights essential to a fair hearing under the Fourteenth Amendment.

Foster v. Illinois: 332 U.S. 134 (1947). Opinion: Frankfurter, J. Dissenting: Black, Douglas, Murphy, and Rutledge, JJ.

The provision of the Sixth Amendment which guarantees to an accused in a criminal prosecution in a federal court the absolute right "to have the assistance of counsel for his defense," is not made applicable by the Fourteenth Amendment to prosecutions in state courts. See *Gideon* v. *Wainwright*, p. 248, below.

Haley v. Ohio: 332 U.S. 596 (1948). Opinion: Douglas, J. Dissenting: Burton, J., Vinson, C.J., and Reed and Jackson, JJ.

A confession of murder by a fifteen-year-old Negro boy after questioning by police for five hours beginning at midnight without benefit of the advice of friends, family, or counsel was involuntary and violative of the due process of the Fourteenth Amendment. This was psychological coercion.

Von Moltke v. Gillies: 332 U.S. 708 (1948). Opinion: Black, J. Dissenting: Burton, J., Vinson, C.J., and Reed, J.

Where a defendant did not competently, intelligently, and with full understanding of the implications waive her constitutional right to counsel, an order should be entered directing her release from further custody under a judgment based on her plea of guilty.

Bute v. Illinois: 333 U.S. 640 (1948). Opinion: Burton, J. Dissenting: Douglas, Black, Murphy, and Rutledge, JJ.

Where there are special circumstances showing that, otherwise, the defendant would not enjoy that fair notice and adequate hearing which constitute the foundation of due process of law in the trial of any criminal charge, the accused has a constitutional right to the assistance of counsel.

Chessman v. Teets, Warden: 354 U.S. 156 (1957). Opinion: Harlan, J. Dissenting: Douglas and Clark, JJ. Abstaining: Warren, C.J.

An accused person is entitled to be represented either in person or by counsel throughout the proceedings for the settlement of the trial record. Further, a refusal on the part of the accused to be represented by counsel at the trial did not constitute a a waiver of his right to counsel at the settlement proceedings.

Moore v. Michigan: 355 U.S. 155 (1957). Opinion: Brennan, J. Dissenting: Burton, Frankfurter, Clark, and Harlan, JJ.

When the accused had several possible defenses involving questions of considerable technical difficulty and where his waiver of counsel and plea of guilty might have been induced by fear of mob violence, the due process clause invalidated his conviction. There is a good chart in the Appendix of this case.

Payne v. Arkansas: 356 U.S. 560 (1958). Opinion: Whittaker, J. Dissenting: Burton and Clark, JJ.

A mentally dull nineteen-year-old Negro with a fifth-grade education was convicted of first-degree murder and sentenced to death after a trial in which a confession was admitted in evidence which was shown by undisputed evidence to have been coerced by fear of mob violence. In spite of other valid evidence, this admission of the coerced confession, over objection of the accused, vitiates the judgment because it violates the due process clause of the Fourteenth Amendment.

Crooker v. California: 357 U.S. 433 (1958). Opinion: Clark, J. Dissenting: Douglas, J., Warren, C.J., and Black and Brennan, JJ.

While denial of a request by an accused for an opportunity to engage counsel in a criminal case violates due process if this makes his subsequent trial lacking in basic fairness, this situation involving a thirty-one-year-old college graduate who had attended law school for a year did not seem to be of this sort. This case was reversed by *Escobedo* v. *Illinois,* p. 249, below.

Cash v. Culver: 358 U.S. 633 (1959). Opinion: Stewart, J. No dissent.

The Florida court's refusal to appoint counsel and the refusal of a motion for a continuance to enable him to obtain counsel was a denial of due process under the Fourteenth Amendment.

Spano v. New York: 360 U.S. 315 (1959). Opinion: Warren, C.J. No dissent.

When an accused person's will was overborne by official pressure, fatigue, and sympathy for the victim's family falsely aroused, his confession was not voluntary and was violative of due process. A forced confession always voids a conviction.

NOTE:

When an accused person in a federal court does not intelligently waive counsel but cannot secure it for financial or other reason, the trial court must see that counsel is secured for the defendant. The due process clause of the Fourteenth Amendment has been interpreted as extending the same broad guarantee in state courts. See *Gideon v. Wainwright,* 372 U.S. 335, 1963, p. 248, below.

THE FIFTH AMENDMENT'S DUE PROCESS CLAUSE

The Fifth Amendment provides that the federal government shall not deprive a person of his life, liberty, or property without due process of law. The same restriction is levied on the states by the Fourteenth Amendment. "Due process" is a nebulous term and subject to definition. It varies from generation to generation in specific meaning but, in general, can be said to embody the concept of fundamental fairness. This includes substantive due process—what is done—as well as procedural due process—how something is done. In *Tot* v. *United States* this notion of essential fairness is brought out by the Court.

Tot v. United States
319 U.S. 463; 63 S.Ct. 1241; 87 L.Ed. 1519 (1943)

(Tot, the petitioner, was convicted of "knowingly, unlawfully, and feloniously" receiving a described firearm which "had been shipped and transported in interstate commerce to the said City of Newark." Tot had previously been convicted of two crimes of violence, a burglary and an assault and battery. Under the terms of the Federal Firearms Act the receipt of a firearm by any person convicted of a crime of violence was a federal offense. Further, the act made possession of a firearm or ammunition by such a person presumptive evidence that these were shipped in interstate commerce. The validity of the act was challenged.)

Vote: 8-0

Mr. Justice Roberts delivered the opinion of the Court:

. . . There remains for decision the question of the power of Congress to create the presumption which § 2 (f) declares, namely, that, from the prisoner's prior conviction of a crime of violence and his present possession of a firearm or ammunition, it shall be presumed (1) that the article was received by him in interstate or foreign commerce, and (2) that such receipt occurred subsequent to July 30, 1938, the effective date of the statute.

The Government argues that the presumption created by the statute meets the tests of due process heretofore laid down by this court. The defendants assert that it fails to meet them because there is no rational connection between the facts proved and the ultimate fact presumed, that the statute is more than a regulation of the order of proof based upon the relative accessibility of evidence to prosecution and defense, and casts an unfair and practically impossible burden of persuasion upon the defendant. . . .

The Government seems to argue that there are two alternative tests of the validity of a presumption created by statute. The first is that there be a rational connection between the facts proved and the fact presumed; the second that of comparative convenience of producing evidence of the ultimate fact. We are of opinion that these are not independent tests but the first is controlling and the second is but a corollary. Under our decisions, a statutory presumption cannot be sustained if there be no rational connection between the fact proved and the ultimate fact presumed, if the inference of the one from proof of the other is arbitrary because of lack of connection between the two in common experience. This is not to say that a valid presumption may not be created upon a view of relation broader than that a jury might take in a specific case. But where the inference is so strained as not to have a reasonable relation to the circumstances of life as we know them it is not competent for the legislature to create it as a rule governing the procedure of courts.

The Government seeks to support the presumption by a showing that, in most states, laws forbid the acquisition of firearms without a record of the transaction or require registration of ownership. From these circumstances it is argued that mere possession tends strongly to indicate that acquisition must have been in an interstate transaction. But we think the conclusion does not rationally follow. Aside from the fact that a number of states have no such laws, there is no presumption that a firearm must have been lawfully acquired or that it was not transferred interstate prior to the adoption of state regulation. Even less basis exists for the inference from mere possession that acquisition occurred subsequent to the effective date of the statute,—July 30, 1938. And, as no state laws or regulations are cited with respect to the acquisition of ammunition, there seems no reasonable ground for a presumption that its purchase or procurement was in interstate rather than in intrastate commerce. It is not too much to say that the presumptions created by the law are violent, and inconsistent with any argument drawn from experience.

Nor can the fact that the defendant has the better means of information, standing alone, justify the creation of such a presumption. In every criminal case the defendant has at least an equal familiarity with the facts and in most a greater familiarity with them than the prosecution. It might, therefore, be argued that to place upon all defendants in criminal cases the burden of going forward with the evidence would be proper. But the argument proves too much. If it were sound, the legislature might validly command that the finding of an indictment, or mere proof of the identity of the accused, should create a presumption of the existence of all the facts essential to guilt. This is not permissible. . . .

Reversed.

Mr. Justice Black concurred, joined by Mr. Justice Douglas:

. . . Compliance with these constitutional provisions, which of course constitute the supreme law of the land, is essential to due process of law, and a conviction obtained without their observance cannot be sustained.

It is unnecessary to consider whether this statute, which puts the defendant against whom no evidence of guilt has been offered in a procedural situation from which he can escape conviction only by testifying, compels him to give evidence against himself in violation of the Fifth Amendment.

Mr. Justice Murphy took no part in the consideration or decision of this case.

RELATED CASES:

Murray's Lessee v. Hoboken Land and Improvement Co.: 18 Howard 272 (1856). Opinion: Curtis, J. No dissent.

Congress may authorize the Treasury Department to fasten a lien upon the lands of a collector of the customs for an amount found to be due the government by accounting officers of the Treasury, provided the alleged debtor has the privilege of bringing the question of his indebtedness before the courts of the United States. Such conduct on the part of the Treasury would constitute neither unauthorized exercise of judicial power by the executive nor a deprivation of liberty or property without due process of law. This case involved the first interpretaiton of due process. Due process is applicable to the legislative branch as well as to the executive and the judiciary.

Yee Hem v. United States: 268 U.S. 178 (1925). Opinion: Sutherland, J. No dissent.

Congress has the power to prohibit the importation of opium and, as a measure reasonably calculated to aid in the enforcement of the prohibition, to make its concealment, with knowledge of its unlawful importation, a crime. Since no lawful purchase could take place in the United States, it was not an illogical inference that the goods had been unlawfully imported.

McNabb v. United States: 318 U.S. 332 (1943). Opinion: Frankfurter, J. Dissenting: Reed, J. Abstaining: Rutledge, J.

The Supreme Court is limited in reviewing convictions in state courts to the enforcement of the "fundamental principles of liberty and justice," which are secured by the Fourteenth Amendment. However, the reviewing power of the Court over convictions brought from federal courts is not confined to the ascertainment of constitutional validity since the Court has general supervision of the administration of criminal justice in the federal courts, both as to procedure and evidence. Here suspects in the shooting of a federal revenue officer were questioned for two days. There was "unnecessary delay."

Rea v. United States: 350 U.S. 214 (1956). Opinion: Douglas, J. Dissenting: Harlan, Reed, Burton, and Minton, JJ.

Where evidence suppressed in a federal court because it was obtained by unlawful search and seizure is used as the basis of a state charge, the federal agent who seized the evidence may be enjoined from transferring it to state authorities or testifying with respect thereto in the state court. This was done on the basis of the Court's supervisory power over law-enforcement agencies.

Griswold v. Connecticut: 381 U.S. 479 (1965). Opinion: Douglas, J. Dissenting: Black, and Stewart, JJ.

The Connecticut birth control statute was held void as a violation of the "right of privacy" under the Ninth Amendment as well as under specific guarantees in the Bill of Rights. This is "within the penumbra of specific guarantees of the Bill of Rights."

In re Gault: 387 U.S. 1 (1967): Opinion: Fortas, J. Dissenting: Stewart, J.

Juveniles have basic constitutional rights that must be recognized. Absent a valid confession, a determination of delinquency and an order of commitment to a state institution cannot be sustained in the absence of sworn testimony subjected to the opportunity for cross-examination in accordance with our law and constitutional requirements.

In re Winship: 397 U.S. 358 (1970). Opinion: Brennan, J. Dissenting: Berger, C.J., and Stewart and Black, JJ.

When a juvenile is involved in a criminal charge there must be proof beyond a reasonable doubt as with an adult.

Eisenstadt v. Baird: 405 U.S. 438 (1972). Opinion: Brennan, J. Dissenting: Burger, C.J. Abstaining: Powell and Rehnquist, JJ.

Following the reasoning of *Griswold* v. *Connecticut* a state cannot prohibit the exhibition, sale, or giving of contraceptives to unmarried individuals. A holding to the contrary would violate the equal protection provision of the Fourteenth Amendment.

Roe v. Wade: 410 U.S. 113 (1973). Opinion: Blackmun, J. Dissenting: White and Rehnquist, JJ.

It is an invasion of privacy contrary to the Ninth and Fourteenth Amendments for a state to prohibit an abortion during the first trimester of pregnancy. Regulation can increase as the pregnancy proceeds to protect the state's interest in preserving life.

NOTE:

Tot was the first case in which an act of Congress was declared unconstitutional following the "revolution" of 1937. Here the Court noted that there must be a rational basis for a presumptive conclusion. In *Tot* a person might well have possession of firearms without their having passed through interstate commerce. On the other hand, in the *Yee Hem* case in which a presumption was made that opium in one's posession was illegally acquired was upheld by the Court since individuals could not lawfully purchase opium in this country.

In discussing due process on the federal level, it should be noted that the contract clause (Article I, Section 10, Clause 1) and the equal protection clause (Fourteenth Amendment, Section 1) apply only to the states. However, the Court in *Lynch* v. *United States* (292 U.S. 571, 1934) held that the due process clause could be used against federal government action where, in a comparable situation, the contract clause would be invoked against the states. And in *Bolling* v. *Sharpe* (347 U.S. 497, 1954) the Court used the due process clause to prohibit federal action when, in the parallel case, the Court had used the equal protection clause to invalidate state action. Nevertheless, the Court made it clear that it did not regard the due process clause as a federal equivalency of the equal protection clause. The Court held that the two are not always "interchangeable phrases."

MILITARY TRIALS

Congress under the Constitution (Article I, Section 8, Clause 14) has the power "to make rules for the government and regulation of the land and naval forces." Under this power Congress has set up the Uniform Code of Military Justice for the governing of the military forces. This is known as military law and is enforced by courts-martial. One of the sections of the UCMJ provided that a person who had committed an offense while he had been a member of the armed forces and had subsequently been discharged could be tried for the offense by court-martial. The validity of such action was questioned in *Toth.*

It might be noted in passing that in addition to *military law*, which is applicable solely to persons in service, there is also *military government,* which prevails in a conquered region, and *martial law,* which applies to all persons, including civilians, who are present in the area involved. Martial law is of two types: (1) *preventive* when military forces simply serve as additional police, and (2) *punitive* or *true* martial law when military men have charge of the courts.

United States ex rel. Toth v. Quarles
350 U.S. 11; 76 S.Ct. 1; 100 L.Ed. 8 (1955)

(After serving with the Air Force in Korea, Robert W. Toth was honorably discharged. He returned home to Pittsburgh and went to work. Five months later he was arrested by military authorities on charges of murder and conspiracy to commit murder while an airman in Korea. At the time of his arrest he had no relationship of any kind with the military. He was taken to Korea to stand trial before a court-martial under authority of a 1950 act of Congress. This action was challenged on the basis that civilian ex-servicemen could not be subjected to trial by court-martial.)

Vote: 6-3

Mr. Justice Black delivered the opinion of the Court:

. . . It has never been intimated by this Court, however, that Article I military jurisdiction could be extended to civilian ex-soldiers who had severed all relationship with the military and its institutions. To allow this extension of military authority would require an extremely broad construction of the language used in the constitutional provision relied on. For given its natural meaning, the power granted Congress "To make Rules" to regulate "the land and naval Forces" would seem to restrict court-martial jurisdiction to persons who are actually members or part of the armed forces. There is a compelling reason for construing the clause this way: any expansion of court-martial jurisdiction like that in the 1950 Act necessarily encroaches on the jurisdiction of federal courts set up under Article III of the Constitution where persons on trial are surrounded with more constitutional safeguards than in military tribunals. . . .

We find nothing in the history or constitutional treatment of military tribunals which entitles them to rank along with Article III courts as adjudicators of the guilt or innocence of people charged with offenses for which they can be deprived of their life, liberty or property. Unlike courts, it is the primary business of armies and navies to fight or be ready to fight wars should the occasion arise. But trial of soldiers to maintain discipline is merely incidental to an army's primary fighting function. To the extent that those responsible for performance of this primary function are diverted from it by the necessity of trying cases, the basic fighting purpose of armies is not served. And conceding to military personnel that high degree of honesty and sense of justice which nearly all of them undoubtedly have, it still remains true that military tribunals have not been and probably never can be constituted in such way that they can have the same kind of qualifications that the Constitution has deemed essential to fair trials of civilians in federal courts. For instance, the Constitution does not provide life tenure for those performing judicial functions in military trials. They are appointed by military commanders and may be removed at will. Nor does the Constitution protect their salaries as it does judicial salaries. Strides have been made toward making courts martial less subject to the will of the executive department which appoints, supervises and ultimately controls them. But from the very nature of things, courts have more independence in passing on the life and liberty of people than do military tribunals.

Moreover, there is a great difference between trial by jury and trial by selected members of the military forces. It is true that military personnel because of their training and experience may be especially competent to try soldiers for infractions of military rules. Such training is no doubt particularly important where an offense charged against a soldier is purely military, such as disobedience of an order, leaving post, etc. But whether right or wrong, the premise underlying the constitutional method for determining guilt or innocence in federal courts is that laymen are better than specialists to perform this task. This idea is inherent in the institution of trial by jury. . . .

Fear has been expressed that if this law is not sustained discharged soldiers may escape punishment altogether for crimes they commit while in the service. But that fear is not warranted and was not shared by the Judge Advocate General of the Army who made a strong statement against passage of the law. He asked Congress to "confer jurisdiction upon Federal courts to try any person for an offense denounced by the [military] code if he is no longer subject thereto. This would be consistent with the fifth amendment of the Constitution." . . . It is conceded that it was wholly within the constitutional power of Congress to follow this suggestion and provide for federal district court trials of discharged soldiers accused of offenses committed while in the armed services. This concession is justified. U.S. Const., Art. III, § 2. . . . There can be no valid argument, therefore, that civilian ex-servicemen must be tried by court-martial or not tried at all. If that is so it is only because Congress has not seen fit to subject them to trial in federal district courts.

None of the other reasons suggested by the Government are sufficient to justify a broad construction of the constitutional grant of power to Congress to regulate the armed forces. That provision itself does not empower Congress to deprive people of trials under Bill of Rights safeguards, and we are not willing to hold that power to circumvent those safeguards should be inferred through the Necessary and Proper Clause. It is impossible to think that the discipline of the Army is going to be disrupted, its morale impaired, or its orderly processes disturbed, by giving ex-servicemen the benefit of a civilian court trial when they are actually civilians. And we are not impressed by the fact that some other countries which do not have our Bill of Rights indulge in the practice of subjecting civilians who were once soldiers to trials by courts-martial instead of trials by civilian courts.

Determining the scope of the constitutional power of Congress to authorize trial by court-martial presents another instance calling for limitation to *the least possible power adequate to the end proposed.* We hold that Congress cannot subject civilians like Toth to trial by court-martial. They, like other civilians, are entitled to have the benefit of safeguards afforded those tried in the regular courts authorized by Article III of the Constitution.

Reversed.

Mr. Justice Reed, with whom Mr. Justice Burton and Mr. Justice Minton joined, dissented:

. . . No question of accommodating the liberty of the citizen to requirements of the military through the interpretation of an ambiguous Act arises. Compare *Ex parte Endo*, 323 U.S. 283. It is not for courts to question the wisdom of the legislation. Its obvious purpose was to assure, insofar as discipline may do so, the proper conduct of our far-flung and numerous military personnel in foreign lands. One need not stress the necessity of orderly conduct by the military whether on domestic or foreign posts for the maintenance of good relations in friendly or vanquished countries. It also seems a reasonable choice that uniform treatment by courts-martial trial of all accused of crimes punishable by the Military Code is preferred for morale and disciplinary purposes to courts-martial trial only for those who remain in the service. This case itself would make a good example of the difficulty of a federal district court trial. . . .

Mr. Justice Minton, whom Mr. Justice Burton joined, dissented:

I agree with the opinion of Mr. Justice Reed, and I would add another reason why I think the judgment should be affirmed.

A civilian not under the jurisdiction of the Military Code has a right to be tried in a civil court for an alleged crime as a civilian. My trouble is that I don't think Toth was a full-fledged civilian. By 50 U.S.C. § 553, Congress had retained jurisdiction to try Toth for a crime he had committed while a soldier and for which admittedly he could have been tried by court-martial if the United States had discovered his crime one minute before discharge.

He was not a full-fledged civilian under his discharge. He was still a soldier to answer in court-martial for the crime he had committed while a soldier. He had a conditional discharge only. The United States clearly reserved the right to charge and try him by court-martial for a crime committed while in the status of a soldier.

RELATED CASES:

United States ex rel. Hirshberg v. Cooke: 336 U.S. 210 (1949). Opinion: Black, J. No dissent.

A Navy court-martial has no jurisdiction to try an enlisted man for a violation of the Articles for the Government of the Navy, committed during a prior enlistment terminated by an honorable discharge, even though he reenlisted on the day following his discharge. After this decision the statute was changed in 1950. Then *Toth* was decided.

Humphrey v. Smith: 336 U.S. 695 (1949). Opinion: Black, J. Dissenting: Murphy, Douglas, and Rutledge, JJ.

The fact of the thorough and impartial investigation required by the Articles of War before the convening of a court-martial is for the military authorities to determine.

Hiatt v. Brown: 339 U.S. 103 (1950). Opinion: Clark, J. No dissent. Abstaining: Douglas, J.

Civil courts can inquire only as to the jurisdiction of courts-martial. Correction of errors is for the military authorities.

O'Callahan v. Parker: 395 U.S. 258 (1969). Opinion: Douglas, J. Dissenting: Harlan, Stewart, and White, JJ.

In order to be tried by a court-martial a crime must be service-connected lest "cases arising in the land and naval forces or in the militia, when in actual service in time of war or public danger," as used in the Fifth Amendment, be expanded to deprive every member of the armed services of the benefits of an indictment by a grand jury and a trial by a jury of his peers. This case arose in Honolulu.

Relford v. Commandant, U.S. Disciplinary Barracks, Ft. Leavenworth: 401 U.S. 355 (1971). Opinion: Blackmun, J. No dissent.

When a serviceman is charged with an offense committed within or at the geographical boundary of a military post and violative of the security of a person or of property there, that offense is "service connected" within the meaning of that requirement as specified in *O'Callaghan* v. *Parker*.

Reid v. Covert
354 U.S. 1; 77 S.Ct. 1222; 1 L.Ed. 2nd 1148 (1957)

(Clarice Covert was accused of killing her husband, a sergeant in the United States Air Force, at an airbase in England. She was not a member of the armed forces but was residing on the base with her husband at the time. She was tried by a court-martial for murder under Article 118 of the Uniform Code of Military

Justice. The jurisdiction of a court-martial over civilian dependents accompanying members of the armed forces outside the United States in a case involving a capital offense was challenged.)

Vote: 6-2

Mr. Justice Black delivered the opinion of the Court:

. . . At the beginning we reject the idea that when the United States acts against citizens abroad it can do so free of the Bill of Rights. The United States is entirely a creature of the Constitution. Its power and authority have no other source. It can only act in accordance with all the limitations imposed by the Constitution. When the Government reaches out to punish a citizen who is abroad, the shield which the Bill of Rights and other parts of the Constitution provide to protect his life and liberty should not be stripped away just because he happens to be in another land. . . .

The language of Article Three, § 2 manifests that constitutional protections for the individual were designed to restrict the United States Government when it acts outside of this country, as well as here at home. After declaring that *all* criminal trials must be by jury, the section states that when a crime is "not committed within any State, the Trial shall be at such Place or Places as the Congress may by Law have directed." If this language is permitted to have its obvious meaning, § 2 is applicable to criminal trials outside of the States as a group without regard to where the offense is committed or the trial held. . . .

. . . The concept that the Bill of Rights and other constitutional protections against arbitrary government are inoperative when they become inconvenient or when expediency dictates otherwise is a very dangerous doctrine and if allowed to flourish would destroy the benefit of a written Constitution and undermine the basis of our government. If our foreign commitments become of such nature that the Government can no longer satisfactorily operate within the bounds laid down by the Constitution, that instrument can be amended by the method which it prescribes. But we have no authority, or inclination, to read exceptions into it which are not there.

. . . The obvious and decisive answer to this, of course, is that no agreement with a foreign nation can confer power on the Congress, or on any other branch of government, which is free from the restraints of the Constitution.

. . . There is nothing in this language which intimates that treaties and laws enacted pursuant to them do not have to comply with the provisions of the Constitution. Nor is there anything in the debates which accompanied the drafting and ratification of the Constitution which even suggests such a result. These debates as well as the history that surrounds the adoption of the treaty provision in Article Six make it clear that the reason treaties were not limited to those made in "pursuance" of the Constitution was so that agreements made by the United States under the Articles of Confederation, including the important peace treaties which concluded the Revolutionary War, would remain in effect. It would be manifestly contrary to the objectives of those who created the Constitution, as well as those who were responsible for the Bill of Rights—let alone alien to our entire constitutional history and tradition—to construe Article Six as permitting the United States to exercise power under an international agreement without observing constitutional prohibitions. In effect, such construction would permit amendment of that document in a manner not sanctioned by Article V. . . .

In summary, we conclude that the Constitution in its entirety applied to the trials of Mrs. Smith and Mrs. Covert. Since their court-martial did not meet the requirements of Article Three, § 2, or the Fifth and Sixth Amendments we are compelled to determine if there is anything *within* the Constitution which authorizes the military trial of dependents accompanying the armed forces overseas.

Article One, § 8, Clause 14, empowers Congress "To make Rules for the Government and Regulation of the land and naval Forces." It has been held that this creates an exception to the normal method of trial in civilian courts as provided by the Constitution and permits Congress to authorize military trial of members of the armed services without all the safeguards given an accused by Article Three and the Bill of Rights. But if the language of Clause 14 is given its natural meaning, the power granted does not extend to civilians—even though they may be dependents living with servicemen on a military base. . . .

It must be emphasized that every person who comes within the jurisdiction of courts-martial is subject to military law—law that is substantially different from the law which governs society. Military law is, in many respects, harsh law which is frequently cast in very sweeping and vague terms. It emphasizes the iron hand and discipline more than it does the even scales of justice. . . .

In summary, "it still remains true that military tribunals have not been and probably never can be constituted in such way that they can have the same kind of qualifications that the Constitution has deemed essential to fair trials of civilians in federal courts." In part this is attributable to the inherent differences in values and attitudes that separate the military establishment from civilian society. In the military, by necessity, emphasis must be placed on the security and order of the group rather than on the value and integrity of the individual. . . .

We should not break faith with this nation's tradition of keeping military power subservient to civilian authority, a tradition which we believe is firmly embodied in the Constitution. The country has remained true to that faith for almost one hundred seventy years. Perhaps no group in the nation has been truer than military men themselves. Unlike the soldiers of many other nations, they have been content to perform their military duties in defense of the nation in every period of need and to perform those duties well without attempting to usurp power which is not theirs under our system of constitutional government.

Reversed and remanded.

Mr. Justice Whittaker took no part in the consideration or decision of these cases.

Mr. Justice Frankfurter, concurred in the result:

. . . The Government, apparently recognizing the constitutional basis for the decision in *Ross*, has, on rehearing, sought to show that civilians in general and civilian dependents in particular have been subject to military order and discipline ever since the colonial period. The materials it has submitted seem too episodic, too meager, to form a solid basis in history, preceding and contemporaneous with the framing of the Constitution, for constitutional adjudication. What has been urged on us falls far too short of proving a well-established practice—to be deemed to be infused into the Constitution—of court-martial jurisdiction, certainly not in capital cases, over such civilians in time of peace.

Mr. Justice Harlan, concurred:

I concur in the result, on the narrow ground that where the offense is capital, Article Two (11) cannot constitutionally be applied to the trial of civilian dependents of members of the armed forces overseas in times of peace. . . .

So far as capital cases are concerned, I think they stand on quite a different footing than other offenses. In such cases the law is especially sensitive to demands for that procedural fairness which inheres in a civilian trial where the judge and trier of fact are not responsive to the command of the convening authority. I do not concede that whatever process is "due" an offender faced with a fine or a prison sentence necessarily satisfies the requirements of the Constitution in a capital case. . . .

Mr. Justice Clark, with whom Mr. Justice Burton joined, dissented:

. . . These women were as much "a part" of the military installation as were their husbands. Upon attack by an enemy they would be so treated; all foreign governments so recognized them at all times; and, in addition, it has been clearly shown, unlike in *Toth*, that "the discipline of the Army is going to be disrupted, its morale impaired, or its orderly processes disturbed" by excluding them from the provisions of the Uniform Code. Every single one of our major military commanders over the world has filed a statement to this effect in this case. We should not substitute our views as to this necessity for those charged with the responsibility of the protection of those far-flung outposts of the free world. The former minority, however, repudiates this underlying basis of the opinion in *Toth*, namely, that where disciplinary measures are necessary to the regulation of the armed forces the Congress does have constitutional power to make rules. In my opinion the rules it has made are necessary to the regulation of the land and naval forces and the means chosen, the Uniform Code, is in no way an unreasonable one. . . .

RELATED CASES:

In re Ross: 140 U.S. 453 (1891). Opinion: Field, J. No dissent.
An American consular court in Japan had jurisdiction over the accused under treaties conferring extraterritorial rights. Constitutional guarantees regarding grand jury indictment and jury trial apply only to citizens and others within the United States. The Constitution can have no operation in another country.

Kinsella v. Krueger: 351 U.S. 470 (1956). Opinion: Clark, J. Dissenting: Warren, C.J., and Black and Douglas, JJ.
A civilian dependent of an American serviceman authorized to accompany him on foreign duty may constitutionally be tried by an American military court-martial in a foreign country for an offense committed there. Failure to provide for indictment by grand jury and trial by a petit jury follows procedure approved by the Court in other types of legislative courts established abroad by Congress. This was reversed by *Reid v. Covert*.

Wilson v. Girard: 354 U.S. 524 (1957). Per Curiam. No dissent. Abstaining: Douglas, J.
There is no constitutional or statutory barrier to the provision of the agreement with Japan under which the United States waived jurisdiction to try an American soldier and agreed to deliver him to Japanese authorities for trial on the charge of causing the death of a Japanese civilian in Japan. The Status of Forces agreement was involved here.

Lee v. Madigan: 358 U.S. 228 (1959). Opinion: Douglas, J. Dissenting: Harlan and Clark, JJ.
In view of the attitude of a free society toward the jurisdiction of military tribunals and our reluctance to give them authority to try people for nonmilitary offenses, any grant to them of power to try people for capital offenses should be construed strictly. Here the offense of conspiracy to commit murder at an army camp in California in 1949 was "in time of peace" even though the war with Germany and Japan had not been legally terminated. Therefore a court-martial had no jurisdiction under the Articles of War.

Grisham v. Hagan: 361 U.S. 278 (1960). Opinion: Clark, J. Dissenting: Whittaker and Stewart, JJ.
Civilian employees of the armed services cannot be tried by court-martial for a capital offense while employed overseas by the United States Army. Here the charge was premeditated murder. This case arose in France.

McElroy v. United States ex rel. Guagliardo: 361 U.S. 281 (1960). Opinion: Clark, J. Dissenting: Frankfurter, Stewart, Harlan, and Whittaker, JJ.

A civilian employee of the Air Force performing the duties of an electrical lineman was convicted by court-martial of larceny and conspiracy to commit larceny from a depot supply house near Casablanca, Morocco. The Court held that civilian employees of the armed forces overseas cannot be made subject to court-martial for noncapital offenses.

Kinsella v. United States ex rel. Singleton: 361 U.S. 234 (1960). Opinion: Clark, J. Dissenting: Frankfurter and Harlan, JJ.

The power of Congress to make rules for the government and regulation of the land and naval forces cannot be expanded by the necessary and proper clause to include prosecution of civilian dependents for noncapital offenses. This case arose in Germany.

NOTE:

In a series of cases the Court has set down that courts-martial have no jurisdiction over any civilians be they discharged service men, wives or dependents of service men, or civilian employees of the armed services and regardless of whether there is a capital or a noncapital offense involved. The five cases of this series make up a fair share of the total of cases decided since 1937 in which acts of Congress have been declared unconstitutional in whole or in part.

CHAPTER VI

OBLIGATION OF CONTRACT

One of the few specific restrictions on the states in the original constitution and one that has been interpreted rather consistently over the years by the Supreme Court is the provision that no state is to pass any law impairing the obligation of contracts. This was originally made a part of the Constitution to keep the states from passing legislation relieving debtors of their obligations. John Marshall then set the principles of interpretation in a series of cases and these have not been seriously breached in the intervening years even though some might feel that the Minnesota Mortgage Case was a departure.

There is no similar restriction on the federal government, evidence that the founding fathers assumed that the economics of the country would be basically in the hands of the states, to keep the states from passing legislation relieving debtors of their obligations.

Trustees of Dartmouth College v. Woodward
4 Wheat. 518; 4 L.Ed. 629 (1819)

(Dartmouth was chartered by the English Crown in 1769. The state legislature of New Hampshire in 1816 by statute attempted a complete reorganization of the government of the College including changing the name to "Dartmouth University." Woodward, secretary-treasurer of the college, had joined the new university movement and had retained the seal, records, and other articles of the college. The trustees of the old college brought an action of trover in the state court against Woodward for the recovery of this property. The state court decided against the college trustees.)

Vote: 5-1

Mr. Chief Justice Marshall delivered the opinion of the Court:

. . . The points for consideration are, 1. Is this contract protected by the Constitution of the United States? 2. Is it impaired by the acts under which the defendant holds? . . .

— A corporation is an artificial being, invisible, intangible, and existing only in contemplation of law. Being the mere creature of law, it possesses only those properties which the charter of its creation confers upon it, either expressly or as incidental to its very existence.—These are such as are supposed best calculated to effect the object for which it was created. Among the most important are immortality, and, if the expression may be allowed, individuality; properties, by which a perpetual succession of many persons are considered as the same, and may act as a single individual. They enable a corporation to manage its own affairs, and to hold property without the perplexing intricacies, the hazardous and endless necessity, of perpetual conveyances for the purpose of transmitting it from hand to hand. It is chiefly for the purpose of clothing bodies of men in succession with these qualities and capacities that corporations were invented and are in use. By these means, a perpetual succession of individuals are capable of acting for the promotion of the particular object, like one immortal being. . . .

. . . They [the donors] are represented by the corporation. The corporation is the assignee of their rights, stands in their place, and distributes their bounty, as they would themselves have distributed it had they been immortal. So with respect to the students who are to derive learning from this source. The corporation is a trustee for them also. Their potential rights, which, taken distributively, are imperceptible, amount collectively to a most important interest. These are, in the aggregate, to be exercised, asserted, and protected by the corporation. . . .

This is plainly a contract to which the donors, the trustees, and the crown (to whose rights and obligations New Hampshire succeeds) were the original parties. It is a contract made on a valuable consideration. It is a contract for the security and disposition of property. It is a contract on the faith of which real and personal estate has been conveyed to the corporation. It is then a contract within the letter of the Constitution, and within its spirit also, unless the fact that the property is invested by the donors in trustees for the promotion of religion and education, for the benefit of persons who are perpetually changing, though the objects remain the same, shall create a particular exception, taking this case out of the prohibition contained in the Constitution.

It is more than possible that the preservation of rights of this description was not particularly in the view of the framers of the Constitution when the clause under consideration was introduced into that instrument. It is probable that interferences of more frequent recurrence, to which the temptation was stronger and of which the mischief was more extensive, constituted the great motive for imposing this restriction on the state legislatures. But although a particular and a rare case may not in itself be of sufficient magnitude to induce a rule, yet it must be governed by the rule, when established, unless some plain and strong reason for excluding it can be given. It is not enough to say that this particular case was not in the mind of the convention when the article was framed, nor of the American people when it was adopted. It is necessary to go farther, and to say that, had this particular case been suggested, the language would have been so varied as to exclude it, or it would have been made a special exception. The case, being within the words of the rule, must be within its operation likewise, unless there be something in the literal construction so obviously absurd, or mischievous, or repugnant to the general spirit of the instrument as to justify those who expound the Constitution in making it an exception. . . .

The opinion of the court, after mature deliberation is, that this is a contract, the obligation of which cannot be impaired without violating the Constitution of the United States. This opinion appears to us to be equally supported by reason and by the former decisions of this court.

2. We next proceed to the inquiry whether its obligation has been impaired by those acts of the Legislature of New Hampshire to which the special verdict refers. . . .

On the effect of this law two opinions cannot be entertained. Between acting directly and acting through the agency of trustees and overseers no essential difference is perceived. The whole power of governing the college is transferred from trustees appointed according to the will of the founder, expressed in the charter, to the executive of New Hampshire. The management and application of the funds of this eleemosynary institution, which are placed by the donors in the hands of trustees named in the charter, and empowered to perpetuate themselves, are placed by this act under the control of the government of the state. The will of the state is substituted for the will of the donors in every essential operation of the college. This is not an immaterial change. The founders of the college contracted, not merely for the perpetual application of the funds which they gave to the objects for which those funds were given, they contracted also to secure that application by the constitution of the corporation. They contracted for a system which should, as far as human foresight can provide, retain forever the government of the literary institution they had formed, in the hands of persons approved by themselves. This system is totally changed. The charter of 1769 exists no longer. It is reorganized, and reorganized in such a manner as to convert a literary institution, moulded according to the will of its founders and placed under the control of private literary men, into a machine entirely subservient to the will of government. This may be for the advantage of this college in particular, and may be for the advantage of literature in general; but it is not according to the will of the donors, and is subversive of that contract on the faith of which their property was given.

Judgment reversed.

Mr. Justice Story concurred:

. . . When a private eleemosynary corporation is thus created by the charter of the crown, it is subject to no other control on the part of the crown, than what is expressly or implicitly reserved by the charter itself. Unless a power be reserved for this purpose, the crown cannot, in virtue of its prorogative, without the consent of the corporation, alter or amend the charter, or divest the corporation of any of its franchises, or add to them, or add to, or diminish, the number of the trustees, or remove any of the members, or change, or control the administration of the charity, or compel the corporation to receive a new charter. This is the uniform language of the authorities, and forms one of the most stubborn, and well settled doctrines of the common law. . . .

Mr. Justice Washington also concurred with the same holding as Mr. Justice Story.

Mr. Justice Duval dissented without opinion.

RELATED CASES:

Fletcher v. Peck: 6 Cr. 87 (1810). Opinion: Marshall, C.J. No dissent.

"When, then, a law is in its nature a contract, when absolute rights have vested under that contract, a repeal of the law cannot divest those rights, and the act of annulling them, if legitimate, is rendered so by a power applicable to the case of every individual in the community." The Court held executed as well as executory contracts protected. This case out of Georgia was the first in which a state law was held void as contrary to the Constitution.

New Jersey v. Wilson: 7 Cr. 164 (1812). Opinion: Marshall, C.J. No dissent.

A state may contract away a portion of its taxing power, and when this privilege is attached by the state to land, and the state does not withdraw the privilege at the time of sale, the purchaser succeeds to this privilege. Otherwise, there would be impairment of the obligation of contract.

Sturges v. Crowninshield: 4 Wheat. 122 (1819). Opinion: Marshall, C. J. No dissent.

State bankruptcy laws cannot be made to apply to contracts previously made since this would, in effect, be a law impairing the obligation of contract. This case arose in New York.

Ogden v. Saunders: 12 Wheat. 213 (1827). Opinion: Johnson, J. Dissenting: Marshall, C.J., and Duval and Story, JJ.

A state bankruptcy law may be applied to contracts made subsequent to the enactment of the statute without violation of the constitutional prohibition of impairment of the obligation of contract. This was Marshall's first dissent in a constitutional law case.

Charles River Bridge v. Warren Bridge: 11 Pet. 420 (1837). Opinion: Taney, C.J. Dissenting: Story and Thompson, JJ.

Charters that involve public grants are to be strictly construed, and "no rights are taken from the public, or given to the corporation, beyond those which the words of the charter, by their natural and proper construction, purport to convey." This case came out of Massachusetts.

Piqua Branch v. Knoop: 16 Howard 369 (1853). Opinion: McLean, J. Dissenting: Catron, Daniel, and Campbell, JJ.

Where by statute a state has required that banks set off 6 per cent of their semi-annual dividends to the use of the state, in lieu of taxes, the state by subsequent statute may not tax the capital stock, surplus, and contingent fund of banks organized under the former act. A bank charter is a legislative contract which cannot be changed without its assent. This is a leading case on the point that taxation is *not* an inalienable power that cannot be bartered away. See *New Jersey* v. *Wilson,* p. 190, above.

Larson v. South Dakota: 278 U.S. 429 (1929). Opinion: Taft, C.J. No dissent.

An exclusive grant by a municipality, under legislative authority of a *ferry* franchise to an individual does not prevent the legislature from subsequently granting the right to another to build a *bridge* near the ferry. A public grant is to be strictly construed. This was a reaffirmation of *Charles River Bridge* v. *Warren Bridge.*

NOTE:

The net result of these cases is that legislative grants of charters to all kinds of private corporations are contracts, and grants of public franchises are to be strictly construed, that is, there is to be no "mind reading" of the legislature; only what is clearly granted has been granted.

Home Building and Loan Assn. v. Blaisdell
290 U.S. 398; 54 S.Ct. 231; 78 L.Ed. 413 (1934)

(A mortgage on the land of Blaisdell was held by the Home Building and Loan Association. By reason of default, the mortgage was foreclosed. The Supreme Court of Minnesota held the action of foreclosure invalid because of the Minnesota statute, "The Minnesota Mortgage Moratorium Law," which provided that when any person is unable to pay or retire a mortgage at the date of redemption, he could, by petitioning a court, be granted a moratorium from a foreclosure sale. This appeal was then taken to the Supreme Court of the United States on the basis that the statute was contrary to the contract clause of the Constitution, as well as contrary to the due process and equal protection clauses of the Fourteenth Amendment.)

Vote: 5-4

Mr. Chief Justice Hughes delivered the opinion of the Court:

. . . In determining whether the provision for this temporary and conditional relief exceeds the power of the state by reason of the clause in the Federal Constitution prohibiting impairment of the obligations of contracts, we must consider the relation of emergency to constitutional power, the historical setting of the contract clause, the development of the jurisprudence of this Court in the construction of that clause, and the principles of construction which we may consider to be established.

Emergency does not create power. Emergency does not increase granted power or remove or diminish the restrictions imposed upon power granted or reserved. The Constitution was adopted in a period of grave emergency. Its grants of power to the Federal Government and its limitations of the power of the states were determined in the light of emergency and they are not altered by emergency. What power was thus granted and what limitations were thus imposed are questions which have always been, and always will be, the subject of close examination under our constitutional system.

While emergency does not create power, emergency may furnish the occasion for the exercise of power. "Although an emergency may not call into life a power which has never lived, nevertheless emergency may afford a reason for the exertion of a living power already enjoyed." *Wilson* v. *New*, 243 U.S. 332. The constitutional question presented in the light of an emergency is whether the power possessed embraces the particular exercise of it in response to particular conditions. Thus, the war power of the Federal Government is not created by the emergency of war, but it is a power given to meet that emergency. It is a power to wage war successfully, and thus it permits the harnessing of the entire energies of the people in a supreme effort to preserve the nation. But even the war power does not remove constitutional limitations safeguarding essential liberties. When the provisions of the Constitution, in grant or restriction, are specific, so particularized as not to admit of construction, no question is presented. Thus, emergency would not permit a state to have more than two Senators in the Congress, or permit the election of a President by a general popular vote without regard to the number of electors to which the states are respectively entitled, or permit the states to "coin money" or "to make anything but gold and silver coin a tender in payment of debts." But where constitutional grants and limitations of power are set forth in general clauses, which afford a broad outline, the process of construction is essential to fill in the details. That is true of the contract clause. . . .

Not only is the constitutional provision qualified by the measure of control which the state retains over remedial processes, but the state also continues to possess authority to safeguard the vital interests of its people. It does not matter that legislation appropriate to that end "has the result of modifying or abrogating contracts already in effect." . . . Not only are existing laws read into contracts in order to fix obligations as between the parties, but the reservation of essential attributes of sovereign power is also read into contracts as a postulate of the legal order. The policy of protecting contracts against impairment presupposes the maintenance of a government by virtue of which contractual relations are worth while,—a government which retains adequate authority to secure the peace and good order of society. This principle of harmonizing the constitutional prohibition with the necessary residuum of state power has had progressive recognition in the decisions of this Court.

. . . The reservation of state power appropriate to such extraordinary conditions may be deemed to be as much a part of all contracts, as is the reservation of state power to protect the public interest in the other situations to which we have referred. And if state power exists to give temporary relief from the enforcement of contracts in the presence of disasters due to physical causes such as fire, flood or earthquake, that power cannot be said to be non-existent when the urgent public need demanding such relief is produced by other and economic causes. . . .

It is no answer to say that this public need was not apprehended a century ago, or to insist that what the provision of the Constitution meant to the vision of that day it must mean to the vision of our time. If by the statement that what the Constitution meant at the time of its adoption it means to-day, it is intended to say that the great clauses of the Constitution must be confined to the interpretation which the framers, with the conditions and outlook of their time, would have placed upon them, the statement carries its own refutation.

It was to guard against such a narrow conception that Chief Justice Marshall uttered the memorable warning: "We must never forget, that it is *a constitution* we are expounding."

Applying the criteria established by our decisions we conclude:

1. An emergency existed in Minnesota which furnished a proper occasion for the exercise of the reserved power of the state to protect the vital interests of the community. . . .

2. The legislation was addressed to a legitimate end, that is, the legislation was not for the mere advantage of particular individuals but for the protection of a basic interest of society.

3. In view of the nature of the contracts in question—mortgages of unquestionable validity—the relief afforded and justified by the emergency, in order not to contravene the constitutional provision, could only be of a character appropriate to that emergency and could be granted only upon reasonable conditions.

4. The conditions upon which the period of redemption is extended do not appear to be unreasonable. . . .

As already noted, the integrity of the mortgage indebtedness is not impaired; interest continues to run; the validity of the sale and the right of a mortgagee-purchaser to title or to obtain a deficiency judgment, if the mortgagor fails to redeem within the extended period, are maintained; and the conditions of redemption, if redemption there be, stand as they were under the prior law. The mortgagor during the extended period is not ousted from possession, but he must pay the rental value of the premises as ascertained in judicial proceedings and this amount is applied to the carrying of the property and to interest upon the indebtedness. . . .

. . . If it be determined, as it must be, that the contract clause is not an absolute and utterly unqualified restriction of the state's protective power, this legislation is clearly so reasonable as to be within the legislative competency.

5. The legislation is temporary in operation. It is limited to the exigency which called it forth. While the postponement of the period of redemption from the foreclosure sale is to May 1, 1935, that period may be reduced by the order of the court under the statute, in case of a change in circumstances, and the operation of the statute itself could not validly outlast the emergency or be so extended as virtually to destroy the contracts.

We are of the opinion that the Minnesota statute as here applied does not violate the contract clause of the Federal Constitution. Whether the legislation is wise or unwise as a matter of policy is a question with which we are not concerned.

What has been said on that point is also applicable to the contention presented under the due process clause. . . .

Nor do we think that the statute denies to the appellant the equal protection of the laws. The classification which the statute makes cannot be said to be an arbitrary one. . . .

Judgment affirmed.

Mr. Justice Sutherland dissented, joined by Mr. Justice VanDevanter, Mr. Justice McReynolds, and Mr. Justice Butler:

. . . The whole aim of construction, as applied to a provision of the Constitution, is to discover the meaning, to ascertain and give effect to the intent, of its framers and the people who adopted it. . . . The necessities which gave rise to the provision, the controversies which preceded, as well as the conflicts of opinion which were settled by its adoption, are matters to be considered to enable us to arrive at a correct result. . . . The history of the times, the state of things existing when the provision was framed and adopted, should be looked to in order to ascertain the mischief and the remedy. . . . As nearly as possible we should place ourselves in the condition of those who framed and adopted it. . . . And if the meaning be at all doubtful the doubt should be resolved, wherever reasonably possible to do so, in a way to forward the evident purpose with which the provision was adopted. . . .

An application of these principles to the question under review removes any doubt, if otherwise there would be any, that the contract impairment clause denies to the several states the power to mitigate hard consequences resulting to debtors from financial or economic exigencies by an impairment of the obligation of contracts of indebtedness. A candid consideration of the history and circumstances which led up to and accompanied the framing and adoption of this clause will demonstrate conclusively that it was framed and adopted with the specific and studied purpose of preventing legislation designed to relieve debtors *especially* in time of financial distress. Indeed, it is not probable that any other purpose was definitely in the minds of those who composed the framers' convention or the ratifying state conventions which followed, although the restriction has been given a wider application upon principles clearly stated by Chief Justice Marshall in the *Dartmouth College* case, 4 Wheat. 518, 644-645. . . .

If it be possible by resort to the testimony of history to put any question of constitutional intent beyond the domain of uncertainty, the foregoing leaves no reasonable ground upon which to base a denial that the clause of the Constitution now under consideration was meant to foreclose state action impairing the obligation of contracts *primarily* and *especially* in respect of such action aimed at giving relief to debtors *in time of emergency*. And if further proof be required to strengthen what already is inexpugnable, such proof will be found in the previous decisions of this court. . . .

The defense of the Minnesota law is made upon grounds which were discountenanced by the makers of the Constitution and have many times been rejected by this court. That defense should not now succeed, because it constitutes an effort to overthrow the constitutional provision by an appeal to facts and circumstances identical with those which brought it into existence. With due regard for the processes of logical thinking, it legitimately cannot be urged that conditions which produced the rule may now be invoked to destroy it. . . .

The Minnesota statute either impairs the obligation of contracts or it does not. If it does not, the occasion to which it relates becomes immaterial, since, then the passage of the statute is the exercise of a normal, unrestricted, state power and requires no special occasion to render it effective. If it does, the emergency no more furnishes a proper occasion for its exercise than if the emergency were nonexistent.

We come back, then, directly, to the question of impairment. As to that, the conclusion reached by the court here seems to be that the relief afforded by the statute does not contravene the constitutional provision because it is of a character appropriate to the emergency and allowed upon what are said to be reasonable conditions. . . .

A statute which materially delays enforcement of the mortgagee's contractual right of ownership and possession does not modify the remedy merely; it destroys, for the period of delay, *all* remedy so far as the enforcement of that right is concerned. The phrase, "obligation of a contract," in the constitutional sense imports a legal duty to perform the specified obligation of that contract, not to substitute and perform, against the will of one of the parties, a different, albeit equally valuable, obligation. And a state, under the contract impairment clause, has no more power to accomplish such a substitution than has one of the parties to the contract against the will of the other. It cannot do so either by acting directly upon the contract, or by bringing about the result under the guise of a statute in form acting only upon the remedy. If it could, efficacy of the constitutional restriction would, in large measure, be made to disappear. . . .

I quite agree with the opinion of the court that whether the legislation under review is wise or unwise is a matter with which we have nothing to do. Whether it is likely to work well or work ill presents a question entirely irrelevant to the issue. The only legitimate inquiry we can make is whether it is constitutional. If it is not, its virtues, if it have any, cannot save it; if it is, its faults cannot be invoked to accomplish its destruction. If the provisions of the Constitution be not upheld when they pinch as well as when they comfort, they may as well be abandoned. Being unable to reach any other conclusion than that the Minnesota statute infringes the constitutional restriction under review, I have no choice but to say so.

RELATED CASES:

Worthen Co. v. Thomas: 292 U.S. 426 (1934). Opinion: Hughes, C.J. No dissent.

In the exercise of police power that affects the obligation of contract, a state must make certain statutory limitations of time or the circumstances of a situation. Here a statute of Arkansas retroactive in effect on life insurance policies and garnishment was held void as impairment of contract.

Worthen Co. v. Kavanaugh: 295 U.S. 56 (1935). Opinion: Cardozo, J. No dissent.

Statutes which so diminish the remedies of holders of bonds of a municipal improvement district with regard to mortgage security for the bonds that the holders are left for some time with no power to enforce the obligation to pay either installments of principal or coupons on the bonds are in violation of the contract clause of the Constitution. This case came out of Arkansas.

Louisville Joint Stock Land Bank v. Radford: 295 U.S. 555 (1935). Opinion: Brandeis, J. No dissent.

A bankruptcy statute cannot deprive a mortgagee of property without just compensation in violation of the Fifth Amendment. Thus, the first Frazier-Lemke Act was held unconstitutional.

Wright v. Vinton Branch of Mountain Trust Bank: 300 U.S. 440 (1937). Opinion: Brandeis, J. No dissent.

Here in a unanimous decision reversing the unanimous decision in *Radford* just eighteen months before, the Court held the revised Frazier-Lemke Act valid. There were no unreasonable modifications of creditors' rights and thus met the Court's objections in *Radford*.

East New York Savings Bank v. Hahn: 326 U.S. 230 (1945). Opinion: Frankfurter, J. Abstaining: Jackson, J.

In sustaining New York's mortgage moratorium the court noted that state police power is a "paramount power" and is so important to the very existence of the state that the power cannot be contracted away. The state police power is an implied condition of every contract and is superior to any rights of individuals under a contract. The Court held that a sudden change in the law might create an emergency.

NOTE:

Home Building and Loan Assn. v. *Blaisdell* reflects a point made by Justice Story in his concurring opinion in the *Dartmouth College* case. That is simply that a state legislature may include in contracts any reservations of the right to change or even to repeal those contracts. In *Blaisdell* the Court went further and noted that every contract is deemed to have been made subject to a proper exercise of the police power of the state. This power is paramount to any rights that might be claimed by individuals under contracts between themselves. This is sometimes referred to as the "doctrine of paramount power."

Stone v. Mississippi
101 U.S. 814; 25 L.Ed. 1079 (1880)

(In 1867 the legislature of Mississippi enacted a statute which chartered the "Mississippi Agricultural and Manufacturing Aid Society," actually a lottery enterprise. In 1868 a new constitution was adopted in convention and ratified by the people in 1869, which prohibited the authorization of lotteries by the state legislature. The validity of the charter was challenged by the Attorney General of Mississippi.)

Vote: 9-0

Mr. Chief Justice Waite delivered the opinion of the Court:

In the present case the question is whether the State of Mississippi, in its sovereign capacity, did by the charter now under consideration bind itself irrevocably by a contract to permit "the Mississippi Agricultural, Educational, and Manufacturing Aid Society," for twenty-five years, "to receive subscriptions, and sell and dispose of certificates of subscription which shall entitle the holders thereof to" "any lands, books, paintings, antiques, scientific instruments or apparatus, or any other property or thing that may be ornamental, valuable, or useful," "awarded to them" "by the casting of lots, or by lot, chance, or otherwise." There can be no dispute but that under this form of words the legislature of the State chartered a lottery company, having all the powers incident to such a corporation, for twenty-five years, and that in consideration thereof the company paid into the State treasury $5,000 for the use of a university, and agreed to pay, and until the commencement of this suit did pay, an annual tax of $1,000 and "one-half of one percent on the amount of receipts derived from the sale of certificates or tickets." If the legislature that granted this charter had the power to bind the people of the State and all succeeding legislatures to allow the corporation to continue its corporate business during the whole term of its authorized existence, there is no doubt about the sufficiency of the language employed to effect that object, although there was an evident purpose to conceal the vice of the transaction by the phrases that were used. Whether the alleged contract exists, therefore, or not, depends on the authority of the legislature to bind the State and the people of the State in that way.

All agree that the legislature cannot bargain away the police power of a State. "Irrevocably grants of property and franchises may be made if they do not impair the supreme authority to make laws for the right government of the State; but no legislature can curtail the power of its successors to make such laws as they may deem proper in matters of police." *Metropolitan Board of Excise* v. *Barrie*, 34 N.Y. 657; *Boyd* v. *Alabama*, 94 U.S. 645. Many attempts have been made in this court and elsewhere to define the police power, but never with entire success. It is always easier to determine whether a particular case comes within the general scope of the power, than to give an abstract definition of the power itself which will be in all respects accurate. No one denies, however, that it extends to all matters affecting the public health or the public morals. . . .

The question is therefore directly presented, whether, in view of these facts, the legislature of a State can, by the charter of a lottery company, defeat the will of the people, authoritatively expressed, in relation to the further continuance of such business in their midst. We think it cannot. No legislature can bargain away the public health or the public morals. The people themselves cannot do it, much less their servants. The supervision of both these subjects of governmental power is continuing in its nature, and they are to be dealt with as the special exigencies of the moment may require. Government is organized with a view to their preservation, and cannot divest itself of the power to provide for them. For this purpose the largest legislative discretion is allowed, and the discretion cannot be parted with any more than the power itself. . . .

But the power of governing is a trust committed by the people to the government, no part of which can be granted away. The people, in their sovereign capacity, have established their agencies for the preservation of the public health and the public morals, and the protection of public and private rights. These several agencies can govern according to their discretion, if within the scope of their general authority, while in power; but they cannot give away nor sell the discretion of those that are to come after them, in respect to matters the government of which, from the very nature of things, must "vary with varying circumstances." They may create corporations, and give them, so to speak, a limited citizenship; but as citizens, limited in their privileges, or otherwise, these creatures of the government creation are subject to such rules and regulations as may from time to time be ordained and established for the preservation of health and morality.

The contracts which the Constitution protects are those that relate to property rights, not governmental. It is not always easy to tell on which side of the line which separates governmental from property rights a particular case is to be put; but in respect to lotteries there can be no difficulty. They are not, in the legal acceptation of the term, *mala in se*, but, as we have just seen, may properly be made *mala prohibita*. They are a species of gambling, and wrong in their influences. They disturb the checks and balances of a well-ordered community. Society built on such a foundation would almost of necessity bring forth a population of speculators and gamblers, living on the expectation of what, "by the casting of lots, or by lot, chance, or otherwise," might be "awarded" to them from the accumulation of others. Certainly the right to suppress them is governmental, to be exercised at all times by those in power, at their discretion. Any one, therefore, who accepted a lottery charter does so with the implied understanding that the people, in their sovereign capacity, and through their properly constituted agencies, may resume it at any time when the public good shall require, and this whether it be paid for or not. All that one can get by such a charter is a suspension of certain governmental rights in his favor, subject to withdrawal at will. He has in legal effect nothing more than a license to enjoy the privilege on the terms named for the specified time, unless it be sooner abrogated by the sovereign power of the State. It is a permit, good as against existing laws but subject to future legislative and constitutional control or withdrawal. . . .

Judgment affirmed.

RELATED CASES:

New Jersey v. Wilson: 7 Cr. 164 (1812). Opinion: Marshall, C.J. No dissent.

A state may bargain away a portion of its taxing power to the extent that land may be exempt and this privilege was here annexed to the land itself.

West River Bridge v. Dix: 6 How. 507 (1848). Opinion: Daniel, J. Dissenting: Wayne, J.

The state may use its right of eminent domain to acquire the franchise rights of a toll bridge company and thereafter convert the bridge into a free public facility. This case arose in Vermont. A franchise is no bar to the power of eminent domain.

Butler v. Pennsylvania: 10 How. 402 (1851). Opinion: Daniel, J. Dissenting: Mc-Lean, J.

Appointment to a public office by state authority does not constitute a contract within the meaning of the contract clause of the Constitution. The office here was Canal Commissioner. Tenure and salary are not contractual in nature.

Piqua Branch of the State Bank v. Knoop: 16 How. 369 (1853). Opinion: McLean, J. Dissenting: Catron, Daniel, and Campbell, JJ.

When a state exempts certain property from taxation and substitutes an agreement for a specific type of levy or tax, the contract is binding, and the rights vested under it must be recognized.

Von Hoffman v. City of Quincy: 4 Wall. 535 (1867). Opinion: Swayne, J. No dissent.

When a special tax has been levied the proceeds of which can be used only for the purpose of paying the interest on bonds, the tax becomes a part of the contract and an attempt to repeal the tax is an impairment of the obligation of contract.

Boston Beer Co. v. Massachusetts: 97 U.S. 25 (1878). Opinion: Bradley, J. No dissent. See p. 221, below.

Fertilizing Co. v. Hyde Park: 97 U.S. 659 (1878). Opinion: Swayne, J. Dissenting: Strong, J. Abstaining: Field, J.

Since contracts are made subject to state police power, a franchise to operate a fertilizer factory did not take from the state "adequate power to protect the public health against the maintenance of nuisances. . . ." Here there was an ordinance prohibiting the transportation of offal through the streets.

Newton v. Commissioners: 100 U.S. 548 (1880). Opinion: Swayne, J. No dissent.

A state cannot contract away its right to locate a county seat since this is a "governmental subject" which cannot properly be made the subject of a contract. The issue was the transfer of the county seat of Mahoning County in Ohio from Canfield to Youngstown.

Manigault v. Springs: 199 U.S. 473 (1905). Opinion: Brown, J. No dissent.

"It is the settled law of this court that the interdiction of statutes impairing the obligation of contracts does not prevent the State from exercising such powers as are vested in it for the promotion of the common weal, or are necessary for the general good of the public, though contracts previously entered into between individuals may thereby be affected." A contract cannot prevent legislation aimed at the public good, here liquor prohibition. This case came out of South Carolina.

Pennsylvania Hospital v. Philadelphia: 245 U.S. 20 (1917). Opinion: White, C.J. No dissent.

A city was not bound by an agreement made which provided that no street would be opened through the hospital grounds.

NOTE:

Given proper conditions and circumstances the police power of a state is not subject to the contract clause. The "general welfare" must take precedence over the rights of individuals. This was particularly obvious in *Home Building and Loan Association* v. *Blaisdell*, 290 U.S. 398 (1934). Thus proper state legislation that affects contracts between individuals is valid. Further, contracts to which the state is a party cannot be construed to have taken from the state its police power should an occasion arise when this power should be exercised.

Two things need to be noted. One, the contract clause covers both executed and executory contracts and public contracts as well as private unless the former are *ultra vires*, as in *Stone* v. *Mississippi*. The other point is that the contract clause is of diminished importance today. Most matters that were originally intended to be covered by it can now be included in today's definition of due process. Edward S. Corwin once observed that the contract clause is "a fifth wheel to the constitutional law coach."

CHAPTER VII

THE FOURTEENTH AMENDMENT

No part of the Constitution, with the possible exception of the Commerce Clause, has been involved in such frequent litigation before the Supreme Court as has the Fourteenth Amendment. A product of the Reconstruction Era, this amendment may illustrate the point that legislation, and particularly that in which the supreme law of the land is concerned, should not be undertaken in time of great emotional stress and instability. The history of the process of its adoption as well as subsequent litigation would seem to point in this direction in spite of the great bulk of cases that has emerged from the past century. The provisions of the Amendment remain today in considerable doubt as to the extent of their meaning, particularly the due process and the equal protection clauses, but perhaps, in our dynamic society, this is a praiseworthy feature.

THE PRIVILEGES OR IMMUNITIES OF UNITED STATES CITIZENSHIP

Exactly what the "privileges or immunities" clause of the Fourteenth Amendment means has never been clear even with the few court decisions of the clause. In *Crandall* v. *Nevada*, 6 Wallace 35 (1868), which was decided March 16, 1868, before the Fourteenth Amendment became effective July 28, 1868, the Court held that the state tax in question there violated the implied guarantees of the original Constitution. In regard to the Fourteenth Amendment generally the Court has consistently held to the point that the prohibitions in the amendment apply only to states and that an individual as an individual cannot violate any of its provisions.

Slaughterhouse Cases*
16 Wall. 36; 21 L.Ed. 394 (1873)

(The first cases brought to the Supreme Court under the Fourteenth Amendment were these. They arose under a Louisiana statute of 1869 regulating the business of slaughtering livestock in New Orleans. The obviously corrupt legislature of the Reconstruction period had granted a monopoly to the facilities of one corporation. Other butchers were to have access to these facilities on payment of a reasonable fee, but the net result was that more than a thousand other persons and companies were prevented from continuing in the business.)

Vote: 5-4

Mr. Justice Miller delivered the opinion of the Court:

* Three cases were involved here. The official title of two of these was *Butchers Benevolent Association of New Orleans* v. *Crescent City Livestock Landing and Slaughterhouse Co.*

. . . The plaintiffs in error accepting this issue, allege that the statute is a violation of the Constitution of the United States in these several particulars:—

That it creates an involuntary servitude forbidden by the thirteenth article of amendment;

That it abridges the privileges and immunities of citizens of the United States;

That it denies to the plaintiffs the equal protection of the laws; and,

That it deprives them of their property without due process of law; contrary to the provisions of the first section of the fourteenth article of amendment. . . .

The next observation is more important in view of the arguments of counsel in the present case. It is, that the distinction between citizenship of the United States and citizenship of a State is clearly recognized and established. Not only may a man be a citizen of the United States without being a citizen of a State, but an important element is necessary to convert the former into the latter. He must reside within the State to make him a citizen of it, but it is only necessary that he should be born or naturalized in the United States to be a citizen of the Union.

It is quite clear, then, that there is a citizenship of the United States, and a citizenship of a State, which are distinct from each other, and which depend upon different characteristics or circumstances in the individual.

We think this distinction and its explicit recognition in this amendment of great weight in this argument, because the next paragraph of this same section, which is the one mainly relied on by the plaintiffs in error, speaks only of privileges and immunities of citizens of the United States, and does not speak of those of citizens of the several States. The argument, however, in favor of the plaintiffs rests wholly on the assumption that the citizenship is the same, and the privileges and immunities guaranteed by the clause are the same.

The language is, "No State shall make or enforce any law which shall abridge the privileges or immunities of citizens of the United States." It is a little remarkable, if this clause was intended as a protection to the citizen of a State against the legislative power of his own State, that the word citizen of the State should be left out when it is so carefully used, and used in contradistinction to citizens of the United States, in the very sentence which preceded it. It is too clear for argument that the change in phraseology was adopted understandingly and with a purpose.

Of the privileges and immunities of the citizen of the United States, and of the privileges and immunities of the citizen of the State, and what they respectively are, we will presently consider; but we wish to state here that it is only the former which are placed by this clause under the protection of the Federal Constitution, and that the latter, whatever they may be, are not intended to have any additional protection by this paragraph of the amendment.

If, then, there is a difference between the privileges and immunities belonging to a citizen of the United States as such, and those belonging to the citizen of the State as such, the latter must rest for their security and protection where they have heretofore rested; for they are not embraced by this paragraph of the amendment. . . .

Having shown that the privileges and immunities relied on in the argument are those which belong to citizens of the States as such, and that they are left to the State governments for security and protection, and not by this article placed under the special care of the Federal government, we may hold ourselves excused from defining the privileges and immunities of citizens of the United States which no State can abridge, until some case involving those privileges may make it necessary to do so.

But lest it should be said that no such privileges and immunities are to be found if those we have been considering are excluded, we venture to suggest some which owe their existence to the Federal Government, its national character, its Constitution, or its laws.

One of these is well described in the case of *Crandall* v. *Nevada*, 6 Wall. 35. It is said to be the right of the citizen of this great country, protected by implied guarantees of its Constitution, "to come to the seat of government to assert any claim he may have upon that government, to transact any business he may have with it, to seek its protection, to share its offices, to engage in administering its functions. He has the right of free access to its seaports, through which all operations of foreign commerce are conducted, to the sub-treasuries, land offices, and courts of justice in the several states". . . .

Another privilege of a citizen of the United States is to demand the care and protection of the Federal government over his life, liberty, and property when on the high seas or within the jurisdiction of a foreign government. Of this there can be no doubt, nor that the right depends upon his character as a citizen of the United States. The right to peaceably assemble and petition for redress of grievances, the privilege of the writ of habeas corpus, are rights of the citizen guaranteed by the Federal Constitution. The right to use the navigable waters of the United States, however they may penetrate the territory of the several States, all rights secured to our citizens by treaties with foreign nations, are dependent upon citizenship of the United States, and not citizenship of a State. One of these privileges is conferred by the very article under consideration. It is that a citizen of the United States, can of his own volition, become a citizen of any State of the Union by a bona fide residence therein, with the same rights as other citizens of that State. To these may be added the rights secured by the thirteenth and fifteenth articles of amendment, and by the other clause of the fourteenth, next to be considered.

The argument has not been much pressed in these cases that the defendant's charter deprives the plaintiffs of their property without due process of law, or that it denies to them the equal protection of the law. The first of these paragraphs has been in the Constitution since the adoption of the Fifth Amendment, as a restraint upon the federal power. It is also to be found in some form of expression in the Constitutions of nearly all of the States, as a restraint upon the power of the States. This law, then, has practically been the same as it now is during the existence of the government, except so far as the present amendment may place the restraining power over the States in this matter in the hands of the Federal government.

We are not without judicial interpretation, therefore, both State and national, of the meaning of this clause. And it is sufficient to say that under no construction of that provision that we have ever seen, or any that we deem admissible, can the restraint imposed by the State of Louisiana upon the exercise of their trade by the butchers of New Orleans be held to be a deprivation of property within the meaning of that provision.

"Nor shall any State deny to any person within its jurisdiction the equal protection of the laws."

In the light of the history of these amendments, and the pervading purpose of them, which we have already discussed, it is not difficult to give a meaning to this clause. The existence of laws in the States where the newly emancipated Negroes resided, which discriminated with gross injustice and hardship against them as a class, was the evil to be remedied by this clause, and by it such laws are forbidden.

If, however, the States did not conform their laws to its requirements, then by the fifth section of the article of amendment Congress was authorized to enforce it by suitable legislation. We doubt very much whether any action of a State not directed by way of discrimination against the Negroes as a class, or on account of their race, will ever be held to come within the purview of this provision. It is so clearly a provision for that race and that emergency, that a strong case would be necessary for its application to any other. But as it is a State that is to be dealt with, and not alone the validity of its laws, we may safely leave that matter until Congress shall have exercised its power, or some case of State oppression, by denial of equal justice in its courts, shall have claimed a decision at our hands. We find no such case in the one before us, and do not deem it necessary to go over the argument again, as it may have relation to this particular clause of the amendment....

Judgment affirmed.

Mr. Justice Field dissented, with the concurrence of Mr. Chief Justice Chase, Mr. Justice Swayne, and Mr. Justice Bradley:

What then, are the privileges and immunities which are secured against abridgement by State legislation?

The terms, privileges and immunities, are not new in the amendment; they were in the Constitution before the amendment was adopted. They are found in the second section of the fourth article, which declares that "the citizens of each State shall be entitled to all privileges and immunities of citizens in the several States," and they have been the subject of frequent consideration in judicial decisions. In *Corfield v. Coryell*, 4 Wash. C.C. 380, Fed. Cas. No. 3,230, Mr. Justice Washington said he had "no hesitation in confining these expressions to those privileges and immunities which were, in their nature, fundamental; which belong of right to citizens of all free governments, and which have at all times been enjoyed by the citizens of the several States which compose the Union, from the time of their becoming free, independent, and sovereign;" and, in considering what those fundamental privileges were, he said that perhaps it would be more tedious than difficult to enumerate them, but that they might be "all comprehended under the following general heads; protection by the government; the enjoyment of life and liberty, with the right to acquire and possess property of every kind, and to pursue and obtain happiness and safety, subject, nevertheless to such restraints as the government may justly prescribe for the general good of the whole." This appears to me to be a sound construction of the clause in question. The privileges and immunities designated are those *which of right belong to the citizens of all free governments*. Clearly among these must be placed the right to pursue a lawful employment in a lawful manner, without other restraint than such as equally affects all persons. In the discussions in Congress upon the passage of the Civil Rights Act repeated reference was made to this language of Mr. Justice Washington. It was cited by Senator Trumbull with the observation that it enumerated the very rights belonging to a citizen of the United States set forth in the first section of the act, and with the statement that all persons born in the United States being declared by the act citizens of the United States, would thenceforth be entitled to the rights of citizens, and that these were the great fundamental rights set forth in the act; and that they were set forth "as appertaining to every freeman"....

This equality of right, with exemption from all disparaging and partial enactments, in the lawful pursuits of life, throughout the whole country, is the distinguishing privilege of citizens of the United States. To them, everywhere, all pursuits, all professions, all avocations are open without other restrictions than such as are imposed equally upon all others of the same age, sex, and condition. The State may prescribe such regulations for every pursuit and calling of life as will promote the public health, secure the good order and advance the general prosperity of society, but when once prescribed, the pursuit or calling must be free to be followed by every citizen who is within the conditions designated, and will conform to the regulations. This is the fundamental idea upon which our institutions rest, and unless adhered to in the legislation of the country our government will be a republic only in name. The Fourteenth Amendment, in my judgment, makes it essential to the validity of the legislation of every State that this equality of right should be respected. How widely this equality has been departed from, how entirely rejected and trampled upon by the act of Louisiana, I have already shown. And it is to be a matter of profound regret that its validity is recognized by a majority of this court, for by it the right of free labor, one of the most sacred and imprescriptible rights of man, is violated. . . . That only is a free government, in the American sense of the term, under which the inalienable right of every citizen to pursue his happiness is unrestrained, except by just, equal, and impartial laws.

Mr. Justice Swayne and Mr. Justice Bradley also filed separate dissenting opinions.

RELATED CASES:

Crandall v. Nevada: 6 Wall. 35 (1868). Opinion: Miller, J. No dissent.

A state cannot impose a tax on persons leaving the state by any common carrier to be collected by the carrier since this would transgress the right of United States citizens to move freely about the country, an implied guarantee.

Colgate v. Harvey: 296 U.S. 404 (1935). Opinion: Sutherland, J. Dissenting: Stone, J.

A state income tax law that levies higher rates on money loaned outside the state than that loaned within the state denies equal protection of the laws and abridges the privilege of United States citizenship to carry on business across state lines. This case out of Vermont is the only one in which the privileges and immunities clause has been held to have been violated. Reversed by *Madden* v. *Kentucky*, below.

Hague v. CIO: 307 U.S. 496 (1939). Opinion: Roberts, J. Dissenting: McReynolds and Butler, JJ.

Municipal ordinances forbidding the distribution of printed matter and the holding of public meetings in streets and other public places without permits are a deprivation of rights under the Constitution. A concurring opinion held the privileges or immunities clause had been violated. See p. 122, above.

Madden v. Kentucky: 309 U.S. 83 (1940). Opinion. Reed, J. Dissenting: Roberts and McReynolds, JJ.

An annual state *ad valorem* tax on bank deposits outside a state at a rate five times that imposed on bank deposits within a state is not invalid in the absence of the most explicit demonstration that the classification "is a hostile and offensive discrimination against particular persons and classes." This decision overruled *Colgate* v. *Harvey*.

Edwards v. California: 314 U.S. 160 (1941). Opinion: Byrnes, J. No dissent.

A state statute making it a misdemeanor for anyone knowingly to bring or assist in bringing into the State a nonresident "indigent person" is invalid as an unconstitutional burden on interstate commerce. The concurring opinion held that the decision should have been based on the "privileges or immunities" clause of the Fourteenth Amendment. The quarantine power is limited to persons and articles which pose a threat to public health and safety. *Edwards* overruled *New York* v. *Miln* (11 Peters 102, 1837) which held valid under the police power a state statute requiring masters of vessels to file lists of arriving passengers. Opinion: Barbour, J. Dissenting: Story, J.

NOTE:

The *Slaughterhouse Cases* were decided only five years after the adoption of the Fourteenth Amendment and were the first interpretation of that amendment. At this time "due process" still basically meant procedure. Substantive due process, by which the "what" of governmental activity as well as the "how" can be questioned, came later although in *Dred Scott* and *Hepburn* v. *Griswold* the court had alluded to substantive due process.

In the rest of the opinion the Court distinguished sharply between the privileges and immunities of state citizenship and of federal citizenship, noting that only the latter were protected from transgression by the states in the Fourteenth Amendment. As to the former, the Court noted that these would be determined as cases arose. In fact, the Court (except for *Colgate* v. *Harvey,* later overruled by *Madden* v. *Kentucky*) has never held a state statute to conflict with the "privileges or immunities" clause of the Fourteenth Amendment. In general, the test of such a privilege is that it be derived from federal law (including, of course, the Constitution) and be the property only of citizens. In this latter respect this provision differs from most of the guarantees of the Constitution which are enjoyed by "persons," citizens and noncitizens alike.

New York v. O'Neill
359 U.S. 1; 79 S.Ct. 564; 3 L.Ed. 2nd 585 (1959)

(O'Neill, a citizen of Illinois, was in Florida to attend a convention. In accordance with a Florida statute entitled "Uniform Law to Secure the Attendance of Witnesses from Within or Without a State in Criminal Proceedings" the Circuit Court of Dade County, Florida, responded to a certificate executed by a judge of the Court of General Sessions, New York County, by summoning O'Neill before it to determine whether he was to be given into the custody of New York authorities to be transported to that state to testify in a grand jury proceeding there. The constitutionality of the statute was challenged.)

Vote: 7-2

Mr. Justice Frankfurter delivered the opinion of the Court:

. . . The Uniform Act as enacted by the Florida Legislature in 1941 was formulated by the National Conference of Commissioners on Uniform State Laws in its present form in 1936. . . . The Uniform Act is reciprocal. It is operative only between States which have enacted it or similar legislation for compelling of witnesses to travel to, and testify in, sister States.

More fundamentally, this case does not involve freedom of travel in its essential sense. At most it represents a temporary interference with voluntary travel. Particularly is this so in an era of jet transportation when vast distances can be traversed in a matter of hours. Respondent was perfectly free to return to Florida after testifying in New York. Indeed, New York was obligated to pay his way back to Florida. Or, after testifying, he could return to Illinois or remain in New York. The privilege of ingress and egress among the States which has been urged in opinions is of hardier stuff. The privilege was to prevent the walling off of States, what has been called the Balkanization of the Nation. The requirement which respondent resists conduces, it merits repetition, toward a free-willed collaboration of independent States. . . .

. . . However, the Florida courts had immediate personal jurisdiction over respondent by virtue of his presence within that State. Insofar as the Fourteenth Amendment is concerned, this gave the Florida courts constitutional jurisdiction to order an act even though that act is to be performed outside of the State. . . .

The primary purpose of this Act is not eleemosynary. It serves a self-protective function for each of the enacting States. By enacting this law the Florida Legislature authorized and enabled Florida courts to employ the procedures of other jurisdictions for the obtaining of witnesses needed in criminal proceedings in Florida. Today forty-two States and Puerto Rico may facilitate criminal proceedings, otherwise impeded by the unavailability of material witnesses, by utilizing the machinery of this reciprocal legislation to obtain such witnesses from without their boundaries. This is not merely altruistic, disinterested enactment.

In any event, to yield to an argument that benefiting other States is beyond the power of a State would completely disregard the inherent implications of our federalism within whose framework our organic society lives and moves and has its being—the abundant and complicated interrelationship between national authority and the States, . . . and between the States *inter sese*. . . .

The manifold arrangements by which the Federal and State Governments collaborate constitute an extensive network of cooperative governmental activities not formulated in the Constitution but not offensive to any of its provisions or prohibitions. . . .

To hold that these and other arrangements are beyond the power of the States and Federal Government because there is no specific empowering provision in the United States Constitution would be to take an unwarrantedly constricted view of state and national powers and would hobble the effective functioning of our federalism. Diffusion of power has its corollary of diffusion of responsibilities with its stimulus to cooperative effort in devising ways and means for making the federal system work. That is not a mechanical structure. It is an interplay of living forces of government to meet the evolving needs of a complex society.

The Constitution of the United States does not preclude resourcefulness of relationships between States on matters as to which there is no grant of power to Congress and as to which the range of authority restricted within an individual State is inadequate. By reciprocal, voluntary legislation the States have invented methods to accomplish fruitful and unprohibited ends. A citizen cannot shirk his duty, no matter how inconvenienced thereby, to testify in criminal proceedings and grand jury investigations in a State where he is found. There is no constitutional provision granting him relief from this obligation to testify even though he must travel to another State to do so. Comity among States, an end particularly to be cherished when the object is enforcement of internal criminal laws, is not to be defeated by an *a priori* restrictive view of state power.

The judgment of the Supreme Court of Florida is reversed and the cause is remanded to that court for proceedings not inconsistent with this opinion.

Reversed and remanded.

Mr. Justice Douglas dissented, with the concurrence of Mr. Justice Black:

The right to free ingress and egress within the country and even beyond the borders is a basic constitutional right, though it is not contained *in haec verba* in the Constitution. . . .

Yet O'Neill is not a fugitive from justice. He carries no criminal taint. He is wanted as a witness in New York. But there is no provision of the Constitution which provides for the extradition of witnesses by the States. That power is today judicially created. But I find no authority on the part of the States to enlarge and expand the power of extradition specifically restricted by the Constitution to criminals. . . . We allow today only what a constitutional amendment could achieve. We in effect amend Article Four, § 2 by construction to add "witnesses" to the group now embraced in Article Four, § 2.

This right of freedom of movement even of the innocent may not be absolute. Perhaps a State could stop a migrant at its borders for health inspection. There may be other narrow and limited qualifications to this right of free ingress and egress which a State may impose. But I know of no power on the part of a State to pick a citizen up and forcibly remove him from its boundaries where there is no basis of extradition. . . .

This is not giving the Constitution a niggardly construction. I urge a liberal construction which will respect the civil rights of the citizens. This right of people to choose such State as they like for their abode, to remain unmolested in their dwellings, and to be protected against being whisked away to another State has been, until today, zealously guarded. Until now, it has been part and parcel of the cherished freedom of movement protected by the constitution.

I would affirm the judgment entered by a unanimous vote of the Florida Supreme Court.

RELATED CASES:

O'Neil v. Vermont: 144 U.S. 323 (1892). Opinion: Blatchford, J. Dissenting: Field, Harlan, and Brewer, JJ.

The provision of the Eighth Amendment prohibiting cruel and unusual punishments does not apply to the states under the privileges or immunities clause of the Fourteenth Amendment.

Maxwell v. Dow: 176 U.S. 581 (1900). Opinion: Peckham, J. Dissenting: Harlan, J.

Only such privileges or immunities are protected by the Fourteenth Amendment as a citizen enjoys by reason of his United States citizenship. Here the Court held state procedure in bringing criminal charges by an information and trial by a jury of eight jurors was not covered by the Amendment. This case arose in Utah.

Mr. Justice Harlan's dissent in *Maxwell* is one of the most elaborate commentaries ever written on the Fourteenth Amendment.

Twining v. New Jersey: 211 U.S. 78 (1908). Opinion: Moody, J. Dissenting: Harlan, J.

The Fifth Amendment provision outlawing self-incrimination is not applied to procedure in state courts either by the due process or the privileges or immunities clause of the Fourteenth Amendment. This decision was reversed by *Griffin* v. *California* (380 U.S. 609, 1965). See p. 261, below.

Adamson v. California: 332 U.S. 46 (1947). Opinion: Reed, J. Dissenting: Black, Douglas, Murphy, and Rutledge, JJ.

The due process clause of the Fourteenth Amendment does not apply the Fifth Amendment to the states so as to protect an accused person from giving testimony under compulsion in state trials. The dissenting opinion by Black with Douglas, Murphy, and Rutledge represented the strongest showing of the pro-incorporation theorists to this time. This case was overruled by *Griffin* v. *California*. See p. 261, below.

NOTE:

New York v. *O'Neill* appears to presume that the states may adopt uniform legislation of this sort—which has the effect of bringing about cooperation between states—without any type of congressional consent such as might be required under Article One, Section 10.

DUE PROCESS OF LAW AND STATE POLICE POWER

The term "due process" is a nebulous thing and the courts will probably never be finished with the task of defining the term in the context in which cases arise. State police power even in its definition as the power to care for the safety, health, morals, and general welfare of persons is a pretty indefinite thing. The attempted application of one indefinite concept to another has produced a series of court cases that has proved to be most interesting and yet at times confusing and disturbing. Much of the economic history of the United States is reflected in these decisions ranging from *Munn* and the other *Granger Cases* to the present time.

Munn v. Illinois
94 U.S. 113; 24 L.Ed. 77 (1877)

(The state of Illinois brought suit against Ira Y. Munn and others, grain ware-housemen in Chicago, for transacting business without a state license contrary to a state statute setting maximum charges for the storage of grain in warehouses. The statute was challenged as violating the provisions of the Constitution vesting in Congress the power to regulate both foreign and interstate commerce, and the due process clause of the Fourteenth Amendment.)

Vote: 7-2

Mr. Chief Justice Waite delivered the opinion of the Court:

. . . When one becomes a member of society, he necessarily parts with some rights or privileges which, as an individual not affected by his relations to others, he might retain. "A body politic," as aptly defined in the preamble of the constitution of Massachusetts, "is a social compact by which the whole people covenants with each citizen, and each citizen with the whole people, that all shall be governed by certain laws for the common good." This does not confer power upon the whole people to control rights which are purely and exclusively private, *Thorpe* v. *R. & B. Railroad Co.*, 27 Vt. 140; but it does authorize the establishment of laws requiring each citizen to so conduct himself, and so use his own property, as not unnecessarily to injure another. This is the very essence of government, and has found expression in the maxim, *sic utere tuo ut alienum non laedas.* From this source came the police powers, which . . . "are nothing more or less than the powers of government inherent in every sovereignty, . . . that is to say, . . . the power to govern men and things." Under these powers the government regulates the conduct of its citizens one towards another, and the manner in which each shall use his own property, when such regulation becomes necessary for the public good. In their exercise it has been customary in England from time immemorial, and in this country from its first colonization, to regulate ferries, common carriers, hackmen, bakers, millers, wharfingers, innkeepers, etc., and in so doing to fix a maximum of charge to be made for services rendered, accomodations furnished, and articles sold. To this day, statutes are to be found in many of the states upon some or all these subjects; and we think it has never yet been successfully contended that such legislation came within any of the constitutional prohibitions against interference with private property. . . .

From this it is apparent that, down to the time of the adoption of the Fourteenth Amendment, it was not supposed that statutes regulating the use, or even the price of the use, of private property necessarily deprived an owner of his property without due process of law. Under some circumstances they may, but not under all. The amendment does not change the law in this particular: it simply prevents the states from doing that which will operate as such a deprivation.

. . . Property does become clothed with a public interest when used in a manner to make it of public consequence, and affect the community at large. When, therefore, one devotes his property to a use in which the public has an interest, he, in effect, grants to the public an interest in that use, and must submit to be controlled by the public for the common good, to the extent of the interest he has thus created. He may withdraw his grant by discontinuing the use; but, so long as he maintains the use, he must submit to the control. . . .

But we need not go further. Enough has already been said to show that, when private property is devoted to a public use, it is subject to public regulation. It remains only to ascertain whether the warehouses of these plaintiffs in error, and the business which is carried on there, come within the operation of this principle.

. . . Undoubtedly, in mere private contracts, relating to matters in which the public has no interest, what is reasonable must be ascertained judicially. But this is because the legislature has no control over such a contract. So, too, in matters which do affect the public interest, as to which legislative control may be exercised, if there are no statutory regulations upon the subject, the courts must determine what is reasonable. The controlling fact is the power to regulate at all. If that exists, the right to establish the maximum of charge, as one of the means of regulation, is implied. In fact, the common-law rule, which requires the charge to be reasonable, is itself a regulation as to price. Without it the owner could make his rates at will, and compel the public to yield to his terms, or forego the use.

But a mere common-law regulation of trade or business may be changed by statute. A person has no property, no vested interest, in any rule of the common law. That is only one of the forms of municipal law, and is no more sacred than any other. Rights of property which have been created by the common law cannot be taken away without due process; but the law itself, as a rule of conduct, may be changed at the will, or even at the whim, of the legislature, unless prevented by constitutional limitations. Indeed, the great office of statutes is to remedy defects in the common law as they are developed, and to adapt it to the changes of time and circumstances. To limit the rate of charge for services rendered in a public employment, or for the use of property in which the public has an interest, is only changing a regulation which existed before. It established no new principle in the law, but only gives a new effect to an old one.

We know that this is a power which may be abused; but that is no argument against its existence. For protection against abuses by legislatures the people must resort to the polls, not to the courts. . . .

We conclude, therefore, that the statute in question is not repugnant to the Constitution of the United States, and that there is no error in the judgment. . . .

Judgment affirmed.

Mr. Justice Field dissented, with the concurrence of Mr. Justice Strong:

I am compelled to dissent from the decision of the court in this case and from the reasons upon which that decision is founded. The principle upon which the opinion of the majority proceeds is, in my judgment, subversive of the rights of private property, heretofore believed to be protected by constitutional guarantees against legislative interference, and is in conflict with the authorities cited in its support. . . .

There is nothing in the character of the business of the defendants as warehouse-men which called for the interference complained of in this case. Their buildings are not nuisances; their occupation of receiving and storing grain infringes upon no rights of others, disturbs no neighborhood, infects not the air, and in no respect prevents others from using and enjoying their property as to them may seem best. The legislation in question is nothing less than a bold assertion of absolute power by the State to control at its discretion the property and business of the citizen, and fix the compensation he shall receive. The will of the legislature is made the condition upon which the owner shall receive the fruits of his property and the just reward of his labor, industry, and enterprise. . . .

It requires no comment to point out the radical differences between the cases of public mills and interest on money, and that of the warehouses in Chicago. No prerogative or privilege of the crown to establish warehouses was ever asserted at the common law. The business of a warehouseman was, at common law, a private business, and is so in its nature. It has no special privileges connected with it, nor did the law ever extend to it any greater protection than it extended to all other private business. No reason can be assigned to justify legislation interfering with the legitimate profits of that business, that would not equally justify an intermeddling with the business of every man in the community, so soon, at least, as his business became generally useful.

I am of the opinion that the judgment of the Supreme Court of Illinois should be reversed.

RELATED CASES:

Davidson v. New Orleans: 96 U.S. 97 (1878). Opinion: Miller, J. No dissent.

The determination of the intent and application of the due process clause of the Fourteenth Amendment is to be "by the gradual process of judicial inclusion and exclusion, as the cases presented for decision shall require. . . ." Here a special assessment by the city for the drainage of swamp lands was upheld. The *Munn* principle is applied here. Business subject to the control of rates or prices is *not* entitled under due process to just compensation.

Railroad Commission Cases: 116 U.S. 307 (1886). Opinion: Waite, C. J. Dissenting: Harlan, J.

A state can regulate the rates of railway transportation within that state's borders. The railroads, however, are entitled to just compensation and the reasonableness of rates is to be determined by judicial review.

Chicago, Milwaukee & St. Paul R. Co. v. Minnesota: 134 U.S. 418 (1890). Opinion: Blatchford, J. Dissenting: Bradley, Gray, and Lamar, JJ.

A railroad company must be permitted to have the question of rates established by a state commissioner subject to judicial investigation or it amounts to lack of due process of law. Here the Court abandoned the *Munn* principle of set rates not subject to judicial review. The reasonableness of a rate must be considered.

Allgeyer v. Louisiana: 165 U.S. 578 (1897). Opinion: Peckham, J. No dissent.

Liberty under the due process clause of the Fourteenth Amendment includes the right of the citizen to be free in the enjoyment of all of his faculties. Thus it means not only freedom of person but also freedom of action. A lawful business must have freedom of contract.

Smyth v. Ames: 169 U.S. 466 (1898). Opinion: Harlan, J. No dissent. Abstaining: Fuller, C.J., and McKenna, J.

Courts may review not only the reasonableness of rates established by a state commission but must also consider the matter of a fair return on the proper value of the property involved. Otherwise, there is confiscation.

Willcox v. Consolidated Gas Co.: 212 U.S. 19 (1909). Opinion: Peckham, J. No dissent.

Where the element of business risk was reduced to a minimum, as in the case of a gas company, a return of 6 per cent was reasonable.

Hope Natural Gas Co. v. Hall: 274 U.S. 284 (1927). Opinion: McReynolds, J. No dissent. Abstaining: Taft, C.J.

It is not a violation of due process for a state to impose an "annual privilege tax" on a business producing natural gas within the state. The tax was computed on the gross proceeds from gas produced within the state. Some of the gas was shipped and sold outside the state.

United Railways and Electric Co. v. West: 280 U.S. 234 (1930). Opinion: Sutherland, J. Dissenting: Brandeis and Stone, JJ.

The "circumstances, locality, and risk" of a situation must all be taken into account in determining what is a fair return on the value of a utility's property.

Federal Power Commission v. Hope Natural Gas Co.: 320 U.S. 591 (1944). Opinion: Douglas, J. Dissenting: Reed, Frankfurter, and Jackson, JJ. Abstaining: Roberts, J.

The total impact of a rate must be considered in determining the justice or reasonableness of that rate, regardless of the method used to reach the particular rate. This decision reversed *Smyth v. Ames*.

NOTE:

Munn v. *Illinois* was the first Fourteenth Amendment case in which the entire court—majority and minority—were concerned with due process. The court proceeded here on the presumption of validity of the statute (the *"Munn* rule" is that of presumed validity) and that judicial review was not available here. In the years following, the court held that a legislature could not provide for unreasonable or confiscatory utility rates and that judicial review should be provided to determine the reasonableness of rates. Later, beginning with *Smyth* v. *Ames*, the Court held at different times various "tests" to determine the reasonableness of a rate such as a fair return on the value of the property, original cost, replacement cost, the cost of operation, market value, prudent investment, and others. Since *Hope Natural Gas* the Court has regarded the "total picture" as the proper guide in determining the reasonableness of rates. *Munn* had made for a drastic expansion in the scope of governmental power over business. Price-fixing was valid if there was a reasonable relation between the business involved and the police power. Anything that was affected with a public interest was subject to the police power. This, of course, was a direct incursion on *laissez-faire*.

Nebbia v. New York
291 U.S. 502; 54 S.Ct. 505; 78 L.Ed. 940 (1934)

(The proprietor of a grocery store in Rochester, New York, Nebbia by name, was found guilty of violation of an order issued by the New York State Milk Control Board. This order had set the selling price of milk, and Nebbia had sold milk below this stipulated price. He appealed his conviction on the grounds that both the state statute and the order of the board issued under it were contrary to the equal protection and due process clauses of the Fourteenth Amendment.)

Vote: 5-4

Mr. Justice Roberts delivered the opinion of the Court:

. . . We think the contention that the discrimination deprives the appellant of equal protection is not well founded. For aught that appears, the appellant purchased his supply of milk from a farmer as do distributors, or could have procured it from a farmer if he so desired. There is therefore no showing that the order placed him at a disadvantage, or in fact affected him adversely, and this alone is fatal to the claim of denial of equal protection. But if it were shown that the appellant is compelled to buy from a distributor, the difference in the retail price he is required to charge his customers, from that prescribed for sales by distributors is not on its face arbitrary or unreasonable, for there are obvious distinctions between the two sorts of merchants which may well justify a difference of treatment, if the legislature possesses the power to control the prices to be charged for fluid milk. . . .

. . . The more serious question is whether, in the light of the conditions disclosed, the enforcement of section 312 (e) denied the appellant the due process secured to him by the Fourteenth Amendment. . . .

Under our form of government the use of property and the making of contracts are normally matters of private and not of public concern. The general rule is that both shall be free of governmental interference. But neither property rights nor contract rights are absolute; for government cannot exist if the citizen may at will use his property to the detriment of his fellows, or exercise his freedom of contract to work them harm. Equally fundamental with the private right is that of the public to regulate it in the common interest. . . .

The Fifth Amendment, in the field of federal activity, and the Fourteenth, as respects state action, do not prohibit governmental regulation for the public welfare. They merely condition the exertion of the admitted power, by securing that the end shall be accomplished by methods consistent with due process. And the guaranty of due process, as has often been held, demands only that the law shall not be unreasonable, arbitrary, or capricious, and that the means selected shall have a real and substantial relation to the object sought to be attained. It results that a regulation valid for one sort of business, or in given circumstances, may be invalid for another sort, or for the same business under other circumstances, because the reasonableness of each regulation depends upon the relevant facts. . . .

We may as well say at once that the dairy industry is not, in the accepted sense of the phrase, a public utility. We think the appellant is also right in asserting that there is in this case no suggestion of any monopoly or monopolistic practice. It goes without saying that those engaged in the business are in no way dependent upon public grants or franchises for the privilege of conducting their activities. But if, as must be conceded, the industry is subject to regulation in the public interest, what constitutional principle bars the state from correcting existing maladjustments by legislation touching prices? We think there is no such principle. The due process clause makes no mention of sales or of prices any more than it speaks of business or contracts or buildings or other incidents of property. The thought seems nevertheless to have persisted that there is something peculiarly sacrosanct about the price one may charge for what he makes or sells, and that, however able to regulate other elements of manufacture or trade, with incidental effect upon price, the state is incapable of directly controlling the price itself. This view was negatived many years ago. *Munn* v. *Illinois*, 94 U.S. 113. . . .

It is clear that there is no closed class or category of businesses affected with a public interest, and the function of courts in the application of the Fifth and Fourteenth Amendments is to determine in each case whether circumstances vindicate the challenged regulation as a reasonable exertion of governmental authority or condemn it as arbitrary or discriminatory. . . . The phrase "affected with a public interest" can, in the nature of things, mean no more than that an industry, for adequate reason, is subject to control for the public good. In several of the decisions of this court wherein the expressions "affected with a public interest," and "clothed with a public use," have been brought forward as the criteria of the validity of price control, it has been admitted that they are not susceptible of definition and form an unsatisfactory test of the constitutionality of legislation directed at business practices or prices. These decisions must rest, finally, upon the basis that the requirements of due process were not met because the laws were found arbitrary in their operation and effect. But there can be no doubt that upon proper occasion and by appropriate measure the state may regulate a business in any of its aspects, including the prices to be charged for the products or commodities it sells.

So far as the requirement of due process is concerned, and in the absence of other constitutional restriction, a state is free to adopt whatever economic policy may reasonably be deemed to promote public welfare, and to enforce that policy by legislation adapted to its purpose. The courts are without authority either to declare such policy, or when it is declared by the legislative arm, to override it. If the laws passed are seen to have a reasonable relation to a proper legislative purpose, and are neither arbitrary nor discriminatory, the requirements of due process are satisfied, and judicial determination to that effect renders a court *functus officio.* . . .

. . . The Constitution does not secure to anyone liberty to conduct his business in such fashion as to inflict injury upon the public at large, or upon any substantial group of the people. Price control, like any other form of regulation, is unconstitutional only if arbitrary, discriminatory, or demonstrably irrelevant to the policy the legislature is free to adopt, and hence an unnecessary and unwarranted interference with individual liberty.

Tested by these considerations we find no basis in the due process clause of the Fourteenth Amendment for condemning the provisions of the Agriculture and Markets Law here drawn into question.

The judgment is affirmed.

Mr. Justice McReynolds dissented, with the concurrence of Mr. Justice Van-Devanter, Mr. Justice Sutherland, and Mr. Justice Butler:

. . . The exigency is of the kind which inevitably arises when one set of men continue to produce more than all others can buy. The distressing result to the producer followed his ill-advised but voluntary efforts. Similar situations occur in almost every business. If here we have an emergency sufficient to empower the legislature to fix sales prices, then whenever there is too much or too little of an essential thing—whether of milk or grain or pork or coal or shoes or clothes—constitutional provisions may be declared inoperative and the "anarchy and despotism" prefigured in *Milligan's* case are at the door. The futility of such legislation in the circumstances is pointed out below. . . .

Is the milk business so affected with public interest that the legislature may prescribe prices for sales by stores? This Court has approved the contrary view; has emphatically declared that a State lacks power to fix prices in similar private businesses. . . .

. . . Assuming that the views and facts reported by the Legislative Committee are correct, it appears to me wholly unreasonable to expect this legislation to accomplish the proposed end—increase of prices at the farm. . . .

Not only does the statute interfere arbitrarily with the rights of the little grocer to conduct his business according to standards long accepted—complete destruction may follow; but it takes away the liberty of twelve million consumers to buy a necessity of life in an open market. . . .

RELATED CASES:

Wolff Packing Co. v. Court of Industrial Relations: 262 U.S. 522 (1923). Opinion: Taft, C.J. No dissent.

The only businesses affected with a public interest are (1) those operating under authority of a public grant of privileges to render public service, such as public utilities; (2) certain occupations with a distinct public interest attached, such as keepers of inns, and (3) those that have such a peculiar relation to the public that the owner has in effect granted the public an interest in that use. Here the packing business was held not to be a business under any of these categories. The packing business is a "private" matter.

Tyson and Bros. v. Banton: 273 U.S. 418 (1927). Opinion: Sutherland, J. Dissenting: Holmes, Brandeis, Stone, and Sanford, JJ.

To be "a business affected with a public interest," the business must have been so devoted to a public use that its use has been granted to the public. The selling of theater tickets is not such a business. See *Gold* v. *DiCarlo*, 380 U.S. 520 (1965).

Ribnik v. McBride: 277 U.S. 350 (1928). Opinion: Frankfurter, J. Dissenting: Stone, Holmes, and Brandeis, JJ.

A statute of New Jersey, attempting to confer on the Commissioner of Labor power to fix the prices which an employment agency can charge for its services is contrary to due process of law, because the business is not one "affected with a public interest." This case was overruled by *Olsen* v. *Nebraska*, below.

Williams v. Standard Oil Co.: 278 U.S. 235 (1929). Opinion: Sutherland, J. Dissenting: Holmes, J.

The sale of gasoline is not a business in the "public interest" category and therefore a Tennessee statute which conferred on a state officer the power to fix the sale price of gasoline is not valid.

New State Ice Co. v. Liebmann: 285 U.S. 262 (1932). Opinion: Sutherland, J. Dissenting: Brandeis and Stone, JJ. Abstaining: Cardozo, J.

Selling ice was held not to be a business affected with a public interest. Therefore, a state statute of Oklahoma, requiring that a person desiring to enter this business secure a state certificate of convenience and necessity, was invalid.

United States v. Rock Royal Co-Op: 307 U.S. 533 (1939). Opinion: Reed, J. Dissenting: Roberts, Butler, and McReynolds, JJ.

An order of the Secretary of Agriculture under the Agricultural Marketing Agreement Act of 1937 for fixing and equalizing minimum prices to be paid producers for milk sold to dealers and disposed of by the latter either in liquid form or as milk products within a marketing area comprising the city of New York and adjacent counties, is within the Constitution. Local prices that affect interstate prices involve interstate commerce. The basic policy of restoring "parity prices" is a definite enough guide.

Olsen v. Nebraska: 313 U.S. 236 (1941). Opinion: Douglas, J. No dissent.

A statute, fixing the maximum compensation that an employment agency may collect, is not a denial of due process of law. The Court in *Olsen* held that the test of affectation with a public interest had been dropped in *Nebbia* v. *New York. Olsen* overruled *Ribnik* v. *McBride*, above.

NOTE:

In *Nebbia* the court dropped the concept of "affected with a public interest" as the basis for its decisions on government regulation cases and held that such regulations depend for their reasonableness upon all of the relevant facts. This marked a departure, and, in a sense, the opinion can be regarded as the beginning of the "New Deal era" from the point of view of the judiciary, a "watershed" case. It involved state rather than federal statutory enactment, but the basic philosophy is that of the New Deal, as McReynolds' dissent obviously indicates.

Lincoln Federal Labor Union v. Northwestern Iron and Metal Company
335 U.S. 525; 69 S.Ct. 251; 93 L.Ed. 212 (1949)

(A statute of the State of North Carolina prohibited an employer from refusing employment to or discharging an employee because of his membership in or lack of membership in a labor union. Also prohibited was a contract between a labor organization and an employer for a closed shop or a union shop. An employer and the officers of a labor union were convicted of a misdemeanor for violation of the statute by entering into such a contract. The "right to work" statute was challenged as violating the First Amendment and the due process and equal protection clauses of the Fourteenth Amendment. A similar statute in Nebraska was also attacked.)

Vote: 9-0

Mr. Justice Black delivered the opinion of the Court:

. . . It is difficult to see how enforcement of this state policy could infringe the freedom of speech of anyone, or deny to anyone the right to assemble or to petition for a redress of grievances. . . .

We deem it unnecessary to elaborate the numerous reasons for our rejection of this contention of appellants. Nor need we appraise or analyze with particularity the rather startling ideas suggested to support some of the premises on which appellants' conclusions rest. There cannot be wrung from a constitutional right of workers to assemble to discuss improvement of their own working standards, a further constitutional right to drive from remunerative employment all other persons who will not, or can not, participate in union assemblies. The constitutional right of workers to assemble, to discuss and formulate plans for furthering their own self interest in jobs cannot be construed as a constitutional guarantee that none shall get and hold jobs except those who will join in the assembly or will agree to abide by the assembly's plans. For where conduct affects the interests of other individuals and the general public, the legality of that conduct must be measured by whether the conduct conforms to valid law, even though the conduct is engaged in pursuant to plans of an assembly.

Second. There is a suggestion though not elaborated in briefs that these state laws conflict with Article One, § 10, of the United States Constitution, insofar as they impair the obligation of contracts made prior to their enactment. That this contention is without merit is now too clearly established to require discussion. . . .

Third. It is contended that the North Carolina and Nebraska laws deny unions and their members equal protection of the laws and thus offend the equal protection clause of the Fourteenth Amendment. . . .

. . . But in identical language these state laws forbid employers to discriminate against union and non-union members. Nebraska and North Carolina thus command equal employment opportunities for both groups of workers. It is precisely because these state laws command equal opportunities for both groups that appellants argue that the constitutionally protected rights of assembly and due process have been violated. For the constitutional protections surrounding these rights are relied on by appellants to support a contention that the Federal Constitution guarantees greater employment rights to union members than to non-union members. This claim of appellants is itself a refutation of the contention that the Nebraska and North Carolina laws fail to afford protection to union members equal to the protection afforded non-union workers.

Fourth. It is contended that these state laws deprive appellants of their liberty without due process of law in violation of the Fourteenth Amendment. Appellants argue that the laws are specifically designed to deprive all persons within the two states of "liberty" (1) to refuse to hire or retain any person in employment because he is or is not a union member, and (2) to make a contract or agreement to engage in such employment discrimination against union or non-union members.

This Court beginning at least as early as 1934, when the *Nebbia* case was decided, has steadily rejected the due process philosophy enunciated in the *Adair-Coppage* line of cases. In doing so it has consciously returned closer and closer to the earlier constitutional principle that states have power to legislate against what are found to be injurious practices in their internal commercial and business affairs, so long as their laws do not run afoul of some specific federal constitutional prohibition, or of some valid federal law. . . . Under this constitutional doctrine the due process clause is no longer to be so broadly construed that the Congress and state legislatures are put in a strait jacket when they attempt to suppress business and industrial conditions which they regard as offensive to the public welfare.

Appellants now ask us to return, at least in part, to the due process philosophy that has been deliberately discarded. Claiming that the Federal Constitution itself affords protection for union members against discrimination, they nevertheless assert that the same Constitution forbids a state from providing the same protection for non-union members. Just as we have held that the due process clause erects no obstacle to block legislative protection of union members, we now hold that legislative protection can be afforded non-union workers.

Affirmed.

Mr. Justice Frankfurter concurred:

... The right of association, like any other right carried to its extreme, encounters limiting principles. . . . At the point where the mutual advantage of association demands too much individual disadvantage, a compromise must be struck. See Dicey, *Law and Public Opinion in England* 465-66 (1905). When that point has been reached—where the intersection should fall—is plainly a question within the special province of the legislature. This Court has given effect to such a compromise in sustaining a legislative purpose to protect individual employees against the exclusionary practices of unions. . . .

Mr. Justice Rutledge concurred:

... I am also in agreement with the Court's decision, but subject to the following reservation. Because no strike has been involved in any of the states of fact, no question has been presented in any of these cases immediately involving the right to strike or concerning the effect of the Thirteenth Amendment. Yet the issues so closely approach touching that right as it exists or may exist under that Amendment that the possible effect of the decisions upon it hardly can be ignored. Strikes have been called throughout union history in defense of the right of union members not to work with nonunion men. If today's decision should be construed to permit a state to foreclose that right by making illegal the concerted refusal of union members to work with nonunion workers, and more especially if the decision should be taken as going so far as to permit a state to enjoin such a strike, I should want a complete and thorough reargument of these cases before deciding so momentous a question.

But the right to prohibit contracts for union security is one thing. The right to force union members to work with nonunion workers is entirely another. Because of this difference, I expressly reserve judgment upon the latter question until it is squarely and inescapably presented. Although this reservation is not made expressly by the Court, I do not understand its opinion to foreclose this question.

Mr. Justice Murphy also concurred.

RELATED CASES:

Adair v. United States: 208 U.S. 161 (1908). Opinion: Harlan, J. Dissenting. McKenna and Holmes, JJ. Abstaining. Moody, J.

It is a violation of due process for Congress to outlaw "yellow dog contracts," an agreement between an employer and an employee by which the employee agrees not to join a labor union. Outlawing these is deemed to infringe on personal liberty and the right of contract.

Coppage v. Kansas: 236 U.S. 1 (1915). Opinion: Pitney, J. Dissenting: Holmes, Day, and Hughes, JJ.

A state statute outlawing "yellow dog contracts" is an unconstitutional infringement of the due process clause of the Fourteenth Amendment. This is deemed violative of personal liberty and the right of private property.

Railway Mail Association v. Corsi: 326 U.S. 88 (1945). Opinion: Reed, J. No dissent.

A state constitution may forbid that a labor organization of government employees deny to any person membership by reason of his race, creed, or color, equal treatment in designation for employment, promotion, or dismissal by any employer. This case arose in New York.

American Federation of Labor v. American Sash and Door Co.: 335 U.S. 538 (1949). Opinion: Black, J. No dissent.

A state legislature (here Arizona) can select one area and prohibit employment discrimination against nonunion workers while not prohibiting discrimination against union workers. This is not a violation of equal protecton.

Garner v. Teamsters, Chauffeurs and Helpers Local Union No. 776 (A.F.L.): 346 U.S. 485 (1953). Opinion: Jackson, J. No dissent.

When Congress has acted in an area in which the Congress evidently considers that uniform regulation is necessary, state legislation is inoperative. Here a Pennsylvania statute duplicated remedies (to be applied in state courts) provided by the National Labor Relations Act.

International Association of Machinists v. Gonzales: 356 U.S. 617 (1958). Opinion: Frankfurter, J. Dissenting: Warren, C.J., and Douglas, J. Abstaining: Black, J.

The National Labor Relations Act does not prohibit suit in a state court by an expelled union member for restoration of his membership and for damages for illegal expulsion.

International Union (UAW-CIO) v. Russell: 356 U.S. 634 (1958). Opinion: Burton, J. Dissenting: Warren, C.J., and Douglas, J. Abstaining: Black, J.

A damage suit in a state court by a nonunion employee kept out of a plant by mass picketing and threats of violence during a strike is not prohibited by the National Labor Relations Act. There was no need to act through the NLRB. The case came out of Alabama.

NOTE:

Lincoln makes clear that the states have the right to regulate to the point of prohibition union security contracts with employers so long as there is no conflict with some superior constitutional or statutory provision. The case is noteworthy for at least two reasons. First, it illustrates how counsel attempts to cover all possible points. Here four points of constitutional attack are made but all fail. Second, the clear reasoning of the Court in the closing paragraph of the opinion is worth more than passing notice.

Euclid v. Ambler Realty Co.
272 U.S. 365; 47 S.Ct. 114; 71 L.Ed. 303 (1926)

(The village of Euclid, Ohio, adopted a zoning ordinance restricting the use of land. The land owned by the Ambler Realty Co. was all zoned residential, and had been held for years for the purpose of developing it for industrial use. Since land for such use is of much greater value than land used for residential purposes, the ordinance was challenged as depriving the company of property without due process of law contrary to the Fourteenth Amendment.)

Vote: 6-3

Mr. Justice Sutherland delivered the opinion of the Court:

. . . The ordinance now under review, and all similar laws and regulations, must find their justification in some aspect of the police power, asserted for the public welfare. The line which in this field separates the legitimate from the illegitimate assumption of power is not capable of precise delimitation. It varies with circumstances and conditions. A regulatory zoning ordinance, which would be clearly valid as applied to the great cities, might be clearly invalid as applied to rural communities. In solving doubts, the maxim *"sic utere tuo ut alienum non laedas,"* which lies at the foundation of so much of the common law of nuisances, ordinarily will furnish a fairly helpful clew. And the law of nuisances, likewise, may be consulted, not for the purpose of controlling, but for the helpful aid of its analogies in the process of ascertaining the scope of the power. Thus the question whether the power exists to forbid the erection of a building of a particular kind or for a particular use, like the question whether a particular thing is a nuisance, is to be determined, not by an abstract consideration of the building or of the thing considered apart, but by considering it in connection with the circumstances and the locality. . . . A nuisance may merely be a right thing in the wrong place, like a pig in the parlor instead of the barnyard. If the validity of the legislative classification for zoning purpose be fairly debatable, the legislative judgment must be allowed to control. . . .

. . . The serious question in the case arises over the provisions of the ordinance excluding from residential districts apartment houses, business houses, retail stores and shops, and other like establishments. This question involves the validity of what is really the crux of the more recent zoning legislation, namely, the creation and maintenance of residential districts, from which business and trade of every sort, including hotels and apartment houses, are excluded. Upon that question this court has not thus far spoken. The decisions of the state courts are numerous and conflicting; but those which broadly sustain the power greatly outnumber those which deny it altogether or narrowly limit it, and it is very apparent that there is a constantly increasing tendency in the direction of the broader view.

What would be the effect of a restraint imposed by one or more of the innumerable provisions of the ordinance, considered apart, upon the value or marketability of the lands, is neither disclosed by the bill nor by the evidence, and we are afforded no basis, apart from mere speculation, upon which to rest a conclusion that it or they would have any appreciable effect upon those matters. Under these circumstances, therefore, it is enough for us to determine, as we do, that the ordinance in its general scope and dominant features, so far as its provisions are here involved, is a valid exercise of authority, leaving other provisions to be dealt with as cases arise directly involving them.

And this is in accordance with the traditional policy of this court. In the realm of constitutional law, especially, this court has perceived the embarrassment which is likely to result from an attempt to formulate rules or decide questions beyond the necessities of the immediate issue. It has preferred to follow the method of a gradual approach to the general by a systematically guarded application and extension of constitutional principles to particular cases as they arise, rather than by out of hand attempts to establish general rules to which future cases must be fitted. This process applies with peculiar force to the solution of questions arising under the due process clause of the Constitution as applied to the exercise of the flexible powers of police, with which we are here concerned.

Decree reversed.

Mr. Justice VanDevanter, Mr. Justice McReynolds, and Mr. Justice Butler dissented without reported opinion.

RELATED CASES:

Chicago, Burlington and Quincy Ry. Co. v. Illinois: 200 U.S. 561 (1906). Opinion: Harlan, J. Dissenting: Brewer, J.

It was not deprivation of property without due process nor denial of equal protection of the laws to force a railroad to move a bridge and culvert and appurtenances in order to care for increased artificial drainage into a creek. The police power covers regulations (here by drainage commissioners) designed to promote the public convenience or the general prosperity.

Reinman v. Little Rock: 237 U.S. 171 (1915). Opinion: Pitney, J. No dissent.

A city ordinance making it unlawful to conduct the business of a livery stable in certain defined portions of that city was not unconstitutional as depriving an owner of a livery stable already established within that district of his property without due process of law or as denying him equal protection of the law.

Hadacheck v. Los Angeles: 239 U.S. 394 (1915). Opinion: McKenna, J. No dissent.

A city ordinance prohibiting the manufacture of bricks within specified limits of the city is not unconstitutional as depriving an owner of a brick factory of his property without due process of law or as denying him equal protection of the laws.

Cusack Co. v. Chicago: 242 U.S. 526 (1917). Opinion: Clarke, J. Dissenting: McKenna, J.

An ordinance of the City of Chicago prohibiting billboards over a certain size in residential areas without securing the written consent of a majority of the property owners on both sides of the street was valid as a proper exercise of the police power. This decision was not as all-inclusive as *Euclid.*

St. Louis Poster Advertising Co. v. City of St. Louis: 249 U.S. 269 (1919). Opinion: Holmes, J. No dissent.

Aesthetic considerations in zoning regulations are secondary to the main consideration of health, morals, and safety.

Village of Belle Terre v. Boraas: 416 U.S. 39 (1974). Opinion: Douglas, J. Dissenting: Brennan and Marshall, JJ.

A municipal ordinance may restrict land use to one-family dwelling houses, that is, houses occupied by no more than two persons not related by blood, adoption, or marriage. The police power includes the power to lay out zones where family values, youth values, and the blessings of quiet seclusion and clean air make the area a sanctuary for people.

NOTE:

Zoning legislation based on the state's power to care for the safety, health, morals, and general welfare of the community has long been regarded as valid. *Euclid* is probably the leading case on this. Only recently has the Court gone beyond the matters of safety, health, and morals to include aesthetic considerations as a proper basis for such legislation.

Berman v. Parker
348 U.S. 26; 75 S.Ct. 98; 99 L.Ed. 27 (1954)

(The District of Columbia Redevelopment Act was challenged as involving improper taking of property. The Act created a land agency with power to prepare a comprehensive plan for the elimination and prevention of slums and substandard housing conditions. The appellants objected to the appropriation of their property for the purposes of this project.)

Vote: 8-0

Mr. Justice Douglas delivered the opinion of the Court:

. . . The power of Congress over the District of Columbia includes all the legislative powers which a state may exercise over its affairs. . . . We deal, in other words, with what traditionally has been known as the police power. An attempt to define its reach or trace its outer limits is fruitless, for each case must turn on its own facts. The definition is essentially the product of legislative determinations addressed to the purposes of government, purposes neither abstractly nor historically capable of complete definition. Subject to specific constitutional limitations, when the legislature has spoken, the public interest has been declared in terms well-nigh conclusive. In such cases the legislature, not the judiciary, is the main guardian of the public needs to be served by social legislation, whether it be Congress legislating concerning the District of Columbia . . . or the States legislating concerning local affairs. . . . This principle admits of no exception merely because the power of eminent domain is involved. The role of the judiciary in determining whether that power is being exercised for a public purpose is an extremely narrow one. . . .

We do not sit to determine whether a particular housing project is or is not desirable. The concept of the public welfare is broad and inclusive. . . . The values it represents are spiritual as well as physical, aesthetic as well as monetary. It is within the power of the legislature to determine that the community should be beautiful as well as healthy, spacious as well as clean, well-balanced as well as carefully patrolled. In the present case, the Congress and its authorized agencies have made determinations that take into account a wide variety of values. It is not for us to reappraise them. If those who govern the District of Columbia decide that the Nation's capital should be beautiful as well as sanitary, there is nothing in the Fifth Amendment that stands in the way.

Once the object is within the authority of Congress, the right to realize it through the exercise of eminent domain is clear. For the power of eminent domain is merely the means to the end. . . . Once the object is within the authority of Congress, the means by which it will be attained is also for Congress to determine. Here one of the means chosen is the use of private enterprise for redevelopment of the area. . . .

It is not for the courts to oversee the choice of the boundary line nor to sit in review on the size of a particular project area. Once the question of the public purpose has been decided, the amount and character of land to be taken for the project and the need for a particular tract to complete the integrated plan rests in the discretion of the legislative branch. . . .

The rights of these property owners are satisfied when they receive that just compensation which the Fifth Amendment exacts as the price of the taking.

The judgment of the District Court, as modified by this opinion, is affirmed.

Affirmed.

(Due to the death of Mr. Justice Jackson, the Court had only eight members sitting at this time.)

NOTE:

Berman v. *Parker* is the case in which the Court definitely first used the concept of aesthetic values as justification for this type of legislative action. While this case arose in the District of Columbia, the federal government there has power comparable to that of each of the states so presumably the same agreement could be used for state action.

Jacobson v. Massachusetts
197 U.S. 11; 25 S.Ct. 358; 49 L.Ed. 643 (1905)

(Under the statutes of Massachusetts, the Board of Health of Cambridge, Mass., adopted a regulation requiring that all persons not recently vaccinated be vaccinated against smallpox. Jacobson was convicted of failure to comply with the regulations. Jacobson claimed a violation of his rights under the Preamble of the Constitution as well as under the guarantees of the Fourteenth Amendment.)

Vote: 7-2

Mr. Justice Harlan delivered the opinion of the Court:

. . . We come, then, to inquire whether any right given or secured by the Constitution is invaded by the statute as interpreted by the state court. The defendant insists that his liberty is invaded when the state subjects him to fine or imprisonment for neglecting or refusing to submit to vaccination; that a compulsory vaccination law is unreasonable, arbitrary, and oppressive, and, therefore, hostile to the inherent right of every freeman to care for his own body and health in such way as to him seems best; and that the execution of such a law against one who objects to vaccination, no matter for what reason, is nothing short of an assault upon his person. But the liberty secured by the Constitution of the United States to every person within its jurisdiction does not import an absolute right in each person to be, at all times and in all circumstances, wholly freed from restraint. There are manifold restraints to which every person is necessarily subject for the common good. On any other basis organized society could not exist with safety to its members. Society based on the rule that each one is a law unto himself would soon be confronted with disorder and anarchy. . . .

Looking at the propositions embodied in the defendant's rejected offers of proof, it is clear that they are more formidable by their number than by their inherent value. Those offers in the main seem to have had no purpose except to state the general theory of those of the medical profession who attach little or no value to vaccination as a means of preventing the spread of smallpox, or who think that vaccination causes other diseases of the body. What everybody knows the court must know, and therefore the state court judicially knew, as this court knows, that an opposite theory accords with the common belief, and is maintained by high medical authority. We must assume that, when the statute in question was passed, the legislature of Massachusetts was not unaware of these opposing theories, and was compelled, of necessity, to choose between them. It was not compelled to commit a matter involving the public health and safety to the final decision of a court or jury. It is no part of the function of a court or a jury to determine which one of two modes was likely to be the most effective for the protection of the public against disease. That was for the legislative department to determine in the light of all the information it had or could obtain. It could not properly abdicate its function to guard the public health and safety. The state legislature proceeded upon the theory which recognized vaccination as at least an effective, if not the best-known, way in which to meet and suppress the evils of a smallpox epidemic that imperilled an entire population. Upon what sound principles as to the relations existing between the different departments of government can the court review this action of the legislature? If there is any such power in the judiciary to review legislative action in respect of a matter affecting the general welfare, it can only be when that which the legislature has done comes within the rule that, if a statute purporting to have been enacted to protect the public health, the public morals, or the public safety, has no real or substantial relation to those objects, or is, beyond all question, a plain, palpable invasion of rights secured by the fundamental law, it is the duty of the courts to so adjudge, and thereby give effect to the Constitution. . . .

Whatever may be thought of the expediency of this statute, it cannot be affirmed to be, beyond question, in palpable conflict with the Constitution. Nor, in view of the methods employed to stamp out the disease of smallpox, can anyone confidently assert that the means prescribed by the state to that end has no real or substantial relation to the protection of the public health and the public safety. . . .

We now decide only that the statute covers the present case, and that nothing clearly appears that would justify this court in holding it to be unconstitutional and inoperative in its application to the plaintiff in error.

The judgment of the court below must be affirmed.

It is so ordered.

Mr. Justice Brewer and Mr. Justice Peckham dissented without opinion.

RELATED CASES:

Boston Beer Co. v. Massachusetts: 97 U.S. 25 (1878). Opinion: Bradley, J. No dissent.

The character of a corporation cannot prevent the state legislature (as an impairment of contract) from prohibiting the sale of liquor. The legislature cannot divest itself of the police power by entering into a contract.

Mugler v. Kansas: 123 U.S. 623 (1887). Opinion: Harlan, J. No dissent.

Here a state prohibition act was sustained but the Court noted that not every statute enacted ostensibly for the promotion of the public welfare is to be regarded as a proper use of the police power. The courts must judge cases as they arise. The effect of liquor is common knowledge, and courts may take judicial notice of this.

Powell v. Pennsylvania: 127 U.S. 678 (1888). Opinion: Harlan, J. Dissenting: Field, J.

In this case a statute prohibiting the manufacture and sale of "oleomargarine butter" was upheld. The Court held that there must be a presumption that the legislature had acted reasonably in passing the statute. This was upheld as a health measure. The state can prevent fraud and misrepresentation.

Buck v. Bell: 274 U.S. 200 (1927). Opinion: Holmes, J. Dissenting: Butler, J.

Compulsory sterilization is valid as an exercise of police power. "The principle that maintains compulsory vaccination is broad enough to cover cutting the Fallopian tubes. . . . Three generations of imbeciles are enough." Bodily privacy was involved. This is an example of substantive due process. The case arose in Virginia.

Liggett Co. v. Baldridge: 278 U.S. 105 (1928). Opinion: Sutherland, J. Dissenting: Holmes and Brandeis, JJ.

A Pennsylvania statute was held invalid as a denial of due process. The statute required every drug store to be operated by a pharmacist and that when drug stores were owned by corporations, associations, or partnerships, all partners or members must be licensed pharmacists. The Court held that there must be some reasonable connection between the legislation and the desired objective. The real purpose of the legislation apparently was to restrict chain drug stores.

Skinner v. Oklahoma: 316 U.S. 535 (1942). Opinion: Douglas, J. No dissent.

Here the Court held void Oklahoma's Habitual Criminal Sterilization Act. Criminals in this instance were defined as those who had been previously convicted two or more times for crimes amounting to felonies involving moral turpitude. The statute was held void on the basis of denial of equal protection in classification of felonies. The exceptions made the classification unreasonable.

NOTE:

Jacobson reiterated the *Munn* rule of "presumed validity." The justices may have been aided in their acceptance of the statute by their obvious approval of the legislative purpose.

Roe v. Wade
410 U.S. 113; 93 S.Ct. 705; 35 L.Ed. 2d 147 (1973)

(Under Texas statutes abortions were prohibited except after medical advice for the purpose of saving the life of the mother. Proceeding under the pseudonym of Jane Roe, a federal class action was instituted against the District Attorney of Dallas County challenging the validity of the statutes. Her life did not appear to be threatened by a continuation of the pregnancy.)

Vote: 7-2

Mr. Justice Blackmun delivered the opinion of the Court:

Jane Roe, a single woman who was residing in Dallas County, Texas, instituted this federal action in March 1970 against the District Attorney of the county. She sought a declaratory judgment that the Texas criminal abortion statutes were unconstitutional on their face, and an injunction restraining the defendant from enforcing the statutes.

Roe alleged that she was unmarried and pregnant; that she wished to terminate her pregnancy by an abortion "performed by a competent, licensed physician, under safe, clinical conditions"; that she was unable to get a "legal" abortion in Texas because her life did not appear to be threatened by the continuation of her pregnancy; and that she could not afford to travel to another jurisdiction in order to secure a legal abortion under safe conditions. She claimed that the Texas statutes were unconstitutionally vague and that they abridged her right of personal privacy, protected by the First, Fourth, Fifth, Ninth, and Fourteenth Amendments. By an amendment to her complaint Roe purported to sue "on behalf of herself and all other women" similarly situated.

A. *Jane Roe.* Despite the use of the pseudonym, no suggestion is made that Roe is a fictitious person. For purposes of her case, we accept as true, and as established, her existence; her pregnant state, as of the inception of her suit in March 1970 and as late as May 21 of that year when she filed an alias affidavit with the District Court; and her inability to obtain a legal abortion in Texas.

Viewing Roe's case as of the time of its filing and thereafter until as late as May, there can be little dispute that it then presented a case or controversy and that, wholly apart from the class aspects, she, as a pregnant single woman thwarted by the Texas criminal abortion laws, had standing to challenge those statutes. . . .

The usual rule in federal cases is that an actual controversy must exist at stages of appellate or certiorari review; and not simply at the date the action is initiated. . . .

But when, as here, pregnancy is a significant fact in the litigation, the normal 266-day human gestation period is so short that the pregnancy will come to term before the usual appellate process is complete. If that termination makes a case moot, pregnancy litigation seldom will survive much beyond the trial stage, and appellate review will be effectively denied. Our law should not be that rigid. Pregnancy often comes more than once to the same woman, and in the general population, if man is to survive, it will always be with us. Pregnancy provides a classic justification for a conclusion of nonmootness. It truly could be "capable of repetition, yet evading review." . . .

We therefore agree with the District Court that Jane Roe had standing to undertake this litigation, that she presented a justiciable controversy, and that the termination of her 1970 pregnancy has not rendered her case moot. . . .

It is thus apparent that at common law, at the time of the adoption of our Constitution, and throughout the major portion of the 19th century, abortion was viewed with less disfavor than under most American statutes currently in effect.

Phrasing it another way, a woman enjoyed a substantially broader right to terminate a pregnancy than she does in most States today. At least with respect to the early stage of pregnancy, and very possibly without such a limitation, the opportunity to make this choice was present in this country well into the 19th century. Even later, the law continued for some time to treat less punitively an abortion procured in early pregnancy. . . .

Three reasons have been advanced to explain historically the enactment of criminal abortion laws in the 19th century and to justify their continued existence.

It has been argued occasionally that these laws were the product of a Victorian social concern to discourage illicit sexual conduct. Texas, however, does not advance this justification in the present case, and it appears that no court or commentator has taken the argument seriously. The appellants and *amici* contend, moreover, that this is not a proper state purpose at all and suggest that, if it were, the Texas statutes are overbroad in protecting it since the law fails to distinguish between married and unwed mothers.

A second reason is concerned with abortion as a medical procedure. When most criminal abortion laws were first enacted, the procedure was a hazardous one for the woman. This was particularly true prior to the development of antisepsis. Antiseptic techniques, of course, were based on discoveries by Lister, Pasteur, and others first announced in 1867, but were not generally accepted and employed until about the turn of the century. Abortion mortality was high. Even after 1900, and perhaps until as late as the development of antibiotics in the 1940's, standard modern techniques such as dilation and curettage were not nearly so safe as they are today. Thus it has been argued that a State's real concern in enacting a criminal abortion law was to protect the pregnant woman, that is, to restrain her from submitting to a procedure that placed her life in serious jeopardy.

Modern medical techniques have altered this situation. Appellants and various *amici* refer to medical data indicating that abortion in early pregnancy, that is, prior to the end of first trimester, although not without its risk, is now relatively safe. Mortality rates for women undergoing early abortions, where the procedure is legal, appear to be as low as or lower than the rates for normal childbirth. Consequently, any interest of the State in protecting the woman from an inherently hazardous procedure, except when it would be equally dangerous for her to forgo it, has largely disappeared. Of course, important state interests in the area of health and medical standards do remain. The State has a legitimate interest in seeing to it that abortion, like any other medical procedure, is performed under circumstances that insure maximum safety for the patient. This interest obviously extends at least to the performing physician and his staff, to the facilities involved, to the availability of after-care, and to adequate provision for any complication or emergency that might arise. The prevalence of high mortality rates at illegal "abortion mills" strengthens, rather than weakens, the State's interest in regulating the conditions under which abortions are performed. Moreover, the risk to the woman increases as her pregnancy continues. Thus the State retains a definite interest in protecting the woman's own health and safety when an abortion is proposed at a late stage of pregnancy.

The third reason is the State's interest—some phrase it in terms of duty—in protecting prenatal life. Some of the argument for this justification rests on the theory that a new human life is present from the moment of conception. The State's interest and general obligation to protect life then extends, it is argued, to prenatal life. Only when the life of the pregnant mother herself is at stake, balanced against the life she carries within her, should the interest of the embryo or fetus not prevail. Logically, of course, a legitimate state interest in this area need not stand or fall on acceptance of the belief that life begins at conception or at some other point prior to live birth. In assessing the State's interest, recognition may be given to the less rigid claim that as long as at least *potential* life is involved, the State may assert interests beyond the protection of the pregnant woman alone. . . .

It is with these interests, and the weight to be attached to them, that this case is concerned.

The Constitution does not explicitly mention any right of privacy. In a line of decisions, however, going back perhaps as far as *Union Pacific R. Co.* v. *Botsford*, 141 U.S. 250, 251 (1891), the Court has recognized that a right of personal privacy, or a guarantee of certain areas or zones of privacy, does exist under the Constitution. In varying contexts the Court or individual Justices have indeed found at least the roots of that right in the First Amendment, *Stanley* v. *Georgia*, 394 U.S. 557, 564 (1969); in the Fourth and Fifth Amendments, *Terry* v. *Ohio*, 392 U.S. 1, 8-9 (1968), *Katz* v. *United States*, 389 U.S. 347, 350 (1967); *Boyd* v. *United States*, 116 U.S. 616 (1886), see *Olmstead* v. *United States*, 277 U.S. 438, 478 (1928) (Brandeis, J., dissenting); in the penumbras of the Bill of Rights, *Griswold* v. *Connecticut*, 381 U.S. 479, 484-485 (1965); in the Ninth Amendment, *id.*, at 486 (Goldberg, J., concurring); or in the concept of liberty guaranteed by the first section of the Fourteenth Amendment, see *Meyer* v. *Nebraska*, 262 U.S. 390, 399 (1923). These decisions make it clear that only personal rights that can be deemed "fundamental" or "implicit in the concept of ordered liberty," *Palko* v. *Connecticut*, 302 U.S. 319, 325 (1937), are included in this guarantee of personal privacy. They also make it clear that the right has some extension to activities relating to marriage, *Loving* v. *Virginia*, 388 U.S. 1, 12 (1967), procreation, *Skinner* v. *Oklahoma*, 316 U.S. 535, 541-542 (1942), contraception, *Eisenstadt* v. *Baird*, 405 U.S. 438, 453-454 (1972); *id.*, at 460, 463-465 (White, J., concurring), family relationships, *Prince* v. *Massachusetts*, 321 U.S. 158, 166 (1944), and child rearing and education, *Pierce* v. *Society of Sisters*, 268 U.S. 510, 535 (1925), *Meyer* v. *Nebraska, supra.*

This right of privacy, whether it be founded in the Fourteenth Amendment's concept of personal liberty and restrictions upon state action, as we feel it is, or, as the District Court determined, in the Ninth Amendment's reservation of rights to the people, is broad enough to encompass a woman's decision whether or not to terminate her pregnancy. The detriment that the State would impose upon the pregnant woman by denying this choice altogether is apparent. Specific and direct harm medically diagnosable even in early pregnancy may be involved. Maternity, or additional offspring, may force upon the woman a distressful life and future. Psychological harm may be imminent. Mental and physical health may be taxed by child care. There is also the distress, for all concerned, associated with the unwanted child, and there is the problem of bringing a child into a family already unable, psychologically and otherwise, to care for it. In other cases, as in this one, the additional difficulties and continuing stigma of unwed motherhood may be involved. All there are factors the woman and her responsible physician necessarily will consider in consultation.

On the basis of elements such as these, appellants and some *amici* argue that the woman's right is absolute and that she is entitled to terminate her pregnancy at whatever time, in whatever way, and for whatever reason she alone chooses. With this we do not agree. Appellants' arguments that Texas either has no valid interest at all in regulating the abortion decision, or no interest strong enough to support any limitation upon the woman's sole determination, is unpersuasive. The Court's decisions recognizing a right of privacy also acknowledge that some state regulation in areas protected by that right is appropriate. As noted above, a state may properly assert important interests in safeguarding health, in maintaining medical standards, and in protecting potential life. At some point in pregnancy, these respective interests become sufficiently compelling to sustain regulation of the factors that govern the abortion decision. The privacy right involved, therefore, cannot be said to be absolute. In fact, it is not clear to us that the claim asserted by some *amici* that one has an unlimited right to do with one's body as one pleases bears a close relationship to the right of privacy previously articulated in the Court's decisions. The Court has refused to recognize an unlimited right of this kind in the past. *Jacobson* v. *Massachusetts*, 197 U.S. 11 (1905) (vaccination); *Buck* v. *Bell*, 274 U.S. 200 (1927) (sterilization).

We therefore conclude that the right of personal privacy includes the abortion decision, but that this right is not unqualified and must be considered against important state interests in regulation. . . .

Although the results are divided, most of these courts have agreed that the right of privacy, however based, is broad enough to cover the abortion decision; that the right, nonetheless, is not absolute and is subject to some limitations; and that at some point the state interests as to protection of health, medical standards, and prenatal life, become dominant. We agree with this approach.

Where certain "fundamental rights" are involved, the Court has held that regulation limiting these rights may be justified only by a "compelling state interest." . . .

The appellee and certain *amici* argue that the fetus is a "person" within the language and meaning of the Fourteenth Amendment. In support of this they outline at length and in detail the well-known facts of fetal development. If this suggestion of personhood is established, the appellant's case, of course, collapses, for the fetus' right to life is then guaranteed specifically by the Amendment. The appellant conceded as much on reargument. On the other hand, the appellee conceded on reargument that no case could be cited that holds that a fetus is a person within the meaning of the Fourteenth Amendment.

The Constitution does not define "person" in so many words. Section 1 of the Fourteenth Amendment contains three references to "person." The first, in defining "citizens," speaks of "persons born or naturalized in the United States." The word also appears both in the Due Process Clause and in the Equal Protection Clause. "Person" is used in other places in the Constitution: in the listing of qualifications for representatives and senators, Art. I, § 2, cl. 2, and § 3, cl. 3; in the Apportionment Clause, Art. I, § 2, cl. 3; in the Migration and Importation provision, Art. I, § 9, cl. 1; in the Emolument Clause, Art. I, § 9, cl. 8; in the Electors provisions, Art. II, § 1, cl. 2, and the superseded cl. 3; in the provision outlining qualifications for the office of President, Art. II, § 1, cl. 5; in the Extradition provisions, Art. IV, § 2, cl. 2, and the superseded Fugitive Slave cl. 3; and in the Fifth, Twelfth, and Twenty-second Amendments as well as in § § 2 and 3 of the Fourteenth Amendment. But in nearly all these instances, the use of the word is such that it has application only postnatally. None indicates, with any assurance, that it has any possible pre-natal application.

All this, together with our observation, *supra*, that throughout the major portion of the 19th century prevailing legal abortion practices were far freer than they are today, persuades us that the word "person," as used in the Fourteenth Amendment, does not include the unborn. This is in accord with the results reached in those few cases where the issue has been squarely presented. . . .

. . . We need not resolve the difficult question of when life begins. When those trained in the respective disciplines of medicine, philosophy, and theology are unable to arrive at any consensus, the judiciary, at this point in the development of man's knowledge, is not in a position to speculate as to the answer.

It should be sufficient to note briefly the wide divergence of thinking on this most sensitive and difficult question. There has always been strong support for the view that life does not begin until live birth. . . .

Perfection of the interests involved, again, has generally been contingent upon live birth. In short, the unborn have never been recognized in the law as persons in the whole sense.

In view of all this, we do not agree that, by adopting one theory of life, Texas may override the rights of the pregnant woman that are at stake. We repeat, however, that the State does have an important and legitimate interest in preserving and protecting the health of the pregnant woman, whether she be a resident of the State or a nonresident who seeks medical consultation and treatment there, and that it has still *another* important and legitimate interest in protecting the potentiality of human life. These interests are separate and distinct. Each grows in substantiality as the woman approaches term and, at a point during pregnancy, each becomes "compelling."

With respect to the State's important and legitimate interest in the health of the mother, the "compelling" point, in the light of present medical knowledge, is at approximately the end of the first trimester. This is so because of the now established medical fact, referred to above at p. 724, that until the end of the first trimester mortality in abortion is less than mortality in normal childbirth. It follows that, from and after this point, a State may regulate the abortion procedure to the extent that the regulation reasonably relates to the preservation and protection of maternal health. . . .

This means, on the other hand, that, for the period of pregnancy prior to this "compelling" point, the attending physician, in consultation with his patient, is free to determine, without regulation by the State, that in his medical judgment the patient's pregnancy should be terminated. If that decision is reached, the judgment may be effectuated by an abortion free of interference by the State.

With respect to the State's important and legitimate interest in potential life, the "compelling" point is at viability. This is so because the fetus then presumably has the capability of meaningful life outside the mother's womb. State regulation protective of fetal life after viability thus has both logical and biological justifications. If the State is interested in protecting fetal life after viability, it may go so far as to proscribe abortion during that period except when it is necessary to preserve the life or health of the mother.

Measured against these standards, Art. 1196 of the Texas Penal Code, in restricting legal abortions to those "procured or attempted by medical advice for the purpose of saving the life of the mother," sweeps too broadly. The statute makes no distinction between abortions performed early in pregnancy and those performed later, and it limits to a single reason, "saving" the mother's life, the legal justification for the procedure. The statute, therefore, cannot survive the constitutional attack made upon it here. . . .

This holding, we feel, is consistent with the relative weights of the respective interests involved, with the lessons and example of medical and legal history, with the lenity of the common law, and with the demands of the profound problems of the present day. The decision leaves the State free to place increasing restrictions on abortion as the period of pregnancy lengthens, so long as those restrictions are tailored to the recognized state interests. The decision vindicates the right of the physician to administer medical treatment according to his professional judgment up to the points where important state interests provide compelling justifications for intervention. Up to those points the abortion decision in all its aspects is inherently, and primarily, a medical decision, and basic responsibility for it must rest with the physician. If an individual practitioner abuses the privilege of exercising proper medical judgment, the usual remedies, judicial and intra-professional, are available.

Our conclusion that Art. 1196, is unconstitutional means, of course, that the Texas abortion statutes, as a unit, must fall. The exception of Art. 1196 cannot be stricken separately, for then the State is left with a statute proscribing all abortion procedures no matter how medically urgent the case.

Although the District Court granted plaintiff Roe declaratory relief, it stopped short of issuing an injunction against enforcement of the Texas statutes. The Court has recognized that different considerations enter into a federal court's decision as to declaratory relief, on the one hand, and injunctive relief, on the other. *Zwickler* v. *Koota*, 389 U.S. 241, 252-255 (1967); *Dombrowski* v. *Pfister*, 380 U.S. 479 (1965). We are not dealing with a statute that, on its face, appears to abridge free expression, an area of particular concern under *Dombrowski* and refined in *Younger* v. *Harris*, 401 U.S., at 50.

We find it unnecessary to decide whether the District Court erred in withholding injunctive relief, for we assume the Texas prosecutorial authorities will give full credence to this decision that the present criminal abortion statutes of that State are unconstitutional.

The judgment of the District Court as to intervenor Hallford is reversed, and Dr. Hallford's complaint in intervention is dismissed. In all other respects the judgment of the District Court is affirmed. Costs are allowed to the appellee.

It is so ordered.

Affirmed in part and reversed in part.

Mr. Justice Rehnquist, dissenting.

The Court's opinion brings to the decision of this troubling question both extensive historical fact and a wealth of legal scholarship. While its opinion thus commands my respect, I find myself nonetheless in fundamental disagreement with those parts of it which invalidate the Texas statute in question, and therefore dissent.

The Court's opinion decides that a State may impose virtually no restriction on the performance of abortions during the first trimester of pregnancy. Our previous decisions indicate that a necessary predicate for such an opinion is a plaintiff who was in her first trimester of pregnancy at some time during the pendency of her law suit. While a party may vindicate his own constitutional rights, he may not seek vindication for the rights of others. *Moose Lodge No. 107* v. *Irvis*, 407 U.S. 163 (1972); *Sierra Club* v. *Morton*, 405 U.S. 727 (1972). The Court's statement of facts in this case makes clear, however, that the record in no way indicates the presence of such a plaintiff. We know only that plaintiff Roe at the time of filing her complaint was a pregnant woman; for aught that appears in this record, she may have been in her *last* trimester of pregnancy as of the date the complaint was filed.

. . . In deciding such a hypothetical lawsuit the Court departs from the long-standing admonition that it should never "formulate a rule of constitutional law broader than is required by the precise facts to which it is to be applied." . . .

. . . I have difficulty in concluding, as the Court does, that the right of "privacy" is involved in this case. Texas by the statute here challenged bars the performance of a medical abortion by a licensed physician on a plaintiff such as Roe. A transaction resulting in an operation such as this is not "private" in the ordinary usage of that word. . . .

. . . But that liberty is not guaranteed absolutely against deprivation, but only against deprivation without due process of law. The test traditionally applied in the area of social and economic legislation is whether or not a law such as that challenged has a rational relation to a valid state objective. . . .

. . . The decision here to break the term of pregnancy into three distinct terms and to outline the permissible restrictions the State may impose in each one, for example, partakes more of judicial legislation than it does of a determination of the intent of the drafters of the Fourteenth Amendment.

The fact that a majority of the States, reflecting after all the majority sentiment in those States, have had restrictions on abortions for at least a century seems to me as strong an indication there is that the asserted right to an abortion is not "so rooted in the traditions and conscience of our people as to be ranked as fundamental," *Snyder* v. *Massachusetts*, 291 U.S. 97, 105 (1934). Even today, when society's views on abortion are changing, the very existence of the debate is evidence that the "right" to an abortion is not so universally accepted as the appellants would have us believe.

Even if one were to agree that the case which the Court decides were here, and that the enunciation of the substantive constitutional law in the Court's opinion were proper, the actual disposition of the case by the Court is still difficult to justify. The Texas statute is struck down *in toto*, even though the Court apparently concedes that at later periods of pregnancy Texas might impose these selfsame statutory limitations on abortion. My understanding of past practice is that a statute found to be invalid as applied to a particular plaintiff, but not unconstitutional as a whole, is not simply "struck down" but is instead declared unconstitutional as before the Court. *Yick Wo* v. *Hopkins*, 118 U.S. 356 (1886); *Street* v. *New York*, 394 U.S. 576 (1969).

For all of the foregoing reasons, I respectfully dissent.

RELATED CASES:

United States v. Vuitch: 402 U.S. 62 (1971). Opinion: Black, J. Dissenting: Harlan, Marshall, and Blackmun, JJ.

A statute of the District of Columbia forbidding abortions unless required to preserve the mother's physical or mental health was held valid. The Court noted that physicians routinely determine such judgments regarding a patient's health while making other contacts.

Doe v. Bolton: 410 U.S. 179 (1973). Opinion: Blackmun, J. Dissenting: White and Rehnquist, JJ.

A Georgia statute required that an abortion be performed in an accredited hospital, that the procedure be approved by the hospital staff abortion committee, that the performing physician's judgment be confirmed by independent examinations of the patient by two other licensed physicians, and that the patient be a resident of Georgia. The Court held all of these requirements void as violative of the rights of both patient and physician under the Fourteenth Amendment.

NOTE:

Due to the complicated argumentation of *Roe* v. *Wade*, the following is offered by way of attempted simplification. In regard to the constitutionality of state statutes prohibiting abortions, the Court held that as to the applicability to a state of the right to life guaranteed specifically by the Fourteenth Amendment, no case can be cited that holds the fetus to be a Fourteenth Amendment "person." The Court noted that "the fetus, at most, represents only the potentiality of life. . . . The unborn have never been recognized in the law as persons in the whole sense." The right to privacy implied in the Constitution "is broad enough to encompass a woman's decision whether or not to terminate her pregnancy." The state has interests as to the protection of health, medical standards, and the potentiality of human life. "These interests are separate and distinct. Each grows in substantiality as the woman approaches term and, at a point during pregnancy, each becomes 'compelling.' " The state's interest in the health of the mother becomes "compelling" at approximately the end of the first trimester. The reason for this is that until that point mortality in abortion is less than mortality in normal childbirth. Up to this point "the attending physician, in consultation with his patient, is free to determine, without regulation by the State, that in his medical judgment the patient's pregnancy should be terminated." After this point, "a State may regulate the abortion procedure to the extent that the regulation reasonably relates to the preservation and protection of maternal health." Finally, the state's interest in potential life becomes "compelling" at viability. "This is so because the fetus then presumably has the capability of meaningful life outside the mother's womb. . . . If the State is interested in protecting fetal life after viability, it may go so far as to proscribe abortion during that period except when it is necessary to preserve the life or health of the mother."

Morehead v. New York ex rel. Tipaldo
298 U.S. 587; 56 S.Ct. 918; 80 L.Ed. 1347 (1936)

(Acting under a statute of the state of New York, the State Industrial Commissioner had prescribed minimum wages for women employees. Tipaldo, manager of a laundry, was convicted and given a jail sentence for failure to obey the order of the commissioner. The substantive power of the state to enact said legislation was challenged.)

Vote: 5-4

Mr. Justice Butler delivered the opinion of the Court:

. . . The state court rightly held that the *Adkins* case controls this one and requires that relator be discharged on the ground that the legislation under which he was indicted and imprisoned is repugnant to the due process clause of the Fourteenth Amendment. . . .

. . . Having regard to the principles applied in the *Adkins* case, the state legislation fixing wages for women was repugnant to the due process clause of the Fourteenth Amendment, we so held and upon the authority of that case affirmed per curiam the decree enjoining its enforcement. It is equally plain that the judgment in the case now before us must also be affirmed.

Mr. Chief Justice Hughes dissented, with the concurrence of Mr. Justice Stone, Mr. Justice Brandeis, and Mr. Justice Cardozo:

I am unable to concur in the opinion in this case. In view of the difference between the statutes involved, I cannot agree that the case should be regarded as controlled by *Adkins* v. *Children's Hospital*, 261 U.S. 525. And I can find nothing in the Federal Constitution which denies to the State the power to protect women from being exploited by overreaching employers through the refusal of a fair wage as defined in the New York Statute and ascertained in a reasonable manner by competent authority. . . .

If liberty of contract were viewed from the standpoint of absolute right, there would be as much to be said against a regulation of the hours of labor of women as against the fixing of a minimum wage. Restriction upon hours is a restriction upon the making of contracts and upon earning power. But the right being a qualified one, we must apply in each case the test of reasonableness in the circumstances disclosed. Here, the special conditions calling for the protection of women, and for the protection of society itself, are abundantly shown. The legislation is not less in the interest of the community as a whole than in the interest of the women employees who are paid less than the value of their services. That lack must be made good out of the public purse. Granted that the burden of the support of women who do not receive a living wage cannot be transferred to employers who pay the equivalent of the service they obtain, there is no reason why the burden caused by the failure to pay that equivalent should not be placed upon those who create it. The fact that the State cannot secure the benefit to society of a living wage for women employees by any enactment which bears unreasonably upon employers does not preclude the State from seeking its objective by means entirely fair both to employers and the women employed.

In the statute before us, no unreasonableness appears. The end is legitimate and the means appropriate. I think that the act should be upheld.

Mr. Justice Stone dissented, with the concurrence of Mr. Justice Brandeis and Mr. Justice Cardozo:

While I agree with all that the Chief Justice has said, I would not make the differences between the present statute and that involved in the *Adkins* Case the sole basis of decision. I attach little importance to the fact that the earlier statute was aimed only at a starvation wage and that the present one does not prohibit such a wage unless it is also less than the reasonable value of the service. Since neither statute compels employment at any wage, I do not assume that employers in one case, more than in the other, would pay the minimum wage if the service were worth less.

The vague and general pronouncement of the Fourteenth Amendment against deprivation of liberty without due process of law is a limitation of legislative power, not a formula for its exercise. It does not purport to say in what particular manner that power shall be exerted. It makes no fine-spun distinctions between methods which the legislature may and which it may not choose to solve a pressing problem of government. It is plain too, that, unless the language of the amendment and the decisions of this Court are to be ignored, the liberty which the amendment protects is not freedom from restraint of all law or of any law which reasonable men may think an appropriate means for dealing with any of those matters of public concern with which it is the business of government to deal. There is grim irony in speaking of the freedom of contract of those who, because of their economic necessities, give their service for less than is needful to keep body and soul together. But if this is freedom of contract no one has ever denied that it is freedom which may be restrained, notwithstanding the Fourteenth Amendment, by a statute passed in the public interest. . . .

It is not for the courts to resolve doubts whether the remedy by wage regulation is as efficacious as many believe, or is better than some other, or is better even than the blind operation of uncontrolled economic forces. The legislature must be free to choose unless government is to be rendered impotent. The Fourteenth Amendment has no more embedded in the Constitution our preference for some particular set of economic beliefs, than it has adopted, in the name of liberty, the system of theology which we may happen to approve.

RELATED CASES:

Lochner v. New York: 198 U.S. 45 (1905). Opinion: Peckham, J. Dissenting: Harlan, White, Holmes, and Day, JJ.

A state statute limiting the hours of employment in bakeries was held to interfere with the right of contract under the Fourteenth Amendment (the due process clause).

Muller v. Oregon: 208 U.S. 412 (1908). Opinion: Brewer, J. No dissent.

A state statute prohibited the employment of any female in any mechanical establishment, factory, or laundry in the state for more than ten hours in any one day. The Court upheld the statute as a proper exercise of state police power and a recognition of the physical difference of women which "justified a difference in legislation." Thus the Court here took "judicial cognizance" of women as the "weaker sex." In this case, Louis D. Brandeis, counsel defending the Oregon law, presented for the first time what came to be known as the "Brandeis brief," a statement presenting the socioeconomic argument. The purpose was to set forth the facts on which a legislature might have reasonably acted. He used both foreign and state laws to bolster his argument. Justice Brewer in his opinion indicated the influence this argumentation had had on the Court's decision.

Bunting v. Oregon: 243 U.S. 426 (1917). Opinion: McKenna, J. Dissenting: White, C.J., VanDevanter and McReynolds, JJ. Abstaining: Brandeis, J.

A state statute required a ten-hour day for all workers in industry with certain exceptions. The Court sustained the act on the basis that it was an exercise of "an admitted power of government" and that nothing in the record indicated that the judgment of the legislature was erroneous as to the propriety of the legislation. This case may be regarded as having overruled *Lochner sub silento.*

Stettler v. O'Hara: 243 U.S. 629 (1917). Per Curiam. No dissent.

A statute of Oregon provided for minimum wages for women. The Court split four to four, which had the effect of sustaining the state Supreme Court's decision in favor of the law as an aid to the protection of the health and morals of women, thus a valid power of the state.

Adkins v. Children's Hospital: 261 U.S. 525 (1923). Opinion: Sutherland, J. Dissenting: Taft, C.J., and Sanford and Holmes, JJ. Abstaining: Brandeis, J.

The District of Columbia Minimum Wage Act was held invalid as contrary to due process (denial of freedom of contract, lack of adequate standards, and no consideration of value of services) under the Fifth Amendment.

NOTE:

Ever since *Adkins in* 1923 the court had consistently held that minimum wage legislation was contrary to freedom of contract as impliedly guaranteed by the "due process" and "liberty" provisions of the Fourteenth Amendment. The court had held in *Adkins* that there was lack of adequate standards in the statute, that the provisions of the statute considered only one party to the contract, and that there was no provision for consideration of the value of the services rendered by the employee in setting the minimum wage.

Justice Brandeis did not take part in *Bunting* and *Stettler* because he had been counsel when the cases began. He did not take part in *Adkins* because his daughter was a member of the District of Columbia Minimum Wage Commission.

In *Morehead* the Court held a New York state minimum wage statute to be the same as the law in question in *Adkins*. However, in the New York law there was a "value of services" standard. This decision was on June 1, 1936. Less than a year later came the *West Coast Hotel* decision on March 29,1937. Justice Roberts switched, "the switch in time that saved nine." (See Charles Leonard, *A Search for a Judicial Philosophy*, Kennikat Press, 1971.)

West Coast Hotel Co. v. Parrish
300 U.S. 379; 57 S.Ct. 578; 81 L.Ed. 703 (1937)

(The state of Washington had by statute prohibited wages below a level adequate for the maintenance of women and minors. A Commission was set up to establish standards of wages and conditions of labor for the protected groups. Elsie Parrish, a chambermaid, brought suit against the hotel to recover the difference between the wages paid her and the minimum wage fixed pursuant to the state law. The statute was attacked as repugnant to the due process clause of the Fourteenth Amendment of the Constitution.)

Vote: 5-4

Mr. Chief Justice Hughes delivered the opinion of the Court:

. . . The principle which must control our decision is not in doubt. The constitutional provision invoked is the due process clause of the Fourteenth Amendment governing the States, as the due process clause invoked in the *Adkins* case governed Congress. In each case the violation alleged by those attacking minimum wage regulation for women is deprivation of freedom of contract. What is this freedom? The Constitution does not speak of freedom of contract. It speaks of liberty and prohibits the deprivation of liberty without due process of law. In prohibiting that deprivation the Constitution does not recognize an absolute and uncontrollable liberty. Liberty in each of its phases has its history and connotation. But the liberty safeguarded is liberty in a social organization which requires the protection of law against the evils which menace the health, safety, morals and welfare of the people. Liberty under the Constitution is thus necessarily subject to the restraints of due process, and regulation which is reasonable in relation to its subject and is adopted in the interests of the community is due process. . . .

With full recognition of the earnestness and vigor with characterize the prevailing opinion in the *Adkins* case, we find it impossible to reconcile that ruling with these well-considered declarations. What can be closer to the public interest that the health of women and their protection from unscrupulous and overreaching employers? And if the protection of women is a legitimate end of the exercise of state power, how can it be said that the requirement of the payment of a minimum wage fairly fixed in order to meet the very necessities of existence is not an admissible means to that end? The legislature of the State was clearly entitled to consider the situation of women in employment, the fact that they are in the class receiving the least pay, that their bargaining power is relatively weak, and that they are the ready victims of those who would take advantage of their necessitous circumstances. The legislature was entitled to adopt measures to reduce the evils of the "sweating system," the exploiting of workers at wages so low as to be insufficient to meet the bare cost of living thus making their very helplessness the occasion of a most injurious competition. The legislature had the right to consider that its minimum wage requirements would be an important aid in carrying out its policy of protection. The adoption of similar requirements by many States evidences a deep-seated conviction both as to the presence of the evil and as to the means adapted to check it. Legislative response to that conviction cannot be regarded as arbitrary or capricious and that is all we have to decide. Even if the wisdom of the policy be regarded as debatable and its effects uncertain, still the legislature is entitled to its judgment.

There is an additional and compelling consideration which recent economic experience has brought into a strong light. The exploitation of a class of workers who are in an unequal position with respect to bargaining power and are thus relatively defenceless against the denial of a living wage is not only detrimental to their health and well being but casts a direct burden for their support upon the community. What these workers lose in wages the taxpayers are called upon to pay. The bare cost of living must be met. We may take judicial notice of the unparalleled demands for relief which arose during the recent period of depression and still continue to an alarming extent despite the degree of economic recovery which has been achieved. It is unnecessary to cite official statistics to establish what is of common knowledge through the length and breadth of the land. While in the instant case no factual brief has been presented, there is no reason to doubt that the State of Washington has encountered the same social problem that is present elsewhere. The community is not bound to provide what is in effect a subsidy for unconscionable employers. The community may direct its law-making power to correct the abuse which springs from their selfish disregard of the public interest. The argument that the legislation in question constitutes an arbitrary discrimination, because it does not extend to men, is unavailing. This Court has frequently held that the legislative authority, acting within its proper field, is not bound to extend its regulation to all cases which it might possibly reach. The legislature "is free to recognize degrees of harm and it may confine its restrictions to those classes of cases where the need is deemed to be clearest." If "the law presumably hits the evil where it is most felt, it is not to be overthrown because there are other instances to which it might have been applied." There is no "doctrinaire requirement" that the legislation should be couched in all embracing terms. . . .

Our conclusion is that the case of *Adkins* v. *Children's Hospital*, 261 U.S. 525, should be, and it is, overruled. The judgment of the Supreme Court of the State of Washington is affirmed.

Mr. Justice Sutherland dissented, with the concurrence of Mr. Justice Van-Devanter, Mr. Justice McReynolds, and Mr. Justice Butler:

. . . The principles and authorities relied upon to sustain the judgment, were considered in *Adkins* v. *Children's Hospital,* 261 U.S. 525, and *Morehead* v. *New York ex rel. Tipaldo*, 298 U.S. 587 and their lack of application to cases like the one in hand pointed out. . . .

Neither the statute involved in the *Adkins* case nor the Washington statute, so far as it is involved here, has the slightest relation to the capacity or earning power of the employee, to the number of hours which constitute the day's work, the character of the place where the work is to be done, or the circumstances or surroundings of the employment. The sole basis upon which the question of validity rests is the assumption that the employee is entitled to receive a sum of money sufficient to provide a living for her, keep her in health and preserve her morals. And as we pointed out at some length in that case (pp. 555-557), the question thus presented for the determination of the board cannot be solved by any general formula prescribed by a statutory bureau, since it is not a composite but an individual question to be answered for each individual, considered by herself. What we said further in that case (pp. 557, 559), is equally applicable here:

"The feature of this statute which, perhaps more than any other, puts upon it the stamp of invalidity is that it exacts from the employer an arbitrary payment for a purpose and upon a basis having no causal connection with his business, or the contract or the work the employee engages to do. The declared basis, as already pointed out, is not the value of the service rendered, but the extraneous circumstance that the employee needs to get a prescribed sum of money to insure her subsistence, health and morals. The ethical right of every worker, man or women, to a living wage may be conceded. One of the declared and important purposes of trade organizations is to secure it. And with that principle and with every legitimate effort to realize it in fact, no one can quarrel; but the fallacy of the proposed method of attaining it is that it assumes that every legitimate employer is bound at all events to furnish it. The moral requirement implicit in every contract of employment, *viz.*, that the amount to be paid and the service to be rendered shall bear to each other some relation of just equivalence, is completely ignored. The necessities of the employee are alone considered and these arise outside of the employment, are the same when there is no employment, and as great in one occupation as in another. . . . A statute requiring an employer to pay in money, to pay at prescribed and regular intervals, to pay the value of the services rendered, even to pay with fair relation to the extent of the benefit obtained from the service, would be understandable. But a statute which prescribes payment without regard to any of these things and solely with relation to circumstances apart from the contract of employment, the business affected by it and the work done under it, is so clearly the product of a naked, arbitrary exercise of power that it cannot be allowed to stand under the Constitution of the United States." . . .

Finally, it may be said that a statute absolutely fixing wages in the various industries at definite sums and forbidding employers and employees from contracting for any other than those designated, would probably not be thought to be constitutional. It is hard to see why the power to fix minimum wages does not connote a like power in respect of maximum wages. And yet, if both powers be exercised in such a way that the minimum and the maximum so nearly approach each other as to become substantially the same, the right to make any contract in respect of wages will have been completely abrogated. . . .

RELATED CASES:

Holden v. Hardy: 169 U.S. 366 (1898). Opinion: Brown, J. Dissenting: Brewer and Peckham, JJ.

A statute of Utah fixed an eight-hour day for the employment of men in underground mines. This was upheld as a proper exercise of state police power in the light of the inequality of employers and employees in the making of labor contracts.

United States v. Darby Lumber Co.: 312 U.S. 100 (1941). Opinion: Stone, J. No dissent.

Here the Court upheld a federal statute prohibiting the shipment in interstate commerce of certain products and commodities produced in the United States under labor conditions which fail to conform to standards set up by the act, and further requiring employers to keep records of the operations of employees. The standards in the act referred to wages, hours, and child labor.

NOTE:

The *West Coast Hotel* decision came after President Franklin Roosevelt's "Court packing" plan and the decision has been credited by some with undermining the Roosevelt packing scheme. The statute here had no "value of services" standard contrary to the New York statute of *Morehead*, so the decision of the Court in *West Coast Hotel* definitely overruled *Adkins*, and probably *sub silento* again, *Lochner*.

Hurtado v. California
110 U.S. 516; 4 S.Ct. 111; 28 L.Ed. 232 (1884)

(Hurtado was charged with first-degree murder by the district attorney in a California County Court by means of an information. Following this, Hurtado was tried by a jury, was found guilty, and was sentenced to death. He challenged the provision of the California state constitution of 1879, under which the proceedings had been carried on, as being contrary to the due process clause of the Fourteenth Amendment. His contention was that indictment by a grand jury was necessary for due process.)

Vote: 7-1

Mr. Justice Matthews delivered the opinion of the Court:

. . . "To what principle, then, are we to resort to ascertain whether this process, enacted by Congress, is due process? To this the answer must be twofold. We must examine the Constitution itself to see whether this process be in conflict with any of its provisions. If not found to be so, we must look to those settled usages and modes of proceeding existing in the common and statute law of England before the emigration of our ancestors, and which are shown not to have been unsuited to their civil and political condition by having been acted on by them after the settlement of this country."

This, it is argued, furnishes an indispensable test of what constitutes "due process of law"; that any proceeding otherwise authorized by law, which is not thus sanctioned by usage, or which supersedes and displaces one that is, cannot be regarded as due process of law.

But this inference is unwarranted. The real syllabus of the passage quoted is, that a process of law, which is not otherwise forbidden, must be taken to be due process of law, if it can show the sanction of settled usage both in England and in this country; but it by no means follows that nothing else can be due process of law. The point in the case cited arose in reference to a summary proceeding, questioned on that account, as not due process of law. The answer was; however exceptional it may be, as tested by definitions and principles of ordinary procedure, nevertheless, this, in substance, has been immemorially the actual law of the land, and, therefore, is due process of law. But to hold that such a characteristic is essential to due process of law, would be to deny every quality of the law but its age, and to render it incapable of progress or improvement. It would be to stamp upon our jurisprudence the unchangeableness attributed to the laws of the Medes and Persians. . . .

It follows that any legal proceeding enforced by public authority, whether sanctioned by age and custom, or newly devised in the discretion of the legislative power, in furtherance of the general public good, which regards and preserves these principles of liberty and justice, must be held to be due process of law. . . .

Tried by these principles, we are unable to say that the substitution for a presentment or indictment by a grand jury of the proceeding by information, after examination and commitment by a magistrate, certifying to the probable guilt of the defendant, with the right on his part to the aid of counsel, and to the crossexamination of the witnesses produced for the prosecution, is not due process of law. It is, as we have seen, an ancient proceeding at common law, which might include every case of an offense of less grade than a felony, except misprision of treason; and in every circumstance of its administration, as authorized by the statute of California, it carefully considers and guards the substantial interest of the prison. It is merely a preliminary proceeding, and can result in no final judgment, except as a consequence of a regular judicial trial, conducted precisely as in cases of indictments. . . .

For these reasons, finding no error therein, the judgment of the Supreme Court of California is affirmed.

Mr. Justice Field took no part in the case.

Mr. Justice Harlan dissented:

. . . The doctrines of the common law respecting the protection of the people in their lives, liberties and property were incorporated into the earlier constitutions of the original States. . . . These fundamental doctrines were subsequently incorporated into the Constitution of the United States. The people were not content with the provision in Section 2 of Article Three, that "the trial of all crimes, except in cases of impeachment, shall be by jury." They desired a fuller and broader enunciation of the fundamental principles of freedom, and therefore demanded that the guaranties of the rights of life, liberty, and property, which experience had proved to be essential to the safety and security of the people, should be placed beyond the danger of impairment or destruction by the general government through legislation by Congress. They perceived no reason why, in respect of those rights, the same limitations should not be imposed upon the general government that had been imposed upon the States by their own Constitutions. Hence, the prompt adoption of the original amendments, by the Fifth of which it is, among other things, provided that "no person shall be deprived of life, liberty, or property, without due process of law." This language is similar to that of the clause of the Fourteenth Amendment now under examination. That similarity was not accidental, but evinces a purpose to impose upon the States the same restrictions, in respect of proceedings involving life, liberty and property, which had been imposed upon the general government.

"Due process of law," within the meaning of the national Constitution, does not import one thing with reference to the powers of the States, and another with reference to the powers of the general government. If particular proceedings conducted under the authority of the general government, and involving life, are prohibited, because not constituting that due process of law required by the Fifth Amendment of the Constitution of the United States, similar proceedings, conducted under the authority of a State, must be deemed illegal as not being due process of law within the meaning of the Fourteenth Amendment. . . .

RELATED CASES:

Murray's Lessee v. Hoboken Land and Improvement Co.: 18 How. 272 (1856). Opinion: Curtis, J. No dissent.

A federal statute authorized the Treasury Department to issue warrants against the property of collectors of federal revenue, who owed funds to the government, without resorting to the courts. The Court held this was not taking property without due process of law. It was not contrary either (1) to constitutional provisions or (2) to historical practice, particularly under English common law. These are regarded as two of the tests of "due process." Another is essential fairness.

Pennoyer v. Neff: 95 U.S. 714 (1878). Opinion: Field, J. Dissenting: Hunt, J.

A judgment against the person is without any validity when rendered by a state court in an action upon a money-demand against a nonresident of the state who was served by publication of the summons but upon whom no personal service of process within the state was made and who did not appear.

Davidson v. New Orleans: 96 U.S. 97 (1878). Opinion: Miller, J. No dissent.

See p. 209, above.

Jordan v. Massachusetts: 225 U.S. 167 (1912). Opinion: Lurton, J. No dissent. Abstaining: Pitney, J.

One convicted by a jury and sentenced to death was not denied due process because after the verdict one of the jurors became insane and the court after an inquiry had in accordance with the established procedure of the state found by a preponderance of the evidence that the juror was of sufficient mental capacity during the trial to act as such. This case was reversed by *Duncan* v. *Louisiana*, 391 U.S. 145 (1968). See p. 168, above.

Walker v. City of Hutchinson: 352 U.S. 112 (1956). Opinion: Black, J. Dissenting: Frankfurter and Burton, JJ. Abstaining: Brennan, J.

Where no reason exists why direct notice cannot be given, notice to a landowner by newspaper publication alone is not sufficient under the due process clause of the Fourteenth Amendment to inform the landowner of a hearing to fix compensation in the condemnation of his property.

NOTE:

Hurtado illustrates nicely the flexibility of due process of law. Since the Constitution specifies that for "a capital, or otherwise infamous crime" the charges are to be presented formally by a grand jury, the federal government can use the information only for misdemeanors. The case also sets forth that indictment is not a "fundamental" right; therefore, it follows that it does not need to be applied in our unincorporated territories nor is it applied to the states under the "Gitlow doctrine."

It needs to be emphasized that while what is time-honored in procedure is regarded properly as "due process," that which is new is not on that fact alone to be regarded as not being "due process." (See interesting article by Charles Fairman, *Stanford Law Review*, December, 1949.)

Palko v. Connecticut
302 U.S. 319; 58 S.Ct. 149; 82 L.Ed. 288 (1937)

(Palko was indicted by the State of Connecticut for murder in the first degree. At a jury trial he was convicted of murder in the second degree and sentenced to life imprisonment. Upon appeal by the state the Supreme Court of Errors ordered a new trial on the basis that there had been error of law to the prejudice of the state. At the second trial, over Palko's objections of double jeopardy, added evidence was admitted and added instructions were given to the jury. This jury returned a verdict of murder in the first degree and Palko was sentenced to death. The whole proceeding was challenged as violating due process of law under the Fourteenth Amendment.)

Vote: 8-1

Mr. Justice Cardozo delivered the opinion of the Court:

. . . We have said that in appellant's view the Fourteenth Amendment is to be taken as embodying the prohibitions of the Fifth. His thesis is even broader. Whatever would be a violation of the original Bill of Rights (Amendments 1 to 8) if done by the federal government is now equally unlawful by force of the Fourteenth Amendment if done by a state. There is no such general rule.

The Fifth Amendment provides, among other things, that no person shall be held to answer for a capital or otherwise infamous crime unless on presentment or indictment of a grand jury. This court has held that, in prosecutions by a state, presentment or indictment by a grand jury may give way to informations at the instance of a public officer. *Hurtado* v. *California*, 110 U.S. 516. . . . The Fifth Amendment provides also that no person shall be compelled in any criminal case to be a witness against himself. This court has said that, in prosecutions by a state, the exemption will fail if the state elects to end it. *Twining* v. *New Jersey*, 211 U.S. 78. . . . The Sixth Amendment calls for a jury trial in criminal cases and the Seventh for a jury trial in civil cases at common law where the value in controversy shall exceed twenty dollars. This court has ruled that consistently with those amendments trial by jury may be modified by a state or abolished altogether. *Walker* v. *Sauvinet*, 92 U.S. 90; *Maxwell* v. *Dow*, 176 U.S. 581. . . . As to the Fourth Amendment, one should refer to *Weeks* v. *United States*, 232 U.S. 383, and as to other provisions of the Sixth, to *West* v. *Louisiana*, 194 U.S. 258.

On the other hand, the due process clause of the Fourteenth Amendment may make it unlawful for a state to abridge by its statutes the freedom of speech which the First Amendment safeguards against encroachment by the Congress (*De Jonge* v. *Oregon*, 299 U.S. 353; *Herndon* v. *Lowry*, 301 U.S. 242) or the like freedom of the press (*Grosjean* v. *American Press Co.*, 297 U.S. 233; *Near* v. *Minnesota*, 283 U.S. 697), or the free exercise of religion (*Hamilton* v. *University of California*, 293 U.S. 245; . . . *Pierce* v. *Society of Sisters*, 268 U.S. 510), or the right of peaceable assembly, without which speech would be unduly trammeled (*De Jonge* v. *Oregon*, 299 U.S. 353; *Herndon* v. *Lowry*, 301 U.S. 242), or the right of one accused of crime to the benefit of counsel (*Powell* v. *Alabama*, 287 U.S. 45). In these and other situations immunities that are valid as against the federal government by force of the specific pledges of particular amendments have been found to be implicit in the concept of ordered liberty, and thus, through the Fourteenth Amendment, become valid as against the states.

The line of division may seem to be wavering and broken if there is a hasty catalogue of the cases on the one side and the other. Reflection and analysis will induct a different view. There emerges the perception of a rationalizing principle which gives to discrete instances a proper order and coherence. The right to trial by jury and the immunity from prosecution except as the result of an indictment may have value and importance. Even so, they are not of the very essence of a scheme of ordered liberty. To abolish them is not to violate a "principle of justice so rooted in the traditions and conscience of our people as to be ranked as fundamental." . . . Few would be so narrow or provincial as to maintain that a fair and enlightened system of justice would be impossible without them. What is true of jury trials and indictments is true also, as the cases show, of the immunity from compulsory self-incrimination. *Twining* v. *New Jersey*, 211 U.S. 78. This too might be lost, and justice still be done. Indeed, today as in the past there are students of our penal system who look upon the immunity as a mischief rather than a benefit, and who would limit its scope or destroy it altogether. . . . The exclusion of these immunities and privileges from the privileges and immunities protected against the action of the states has not been arbitrary or casual. It has been dictated by a study and appreciation of the meaning, the essential implications, of liberty itself.

We reach a different plane of social and moral values when we pass to the privileges and immunities that have been taken over from the earlier articles of the federal Bill of Rights and brought within the Fourteenth Amendment by a process of absorption. These in their origin were effective against the federal government alone. If the Fourteenth Amendment has absorbed them, the process of absorption has had its source in the belief that neither liberty nor justice would exist if they were sacrificed. *Twining* v. *New Jersey, supra.* This is true, for illustration, of freedom of thought and speech. Of that freedom one may say that it is the matrix, the indispensable condition, of nearly every other form of freedom. With rare aberrations a pervasive recognition of that truth can be traced in our history, political and legal. So it has come about that the domain of liberty, withdrawn by the Fourteenth Amendment from encroachment by the states, has been enlarged by latter-day judgments to include liberty of the mind as well as liberty of action. . . .

Our survey of the cases serves, we think, to justify the statement that the dividing line between them, if not unfaltering throughout its course, has been true for the most part to a unifying principle. On which side of the line the case made out by the appellant has appropriate location must be the next inquiry and the final one. Is that kind of double jeopardy to which the statute has subjected him a hardship so acute and shocking that our policy will not endure it? Does it violate those "fundamental principles of liberty and justice which lie at the base of all our civil and political institutions?" . . . The answer surely must be "no." What the answer would have to be if the state were permitted after a trial free from error to try the accused over again or to bring another case against him, we have no occasion to consider. We deal with the statute before us and no other. The state is not attempting to wear the accused out by a multitude of cases with accumulated trials. It asks no more than this, that the case against him shall go on until there shall be a trial free from the corrosion of substantial legal error. . . . This is not cruelty at all, nor even vexation in any immoderate degree. If the trial had been infected with error adverse to the accused, there might have been review at his instance, and as often as necessary to purge the vicious taint. A reciprocal privilege, subject at all times to the discretion of the presiding judge . . . , has now been granted to the state. There is here no seismic innovation. The edifice of justice stands, in its symmetry, to many, greater than before.

2. The conviction of appellant is not in derogation of any privileges or immunities that belong to him as a citizen of the United States. . . .

Maxwell v. *Dow, supra*, gives all the answer that is necessary.

The judgment is affirmed.

Mr. Justice Butler dissented without opinion.

RELATED CASES:

Barron v. Baltimore: 7 Pet. 243 (1833). Opinion: Marshall, C. J. No dissent.

Provisions of the Constitution (here the Fifth Amendment) phrased in general terms apply only to the federal government and not to the states.

Maxwell v. Dow: 176 U.S. 581 (1900). Opinion: Peckham, J. Dissenting: Harlan, J.

Indictment by grand jury and trial by a jury of twelve are not guaranteed in state courts by either the due process or the privileges or immunities provisions of the Fourteenth Amendment.

Patterson v. Colorado: 205 U.S. 454 (1907). Opinion: Holmes, J. Dissenting: Harlan and Brewer, JJ.

There is no violation of the Fourteenth Amendment where a state court justice convicts a person of contempt for publication of certain articles and a cartoon which, it was charged, reflected upon the motives and conduct of the state supreme court in cases still pending and were intended to embarrass the court in the impartial administration of justice.

Twining v. New Jersey: 211 U.S. 78 (1908). Opinion: Moody, J. Dissenting: Harlan, J.

Neither the privileges or immunities guarantee nor the due process clause of the Fourteenth Amendment protects against self-incrimination in the state courts. This case was reversed by *Griffin* v. *California,* p. 261, below.

Gitlow v. New York: 268 U.S. 652 (1925). Opinion: Sanford, J. Dissenting: Holmes and Brandeis, JJ.

Where there is presented not merely the abstract doctrine of overthrowing organized government by force, violence, or unlawful means but rather advocacy of action to that end, state statutes may restrict the activity. Also, in this case the Court for the first time held that freedom of speech and press in the First Amendment are applied to the states by the due process clause of the Fourteenth Amendment.

Cassell v. Texas: 339 U.S. 282 (1950). Opinion: Reed, J. Dissenting: Jackson, J. Abstaining: Douglas, J.

The choice by jury commissioners of grand jurors only from acquaintances, and the statement by the commissioners that they knew no eligible Negroes in an area where Negroes made up a large proportion of the population, was discriminatory.

Stein v. New York: 346 U.S. 156 (1953). Opinion: Jackson, J. Dissenting: Douglas and Black, JJ.

Permitting jury determination of the voluntariness of a confession and conviction by the jury on other evidence is not contrary to the Fourteenth Amendment. This decision was overruled by *Jackson* v. *Denno,* p. 257, below.

Thompson v. City of Louisville: 362 U.S. 199 (1960). Opinion: Black, J. No dissent.

This case went to the Supreme Court by certiorari to the Police Court of Louisville, Kentucky. The decision held that the convictions were so totally devoid of evidentiary support as to render the convictions invalid under the due process clause of the Fourteenth Amendment. The charge was loitering and disorderly conduct. This possibly was the first time that a state criminal conviction was overturned by the Court for lack of evidence.

Benton v. Maryland: 395 U.S. 784 (1969). Opinion: Marshall, J. Dissenting: Harlan and Stewart, JJ.

John Benton had been tried in a Maryland state court on charges of burglary and larceny and the jury found him not guilty of larceny but convicted him on the burglary count. On a second trial Benton was again charged with both larceny and burglary and it was on this point that Benton objected to the retrial on the larceny count since he argued that because the first jury had found him not guilty of larceny, retrial would violate the constitutional prohibition against subjecting persons to double jeopardy for the same offense. The Court agreed and held that "the double jeopardy prohibition of the Fifth Amendment represents a fundamental ideal in our constitutional heritage, and that it should apply to the States through the Fourteenth Amendment. Insofar as it is inconsistent with this holding, *Palko* v. *Connecticut* is overruled."

Ashe v. Swenson: 397 U.S. 436 (1970). Opinion: Stewart, J. Dissenting: Burger, C.J.

After an accused person had been on trial for the robbery of one of six participants in a poker game and found not guilty due to insufficient evidence, chiefly on the matter of identification, subsequent trial for the robbery of another participant in the game was double jeopardy.

NOTE:

The remarkable feature of *Palko* is its very successful effort to clarify the distinction between "formal" and "fundamental" rights. The "litany" of specific rights is not up to date but the line of demarcation that divides the categories has seldom been better explained. While the idea of such a division of constitutional guarantees was first enunciated by the Court in the *Insular* cases, the first application of the concept to the states came in *Gitlow* in 1925. Only three years before in *Prudential Insurance Co.* v. *Cheek* (259 U.S. 530, 1922) the Court had specifically refused to use the Fourteenth Amendment to apply free speech restrictions to the states. However, in 1923 in *Meyer* v. *Nebraska* (262 U.S. 390, 1923) and in *Pierce* v. *Society of Sisters* (268 U.S. 510, 1925), decided only a week before *Gitlow*, there was some evidence that the Court was taking a broader view of the "liberty" guaranteed against state action in the Fourteenth Amendment.

To the rights classified as "fundamental" in *Palko* should be added those concerning search and seizure (*Mapp* v. *Ohio*, 367 U.S. 643, 1961), cruel and unusual punishment (*Robinson* v. *California*, 370 U.S. 660, 1962), counsel in all cases (*Gideon* v. *Wainwright*, 372 U.S. 335, 1963), self-incrimination (*Malloy* v. *Hogan*, 378 U.S. 1, 1964 and *Murphy* v. *Waterfront Commission of New York Harbor*, 378 U.S. 52, 1964), a speedy and public trial (*Klopfer* v. *North Carolina*, 386 U.S. 213, 1967), an impartial jury (*Parker* v. *Gladden*, 385 U.S. 363, 1966), trial by jury in all criminal cases (*Duncan* v. *Louisiana*, 391 U.S. 145, 1968), to be confronted with witnesses (*Pointer* v. *Texas*, 380 U.S. 400, 1965), compulsory process for obtaining witnesses (*Washington* v. *Texas*, 388 U.S. 14, 1967), and double jeopardy (*Benton* v. *Maryland*, 395 U.S. 784, 1969). Again the flexibility inherent in the constitution is emphasized.

The principle explained in *Palko* has sometimes been referred to as the "absorptionist theory," by which certain basic rights have come within the Court's definition of "liberty." One school of thought holds that the entire Bill of Rights should be thus assimilated and applied to the states. At least two dangers of the adoption of such a policy need to be noted. One of these is that experimentation or improvement in judicial procedure by the state courts (such as the use of the information) would be greatly hampered if not stifled. Also, all kinds of difficulties would arise in the state courts where cases without number could be reopened under the "new dispensation." Most of the new rules the Court has refused to apply retroactively. See *Johnson* v. *New Jersey,* p. 257, below.

Louisiana ex rel. Francis v. Resweber
329 U.S. 459; 67 S.Ct. 374; 91 L.Ed. 422 (1947)

(A Negro citizen of Louisiana, Willie Francis, was sentenced to be electrocuted after conviction for murder. A death warrant was issued and Francis was prepared for execution on May 3, 1946. He was placed in the electric chair with the authorized witnesses present. When the switch was turned on, death did not result because of mechanical difficulties. Then a new death warrant was issued by the governor with the execution set for May 9, 1946. This action was challenged as involving double jeopardy and cruel and unusual punishment under the due process clause of the Fourteenth Amendment as well as a denial of equal protection.)

Vote: 5-4

Mr. Justice Reed delivered the opinion of the Court:

. . . *First.* Our minds rebel against permitting the same sovereignty to punish an accused twice for the same offense. . . . But where the accused successfully seeks review of a conviction, there is no double jeopardy upon a new trial. . . . Even where a state obtains a new trial after conviction because of errors, while an accused may be placed on trial a second time, it is not the sort of hardship to the accused that is forbidden by the Fourteenth Amendment. . . . As this is a prosecution under state law, so far as double jeopardy is concerned, the *Palko* case is decisive. For we see no difference from a constitutional point of view between a new trial for error of law at the instance of the state that results in a death sentence instead of imprisonment for life and an execution that follows a failure of equipment. When an accident, with no suggestion of malevolence, prevents the consummation of a sentence, the state's subsequent course in the administration of its criminal law is not affected on that account by any requirement of due process under the Fourteenth Amendment. We find no double jeopardy here which can be said to amount to a denial of federal due process in the proposed execution.

Second. We find nothing in what took place here which amounts to cruel and unusual punishment in the constitutional sense. The case before us does not call for an examination into any punishments except that of death. . . . The traditional humanity of modern Anglo-American law forbids the infliction of unnecessary pain in the execution of the death sentence. Prohibition against the wanton infliction of pain has come into our law from the Bill of Rights of 1688. The identical words appear in our Eighth Amendment. The Fourteenth would prohibit by its due process clause execution by a state in a cruel manner.

Petitioner's suggestion is that because he once underwent the psychological strain of preparation for electrocution, now to require him to undergo this preparation again subjects him to a lingering or cruel and unusual punishment. Even the fact that petitioner has already been subjected to a current of electricity does not make his subsequent execution any more cruel in the constitutional sense than any other execution. The cruelty against which the Constitution protects a convicted man is cruelty inherent in the method of punishment, not the necessary suffering involved in any method employed to extinguish life humanely. The fact that an unforeseeable accident prevented the prompt consummation of the sentence cannot, it seems to us, add an element of cruelty to a subsequent execution. There is no purpose to inflict unnecessary pain nor any unnecessary pain involved in the proposed execution.

The situation of the unfortunate victim of this accident is just as though he had suffered the identical amount of mental anguish and physical pain in any other occurrence, such as, for example, a fire in the cell block. We cannot agree that the hardship imposed upon the petitioner rises to that level of hardship denounced as denial of due process because of cruelty.

Third. The Supreme Court of Louisiana also rejected petitioner's contention that death inflicted after his prior sufferings would deny him the equal protection of the laws, guaranteed by the Fourteenth Amendment. This suggestion in so far as it differs from the due process argument is based on the idea that execution, after an attempt at execution has failed, would be a more severe punishment than is imposed upon others guilty of a like offense. That is, since others do not go through the strain of preparation for execution a second time or have not experienced a non-lethal current in a prior attempt at execution, as petitioner did, to compel petitioner to submit to execution after these prior experiences denies to him equal protection. Equal protection does not protect a prisoner against even illegal acts of officers in charge of him, much less against accidents during his detention for execution. . . . Laws cannot prevent accidents nor can a law equally protect all against them. So long as the law applies to all alike, the requirements of equal protection are met. We have no right to assume that Louisiana singled out Francis for a treatment other than that which has been or would generally be applied. . . .

Mr. Justice Frankfurter concurred:

. . . I cannot bring myself to believe that for Louisiana to leave to executive clemency, rather than to require, mitigation of a sentence of death duly pronounced upon conviction of murder because a first attempt to carry it out was an innocent misadventure, offends a principle of justice "rooted in the traditions and conscience of our people". . . . Short of the compulsion of such a principle, this Court must abstain from interference with State action no matter how strong one's personal feeling of revulsion against a State's insistence on its pound of flesh. One must be on guard against finding in personal disapproval a reflection of more or less prevailing condemnation. Strongly drawn as I am to some of the sentiments expressed by my brother Burton, I cannot rid myself of the conviction that were I to hold that Louisiana would transgress the Due Process Clause if the State were allowed, in the precise circumstances before us, to carry out the death sentence, I would be enforcing my private view rather than that consensus of society's opinion which, for purposes of due process, is the standard enjoined by the Constitution. . . .

Mr. Justice Burton dissented, with the concurrence of Mr. Justice Douglas, Mr. Justice Murphy and Mr. Justice Rutledge:

. . . In determining whether the proposed procedure is unconstitutional, we must measure it against a lawful electrocution. The contrast is that between instantaneous death and death by installments—caused by electric shocks administered after one or more intervening periods of complete consciousness of the victim. Electrocution, when instantaneous, *can* be inflicted by a state in conformity with the due process of law. . . . The Supreme Court of Louisiana has held that electrocution, in the manner prescribed in its statute, is more humane than hanging. . . .

The all-important consideration is that the execution shall be so instantaneous and substantially painless that the punishment shall be reduced, as nearly as possible, to no more than that of death itself. Electrocution has been approved only in a form that eliminates suffering.

. . . How many deliberate and intentional reapplications of electric current does it take to produce a cruel, unusual and unconstitutional punishment? While five applications would be more cruel and unusual than one, the uniqueness of the present case demonstrates that, today, two separated applications are sufficiently "cruel and unusual" to be prohibited. If five attempts would be "cruel and unusual," it would be difficult to draw the line between two, three, four and five. It is not difficult, however, as we here contend, to draw the line between the one continuous application prescribed by statute and any other application of the current.

Lack of intent that the first application be less than fatal is not material. The intent of the executioner cannot lessen the torture or excuse the result. It was the statutory duty of the state officials to make sure that there was no failure. The procedure in this case contrasts with common knowledge of precautions generally taken elsewhere to insure against failure of electrocutions. . . .

. . . On that record, denial of relief means that the proposed repeated, and at least second, application to the relator of an electric current sufficient to cause death is not, under present circumstances, a cruel and unusual punishment violative of due process of law. It exceeds any punishment prescribed by law. There is no precedent for it. What then is it, if it be not cruel, unusual and unlawful? . . .

The remand of this cause to the Supreme Court of Louisiana in the manner indicated does not mean that the relator necessarily is entitled to a complete release. It means merely that the courts of Louisiana must examine the facts both as to the actual nature of the punishment already inflicted and that proposed to be inflicted and, if the proposed punishment amounts to a violation of due process of law under the Constitution of the United States, then the State must find some means of disposing of this case that will not violate that Constitution.

For the reasons stated, we are unable to concur in the judgment of this Court which affirms the judgment below.

RELATED CASES:

Hoag v. New Jersey: 356 U.S. 464 (1958). Opinion: Harlan, J. Dissenting: Warren, C.J., and Douglas and Black, JJ. Abstaining: Brennan, J.

Robbery of four persons at the same time can be construed as four separate offenses which may be tried consecutively. However, prosecution for each robbery at a different trial might unduly harass an accused. The question under the due process clause of the Fourteenth Amendment is whether multiple trials result in "fundamental unfairness." See *Ashe* v. *Swenson*, below.

Ciucci v. Illinois: 356 U.S. 571 (1958). Per Curiam. Dissenting: Douglas, Brennan, and Black, JJ., and Warren, C.J.

Where there was a multiple murder, the state may prosecute these as individual offenses at separate trials. The state, without violation of due process, may utilize all relevant evidence at each of these trials in the absence of proof establishing that such a course of action entailed fundamental unfairness.

Robinson v. California: 370 U.S. 660 (1962). Opinion: Stewart, J. Dissenting: Clark and White, JJ. Abstaining: Frankfurter, J.

A state statute that made it a criminal offense for a person to be "addicted to the use of narcotics" and this "even though he has never touched any narcotic drug within the State or been guilty of any irregular behavior there" was void as inflicting cruel and unusual punishment in violation of the Fourteenth Amendment. What the Court most certainly appeared to be saying was that this portion of the Eighth Amendment is to be added to those portions of the Bill of Rights made applicable to the states by means of the Fourteenth Amendment. The Court regarded addiction as an illness rather than as a crime.

Ashe v. Swenson: 397 U.S. 436 (1970). Opinion: Stewart, J. Dissenting: Burger, C.J.

Here six poker players were the victims of robbery. Ashe, one of the accused, was tried for the robbery of one victim. He was found not guilty. Later he was brought to trial for the robbery of another of the victims. This time he was found guilty and he charged double jeopardy. The Court agreed, noting that the name of the victim had no bearing on the issue since the jury in the first trial had determined that Ashe was not one of the robbers.

NOTE:

In *Resweber* the Court came close to incorporating the cruel and unusual punishment provisions of the Eighth Amendment in the due process clause of the Fourteenth Amendment. This incorporation appears to have been definitely accomplished in *Robinson* v. *California*, 370 U.S. 660 (1962). The applicability of the double jeopardy provision of the Fifth Amendment was also brought into question but left by *Resweber* without decision, so that the doctrine of *Palko* remained undisturbed on that point. In 1969 the Court overruled *Palko* in *Benton* v. *Maryland* 395 U.S. 784.

Powell v. Alabama
287 U.S. 45; 53 S.Ct. 55; 77 L.Ed. 158 (1932)

(This was the first of the famous "*Scottsboro* cases." Powell was one of nine Negro boys who were indicted for the rape of two white girls. Six days after the date of the crime they were tried in a community where the attitude was one of great hostility. The accused were not represented by counsel, the judge simply appointed "all members of the bar" to defend them. The proceedings were challenged as denying due process to the defendants.)

Vote: 7-2

Mr. Justice Sutherland delivered the opinion of the Court:

. . . *First*. The record shows that immediately upon the return of the indictment defendants were arraigned and pleaded not guilty. Apparently they were not asked whether they had, or were able to employ, counsel, or wished to have counsel appointed; or whether they had friends or relatives who might assist in that regard if communicated with. That it would not have been an idle ceremony to have given the defendants reasonable opportunity to communicate with their families and endeavor to obtain counsel is demonstrated by the fact that very soon after conviction, able counsel appeared in their behalf.

It is hardly necessary to say that, the right to counsel being conceded, a defendant should be afforded a fair opportunity to secure counsel of his own choice. Not only was that not done here, but such designation of counsel as was attempted was either so indefinite or so close upon the trial as to amount to a denial of effective and substantial aid in that regard. This will be amply demonstrated by a brief review of the record. . . .

Nor do we think the situation was helped by what occurred on the morning of the trial. At that time, as appears from the colloquy printed above, Mr. Roddy stated to the court that he did not appear as counsel, but that he would like to appear along with counsel that the court might appoint; that he had not been given an opportunity to prepare the case; that he was not familiar with the procedure in Alabama, but merely came down as a friend of the people who were interested; that he thought the boys would be better off if he should step entirely out of the case. Mr. Moody, a member of the local bar, expressed a willingness to help Mr. Roddy in anything he could do under the circumstances. To this the court responded: "All right, all the lawyers that will; of course I would not require a lawyer to appear if——." And Mr. Moody continued, "I am willing to do that for him as a member of the bar; I will go ahead and help do anything I can do." With this dubious understanding, the trials immediately proceeded. The defendants, young, ignorant, illiterate, surrounded by hostile sentiment, haled back and forth under guard of soldiers, charged with an atrocious crime regarded with especial horror in the community where they were to be tried, were thus put in peril of their lives within a few moments after counsel for the first time charged with any degree of responsibility began to represent them.

It is not enough to assume that counsel thus precipitated into the case thought there was no defense, and exercised their best judgment in proceeding to trial without preparation. Neither they nor the court could say what a prompt and thoroughgoing investigation might disclose as to the facts. No attempt was made to investigate. No opportunity to do so was given. Defendants were immediately hurried to trial. . . . Under the circumstances disclosed, we hold that defendants were not accorded the right of counsel in any substantial sense. To decide otherwise, would simply be to ignore actualities. . . .

Second. The Constitution of Alabama provides that in all criminal prosecutions the accused shall enjoy the right to have the assistance of counsel; and a state statute requires the court in a capital case, where the defendant is unable to employ counsel, to appoint counsel for him. The state supreme court held that these provisions had not been infringed, and with that holding we are powerless to interfere. The question, however, which is our duty, and within our power, to decide, is whether the denial of the assistance of counsel contravenes the due process clause of the Fourteenth Amendment to the federal Constitution. . . .

. . . While the question has never been categorically determined by this court, a consideration of the nature of the right and a review of the expressions of this and other courts, makes it clear that the right to the aid of counsel is of this fundamental character.

It has never been doubted by this court, or any other so far as we know, that notice and hearing are preliminary steps essential to the passing of an enforceable judgment, and that they, together with a legally competent tribunal having jurisdiction of the case, constitute basic elements of the constitutional requirement of due process of law. . . .

What, then, does a hearing include? Historically and in practice, in our own country at least, it has always included the right to the aid of counsel when desired and provided by the party asserting the right. The right to be heard would be, in many cases, of little avail if it did not comprehend the right to be heard by counsel. Even the intelligent and educated layman has small and sometimes no skill in the science of law. If charged with crime, he is incapable, generally, of determining for himself whether the indictment is good or bad. He is unfamiliar with the rules of evidence. Left without the aid of counsel, he may be put on trial without a proper charge, and convicted upon incompetent evidence, or evidence irrelevant to the issue or otherwise inadmissible. He lacks both the skill and knowledge adequately to prepare his defense, even though he have a perfect one. He requires the guiding hand of counsel at every step in the proceedings against him. Without it, though he be not guilty, he faces the danger of conviction because he does not know how to establish his innocence. If that be true of men of intelligence, how much more true is it of the ignorant and illiterate, or those of feeble intellect. If in any case, in civil or criminal, a state or federal court were arbitrarily to refuse to hear a party by counsel, employed by and appearing for him, it reasonably may not be doubted that such a refusal would be a denial of a hearing, and, therefore, of due process in the constitutional sense. . . .

In the light of the facts outlined in the forepart of this opinion—the ignorance and illiteracy of the defendants, their youth, the circumstances of public hostility, the imprisonment and the close surveillance of the defendants by the military forces, the fact that their friends and families were all in other states and communication with them necessarily difficult, and above all that they stood in deadly peril of their lives—we think the failure of the trial court to give them reasonable time and opportunity to secure counsel was a clear denial of due process.

But passing that, and assuming their inability, even if opportunity had been given, to employ counsel, as the trial court evidently did assume, we are of opinion that, under the circumstances just stated, the necessity of counsel was so vital and imperative that the failure of the trial court to make an effective appointment of counsel was likewise a denial of due process within the meaning of the Fourteenth Amendment. Whether this would be so in other criminal prosecutions, or under other circumstances, we need not determine. All that is necessary now to decide, as we do decide, is that in a capital case, where the defendant is unable to employ counsel, and is incapable adequately of making his own defense because of ignorance, feeblemindedness, illiteracy, or the like, it is the duty of the court, whether requested or not, to assign counsel for him as a necessary requisite of due process of law; and that duty is not discharged by an assignment at such a time or under such circumstances as to preclude the giving of effective aid in the preparation and trial of the case. To hold otherwise would be to ignore the fundamental postulate, already adverted to, "that there are certain immutable principles of justice which inhere in the very idea of free government which no member of the Union may disregard." . . . In a case such as this, whatever may be the rule in other cases, the right to have counsel appointed, when necessary, is a logical corollary from the constitutional right to be heard by counsel. . . .

The judgments must be reversed, and the causes remanded for further proceedings not inconsistent with this opinion.

Judgments reversed.

Mr. Justice Butler dissented, with the concurrence of Mr. Justice McReynolds:

If correct, the ruling that the failure of the trial court to give petitioners time and opportunity to secure counsel was denial of due process is enough, and with this the opinion should end. But the Court goes on to declare that "the failure of the trial court to make an effective appointment of counsel was likewise a denial of due process within the meaning of the Fourteenth Amendment." This is an extension of federal authority into a field hitherto occupied exclusively by the several states. Nothing before the Court calls for a consideration of the point. It was not suggested below and petitioners do not ask for its decision here. The Court, without being called upon to consider it, adjudges without a hearing an important constitutional question concerning criminal procedure in state courts. . . .

RELATED CASES:

Norris v. Alabama: 294 U.S. 587 (1935). Opinion: Hughes, C.J. No dissent. Abstaining: McReynolds, J.

Exclusion of all Negroes from a grand jury by which a Negro is indicted, or from the petit jury by which he is tried for the offense, resulting from systematic and arbitrary exclusion of Negroes from the jury lists solely because of their race or color, is a denial of the equal protection of the laws guaranteed by the Fourteenth Amendment. This was the second "Scottsboro Case." This was not provided by statute but was practiced.

Betts v. Brady: 316 U.S. 455 (1942). Opinion: Roberts, J. Dissenting: Black, Douglas, and Murphy, JJ.

Due process does not obligate a state to furnish counsel in every case. Most states do not consider appointment of counsel a fundamental right, essential to a fair trial.

This is usually regarded as a matter of legislative policy. Here, a case of robbery in a Maryland court, the circumstances seemed not such as to require counsel. This decision was overruled by *Gideon* v. *Wainwright,* p. 248.

Rice v. Olson: 324 U.S. 786 (1945). Opinion: Black, J. Dissenting: Frankfurter, Roberts, and Jackson, JJ.

An allegation by a party convicted in a state court of burglary that the trial court failed to advise him of his constitutional rights to counsel and to call witnesses may show a prima facie violation of his right to counsel in a petition by him for writ of habeas corpus. He cannot be held to have waived his constitutional right to counsel because he entered a plea of guilty.

Canizio v. New York: 327 U.S. 82 (1946). Opinion: Black, J. Dissenting: Murphy and Rutledge, JJ. Abstaining: Jackson, J.

The accused did not have counsel during the trial until two days before he was sentenced. The Court held that this counsel had "ample time to take advantage of every defense which would have been available to him originally."

DeMeerleer v. Michigan: 329 U.S. 663 (1947). Opinion: Per Curiam. No dissent.

When a seventeen-year-old boy was arraigned, tried, convicted of first-degree murder, and sentenced to life imprisonment, all on the same day and without counsel throughout, there was denial of due process.

Townsend v. Burke: 334 U.S. 736 (1948). Opinion: Jackson, J. Dissenting: Vinson, C.J., and Reed and Burton, JJ.

Here Pennsylvania had found Townsend guilty of burglary and robbery without benefit of counsel. Due process requires counsel when necessary to make sure "that the conviction and sentence were not predicated on misinformation or misreading of court records."

Chandler v. Fretag: 348 U.S. 3 (1954). Opinion: Warren, C.J. No dissent.

An accused must be given the opportunity to secure counsel or there is a denial of due process under the Fourteenth Amendment. "Regardless of whether petitioner would have been entitled to the appointment of counsel, his right to be heard through his own counsel was unqualified." Involved here was an uneducated middle-aged Negro. The case arose in Tennessee. The charge was housebreaking.

Chessman v. Teets, Warden: 354 U.S. 156 (1957). Opinion: Harlan, J. Dissenting: Burton, Douglas, and Clark, JJ. Abstaining: Warren, C.J.

Refusal of an accused to be represented by counsel at the trial does not constitute a waiver of his right to counsel at the settlement proceedings.

Moore v. Michigan: 355 U.S. 155 (1957). Opinion: Brennan, J. Dissenting: Frankfurter, Harlan, Burton, and Clark, JJ.

Where a person convicted of murder in a state court has not intelligently and understandingly waived the benefit of counsel and where the circumstances show that his rights could not have been fairly protected without counsel, there is denial of due process under the Fourteenth Amendment. Involved was a seventeen-year old Negro with a seventh grade education.

Blackburn v. Alabama: 361 U.S. 199 (1960). Opinion: Warren, C. J. No dissent.

Where the involuntariness of a confession (here to a charge of robbery) is conclusively demonstrated at any stage of a trial, the defendant is deprived of due process by its use in obtaining his conviction. Here the accused was probably insane and incompetent at the time he allegedly confessed. He had been questioned eight or nine hours.

NOTE:

Powell was the first "Scottsboro case" and was the case which applied to the states the guarantee of counsel provision of the Sixth Amendment if certain circumstances are present. (The second "Scottsboro case" was *Norris* v. *Alabama,* 294

U.S. 587, 1935.) It must be carefully noted that the Sixth Amendment provision of counsel had not at this time been incorporated into the Fourteenth and thus made applicable to the states except under certain circumstances and considerations. This the Court made clear in *Betts* v. *Brady*, 316 U.S. 455 (1942). The Fourteenth Amendment's due process clause had been invoked to outlaw self-incrimination activities by a state insofar as that might be involved in a coerced confession. This, however, was simply part of the application of due process—defined as "essential fairness"—and included also the guarantee of a fair jury trial. As the Court has noted, a denial by a state of rights or privileges specifically embodied in various of the first eight amendments may, in certain circumstances, or in connection with other elements, operate, in a given case, to deprive a person of due process of law in violation of the Fourteenth Amendment.

It was not until *Gideon* v. *Wainwright*, 372 U.S. 335 (1963) that the Court applied the guarantee of counsel in the Sixth Amendment to all cases in the state courts, capital and noncapital alike. The so-called "Gitlow doctrine" was thus given further extension.

Gideon v. Wainwright
372 U.S. 335; 83 S.Ct. 792; 9 L.Ed. 2d 799 (1963)

(Clarence Earl Gideon was charged in a Florida state court with having broken and entered a poolroom with intent to commit a misdemeanor. This is a noncapital felony under Florida law. He appeared in court without funds and without counsel and asked the court to appoint counsel for him. This was denied because the law of Florida permitted appointment of counsel for indigent defendants only in capital cases. He conducted his own defense, was convicted and sentenced to prison. Subsequently he applied for a writ of habeas corpus on the ground that the trial court's refusal to appoint counsel denied him rights under the Constitution. The state Supreme Court denied all relief.)

Vote: 9-0

Mr. Justice Black delivered the opinion of the Court:

. . . Treating due process as "a concept less rigid and more fluid than those envisaged in other specific and particular provisions of the Bill of Rights," the Court held that refusal to appoint counsel under the particular facts and circumstances in the *Betts* case was not so "offensive to the common and fundamental ideas of fairness" as to amount to a denial of due process. Since the facts and circumstances of the two cases are so nearly indistinguishable, we think the *Betts* v. *Brady* holding if left standing would require us to reject Gideon's claim that the Constitution guarantees him the assistance of counsel. Upon full reconsideration we conclude that *Betts* v. *Brady* should be overruled. . . .

. . . Not only these precedents but also reason and reflection require us to recognize that in our adversary system of criminal justice, any person haled into court, who is too poor to hire a lawyer, cannot be assured a fair trial unless counsel is provided for him. This seems to us to be an obvious 'truth. Governments, both state and federal, quite properly spend vast sums of money to establish machinery to try defendants accused of crime. Lawyers to prosecute are everywhere deemed essential to protect the public's interest in an orderly society. Similarly, there are few defendants charged with crime, few indeed, who fail to hire the best lawyers they can get to prepare and present their defenses. That government hires lawyers to prosecute and defendants who have the money hire lawyers to defend are the strongest indications of the widespread belief that lawyers in criminal courts are necessities, not luxuries. The right of one charged with crime to counsel may not be deemed fundamental and essential to fair trials in some countries, but it is in ours. From the very beginning, our state and national constitutions and laws have laid great emphasis on procedural and substantive safeguards designed to assure fair trials before impartial tribunals in which every defendant stands equal before the law. This noble ideal cannot be realized if the poor man charged with crime has to face his accusers without a lawyer to assist him. . . .

Reversed.

Mr. Justice Harlan concurred:

. . . In agreeing with the Court that the right to counsel in a case such as this should now be expressly recognized as a fundamental right embraced in the Fourteenth Amendment, I wish to make a further observation. When we hold a right or immunity, valid against the Federal Government, to be "implicit in the concept of ordered liberty" and thus valid against the States, I do not read our past decisions to suggest that by so holding, we automatically carry over an entire body of federal law and apply it in full sweep to the States. Any such concept would disregard the frequently wide disparity between the legitimate interests of the States and of the Federal Government, the divergent problems that they face, and the significantly different consequences of their actions. Cf. *Roth* v. *United States*, 354 U.S. 476, 496-508 (separate opinion of this writer). In what is done today I do not understand the Court to depart from the principles laid down in *Palko* v. *Connecticut*, 302 U.S. 319, or to embrace the concept that the Fourteenth Amendment "incorporates" the Sixth Amendment as such.

On these premises I join in the judgment of the Court.

RELATED CASES:

Lane v. Brown: 372 U.S. 477 (1963). Opinion: Stewart, J. No dissent.

Where a Public Defender who thinks that an appeal would be unsuccessful can cut off the appeal of an indigent in a criminal case there has been denial of due process.

Draper v. Washington: 372 U.S. 487 (1963). Opinion: Goldberg, J. Dissenting: White, Clarke, Harlan and Stewart.

The determination of a trial judge that an indigent's appeal in a criminal case is frivolous is an inadequate substitute for the full appellate review available to non-indigents when the effect of that finding is to prevent an appellate examination based upon a sufficiently complete record of the trial proceedings themselves.

Argersinger v. Hamlin: 407 U.S. 25 (1972). Opinion: Douglas, J. No dissent.

This is a sequel to *Gideon* v. *Wainwright*, 372 U.S. 335 (1963). Counsel is necessary in any trial for any offense, whether classified as petty, misdemeanor, or felony, involving the possibility of imprisonment. In "assembly-line justice" to which misdemeanor defendants are frequently subjected counsel is needed so that the accused will know what is going on and the possible penalties. There may be "a knowing and intelligent" waiver. Charges not involving imprisonment are not affected by this decision.

Escobedo v. Illinois
378 U.S. 478; 84 S.Ct. 1758; 12 L.Ed. 2d 977 (1964)

(Danny Escobedo, a twenty-two-year-old of Mexican extraction, was arrested in Chicago with his sister and taken to police headquarters for interrogation in connection with the fatal shooting, about eleven days before, of his brother-in-law. He had been arrested shortly after the shooting, but had made no statement, and was released after his lawyer obtained a writ of habeas corpus from a state court. Petitioner made several requests to see his lawyer, who, though present in the building, and despite persistent efforts, was refused access to his client. Petitioner was not advised by the police of his right to remain silent and, after persistent questioning by the police, made a damaging statement to an Assistant State's Attorney which was admitted at the trial. Convicted of murder, he appealed to the State Supreme Court, which affirmed the conviction.)

Vote: 5-4

Mr. Justice Goldberg delivered the opinion of the Court:

The critical question in this case is whether, under the circumstances, the refusal by the police to honor petitioner's request to consult with his lawyer during the course of an interrogation constitutes a denial of "the Assistance of Counsel" in violation of the Sixth Amendment to the Constitution as "made obligatory upon the States by the Fourteenth Amendment," *Gideon* v. *Wainwright*, 372 U.S. 335, 342, and thereby renders inadmissible in a state criminal trial any incriminating statement elicited by the police during the interrogation. . . .

Notwithstanding repeated requests by each, petitioner and his retained lawyer were afforded no opportunity to consult during the course of the entire interrogation. At one point, as previously noted, petitioner and his attorney came into each other's view for a few moments but the attorney was quickly ushered away. Petitioner testified "that he heard a detective telling the attorney the latter would not be allowed to talk to [him] 'until they were done' " and that he heard the attorney being refused permission to remain in the adjoining room. A police officer testified that he had told the lawyer that he could not see petitioner until "we were through interrogating" him.

There is testimony by the police that during the interrogation, petitioner, a 22-year-old of Mexican extraction with no record of previous experience with the police, "was handcuffed" in a standing position and that he "was nervous, he had circles under his eyes and he was upset" and was "agitated" because "he had not slept well in over a week."

It is undisputed that during the course of the interrogation Officer Montejano, who "grew up" in petitioner's neighborhood, who knew his family, and who uses "Spanish language in [his] police work," conferred alone with petitioner "for about a quarter of an hour. . . ." Petitioner testified that the officer said to him "in Spanish that my sister and I could go home if I pinned it on Benedict DiGerlando," that "he would see to it that we would go home and be held only as witnesses, if anything, if we had made a statement against DiGerlando . . . , that we would be able to go home that night." Petitioner testified that he made the statement in issue because of this assurance. Officer Montejano denied offering any such assurance. . . .

Petitioner, a layman, was undoubtedly unaware that under Illinois law an admission of "mere" complicity in the murder plot was legally as damaging as an admission of firing of the fatal shots. *Illinois* v. *Escobedo*, 28 Ill. 2d 41, 190 N.E. 2d 825. The "guiding hand of counsel" was essential to advise petitioner of his rights in this delicate situation. *Powell* v. *Alabama*, 287 U.S. 45, 69. This was the "stage when legal aid and advice" were most critical to petitioner. . . .

We hold, therefore, that where, as here, the investigation is no longer a general inquiry into an unsolved crime but has begun to focus on a particular suspect, the suspect has been taken into police custody, the police carry out a process of interrogations that lends itself to eliciting incriminating statements, the suspect has requested and been denied an opportunity to consult with his lawyer, and the police have not effectively warned him of his absolute constitutional right to remain silent, the accused has been denied "the Assistance of Counsel" in violation of the Sixth Amendment to the Constitution as "made obligatory upon the States by the Fourteenth Amendment," *Gideon* v. *Wainwright*, 372 U.S., at 342, and that no statement elicited by the police during the interrogation may be used against him at a criminal trial. . . .

Nothing we have said today affects the powers of the police to investigate "an unsolved crime," *Spano* v. *New York*, 360 U.S. 315, 327 (Stewart, J., concurring), by gathering information from witnesses and by other "proper investigative efforts." *Haynes* v. *Washington*, 373 U.S. 503, 519. We hold only that when the process shifts from investigatory to accusatory—when its focus is on the accused and its purpose is to elicit a confession—our adversary system begins to operate, and, under the circumstances here, the accused must be permitted to consult with his lawyer.

The judgment of the Illinois Supreme Court is reversed and the case remanded for proceedings not inconsistent with this opinion.

Reversed and remanded.

Mr. Justice Stewart dissented:

. . . The confession which the Court today holds inadmissible was a voluntary one. It was given during the course of a perfectly legitimate police investigation of an unsolved murder. The Court says that what happened during this investigation "affected" the trial. I had always supposed that the whole purpose of a police investigation of a murder was to "affect" the trial of the murderer, and that it would be only an incompetent, unsuccessful, or corrupt investigation which would not do so. The Court further says that the Illinois police officers did not advise the petitioner of his "constitutional rights" before he confessed to the murder. This Court has never held that the Constitution requires the police to give any "advice" under circumstances such as these.

Supported by no stronger authority than its own rhetoric, the Court today converts a routine police investigation of an unsolved murder into a distorted analogue of a judicial trial. It imports into this investigation constitutional concepts historically applicable only after the onset of formal prosecutorial proceedings. By doing so, I think the Court perverts those precious constitutional guarantees, and frustrates the vital interests of society in preserving the legitimate and proper function of honest and purposeful police investigation. . . .

Mr. Justice White dissented, joined by Mr. Justice Clark and Mr. Justice Stewart:

. . . By abandoning the voluntary-involuntary test for admissibility of confessions, the Court seems driven by the notion that it is uncivilized law enforcement to use an accused's own admissions against him at his trial. It attempts to find a home for this new and nebulous rule of due process by attaching it to the right to counsel guaranteed in the federal system by the Sixth Amendment and binding upon the States by virtue of the due process guarantee of the Fourteenth Amendment. *Gideon* v. *Wainwright, supra.* The right to counsel now not only entitles the accused to counsel's advice and aid in preparing for trial but stands as an impenetrable barrier to any interrogation once the accused has become a suspect. From that very moment apparently his right to counsel attaches, a rule wholly unworkable and impossible to administer unless police cars are equipped with public defenders and undercover agents and police informants have defense counsel at their side. I would not abandon the Court's prior cases defining with some care and analysis the circumstances requiring the presence or aid of counsel and substitute the amorphous and wholly unworkable principle that counsel is constitutionally required whenever he would or could be helpful. . . .

Under this new approach one might just as well argue that a potential defendant is constitutionally entitled to a lawyer before, not after, he commits a crime, since it is then that crucial incriminating evidence is put within the reach of the Government by the would-be accused. Until now there simply has been no right guaranteed by the Federal Constitution to be free from the use at trial of a voluntary admission made prior to indictment. . . .

Today's decision cannot be squared with other provisions of the Constitution which, in my view, define the system of criminal justice this Court is empowered to administer. . . .

RELATED CASES:

Haynes v. Washington: 373 U.S. 503 (1963). Opinion: Goldberg, J. Dissenting: Clark, Harlan, Stewart, and White, JJ.

The accused was convicted of robbery after he had been held incommunicado until some five or seven days after his arrest, by which time a written and signed confession had been secured from him. The Court held a confession obtained by police through the use of threats is violative of due process, a coerced confession, and that the question in each case is whether the defendant's will was overborne at the time he confessed. The conviction was reversed.

Massiah v. United States: 377 U.S. 201 (1964). Opinion: Stewart, J. Dissenting: White, Clark, and Harlan, JJ.

An accused person was denied the basic protection of the Sixth Amendment when there was used against him at his trial evidence of his own incriminating words which federal agents had deliberately elicited from him (here by means of a hidden radio transmitter) after he had been indicted and in the absence of his counsel. This was electronic eavesdropping with the radio transmitter under the front seat of the car.

Pointer v. Texas: 380 U.S. 400 (1965). Opinion: Black, J. No dissent.

The Sixth Amendment's right of an accused to confront the witnesses against him is likewise a fundamental right for the kind of fair trial which is this country's constitutional goal and is made obligatory upon the states by the Fourteenth Amendment. A transcript of the testimony at the pretrial hearing was introduced at the trial because the witness had left the state.

Estes v. Texas: 381 U.S. 532 (1965). Opinion: Clark, J. Dissenting: Stewart, Black, Brennan, and White, JJ.

The potential impact of televised trial proceedings on the jurors, witnesses, the trial judge, and the defendant can strip the accused of a fair trial. This may change in the future but this judgment had to be based on the current situation.

Sheppard v. Maxwell: 384 U.S. 333 (1966). Opinion: Clark, J. Dissenting: Black, J.

Dr. Samuel H. Sheppard did not receive a fair trial consistent with the due process clause of the Fourteenth Amendment because of the trial judge's failure to protect the defendant from the massive, pervasive, and prejudicial publicity that attended his prosecution. There was a "carnival atmosphere."

Parker v. Gladden: 385 U.S. 363 (1966). Opinion: Per Curiam. Dissenting: Harlan, J.

The Sixth Amendment's provision for an impartial jury is applied to the states by means of the Fourteenth Amendment. The case came out of Oregon where Parker had been convicted of second-degree murder.

Klopfer v. North Carolina: 386 U.S. 213 (1967). Opinion: Warren, C.J. No dissent.

The right to a speedy trial is guaranteed by the Sixth Amendment and applied to the states by the Fourteenth. This right is as fundamental as any of the rights secured by the Sixth Amendment. This is borne out by the history of the right and its reception in this country.

Washington v. Texas: 388 U.S. 14 (1967). Opinion: Warren, C.J. No dissent.

Just as an accused has the right to confront the prosecution's witnesses for the purpose of challenging their testimony he has the right to present his own witnesses to establish a defense. This is a fundamental right of the Sixth Amendment and is applicable to the states.

Miranda v. Arizona
384 U.S. 436; 86 S.Ct. 1602; 16 L.Ed. 2d 694 (1966)

(Four cases were decided by the Court at one time but in the principal case Ernesto Miranda while in police custody in Phoenix was questioned by police officers, detectives, or a prosecuting attorney in a room in which he was cut off from the outside world. None of the defendants was given a full and effective warning of his rights at the outset of the interrogation process. In all four cases the questioning elicited oral admissions, and in three of them signed statements as well, which were admitted at their trials. All defendants were convicted and all convictions, except one from California, were affirmed on appeal.)

Vote: 5-4

Mr. Chief Justice Warren delivered the opinion of the Court:

The cases before us raise questions which go to the roots of our concepts of American criminal jurisprudence: the restraints society must observe consistent with the Federal Constitution in prosecuting individuals for crime. More specifically, we deal with the admissibility of statements obtained from an individual who is subjected to custodial police interrogation and the necessity for procedures which assure that the individual is accorded his privilege under the Fifth Amendment to the Constitution not to be compelled to incriminate himself.

We dealt with certain phases of this problem recently in *Escobedo* v. *Illinois*, 378 U.S. 478 (1964). There, as in the four cases before us, law enforcement officials took the defendant into custody and interrogated him in a police station for the purpose of obtaining a confession. The police did not effectively advise him of his right to remain silent or of his right to consult with his attorney. Rather, they confronted him with an alleged accomplice who accused him of having perpetrated a murder. When the defendant denied the accusation and said "I didn't shoot Manuel, you did it," they handcuffed him and took him to an interrogation room. There, while handcuffed and standing, he was questioned for four hours until he confessed. During this interrogation, the police denied his request to speak to his attorney, and they prevented his retained attorney, who had come to the police station, from consulting with him. At his trial, the State, over his objection, introduced the confession against him. We held that the statements thus made were constitutionally inadmissible. . . .

We start here, as we did in *Escobedo*, with the premise that our holding is not an innovation in our jurisprudence, but is an application of principles long recognized and applied in other settings. . . .

Our holding will be spelled out with some specificity in the pages which follow but briefly stated it is this: the prosecution may not use statements, whether exculpatory or inculpatory, stemming from custodial interrogation of the defendant unless it demonstrates the use of procedural safeguards effective to secure the privilege against self-incrimination. By custodial interrogation, we mean questioning initiated by law enforcement officers after a person has been taken into custody or otherwise deprived of his freedom of action in any significant way. As for the procedural safeguards to be employed, unless other fully effective means are devised to inform accused persons of their right of silence and to assure a continuous opportunity to exercise it, the following measures are required. Prior to any questioning, the person must be warned that he has a right to remain silent, that any statement he does make may be used as evidence against him, and that he has a right to the presence of an attorney, either retained or appointed. The defendant may waive effectuation of these rights, provided the waiver is made voluntarily, knowingly and intelligently. If, however, he indicates in any manner and at any stage of the process that he wishes to consult with an attorney before speaking there can be no questioning. Likewise, if the individual is alone and indicates in any manner that he does not wish to be interrogated, the police may not question him. The mere fact that he may have answered some questions or volunteered some statements on his own does not deprive him of the right to refrain from answering any further inquiries until he has consulted with an attorney and thereafter consents to be questioned.

I.

The constitutional issue we decide in each of these cases is the admissibility of statements obtained from a defendant questioned while in custody and deprived of his freedom of action. In each, the defendant was questioned by police officers, detectives, or a prosecuting attorney in a room in which he was cut off from the outside world. In none of these cases was the defendant given a full and effective warning of his rights at the outset of the interrogation process. In all the cases, the questioning elicited oral admissions, and in three of them, signed statements as well which were admitted at their trials. They all thus share salient features—incommunicado interrogation of individuals in a police-dominated atmosphere, resulting in self-incriminating statements without full warnings of constitutional rights. . . .

In the cases before us today, given this background, we concern ourselves primarily with this interrogation atmosphere and the evils it can bring. In No. 759, *Miranda* v. *Arizona*, the police arrested the defendant and took him to a special interrogation room where they secured a confession. In No. 760, *Vignera* v. *New York*, the defendant made oral admissions to the police after interrogation in the afternoon, and then signed an inculpatory statement upon being questioned by an assistant district attorney later the same evening. In No. 761, *Westover* v. *United States*, the defendant was handed over to the Federal Bureau of Investigation by local authorities after they had detained and interrogated him for a lengthy period, both at night and the following morning. After some two hours of questioning, the federal officers had obtained signed statements from the defendant. Lastly, in No. 584, *California* v. *Stewart*, the local police held the defendant five days in the station and interrogated him on nine separate occasions before they secured his inculpatory statement. . . .

From the foregoing, we can readily perceive an intimate connection between the privilege against self-incrimination and police custodial questioning. It is fitting to turn to history and precedent underlying the Self-Incrimination Clause to determine its applicability in this situation.

II.

We sometimes forget how long it has taken to establish the privilege against self-incrimination, the sources from which it came and the fervor with which it was defended. Its roots go back into ancient times. . . .

At the outset, if a person in custody is to be subjected to interrogation, he must first be informed in clear and unequivocal terms that he has the right to remain silent. For those unaware of the privilege, the warning is needed simply to make them aware of it—the threshold requirement for an intelligent decision as to its exercise. More important, such a warning is an absolute prerequisite in overcoming the inherent pressures of the interrogation atmosphere. It is not just the subnormal or woefully ignorant who succumb to an interrogator's imprecations, whether implied or expressly stated, that the interrogation will continue until a confession is obtained or that silence in the face of accusation is itself damning and will bode ill when presented to a jury. Further, the warning will show the individual that his interrogators are prepared to recognize his privilege should he choose to exercise it. . . .

The warning of the right to remain silent must be accompanied by the explanation that anything said can and will be used against the individual in court. This warning is needed in order to make him aware not only of the privilege, but also of the consequences of forgoing it. It is only through an awareness of these consequences that there can be any assurance of real understanding and intelligent exercise of the privilege. Moreover, this warning may serve to make the individual more acutely aware that he is faced with a phase of the adversary system—that he is not in the presence of persons acting solely in his interest.

The circumstances surrounding in-custody interrogation can operate very quickly to overbear the will of one merely made aware of his privilege by his interrogators. Therefore, the right to have counsel present at the interrogation is indispensable to the protection of the Fifth Amendment privilege under the system we delineate today. . . .

The presence of counsel at the interrogation may serve several significant subsidiary functions as well. If the accused decides to talk to his interrogators, the assistance of counsel can mitigate the dangers of untrustworthiness. With a lawyer present the likelihood that the police will practice coercion is reduced, and if coercion is nevertheless exercised the lawyer can testify to it in court. The presence of a lawyer can also help to guarantee that the accused gives a fully accurate statement to the police and that the statement is rightly reported by the prosecution at trial. . . .

An individual need not make a pre-interrogation request for a lawyer. While such request affirmatively secures his right to have one, his failure to ask for a lawyer does not constitute a waiver. . . .

Accordingly we hold that an individual held for interrogation must be clearly informed that he has the right to consult with a lawyer and to have the lawyer with him during interrogation under the system for protecting the privilege we delineate today. As with the warnings of the right to remain silent and that anything stated can be used in evidence against him, this warning is an absolute prerequisite to interrogation. . . .

If an individual indicates that he wishes the assistance of counsel before any interrogation occurs, the authorities cannot rationally ignore or deny his request on the basis that the individual does not have or cannot afford a retained attorney. The financial ability of the individual has no relationship to the scope of the rights involved here. The privilege against self-incrimination secured by the Constitution applies to all individuals. The need for counsel in order to protect the privilege exists for the indigent as well as the affluent. . . .

In order fully to apprise a person interrogated of the extent of his rights under this system then, it is necessary to warn him not only that he has the right to consult with an attorney, but also that if he is indigent a lawyer will be appointed to represent him. Without this additional warning, the admonition of the right to consult with counsel would often be understood as meaning only that he can consult with a lawyer if he has one or has the funds to obtain one. . . .

If the interrogation continues without the presence of an attorney and a statement is taken, a heavy burden rests on the government to demonstrate that the defendant knowingly and intelligently waived his privilege against self-incrimination and his right to retained or appointed counsel.

. . . Moreover, where in-custody interrogation is involved, there is no room for the contention that the privilege is waived if the individual answers some questions or gives some information on his own prior to invoking his right to remain silent when interrogated. . . .

The principles announced today deal with the protection which must be given to the privilege against self-incrimination when the individual is first subjected to police interrogation while in custody at the station or otherwise deprived of his freedom of action in any way. It is at this point that our adversary system of criminal proceedings commences, distinguishing itself at the outset from the inquisitorial system recognized in some countries. Under the system of warnings we delineate today or under any other system which may be devised and found effective, the safeguards to be erected about the privilege must come into play at this point. . . .

To summarize, we hold that when an individual is taken into custody or otherwise deprived of his freedom by the authorities and is subjected to questioning, the privilege against self-incrimination is jeopardized. Procedural safeguards must be employed to protect the privilege, and unless other fully effective means are adopted to notify the person of his right of silence and to assure that the exercise of the right will be scrupulously honored, the following measures are required. He must be warned prior to any questioning that he has the right to remain silent, that anything he says can be used against him in a court of law, that he has the right to the presence of an attorney, and that if he cannot afford an attorney one will be appointed for him prior to any questioning if he so desires. Opportunity to exercise these rights must be afforded to him throughout the interrogation. After such warnings have been given, and such opportunity afforded him, the individual may knowingly and intelligently waive these rights and agree to answer questions or make a statement. But unless and until such warnings and waiver are demonstrated by the prosecution at trial, no evidence obtained as a result of interrogation can be used against him. . . .

We reverse. From the testimony of the officers and by the admission of respondent, it is clear that Miranda was not in any way apprised of his right to consult with an attorney and to have one present during the interrogation, nor was his right not to be compelled to incriminate himself effectively protected in any other manner. Without these warnings the statements were inadmissible. The mere fact that he signed a statement which contained a typed-in clause stating that he had "full knowledge" of his "legal rights" does not approach the knowing and intelligent waiver required to relinquish constitutional rights. . . .

Mr. Justice Clark dissented:

. . . Rather than employing the arbitrary Fifth Amendment rule which the Court lays down I would follow the more pliable dictates of Due Process Clauses of the Fifth and Fourteenth Amendments which we are accustomed to administering and which we know from our cases are effective instruments in protecting persons in police custody. In this way we would not be acting in the dark nor in one full sweep changing the traditional rules of custodial interrogation which this Court has for so long recognized as a justifiable and proper tool in balancing individual rights against the rights of society. It will be soon enough to go further when we are able to appraise with somewhat better accuracy the effect of such a holding. . . .

Mr. Justice Harlan dissented, joined by Mr. Justice Stewart and Mr. Justice White:

. . . To incorporate this notion into the Constitution requires a strained reading of history and precedent and a disregard of the very pragmatic concerns that alone may on occasion justify such strains. I believe that reasoned examination will show that the Due Process Clauses provided an adequate tool for coping with confessions and that, even if the Fifth Amendment privilege against self-incrimination be invoked, its precedents taken as a whole do not sustain the present rules. Viewed as a choice based on pure policy, these new rules prove to be a highly debatable if not one-sided appraisal of the competing interests, imposed over widespread objection, at the very time when judicial restraint is most called for by the circumstances.

Mr. Justice White dissented, joined by Mr. Justice Harlan and Mr. Justice Stewart:

The proposition that the privilege against self-incrimination forbids in-custody interrogation without the warnings specified in the majority opinion and without a clear waiver of counsel has no significant support in the history of the privilege or in the language of the Fifth Amendment. As for the English authorities and the common-law history, the privilege, firmly established in the second half of the seventeenth century, was never applied except to prohibit compelled judicial interrogations. . . .

Our own constitutional provision provides that no person "shall be compelled in any criminal case to be a witness against himself." These words, when "[c]onsidered in the light to be shed by grammar and the dictionary . . . appear to signify simply that nobody shall be compelled to give oral testimony against himself in a criminal proceeding under way in which he is defendant." Corwin, The Supreme Court's Construction of the Self-Incrimination Clause, 29 Mich. L. Rev. 1, 2. . . .

But if the Court is here and now to announce new and fundamental policy to govern certain aspects of our affairs, it is wholly legitimate to examine the mode of this or any other constitutional decision in this Court and to inquire into the advisability of its end product in terms of the long-range interest of the country. . . .

RELATED CASES:

Jackson v. Denno: 378 U.S. 368 (1964). Opinion: White, J. Dissenting: Clark, Harlan, Stewart, and Black, JJ.

A defendant in a criminal case is deprived of due process of law if his conviction is founded, in whole or in part, upon an involuntary confession, without regard for the truth or falsity of the confession and even though there is ample evidence aside from the confession to support the conviction. The voluntariness of the confession must be determined prior to admission in evidence. This case overruled *Stein* v. *New York*, p. 239, above.

Johnson v. New Jersey: 384 U.S. 719 (1966). Opinion: Warren, C.J. Dissenting: Black and Douglas, JJ.

Where there has been retroactive application of a new rule this has been justified bceause the rule affected the very integrity of the fact-finding process and averted the clear danger of convicting the innocent. The Court refused to apply *Escobedo* and *Miranda* retroactively. This would seriously disrupt the administration of our criminal laws, the Court held.

Illinois v. Allen: 397 U.S. 337 (1970). Opinion: Black, J. No dissent.

An accused loses his right to be present throughout his trial by disruptive, stubbornly defiant conduct. Judges have discretion to meet the circumstances of each case—bind and gag, cite for contempt, remove from the courtroom.

Lego v. Twomey, Warden: 404 U.S. 477 (1972). Opinion: White, J. Dissenting: Brennan, Douglas, and Marshall, JJ. Abstaining: Powell and Rehnquist, JJ.

The judge rather than the jury determines the admissibility of evidence and there is no requirement that the voluntary character of a confession be submitted to a jury for its separate consideration. The judge presumably acts reliably.

NOTE:

The three cases of *Gideon, Escobedo,* and *Miranda* represent a new high in standards set by the Supreme Court in interpreting and applying the requirement of counsel in criminal cases. The Court has long recognized the importance of the guarantee of counsel but these and allied cases push the point where the right to counsel is effective back almost to the point of arrest. Involved also here is the matter of coerced confessions and the two guarantees have been almost merged. See *Massiah* v. *United States*, 377 U.S. 201 (1964). The decisions in these cases have aroused much bitter criticism of the Court.

The Court on the whole has refused to make the new interpretations retroactive except where the "integrity of the fact-finding process" has been seriously questioned and there has been the danger of an innocent person being convicted. See *Linkletter* v. *Walker*, 381 U.S. 618 (1965), *Tehan* v. *Shott*, 382 U.S. 406 (1966), *Johnson* v. *New Jersey*, 384 U.S. 719 (1966), and *DeStefano* v. *Woods*, 392 U.S. 631 (1968).

Fay v. New York
332 U.S. 261; 67 S.Ct. 1613; 91 L.Ed. 2043 (1947)

(A "blue ribbon" jury found Fay and another, Bore, guilty of conspiracy to extort and of extortion. The question before the Court was whether a warranted conviction by a jury individually accepted as fair and unbiased should be set aside on the ground that the make-up of the panel from which they were drawn unfairly narrowed the choice of jurors and denied defendants due process of law or equal protection of the laws in violation of the Fourteenth Amendment.)

Vote: 5-4

Mr. Justice Jackson delivered the opinion of the Court:

. . . The special jury is not one brought into existence for this particular case nor for any special class of offenses or type of accused. It is part of the regular machinery of trial in counties of one million or more inhabitants. In its sound discretion the court may order trial by special jury on application of either party in a civil action and by either the prosecution or defense in criminal cases. The motion may be granted only on a showing that "by reason of the importance or intricacy of the case, a special jury is required" or "the issue to be tried has been so widely commented upon . . . that an ordinary jury cannot without delay and difficulty be obtained" or that for any other reason "the due, efficient and impartial administration of justice in the particular case would be advanced by the trial of such an issue by a special jury". . . .

. . . Well has it been said of our power to limit state action that "To stay experimentation in things social and economic is a grave responsibility. Denial of the right to experiment may be fraught with serious consequences to the nation. It is one of the happy incidents of the federal system that a single courageous state may, if its citizens choose, serve as a laboratory; and try novel social and economic experiments without risk to the rest of the country." Mr. Justice Brandeis, dissenting in *New State Ice Co.* v. *Liebmann*, 285 U.S. 262, 311.

As there is no violation of a federal statute alleged, the challenge to this judgment under the due process clause must stand or fall on a showing that these defendants have had a trial so unfair as to amount to a taking of their liberty without due process of law. On this record we think that showing has not been made.

Affirmed.

Mr. Justice Murphy dissented, with the concurrence of Mr. Justice Black, Mr. Justice Douglas, and Mr. Justice Rutledge:

The equal protection clause of the Fourteenth Amendment prohibits a state from convicting any person by use of a jury which is not impartially drawn from a cross-section of the community. That means that juries must be chosen without systematic and intentional exclusion of any otherwise qualified group of individuals. . . . Only in that way can the democratic traditions of the jury system be preserved. . . . It is because I believe that this constitutional standard of jury selection has been ignored in the creation of the so-called "blue ribbon" jury panel in this case that I am forced to dissent. . . .

. . . If the constitutional right to a jury impartially drawn from a cross-section of the community has been violated, we should vindicate that right even though the effect of the violation has not yet put in a tangible appearance. Otherwise that right may be irretrievably lost in a welter of evidentiary rules.

Since this "blue ribbon" panel falls short of the constitutional standard of jury selection, the judgments below should be reversed.

RELATED CASES:

Spies v. Illinois: 123 U.S. 131 (1887). Opinion: White, C.J. No dissent.

A statute interpreted to mean that a juror in a criminal case is not disqualified because he has formed an opinion on the case through newspaper accounts or rumors, if he is able to base his verdict only upon the account given by the witnesses under oath, does not deprive an accused of the right to trial by impartial jury.

Moore v. New York: 333 U.S. 565 (1948). Opinion: Jackson, J. Dissenting: Murphy, Black, and Douglas, JJ.

Where the record of a case fails to show proof of systematic, intentional, and deliberate exclusion of Negroes from jury duty, there is no violation of due process or of equal protection of the laws.

Brown v. Allen: 344 U.S. 443 (1953). Opinion: Reed, J. Dissenting: Frankfurter, Black, and Douglas, JJ.

In a North Carolina case the Court held that the use, nondiscriminantly as to race, of the tax lists as the source of jury lists, does not violate the Fourteenth Amendment. Here there had been a good faith effort to secure competent juries.

See "Related Cases" under *Patton* and *Thiel,* pp. 168 and 171, above.

NOTE:

Fay, in effect, reiterates the principle that due process does not require that different groups or different races be represented on a jury. Too, there was no showing of discrimination to offend equal protection. Thus, a "blue ribbon" jury, which involves the selection of jurors with special qualifications, is valid. However, the Court has given some indication in recent years that it might want to take a "second look" at the "blue ribbbon" jury arrangement. The "blue ribbon" jury was abolished in New York in 1965.

Adamson v. California
332 U.S. 46; 67 S.Ct. 1672; 91 L.Ed. 1903 (1947)

(A citizen of the United States, Adamson, was convicted by a jury of murder in the first degree and without recommendation of mercy. Under the California Constitution the failure of a defendant to explain or deny evidence against him may be commented on by the court and by counsel and may be considered by both the court and the jury. Adamson did not testify. These provisions of the California Constitution were challenged as abridging the guarantee against self-incrimination and of due process.)

Vote: 5-4

Mr. Justice Reed delivered the opinion of the Court:

. . . A right to a fair trial is a right admittedly protected by the Due Process Clause of the Fourteenth Amendment. Therefore, appellant argues, the Due Process Clause of the Fourteenth Amendment protects his privilege against self-incrimination. The Due Process Clause of the Fourteenth Amendment, however, does not draw all the rights of the federal Bill of Rights under its protection. That contention was made and rejected in *Palko* v. *Connecticut*, 302 U.S. 319, 323. It was rejected with citation of the cases excluding several of the rights, protected by the Bill of Rights, against infringement by the National Government. Nothing has been called to our attention that either the framers of the Fourteenth Amendment or the states that adopted intended its Due Process Clause to draw within its scope the earlier amendments to the Constitution. *Palko* held that such provisions of the Bill of Rights as were "implicit in the concept of ordered liberty," 302 U.S. at page 325 . . . became secure from state interference by the clause. But it held nothing more.

Specifically, the Due Process Clause does not protect by virtue of its mere existence the accused's freedom from giving testimony by compulsion in state trials that is secured to him against federal interference by the Fifth Amendment. . . .

. . . When evidence is before a jury that threatens conviction, it does not seem unfair to require him to choose between leaving the adverse evidence unexplained and subjecting himself to impeachment through disclosure of former crimes. . . .

We find no other error that gives ground for our intervention in California's administration of criminal justice.

Affirmed.

Mr. Justice Frankfurter concurred:

. . . And so, when, as in a case like the present, a conviction in a State court is here for review under a claim that a right protected by the Due Process Clause of the Fourteenth Amendment has been denied, the issue is not whether an infraction of one of the specific provisions of the first eight Amendments is disclosed by the record. The relevant question is whether the criminal proceedings which resulted in conviction deprived the accused of the due process of law to which the United States Constitution entitled him. . . .

Mr. Justice Murphy dissented, with the concurrence of Mr. Justice Rutledge:

. . . I agree that the specific guarantees of the Bill of Rights should be carried over intact into the first section of the Fourteenth Amendment. But I am not prepared to say that the latter is entirely and necessarily limited by the Bill of Rights. Occasions may arise where a proceeding falls so far short of conforming to fundamental standards of procedure as to warrant constitutional condemnation in terms of a lack of due process despite the absence of a specific provision in the Bill of Rights. . . .

Mr. Justice Black dissented, with the concurrence of Mr. Justice Douglas:

. . . My study of the historical events that culminated in the Fourteenth Amendment, and the expressions of those who sponsored and favored, as well as those who opposed its submission and passage, persuades me that one of the chief objects that the provisions of the Amendment's first section, separately, and as a whole, were intended to accomplish was to make the Bill of Rights, applicable to the states. With full knowledge of the import of the *Barron* decision, the framers and backers of the Fourteenth Amendment proclaimed its purpose to be to overturn the constitutional rule that case had announced. This historical purpose has never received full consideration or exposition in any opinion of this Court interpreting the Amendment. . . .

For this reason, I am attaching to this dissent, an appendix which contains a resume, by no means complete, of the Amendment's history. In my judgment that history conclusively demonstrates that the language of the first section of the Fourteenth Amendment, taken as a whole, was thought by those responsible for its submission to the people, and by those who opposed its submission, sufficiently explicit to guarantee that thereafter no state could deprive its citizens of the privileges and protections of the Bill of Rights. Whether this Court ever will, or whether it now should, in the light of past decisions, give full effect to what the Amendment was intended to accomplish is not necessarily essential to a decision here. However that may be, our prior decisions, including *Twining*, do not prevent our carrying out that purpose, at least to the extent of making applicable to the states, not a mere part, as the Court has, but the full protection of the Fifth Amendment's provision against compelling evidence from an accused to convict him of crime. And I further contend that the "natural law" formula which the Court uses to reach its conclusion in this case should be abandoned as an incongruous excrescence on our Constitution. I believe that formula to be itself a violation of our Constitution, in that it subtly conveys to courts, at the expense of legislatures, ultimate power over public policies in fields where no specific provision of the Constitution limits legislative power. And my belief seems to be in accord with the views expressed by this Court, at least for the first two decades after the Fourteenth Amendment was adopted. . . .

RELATED CASES:

Twining v. New Jersey: 211 U.S. 78 (1908). Opinion: Moody, J. Dissenting: Harlan, J.
    See p. 261, above. Harlan's dissent in *Twining* reiterated the "absorbtionist" argument of his dissents in *Maxwell* v. *Dow* and *Hurtado*.

Palko v. Connecticut: 302 U.S. 319 (1937). Opinion: Cardozo, J. Dissenting: Butler, J.
    There may be provision in state law for appeal by the state of a decision in a criminal case where the verdict of guilty has applied to a lesser offense. The double jeopardy provisions of the Fifth Amendment are not applied to the states by virtue of the Fourteenth Amendment. Further, there could be no charge of lack of due process unless the first trial was without error. But see *Benton* v. *Maryland*, 395 U.S. 784 (1969), p. 240, above.

Griffin v. California: 380 U.S. 609 (1965). Opinion: Douglas, J. Dissenting: Stewart and White, JJ. Abstaining: Warren, C.J.
    The guarantee against self-incrimination includes prohibition against either comment by the prosecution on the accused's silence or instructions by the court that such silence is evidence of guilt. Therefore the jury cannot take into consideration the failure of the defendant to testify. This decision reversed *Twining* v. *New Jersey*, 211 U.S. 78 (1908) and *Adamson* v. *California*, 332 U.S. 46 (1947).
    See *Malloy* v. *Hogan*, p. 151, above.

NOTE:

    Mr. Justice Black's dissent in *Adamson* is one of the strongest argumentations of the case for the application of the entire Bill of Rights to the states by means of the Fourteenth Amendment ever presented. Three justices agreed with him, the "high water mark" of the movement. Therefore, due process is still not "a shorthand summary for the first eight amendments," as Mr. Justice Frankfurter put it in his very capable concurring opinion in *Adamson* in which he answered Black. But by the cumulative process the "absorptionists" of *Adamson* appear to have won. See Note following *Palko*, p. 240, above.

Wolf v. Colorado
338 U.S. 25; 69 S.Ct. 1359; 93 L.Ed. 1782 (1949)

(Police officers went to the office of a physician and, without a warrant, took his appointment book. From this source they obtained the names of patients who testified against the physician. Subsequently he was found guilty of illegal practice. The Court on *certiorari* had to determine whether a conviction in a state court for a state offense denies due process under the Fourteenth Amendment when the evidence used for conviction was obtained under circumstances that would have rendered it inadmissible in a prosecution for violation of a federal law in a federal court as violative of the guarantee of search and seizure under the Fourth Amendment as applied in *Weeks* v. *United States*, 232 U.S. 383.)

Vote: 6-3

Mr. Justice Frankfurter delivered the opinion of the Court:

. . . To rely on a tidy formula for the easy determination of what is a fundamental right for purposes of legal enforcement may satisfy a longing for certainty but ignores the movements of a free society. It belittles the scale of the conception of due process. The real clue to the problem confronting the judiciary in the application of the Due Process Clause is not to ask where the line is once and for all to be drawn but to recognize that it is for the Court to draw it by the gradual and empiric process of "inclusion and exclusion." *Davidson* v. *New Orleans*, 96 U.S. 97, 104. This was the Court's insight when first called upon to consider the problem; to this insight the Court has on the whole been faithful as case after case has come before it since *Davidson* v. *New Orleans* was decided.

The security of one's privacy against arbitrary intrusion by the police—which is at the core of the Fourth Amendment—is basic to a free society. It is therefore implicit in "the concept of ordered liberty" and as such enforceable against the States through the Due Process Clause. The knock at the door, whether by day or by night, as a prelude to a search, without authority of law but solely on the authority of the police, did not need the commentary of recent history to be condemned as inconsistent with the conception of human rights enshrined in the history and the basic constitutional documents of English-speaking peoples.

Accordingly, we have no hesitation in saying that were a State affirmatively to sanction such police incursion into privacy it would run counter to the guaranty of the Fourteenth Amendment. But the ways of enforcing such a basic right raise questions of a different order. How such arbitrary conduct should be checked, what remedies against it should be afforded, the means by which the right should be made effective, are all questions that are not to be so dogmatically answered as to preclude the varying solutions which spring from an allowable range of judgment on issues not susceptible of quantitative solution.

In *Weeks* v. *United States, supra*, this Court held that in a federal prosecution the Fourth Amendment barred the use of evidence secured through an illegal search and seizure. This ruling was made for the first time in 1914. It was not derived from the explicit requirements of the Fourth Amendment; it was not based on legislation expressing Congressional policy in the enforcement of the Constitution. The decision was a matter of judicial implication. Since then it has been frequently applied and we stoutly adhere to it. But the immediate question is whether the basic right to protection against arbitrary intrusion by the police demands the exclusion of logically relevant evidence obtained by an unreasonable search and seizure because, in a federal prosecution for a federal crime, it would be excluded. As a matter of inherent reason, one would suppose this to be an issue as to which men with complete devotion to the protection of the right of privacy might give different answers. When we find that in fact most of the English-speaking world does not regard as vital to such protection the exclusion of evidence thus obtained, we must hesitate to treat this remedy as an essential ingredient of the right. The contrariety of views of the States is particularly impressive in view of the careful reconsideration which they have given the problem in the light of the *Weeks* decision. . . .

We hold, therefore, that in a prosecution in a State court for a State crime the Fourteenth Amendment does not forbid the admission of evidence obtained by an unreasonable search and seizure. And though we have interpreted the Fourth Amendment to forbid the admission of such evidence, a different question would be presented if Congress under its legislative powers were to pass a statute purporting to negate the *Weeks* doctrine. We would then be faced with the problem of the respect to be accorded the legislative judgment on an issue as to which, in default of that judgment, we have been forced to depend upon our own. Problems of a converse character, also not before us, would be presented should Congress under Section 5 of the Fourteenth Amendment undertake to enforce the rights there guaranteed by attempting to make the *Weeks* doctrine binding upon the States.

Affirmed.

(The Appendix of the opinion includes a listing of the states of the Union and their attitudes on the *Weeks* doctrine. Australia, Canada, England, India, and Scotland are also included.)

Mr. Justice Black concurred:

. . . I agree with the conclusion of the Court that the Fourth Amendment's prohibition of "unreasonable searches and seizures" is enforceable against the states. Consequently, I should be for reversal of this case if I thought the Fourth Amendment not only prohibited "unreasonable searches and seizures," but also, of itself, barred the use of evidence so unlawfully obtained. But I agree with what appears to be a plain implication of the Court's opinion that the federal exclusionary rule is not a command of the Fourth Amendment but is a judicially created rule of evidence which Congress might negate. . . . This leads me to concur in the Court's judgment of affirmance.

It is not amiss to repeat my belief that the Fourteenth Amendment was intended to make the Fourth Amendment in its entirety applicable to the states. The Fourth Amendment was designed to protect people against unrestrained searches and seizures by sheriffs, policemen and other law enforcement officers. Such protection is an essential in a free society. . . .

Mr. Justice Rutledge dissented, joined by Mr. Justice Murphy:

. . . As Congress and this Court are, in my judgment, powerless to permit the admission in federal courts of evidence seized in defiance of the Fourth Amendment, so I think state legislators and judges—if subject to the Amendment, as I believe them to be—may not lend their offices to the admission in state courts of evidence thus seized. Compliance with the Bill of Rights betokens more than lip service.

The Court makes the illegality of this search and seizure its inarticulate premise of decision. I acquiese in that premise and think the conviction should be reversed.

Mr. Justice Murphy dissented, joined by Mr. Justice Rutledge:

. . . The conclusion is inescapable that but one remedy exists to deter violations of the search and seizure clause. That is the rule which excludes illegally obtained evidence. Only by exclusion can we impress upon the zealous prosecutor that violation of the Constitution will do him no good. And only when that point is driven home can the prosecutor be expected to emphasize the importance of observing constitutional demands in his instructions to the police. . . .

I cannot believe that we should decide due process questions by simply taking a poll of the rules in various jurisdictions, even if we follow the *Palko* "test." Today's decision will do inestimable harm to the cause of fair police methods in our cities and states. Even more important, perhaps, it must have tragic effect upon public respect for our judiciary. For the Court now allows what is indeed shabby business: lawlessness by officers of the law.

Since the evidence admitted was secured in violation of the Fourth Amendment, the judgment should be reversed.

Mr. Justice Douglas also dissented.

RELATED CASES:

Cassell v. Texas: 339 U.S. 282 (1950). Opinion: Reed, J. Dissenting: Jackson, J. Abstaining: Douglas, J.

In a dissenting opinion in the case (the decision holding that there had been discrimination against Negroes in the selection of a grand jury) Mr. Justice Jackson noted, "I would treat this as a case where the irregularity is not shown to have harmed this defendant, and affirm the conviction. But in this and similar cases, I would send a copy of the record to the Department of Justice for investigation as to whether there have been violations of the statute and if so, for prosecution." The jury commissioners were chosen from personal acquaintances and did not know the Negroes well.

Irvine v. California: 347 U.S. 128 (1954). Opinion: Jackson, J. Dissenting: Black, Douglas, Frankfurter, and Burton, JJ.

Evidence secured by officers by "trespass and probably a burglary" may be entered in a prosecution in a state court for a state offense. "We adhere to *Wolf* as stating the law of search-and-seizure cases and decline to introduce vague and subjective distinctions."

McKeiver v. Pennsylvania: 403 U.S. 528 (1971). Opinion: Blackmun, J. Dissenting: Douglas, Black, and Marshall, JJ.

In the case of a sixteen-year-old charged with acts of juvenile delinquency that under Pennsylvania law are felonies, the Court denied jury trial. It was held that juvenile court proceedings have not yet been held to be "criminal prosecution" within the meaning and reach of the Sixth Amendment made applicable to the states by the Fourteenth Amendment. In juvenile proceedings the applicable due process is fundamental fairness. To require a jury trial as a constitutional precept might make the juvenile proceeding into a fully adversary process. There would seem to be little need for the separate existence of a juvenile court system if the criminal adjudicative process of the "adult" court system is to be superimposed.

NOTE:

The net result of *Wolf* is that unreasonable searches and seizures are forbidden but the evidence thus secured may be admitted in state courts. This, of course, was modified by *Mapp* v. *Ohio*, 367 U.S. 643, 1961. *Wolf* is an unusual case in that the Court set forth a very specific point— that the security of one's privacy against arbitrary intrusion by the police is basic to a free society, in other words, is "fundamental"—but, having set down this doctrine, refused to proceed to the implementation or enforcement of it by the exclusion of evidence thus illegally secured. The case, as noted, is no longer controlling. See *Frank* v. *Maryland* and *Camara* v. *Municipal Court,* p. 127, above.

Mapp v. Ohio
367 U.S. 643; 81 S.Ct. 1684; 6 L.Ed. 2nd 1081 (1961)

(Police officers in Cleveland requested that they be admitted to the Mapp residence in order to search for a fugitive who was reportedly hiding in the home. Further, the police had word that a large amount of policy paraphernalia was hidden there. The officers proceeded to enter the house forcefully without a warrant, and to search the entire house from basement to second floor. The obscene materials for possession of which the defendant was ultimately convicted were discovered in the course of that widespread search. The use in the state court of the evidence thus obtained was challenged.)

Vote: 6-3

Mr. Justice Clark delivered the opinion of the Court:

. . . Seventy-five years ago, in *Boyd* v. *United States*, 116 U.S. 616, 630, 1886, considering the Fourth and Fifth Amendments as running "almost into each other" on the facts before it, this Court held that the doctrines of those Amendments "apply to all invasions on the part of the government and its employes of the sanctity of a man's home and the privacies of life. . . ."

Less than 30 years after *Boyd*, this Court, in *Weeks* v. *United States*, 232 U.S. 383, 1914, stated that "the 4th Amendment . . . put the courts of the United States and Federal officials, in the exercise of their power and authority, under limitations and restraints [and] forever secure[d] the people, their persons, houses, papers, and effects, against all unreasonable searches and seizures under the guise of law . . . and the duty of giving to it force and effect is obligatory upon all entrusted under our Federal system with the enforcement of the laws". . . .

In 1949, 35 years after *Weeks* was announced, this Court, in *Wolf* v. *People of State of Colorado, supra*, again for the first time, discussed the effect of the Fourth Amendment upon the States through the operation of the Due Process Clause of the Fourteenth Amendment. It said: "[W]e have no hesitation in saying that were a State affirmatively to sanction such police incursion into privacy it would run counter to the guaranty of the Fourteenth Amendment." Nevertheless, after declaring that the "security of one's privacy against arbitrary intrusion by the police" is "implicit in the 'concept of ordered liberty' and as such enforceable against the States through the Due Process Clause," cf. *Palko* v. *State of Connecticut*, 302 U.S. 319, 1937, and announcing that it "stoutly adhere[d]" to the *Weeks* decision, the Court decided that the *Weeks* exclusionary rule would not then be imposed upon the States as "an essential ingredient of the right." 338 U.S. at pages 27-29. The Court's reasons for not considering essential to the right to privacy, as a curb imposed upon the States by the Due Process Clause, that which decades before had been posited as part and parcel of the Fourth Amendment's limitation upon federal encroachment of individual privacy, were bottomed on factual considerations.

. . . Today we once again examine *Wolf's* constitutional documentation of the right to privacy free from unreasonable state intrusion, and, after its dozen years on our books, are led by it to close the only courtroom door remaining open to evidence secured by official lawlessness in flagrant abuse of that basic right, reserved to all persons as a specific guarantee against that very same unlawful conduct. We hold that all evidence obtained by searches and seizures in violation of the Constitution is, by that same authority, inadmissible in a state court.

Since the Fourth Amendment's right of privacy has been declared enforceable against the States through the Due Process Clause of the Fourteenth, it is enforceable against them by the same sanction of exclusion as is used against the Federal Government. . . .

Moreover, our holding that the exclusionary rule is an essential part of both the Fourth and Fourteenth Amendments is not only the logical dictate of prior cases, but it also makes very good sense. There is no war between the Constitution and common sense. . . .

The ignoble shortcut to conviction left open to the State tends to destroy the entire system of constitutional restraints on which the liberties of the people rest. Having once recognized that the right to privacy embodied in the Fourth Amendment is enforceable against the States, and that the right to be secure against rude invasions of privacy by state officers is, therefore, constitutional in origin, we can no longer permit that right to remain an empty promise. Because it is enforceable in the same manner and to like effect as other basic rights secured by the Due Process Clause, we can no longer permit it to be revocable at the whim of any police officer who, in the name of law enforcement itself, chooses to suspend its enjoyment. Our decision, founded on reason and truth, gives to the individual no more than that which the Constitution guarantees him, to the police officer no less than that to which honest law enforcement is entitled, and, to the courts, that judicial integrity so necessary in the true administration of justice.

The judgment of the Supreme Court of Ohio is reversed and the cause remanded for further proceedings not inconsistent with this opinion.

Reversed and remanded.

Mr. Justice Black concurred:

. . . I am still not persuaded that the Fourth Amendment, standing alone, would be enough to bar the introduction into evidence against an accused of papers and effects seized from him in violation of its commands. For the Fourth Amendment does not itself contain any provision expressly precluding the use of such evidence, and I am extremely doubtful that such a provision could properly be inferred from nothing more than the basic command against unreasonable searches and seizures. Reflection on the problem, however, in the light of cases coming before the Court since Wolf, has led me to conclude that when the Fourth Amendment's ban against unreasonable searches and seizures is considered together with the Fifth Amendment's ban against compelled self-incrimination, a constitutional basis emerges which not only justifies but actually requires the exclusionary rule. . . .

Mr. Justice Douglas concurred:

. . . The only remaining remedy, if exclusion of the evidence is not required, is an action of trespass by the homeowner against the offending officer. Mr. Justice Murphy showed how onerous and difficult it would be for the citizen to maintain that action and how meagre the relief even if the citizen prevails. 338 U.S. 42-44. The truth is that trespass actions against officers who make unlawful searches and seizures are mainly illusory remedies.

. . . Once evidence, inadmissible in a federal court, is admissible in a state court a "double standard" exists which, as the Court points out, leads to "working arrangements" that undercut federal policy and reduce some aspects of law enforcement to shabby business. The rule that supports that practice does not have the force of reason behind it.

Mr. Justice Harlan, whom Mr. Justice Frankfurter and Mr. Justice Whittaker joined, dissented:

In overruling the *Wolf* case the Court, in my opinion, has forgotten the sense of judicial restraint which, with due regard for *stare decisis*, is one element that should enter into deciding whether a past decision of this Court should be overruled. Apart from that I also believe that the *Wolf* rule represents sounder Constitutional doctrine than the new rule which now replaces it.

From the Court's statement of the case one would gather that the central, if not controlling, issue on this appeal is whether illegally state-seized evidence is Constitutionally admissable in a state prosecution, an issue which would of course face us with the need for re-examining *Wolf*. However, such is not the situation. For, although that question was indeed raised here and below among the appellant's subordinate points, the new and pivotal issue brought to the Court by this appeal is whether § 2905.34 of the Ohio Revised Code making criminal the *mere* knowing possession or control of obscene material, and under which appellant has been convicted, is consistent with the rights of free thought and expression assured against state action by the Fourteenth Amendment. That was the principal issue which was decided by the Ohio Supreme Court, which was tendered by appellant's Jurisdictional Statement, and which was briefed and argued in this Court.

In this posture of things, I think it fair to say that five members of this Court have simply "reached out" to overrule *Wolf*. With all respect for the views of the majority, and recognizing that *stare decisis* carries different weight in Constitutional adjudication than it does in nonconstitutional decision, I can perceive no justification for regarding this case as an appropriate occasion for re-examining *Wolf*. . . .

RELATED CASES:

Boyd v. United States: 116 U.S. 616 (1886). Opinion: Bradley, J. No dissent.
The Fifth and Fourth Amendments "run almost into each other" since compulsory production of the private books and papers of the owner of goods sought to be forfeited in such a suit is compelling him to be a witness against himself and is an unreasonable search and seizure.

Weeks v. United States: 232 U.S. 383 (1914). Opinion: Day, J. No dissent.
Evidence secured by unreasonable search and seizure is excluded from use in a federal criminal trial. This is a rule of evidence adopted by the Court rather than an integral part of the search and seizure guarantee. See p. 139, above.

McNabb v. United States: 318 U.S. 332 (1943). Opinion: Frankfurter, J. Dissenting: Reed, J. Abstaining: Rutledge, J.
An accused person must be taken "without unnecessary delay" before a committing magistrate. If this is not done, a confession secured from the prisoner is not admissible in a federal court. This rule was enunciated by the Court under its general supervisory power over the federal courts. Here a federal revenue officer had been shot.

Stefanelli v. Minard: 342 U.S. 117 (1951). Opinion: Frankfurter, J. Dissenting: Douglas, J. Abstaining: Minton, J.
Federal courts should refuse to intervene in state criminal proceedings to suppress the use of evidence even when claimed to have been secured by unlawful search and seizure. Here New Jersey had indicted Stefanelli for bookmaking on the basis of such evidence.

Mallory v. United States: 354 U.S. 449 (1957). Opinion: Frankfurter, J. No dissent.
This case reversed a conviction for rape in a Federal District Court. The accused was arrested in early afternoon and held near numerous committing magistrates but was not taken before one until the next day. He confessed about 9:30 P.M. on the day of his arrest but was not told of his right to counsel, his right to remain silent, or his right to a preliminary examination before a magistrate.

Ker v. California: 374 U.S. 23 (1963). Opinion: Clark, J. Dissenting: Brennan, J., Warren, C.J., and Goldberg and Douglas, JJ.
Where information within the knowledge of police officers at the time of arrest without a warrant clearly furnished grounds for a reasonable belief that an offense had been or was being committed, the entry and search of the apartment was not unreasonable under the standards of the Fourth Amendment as applied to the states through the Fourteenth Amendment. Involved here was possession of marihuana.

Preston v. United States: 376 U.S. 364 (1964). Opinion: Black, J. No dissent.

Search of an autotmobile without a warrant at a time subsequent to arrest is too remote in time or place to have been made as incidental to the arrest and thus fails to meet the test of reasonableness under the Fourth Amendment rendering the evidence obtained as a result of the search inadmissible. Preston had been arrested for vagrancy. Hours later evidence was found in his car of conspiracy to rob a federally insured bank.

Rugendorf v. United States: 376 U.S. 528 (1964). Opinion: Clark, J. Dissenting: Douglas, Brennan, and Goldberg, JJ., and Warren, C.J.

A search warrant may be issued by a United States Commissioner when there is substantial basis for him to conclude that stolen property is in a home. No more is required for a showing of probable cause. This was based partly on statements of informants. Furs were involved here. United States Commissioners are now known as "Magistrates."

Aquilar v. Texas: 378 U.S. 108 (1964). Opinion: Goldberg, J. Dissenting: Clark, Black, and Stewart, JJ.

A search warrant was improperly issued when founded on an affidavit alleging belief that the contraband would be found because of information supplied by an unidentified informant without any supporting facts. The Court held that this affidavit secured by two Houston police officers was invalid because there was lack of probable cause from the facts or circumstances presented.

Stanford v. Texas: 379 U.S. 476 (1965). Opinion: Stewart, J. No dissent.

Under a warrant for the search of a home for books, pamphlets, and other written instruments concerning the Communist Party of Texas two thousand items were seized. The Court held that this was the kind of warrant which it was the purpose of the Fourth Amendment to forbid—a general warrant. The Fourth Amendment requires precision in describing the place to be searched and the person or things to be seized. After a five-hour search such things as insurance policies and household bills were taken.

Linkletter v. Walker: 381 U.S. 618 (1965). Opinion: Clark, J. Dissenting: Black and Douglas, JJ.

The Constitution neither prohibits nor requires retrospective effect be given to a new rule. To make the rule of *Mapp* v. *Ohio* retrospective would tax the administration of justice to the utmost, the Court held. There is no likelihood of unreliability or coercion present in a search and seizure case.

Lewis v. United States: 385 U.S. 206 (1966). Opinion: Warren, C.J. Dissenting: Douglas, J.

When a home is converted into a commercial center to which outsiders are invited for purposes of transacting unlawful business, that business is entitled to no greater sanctity than if it were carried on in a store or other public place.

Terry v. Ohio: 392 U.S. 1 (1968). Opinion: Warren, C.J. Dissenting: Douglas, J.

Where a police officer has reasonable grounds to believe that a suspect is armed and dangerous and it is necessary for the protection of himself and others to take swift measures to discover the true facts and neutralize the threat of harm the officer may search the suspect. The search must be confined in scope to an intrusion reasonably designed to discover guns, knives, clubs, or other hidden instruments. Such a search is reasonable under the Fourth Amendment and any weapons seized may be introduced in evidence. The procedure is called "patting down." Here warrant procedure is not practical.

Sibron v. New York: 392 U.S. 40 (1968). Opinion: Warren, C.J. Dissenting: Black, J.

Where a search of a suspect by a police officer is not reasonably limited in scope to the accomplishment of the only goal which might conceivably have justified its inception—the protection of the officer by disarming a potentially dangerous man—the search is a violation of the Fourth Amendment. This is "stop and frisk" procedure.

Chambers v. Maroney: 399 U.S. 42 (1970). Opinion: White, J. Dissenting: Harlan, J. Abstaining: Blackmun, J.

Search and seizure of an automobile without a warrant is permissible when the search is made as a part of a valid arrest which was undertaken because of probable cause to believe the accused had committed a felony. This is true even though the search takes place some time after arrest when the car might have seen searched at the time of arrest.

Adams v. Williams: 407 U.S. 143 (1972). Opinion: Rehnquist, J. Dissenting: Douglas, Marshall, and Brennan, JJ.

Where a tip to a police officer by a reliable informant has proved correct (here possession of a gun and narcotics), there is probable cause for arrest. When the proper arrest takes place in a car, both the person and the car may be searched incident to the arrest and the fruits of the search may be admitted at the trial. An officer can conduct a limited protective search for concealed weapons when he has reason to believe the suspect is armed and dangerous.

NOTE:

Mapp, a truly leading case, marks the acceptance by the Court of the *Weeks* rule of exclusion of evidence secured by unreasonable search and seizure in state courts as well as federal. This came only after years of inconclusiveness best illustrated by the *Wolf* v. *Colorado* case in which the Court said "yes" but then "no." *Mapp*, of course, represents a still further extension of the "Gitlow doctrine," this time applying the Fourth Amendment to the states by means of the "liberty" and "due process" provisions of the Fourteenth Amendment. *Terry* and *Sibron* represent the latest view of the Court in "stop and frisk" situations.

Breithaupt v. Abram
352 U.S. 432; 77 S.Ct. 408; 1 L.Ed. 2nd 448 (1957)

(Breithaupt was driving a pickup truck on a state highway in New Mexico when he was involved in a collision which resulted in the deaths of three persons, and he was seriously injured. A pint whisky bottle, almost empty, was found in the glove compartment of the truck. Breithaupt was taken to a hospital and, while he was unconscious in the emergency room, a physician, at the request of a state patrolman, took a sample of his blood. Laboratory analysis showed that it contained about .17% alcohol. Subsequently Breithaupt was charged with involuntary manslaughter, and at the trial an expert testified that a person with .17% alcohol in his blood was under the influence of intoxicating liquor. The resulting conviction was challenged on the basis that the involuntary blood test deprived him of due process of law under the Fourteenth Amendment.)

Vote: 6-3

Mr. Justice Clark delivered the opinion of the Court:

. . . Petitioner relies on the proposition that "the generative principles" of the Bill of Rights should extend the protection of the Fourth and Fifth Amendments to his case through the Due Process Clause of the Fourteenth Amendment. But *Wolf* v. *Colorado*, 338 U.S. 25 (1949), answers this contention in the negative. . . . New Mexico has rejected, as it may, the exclusionary rule set forth in *Weeks*. . . . Therefore, the rights petitioner claims afford no aid to him here for the fruits of the violations, if any, are admissible in the State's prosecution.

Petitioner's remaining and primary assault on his conviction is not so easily unhorsed. He urges that the conduct of the state officers here offends that "sense of justice" of which we spoke in *Rochin* v. *California*, 342 U.S. 165 (1952). In that case state officers broke into the home of the accused and observed him place something in his mouth. The officers forced open his mouth after considerable struggle in an unsuccessful attempt to retrieve whatever was put there. A stomach pump was later forcibly used and among the matter extracted from his stomach were found narcotic pills. As we said there, "this course of proceeding by agents of government to obtain evidence is bound to offend even hardened sensibilities." *Id.*, at 172. We set aside the conviction because such conduct "shocked the conscience" and was so "brutal" and offensive that it did not comport with traditional ideas of fair play and decency. We therefore found that the conduct was offensive to due process. But we see nothing comparable here to the facts in *Rochin*.

Basically the distinction rests on the fact that there is nothing "brutal" or "offensive" in the taking of a sample of blood when done, as in this case, under the protective eye of a physician. To be sure, the driver here was unconscious when the blood was taken, but the absence of conscious consent, without more, does not necessarily render the taking a violation of a constitutional right; and certainly the test as administered here would not be considered offensive by even the most delicate. Furthermore, due process is not measured by the yardstick of personal reaction or the sphygmogram of the most sensitive person, but by that whole community sense of "decency and fairness" that has been woven by common experience into the fabric of acceptable conduct. It is on this bedrock that this Court has established the concept of due process. The blood test procedure has become routine in our everyday life. It is a ritual for those going into the military service as well as those applying for marriage licenses. Many colleges require such tests before permitting entrance and literally millions of us have voluntarily gone through the same, though a longer, routine in becoming blood donors. Likewise, we note that a majority of our States have either enacted statutes in some form authorizing tests of this nature or permit findings so obtained to be admitted in evidence. We therefore conclude that a blood test taken by a skilled technician is not such "conduct that shocks the conscience," *Rochin, supra*, at 172, nor such a method of obtaining evidence that it offends a "sense of justice," *Brown* v. *Mississippi*, 297 U.S. 278, 285-286 (1936). This is not to say that the indiscriminate taking of blood under different conditions or by those not competent to do so may not amount to such "brutality" as would come under the *Rochin* rule. The chief law-enforcement officer of New Mexico, while at the Bar of this Court, assured us that every proper medical precaution is afforded an accused from whom blood is taken.

The test upheld here is not attacked on the ground of any basic deficiency or of injudicious application, but admittedly is a scientifically accurate method of detecting alcoholic content in the blood, thus furnishing an exact measure upon which to base a decision as to intoxication. Modern community living requires modern scientific methods of crime detection lest the public go unprotected. The increasing slaughter on our highways, most of which should be avoidable, now reaches the astounding figures only heard of on the battlefield. The States, through safety measures, modern scientific methods, and strict enforcement of traffic laws, are using all reasonable means to make automobile driving less dangerous.

As against the right of an individual that his person be held inviolable, even against so slight an intrusion as involved in applying a blood test of the kind to which millions of Americans submit as a matter of course nearly every day, must be set the interests of society in the scientific determination of intoxication, one of the great causes of the mortal hazards of the road. And the more so since the test likewise may establish innocence, thus affording protection against the treachery of judgment based on one or more of the senses. Furthermore, since our criminal law is to no small extent justified by the assumption of deterrence, the individual's right to immunity from such invasion of the body as is involved in a properly safeguarded blood test is far outweighed by the value of its deterrent effect due to public realization that the issue of driving while under the influence of alcohol can often by this method be taken out of the confusion of conflicting contentions.

For these reasons the judgment is affirmed.

Mr. Chief Justice Warren, with whom Mr. Justice Black and Mr. Justice Douglas joined, dissented:

The judgment in this case should be reversed if *Rochin* v. *California*, 342 U.S. 165, is to retain its vitality and stand as more than an instance of personal revulsion against particular police methods. I cannot agree with the Court when it says, "we see nothing comparable here to the facts in *Rochin*." It seems to me the essential elements of the cases are the same and the same result should follow.

There is much in the Court's opinion concerning the hazards on our nation's highways, the efforts of the States to enforce the traffic laws and the necessity for the use of modern scientific methods in the detection of crime. Everyone can agree with these sentiments, and yet they do not help us particularly in determining whether this case can be distinguished from *Rochin*. That case grew out of police efforts to curb the narcotics traffic, in which there is surely a state interest of at least as great magnitude as the interest in highway law enforcement. Nor does the fact that many States sanction the use of blood test evidence differentiate the cases. At the time *Rochin* was decided illegally obtained evidence was admissible in the vast majority of States. In both *Rochin* and this case the officers had probable cause to suspect the defendant of the offense of which they sought evidence. In *Rochin* the defendant was known as a narcotics law violator, was arrested under suspicious circumstances and was seen by the officers to swallow narcotics. In neither case, of course, are we concerned with the defendant's guilt or innocence. The sole problem is whether the proceeding was tainted by a violation of the defendant's constitutional rights.

In reaching its conclusion that in this case, unlike *Rochin*, there is nothing "brutal" or "offensive" the Court has not kept separate the component parts of the problem. Essentially there are two: the character of the invasion of the body and the expression of the victim's will; the latter may be manifested by physical resistance. Of course, one may consent to having his blood extracted or his stomach pumped and thereby waive any due process objection. In that limited sense the expression of the will is significant. But where there is no affirmative consent, I cannot see that it should make any difference whether one states unequivocally that he objects or resorts to physical violence in protest or is in such condition that he is unable to protest. The Court, however, states that "the absence of conscious consent, without more, does not necessarily render the taking a violation of a constitutional right." This implies that a different result might follow if petitioner had been conscious and had voiced his objection. I reject the distinction.

. . . I cannot accept an analysis that would make physical resistance by a prisoner a prerequisite to the existence of his constitutional rights.

Apart from the irrelevant factor of physical resistance, the techniques used in this case and in *Rochin* are comparable. In each the operation was performed by a doctor in a hospital. In each there was an extraction of body fluids. Neither operation normally causes any lasting ill effects. . . .

Only personal reaction to the stomach pump and the blood test can distinguish them. To base the restriction which the Due Process Clause imposes on state criminal procedures upon such reactions is to build on shifting sands. We should in my opinion, hold that due process means at least that law-enforcement officers in their efforts to obtain evidence from persons suspected of crime must stop short of bruising the body, breaking skin, puncturing tissue or extracting body fluids, whether they contemplate doing it by force or by stealth.

Viewed according to this standard, the judgment should be reversed.

Mr. Justice Douglas, with whom Mr. Justice Black joined, dissented:

The Court seems to sanction in the name of law enforcement the assault made by the police on this unconscious man. If law enforcement were the chief value in our constitutional scheme, then due process would shrivel and become of little value in protecting the rights of the citizen. But those who fashioned the Constitution put certain rights out of the reach of the police and preferred other rights over law enforcement. . . .

And if the decencies of a civilized state are the test, it is repulsive to me for the police to insert needles into an unconscious person in order to get the evidence necessary to convict him, whether they find the person unconscious, give him a pill which puts him to sleep, or use force to subdue him. The indignity to the individual is the same in one case as in the other, for in each is his body invaded and assaulted by the police who are supposed to be the citizen's protector.

I would reverse the judgment of conviction.

RELATED CASES:

Brown v. Mississippi: 297 U.S. 278 (1936). Opinion: Hughes, C. J. No dissent.

A conviction of murder based solely on confessions admittedly obtained under torture cannot stand. "Because a state may dispense with a jury trial, it does not follow that it may substitute trial by ordeal. The rack and torture chamber may not be substituted for the witness stand." This is sometimes referred to as the "third degree case." The trial was "a mere pretence." Three Negroes were involved.

Feldman v. United States: 322 U.S. 487 (1944). Opinion: Frankfurter, J. Dissenting: Black, J.

When a state has extracted evidence under a state immunity statute, there is no bar to the federal government using this testimony in a prosecution in a federal court for a federal offense. A state by its actions cannot "restrict the operations of the National Government within its sphere." This involved the supremacy of national law. There can be no "complicity" of federal officers in a state case. This is required by our system of "dual sovereignties."

Knapp v. Schweitzer: 357 U.S. 371 (1958). Opinion: Frankfurter, J. Dissenting: Warren, C.J., and Black and Douglas, JJ.

Refusal of a person to answer after being granted immunity under a state statute may validly result in citation for contempt in state court. The possibility that answering might subject him to federal prosecution for violation of a federal statute will not excuse him from answering. The Fifth Amendment applies only to the federal government. See *Malloy* v. *Hogan*, 378 U.S. 1 (1964) and *Murphy* v. *Waterfront Commission*, 378 U.S. 52 (1964), pp. 151 and 240 respectively, above. This case reiterated *Feldman*.

Schmerber v. California: 384 U.S. 757 (1966). Opinion: Brennan, J. Dissenting: Warren, C.J., and Black, Douglas, and Fortas, JJ.

The privilege against self-incrimination protects an accused only from being compelled to testify against himself or otherwise provide the state with evidence of a testimonial or communicative nature. The withdrawal of blood even against the objections of the defendant and use of the analysis did not involve compulsion of these ends. This was not violative of either search and seizure or of self-incrimination.

United States v. Dionisio: 410 U.S. 1 (1973). Opinion: Stewart, J. Dissenting: Brennan, Douglas, and Marshall, JJ.

A grand jury subpoena called for voice exemplars so that they could be compared with recorded conversations that had been received. The Court upheld the subpoenas noting that the voice recordings were to be used solely to measure the physical properties of the witnesses' voices, not for the testimonial or communicative content of what was to be said. "No person can have a reasonable expectation that others will not know the sound of his voice, any more than he can reasonably expect that his face will be a mystery to the world." There is no Fourth Amendment protection for such disclosure.

NOTE:

Breithaupt illustrates the difficulty that faced the Court as long as *Wolf* v. *Colorado* was law. With *Mapp* such dilemmas should be at least reduced to a minimum. Now at least it is clear that the search and seizure guarantee is as applicable to state as to federal procedure. Beyond this there will remain, of course, the matter of fundamental fairness that is involved in the concept of essential justice under due process.

For the sake of a more adequate comparison, it is unfortunate that in both *Breithaupt* and *Rochin* the accused was not either conscious or unconscious. As is so often true of dissenting opinions, the dissent in *Breithaupt* seems to make much sense. In the more recent *Schmerber* case the accused was conscious and objected to the test but the Court reaffirmed *Breithaupt* thus confirming it as the controlling case in the matter.

Chambers v. Florida
309 U.S. 227; 60 S.Ct. 472; 84 L.Ed. 716 (1940)

(Chambers and others, Negroes, were accused of the robbery and murder of Robert Darey, white, in Pompano, Florida. They were then removed to the Dade County Jail at Miami as a safeguard against mob violence. For a period of a week they were questioned continuously and denied constantly their guilt. At the end of the week, after an all-night questioning period, all confessed. These "sunrise" confessions were used to obtain convictions. This procedure was challenged as a violation of due process of law under the Fourteenth Amendment.)

Vote: 8-0

Mr. Justice Black delivered the opinion of the Court:

. . . This requirement—of conforming to fundamental standards of procedure in criminal trials—was made operative against the States by the Fourteenth Amendment. Where one of several accused had limped into the trial court as a result of admitted physical mistreatment inflicted to obtain confessions upon which a jury had returned a verdict of guilty of murder, this Court recently declared, *Brown* v. *Mississippi* . . . , that "It would be difficult to conceive of methods more revolting to the sense of justice than those taken to procure the confessions of these petitioners, and the use of the confession thus obtained as the basis for conviction and sentence was a clear denial of due process."

Here, the record develops a sharp conflict upon the issue of physical violence and mistreatment, but shows, without conflict, the dragnet methods of arrest on suspicion without warrant, and the protracted questioning and cross questioning of these ignorant young colored tenant farmers by State officials ond other white citizens, in a fourth floor jail room, where as prisoners they were without friends, advisers or counselors, and under circumstances calculated to break the strongest nerve and the stoutest resistance. Just as our decision in *Brown* v. *Mississippi* was based upon the fact that the confessions were the result of compulsion, so in the present case, the admitted practices were such as to justify the statement that "The undisputed facts showed that compulsion was applied."

For five days petitioners were subjected to interrogations culminating in Saturday's (May 20th) all night examination. Over a period of five days they steadily refused to confess and disclaimed any guilt. The very circumstances surrounding their confinement and their questioning without any formal charges having been brought, were such as to fill petitioners with terror and frightful misgivings. Some were practical strangers in the community; three were arrested in a one-room farm tenant house which was their home; the haunting fear of mob violence was around them in an atmosphere charged with excitement and public indignation. From virtually the moment of their arrest until their eventual confessions they never knew just when anyone would be called back to the fourth floor room, and there, surrounded by his accusers and others, interrogated by men who held their very lives —so far as these ignorant petitioners could know—in the balance. The rejection of petitioner Woodward's first "confession," given in the early hours of Sunday morning, because it was found wanting, demonstrates the relentless tenacity which "broke" petitioners' will and rendered them helpless to resist their accusers further. To permit human lives to be forfeited upon confessions thus obtained would make of the constitutional requirement of due process of law a meaningless symbol.

We are not impressed by the argument that law enforcement methods such as those under review are necessary to uphold our laws. The Constitution proscribes such lawless means irrespective of the end. And this argument flouts the basic principle that all people must stand on an equality before the bar of justice in every American court. Today, as in ages past, we are not without tragic proof that the exalted power of some governments to punish manufactured crime dictatorially is the handmaid of tyranny. Under our constitutional system, courts stand against any winds that blow as havens of refuge for those who might otherwise suffer because they are helpless, weak, outnumbered, or because they are non-conforming victims of prejudice and public excitement. Due process of law, preserved for all by our Constitution, commands that no such practice as that disclosed by this record shall send any accused to his death. No higher duty, no more solemn responsibility, rests upon this Court, than that of translating into living law and maintaining this constitutional shield deliberately planned and inscribed for the benefit of every human being subject to our Constitution—of whatever race, creed or persuasion.

The Supreme Court of Florida was in error and its judgment is reversed.

Mr. Justice Murphy took no part in the consideration or decision of this case.

RELATED CASES:

Lisenba v. California: 314 U.S. 219 (1941). Opinion: Roberts, J. Dissenting: Black and Douglas, JJ.

When questioning by relays of officers went on continually for two days and nights but the confession did not occur until ten days later, there was no denial of due process, and the evidence so secured could be used. Questioning for extended periods does not necessarily mean lack of due process.

Ward v. Texas: 316 U.S. 547 (1942). Opinion: Byrnes, J. No dissent.

Where law enforcement officers arrest an individual without a warrant, accuse him of murder, incarcerate him and by means of persistent questioning coerce him to confess, the use of the confession at trial will void a conviction.

Ashcraft v. Tennessee: 322 U.S. 143 (1944). Opinion: Black, J. Dissenting: Jackson, Roberts, and Frankfurter, JJ.

Thirty-six hours of continuous questioning by officers using powerful electric lights that results in a confession "is so inherently coercive that its very existence is irreconcilable with the possession of mental freedom by a lone suspect against whom its full coercive force is brought to bear." There was no physical abuse.

NOTE:

Chambers is again illustrative of the concern the Court has for circumstances surrounding cases that come before it. Here psychological coercion was held to be violative of due process. Either physical or psychological coercion is contrary to the "essential justice" guaranteed by the Fourteenth Amendment against transgression by the states.

Winters v. New York
333 U.S. 507; 68 S.Ct. 665; 92 L.Ed. 840 (1948)

(Winters, a New York City bookdealer, was convicted of having in his possession with intent to sell certain magazines claimed to violate a portion of the New York Penal Law. This part prohibits such activity in regard to publications "principally made up of criminal news, police reports, or accounts of criminal deeds, or pictures, or stories of deeds of bloodshed, lust or crime." This was challenged as being contrary to the right of freedom of speech and press made applicable to the states by the Fourteenth Amendment.)

Vote: 6-3

Mr. Justice Reed delivered the opinion of the Court:

. . . Acts of gross and open indecency or obscenity, injurious to public morals, are indictable at common law, as violative of the public policy that requires from the offender retribution for acts that flaunt accepted standards of conduct. . . . When a legislative body concludes that the mores of the community call for an extension of the impermissible limits, an enactment aimed at the evil is plainly within its power, if it does not transgress the boundaries fixed by the Constitution for freedom of expression. The standards of certainty in statutes punishing for offenses is higher than in those depending primarily upon civil sanction for enforcement. The crime "must be defined with appropriate definiteness." *Cantwell* v. *Connecticut,* 310 U.S. 296; *Pierce* v. *United States,* 314 U.S. 306, 311. There must be ascertainable standards of guilt. Men of common intelligence cannot be required to guess at the meaning of the enactment. The vagueness may be from uncertainty in regard to persons within the scope of the act, . . . or in regard to the applicable tests to ascertain guilt. . . .

The subsection of New York Penal Law, as now interpreted by the Court of Appeals, prohibits distribution of a magazine principally made up of criminal news or stories of deeds of bloodshed or lust, so massed as to become vehicles for inciting violent and depraved crimes against the person. But even considering the gloss put upon the literal meaning by the Court of Appeals' restriction of the statute to collections of stories "so massed as to become vehicles for inciting violent and depraved crimes against the person . . . not necessarily . . . sexual passion," we find the specification of publications, prohibited from distribution, too uncertain and indefinite to justify the conviction of this petitioner. Even though all detective tales and treatises on criminology are not forbidden, and though publications made up of criminal deeds not characterized by bloodshed or lust are omitted from the interpretation of the Court of Appeals, we think fair use of collections of pictures and stories would be interdicted because of the utter impossibility of the actor or the trier to know where this new standard of guilt would draw the line between the allowable and the forbidden publications. No intent or purpose is required—no indecency or obscenity in any sense heretofore known to the law. . . .

The Statute as construed by the Court of Appeals does not limit punishment to the indecent and obscene, as formerly understood. When stories of deeds of bloodshed, such as many in the accused magazines, are massed so as to incite to violent crimes, the statute is violated. It does not seem to us that an honest distributor of publications could know when he might be held to have ignored such a prohibition. Collections of tales of war horrors, otherwise unexceptionable, might well be found to be "massed" so as to become "vehicles for inciting violent and depraved crimes." Where a statute is so vague as to make criminal an innocent act, a conviction under it cannot be sustained. . . .

Reversed.

Mr. Justice Frankfurter dissented, with the concurrence of Mr. Justice Jackson and Mr. Justice Burton:

. . . The action of this Court today in invalidating legislation having the support of almost half the States of the Union rests essentially on abstract notions about "indefiniteness." The Court's opinion could have been written by one who had never read the issues of "Headquarters Detective" which are the basis of the prosecution before us, who had never deemed their contents as relevant to the form in which the New York legislation was cast, had never considered the bearing of such "literature" on juvenile delinquency, in the allowable judgment of the legislature. Such abstractions disregard the considerations that may well have moved and justified the State in not being more explicit than these state enactments are. . . .

. . . The essence of the Court's decision is that it gives publications which have "nothing of any possible value to society" constitutional protection but denies to the States the power to prevent the grave evils to which, in their rational judgment, such publications give rise. The legislatures of New York and the other States were concerned with these evils and not with neutral abstractions of harmlessness. Nor was the New York Court of Appeals merely resting, as it might have done, on a deep-seated conviction as to the existence of an evil and as to the appropriate means for checking it. That court drew on its experience, as revealed by "many recent records" of criminal convictions before it, for its understanding of the practical concrete reasons that led the legislatures of a score of States to pass the enactments now here struck down. . . .

The Court has been led into error, if I may respectfully suggest, by confusing want of certainty as to the outcome of different prosecutions for similar conduct, with want of definiteness in what the law prohibits. But diversity in result for similar conduct in different trials under the same statute is an unavoidable feature of criminal justice. So long as these diversities are not designed consequences but due merely to human fallibility, they do not deprive persons of due process of law. . . .

RELATED CASES:

Moore v. Dempsey: 261 U.S. 86 (1923). Opinion: Holmes, J. Dissenting: McReynolds and Sutherland, JJ.

Where the atmosphere of a trial involves intimidation and threats of mob violence, there is denial of due process. Here, under such circumstances, five Negroes were convicted of first-degree murder of a white man and sentenced to death in Arkansas. The trial lasted forty-five minutes. The jury verdict was in five minutes.

Connally v. General Construction Co.: 269 U.S. 385 (1926). Opinion: Sutherland, J. No dissent.

The "vice of vagueness" was also present in an Oklahoma statute that made criminal paying employees "less than the current rate of per diem wages in the locality where the work is performed." Where one must guess at the meaning of a statute, there is a violation of due process.

Tumey v. Ohio: 273 U.S. 510 (1927). Opinion: Taft, C.J. No dissent.

When the presiding judge in a court will be paid only if the defendant is found guilty, there is a violation of due process under the Fourteenth Amendment. Here the mayor of a small town was to be paid $12. This was a liquor bootlegging case.

Lanzetta v. New Jersey: 306 U.S. 451 (1939). Opinion: Butler, J. Abstaining: Frankfurter, J. No dissent.

Crimes must be clearly defined or the statutes will be declared void because of vagueness. Here "gangsters" were subjected to penalties without a proper definition of the term.

In re Oliver: 333 U.S. 257 (1948). Opinion: Black, J. Dissenting: Frankfurter and Jackson, JJ.

In Michigan a "one-man grand jury" proceeding in which the "jury" also served as trial judge in a secret proceeding without counsel or definite charges or a confrontation of witnesses was held unconstitutional. The grand jury was investigating gambling. The conviction was apparently for contempt of court.

Burstyn v. Wilson: 343 U.S. 495 (1952). Opinion: Clark, J. No dissent.

Movies are an aspect of free speech and press as completely as newspapers. Too, the "sacrilege" standard applied in the case was too vague.

Ward v. Village of Monroeville, Ohio: 409 U.S. 57 (1972). Opinion: Brennan, J. Dissenting: White and Rehnquist, JJ.

Where a mayor holds court and a major part of the income of his city is derived from fines, forfeitures, costs, and fees imposed by his court there is a lack of due process of law. The mayor's responsibilities for village finances might make him partisan to maintain the high level of contribution from the mayor's court.

NOTE:

Winters exemplifies action by the Court voiding a statute as a result of the "vice of vagueness." When a statute requires one to guess as to its meaning, due process has been violated. Obscenity statutes offer a peculiar difficulty in phrasing the provisions so that there is precision in the expressed intention of what publications are to be affected by the legislation. There is no "rule of thumb" by which one can set down the rather nebulous line that separates the "sufficiently definite" statute from the "too vague" statute, but there is a line. Also, abridgment of freedom of speech was at least persuasive here. The statute verges on prior restraint.

Wieman v. Updegraff
344 U.S. 183; 73 S.Ct. 215; 97 L.Ed. 216 (1952)

(The state of Oklahoma had required by statute that all state officers and employees should take a loyalty oath. Certain members of the faculty and staff of Oklahoma Agricultural and Mechanical College failed to observe the statutory requirement. Updegraff, a citizen and taxpayer, brought this suit to enjoin state officials from paying further compensation to employees who had not subscribed to the oath. The statute was attacked as violating the due process clause of the Fourteenth Amendment.)

Vote: 8-0

Mr. Justice Clark delivered the opinion of the Court:

. . . We are thus brought to the question touched on in *Garner, Adler,* and *Gerende*: whether the Due Process Clause permits a state, in attempting to bar disloyal individuals from its employ, to exclude persons solely on the basis of organizational membership, regardless of their knowledge concerning the organizations to which they had belonged. For, under the statute before us, the fact of membership alone disqualifies. If the rule be expressed as a presumption of disloyalty, it is a conclusive one.

But membership may be innocent. A state servant may have joined a proscribed organization unaware of its activities and purposes. In recent years, many completely loyal persons have severed organizational ties after learning for the first time of the character of groups to which they had belonged. "They had joined, [but] did not know what it was, they were good, fine young men and women, loyal Americans, but they had been trapped into it—because one of the great weaknesses of all Americans, whether adult or youth, is to join something." (Testimony of J. Edgar Hoover, Hearings before House Committee on Un-American Activities on H.R. 1884 and H.R. 2122, 80th Cong., 1st Sess. 46.) At the time of affiliation, a group itself may be innocent, only later coming under the influence of those who would turn it toward illegitimate ends. Conversely, an organization formerly subversive and therefore designated as such may have subsequently freed itself from the influences which originally led to its listing.

There can be no dispute about the consequences visited upon a person excluded from public employment on disloyalty grounds. In view of the community, the stain is a deep one; indeed, it has become a badge of infamy. Especially is this so in time of cold war and hot emotions when "each man begins to eye his neighbor as a possible enemy." Yet under the Oklahoma Act, the fact of association alone determines disloyalty and disqualification; it matters not whether association existed innocently or knowingly. To thus inhibit individual freedom of movement is to stifle the flow of democratic expression and controversy at one of its chief sources. We hold that the distinction observed between the case at bar and *Garner, Adler,* and *Gerende* is decisive. Indiscriminate classification of innocent with knowing activity must fall as an assertion of arbitrary power. The oath offends due process.

. . . We need not pause to consider whether an abstract right to public employment exists. It is sufficient to say that constitutional protection does extend to the public servant whose exclusion pursuant to a statute is patently arbitrary or discriminatory. . . .

Reversed.

Mr. Justice Jackson, not having heard the argument, took no part in the consideration or decision of this case.

Mr. Justice Burton concurred without opinion.

Mr. Justice Black concurred, joined by Mr. Justice Douglas:

I concur in all the Court says in condemnation of Oklahoma's test oath. I agree that the State Act prescribing that test oath is fatally offensive to the due process guarantee of the United States Constitution. . . .

It seems self-evident that all speech criticizing government rulers and challenging current beliefs may be dangerous to the status quo. With full knowledge of this danger the Framers rested our First Amendment on the premise that the slightest suppression of thought, speech, press, or public assembly is still more dangerous. This means that individuals are guaranteed an undiluted and unequivocal right to express themselves on questions of current public interest. It means that Americans discuss such questions as of right and not on sufferance of legislatures, courts or any other governmental agencies. It means that courts are without power to appraise and penalize utterances upon their motion that these utterances are dangerous. In my view this uncompromising interpretation of the Bill of Rights is the one that must prevail if its freedoms are to be saved. Tyrannical totalitarian governments cannot safely allow their people to speak with complete freedom. I believe with the Framers that our free Government can.

Mr. Justice Frankfurter, whom Mr. Justice Douglas joined, concurred:

. . . It is the special task of teachers to foster those habits of open-mindedness and critical inquiry which alone make for responsible citizens, who, in turn, make possible an enlightened and effective public opinion. Teachers must fulfill their function by precept and practice, by the very atmosphere which they generate; they must be exemplars of open-mindedness and free inquiry. They cannot carry out their noble task if the conditions for the practice of a responsible and critical mind are denied to them. . . .

RELATED CASES:

Bryant v. Zimmerman: 278 U.S. 63 (1928). Opinion: Van Devanter, J. Dissenting: McReynolds, J.

To require associations having an oath-bound membership to file with a state officer sworn copies of their constitutions, oaths of membership, etc., with lists of their members and officers, and to provide that persons who become or remain members or attend meetings knowing that such requirement has not been complied with shall be arrested and punished is a reasonable exercise of the police power and not a violation of such persons' liberty under the due process clause of the Fourteenth Amendment. The Ku Klux Klan was involved here.

Snyder v. Massachusetts: 291 U.S. 97 (1934). Opinion: Cardozo, J. Dissenting: Roberts, Brandeis, Sutherland, and Butler, JJ.

Under the Fourteenth Amendment a state cannot set up procedure in criminal cases that "offends some principle of justice so rooted in the traditions and conscience of our people as to be ranked as fundamental." Here the jury visited the scene of the crime in the defendant's absence, but accompanied by the judge and counsel.

Chaplinsky v. New Hampshire: 315 U.S. 568 (1942). Opinion: Murphy, J. No dissent.

A state can prohibit name calling on the street when the speech is likely to cause a breach of the peace by provoking the person addressed to acts of violence.

Gerende v. Board of Supervisors of Elections: 341 U.S. 56 (1951). Per Curiam. No dissent.

A decision of the highest court of Maryland upholding the validity of a Maryland law construed as requiring that in order for a candidate for public office to obtain a place on the ballot he must swear that he is not engaged "in one way or another in the attempt to overthrow the government *by force or violence*," and that he is not knowingly a member of an organization engaged in such an attempt, was affirmed by the Supreme Court on the understanding that an affidavit in those terms fully satisfied the requirement. This decision was overruled by *Baggett* v. *Bullitt*, 377 U.S. 360 (1964). See p. 282, below.

Adler v. Board of Education: 342 U.S. 485 (1952). Opinion: Minton, J. Dissenting: Black, Frankfurter, and Douglas, JJ.

A finding that a person is unfit and is disqualified from employment in the public school system because of membership in a listed organization is not a denial of speech and assembly. But see *Keyishian* v. *Board of Regents,* 385 U.S. 589 (1967), p. 77, above. See *Adler,* p. 75, above.

Griffin v. Illinois: 351 U.S. 12 (1956). Opinion: Black, J. Dissenting: Burton, Minton, Reed, and Harlan, JJ.

In criminal trials, including noncapital charges, a state cannot discriminate on account

of poverty. Here there was a requirement that, on appeal, the accused pay for a steno-
graphic transcript of the trial proceedings. As an indigent, this barred his appeal. The
state provided free transcripts only for review of constitutional questions and to indigent
defendants under death sentence. This virtually made financial ability the basis for appeal.
This denied equal protection since there must be "essential fairness."

Beilan v. Board of Public Education: 357 U.S. 399 (1958). Opinion: Burton, J. Dissenting:
Douglas, Black, and Brennan, JJ., and Warren, C.J.

Basically the same principle was involved here as in *Lerner* v. *Casey*, below. Here a
public school teacher was dismissed for refusal to answer questions in a hearing conducted
by the school authorities. Here Communist associational activity was involved in Philadelphia.

NAACP v. Alabama: 357 U.S. 449 (1958). Opinion: Harlan, J. No dissent.

A state court order compelling a state branch of the NAACP to disclose its membership lists, even when made pursuant to state action to oust the association from the state
for carrying on the activities of a foreign corporation without being duly qualified, is
likely to constitute an effective restraint on the members' freedom of association. Freedom
of association is an inseparable aspect of the "liberty" provision of the due process clause
of the Fourteenth Amendment. Here the initial exertion of power was by the state even
though there were later "private community pressures."

Lerner v. Casey: 357 U.S. 468 (1958). Opinion: Harlan, J. Dissenting: Warren, C.J.,
and Douglas, Black, and Brennan, JJ.

A conductor, on a city-owned subway, could be discharged for refusal to answer
questions at a hearing conducted by city authorities since this lack of frankness could
be regarded as marking him a person of doubtful trust and reliability, a "security risk."
The questions were about Communist Party membership. The case arose in New York
City.

Speiser v. Randall: 357 U.S. 513 (1958). Opinion: Brennan, J. Dissenting: Clark, J.
Abstaining: Warren, C.J.

Enforcement by a state of a statutory requirement that a taxpayer take an oath
that he does not criminally advocate the overthrow of the federal or state government
by force, violence, or other unlawful means or advocate the support of a foreign government against the United States in the event of hostilities, as a prerequisite to the
right to a veterans tax exempion, is a denial of free speech wihout due process of law
since it places the burdens of proof and persuasion on the taxpayer. It is valid in ordinary
tax cases to require taxpayers to prove their statements but here free speech was
involved. The case came out of California.

NOTE:

Scienter, or knowledge of the nature of the organization, was held in *Wieman*
to be the requirement of a legitimate statute rather than mere "guilt by association."

See also *Cramp* v. *Board of Public Instruction of Orange County* (Florida), 368
U.S. 278 (1961), p. 76, above.

Garner v. Board of Public Works
341 U.S. 716; 71 S.Ct. 909; 95 L.Ed. 1317 (1951)

(An ordinance of the city of Los Angeles provided that each employee of the
city must take an oath that he had not been during the previous five years, was not,
and would not be during his term of service to the city a member of a subversive
organization. Further, every employee was required to execute an affidavit stating
whether he was or ever had been a member of the Communist Party or of the

Communist Political Association, and if he was or had been such a member, he was to state the dates when he became and during which he remained a member. This measure was challenged as *ex post facto* legislation, as constituting a bill of attainder, and as denying due process.)

Vote: 5-4

Mr. Justice Clark delivered the opinion of the Court:

. . . We think that a municipal employer is not disabled because it is an agency of the State from inquiring of its employees as to matters that may prove relevant to their fitness and suitability for the public service. Past conduct may well relate to present fitness; past loyalty may have a reasonable relationship to present and future trust. Both are commonly inquired into in determining fitness for both high and low positions in private industry and are not less relevant in public employment. The affidavit requirement is valid. . . .

The ordinance would be *ex post facto* if it imposed punishment for past conduct lawful at the time it was engaged in. Passing for the moment the question whether separation of petitioners from their employment must be considered as punishment, the ordinance clearly is not *ex post facto*. The activity covered by the oath had been proscribed by the Charter in the same terms, for the same purpose, and to the same effect over seven years before, and two years prior to the period embraced in the oath. Not the law but the fact was posterior.

Bills of attainder are "legislative acts . . . that apply either to named individuals or to easily ascertainable members of a group in such a way as to inflict punishment on them without a judicial trial . . . ." *United States* v. *Lovett*, 328 U.S. 303, 315, 1946. Punishment is a prerequisite. See concurring opinion in *Lovett, supra*, 328 U.S. at pages 318, 324. Whether legislative action curtailing a privilege previously enjoyed amounts to punishment depends upon "the circumstances attending and the causes of the deprivation." *Cummings* v. *State of Missouri*, 4 Wall. 277, 320, 1867. We are unable to conclude that punishment is imposed by a general regulation which merely provides standards of qualification and eligibility for employment. . . .

Nor are we impressed by the contention that the oath denies due process because its negation is not limited to affiliations with organizations known to the employee to be in the proscribed class. We have no reason to suppose that the oath is or will be construed by the City of Los Angeles or by California courts as affecting adversely those persons who during their affiliation with a proscribed organization were innocent of its purpose, or those who severed their relations with any such organization when its character became apparent, or those who were affiliated with organizations which at one time or another during the period covered by the ordinance were engaged in proscribed activity but not at the time of affiant's affiliation. We assume that scienter is implicit in each clause of the oath. As the city has done nothing to negative this interpretation, we take for granted that the ordinance will be so read to avoid raising difficult constitutional problems which any other application would present. . . . It appears from correspondence of record between the city and petitioners that although the city welcomed inquiry as to its construction of the oath, the interpretation upon which we have proceeded may not have been explicitly called to the attention of petitioners before their refusal. We assume that if our interpretation of the oath is correct the City of Los Angeles will give those petitioners who heretofore refused to take the oath an opportunity to take it as interpreted and resume their employment.

The judgment as to Pacifico and Schwartz is affirmed. The judgment as to the remaining petitioners is affirmed on the basis of the interpretation of the ordinance which we have felt justified in assuming.

Affirmed.

Mr. Justice Frankfurter concurred in part and dissented in part:

The Constitution does not guarantee public employment. City, State and Nation are not confined to making provisions appropriate for securing competent professional discharge of the functions pertaining to diverse governmental jobs. They may also assure themselves of fidelity to the very presuppositions of our scheme of government on the part of those who seek to serve it. No unit of government can be denied the right to keep out of its employ those who seek to overthrow the government by force or violence, or are knowingly members of an organization engaged in such endeavor. . . .

Mr. Justice Burton, dissented in part and concurred in part:

I cannot agree that under our decisions the oath is valid. . . . The oath is so framed as to operate retrospectively as a perpetual bar to those employees who held certain views at any time since a date five years preceding *the effective date of the ordinance.* It leaves no room for a change of heart. It calls for more than a profession of present loyalty or promise of future attachment. It is not limited in retrospect to any period measured by reasonable relation to the present. In time this ordinance will amount to the requirement of an oath that the affiant has *never* done any of the proscribed acts. . . .

Mr. Justice Douglas, with whom Mr. Justice Black joined, dissented:

. . . Petitioners were disqualified from office not for what they are today, not because of any program they currently espouse . . . not because of standards related to fitness for the office . . . but for what they once advocated. They are deprived of their livelihood by legislative act, not by judicial processes. We put the case in the aspect most invidious to petitioners. Whether they actually advocated the violent overthrow of Government does not appear. But here, as in the *Cummings* case, the vice is in the presumption of guilt which can only be removed by the expurgatory oath. That punishment, albeit conditional, violates here as it did in the *Cummings* case the constitutional prohibition against bills of attainder. Whether the ordinance also amounts to an *ex post facto* law is a question we do not reach.

RELATED CASES:

Baggett v. Bullitt: 377 U.S. 360 (1964). Opinion: White, J. Dissenting: Clark and Harlan, JJ.

Here a Washington state loyalty oath statute was declared void because of vagueness. The requirement was held not open to one or a few interpretations but to an indefinite number. This decision overruled *Gerende* v. *Board of Supervisors of Elections*, 341 U.S. 56 (1951), p. 279, above.

Elfbrandt v. Russell: 384 U.S. 11 (1966). Opinion: Douglas, J. Dissenting: White, Harlan, Clark, and Stewart, JJ.

The freedom of association guaranteed by the First Amendment protects those who join an organization but do not share its unlawful purposes and who do not participate in its unlawful activities. There must be a "specific interest" to further the illegal aims of the organization. Here the Arizona loyalty oath law was held void.

NOTE:

Knowledge of the subversive character of organizations of which one is a member as a basis for denial of public employment was in *Garner* held necessary again. This requirement of knowledge—scienter—may be implicit in the statute rather than expressed. The Court made the point that the way one has conducted himself in the past may well bear a reasonable relationship to present fitness—the "professional standards" test.

Slochower v. Board of Higher Education of the City of New York
350 U.S. 551; 76 S.Ct. 637; 100 L.Ed. 692 (1956)

(Harry Slochower had been summarily discharged from his position as associate professor at Brooklyn College, an institution maintained by the City of New York, after he had invoked the privilege against self-incrimination under the Fifth Amendment before an investigating committee of the United States Senate, the Internal Security Subcommittee of the Committee on the Judiciary. The removal was in pursuance of a provision of the city's charter that whenever an employe of the city utilized the privilege against self-incrimination to avoid answering a question relating to his official conduct, he was to be immediately removed and ineligible to any further election or appointment to city office. Slochower challenged the charter provision as violative of both the due process and the privileges or immunities clauses of the Fourteenth Amendment.)

Vote: 5-4

Mr. Justice Clark delivered the opinion of the Court:

. . . At the outset we must condemn the practice of imputing a sinister meaning to the exercise of a person's constitutional right under the Fifth Amendment. The right of an accused person to refuse to testify, which had been in England merely a rule of evidence, was so important to our forefathers that they raised it to the dignity of a constitutional enactment, and it has been recognized as "one of the most valuable prerogatives of the citizen." *Brown* v. *Walker*, 161 U.S. 591, 610. We have reaffirmed our faith in this principle recently in *Quinn* v. *United States*, 349 U.S. 155. In *Ullmann* v. *United States*, 350 U.S. 422, we scored the assumption that those who claim this privilege are either criminals or perjurers. The privilege against self-incrimination would be reduced to a hollow mockery if its exercise could be taken as equivalent either to a confession of guilt or a conclusive presumption of perjury. As we pointed out in *Ullmann*, a witness may have a reasonable fear of prosecution and yet be innocent of any wrongdoing. The privilege serves to protect the innocent who otherwise might be ensnared by ambiguous circumstances. . . .

It is one thing for the city authorities themselves to inquire into Slochower's fitness, but quite another for his discharge to be based entirely on events occurring before a federal committee whose inquiry was announced as not directed at "the property, affairs, or government of the city, or . . . official conduct of city employees." In this respect the present case differs materially from *Garner*, where the city was attempting to elicit information necessary to determine the qualifications of its employees. Here, the Board had possessed the pertinent information for 12 years, and the questions which Professor Slochower refused to answer were admittedly asked for a purpose wholly unrelated to his college functions. On such a record the Board cannot claim that its action was part of a bona fide attempt to gain needed and relevant information.

Without attacking Professor Slochower's qualification for his position in any manner, and apparently with full knowledge of the testimony he had given some 12 years before at the state committee hearing, the Board seized upon his claim of privilege before the federal committee and converted it through the use of § 903 into a conclusive presumption of guilt. Since no inference of guilt was possible from the claim before the federal committee, the discharge falls of its own weight as wholly without support. There has not been the "protection of the individual against arbitrary action" which Mr. Justice Cardozo characterized as the very essence of due process. . . .

This is not to say that Slochower has a constitutional right to be an associate professor of German at Brooklyn College. The State has broad powers in the selection and discharge of its employees, and it may be that proper inquiry would show Slochower's continued employment to be inconsistent with a real interest of the State. But there has been no such inquiry here. We hold that summary dismissal of appellant violates due process of law.

The judgment is reversed and the cause is remanded for further proceedings not inconsistent with this opinion.

Reversed and remanded.

Mr. Justice Black and Mr. Justice Douglas joined the Court's judgment and opinion, but also adhered to the views expressed in their dissents in *Adler* v. *Board of Education of City of New York*, and *Garner* v. *Board of Public Works of City of Los Angeles, supra*, and to their concurrences in *Wieman* v. *Updegraff, supra*.

Mr. Justice Reed, with whom Mr. Justice Burton and Mr. Justice Minton joined, dissented:

. . . The Court finds it a denial of due process to discharge an employee merely because he relied upon the Fifth Amendment plea of self-incrimination to avoid answering questions which he would be otherwise required to answer. We assert the contrary—the city does have reasonable ground to require its employees either to give evidence regarding facts of official conduct within their knowledge or to give up the positions they hold. . . .

Mr. Justice Harlan dissented:

. . . In effect, what New York has done is to say that it will not employ teachers who refuse to cooperate with public authorities when asked questions relating to official conduct. . . . Moreover, I think that a State may justifiably consider that teachers who refuse to answer questions concerning their official conduct are no longer qualified for public school teaching, on the ground that their refusal to answer jeopardizes the confidence that the public should have in its school system. On either view of the statute, I think Dr. Slochower's discharge did not violate due process. . . .

RELATED CASES:

Keyishian v. Board of Regents: 385 U.S. 589 (1967). Opinion: Brennan, J. Dissenting: Clark, Harlan, Stewart, and White, JJ.

Public employment, including academic employment, cannot be conditioned upon the surrender of constitutional rights which could not be abridged by direct government action. Mere knowing membership without a specific intent to further the unlawful aims of an organization is not a constitutionally adequate basis for exclusion from such positions. This case arose in New York.

NOTE:

No legal effect can be given to any presumption that the plea of possible incrimination under the Fifth Amendment indicates guilt on the part of the person making the plea. However, local government units may take the plea as a "take-off" point from which to conduct a hearing. Also lack of cooperation in answering questions at a hearing may be interpreted as indicative of "incompetence" or "unreliability." See *Keyishian,* p. 77, above. The "absolutists" believe that the First Amendment gives unlimited license to talk.

Konigsberg v. State Bar of California
366 U.S. 36; 81 S.Ct. 997; 6 L.Ed. 2nd 105 (1961)

(This case is a sequel to *Konigsberg* v. *State Bar of California*, 353 U,S. 252 (1957), in which the Supreme Court reversed the state's initial refusal of Konigsberg's application for admission to the bar. Under California law the State Supreme Court may admit to the practice of law any applicant whose qualifications have been certified to it by the California Committee of Bar Examiners. The Committee had declined to certify Konigsberg on the ground that his refusal repeatedly to answer the Committee's questions as to his past or present membership in the Communist Party had obstructed a full investigation into his qualifications. He claimed that it was unconstitutionally arbitrary for the state to deny him admission to the bar because of his refusal to answer these questions.)

Vote: 5-4

Mr. Justice Harlan delivered the opinion of the Court:

. . . In the absence of the slightest indication of any purpose on the part of the State to evade the Court's prior decision, principles of finality protecting the parties to this state litigation are, within broad limits of fundamental fairness, solely the concern of California law. . . . In this instance they certainly have not been transgressed by the State merely taking further action in this essentially administrative type of proceeding.

We think it clear that the Fourteenth Amendment's protection against arbitrary state action does not forbid a State from denying admission to a bar applicant so long as he refuses to provide unprivileged answers to questions having a substantial relevance to his qualifications. An investigation of this character, like a civil suit, requires procedural as well as substantive rules. . . .

There remains the question as to whether Konigsberg was adequately warned of the consequences of his refusal to answer. At the outset of the renewed hearings the Chairman of the Committee stated:

"As as result of our two-fold purpose [to investigate and reach determinations], particularly our function of investigation, we believe it will be necessary for you, Mr. Konigsberg, to answer our material questions or our investigation will be obstructed. We would not then as a result be able to certify you for admission." . . .

The record thus leaves no room for doubt on the score of "warning," and petitioner does not indeed contend to the contrary.

Finally, petitioner argues that, in any event, he was privileged not to respond to questions dealing with Communist Party membership because they unconstitutionally impinged upon rights of free speech and association protected by the Fourteenth Amendment.

At the outset we reject the view that freedom of speech and association . . . as protected by the First and Fourteenth Amendments, are "absolutes," not only in the undoubted sense that where the constitutional protection exists it must prevail, but also in the sense that the scope of that protection must be gathered solely from a literal reading of the First Amendment. . . .

Nor is the state interest in this respect insubstantially related to the right which California claims to inquire about Community Party membership. This Court has long since recognized the legitimacy of a statutory finding that membership in the Communist Party is not unrelated to the danger of use for such illegal ends of powers given for limited purposes. . . .

As regards the questioning of public employees relative to Communist Party membership it has already been held that the interest in not subjecting speech and association to the deterrence of subsequent disclosure is outweighed by the State's interest in ascertaining the fitness of the employee for the post he holds, and hence that such questioning does not infringe constitutional protections. . . . With respect to this same question of Communist Party membership, we regard the State's interest in having lawyers who are devoted to the law in its broadest sense, including not only its substantive provisions, but also its procedures for orderly change, as clearly sufficient to outweigh the minimal effect upon free association occasioned by compulsory disclosure in the circumstances here presented. . . .

The judgment of the Supreme Court of California is affirmed.

Affirmed.

Mr. Justice Black, with whom The Chief Justice and Mr. Justice Douglas concurred, dissented:

. . . In this situation, it seems to me that Konigsberg has been rejected on a ground that is not supported by any authoritatively declared rule of law for the State of California. This alone would be enough for me to vote to reverse the judgment. There are other reasons, however.

Konigsberg's objection to answering questions as to whether he is or was a member of the Communist Party has, from the very beginning, been based upon the contention that the guarantees of free speech and association of the First Amendment as made controlling upon the States by the Fourteenth Amendment preclude California from denying him admission to its Bar for refusing to answer such questions. In this I think Konigsberg has been correct. California has apparently not even attempted to make actual present membership in the Communist Party a bar to the practice of law, and even if it had, I assume it would not be contended that such a law could be applied to conduct that took place before the law was passed. For such an application would, I think, not only be a clear violation of the *ex post facto* provision of the Federal Constitution, but would also constitute a bill of attainder squarely within this Court's holdings in *Cummings* v. *State of Missouri* and *Ex parte Garland*. And yet it seems to me that this record shows, beyond any shadow of a doubt, that the reason Konigsberg has been rejected is because the Committee suspects that he was at one time a member of the Communist Party. I agree with the implication of the majority opinion that this is not an adequate ground to reject Konigsberg and that it could not be constitutionally defended. . . .

Mr. Justice Brennan, with whom The Chief Justice joined, dissented.

. . . The Committee did not come forward, in the proceeding we passed upon in 353 U.S. 252 nor in the subsequent proceeding, with evidence to show that Konigsberg unlawfully advocated the overthrow of the government. Under our decision in *Speiser* v. *Randall*, 357 U.S. 513, the Fourteenth Amendment therefore protects Konigsberg from being denied admission to the Bar for his refusal to answer the questions. . . .

RELATED CASES:

Schware v. New Mexico Board of Bar Examiners: 353 U.S. 232 (1957). Opinion: Black, J. No dissent. Abstaining: Whittaker, J.

Qualifications set by a state for admission to the bar must have a rational connection with the applicant's fitness or capacity to practice law. In applying these standards there must be a basis for an official finding that the applicant does not meet the standards or the action will contravene the due process clause of the Fourteenth Amendment. It cannot be automatically inferred that all members of the party had illegal aims and engaged in illegal activities. Schware had been a member of the Communist Party.

In re Anastaplo: 366 U.S. 82 (1961). Opinion: Harlan, J. Dissenting: Black, Brennan, and Douglas, JJ., and Warren, C.J.

The exclusion of a petitioner from admission to the bar on the ground that he had obstructed the Illinois Committee on Character and Fitness in the performance of its duties because of his refusal to answer questions relating to his membership in the Communist Party was not arbitrary or discriminatory. There was no derogatory information. He was stubborn even though he had been warned.

Cohen v. Hurley: 366 U.S. 117 (1961). Opinion: Harlan, J. Dissenting: Brennan, Douglas, and Black, JJ., and Warren, C.J.

Disbarment of a lawyer solely because of his refusal to cooperate in the efforts of a court to expose unethical conduct, and without any independent evidence of wrongdoing on his part, was not arbitrary, irrational, or discriminatory contrary to due process. The Fourteenth Amendment did not give a federal constitutional right not to be required to incriminate oneself in state proceedings. The unethical conduct was "ambulance chasing." The case arose in New York.

Spevack v. Klein: 385 U.S. 511 (1967). Opinion: Douglas, J. Dissenting: Harlan, Clark, Stewart, and White, JJ.

The self-incrimination clause of the Fifth Amendment has been absorbed in the Fourteenth and it extends its protection to lawyers as well as to other individuals, and it should not be watered down by imposing the dishonor of disbarment and the deprivation of a livelihood as a price for asserting it. Spevack refused to answer questions in a disciplinary proceeding. This case overruled *Cohen* v. *Hurley*, above.

See also *Malloy* v. *Hogan*, p. 151, above.

Baird v. State Bar of Arizona: 401 U.S. 1 (1971). Opinion: Black, J. Dissenting: Blackmun, Harlan, and White, JJ., and Burger, C.J.

A state cannot exclude a person from the practice of law solely because he is a member of a particular political organization (here the Communist Party) or because he holds certain beliefs.

Law Students Civil Rights Research Council, Inc. v. Wadmond: 401 U.S. 154 (1971). Opinion: Stewart, J. Dissenting: Black, Douglas, Marshall, and Brennan, JJ.

A state (here New York) may require that an applicant for admission to the bar furnish proof that he believes in the form of government of the United States and is loyal to such government.

NOTE:

The historically close relationship of the state to the legal profession undoubtedly is at the basis of *Konigsberg.* Certainly other professions would not be similarly restricted by the state.

By way of conclusion, in the application of specific guarantees of the federal Bill of Rights to the states there are two possible tests. One is the determination by the Court that a particular guarantee is "fundamental." The other is a determination by the Court that under the peculiar circumstances of a case one or more of the specific guarantees must be applied in order to provide essential justice or fairness, in other words, due process.

The effective difference between the two tests is fairly obvious. Under the definition-of-liberty test, where the Court distinguishes between "formal" and "fundamental" rights, the inclusion of a specific guarantee means that henceforth that provision of the Constitution is to be as applicable in the areas of state operations as it is in regard to federal matters. In the second type of test, where the Court determines that a particular procedure denies essential justice and is thus violative of due process, there is much more flexibility involved while at the same time rights are safeguarded. Here the particular provisions are not henceforth to be applied rigidly at all times but only when under a given set of circumstances there will be a lack of essential fairness.

CHAPTER VIII

EQUAL PROTECTION OF THE LAWS

Ever since the adoption of the Fourteenth Amendment the question of the real meaning of the equal protection provisions of that amendment have been in process of evolution. Even today the process continues. From the time of Mr. Justice Miller's observation in the *Slaughterhouse Cases* in 1873 that "We doubt very much whether any action of a state not directed by way of discrimination against the Negroes as a class, or on account of their race, will ever be held to come within the purview of this provision" through the years when corporations were the chief beneficiaries of this guarantee against unreasonable classification and discrimination to the present time when Negroes are the ones mostly involved in cases under this provision, the court has wound a weary way.

CLASSIFICATION AND EQUAL PROTECTION

The inscription on the frieze of the Supreme Court building, "Equal Justice Under Law," is not a bad restatement in brief of the equal protection provision of the Fourteenth Amendment. Persons who are in basically the same circumstances and situation are not to be treated differently in law. This does not preclude classification of persons, property, size, location, or occupations. Indeed the circumstances at a particular time and place may require classification in order to bring about justice. Thus women may be treated differently in the law from men, children from adults. Reasonable distinctions may be made validly, and this matter has probably nowhere been more obvious than in the exercise of the taxing power.

Allied Stores of Ohio, Inc. v. Bowers
358 U.S. 522; 79 S.Ct. 437; 3 L.Ed. 2nd 480 (1959)

(The Allied Stores of Ohio challenged the validity of an *ad valorem* state tax on the contents of its warehouses. The company owns and operates department stores in Ohio. Merchandise is transferred as needed to the stores from these warehouses. Sometimes goods are delivered directly from a warehouse to a customer. The tax in question was alleged to deny equal protection of the laws under the Fourteenth Amendment because Ohio exempted from such taxation merchandise belonging to nonresidents "if held in a storage warehouse for storage only.")

Vote: 8-0

Mr. Justice Whittaker delivered the opinion of the Court:

. . . Does the proviso exempting "merchandise or agricultural products belonging to a nonresident . . . if held in a storage warehouse for storage only" deny to appellant, a resident of the State, the equal protection of the laws within the meaning of the Fourteenth Amendment? The applicable principles have been often stated and are entirely familiar. The States have a very wide discretion in the laying of their taxes. When dealing with their proper domestic concerns, and not trenching upon the prerogatives of the National Government or violating the guaranties of the Federal Constitution, the States have the attribute of sovereign powers in devising their fiscal systems to ensure revenue and foster their local interests. Of course, the States, in the exercise of their taxing power, are subject to the requirements of the Equal Protection Clause of the Fourteenth Amendment. But that clause imposes no iron rule of equality, prohibiting the flexibility and variety that are appropriate to reasonable schemes of state taxation. The State may impose different specific taxes upon different trades and professions and may vary the rate of excise upon various products. It is not required to resort to close distinctions or to maintain a precise, scientific uniformity with reference to composition, use or value. . . . "To hold otherwise would be to subject the essential taxing power of the State to an intolerable supervision, hostile to the basic principles of our Government and wholly beyond the protection which the general clause of the Fourteenth Amendment was intended to assure." *Ohio Oil Co.* v. *Conway, supra*, 281 U.S., at 159.

But there is a point beyond which the State cannot go without violating the Equal Protection Clause. The State must proceed upon a rational basis and may not resort to a classification that is palpably arbitrary. The rule often has been stated to be that the classification "must rest upon some ground of difference having a fair and substantial relation to the object of the legislation." . . .

Coming directly to the concrete problem now before us, it has repeatedly been held and appears to be entirely settled that a statute which encourages the location within the State of needed and useful industries by exempting them, though not also others, from its taxes is not arbitrary and does not violate the Equal Protection Clause of the Fourteenth Amendment. . . .

In the light of the law thus well settled, how stands appellant's case? We cannot assume that state legislative enactments were adopted arbitrarily or without good reason to further some legitimate policy of the State. What were the special reasons, motives or policies of the Ohio Legislature for adopting the questioned proviso we do not know with certainty, nor is it important that we should, . . . for a state legislature need not explicitly declare its purpose. But it is obvious that it may reasonably have been the purpose and policy of the State Legislature, in adopting the proviso, to encourage the construction or leasing and operation of warehouses in Ohio by nonresidents with the attendant benefits to the State's economy, or to stimulate the market for merchandise and agricultural products produced in Ohio by enabling nonresidents to purchase and hold them in the State for storage only, free from taxes, in anticipation of future needs. Other similar purposes reasonably may be conceived. Therefore, we cannot say that the discrimination of the proviso which exempted only the "merchandise or agricultural products belonging to a nonresident . . . if held in a storage warehouse for storage only" was not founded upon a reasonable distinction, or difference in state policy, or that no state of facts reasonably can be conceived to sustain it. For those reasons, it cannot be said, in the light of the settled law as shown by the cases cited, that the questioned proviso was invidious or palpably arbitrary and denied appellant the equal protection of the laws within the meaning of the Fourteenth Amendment.

Mr. Justice Stewart took no part in the consideration or decision of this case.

RELATED CASES:

State Board of Tax Commissioners of Indiana v. Jackson: 283 U.S. 527 (1931). Opinion: Roberts, J. Dissenting: Sutherland, VanDevanter, McReynolds, and Butler, JJ.

A chain store tax graduated according to the number of stores owned is valid. This classification is justified on the basis of the differences in the organization, management and method of operation of chain stores compared with other types of stores. The Court held that the discrimination was based on a reasonable distinction.

Great Atlantic and Pacific Tea Co., v. Grosjean: 301 U.S. 412 (1937). Opinion: Roberts, J. Dissenting: Sutherland, J. Abstaining: VanDevanter and Stone, JJ.
   Here Louisiana's chain store tax was held valid. Even stores outside the state were counted.

Shapiro v. Thompson: 394 U.S. 618 (1969): Opinion: Brennan, J. Dissenting: Warren, C.J., and Black and Harlan, JJ.
   The Connecticut statutory prohibition of welfare benefits to state residents of less than a year created a classification which denied equal protection of the laws because this was not shown to be necessary to promote a *compelling* governmental interest. Also, since the Constitution guarantees the right of interstate movement, the purpose of deterring the migration of indigents into a state is impermissible. This same decision involved statutory provisions from Connecticut and the District of Columbia. In the latter instance the Court held that there was violation of the due process clause of the Fifth Amendment.

Lehnhausen v. Lake Shore Auto Parts Co.: 410 U.S. 356 (1973). Opinion: Douglas, J. No dissent.
   The Illinois personal property tax exempts all personal property owned by individuals but retains such taxes as to personal property owned by corporations or other "non-individuals." In the field of taxation the states have large leeway in making classifications and drawing lines which in their judgment produce reasonable systems of taxation. The arrangement was upheld.

NOTE:

   Classification for purposes of taxation does not violate the equal protection clause if there is a reasonable basis for the state's policy of differentiation. Where the discrimination involves nonresidents of the state, there must be solid reasons beyond mere difference of residence. Throughout the litany of the cases dealing with classification and equal protection is the basic concept of reasonableness. Any arbitrary classification is inherently bad. Various forms of taxation, labor legislation, a legal distinction between industries and occupations, and other legislative matters have been upheld where there has been a real and reasonable distinction between the classes.

RACE AND EQUAL PROTECTION

   Belatedly the prediction of Mr. Justice Miller has come true and today the prime concern of the Court in connection with the interpretation of the equal protection provision of the Fourteenth Amendment is in connection with racial matters. This has been increasingly true so that today it is a rare case before the Court involving equal protection that does not have racial overtones. The scope of these cases has been broad, ranging from court procedure through property rights to transportation and education, and the trend shows no signs of slackening.

Norris v. Alabama
294 U.S. 587; 55 S.Ct. 579; 79 L.Ed. 1074 (1935)

(This was the second "Scottsboro case," the sequel to *Powell* v. *Alabama*. See p. 244, above. Nine Negro boys, Norris among them, were indicted in March, 1931, in Jackson County, Alabama, for the crime of rape. A motion for a change of venue was granted, and the trial was conducted in Morgan County. The validity of the proceedings was questioned since both the grand and petit juries had been chosen to the exclusion of Negroes. This was claimed to be a violation of the guarantee of equal protection of the laws.)

Vote: 8-0

Mr. Chief Justice Hughes delivered the opinion of the Court:

First. There is no controversy as to the constitutional principle involved. . . . This Court thus stated the principle in *Carter* v. *Texas*, 177 U.S. 442, in relation to exclusion from service on grand juries: "Whenever by any action of a State, whether through its legislature, through its courts, or through its executive or administrative officers, all persons of the African race are excluded, solely because of their race or color, from serving as grand jurors in the criminal prosecution of a person of the African race, the equal protection of the laws is denied to him, contrary to the Fourteenth Amendment . . . ." The principle is equally applicable to a similar exclusion of Negroes from service on petit juries. . . . And although the state statute defining the qualifications of jurors may be fair on its face, the Constitutional provision affords protection against action of the State through its administrative officers in effecting the prohibited discrimination. . . .

The question is of the application of this established principle to the facts disclosed by the record. That the question is one of fact does not relieve us of the duty to determine whether in truth a federal right has been denied. When a federal right has been specially set up and claimed in a state court, it is our province to inquire not merely whether it was denied in express terms but also whether it was denied in substance and effect. . . .

Defendant adduced evidence to support the charge of unconstitutional discrimination in the actual administration of the statute in Jackson County. The testimony, as the state court said, tended to show that "in a long number of years no Negro had been called for jury service in that county." It appeared that no Negro had served on any grand or petit jury in that county within the memory of witnesses who had lived there all their lives. Testimony to that effect was given by men whose ages ran from fifty to seventy-six years. Their testimony was uncontradicted. It was supported by the testimony of officials. The clerk of the jury commission and the clerk of the circuit court had never known of a Negro serving on a grand jury in Jackson County. The court reporter, who had not missed a session in that county in twenty-four years, and two jury commissioners testified to the same effect. One of the latter, who was a member of the commission which made up the jury roll for the grand jury which found the indictment, testified that he had "never known of a single instance where any Negro sat on any grand or petit jury in the entire history of that county."

That testimony in itself made out a prima facie case of the denial of the equal protection which the Constitution guarantees. . . .

The state court rested its decision upon the ground that even if it were assumed that there was no name of a Negro on the jury roll, it was not established that race or color caused the omission. The court pointed out that the statute fixed a high standard of qualifications for jurors . . . and that the jury commission was vested with a wide discretion. The court adverted to the fact that more white citizens possessing age qualifications had been omitted from the jury roll than the entire Negro population of the county, and regarded the testimony as being to the effect that "the matter of race, color, politics, religion or fraternal affiliations" had not been discussed by the commission and had not entered into their consideration, and that no one had been excluded because of race or color. . . .

We are of the opinion that the evidence required a different result from that reached in the state court. We think that the evidence that for a generation or longer no Negro had been called for service on any jury in Jackson County, that there were Negroes qualified for jury service, that according to the practice of the jury commission their names would normally appear on the preliminary list of male citizens of the requisite age but that no names of Negroes were placed on the jury roll, and the testimony with respect to the lack of appropriate consideration of the qualifications of Negroes, established the discrimination which the Constitution forbids. The motion to quash the indictment upon that ground should have been granted. . . .

Within the memory of witnesses, long resident there, no Negro had ever served on a jury in that county or had been called for such service. Some of these witnesses were over fifty years of age and had always lived in Morgan County. Their testimony was not contradicted. A clerk of the circuit court, who had resided in the county for thirty years, and who had been in office for over four years, testified that during his official term approximately 2500 persons had been called for jury service and that not one of them was a Negro; that he did not recall "ever seeing any single person of the colored race serve on any jury in Morgan County."

There was abundant evidence that there were a large number of Negroes in the county who were qualified for jury service. Men of intelligence, some of whom were college graduates, testified to long lists (said to contain nearly 200 names) of such qualified Negroes, including many business men, owners of real property and householders. When defendant's counsel proposed to call many additional witnesses in order to adduce further proof of qualifications of Negroes for jury service, the trial judge limited the testimony, holding that the evidence was cumulative.

We find no warrant for a conclusion that the names of any of the Negroes as to whom this testimony was given, or of any other Negroes, were placed on the jury rolls. No such names were identified. The evidence that for many years no Negro had been called for jury service itself tended to show the absence of the names of Negroes from the jury rolls, and the State made no effort to prove their presence. . . .

For this long-continued, unvarying, and wholesale exclusion of Negroes from jury service we find no justification consistent with the constitutional mandate. . . .

Reversed.

Mr. Justice McReynolds took no part in the hearing or decision of this case.

RELATED CASES:

Strauder v. West Virginia: 100 U.S. 303 (1880). Opinion: Strong, J. Dissenting: Field and Clifford, JJ.

A state statute that provided for juries to be made up exclusively of white men was declared invalid under the Fourteenth Amendment.

Virginia v. Rives: 100 U.S. 313 (1880). Opinion: Strong, J. No dissent.

Where there is no state statutory discrimination and there have been no Negroes on juries purely by chance, there is no discrimination. A Negro does not have the right to have Negroes on a jury.

Ex parte Virginia: 100 U.S. 339 (1880). Opinion: Strong, J. Dissenting: Field and Clifford, JJ.

A state judge's indictment was upheld under federal law forbidding the exclusion of Negroes from juries because of race, color, or previous condition of servitude as a denial of equal protection.

Smith v. Texas: 311 U.S. 128 (1940). Opinion: Black, J. No dissent.

The conviction of a Negro upon an indictment returned by the grand jury of a county in which, at the time of such return and long prior thereto, Negroes were intentionally and systematically excluded from grand jury service, solely on account of their race and color denies to him the equal protection of the laws. There was the inference of discrimination from the facts of unequal treatment.

Hill v. Texas: 316 U.S. 400 (1942). Opinion: Stone, C.J. No dissent.
When no Negroes have served on a grand jury for sixteen years when there are presumably many Negroes qualified to serve, there is a prima facie case of discrimination with the burden of rebuttal on the state.

Akins v. Texas: 325 U.S. 398 (1945). Opinion: Reed, J. Dissenting: Stone, C.J., and Black and Murphy, JJ.
When there is Negro representation on juries even though it is far out of proportion to the actual number of Negroes resident in the area, there is technical compliance within the equal protection requirement. Here there was one Negro each on the grand jury and petit jury. Proportional representation was not necessary.

Patton v. Mississippi: 332 U.S. 463 (1947). Opinion: Black, J. No dissent.
The burden of proof is on the state to justify the exclusion of Negroes from juries when this exclusion has continued for thirty years. This was true even though administrative practice was responsible.

Avery v. Georgia: 345 U.S. 559 (1953). Opinion: Vinson, C.J. No dissent. Abstaining: Jackson, J.
It is a denial of equal protection when the arrangement for drawing jurors provides that the names of white persons are to be on white paper and the names of Negroes on yellow tickets. With no Negroes having been chosen, there is a prima facie case of discrimination. The burden was on the state then to overcome it.

Hernandez v. Texas: 347 U.S. 475 (1954). Opinion: Warren, C.J. No dissent.
The "rule of exclusion" was here applied to persons of Mexican or Latin American descent. When no such persons had served on a jury in a county for twenty-five years where a sizable percentage of the population of the county was of such descent, there is a prima facie case of discrimination. Where no reasonable classification, the exclusion was void.

Eubanks v. Louisiana: 356 U.S. 584 (1958). Opinion: Black, J. No dissent.
When a jury selection plan operates in such a way as always to result in the complete and long-continued exclusion of any representative at all from a large group of Negroes, there is a denial of equal protection of the laws guaranteed by the Fourteenth Amendment.

Carter v. Jury Commissioners of Greene County: 396 U.S. 320 (1970). Opinion: Stewart, J. Dissenting: Douglas, J.
With the population of Greene County, Alabama, about 65 percent Negro, those on the jury roll constituted only 32 percent. The Court denied that the statute was unconstitutional on its face. Negroes are not entitled to proportional representation by race. All of the members of the jury commission were white.

NOTE:

Norris was the second "Scottsboro case." Discrimination was inferred from the historical facts surrounding the trial. There is no implication here that a defendant Negro has the right to have members of his race on the jury. All that is guaranteed is that no purposeful discrimination against Negroes is to be present in the selection of a jury. Actually color is not to be consciously taken into account even if Negroes be thereby favored.

Certain classes of persons can be legally excluded from service on juries. This has been held to be action in accordance with the general welfare. This includes physicians, teachers, lawyers, clergy, dentists, and other professionals. Presumably such service would interfere with their work. See *Rawlins* v. *Georgia*, 201 U.S. 638 (1906).

Shelley v. Kraemer
334 U.S. 1; 68 S.Ct. 836; 92 L.Ed. 1161 (1948)

(Restrictive covenants, which have as their purpose the exclusion of persons of a designated race or color from the ownership or occupancy of real property in specified locations, were involved here. Shelley, a Negro, had purchased property in St. Louis covered by a restrictive covenant that barred Negroes. The Supreme Court of Missouri, at the request of owners of other property subject to the restrictive covenant, ordered the Negroes to vacate the property they had recently acquired. This state court order was challenged as a violation of the equal protection clause of the Fourteenth Amendment. A companion case out of Detroit, *Sipes* v. *McGhee*, was decided at the same time.)

Vote: 6-0

Mr. Chief Justice Vinson delivered the opinion of the Court:

. . . It is well, at the outset, to scrutinize the terms of the restrictive agreements involved in these cases. In the Missouri case, the covenant declares that no part of the affected property shall be "occupied by any person not of the Caucasian race, it being intended hereby to restrict the use of said property . . . against the occupancy as owners or tenants of any portion of said property for resident or other purpose by people of the Negro or Mongolian race." Not only does the restriction seek to proscribe use and occupancy of the affected properties by members of the excluded class, but as construed by the Missouri courts, the agreement requires that title of any person who uses his property in violation of the restriction shall be divested. . . .

It cannot be doubted that among the civil rights intended to be protected from discriminatory state action by the Fourteenth Amendment are the rights to acquire, enjoy, own and dispose of property. Equality in the enjoyment of property rights was regarded by the framers of that Amendment as an essential pre-condition to the realization of other basic civil rights and liberties which the Amendment was intended to guarantee. Thus, Sec. 1978 of the Revised Statutes, derived from Sec. 1 of the Civil Rights Act of 1866 which was enacted by Congress while the Fourteenth Amendment was also under consideration provides:

"All citizens of the United States shall have the same right, in every State and Territory, as is enjoyed by white citizens thereof to inherit, purchase, lease, sell, hold, and convey real and personal property." This Court has given specific recognition to the same principle. *Buchanan* v. *Warley*, 245 U.S. 60 (1917). . . .

Since the decision of this Court in the *Civil Rights Cases*, 109 U.S. 3 (1883), the principle has become firmly embedded in our constitutional law that the action inhibited by the first section of the Fourteenth Amendment is only such action as may fairly be said to be that of the States. That Amendment erects no shield against merely private conduct, however discriminatory or wrongful.

We conclude, therefore, that the restrictive agreements standing alone cannot be regarded as a violation of any rights guaranteed to petitioners by the Fourteenth Amendment. So long as the purposes of those agreements are effectuated by voluntary adherence to their terms, it would appear clear that there has been no action by the State and the provisions of the Amendment have not been violated. . . .

But here there was more. These are cases in which the purposes of the agreements were secured only by judicial enforcement by state courts of the restrictive terms of the agreements. The respondents urged that judicial enforcement of private agreements does not amount to state action; or in any event, the participation of the States is so attenuated in character as not to amount to state action within the meaning of the Fourteenth Amendment. Finally, it is suggested, even if the States in these cases may be deemed to have acted in the constitutional sense, their action did not deprive petitioners of rights guaranteed by the Fourteenth Amendment. We move to a consideration of these matters.

That the action of state courts and of judicial officers in their official capacities is to be regarded as action of the State within the meaning of the Fourteenth Amendment, is a proposition which has long been established by decisions of this Court. . . .

The short of the matter is that from the time of the adoption of the Fourteenth Amendment until the present, it has been the consistent ruling of this Court that the action of the States to which the Amendment has reference, includes action of the state courts and state judicial officials. Although, in construing the terms of the Fourteenth Amendment, differences have from time to time been expressed as to whether particular types of state action may be said to offend the Amendment's prohibitory provisions, it has never been suggested that state court action is immunized from the operation of those provisions simply because the act is that of the judicial branch of the state government.

Against this background of judicial construction, extending over a period of some three-quarters of a century, we are called upon to consider whether enforcement by state courts of the restrictive agreements in these cases may be deemed to be the acts of those States; and, if so, whether that action has denied these petitioners the equal protection of the laws which the Amendment was intended to insure.

We have no doubt that there has been state action in these cases in the full and complete sense of the phrase. The undisputed facts disclose that petitioners were willing purchasers of properties upon which they desired to establish homes. The owners of the properties were willing sellers; and contracts of sale were accordingly consummated. It is clear that but for the active intervention of the state courts, supported by the full panoply of state power, petitioners would have been free to occupy the properties in question without restraint.

These are not cases, as has been suggested, in which the States have merely abstained from action, leaving private individuals free to impose such discriminations as they see fit. Rather, these are cases in which the States have made available to such individuals the full coercive power of government to deny to petitioners, on the grounds of race or color, the enjoyment of property rights in premises which petitioners are willing and financially able to acquire and which the grantors are willing to sell. The difference between judicial enforcement and non-enforcement of the restrictive covenants is the difference to petitioners between being denied rights of property available to other members of the community and being accorded full enjoyment of those rights on an equal footing. . . .

We hold that in granting judicial enforcement of the restrictive agreements in these cases, the States have denied petitioners the equal protection of the laws and that, therefore, the action of the state courts cannot stand.

Reversed.

Mr. Justice Reed, Mr. Justice Jackson, and Mr. Justice Rutledge took no part in the hearing or decision of these cases.

RELATED CASES:

Buchanan v. Warley: 245 U.S. 60 (1917). Opinion: Day, J. No dissent.

A city ordinance of Louisville which prohibited "block busting" violated the Fourteenth

Amendment as it prevented the seller from disposing of his property as he desired and prevented the purchaser from occupying his property. Both of these factors are significant elements of the right of property.

Corrigan v. Buckley: 271 U.S. 323 (1926). Opinion: Sanford, J. No dissent.

This case involved restrictive covenants as applied to property in the District of Columbia. The suit was by one owner against another owner to prevent his breaking the covenant. The Court held that the due process clause of the Fifth Amendment did not apply since it "is a limitation only upon the powers of the general government, and is not directed against the action of individuals." It does not apply to private covenants.

Harmon v. Tyler: 273 U.S. 668 (1927). Per Curiam. No dissent.

In a *per curiam* opinion the Supreme Court here affirmed a Fourth Circuit Court of Louisiana on the authority of *Buchanan* v. *Warley*, 245 U.S. 60 (1917).

City of Richmond v. Deans: 281 U.S. 704 (1930). Per Curiam. No dissent.

In a *per curiam* opinion the Supreme Court here affirmed a Fourth Circuit Court of Appeals decree which held as a violation of the Fourteenth Amendment's due process clause a city zoning ordinance prohibiting a person from using as a residence any building on any street between intersecting streets where a majority of residences on such street are occupied by those with whom the person is forbidden to intermarry.

Hurd v. Hodge: 334 U.S. 24 (1948). Opinion: Vinson, C.J. No dissent. Abstaining: Reed, Jackson, and Rutledge, JJ.

In another District of Columbia restrictive covenant case the Court held that federal courts could not enforce the covenants since this would deny "rights intended by Congress to be protected by the Civil Rights Act." Also, the Court held that for a federal court to enforce an agreement that the state courts could not enforce would be contrary to federal public policy.

Dorsey v. Stuyvesant Town Corp.: 339 U.S. 981 (1950). Per Curiam. Dissenting: Black and Douglas, JJ.

Where a state law aided a private corporation in a housing development (here by condemning the land and granting certain tax exemptions), later discrimination against Negroes in the selection of tenants on the part of the private corporation did not amount to state action and thus did not violate the Fourteenth Amendment.

City of Birmingham v. Monk: 341 U.S. 940 (1951). Per Curiam. No dissent.

In this case the Supreme Court denied *certiorari* to the Fifth Circuit Court of Appeals which had held that an ordinance making it unlawful for Negroes to reside in areas zoned white-residential and for whites to reside in areas zoned Negro-residential, and declaring it a misdemeanor for Negroes to live in a white area, was not a legitimate exercise of state police power.

Barrows v. Jackson: 346 U.S. 249 (1953). Opinion: Minton, J. Dissenting: Vinson, C.J. Abstaining: Reed and Jackson, JJ.

In this case out of California the Court held that a state court could not entertain a suit for damages to enforce a restrictive covenant against a co-covenantor. California could not enforce the covenant by equity or by statutory provision. Thus would be state action. The property owner maintained that the value of the property had dropped.

Leeper v. Charlotte Park Commission: 350 U.S. 983 (1956). Per Curiam. No dissent.

Where real property is conveyed to a city for park and recreational purposes for exclusive use by members of the white race, if this condition is not followed the courts may enforce the provision that the land will then revert to the grantor or his heirs. This case arose in North Carolina.

Pennsylvania v. Philadelphia (Pennsylvania vs. Board of Directors of City Trusts of City of Philadelphia): 353 U.S. 230 (1957). Per Curiam. No dissent.

When a city is trustee of a fund under the terms of a will and discrimination is practiced in the administration of the trust, this amounts to discrimination by an agency of the state and is unconstitutional. Involved here was Girard College. In a subsequent hearing of this case (357 U.S. 570, 1958), after a private board was substituted for the city board, the Fourteenth Amendment was held not applicable. In spite of this holding, the college was later ordered to integrate. *Commonwealth of Pennsylvania* v. *Revelle W. Brown*, 392 F. 2d 120 (1968). The Court of Appeals reinterpreted the will "in this changed world."

Evans v. Newton: 382 U.S. 296 (1966). Opinion: Douglas, J. Dissenting: Black, Harlan, and Stewart, JJ.

A tract of land was left to the city of Macon, Georgia, as a park for white people to be controlled by a white Board of Managers. They resigned when it was alleged in court that they were violating federal law by enforcing the racial restrictions. Private trustees were appointed to carry out the testator's instructions. The Court held the actions of the private trustees to be "state action" subject to the equal protection requirements of the Fourteenth Amendment, as the park still had its character as a public facility.

Reitman v. Mulkey: 387 U.S. 369 (1967). Opinion: White, J. Dissenting: Harlan, Black, Clark, and Stewart, JJ.

A provision of the California Constitution forbidding open housing legislation by the state or any of its subdivisions involved the state in racial discrimination and was thus invalid. This was known as "Proposition 14" and guaranteed the right to sell, lease, rent (or not) to a person of one's choosing. It served to authorize racial discrimination.

Jones v. Alfred H. Mayer Co.: 392 U.S. 409 (1968). Opinion: Stewart, J. Dissenting: Harlan and White, JJ.

The Civil Rights Act of 1866 enacted by Congress under its power to enforce the Thirteenth Amendment bars all racial discrimination, private as well as public, in the sale or rental of property. The statute does not include discrimination based on grounds of religion or national origin. Congress has the power to determine what are the badges and incidents of slavery. Among these are restraints on the same right to inherit, purchase, lease. sell, and convey property as is enjoyed by white citizens. This case arose in Missouri.

Hunter v. Erickson: 393 U.S. 385 (1969). Opinion: White, J. Dissenting: Black, J.

A provision of the charter of Akron, Ohio, that requires any ordinance enacted by the city council that regulates the use, sale, advertisement, transfer, listing, assignment, lease, sublease, or financing of real property on the basis of race, color, religion, national origin, or ancestry to first be approved by a majority of the voters violates the equal protection clause of the Fourteenth Amendment. The law's impact places special burdens on racial minorities.

Evans v. Abney: 396 U.S. 435 (1970). Opinion: Black, J. Dissenting: Douglas and Brennan, JJ.

When a tract of land has been willed to a city for the exclusive use of white people, the city may legally permit the property to revert to the heirs of the deceased. This case arose in Macon, Georgia.

Moose Lodge No. 107 v. Irvis: 407 U.S. 163 (1972). Opinion: Rehnquist, J. Dissenting: Douglas, Brennan, and Marshall, JJ.

Racial discrimination by a private club that holds a state liquor license does not implicate the state in the discrimination. State-furnished services include a wide range from fire protection to utilities and to hold that because a private entity that discriminates and that receives any sort of benefit from the state "would utterly emasculate the distinction between private as distinguished from State conduct." To come within the constitutional prohibition the state must have "significantly involved itself with invidious discriminations." This case came out of Harrisburg, Pennsylvania.

NOTE:

Shelley does not invalidate restrictive covenants. Such arrangements may still be made between private individuals. All that is changed is that neither federal nor state courts may be used as means of enforcement of such agreements. The equal protection provision of the Fourteenth Amendment is not applicable to private persons, natural or legal. There must be state action in order for the Fourteenth Amendment to be applicable, and the Court in *Shelley* was holding that any action by a state court by way of enforcement of restrictive covenants would amount to state participation. In other words, in a matter in which the state legislature could not act under the Fourteenth Amendment, the state courts could not act.

What has been regarded by some as a sort of "reverse Gitlow doctrine" resulted from the Court in *Hurd* v. *Hodge*, 334 U.S. 24 (1948) and *Bolling* v. *Sharpe*, 347 U.S. 497 (1954) holding that the due process clause of the Fifth Amendment has the same effect on federal action as does the equal protection provision of the Fourteenth Amendment on state action. Thus there has been something of a nationalizing of the equal protection guarantee.

Just what change *Jones* v. *Mayer* makes in the legal status of restrictive covenants is not entirely clear. The very existence of such a "conspiracy" to violate the law might be held illegal by the Court, but it would be difficult for such a ruling to affect informal agreements of this sort, as a practical matter. Of course, since *Shelley* such agreements no matter how formal have had only psychological effect.

Plessy v. Ferguson
163 U.S. 537; 16 S.Ct. 1138; 41 L.Ed. 256 (1896)

(Plessy was a citizen of Louisiana with one-eighth Negro blood. He refused to obey the order of the conductor of a train to sit in the Negro car. He was arrested for violation of a Louisiana state statute which required separate accommodations for white and colored passengers on railroads in the state. Plessy claimed that the statute was contrary to the Thirteenth and Fourteenth Amendments.)

Vote: 7-1

Mr. Justice Brown delivered the opinion of the Court:

... The object of the [Fourteenth] Amendment was undoubtedly to enforce the absolute equality of the two races before the law, but in the nature of things it could not have been intended to abolish distinctions based upon color, or to enforce social, as distinguished from political, equality, or a commingling of the two races upon terms unsatisfactory to either. Laws permitting, and even requiring, their separation in places where they are liable to be brought into contact do not necessarily imply the inferiority of either race to the other, and have been generally, if not universally, recognized as within the competency of the state legislatures in the exercise of their police power. The most common instance of this is connected with the establishment of separate schools for white and colored children, which has been held to be a valid exercise of the legislative power even by courts of States where the political rights of the colored race have been longest and most earnestly enforced. ...

So far, then, as a conflict with the Fourteenth Amendment is concerned, the case reduces itself to the question whether the statute of Louisiana is a reasonable regulation, and with respect to this there must necessarily be a large discretion on the part of the legislature. In determining the question of reasonableness it is at liberty to act with reference to the established customs and traditions of the people, and with a view to the promotion of their comfort, and the preservation of the public peace and good order. Gauged by this standard, we cannot say that a law which authorizes or even requires the separation of the two races in public conveyances is unreasonable, or more obnoxious to the Fourteenth Amendment than the acts of Congress requiring separate schools for colored children in the District of Columbia, the constitutionality of which does not seem to have been questioned, or the corresponding acts of State legislatures.

We consider the underlying fallacy of the plaintiff's argument to consist in the assumption that the enforced separation of the two races stamps the colored race with a badge of inferiority. If this be so, it is not by reason of anything found in the act, but solely because the colored race chooses to put that construction upon it. The argument necessarily assumes that if, as has been more than once the case, and is not unlikely to be so again, the colored race should become the dominant power in the state legislature, and should enact a law in precisely similar terms, it would thereby relegate the white race to an inferior position. We imagine that the white race, at least, would not acquiesce in this assumption. The argument also assumes that social prejudices may be overcome by legislation, and that equal rights cannot be secured to the Negro except by an enforced commingling of the two races. We cannot accept this proposition. If the two races are to meet on terms of social equality, it must be the result of natural affinities, a mutual appreciation of each other's merits and a voluntary consent of individuals. . . . Legislation is powerless to eradicate racial instincts or to abolish distinctions based upon physical differences, and the attempt to do so can only result in accentuating the difficulties of the present situation. If the civil and political rights of both races be equal, one cannot be inferior to the other civilly or politically. If one race be inferior to the other socially, the Constitution of the United States cannot put them upon the same plane. . . .

The judgment of the court below is therefore affirmed.

Mr. Justice Harlan dissented:*

. . . The white race deems itself to be the dominant race in this country. And so it is, in prestige, in achievement, in education, in wealth and in power. So, I doubt not, that it will continue to be for all time, if it remains true to its great heritage and holds fast to the principles of constitutional liberty. But in view of the Constitution, in the eye of the law, there is in this country no superior, dominant, ruling class of citizens. There is no caste here. Our Constitution is color-blind, and neither knows nor tolerates classes among citizens. In respect of civil rights, all citizens are equal before the law. The humblest is the peer of the most powerful. The law regards man as man, and takes no account of his surroundings or of his color when his civil rights as guaranteed by the supreme law of the land are involved. It is, therefore, to be regretted that this high tribunal, the final expositor of the fundamental law of the land, has reached the conclusion that it is competent for a State to regulate the enjoyment by citizens of their civil rights solely upon the basis of race.

In my opinion, the judgement this day rendered will, in time, prove to be quite as pernicious as the decision made by this tribunal in the *Dred Scott* case. It was adjudged in that case that the descendants of Africans who were imported into this country and sold as slaves were not included nor intended to be included under the word "citizens" in the Constitution, and could not claim any of the rights and privileges which that instrument provided for and secured to citizens of the United States; that at the time of the adoption of the Constitution they were "considered as a subordinate and inferior class of beings, who had been subjugated by the

* Grandfather of the late Justice Harlan.

dominant race, and whether emancipated or not, yet remained subject to their authority, and had no rights or privileges but such as those who held the power and the government might choose to grant them." 19 How. 393. The recent amendments of the Constitution, it was supposed, had eradicated these principles from our institutions. But it seems that we have yet, in some of the states, a dominant race, a superior class of citizens, which assumes to regulate the enjoyment of civil rights, common to all citizens, upon the basis of race. The present decision. it may well be apprehended, will not only stimulate aggressions, more or less brutal and irritating, upon the admitted rights of colored citizens of the United States and the States in which they respectively reside and whose privileges and immunities, as citizens, the States are forbidden to abridge. Sixty millions of whites are in no danger from the presence here of eight millions of blacks. The destinies of the two races in this country are indissolubly linked together, and the interests of both require that the common government of all shall not permit the seeds of race hate to be planted under the sanction of law. What can more certainly arouse race hate, what more certainly create and perpetuate a feeling of distrust between these races, than State enactments which in fact proceed on the ground that colored citizens are so inferior and degraded that they cannot be allowed to sit in public coaches occupied by white citizens? That, as all will admit, is the real meaning of such legislation as was enacted in Louisiana. . . .

I am of opinion that the statute of Louisiana is inconsistent with the personal liberty of citizens, white and black, in that State, and hostile to both the spirit and letter of the Constitution of the United States. If laws of like character should be enacted in the several States of the Union, the effect would be in the highest degree mischievous. Slavery as an institution tolerated by law would, it is true, have disappeared from our country, but there would remain a power in the States, by sinister legislation, to interfere with the full enjoyment of the blessings of freedom; to regulate civil rights, common to all citizens, upon the basis of race; and to place in a condition of legal inferiority a large body of American citizens, now constituting a part of the political community, called the people of the United States, for whom and by whom, through representatives, our government is administered. Such a system is inconsistent with the guarantee given by the Constitution to each State of a republican form of government, and may be stricken down by congressional action, or by the courts in the discharge of their solemn duty to maintain the supreme law of the land, anything in the Constitution or laws of any State to the contrary notwithstanding.

For the reasons stated, I am constrained to withhold my assent from the opinion and judgment of the majority.

Mr. Justice Brewer took no part in the hearing or decision of this case.

RELATED CASES:

Hall v. DeCuir: 95 U.S. 485 (1878). Opinion: Waite, C.J. No dissent.

Here the Court held that a Louisiana statute passed during the Reconstruction period and prohibiting segregation on public carriers invaded a field reserved for Congress since the matter required uniformity of practice so as not to be a burden on interstate commerce. Here the carrier was a steamboat on the Mississippi River.

Louisville, New Orleans and Texas Railroad Co. v. Mississippi: 133 U.S. 587 (1890). Opinion: Brewer, J. Dissenting: Harlan and Bradley, JJ.

A state statute requiring segregation on common carriers was upheld as applying only to intrastate commerce.

McCabe v. Atchison, Topeka and Santa Fe Railway Co.: 235 U.S. 151 (1914). Opinion: Hughes, J. No dissent.

An Oklahoma statute that permitted railroads to provide Pullman and dining cars for the exclusive use of whites while not providing them on demand for Negroes was not the "substantial equality" required by the Interstate Commerce Act. This was known as the "separate coach" law of 1907.

Mitchell v. United States: 313 U.S. 80 (1941). Opinion: Hughes, C.J. No dissent.
Denial of Pullman accommodations to Negroes is unjust discrimination under the Interstate Commerce Act as well as contrary to the substantial equality demanded by the Fourteenth Amendment. Mitchell was a Negro Congressman from Illinois.

Morgan v. Virginia: 328 U.S. 373 (1946). Opinion: Reed, J. Dissenting: Burton, J. Abstaining: Jackson, J.
A state statute requiring segregation on all buses, both interstate and intrastate, was held invalid. Seating arrangements on interstate buses requires a uniform rule so as to avoid a burden on interstate commerce. The statute required whites to be seated in front and Negroes in the rear. The route was from Virginia to Baltimore.

Bob-Lo Excursion Co. v. Michigan: 333 U.S. 28 (1948). Opinion: Rutledge, J. Dissenting: Jackson, J., and Vinson, C.J.
Here the Michigan Civil Rights Act had been applied against a Detroit amusement park company which operated an excursion steamer to its park on an island on the Canadian side of the Detroit River. The company had refused transportation to a Negro girl maintaining that the state law did not apply since this was foreign commerce. The Court upheld the law since the commerce was only technically foreign and actually "highly local." The Court held that Bois Blanc Island, only 15 miles from Detroit, was in many ways an "adjunct of the city of Detroit."

Henderson v. United States (Henderson v. Southern Railway Co.): 339 U.S. 816 (1950). Opinion: Burton, J. No dissent. Abstaining: Clark, J.
Here the Court held that the Interstate Commerce Act was violated by the segregation of Negroes within dining cars, since the Act forbade undue prejudice or disadvantage. This decision relied on *Mitchell.*

Gayle v. Browder: 352 U.S. 903 (1956). Per Curiam. No dissent.
An ordinance of Montgomery and an Alabama statute that required segregation on intrastate buses was held to be contrary to the equal protection and due process clauses of the Fourteenth Amendment.

Speed v. City of Tallahassee: 356 U.S. 913 (1958). Per Curiam. No dissent.
Bus drivers may be empowered to seat passengers for nonracial reasons.

NOTE:

Plessy is the famous 1896 decision that was in principle reversed by the Court in *Brown* v. *Board of Education.* The "separate but equal" principle was followed in the intervening years in a variety of cases and, in fact, has not yet been specifically overruled as applied to the situation to which it originally referred. Great interest is today attached to the dissenting opinion of Mr. Justice Harlan, which has been given a rather prophetic dignity.

Sweatt v. Painter
339 U.S. 629; 70 S.Ct. 848; 94 L.Ed. 1114 (1950)

(Heman Sweatt's application for admission to the University of Texas Law School was rejected solely because he was a Negro. The state courts had noted that a newly established law school for Negroes was available. However, Sweatt maintained that the new school was not on a par academically with the Law School of the University of Texas, and that his denial of admission was a denial of equal protection.)

Vote: 9-0

Mr. Chief Justice Vinson delivered the opinion of the Court:

... Whether the University of Texas Law School is compared with the original or the new law school for Negroes, we cannot find substantial equality in the educational opportunities offered white and Negro law students by the State. In terms of number of the faculty, variety of courses and opportunity for specialization, size of the student body, scope of the library, availability of law review and similar activities, the University of Texas Law School is superior. What is more important, the University of Texas Law School possesses to a far greater degree those qualities which are incapable of objective measurement but which make for greatness in a law school. Such qualities, to name but a few, include reputation of the faculty, experience of the administration, position and influence of the alumni, standing in the community, traditions and prestige. It is difficult to believe that one who had a free choice between these law schools would consider the question close.

Moreover, although the law is a highly learned profession, we are well aware that it is an intensely practical one. The law school, the proving ground for legal learning and practice, cannot be effective in isolation from the individuals and institutions with which the law interacts. Few students and no one who has practiced law would choose to study in an academic vacuum, removed from the interplay of ideas and the exchange of views with which the law is concerned. The law school to which Texas is willing to admit petitioner excludes from its student body members of the racial groups which number 85% of the population of the State and include most of the lawyers, witnesses, jurors, judges and other officials with whom petitioner will inevitably be dealing when he becomes a member of the Texas Bar. With such a substantial and significant segment of society excluded, we cannot conclude that the education offered petitioner is substantially equal to that which he would receive if admitted to the University of Texas Law School. . . .

In accordance with these cases, petitioner may claim his full constitutional right: legal education equivalent to that offered by the State to students of other races. Such education is not available to him in a separate law school as offered by the State. We cannot, therefore, agree with respondents that the doctrine of *Plessy* v. *Ferguson*, 163 U.S. 537 (1896), requires affirmance of the judgment below. Nor need we reach petitioner's contention that *Plessy* v. *Ferguson* should be reexamined in the light of contemporary knowledge respecting the purposes of the Fourteenth Amendment and the effects of racial segregation.

We hold that the Equal Protection Clause of the Fourteenth Amendment requires that petitioner be admitted to the University of Texas Law School. The judgment is reversed and the cause is remanded for proceedings not inconsistent with this opinion.

Reversed.

RELATED CASES:

Cumming v. Richmond County Board of Education: 175 U.S. 528 (1899). Opinion: Harlan, J. No dissent.

A Georgia school board's discontinuance of a Negro high school while continuing the high school for whites was held valid on the basis of lack of county finances. The Court held that closing the white school would not help the Negroes. Further, private schools were available for Negroes at no additional cost to them. Finally, since education is primarily a state matter, there should be intervention only when constitutional rights are clearly violated.

Berea College v. Kentucky: 211 U.S. 45 (1908). Opinion: Brewer, J. Dissenting: Harlan and Day, JJ.

Because of its power to control corporations, a state may require a private school not to integrate its student body. The statute was, in effect, an amendment to the corporate charter.

Gong Lum v. Rice: 275 U.S. 78 (1927). Opinion: Taft, C.J. No dissent.

The Court held that it was not denial of equal protection to require a Chinese girl to attend a Negro school instead of a white school. The Court held that this had been decided many times. The case arose in Mississippi.

Missouri ex rel. Gaines v. Canada: 305 U.S. 337 (1938). Opinion: Hughes, C.J. Dissenting: McReynolds, J.

A state cannot exclude Negroes from its law school by offering to pay the tuition of Negroes at law schools in neighboring states. The Court held that a state can give equal protection only where its laws operate, within its own jurisdiction. The contention of Gaines, Negro, against S. W. Canada, Registrar of the University of Missouri, was thus upheld.

Sipuel v. Board of Regents of the University of Oklahoma: 332 U.S. 631 (1948). Per Curiam. No dissent.

A Negro woman was held to be denied equal protection when denied admission to the Law School of the University of Oklahoma.

Fisher v. Hurst: 333 U.S. 147 (1948). Per Curiam. Dissenting: Murphy and Rutledge, JJ.

Miss Sipuel here brought suit in her married name of Fisher. The Court refused to issue a writ of mandamus to the Supreme Court of Oklahoma when it had issued an order directing that no students be admitted to the law school until appellant had also been admitted to either the existing state law school or a separate one provided for her.

McLaurin v. Oklahoma State Regents: 339 U.S. 637 (1950). Opinion: Vinson, C.J. No dissent.

Segregated practices in a graduate school requiring a certain separation in classrooms, library, and cafeteria deny equal protection. They "impair and inhibit his ability to study, to engage in discussions and exchange views with other students, and, in general, to learn his profession."

Palmer v. Thompson: 403 U.S. 217 (1971). Opinion: Black, J. Dissenting: Douglas, White, Brennan, and Marshall, JJ.

It is purely a discretionary matter for a city (here Jackson, Mississippi) to decide whether it wishes to have public swimming pools or not, but tax-supported swimming pools cannot be denied to one group because of color and supplied to another group.

San Antonio Independent School District v. Rodriguez: 411 U.S. 1 (1973). Opinion: Powell, J. Dissenting: Brennan, White, Douglas, and Marshall, JJ.

The Texas system of financing public education by the use of the property tax does not infringe on a fundamental right either explicitly or implicitly protected by the Constitution. Education is not a right protected under the Constitution. There is no evidence that the tax system discriminates against "poor" people or that it results in the absolute deprivation of education. At least where wealth is concerned, the equal protection clause does not require absolute equality or precisely equal advantages. Decisions as to the raising and disposition of public revenues for local purposes should be made by local authorities who presumably possess the expertise and the familiarity with local problems. Mexican-Americans were living in a school district with a low property tax base.

NOTE:

In a series of cases the Court had become more and more insistent that the "separate but equal" formula should involve more equality if not less separateness.

Sweatt v. *Painter* simply continued this "parade." Here again the facilities were held not to be equal and the state was ordered to give such "equal protection." Segregation was still not considered to be violative of equal protection.

Brown v. Board of Education of Topeka
347 U.S. 483; 74 S.Ct. 686; 98 L.Ed. 873 (1954)

(This case from Kansas was decided along with companion cases from South Carolina, Virginia, and Delaware. All of the cases involved the same basic question —admission to public schools on a nonsegregated basis. The Negro children involved were of elementary or high school age or both. The segregation provisions were on a state constitutional or statutory basis except in Kansas where there were only statutory provisions. The question for the Court to decide was whether segregation of children in public schools solely on the basis of race is forbidden under the equal protection provision of the Fourteenth Amendment even though the physical facilities and other "tangible" factors might be equal for both whites and Negroes.)

Vote: 9-0

Mr. Chief Justice Warren delivered the opinion of the Court:

. . . In the first cases in this Court construing the Fourteenth Amendment, decided shortly after its adoption, the Court interpreted it as proscribing all state-imposed discriminations against the Negro race. The doctrine of "separate but equal" did not make its appearance in this Court until 1896 in the case of *Plessy* v. *Ferguson* involving not education but transportation. American courts have since labored with the doctrine for over half a century. In this Court, there have been six cases involving the "separate but equal" doctrine in the field of public education. In *Cumming* v. *Board of Education of Richmond County*, 175 U.S. 528, and *Gong Lum* v. *Rice*, 275 U.S. 78, the validity of the doctrine itself was not challenged. In more recent cases, all on the graduate school level, inequality was found in that specific benefits enjoyed by white students were denied to Negro students of the same educational qualifications. *State of Missouri ex rel. Gaines* v. *Canada*, 305 U.S. 337; *Sipuel* v. *Board of Regents of University of Oklahoma*, 332 U.S. 631; *Sweatt* v. *Painter*, 339 U.S. 629; *McLaurin* v. *Oklahoma State Regents*, 339 U.S. 637. In none of these cases was it necessary to reexamine the doctrine to grant relief to the Negro plaintiff. And in *Sweatt* v. *Painter* the Court expressly reserved decision on the question whether *Plessy* v. *Ferguson* should be held inapplicable to public education.

In the instant cases, that question is directly presented. Here, unlike *Sweatt* v. *Painter*, there are findings below that the Negro and white schools involved have been equalized, or are being equalized, with respect to buildings, curricula, qualifications and salaries of teachers, and other "tangible" factors. Our decision, therefore, cannot turn on merely a comparison of these tangible factors in the Negro and white schools involved in each of the cases. We must look instead to the effect of segregation itself on public education.

In approaching this problem, we cannot turn the clock back to 1868 when the Amendment was adopted, or even to 1896 when *Plessy* v. *Ferguson* was written. We must consider public education in the light of its full development and its present place in American life throughout the Nation. Only in this way can it be determined if segregation in public schools deprives these plaintiffs of the equal protection of the laws.

Today, education is perhaps the most important function of state and local governments. Compulsory school attendance laws and the great expenditures for education both demonstrate our recognition of the importance of education to our democratic society. It is required in the performance of our most basic public responsibilities, even service in the armed forces. It is the very foundation of good citizenship. Today it is a principal instrument in awakening the child to cultural values, in preparing him for later professional training, and in helping him to adjust normally to his environment. In these days, it is doubtful that any child may reasonably be expected to succeed in life if he is denied the opportunity of an education. Such an opportunity, where the state has undertaken to provide it, is a right which must be made available to all on equal terms.

We come then to the question presented: Does segregation of children in public schools solely on the basis of race, even though the physical facilities and other "tangible" factors may be equal, deprive the children of the minority group of equal educational opportunities? We believe that it does.

In *Sweatt* v. *Painter*, in finding that a segregated law school for Negroes could not provide them equal educational opportunities, this Court relied in large part on "those qualities which are incapable of objective measurement but which make for greatness in a law school." In *McLaurin* v. *Oklahoma State Regents*, the Court, in requiring that a Negro admitted to a white graduate school be treated like all other students, again resorted to intangible considerations: ". . . his ability to study, to engage in discussions and exchange views with other students, and, in general, to learn his profession." Such considerations apply with added force to children in grade and high schools. To separate them from others of similar age and qualifications solely because of their race generates a feeling of inferiority as to their status in the community that may affect their hearts and minds in a way unlikely ever to be undone. The effect of this separation on their educational opportunities was well stated by a finding in the Kansas case by a court which nevertheless felt compelled to rule against the Negro plaintiffs:

"Segregation of white and colored children in public schools has a detrimental effect upon the colored children. The impact is greater when it has the sanction of the law; for the policy of separating the races is usually interpreted as denoting the inferiority of the Negro group. A sense of inferiority affects the motivation of a child to learn. Segregation with the sanction of law, therefore, has a tendency to retard the educational and mental development of Negro children and to deprive them of some of the benefits they would receive in a racially integrated school system." Whatever may have been the extent of psychological knowledge at the time of *Plessy* v. *Ferguson*, this finding is amply supported by modern authority. Any language in *Plessy* v. *Ferguson* contrary to this finding is rejected.

We conclude that in the field of public education the doctrine of "separate but equal" has no place. Separate educational facilities are inherently unequal. Therefore, we hold that the plaintiffs and others similarly situated for whom the actions have been brought are, by reason of the segregation complained of, deprived of the equal protection of the laws guaranteed by the Fourteenth Amendment. This disposition makes unnecessary any discussion whether such segregation also violates the Due Process Clause of the Fourteenth Amendment. . . .

RELATED CASES:

Bolling v. Sharpe: 347 U.S. 497 (1954). Opinion: Warren, C.J. No dissent.

Segregation imposes on Negro children of the District of Columbia a burden that constitutes an arbitrary deprivation of their liberty in violation of the due process clause of the Fifth Amendment. This involved substantive due process, here the equivalency of "equal protection."

Brown v. Board of Education: 349 U.S. 294 (1955). Opinion: Warren, C.J. No dissent.

The lower courts should issue such orders and decrees necessary and proper pursuant to their equity power to admit blacks to all public schools on a nondiscriminatory basis "with all deliberate speed," and considering the different and varied circumstances and factual situations before them.

Baltimore City v. Dawson: 350 U.S. 877 (1955). Per Curiam. No dissent.

The Court here, without a written opinion, applied the desegregation principle to public beaches.

Holmes v. Atlanta: 350 U.S. 879 (1955). Per Curiam. No dissent.

Here the principle was applied to public golf courses.

Florida ex rel. Hawkins v. Board of Control: 350 U.S. 413 (1956). Per Curiam. No dissent.

Even though Florida had a "substantially equal" law school for Negroes, Hawkins was entitled to "prompt admission" to the white law school.

Aaron v. Cooper: 357 U.S. 566 (1958). Per Curiam. No dissent.

Where a federal District Court entered an order authorizing public school officials to suspend for a specified time a plan of racial integration previously approved both by that court and the Court of Appeals, and where parties applied to the Court of Appeals for a stay of the order, the Supreme Court denied *certiorari* on the assumption that the Court of Appeals would act upon the application for a stay or for appeal in ample time to permit arrangements to be made for the next school year.

Shuttlesworth v. Birmingham Board of Education: 358 U.S. 101 (1958). Per Curiam. No dissent.

Here the Court upheld placement of pupils in schools "upon a basis of individual merit without regard to their race or color."

Slade v. Board of Education of Hartford County: 357 U.S. 906 (1958). Per Curiam. No dissent.

A plan by the local school board in Michigan for the gradual integration of schools was attacked by the NAACP as being too slow. The Court refused to tamper with the situation.

Griffin v. County School Board of Prince Edward County: 377 U.S. 218 (1964). Opinion: Black, J. No dissent.

For the county board to close public schools while at the same time tuition grants and tax concessions are made to assist white children in private segregated schools is a denial of equal protection under the Fourteenth Amendment. The Court noted that a lower federal court could order the county board to levy taxes to operate a public school system in the county. This case arose in Virginia.

Green v. County School Board of New Kent County, Virginia: 391 U.S. 430 (1968). Opinion: Brennan, J. No dissent.

School boards must formulate positive plans that promise realistically to bring about promptly a unitary, nonracial, nondiscriminatory school system. In the same vein on the same day the Court also decided *Raney* v. *Board of Education of Gould School District* (Arkansas), 391 U.S. 443 (1968)—freedom of choice plans void—and *Monroe* v. *Board of Commissioners of the City of Jackson* (Tennessee), 391 U.S. 450 (1968)—freedom of transfer rejected.

United States v. Montgomery County Board of Education: 395 U.S. 225 (1969). Opinion: Black, J. No dissent.

A U.S. District Court order to the local school board setting a ratio of white to Negro teachers in each school in the district was held valid as implementing a desegregated system. This case came out of Alabama.

Swann v. Charlotte-Mecklenburg Board of Education: 402 U.S. 1 (1971). Opinion: Burger, C.J. No dissent.

When the school authorities do not carry out their obligation to establish acceptable remedies for violations of the equal protection guarantee the federal District Court has broad power to devise a remedy that will assure a unitary school system. Included here may be the use of mathematical ratios and bus transportation as tools of school desegregation. This case arose in Mecklenburg County, North Carolina.

North Carolina State Board v. Swann: 402 U.S. 43 (1971). Opinion: Burger, C.J. No dissent.

A state statute prohibiting the involuntary bussing of students to bring about a balance or a ratio of race, religion, or national origins is void since it operates to affect adversely the operation of a unitary school system or the disestablishment of a dual school system. The statute is not required to be "color blind" since this would militate against the elimination of a dual school system.

Graham v. Richardson: 403 U.S. 365 (1971). Opinion: Blackmun, J. No dissent.

A state (here Arizona) cannot deny equal protection of the laws to any person (including lawfully admitted aliens as well as citizens) within its jurisdiction. A state has discretion to classify persons on a reasonable basis but there can be no "special public interest" in tax revenues to which aliens have contributed on an equal basis with the citizens of the state. Therefore a state cannot deny welfare benefits to an alien who has not resided in the United States for a set period of years.

NOTE:

Brown v. *Board of Education* is one of the most momentous decisions handed down by the Court in this century. Its ultimate effects, for good or evil, can only be imagined. It is, incidentally, an excellent example of the fact that a decision by the Court is technically applicable only to the parties before the Court. As *Bolling* v. *Sharpe* proves, in certain instances the due process clause can be used as an effective substitute for the equal protection clause. Several points distinguish the opinion. Among these are the absence of precedents and the use of sociological evidence. After the original decision in 1954, the Court held a subsequent hearing in 1955 and handed down a "mandate decision" to implement the carrying out of its original judgment (*Brown* v. *Board*, 349 U.S. 294).

As already noted, the Court's decision in *Bolling* following that in *Hurd* v. *Hodge* (334 U.S. 24, 1948) has been regarded as nationalizing the equal protection clause of the Fourteenth Amendment in that the due process clause of the Fifth Amendment has been found capable of broad enough interpretation to include the basic concepts involved in "equal protection."

Two points in connection with *Brown* (and as borne out in subsequent cases) need emphasis. The first of these is that the Court did not mandate integration but simply outlawed segregation on a racial basis, and, secondly, this segregation thus outlawed was that *solely* on a basis of race. This point the Court emphasized repeatedly in the course of the opinion in *Brown*. In very recent cases the Court had held that integration must be positively sought. Thus the Court is departing from its original posture in *Brown* and subsequent cases. What will be the effects of this remains to be seen. See *Green* v. *County School Board, Raney* v. *Board*, and *Monroe* v. *Board* in "Related Cases" above, p. 306.

Milliken v. Bradley
418 U.S. 717; 94 S.Ct. 3112; 41 L.Ed. 2d 1069 (1974)

(Ronald Bradley and others of the Detroit NAACP brought a class action suit against Governor William Milliken, the state and city boards of education, and

others claiming racial segregation as a result of school district zone boundaries. The lower courts approved a regional plan including the city and a number of suburbs.)
    Vote: 5-4
    Mr. Chief Justice Burger delivered the opinion of the Court.
    We granted certiorari in these consolidated cases to determine whether a federal court may impose a multidistrict, areawide remedy to a single district *de jure* segregation problem absent any finding that the other included school districts have failed to operate unitary school systems within their districts, absent any claim or finding that the boundary lines of any affected school district were established with the purpose of fostering racial segregation in public schools, absent any finding that the included districts committed acts which effected segregation within the other districts, and absent a meaningful opportunity for the included neighboring school districts to present evidence or be heard on the propriety of a multidistrict remedy or on the question of constitutional violations by those neighboring districts.
    . . . Viewing the record as a whole, it seems clear that the District Court and the Court of Appeals shifted the primary focus from a Detroit remedy to the metropolitan area only because of their conclusion that total desegregation of Detroit would not produce the racial balance which they perceived as desirable. Both courts proceeded on an assumption that the Detroit schools could not be truly desegregated—in their view of what constituted desegregation—unless the racial composition of the student body of each school substantially reflected the racial composition of the population of the metropolitan area as a whole. The metropolitan area was then defined as Detroit plus 53 of the outlying school districts. . . .
    . . . Boundary lines may be bridged where there has been a constitutional violation calling for inter-district relief, but, the notion that school district lines may be casually ignored or treated as a mere administrative convenience is contrary to the history of public education in our country. No single tradition in public education is more deeply rooted than local control over the operation of schools; local autonomy has long been thought essential both to the maintenance of community concern and support for public schools and to quality of the educational process. . . .
    . . . Of course, no state law is above the Constitution. School district lines and the present laws with respect to local control, are not sacrosanct and if they conflict with the Fourteenth Amendment federal courts have a duty to prescribe appropriate remedies. See, *e.g., Wright* v. *Council of City of Emporia*, 407 U.S. 451; *United States* v. *Scotland Neck City Board of Education*, 407 U.S. 484 (state or local officials prevented from carving out a new school district from an existing district that was in process of dismantling a duel school system); cf. *Haney* v. *County Board of Education of Sevier County*, 429 F.2d 364 (State contributed to separation of races by drawing of school district lines); *United States* v. *Texas*, 321 F. Supp, 1043, cert. denied, sub nom. *Edgar* v. *United States*, 404 U.S. 1016 (one or more school districts created and maintained for one race). But our prior holdings have been confined to violations and remedies within a single school district. We therefore turn to address, for the first time, the validity of a remedy mandating cross-district or inter-district consolidation to remedy a condition of segregation found to exist in only one district.
    The controlling principle consistently expounded in our holdings is that the scope of the remedy is determined by the nature and extent of the constitutional violation. *Swann, supra*, 402 U.S., at 16, 91 S.Ct., at 1276. Before the school districts may be set aside by consolidating the separate units for remedial purposes or by imposing a cross-district remedy, it must first be shown that there has been a constitutional violation within one district that produces a significant segregative effect

in another district. Specifically it must be shown that racially discriminatory acts of the state or local school districts, or of a single school district have been a substantial cause of inter-district segregation. Thus an inter-district remedy might be in order where the racially discriminatory acts of one or more school districts caused racial segregation in an adjacent district, or where district lines have been deliberately drawn on the basis of race. In such circumstances an inter-district remedy would be appropriate to eliminate the inter-district segregation directly caused by the constitutional violation. Conversely, without an inter-district violation and inter-district effect, there is no constitutional wrong calling for an inter-district remedy.

The record before us, voluminous as it is, contains evidence of *de jure* segregated conditions only in the Detroit schools; indeed, that was the theory on which the litigation was initially based and on which the District Court took evidence. See p. 3123, *supra*. With no showing of significant violation by the 53 outlying school districts and no evidence of any inter-district violation or effect, the court went beyond the original theory of the case as framed by the pleadings and mandated a metropolitan area remedy. To approve the remedy ordered by the court would impose on the outlying districts, not shown to have committed any constitutional violation, a wholly impermissible remedy based on a standard not hinted at in *Brown I* and *II* or any holding of this Court.

The constitutional right of the Negro respondents residing in Detroit is to attend a unitary school system in that district. Unless petitioners drew the district lines in a discriminatory fashion, or arranged for white students residing in the Detroit district to attend schools in Oakland and Macomb Counties, they were under no constitutional duty to make provisions for Negro students to do so. The view of the dissenters, that the existence of a dual system *in Detroit* can be made the basis for a decree requiring cross-district transportation of pupils cannot be supported on the grounds that it represents merely the devising of a suitably flexible remedy for the violation of rights already established by our prior decisions. It can be supported only by drastic expansion of the constitutional right itself, an expansion without any support in either constitutional principle or precedent.

In reversing the decision of the Court of Appeals this Court is in no way turning its back on the proscription of state-imposed segregation first voiced in *Brown* v. *Board of Education*, 347 U.S. 483, or on the delineation of remedial powers and duties most recently expressed in *Swann* v. *Charlotte-Mecklenburg Board of Education*, 402 U.S. 1. In *Swann* the Court addressed itself to the range of equitable remedies available to the courts to effectuate the desegregation mandated by *Brown* and its progeny, noting that the task in choosing appropriate relief is "to correct . . . the condition that offends the Constitution," and that "the nature of the violation determines the scope of the remedy. . . ." 402 U.S., at 16.

The disposition of this case thus falls squarely under these principles. The only "condition that offends the Constitution" found by the District Court in this case is the existence of officially supported segregation in and among public schools in Detroit itself. There were no findings that the differing racial composition between schools in the city and in the outlying suburbs was caused by official activity of any sort. It follows that the decision to include in the desegregation plan pupils from school districts outside. Detroit was not predicated upon any constitutional violation involving those school districts. By approving a remedy that would reach beyond the limits of the city of Detroit to correct a constitutional violation found to have occurred solely within that city the Court of Appeals thus went beyond the governing equitable principles established in this Court's decisions.

Reversed and remanded.

Mr. Justice Douglas, dissenting.

. . . The issue is not whether there should be racial balance but whether the State's use of various devices that end up with black schools and white schools brought the Equal Protection Clause into effect. Given the State's control over the educational system in Michigan, the fact that the black schools are in one district and the white schools are in another is not controlling—either constitutionally or equitably.

Mr. Justice White, with whom Mr. Justice Douglas, Mr. Justice Brennan, and Mr. Justice Marshall join, dissenting.

Regretfully, and for several reasons, I can join neither the Court's judgment nor its opinion. The core of my disagreement is that deliberate acts of segregation and their consequences will go unremedied, not because a remedy would be infeasible or unreasonable in terms of the usual criteria governing school desegregation cases, but because an effective remedy would cause what the Court considers to be undue administrative inconvenience to the State. The result is that the State of Michigan, the entity at which the Fourteenth Amendment is directed, has successfully insulated itself from its duty to provide effective desegregation remedies by vesting sufficient power over its public schools in its local school districts. If this is the case in Michigan, it will be the case in most States.

In sum, several factors in this case coalesce to support the District Court's ruling that it was the State of Michigan itself, not simply the Detroit Board of Education, which bore the obligation of curing the condition of segregation within the Detroit city schools. The actions of the State itself directly contributed to Detroit's segregation. Under the Fourteenth Amendment, the State is ultimately responsible for the actions of its local agencies. And finally, given the structure of Michigan's educational system, Detroit's segregation cannot be viewed as the problem of an independent and separate entity. Michigan operates a single statewide system of education, a substantial part of which was shown to be segregated in this case.

RELATED CASES:

See pp. 305-306, above.

> ## Civil Rights Cases
> ### 109 U.S. 3; 3 S.Ct. 18; 27 L.Ed. 835 (1883)

(Certain Negroes had been refused admission to hotels, theaters, and railroad "ladies' cars" by the owners of these facilities. An act of Congress forbade discrimination. The arrest of these private owners was challenged on the basis that the Fourteenth Amendment does not prohibit discriminatory activity on the part of private citizens.)

Vote: 8-1

Mr. Justice Bradley delivered the opinion of the Court:

. . . The first section of the Fourteenth Amendment, which is the one relied on, after declaring who shall be citizens of the United States, and of the several states, is prohibitory in its character, and prohibitory upon the States. It declares that: "No State shall make or enforce any law which shall abridge the privileges or immunities of citizens of the United States; nor shall any State deprive any person of life, liberty or property without due process of law; nor deny to any person within its jurisdiction the equal protection of the laws." It is State action of a particular character that is prohibited. Individual invasion of individual rights is not the subject-matter of the Amendment. It has a deeper and broader scope. It nullifies and makes void all State legislation, and State action of every kind, which impairs the privileges and immunities of citizens of the United States, or which injures them in life, liberty or property without due process of law, or which denies to any of them the equal protection of the laws. It not only does this, but, in order that the national will, thus declared, may not be a mere *brutum fulmen*, the last section of the Amendment invests Congress with power to enforce it by appropriate legislation. To enforce what? To enforce the prohibition. To adopt appropriate legislation for correcting the effects of such prohibited State laws and State Acts, and thus to render them effectually null, void and innocuous. This is the legislative power conferred upon Congress, and this is the whole of it. It does not invest Congress with power to legislate upon subjects which are within the domain of State legislation; but to provide modes of relief against State legislation, or State action, of the kind referred to. It does not authorize Congress to create a code of municipal law for the regulation of private rights; but to provide modes of redress against the operation of State laws, and the action of State officers, executive or judicial, when these are subversive of the fundamental rights specified in the Amendment. Positive rights and privileges are undoubtedly secured by the Fourteenth Amendment; but they are secured by way of prohibition against State laws and State proceedings affecting those rights and privileges, and by power given to Congress to legislate for the purpose of carrying such prohibition into effect; and such legislation must, necessarily, be predicated upon such supposed State laws or State proceedings, and be directed to the correction of their operation and effect. . . .

And so in the present case, until some State law has been passed, or some State action through its officers or agents has been taken, adverse to the rights of citizens sought to be protected by the Fourteenth Amendment, no legislation of the United States under said Amendment, nor any proceedings under such legislation, can be called into activity; for the prohibitions of the Amendment are against State laws and acts done under State authority. Of course, legislation may and should be provided in advance to meet the exigency when it arises; but it should be adapted to the mischief and wrong which the Amendment was intended to provide against; and that is, State laws, or State action of some kind, adverse to the rights of the citizens secured by the Amendment. Such legislation cannot properly cover the whole domain of rights appertaining to life, liberty and property, defining them and providing for their vindication. That would be to establish a code of municipal law regulative of all private rights between man and man in society. It would be to make Congress take the place of the State Legislatures and to supersede them. It is absurd to affirm that, because of the rights of life, liberty and property, which include all civil rights that men have, are, by the Amendment, sought to be protected against invasion on the part of the State without due process of law, Congress may, therefore, provide due process of law for their vindication in every case; and that, because the denial by a State to any persons, of the equal protection of the laws, is prohibited by the Amendment, therefore Congress may establish laws for their equal protection. In fine, the legislation which Congress is authorized to adopt in this behalf is not general legislation upon the rights of the citizen, but corrective legislation, that is, such as may be necessary and proper for counteracting such laws as the States may adopt or enforce, and which, by the Amendment, they are prohibited from making or enforcing, or such acts and proceedings as the States may commit or take, and which, by the Amendment, they are prohibited from committing or taking. . . .

On the whole we are of opinion, that no countenance of authority for the passage of the law in question can be found in either the Thirteenth or Fourteenth Amendment of the Constitution; and no other ground of authority for its passage being suggested, it must necessarily be declared void, at least so far as its operation in the several States is concerned. . . .

Mr. Justice Harlan dissented:

The opinion in these cases proceeds, it seems to me, upon grounds entirely too narrow and artificial. I cannot resist the conclusion that the substance and spirit of the recent amendments of the Constitution have been sacrificed by a subtle and ingenious verbal criticism. "It is not the words of the law but the internal sense of it that makes the law: the letter of the law is the body; the sense and reason of the law is the soul." Constitutional provisions, adopted in the interest of liberty, and for the purpose of securing, through national legislation, if need be, rights inhering in a state of freedom, and belonging to American citizenship, have been so construed as to defeat the ends the people desired to accomplish, which they attempted to accomplish and which they supposed they had accomplished by changes in their fundamental law. . . .

In every material sense applicable to the practical enforcement of the Fourteenth Amendment, railroad corporations, keepers of inns, and managers of places of public amusement are agents or instrumentalities of the States, because they are charged with duties to the public, and are amenable, in respect of their duties and functions, to governmental regulation. It seems to me that, within the principle settled in *Ex parte Virginia*, a denial, by these instrumentalities of the State, to the citizen, because of his race, of that equality of civil rights secured to him by law, is a denial by the State, within the meaning of the Fourteenth Amendment. . . .

RELATED CASES:

Logan v. United States: 114 U.S. 263 (1892). Opinion: Waite, C.J. No dissent.

The federal government has the right and the duty to protect prisoners in its custody against mob action. Moreover, the prisoners have the right "secured to them by the Constitution and laws of the United States" to be protected.

Burton v. Wilmington Parking Authority: 365 U.S. 715 (1951). Opinion: Clark, J. Dissenting: Frankfurter, Harlan, and Whittaker, JJ.

Discrimination based on race carried out by a privately owned and operated restaurant which leased space in a publicly owned and operated building contravened the equal protection clause of the 14th Amendment since this was held to be "state action."

McLaughlin v. Florida: 379 U.S. 184 (1964). Opinion: White, J. No dissent.

A Florida statute which made it a crime for a couple made up of a white and a Negro habitually to live in and occupy in the nighttime the same room while the same conduct when engaged in by any other type of couple is not penalized was held to be an invidious racial discrimination forbidden by the equal protection clause.

Heart of Atlanta Motel, Inc. v. United States: 379 U.S. 241 (1965). Opinion: Clark, J. No dissent.

The owner of a large motel in Atlanta, which restricted its clientele to white persons brought suit for a declaratory judgment and for an injunction to restrain the enforcement of the Civil Rights Act of 1964. The owner admitted that approximately three-fourths of its registered guests came from outside the state. The Court upheld the Act noting that "the power of Congress to promote interstate commerce also includes the power to regulate the local incidents thereof, including local activities in both the States of origin and destination, which might have a substantial and harmful effect upon that commerce. . . ."

Shuttlesworth v. The City of Birmingham: 394 U.S. 147 (1969). Opinion: Stewart, J. Abstaining: Marshall, J.

A Negro minister who helped lead Negroes in an orderly civil rights march in Birmingham, Alabama, was arrested and convicted for violating a city ordinance which prohibited participating in any parade or procession on city streets without first obtaining a permit from the City Commission. The Court declared the ordinance void noting that "our decisions have also made clear that picketing and parading may nonetheless constitute methods of expression, entitled to First Amendment protection. . . ."

Hamm v. City of Rock Hill: 379 U.S. 306 (1964). Opinion: Clark, J. Dissenting: Black, Harlan, White, and Stewart, JJ.

Convictions for conduct no longer unlawful must be nullified, if under direct review at the time. Here the Civil Rights Act of 1964 ran counter to state trespass statutes.

Adderley v. Florida: 385 U.S. 39 (1966). Opinion: Black, J. Dissenting: Douglas, Brennan, and Fortas, JJ., and Warren, C.J.

A state trespass statute applies to a demonstration on the premises of a jail, which is built for security purposes and is not open to the public.

Loving v. Virginia: 388 U.S. 1 (1967). Opinion: Warren, C.J. No dissent.

Virginia's statute banning interracial marriages restricts freedom to marry solely because of racial classification and thus violates the central meaning of the equal protection clause as well as the due process clause of the Fourteenth Amendment. Marriage is one of the basic rights of man fundamental to our very existence and survival. Such statutes are known as miscegenation statutes.

Walker v. City of Birmingham: 388 U.S. 307 (1967). Opinion: Stewart, J. Dissenting: Warren, C.J., and Douglas, Brennan, and Fortas, JJ.

There can be no bypassing of orderly judicial review of a temporary injunction before disobeying it. The injunction enjoined participation in or encouragement of mass street parades without a permit as required by city ordinance.

NOTE:

The decision in the *Civil Rights Cases* set the pattern for the view of the Fourteenth Amendment that it applied only to state action and not to private actions. This decision and some others of the same period have sometimes been referred to as the Second Civil War, this one won by the South in the Supreme Court.

Earlier in *United States* v. *Cruikshank* (92 U.S. 542, 1876) the Court had noted that the Fourteenth Amendment "adds nothing to the rights of one citizen as against another. It simply furnishes a federal guaranty against any encroachment by the States upon the fundamental rights which belong to every citizen as a member of society." More recent cases have obviously taken a much more liberal view of the meaning of the Fourteenth Amendment.

Screws v. United States
325 U.S. 91; 65 S.Ct. 1031; 89 L.Ed. 1495 (1945)

(A county sheriff in Georgia by the name of Screws, with the aid of a policeman and a deputy, arrested a Negro on a warrant charging him with the theft of a tire. When they arrived at the Courthouse, the officers proceeded to beat the Negro, claiming that he had reached for a gun. He was rendered unconscious and died at a hospital within an hour. The officers were charged with violation of the Federal Criminal Code, Section 20 (now Title 18 U.S.C. 242), which makes a federal offense of willfully depriving a person, under color of law, of his rights, privileges, or immunities guaranteed by the Constitution and laws of the United States. The case involved the question of whether Congress has the power to provide for the punishment of state officials for violation of federal civil rights.)

Vote: 5-4

Mr. Justice Douglas delivered the opinion of the Court:

. . . We hesitate to say that when Congress sought to enforce the Fourteenth

Amendment in this fashion it did a vain thing. We hesitate to conclude that for 80 years this effort of Congress, renewed several times, to protect the important rights of the individual guaranteed by the Fourteenth Amendment has been an idle gesture. Yet if the Act falls by reason of vagueness so far as due process of law is concerned, there would seem to be a similar lack of specificity when the privileges and immunities clause . . . and the equal protection clause . . . of the Fourteenth Amendment are involved. Only if no construction can save the Act from this claim of unconstitutionality are we willing to reach that result. We do not reach it, for we are of the view that if § 20 is confined more narrowly than the lower courts confined it, it can be preserved as one of the sanctions to the great rights which the Fourteenth Amendment was designed to secure. . . .

The difficulty here is that this question of intent was not submitted to the jury with the proper instructions. The court charged that petitioners acted illegally if they applied more force than was necessary to make the arrest effectual or to protect themselves from the prisoner's alleged assault. But in view of our construction of the word "willfully" the jury should have been further instructed that it was not sufficient that petitioners had a generally bad purpose. To convict it was necessary for them to find that petitioners had the purpose to deprive the prisoner of a constitutional right, e.g. the right to be tried by a court rather than by ordeal. And in determining whether that requisite bad purpose was present the jury would be entitled to consider all the attendant circumstances—the malice of petitioners, the weapons used in the assault, its character and duration, the provocation, if any, and the like. . . .

It is said, however, that petitioners did not act "under color of any law" within the meaning of § 20 of the Criminal Code. We disagree. We are of the view that petitioners acted under "color" of law in making the arrest of Robert Hall and in assaulting him. They were officers of the law who made the arrest. By their own admissions they assaulted Hall in order to protect themselves and to keep their prisoner from escaping. It was their duty under Georgia law to make the arrest effective. Hence, their conduct comes within the statute.

. . . It is clear that under "color" of law means under "pretense" of law. Thus acts of officers in the ambit of their personal pursuits are plainly excluded. Acts of officers who undertake to perform their official duties are included whether they hew to the line of their authority or overstep it. . . .

Reversed.

Mr. Justice Murphy dissented:

. . . It is unnecessary to send this case back for a further trial on the assumption that the jury was not charged on the matter of the willfulness of the state officials, an issue that was not raised below or before us. The evidence is more than convincing that the officials willfully, or at least with wanton disregard of the consequences, deprived Robert Hall of his life without due process of law. A new trial could hardly make that fact more evident; the failure to charge the jury on willfulness was at most an inconsequential error. Moreover, the presence or absence of willfulness fails to decide the constitutional issue raised before us. Section 20 is very definite and certain in its reference to the right to life as spelled out in the Fourteenth Amendment quite apart from the state of mind of the state officials. A finding of willfulness can add nothing to the clarity of that reference. . . .

Mr. Justice Roberts, Mr. Justice Frankfurter, and Mr. Justice Jackson dissented:

. . . The debates in Congress are barren of any indication that the supporters of the legislation now before us had the remotest notion of authorizing the National Government to prosecute State officers for conduct which their State had made a State offense where the settled custom of the State did not run counter to formulated law.

Were it otherwise it would indeed be surprising. It was natural to give the shelter of the Constitution to those basic human rights for the vindication of which the successful conduct of the Civil War was the end of a long process. And the extension of federal authority so as to guard against evasion by any State of these newly created federal rights was an obvious corollary. But to attribute to Congress the making overnight of a revolutionary change in the balance of the political relations between the National Government and the States without reason, is a very different thing. And to have provided for the National Government to take over the administration of criminal justice from the States to the extent of making every lawless action of the policeman on the beat or in the station house, whether by way of third degree or the illegal ransacking for evidence in a man's house . . . , a federal offense, would have constituted a revolutionary break with the past overnight. . . .

. . . The matter concerns policies inherent in our federal system and the undesirable consequences of federal prosecution for crimes which are obviously and predominantly State crimes no matter how much sophisticated argumentation may give them the appearance of federal crimes. Congress has not expressed a contrary purpose, either by the language of its legislation or by anything appearing in the environment out of which its language came. The practice of government for seventy-five years likewise speaks against it. Nor is there a body of judicial opinion which bids us find in the unbridled excess of a State officer, constituting a crime under his State law, action taken "under color of law" which federal law forbids.

. . . In the absence of clear direction by Congress we should leave to the States the enforcement of their criminal law, and not relieve States of the responsibility for vindicating wrongdoing that is essentially local or weaken the habits of local law enforcement by tempting reliance on federal authority for an occasional unpleasant task of local enforcement. . . .

RELATED CASES:

Williams v. United States: 341 U.S. 97 (1951). Opinion: Douglas, J. Dissenting: Black, Minton, Frankfurter, and Jackson, JJ.

A private detective also serving as a deputy police officer beat four suspects until they confessed. He was convicted for violation of Sec. 242 of the federal Code for depriving persons, under color of law, of the right to be tried by due process of law under the Fourteenth Amendment. However, in *United States* v. *Williams*, 341 U.S. 70, the Court had held that the detective could not be prosecuted under Sec. 241 of the Code since only rights and privileges of United States citizenship are protected therein. The appendix of this case has a good, concise history of changes in the language of federal criminal statutes.

Collins v. Hardyman: 341 U.S. 651 (1951). Opinion: Jackson, J. Dissenting: Burton, Black, and Douglas, JJ.

The Court held that there was no conspiracy but a "lawless political brawl" in an attempt to break up a meeting. Therefore the constitutionality of federal legislation directed against persons who conspire to deprive persons of equal protection or equal privileges and immunities was not ruled upon. (Title 42, Sec. 1985.)

Griffin v. Maryland: 378 U.S. 130 (1964). Opinion: Warren, C.J. Dissenting: Harlan, Black, and White, JJ.

The action of an individual who, as a deputy sheriff possessing state authority, purports to act pursuant to that authority, is state action. It is immaterial that he could have taken the same action in a purely private capacity or that his actions were not authorized by state law.

United States v. Price: 383 U.S. 787 (1966). Opinion: Fortas, J. No dissent.

The Federal Criminal Code includes a person who acts "under color of law" even though he is not an officer of a state. It is enough that he is a willful participant in joint activity with the state or its agents. This part of the code is a holdover from Reconstruction days. This case came out of Philadelphia, Neshoba County, Mississippi.

NOTE:

Screws, Benanti v. *United States,* and *United States* v. *Classic* are examples of the application to state officials of the provisions of federal laws. The Court has made "under color of" and "under pretense of" state law mutually interchangeable terms in its interpretation of the applicable federal criminal statute. However, the constitutional difficulties involved in applying such federal criminal legislation to individuals are very obvious.

ALIENS AND EQUAL PROTECTION

The discrimination that the Fourteenth Amendment wars against has found expression in statutes directed not only at Negroes but also at aliens. Foremost among these have been those discriminating against aliens in specified occupations and in the matter of land ownership. Over the years the Court has attempted to uphold legislative enactments if there appeared to be a reasonable basis for the acts of the legislatures. The benefit of the doubt has sometimes been given to legislatures on the basis of varying local conditions. The crucial point is the presence of a reasonable basis for the classification or distinction. Recent decisions have taken the point of view that the permissible area of state statutory discrimination against aliens as a class is a very narrow one.

Truax v. Raich
239 U.S. 33; 36 S.Ct. 7; 60 L.Ed. 131 (1915)

(A statute of the state of Arizona provided that an employer of more than five workers at any one time must have not less than eighty percent of them "qualified electors or native-born citizens of the United States or some sub-division thereof." Mike Raich was a native of Austria and not a qualified elector. After the adoption of the statute, Raich was informed by his employer, William Truax, that, because of the requirement, Raich was discharged. Raich then filed a bill to restrain Truax from taking this action asserting that the statute deprived him of equal protection of the laws under the Fourteenth Amendment.)

Vote: 8-1

Mr. Justice Hughes delivered the opinion of the Court:

. . . It is sought to justify this act as an exercise of the power of the State to make reasonable classifications in legislating to promote the health, safety, morals and welfare of those within its jurisdiction. But this admitted authority, with the broad range of legislative discretion that it implies, does not go so far as to make it possible for the State to deny to lawful inhabitants, because of their race or nationality, the ordinary means of earning a livelihood. It requires no argument to show that the right to work for a living in the common occupations of the community is of the very essence of the personal freedom and opportunity that it was the purpose of the Amendment to secure. . . . If this could be refused solely upon the ground of race or nationality, the prohibition of the denial to any person of the equal protection of the laws would be a barren form of words. It is no answer to say, as it is argued, that the act proceeds upon the assumption that "the employment of aliens unless restrained was a peril to the public welfare." The discrimination against aliens in the wide range of employments to which the act relates is made an end in itself and thus the authority to deny to aliens, upon the mere fact of their alienage, the right to obtain support in the ordinary fields of labor is necessarily involved. It must also be said that reasonable classification implies action consistent with the legitimate interests of the State, and it will not be disputed that these cannot be so broadly conceived as to bring them into hostility to exclusive Federal power. The authority to control immigration—to admit or exclude aliens—is vested solely in the Federal Government. . . . The assertion of an authority to deny to aliens the opportunity of earning a livelihood when lawfully admitted to the State would be tantamount to the assertion of the right to deny them entrance and abode, for in ordinary cases they cannot live where they cannot work. And if such a policy were permissible, the practical result would be that those lawfully admitted to the country under the authority of the Acts of Congress, instead of enjoying in a substantial sense and in their full scope the privileges conferred by the admission, would be segregated in such of the States as chose to offer hospitality.

. . . The discrimination is against aliens as such in competition with citizens in the described range of enterprises and in our opinion it clearly falls under the condemnation of the fundamental law.

Order affirmed.

Mr. Justice McReynolds dissented:

It seems to me plain that this is a suit against a state to which the Eleventh Amendment declares "the judicial power of the United States shall not be construed to extend."

RELATED CASES:

McCready v. Virginia: 94 U.S. 391 (1877). Opinion: Waite, C.J. No dissent.

The trusteeship of the state in regard to fish and game may be legally expanded by the state to empower it to prohibit not only aliens but also citizens of other states of the United States fishing for oysters in waters of the state.

Yick Wo v. Hopkins: 118 U.S. 356 (1886). Opinion: Matthews, J. No dissent.

An ordinance of San Francisco requiring a permit for the establishment of a laundry while fair on its face was administered in such discriminatory fashion as to deny equal protection of the laws.

Patsone v. Pennsylvania: 232 U.S. 138 (1914). Opinion: Holmes, J. Dissenting: White, C.J.

A state may prohibit aliens hunting wild game therein since the state is serving in the guise of guardian or trustee for the collective rights of the state's citizens.

Heim v. McCall: 239 U.S. 175 (1915). Opinion: McKenna, J. No dissent.

A state may legally include in its contracts for public works provisions forbidding contractors to employ aliens subject to a penalty of forfeiture of contract. A state may give preference to its own citizens.

Ohio ex rel. Clarke v. Deckebach: 274 U.S. 392 (1927). Opinion: Stone, J. No dissent.

A state may deny an alien a license to operate a pool and billiard room. There is the possibility of a rational basis for such a legislative judgment in this situation and "we have no such knowledge of local conditions as would enable us to say that it is clearly wrong."

NOTE:

Truax did two things. It reiterated federal supremacy in the field of admission and control of aliens and it noted that a state cannot under guise of the exercise of police power deny to an alien the ordinary means of earning a livelihood. This is a denial of equal protection of the laws. In certain other areas of the exercise of police power and in such matters as the custody and dispersal of the property of the state's citizens, a state may probably treat aliens in a different manner from citizens within narrow limits.

Oyama v. California
332 U.S. 633; 68 S.Ct. 269; 92 L.Ed. 249 (1948)

(Aliens ineligible for citizenship were forbidden to acquire, own, occupy, lease, or transfer agricultural land by the terms of the California Alien Land Laws. A Japanese citizen not eligible for citizenship, Kajiro Oyama, purchased six acres of land in 1934 which he then deeded to his son, Fred, a six-year-old American citizen by birth. Six months later the father petitioned a court that he be appointed Fred's guardian, and the court entered the order. In 1942 the Oyama family was evacuated from the Coast to a relocation center. In 1944, while the family was still restrained from returning home, the state petitioned the court to escheat the land on the contention that there had been intent to violate and evade the California statute. This statute was attacked as violating equal protection under the Fourteenth Amendment.)

Vote: 6-3

Mr. Chief Justice Vinson delivered the opinion of the Court:

. . . We agree with petitioner's first contention, that the Alien Land Law, as applied in this case, deprives Fred Oyama of the equal protection of California's laws and of his privileges as an American citizen. In our view of the case, the State has discriminated against Fred Oyama; the discrimination is based solely on his parents' country of origin; and there is absent the compelling justification which would be needed to sustain discrimination of that nature.

. . . The California law points in one direction for minor citizens like Fred Oyama, whose parents cannot be naturalized, and in another for all other children —for minor citizens whose parents are either citizens or eligible aliens, and even for minors who are themselves aliens though eligible for naturalization.

In the first place, for most minors California has the customary rule that where a parent pays for a conveyance to his child there is a presumption that a gift was intended; there is no presumption of a resulting trust, no presumption that the minor takes the land for the benefit of his parent. . . . Thus the burden of proving that there was in fact no completed bona fide gift falls to him who would attack its validity.

Fred Oyama, on the other hand, faced at the outset the necessity of overcoming a statutory presumption that conveyances financed by his father and recorded in Fred's name were not gifts at all. Something very akin to a resulting trust *was* presumed and, at least *prima facie*, Fred *was* presumed to hold title for the benefit of his parent.

In the second place, when it came to rebutting this statutory presumption, Fred Oyama ran into other obstacles which, so far as we can ascertain, do not beset the path of most minor donees in California.

. . . The fact that the father attached no strings to the transfer was taken to indicate that he meant, in effect, to acquire the beneficial ownership himself. . . .

Furthermore, Fred Oyama had to counter evidence that his father was remiss in his duties as guardian. . . .

The cumulative effect, we believe, was clearly to discriminate against Fred Oyama. He was saddled with an onerous burden of proof which need not be borne by California children generally. The statutory presumption and the two ancillary inferences, which would not be used against most children, were given such probative value as to prevail in the face of a deed entered in the public records, four court orders recognizing Fred Oyama as the owner of the land, several newspaper notices to the same effect, and testimony that business transactions regarding the land were generally understood to be on his behalf. In short, Fred Oyama lost his gift, irretrievably and without compensation, solely because of the extraordinary obstacles which the State set before him. . . .

There remains the question whether discrimination between citizens on the basis of their racial descent, as revealed in this case, is justifiable. Here we start with the proposition that only the most exceptional circumstances can excuse discrimination on that basis in the face of the equal protection clause and a federal statute giving all citizens the right to own land. . . .

The only justification urged upon us by the State is that the discrimination is necessary to prevent evasion of the Alien Land Law's prohibition against the ownership of agricultural land by ineligible aliens. This reasoning presupposes the validity of that prohibition, a premise which we deem it unnecessary and therefore inappropriate to reexamine in this case. But assuming, for purposes of argument only, that the basic prohibition is constitutional, it does not follow that there is no constitutional limit to the means which may be used to enforce it. In the light most favorable to the State, this case presents a conflict between the State's right to formulate a policy of landholding within its bounds and the right of American citizens to own land anywhere in the United States. When these two rights clash, the rights of a citizen may not be subordinated merely because of his father's country of origin.

Since the view we take of petitioners' first contention requires reversal of the decision below, we do not reach their other contentions: that the Alien Land Law denies ineligible aliens the equal protection of the laws, and that failure to apply any limitations period to escheat actions under that law takes property without due process of law.

Reversed.

Mr. Justice Black, with whom Mr. Justice Douglas agreed, concurred:

. . . I should prefer to reverse the judgment on the broader grounds that the basic provisions of the California Alien Land Law violate the equal protection clause of the Fourteenth Amendment and conflict with federal laws and treaties governing the immigration of aliens and their rights after arrival in this country. . . .

. . . If there is any one purpose of the Fourteenth Amendment that is wholly outside the realm of doubt, it is that the Amendment was designed to bar States from denying to some groups, on account of their race or color, any rights, privileges, and opportunities accorded to other groups. I would now overrule the previous decisions of this Court that sustained state land laws which discriminate against people of Japanese origin residing in this country.

. . . Although Japanese are not permitted to become citizens by the ordinary process of naturalization, still Congress permitted the admission of some Japanese into this country. . . . California should not be permitted to erect obstacles designed to prevent the immigration of people whom Congress has authorized to come into and remain in the country. . . .

Mr. Justice Murphy, with whom Mr. Justice Rutledge joined, concurred:

. . . The Alien Land Law, in short, was designed to effectuate a purely racial discrimination, to prohibit a Japanese alien from owning or using agricultural land solely because he is a Japanese alien. It is rooted deeply in racial, economic and social antagonisms. The question confronting us is whether such a statute, viewed against the background of racism, can mount the hurdle of the equal protection clause of the Fourteenth Amendment. Can a state disregard in this manner the historic ideal that those within the borders of this nation are not to be denied rights and privileges because they are of a particular race? I say that it cannot.

The equal protection clause is too clear to admit of any other conclusion. It provides that no state shall "deny to any person within its jurisdiction the equal protection of the laws." The words "any person" have sufficient scope to include resident aliens, whether eligible for citizenship or not. . . . The concept of equal protection . . . may in rare cases permit a state to single out a class of persons, such as ineligible aliens, for distinctive treatment. The crucial test in these exceptional instances is whether there is a rational basis for the particular kind of discrimination involved. . . .

Such a rational basis is completely lacking where, as here, the discrimination stems directly from racial hatred and intolerance. . . .

Mr. Justice Reed, with whom Mr. Justice Burton joined, dissented:

The Court's opinion assumes *arguendo* that the California Alien Land Laws are constitutional. As we read the opinion, it holds that the Alien Land Laws of California, as here applied, discriminate in an unconstitutional manner against an America citizen—a son born in the United States to resident parents of Japanese nationality. From this holding we dissent. . . .

Discrimination in the sense of placing more burdens upon some than upon others is not in itself unconstitutional. If all types of discrimination were unconstitutional, our society would be incapable of legislation upon many important and vital questions. All reasonable classification puts its subjects into different categories where they may have advantages or disadvantages that flow from their positions. The grouping of all those who take land as grantees, in a transaction in which an ineligible alien pays the consideration, in a class subject to the statutory presumption of § 9 and other inferences which are reasonably related to the transfer, should not be struck down as unconstitutional. Unless the California Land Laws are to be held unconstitutional, we think the presumption and its resulting effects must be accepted as legal.

Mr. Justice Jackson dissented:

I am unable to see how this Court logically can set aside this judgment unless it is prepared to invalidate the California Alien Land Laws, on which it is based. If this judgment of escheat seems harsh as to the Oyamas, it is only because it faithfully carries out a legislative policy, the validity of which this Court does not question. . . .

RELATED CASES:

Terrace v. Thompson: 263 U.S. 197 (1923). Opinion: Butler, J. Dissenting: McReynolds and Brandeis, JJ. Abstaining: Sutherland, J.

A state may prohibit the sale or lease of agricultural land to aliens who have not declared an intention of acquiring citizenship. This is a reasonable exercise of state police power based on the importance of "the quality and allegiance of those who own, occupy and use the farm lands within its borders. . . ." The case arose in the state of Washington.

Cockrill v. California: 268 U.S. 258 (1925). Opinion: Butler, J. No dissent.

The statutory presumption of the California Alien Land Law—that a conveyance to a United States citizen in which the consideration is paid by an alien not eligible for United States citizenship is presumptive evidence that the conveyance was made to avoid the law's proscription against conveyances to such aliens—is consistent with the due process and equal protection clauses of the Fourteenth Amendment.

Takahashi v. Fish and Game Commission: 334 U.S. 410 (1948). Opinion: Black, J. Dissenting: Reed and Jackson, JJ.

A state cannot forbid the issuance of fishing licenses to persons ineligible to citizenship. A state is not free to use in its statutes a formula of classification used by the federal government in immigration and naturalization statutes. Any legislation applicable to aliens as a class must be within narrow limits. Otherwise there is denial of equal protection. This case was decided six months after *Oyama*.

NOTE:

Oyama casts doubt on the validity of other alien land legislation. Even in the area of state interest in fish and wild game the Court's decisions have indicated a trend to real modification of the traditional rule. *Takahashi* is a good example of this. The "proprietary interest" doctrine appears to have come upon bad times. See *Toomer* v. *Witsell*, 334 U.S. 385 (1948).

PEONAGE

While it involves the Thirteenth rather than the Fourteenth Amendment, this appears a good place to mention the matter of peonage. Actually the Thirteenth Amendment is the only liberty guarantee of the Constitution that applies directly to individuals. The federal Antipeonage Act, passed by Congress under its power to enforce the Thirteenth Amendment, provides that any person who subjects another to involuntary servitude is guilty of a federal crime. The Amendment applies directly to states and a number of state statutes dealing primarily with compulsory service based on debt have been challenged before the Court on this basis.

Pollock v. Williams
322 U.S. 4; 64 S.Ct. 792; 88 L.Ed. 1095 (1944)

(Pollock attacked the validity of a Florida statute making it a misdemeanor to induce advances of money with intent to defraud by a promise to perform labor and further making failure to perform labor for which money has been obtained *prima facie* evidence of intent to defraud. He was arrested for taking a $5 advance with intent to defraud and pleaded guilty before a county judge. The state circuit court held the statute in question unconstitutional and discharged Pollock. The Supreme Court of Florida reversed, holding that the presumption mentioned above had not played any part in the case since the defendant had pleaded guilty.)

Vote: 7-2

Mr. Justice Jackson delivered the opinion of the Court:

. . . It is true that in each opinion dealing with statutes of this type this Court has expressly recognized the right of the state to punish fraud, even in matters of this kind, by statutes which do not either in form or in operation lend themselves to sheltering the practice of peonage. Deceit is not put beyond the power of the state because the cheat is a laborer nor because the device for swindling is an agreement to labor. But when the state undertakes to deal with this specialized form of fraud, it must respect the constitutional and statutory command that it may not make failure to labor in discharge of a debt any part of a crime. It may not directly or indirectly comand involuntary servitude, even if it was voluntarily contracted for. . . .

We impute to the legislature no intention to oppress, but we are compelled to hold that the Florida Act of 1919 as brought forward on the statutes as § § 817.09 and 817.10 of the Statutes of 1941, F.S.A. are, by virtue of the Thirteenth Amendment and the Antipeonage Act of the United States, null and void. The judgment of the court below is reversed and the cause is remanded for further proceedings not inconsistent with this opinion.

Mr. Justice Reed dissented, with the concurrence of Mr. Chief Justice Stone:

However much peonage may offend our susceptibilities, and however great our distaste for a statute which is capable of use as a means of imposing peonage on the working man, the present statute is, in this Court, no more immune than any other which a state may enact, from the salutary requirement that its constitutionality must be presumed, and that the burden rests on him who assails it, on constitutional grounds, to show that it is either unconstitutional on its face or that it has been or will be in fact so applied as to deny his constitutional rights. . . .

. . . The presumption of constitutionality of statutes is a safeguard wisely conceived to keep courts within constitutional bounds in the exercise of their extraordinary power of judicial review. It should not be disregarded here. . . .

RELATED CASES:

Robertson v. Baldwin: 165 U.S. 275 (1897). Opinion: Brown, J. Dissenting: Harlan, J.

The Court held that seamen who contract for a voyage aboard ship and later "jump ship" may be legally arrested and returned to the ship without violating the Thirteenth Amendment. Seamen's work is of a semipublic character and also seamen have long been regarded as exceptional in regard to conditions requiring continued service for a specified time.

Clyatt v. United States: 197 U.S. 207 (1905). Opinion: Brewer, J. No dissent.

The Thirteenth Amendment grants to Congress power to enforce the prohibition against involuntary servitude, including peonage (a status or condition of compulsory service based upon the indebtedness of the peon to the master) and to punish persons holding another in peonage. Here an Alabama antipeonage statute was held valid.

Bailey v. Alabama: 219 U.S. 219 (1911). Opinion: Hughes, J. Dissenting: Holmes and Lurton, JJ.

A state cannot provide by statute that any person who enters into a contract for services and is given an advance of money or property, and failing to perform the services or to return the money or property is to be regarded as guilty of theft, the action being regarded as prima facie evidence of intent to injure or defraud. This is contrary to the Thirteenth Amendment. This is probably the leading peonage case in spite of the date of the case. It required work for another person as an alternative to jail. The essence of "peonage" is compulsory service in payment of debt.

United States v. Reynolds: 235 U.S. 133 (1914). Opinion: Day, J. No dissent. Abstaining: McReynolds, J.

An Alabama statute permitted a convicted person to have another pay his fine on the proviso that the convicted person work for this party for a specified period of time. If this agreement was not carried out, the convicted person could be fined the amount of the damages and compelled to work out the amount. This the Court held violated both the Thirteenth Amendment and the federal Antipeonage Act.

Butler v. Perry: 240 U.S. 328 (1916). McReynolds, J. No dissent.

A Florida statute that required all able-bodied citizens to work a specified number of days in the repair of roads and bridges each year as a substitute for the payment of road taxes was held not unconstitutional.

Selective Draft Law Cases (Arver v. United States): 245 U.S. 366 (1918). Opinion: White, C.J. No dissent.

Conscription for military service is not contrary to the Thirteenth Amendment. ". . . We are constrained to the conclusion that the contention to that effect is refuted by its mere statement."

Taylor v. Georgia: 315 U.S. 25 (1942). Opinion: Byrnes, J. No dissent. Abstaining: Roberts, J.

The Court held that, under the statute, "one who has received an advance on a contract for services which he is unable to repay is bound by the threat of penal sanctions to remain at his employment until the debt has been discharged. Such coerced labor is peonage" and contrary to the Thirteenth Amendment.

Jones v. Alfred H. Mayer Co.: 392 U.S. 409 (1968). Opinion: Stewart, J. Dissenting: Harlan and White, JJ.

See p. 297, above.

NOTE:

On the modern scene peonage is the nearest example we have of the slavery that once flourished on this continent. Peonage is the status of compulsory service which has its basis in the indebtedness of an individual to one who is his de facto master. With some exceptions, such as service on juries, on highway work, and in the military, a person cannot be forced to labor under threat of criminal punishment. Jackson's opinion in *Pollock* contains a valuable account of peonage in the lumber camps of Maine and elsewhere.

Most state constitutions specifically forbid imprisonment for debt. What a state cannot do directly under federal or state constitutions it may not do indirectly.

CHAPTER IX

ELECTORAL RIGHTS

One of the most basic of the privileges of citizenship is that of participation in free and fair elections. In no other way can our claim to democracy be made effective. Only when the officials of government are reminded periodically that the electorate is ultimately in control can there be assurance of true consideration of the welfare of the whole people.

THE STATES AND VOTING

The basic determination of who possesses suffrage is a matter for the states to determine. The Fifteenth, Fourteenth, and Nineteenth amendments have somewhat limited this discretion of the states, but this is still a matter of prime state concern. This is not to say that the federal government is excluded from the field, and over a period of years the Court has been occupied attempting to determine the exact extent to which state power over the entire field of voting has been delimited by these amendments, which, as indicated, basically act as a negative on certain state suffrage activities while leaving the positive determinations of voting to the states.

In Article One, Section 4, Congress is empowered to determine the times, places, and manner of holding congressional elections. Congress has seen fit to determine only the times and the manner. However, recent decisions of the Supreme Court have upheld congressional regulation of primaries as well as elections. The legal arguments over this have had a long and stormy history. In 1921 in *Newberry* the Court held that a party primary was not an election in a constitutional sense and that therefore Congress could not control primaries. Following this the Texas legislature prohibited the participation of Negroes in that state's Democratic Party primaries. In *Nixon* v. *Herndon* the Court held this violative of the equal protection clause of the Fourteenth Amendment. Then the Texas legislature empowered the executive committee of a party to determine qualifications for voting in that party's primary. The Democratic Party committee thereupon restricted participation in its primary to white Democrats. In *Nixon* v. *Condon* the Court voided this as being in effect state action and subject to the equal protection clause.

In a new approach the state convention of the Texas Democratic Party adopted a resolution in 1932 providing that only white citizens qualified to vote should be eligible for membership in the Democratic Party and entitled to take part in its activities and deliberations. This action the Court in *Grovey* v. *Townsend* upheld as legal. The reasoning was that the voluntary action of the state party convention did not involve the state government while determination by the party's executive committee acting under authority of a state statute did involve the state and did therefore invoke constitutional restrictions. A few years later the Supreme Court decided the *Classic* and *Allwright* cases.

United States v. Classic
313 U.S. 299; 61 S.Ct. 1031; 85 L.Ed. 1368 (1941)

(As in many states, Louisiana statutes provide for a primary election, at public expense, to nominate candidates for Representatives in Congress. In such a primary, Classic and others, Commissioners of Elections, willfully altered and falsely counted and certified the ballots of voters cast in the primary election. They were convicted of violation of the Federal Criminal Code which prohibits attempts to deprive citizens of their rights or privileges under the Constitution or laws of the United States. The Court had before it the question whether voting in such a primary and having one's vote counted is a constitutional right under the Criminal Code.)

Vote: 5-3

Mr. Justice Stone delivered the opinion of the Court:

. . . The primary in Louisiana is an integral part of the procedure for the popular choice of Congressmen. The right of qualified voters to vote at the congressional primary in Louisiana and to have their ballots counted is thus the right to participate in that choice.

We come then to the question whether that right is one secured by the Constitution. Section 2 of Article One commands that Congressmen shall be chosen by the people of the several states by electors, the qualifications of which it prescribes. The right of the people to choose, whatever its appropriate constitutional limitations, where in other respects it is defined, and the mode of its exercise is prescribed by state action in conformity to the Constitution, is a right established and guaranteed by the Constitution and hence is one secured by it to those citizens and inhabitants of the state entitled to exercise the right. . . . While, in a loose sense, the right to vote for representatives in Congress is sometimes spoken of as a right derived from the states, . . . this statement is true only in the sense that the states are authorized by the Constitution, to legislate on the subject as provided by Section 2 of Article One, to the extent that Congress has not restricted state action by the exercise of its powers to regulate elections under Section 4 and its more general power under Article One, Section 8, Clause 18 of the Constitution "to make all laws which shall be necessary and proper for carrying into execution the foregoing powers". . . .

Obviously included within the right to choose, secured by the Constitution, is the right of qualified voters within a state to cast their ballots and have them counted at congressional elections. This Court has consistently held that this is a right secured by the Constitution. . . . And since the constitutional command is without restriction or limitation, the right, unlike those guaranteed by the Fourteenth and Fifteenth Amendments, is secured against the action of individuals as well as of states. . . .

But we are now concerned with the question whether the right to choose at a primary election, a candidate for election as representative, is embraced in the right to choose representatives secured by Article One, Section 2. We may assume that the framers of the Constitution in adopting that section, did not have specifically in mind the selection and elimination of candidates for Congress by the direct primary any more than they contemplated the application of the commerce clause to interstate telephone, telegraph and wireless communication which are concededly within it. But in determining whether a provision of the Constitution applies to a new subject matter, it is of little significance that it is one with which the framers were not familiar. For in setting up an enduring framework of government they undertook to carry out for the indefinite future and in all the vicissitudes of the changing affairs of men, those fundamental purposes which the instrument itself discloses. Hence we read its words, not as we read legislative codes which are subject to continuous revision with the changing course of events, but as the revelation of the great purposes which were intended to be achieved by the Constitution as a continuing instrument of government. . . . If we remember that "it is a Constitution we are expounding," we cannot rightly prefer, of the possible meanings of its words, that which will defeat rather than effectuate the constitutional purpose.

That the free choice by the people of representatives in Congress, subject only to the restrictions to be found in Sections 2 and 4 of Article One and elsewhere in the Constitution, was one of the great purposes of our constitutional scheme of government cannot be doubted. We cannot regard it as any the less the constitutional purpose or its words as any the less guaranteeing the integrity of that choice when a state, exercising its privilege in the absence of congressional action, changes the mode of choice from a single step, a general election, to two, of which the first is the choice at a primary of those candidates from whom, as a second step, the representative in Congress is to be chosen at the election.

Nor can we say that that choice which the Constitution protects is restricted to the second step because Section 4 of Article One, as a means of securing a free choice of representatives by the people, has authorized Congress to regulate the manner of elections, without making any mention of primary elections. For we think that the authority of Congress, given by Section 4, includes the authority to regulate primary elections when, as in this case, they are a step in the exercise by the people of their choice of representatives in Congress. . . .

. . . The right to participate in the choice of representatives for Congress includes, as we have said, the right to cast a ballot and to have it counted at the general election whether for the successful candidate or not. Where the state law has made the primary an integral part of the procedure of choice, or where in fact the primary effectively controls the choice, the right of the elector to have his ballot counted at the primary, is likewise included in the right protected by Article One, Section 2. . . .

If a right secured by the Constitution may be infringed by the corrupt failure to include the vote at a primary in the official count, it is not significant that the primary, like the voting machine, was unknown when Section 19 was adopted. Abuse of either may infringe the right and therefore violate Section 19. . . .

The right of the voters at the primary to have their votes counted is, as we have stated, a right or privilege secured by the Constitution, and to this Section 20 also gives protection. The alleged acts of appellees were committed in the course of their performance of duties under the Louisiana statute requiring them to count the ballots, to record the result of the count, and to certify the result of the election. Misuse of power, possessed by virtue of state law, is action taken "under color of" state law. . . . Here the acts of appellees infringed the constitutional right and deprived the voters of the benefit of it within the meaning of Section 20. . . .

Reversed.

Mr. Chief Justice Hughes took no part in the hearing or decision of this case.

Mr. Justice Douglas dissented, with the concurrence of Mr. Justice Black and Mr. Justice Murphy:

. . . I agree with most of the views expressed in the opinion of the Court. And it is with diffidence that I dissent from the result there reached.

The disagreement centers on the meaning of § 19 of the Criminal Code, which protects every right secured by the Constitution. The right to vote at a final Congressional election and the right to have one's vote counted in such an election have been held to be protected by §19. . . . Yet I do not think that the principles of those cases should be, or properly can be, extended to primary elections. To sustain this indictment we must so extend them. But when we do, we enter perilous territory.

. . . We should ever be mindful that "before a man can be punished, his case must be plainly and unmistakably within the statute." *United States* v. *Lacher*, 134 U.S. 624, 628. That admonition is reemphasized here by the fact that § 19 imposes not only a fine of $5,000 and ten years in prison, but also makes him who is convicted "ineligible to any office, or place of honor, profit or trust created by the Constitution or laws of the United States." It is not enough for us to find in the vague penumbra of a statute some offense about which Congress could have legislated, and then to particularize it as a crime because it is highly offensive. . . . Civil liberties are too dear to permit conviction for crimes which are only implied and which can be spelled out only by adding inference to inference.

Section 19 does not purport to be an exercise by Congress of its power to regulate primaries. It merely penalizes conspiracies "to injure, oppress, threaten, or intimidate any citizen in the free exercise or enjoyment of any right or privilege secured to him by the Constitution or laws of the United States." Thus, it does no more than refer us to the Constitution for the purpose of determining whether or not the right to vote in a primary is secured. Hence we must do more than find in the Constitution the power of Congress to afford that protection. We must find that protection on the face of the Constitution itself. . . .

Article One, § 4 specifies the machinery whereby the times, places and manner of holding elections shall be established and controlled. Article One, § 2 provides that representatives shall be "chosen" by the people. But for purposes of the criminal law as contrasted to the interpretation of the Constitution as the source of the implied power of Congress, I do not think that those provisions in absence of specific legislation by Congress protect the primary election or the nominating convention. While they protected the right to vote, and the right to have one's vote counted, at the final election, as held in the *Yarbrough* and *Mosley* cases, they certainly do not *per se* extend to all acts which in their indirect or incidental effect restrain, restrict, or interfere with that choice. . . .

RELATED CASES:

Minor v. Happersett: 21 Wall. 162 (1875). Opinion: Waite, C.J. No dissent.

The Court held that "the Constitution of the United States does not confer the right of suffrage upon any one, and that the Constitution and laws of the several States which commit that important trust to men alone are not necessarily void." Therefore, suffrage was held not to be a privilege of United States citizenship. Suffrage for women was not required for a republican form of government.

Ex parte Yarbrough: 110 U.S. 651 (1884). Opinion: Miller, J. No dissent.

Congress has the right to protect the privilege to vote for members of Congress since this is a right that flows from Article One of the Constitution for those who meet the qualifications for voting for members of "the most numerous branch of the State legislature."

Newberry v. United States: 256 U.S. 232 (1921). Opinion: McReynolds, J. Dissenting: White, C.J., and Pitney, Brandeis, and Clarke, JJ.

The power of Congress over elections does not include the regulation of primaries. The direct primary was unknown to the Constitution and is not truly an election. This case came out of the Newberry-Henry Ford senatorial election in Michigan.

Burroughs v. United States: 290 U.S. 534 (1934). Opinion: Sutherland, J. Dissenting: McReynolds, J.

Congress has power to legislate to safeguard elections; therefore the Corrupt Practices Act of 1925, requiring detailed financial reports from committees set up to influence the election of Presidential electors is valid.

Breedlove v. Suttles: 302 U.S. 277 (1937). Opinion: Butler, J. No dissent.
A state poll tax as a precondition to voting does not deny equal protection nor does if violate the Fifteenth or Nineteenth·Amendments.

United States v. Raines: 362 U.S. 17 (1960). Opinion: Brennan, J. No dissent.
Discrimination by state officials, within the course of their official duties, against the voting rights of citizens, on grounds of race or color, is subject to the ban of the Fifteenth Amendment and legislation designed to deal with such discrimination is appropriate legislation under it. Involved here was the Registration-Civil Rights Act of 1951 which also included the Civil Rights Commission. The case arose in Georgia.

Harman v. Forssenius: 380 U.S. 528 (1965). Opinion: Warren, C.J. No dissent.
For federal elections the Twenty-fourth Amendment abolished the poll tax as a prerequisite for voting and no equivalent or milder substitute may be imposed. Here the substitute under Virginia law was the filing of a witnessed or notarized certificate of residence six months before the federal election. This was a burdensome requirement. The state could not impose a substitute for the poll tax.

South Carolina v. Katzenbach: 383 U.S. 301 (1966). Opinion: Warren, C.J. Dissenting: Black, J.
The Voting Rights Act of 1965 providing for a temporary suspension of a state's voting tests or devices, review of new voting rules, and federal examiners to qualify applicants for registration are means Congress may use to effectuate the constitutional prohibition of racial discrimination in voting. The Fifteenth Amendment supersedes contrary exertions of state power.

Harper v. Virginia State Board of Elections: 383 U.S. 663 (1966). Opinion: Douglas J. Dissenting: Black, Harlan, and Stewart, JJ.
A state violates the equal protection clause of the Fourteenth Amendment whenever it makes the affluence of the voter or payment of any fee an electoral standard. Voter qualifications have no relation to the payment of a tax. This decision overruled in part *Breedlove* v. *Suttles*, 302 U.S. 277 (1937). Poll tax is void in state elections.

Katzenbach v. Morgan: 384 U.S. 641 (1966). Opinion: Brennan, J. Dissenting: Harlan and Stewart, JJ.
The Voting Rights Act of 1965 prohibits the enforcement of state literacy tests in the case of persons who have successfully completed the sixth primary grade in American-flag schools. This was upheld under the equal protection clause against the effort of New York to enforce its literacy test in the case of persons who had attended school in Puerto Rico.

Oregon v. Mitchell: 400 U.S. 112 (1970). Opinion: Black, J. Dissenting: Burger, C.J., Harlan, Stewart, and Blackmun.
Congress has ultimate power over congressional and presidential elections. Congress thus may permit eighteen-year-old citizens to vote in such elections and may prohibit states disqualifying voters for not meeting residency requirements in such elections. Congress may ban literacy tests in all elections, state and federal, under the enforcement provisions of the Fourteenth and Fifteenth amendments. The subsequent adoption of the Twenty-sixth Amendment made much of this decision of historical interest only.

Dunn v. Blumstein: 405 U.S. 330 (1972). Opinion: Marshall. Dissenting: Burger, C.J. Abstaining: Powell and Rehnquist, JJ.
Tennessee's durational residence laws were held discriminatory and thus violative of the equal protection clause unless the state could prove them *necessary* to promote a compelling governmental interest. The Court suggested that thirty days might be an adequate residential period for the state to complete election administrative tasks,

particularly those necessary to prevent fraud. Residence requirements as a means to insure minimum knowledge of the issues on the part of voters was held to be a requirement of knowledge imposed on only some citizens and thus a denial of equal protection.

NOTE:

See Note following *Smith* v. *Allwright,* p. 331.

Smith v. Allwright
321 U.S. 649; 64 S.Ct. 757; 88 L.Ed. 987 (1944)

(A Negro citizen of Texas, Lonnie E. Smith, brought suit for damages against election judges because of their refusal to provide him with a ballot so that he might vote in the Democratic primary election of 1940 at which time candidates for the Senate and House of Representatives of the United States Congress were to be nominated as were officers of the state government. Since Smith had fulfilled all legal requirements for voting, the refusal of a ballot was based solely on his race and color. Since the Democratic Party of Texas in state convention had adopted a resolution restricting membership in the party to white persons, this fact was advanced as a defense by the election officers. The question before the court was whether this convention's resolution was purely private action or was the convention acting as an agent of the state.)

Vote: 8-1

Mr. Justice Reed delivered the opinion of the Court:

. . . Primary elections are conducted by the party under state statutory authority. The county executive committee selects precinct election officials and the county, district or state executive committees, respectively, canvass the returns. These party committees or the state convention certify the party's candidates to the appropriate officers for inclusion on the official ballot for the general election. No name which has not been so certified may appear upon the ballot for the general election as a candidate of a political party. No other name may be printed on the ballot which has not been placed in nomination by qualified voters who must take oath that they did not participate in a primary for the selection of a candidate for the office for which the nomination is made.

The state courts are given exclusive original jurisdiction of contested elections and of mandamus proceedings to compel party officers to perform their statutory duties.

We think that this statutory system for the selection of party nominees for inclusion on the general election ballot makes the party which is required to follow these legislative directions an agency of the State insofar as it determines the participants in a primary election. The party takes its character as a state agency from the duties imposed upon it by state statutes; the duties do not become matters of private law because they are performed by a political party. The plan of the Texas primary follows substantially that of Louisiana, with the exception that in Louisiana the State pays the cost of the primary while Texas assesses the cost against candidates. In numerous instances, the Texas statutes fix or limit the fees to be charged. Whether paid directly by the State or through state requirements, it is state action which compels. When primaries become a part of the machinery for choosing officials, state and national, as they have here, the same tests to determine the character of discrimination or abridgement should be applied to the primary as are applied to the general election. If the State requires a certain electoral procedure, prescribes a general election ballot made up of party nominees so chosen and limits the choice of the electorate in general elections for state offices, practically speaking, to those whose names appear on such a ballot, it endorses, adopts and enforces the discrimination against Negroes, practiced by a party entrusted by Texas law with the determination of the qualifications of participants in the primary. This is state action within the meaning of the Fifteenth Amendment. . . .

The United States is a constitutional democracy. Its organic law grants to all citizens a right to participate in the choice of elected officials without restrictions by any State because of race. This grant to the people of the opportunity for choice is not to be nullified by a state through casting its electoral process in a form which permits a private organization to practice racial discrimination in the election. Constitutional rights would be of little value if they would be thus indirectly denied. . . .

. . . Here we are applying, contrary to the recent decision in *Grovey* v. *Townsend*, the well-established principle of the Fifteenth Amendment, forbidding the abridgement by a State of a citizen's right to vote. *Grovey* v. *Townsend* is overruled.

Judgment reversed.

Mr. Justice Roberts dissented:

. . . The reason·for my concern is that the instant decision, overruling that announced about nine years ago, tends to bring adjudications of this tribunal into the same class as a restricted railroad ticket, good for this day and train only. I have no assurance, in view of current decisions, that the opinion announced today may not shortly be repudiated and overruled by justices who deem they have new light on the subject. . . .

It is regrettable that in an era marked by doubt and confusion, an era whose greatest need is steadfastness of thought and purpose, this court, which has been looked to as exhibiting consistency in adjudication and a steadiness which would hold the balance even in the face of temporary ebbs and flows of opinions, should now itself become the breeder of fresh doubt and confusion in the public mind as to the stability of our institutions.

[Roberts had written the opinion in *Grovey* v. *Townsend*, so this may well be an example of "personal loyalty" to the precedents of the Court.]

RELATED CASES:

Williams v. Mississippi: 170 U.S. 213 (1898). Opinion: McKenna, J. No dissent.

A state statute requiring persons desiring to vote to show a receipt for the payment of poll tax as well as the ability to read, understand, and interpret reasonably the state constitution was held not to deny the privilege of voting on the basis of race or color. There was no discrimination.

Guinn v. United States: 238 U.S. 347 (1915). Opinion: White, C.J. No dissent. Abstaining: McReynolds, J.

An Oklahoma statute established literacy tests for voting but exempted from the test those persons who were themselves, or whose ancestors were, entitled to vote on January 1, 1866. This was the so-called "grandfather clause." The Court held this to be in violation of the equal protection of the Fifteenth Amendment.

Nixon v. Herndon: 273 U.S. 536 (1927). Opinion: Holmes, J. No dissent.

A Texas statute prohibiting participation by Negroes in Democratic Party primaries violated the equal protection clause of the Fourteenth Amendment. This was known as the White Primary Law.

Nixon v. Condon: 286 U.S. 73 (1932). Opinion: Cardozo, J. Dissenting: McReynolds, VanDevanter, Sutherland, and Butler, JJ.

When a Texas state statute empowers the State Executive Committee of a party to prescribe the qualifications of that party's members for voting or other participation, and a resolution of that committee bars Negroes from the primaries, that action is action by the Committee as representative of the state in the discharge of the state's authority. Since the state could not deny equal protection, this was an unconstitutional act. The state authorized the discrimination.

Grovey v. Townsend: 295 U.S. 45 (1935). Opinion: Roberts, J. No dissent.
    A resolution of the Texas state convention of the Democratic Party resulted in barring all Negroes from the Democratic Party primaries. The Court held a state convention of a party to be a private organization and not an organization of the state. Therefore, there was no basis for applying the Fourteenth and Fifteenth Amendments. This was held *not* to be the result of state action.

Lane v. Wilson: 307 U.S. 268 (1939). Opinion: Frankfurter, J. Dissenting: McReynolds and Butler, JJ. Abstaining: Douglas, J.
    An Oklahoma statute in 1916 provided for a registration period for voting of twelve days but exempted from the registration those who had voted in the 1914 election when the "grandfather clause" was effective. The Court held that the provisions of the law as well as the practical difficulties in the administration of the law amounted to discrimination under the Fifteenth Amendment. Sophisticated as well as simple-minded modes of discrimination were nullified.

Rice v. Elmore: 333 U.S. 875 (1948). Per Curiam. No dissent.
    South Carolina repealed all statutes dealing with party primaries to the end that the Democratic primary might be regarded as a "private club" and could bar Negroes. However, because of the basic use of the primary for the nomination of candidates for federal and state offices, this was held to violate the Fourteenth and Fifteenth Amendments.

Schnell v. Davis: 336 U.S. 933 (1949). Per Curiam. Dissenting: Reed, J.
    An amendment to the Alabama state constitution (the "Boswell Amendment") required that voters be able to understand and explain any article of the federal Constitution to the satisfaction of local election officials. The Court agreed that the purpose of this was to disfranchise Negroes and was therefore contrary to the Fifteenth Amendment.

Terry v. Adams: 345 U.S. 461 (1953). Opinion: Black, J. Dissenting: Minton, J.
    A Texas county political organization that excluded Negroes, the Jaybird Democratic Association, was not state controlled but held its own primaries and the winners then entered the regular Democratic primaries. The record showed that in sixty years their candidates always won. The Court held that the Jaybird primary was an integral part of the county's elective process and therefore the exclusion of Negroes was contrary to the Fifteenth Amendment.

American Party of Texas v. White: 415 U.S. 767 (1974). Opinion: White, J. Dissenting: Douglas, J.
    A state may require political parties to nominate candidates through the process of precinct, county, and state conventions. However, a state cannot print on absentee ballots only the two major established parties, the Democrats and the Republicans. This is arbitrary discrimination violative of the equal protection clause.

NOTE:

    The central point in the "new" white primary cases of *Classic* and *Allwright* is that state primaries presumably have been identified with the total electoral process with the whole being under state direction, including political parties that might be involved, and thus the whole being subject to Constitutional restrictions on the states. There remains for future clarification the exact extent of the term "integral part" when used in reference to primaries in the electoral process. The Court may some day hold that certain state primaries are not such part of the electoral processes of those states.

THE COURTS AND REPRESENTATION PROBLEMS

Almost from the beginning of the Supreme Court's history the Court has refused to take cases that involved what the Court has characterized as "political" questions. These are matters that are essentially the function of the political or policy-determining units of government, specifically the executive and the legislature. Prominent among these "political" questions has been the matter of the apportionment of state legislatures. The leading case on this has been *Colegrove* v. *Green*, even though it dealt specifically with Congressional districting rather than state legislative districting, and the Court used *Colegrove* as a precedent in a number of suits. Then came the "straw in the wind" of *Gomillion* v. *Lightfoot* in 1960 and the reversal of *Colegrove*'s philosophy in *Baker* v. *Carr* in 1962.

Colegrove v. Green
328 U.S. 549; 66 S.Ct. 1198; 90 L.Ed. 1432 (1946)

(Suit was brought by residents of a Congressional district in Illinois with a larger population than other districts in the state to restrain the officials of the state from carrying on an election in which Representatives were to be elected from these districts. The contention was that the Congressional districts lacked compactness of territory and approximate equality of population.)

Vote: 4-3

Mr. Justice Frankfurter delivered the opinion of the Court:

. . . We are of opinion that the petitioners ask of this Court what is beyond its competence to grant. This is one of those demands on judicial power which cannot be met by verbal fencing about "jurisdiction." It must be resolved by considerations on the basis of which this Court, from time to time, has refused to intervene in controversies. It has refused to do so because due regard for the effective working of our Government revealed this issue to be of a peculiarly political nature and therefore not meet for judicial determination.

. . . The short of it is that the Constitution has conferred upon Congress exclusive authority to secure fair representation by the States in the popular House and left to that House determination whether States have fulfilled their responsibility. If Congress failed in exercising its powers, whereby standards of fairness are offended, the remedy ultimately lies with the people. Whether Congress faithfully discharges its duty or not, the subject has been committed to the exclusive control of Congress. An aspect of government from which the judiciary, in view of what is involved, has been excluded by the clear intention of the Constitution cannot be entered by the federal courts because Congress may have been in default in exacting from States obedience to its mandate. . . .

To sustain this action would cut very deep into the very being of Congress. Courts ought not to enter this political thicket. The remedy for unfairness in districting is to secure State legislatures that will apportion properly, or to invoke the ample powers of Congress. The Constitution has many commands that are not enforceable by courts because they clearly fall outside the conditions and purposes that circumscribe judicial action. Thus, "on Demand of the executive Authority," Article Four, Section 2, of a State it is the duty of a sister State to deliver up a fugitive from justice. But the fulfillment of this duty cannot be judicially enforced. *Kentucky* v. *Dennison*, 24 How. 66. The duty to see to it that the laws are faithfully executed cannot be brought under legal compulsion. *Mississippi* v. *Johnson*, 4 Wall. 475. Violation of the great guaranty of a republican form of government in States cannot be challenged in the courts. *Pacific Teleph. & Teleg. Co.* v. *Oregon*, 223 U.S.

118. The Constitution has left the performance of many duties in our governmental scheme to depend on the fidelity of the executive and legislative action and, ultimately, on the vigilance of the people in exercising their political rights.

Dismissal of the complaint is affirmed.

Mr. Justice Jackson did not sit in this case because of his attendance at the Nuremberg War Crimes trials.

Chief Justice Stone had died shortly before the decision.

Mr. Justice Rutledge concurred:

. . . Assuming that the controversy is justiciable, I think the cause is of so delicate a character, in view of the considerations above noted, that the jurisdiction should be exercised only in the most compelling circumstances.

As a matter of legislative attention, whether by Congress or the General Assembly, the case made by the complaint is strong. But the relief it seeks pitches this Court into delicate relation to the functions of state officials and Congress, compelling them to take action which heretofore they have declined to take voluntarily or to accept the alternative of electing representatives from Illinois at large in the forthcoming elections.

The shortness of the time remaining makes it doubtful whether action could, or would, be taken in time to secure for petitioners the effective relief they seek. To force them to share in an election at large might bring greater equality of voting right. It would also deprive them and all other Illinois citizens of representation by districts which the prevailing policy of Congress commands. . . .

The right here is not absolute. And the cure sought may be worse than the disease. . . .

Mr. Justice Black dissented, with the concurrence of Mr. Justice Douglas and Mr. Justice Murphy:

. . . It is difficult for me to see why the 1901 State Apportionment Act does not deny appellants equal protection of the laws. The failure of the Legislature to reapportion the Congressional election districts for forty years, despite census figures indicating great changes in the distribution of the population, has resulted in election districts the population of which range from 112,000 to 900,000. One of the appellants lives in a district of more than 900,000 people. His vote is consequently much less effective than that of each of the citizens living in the district of 112,000. And such a gross inequality in the voting power of citizens irrefutably demonstrates a complete lack of effort to make an equitable apportionment. The 1901 State Apportionment Act if applied to the next election would thus result in a wholly indefensible discrimination against appellants and all other voters in heavily populated districts. The equal protection clause of the Fourteenth Amendment forbids such discrimination. It does not permit the States to pick out certain qualified citizens or groups of citizens and deny them the right to vote at all. . . . No one would deny that the equal protection clause would also prohibit a law that would expressly give certain citizens a half-vote and others a full vote. The probable effect of the 1901 State Apportionment Act in the coming election will be that certain citizens, and among them the appellants, will in some instances have votes only one-ninth as effective in choosing representatives to Congress as the votes of other citizens. Such discriminatory legislation seems to me exactly the kind that the equal protection clause was introduced to prohibit. . . .

RELATED CASES:

Fergus v. Marks: 321 Ill. 510 (1926). Opinion: Heard, J. No dissent.

State courts cannot compel a state legislature to reapportion the state into districts from which members of the state Senate will be elected. Such actions would be violations of the constitutionally imposed separation of powers. The legislature "is responsible to the people for a failure to perform that duty."

Cook v. Fortson: 329 U.S. 675 (1946). Per Curiam. Dissenting: Black, Murphy, and Rutledge, JJ.

In this case the Supreme Court directed a district court to dismiss a petition by a candidate who had received the majority of the popular vote in an election. The petitioner was seeking to enjoin compliance with the Georgia county unit rule in selecting a party nominee for Congress.

MacDougall v. Green: 335 U.S. 281 (1948). Per Curiam. No dissent.

An Illinois statute that requires a distribution of signatures of voters on a petition to nominate candidates for a new political party among at least fifty counties of the state is not a denial of equal protection or due process. The party involved was the Progressive Party. The case was reversed by *Moore* v. *Ogilvie*, below.

South v. Peters: 339 U.S. 276 (1950). Opinion: Per Curiam. Dissenting: Douglas and Black, JJ.

In Georgia, a county unit system allots each county a number of votes that range from two to six depending on population. The distribution amounts to discrimination in favor of the rural counties and resultant discrimination against urban Negro populations. Within each county the "electoral vote" goes to the candidate who receives the greatest popular vote. The Court refused to rule on the legality of this system holding that this was a political issue "arising from a state's geographical distribution of electoral strength among its political subdivisions."

Moore v. Ogilvie: 394 U.S. 814 (1969). Opinion: Douglas, J. Dissenting: Stewart and Harlan, JJ.

An Illinois statute which provides that nominating petitions for independent candidates must include 200 signatures from each of at least 50 of the state's 102 counties applied a rigid, arbitrary formula to sparsely settled counties and populous counties alike and thus discriminated against the residents of the populous counties in the exercise of their political rights in violation of the equal protection clause of the Fourteenth Amendment. This decision overruled *MacDougall* v. *Green*, above.

NOTE:

Colegrove reiterates the traditional view of the Court that reapportionment and redistricting of legislative bodies is a political matter and not a justiciable question. The case is notable for Frankfurter's observation that the Court should not get involved in the "political thicket" and for Black's dissent in which he maintained that deliberate legislative discrimination in a matter such as this was denial of equal protection. Sixteen years later in *Baker* v. *Carr* their views were unchanged but their majority and minority positions were reversed. Mr. Justice Rutledge voted with the majority in *Colegrove* because he thought this view was the lesser of two evils. The presumption of the Court seemed to be that Congress under Article One, Section 4 has the power to redistrict states.

Baker v. Carr
369 U.S. 186; 82 S.Ct. 691; 7 L.Ed. 2nd 663 (1962)

(This was a civil action brought to redress an alleged deprivation of federal constitutional rights. A 1901 statute of Tennessee had been the most recent apportionment of members of the state's General Assembly, and the contention was that this did not provide for a proper representation of the voters of the state. The constitution of the state provides for decennial reapportionment. Because of the growth and redistribution of the state's population after 1901, the apportionment in force was challenged as denying equal protection to voters under the Fourteenth Amendment. The Federal District Court dismissed the case for lack of jurisdiction of the subject matter.)

Vote: 6-2

Mr. Justice Brennan delivered the opinion of the Court:

. . . In light of the District Court's treatment of the case, we hold today only (a) that the court possessed jurisdiction of the subject matter; (b) that a justiciable cause of action is stated upon which appellants would be entitled to appropriate relief; and (c) because appellees raise the issue before this Court, that the appellants have standing to challenge the Tennessee apportionment statutes. Beyond noting that we have no cause at this stage to doubt the District Court will be able to fashion relief if violations of constitutional rights are found, it is improper now to consider what remedy would be most appropriate if appellants prevail at the trial.

[*Jurisdiction of the Subject Matter.*] The District Court was uncertain whether our cases withholding federal judicial relief rested upon a lack of federal jurisdiction or upon the inappropriateness of the subject matter for judicial consideration —what we have designated "nonjusticiability." The distinction between the two grounds is significant. In the instance of nonjusticiability, consideration of the cause is not wholly and immediately foreclosed; rather, the Court's inquiry necessarily proceeds to the point of deciding whether the duty asserted can be judicially identified and its breach judicially determined, and whether protection for the right asserted can be judicially molded. In the instance of lack of jurisdiction the cause either does not "arise under" the Federal Constitution, laws or treaties (or fall within one of the other enumerated categories of Article Three, § 2), or is not a "case or controversy" within the meaning of that section; or the cause is not one described by any jurisdictional statute. Our conclusion . . . that this cause presents no nonjusticiable "political question" settles the only possible doubt that it is a case or controversy. Under the present heading of "Jurisdiction of the Subject Matter" we hold only that the matter set forth in the complaint does arise under the Constitution and is within 28 U.S.C. § 1343. . . .

Article Three, §2 of the Federal Constitution provides that "the judicial Power shall extend to all Cases, in Law and Equity, arising under this Constitution, the Laws of the United States, and Treaties made, or which shall be made, under their Authority . . ." It is clear that the cause of action is one which "arises under" the Federal Constitution. The complaint alleges that the 1901 statute effects an apportionment that deprives the appellants of the equal protection of the laws in violation of the Fourteenth Amendment. . . .

Since the complaint plainly sets forth a case arising under the Constitution, the subject matter is within the federal judicial power defined in Article Three, § 2, and so within the power of Congress to assign to the jurisdiction of the District Courts. Congress has exercised that power in 28 U.S.C. § 1343(3). . . .

"The district courts shall have original jurisdiction of any civil action authorized by law to be commenced by any person . . . to redress the deprivation, under color of any State law, statute, ordinance, regulation, custom or usage, of any right, privilege or immunity secured by the Constitution of the United States. . . ."

We hold that the District Court has jurisdiction of the subject matter of the federal constitutional claim asserted in the complaint.

[*Standing.*] A federal court cannot "pronounce any statute, either of a state or of the United States, void, because irreconcilable with the constitution, except as it is called upon to adjudge the legal rights of litigants in actual controversies." *Liverpool, N. Y. & P. Steamship Co.* v. *Commissioners of Emigration*, 113 U.S. 33, 39. Have the appellants alleged such a personal stake in the outcome of the controversy as to assure that concrete adverseness which sharpens the presentation of issues upon which the court so largely depends for illumination of difficult constitutional questions? This is the gist of the question of standing. It is, of course, a question of federal law.

The complaint was filed by residents of Davidson, Hamilton, Knox, Montgomery, and Shelby Counties. Each is a person allegedly qualified to vote for members of the General Assembly representing his county. These appellants sued "on their own behalf and on behalf of all qualified voters of their respective counties, and further, on behalf of all voters of the State of Tennessee who are similarly situated. . . ." The appellees are the Tennessee Secretary of State, Attorney General, Coordinator of Elections, and members of the State Board of Elections; the members of the State Board are sued in their own right and also as representatives of the County Election Commissioners whom they appoint.

We hold that the appellants do have standing to maintain this suit. Our decisions plainly support this conclusion. Many of the cases have assumed rather than articulated the premise in deciding the merits of similar claims. And *Colegrove* v. *Green,* *supra,* squarely held that voters who allege facts showing disadvantage to themselves as individuals have standing to sue. A number of cases decided after *Colegrove* recognized the standing of the voters there involved to bring those actions. . . .

[*Justiciability.*] In holding that the subject matter of this suit was not justiciable, the District Court relied on *Colegrove* v. *Green, supra,* and subsequent *per curiam* cases. The court stated: "From a review of these decisions there can be no doubt that the federal rule . . . is that the federal courts . . . will not intervene in cases of this type to compel legislative reapportionment." 179 F.Supp. at 826. We understand the District Court to have read the cited cases as compelling the conclusion that since the appellants sought to have a legislative apportionment held unconstitutional, their suit presented a "political question" and was therefore nonjusticiable. We hold that this challenge to an apportionment presents no nonjusticiable "political question." The cited cases do not hold the contrary.

. . . The nonjusticiability of a political question is primarily a function of the separation of powers. Much confusion results from the capacity of the "political question" label to obscure the need for case-by-case inquiry. Deciding whether a matter has in any measure been committed by the Constitution to another branch of government, or whether the action of that branch exceeds whatever authority has been committed, is itself a delicate exercise in constitutional interpretation, and is a responsibility of this Court as ultimate interpreter of the Constitution. . . .

. . . The question here is the consistency of state action with the Federal Constitution. We have no question decided, or to be decided, by a political branch of government coequal with this Court. Nor do we risk embarrassment of our government abroad, or grave disturbance at home if we take issue with Tennessee as to the constitutionality of her action here challenged. Nor need the appellants, in order to succeed in this action, ask the Court to enter upon policy determinations for which judicially manageable standards are lacking. Judicial standards under the Equal Protection Clause are well developed and familiar, and it has been open to courts since the enactment of the Fourteenth Amendment to determine, if on the particular facts they must, that a discrimination reflects *no* policy, but simply arbitrary and capricious action.

We conclude that the complaint's allegations of a denial of equal protection present a justiciable constitutional cause of action upon which appellants are entitled to a trial and a decision. The right asserted is within the reach of judicial protection under the Fourteenth Amendment.

The judgment of the District Court is reversed and the cause is remanded for further proceedings consistent with this opinion.

Reversed and remanded.

Mr. Justice Whittaker did not participate in the decision of this case.

Mr. Justice Douglas concurred:

There is no doubt that the federal courts have jurisdiction of controversies concerning voting rights. The Civil Rights Act gives them authority to redress the deprivation "under color of any state law" of any "right, privilege or immunity secured by the Constitution of the United States or by any Act of Congress providing for equal rights of citizens. . . ."

With the exceptions of *Colegrove* v. *Green*, 328 U.S. 549; *MacDougall* v. *Green*, 335 U.S. 281; *South* v. *Peters*, 339 U.S. 276, and the decisions they spawned, the Court has never thought that protection of voting rights was beyond judicial cognizance. Today's treatment of those cases removes the only impediment to judicial cognizance of the claims stated in the present complaint.

The justiciability of the present claims being established, any relief accorded can be fashioned in the light of well-known principles of equity.

Mr. Justice Clark concurred:

. . . Although I find the Tennessee apportionment statute offends the Equal Protection Clause, I would not consider intervention by this Court into so delicate a field if there were any other relief available to the people of Tennessee. But the majority of the people of Tennessee have no "practical opportunities for exerting their political weight at the polls" to correct the existing "invidious discrimination." Tennessee has no initiative and referendum. I have searched diligently for other "practical opportunities" present under the law. I find none other than through the federal courts. The majority of the voters have been caught up in a legislative strait jacket. Tennessee has an "informed, civically militant electorate" and "an aroused popular conscience," but it does not sear "the conscience of the people's representatives." This is because the legislative policy has riveted the present seats in the Assembly to their respective constituencies, and by the votes of their incumbents a reapportionment of any kind is prevented. The people have been rebuffed at the hands of the Assembly; they have tried the constitutional convention route, but since the call must originate in the Assembly it, too, has been fruitless. They have tried Tennessee courts with the same result, and Governors have fought the tide only to flounder. It is said that there is recourse in Congress and perhaps that may be, but from a practical standpoint this is without substance. To date Congress has never undertaken such a task in any State. We therefore must conclude that the people of Tennessee are stymied and without judicial intervention will be saddled with the present discrimination in the affairs of their state government. . . .

. . . It is well for this Court to practice self-restraint and discipline in constitutional adjudication, but never in its history have those principles received sanction where the national rights of so many have been so clearly infringed for so long a time. National respect for the courts is more enhanced through the forthright enforcement of those rights rather than by rendering them nugatory through the interposition of subterfuges. In my view the ultimate decision today is in the greatest tradition of this Court.

Mr. Justice Stewart concurred:

The separate writings of my dissenting and concurring Brothers stray so far from the subject of today's decision as to convey, I think, a distressingly inaccurate impression of what the Court decides. For that reason, I think it appropriate, in joining the opinion of the Court, to emphasize in a few words what the opinion does and does not say.

The Court today decides three things and no more: "(a) that the court possessed jurisdiction of the subject matter; (b) that a justiciable cause of action is stated upon which appellants would be entitled to appropriate relief; and (c) . . . that the appellants have standing to challenge the Tennessee apportionment statutes". . . .

. . . But the merits of this case are not before us now. The defendants have not yet had an opportunity to be heard in defense of the State's system of apportionment; indeed, they have not yet even filed an answer to the complaint. As in other cases, the proper place for the trial is in the trial court, not here.

Mr. Justice Frankfurter, whom Mr. Justice Harlan joined, dissented:

The Court today reverses a uniform course of decision established by a dozen cases, including one by which the very claim now sustained was unanimously rejected only five years ago. The impressive body of rulings thus cast aside reflected the equally uniform course of our political history regarding the relationship between population and legislative representation—a wholly different matter from denial of the franchise to individuals because of race, color, religion or sex. Such a massive repudiation of the experience of our whole past in asserting destructively novel judicial power demands a detailed analysis of the role of this Court in our constitutional scheme. Disregard of inherent limits in the effective exercise of the Court's "judicial Power" not only presages the futility of judicial intervention in the essentially political conflict of forces by which the relation between population and representation has time out of mind been and now is determined. It may well impair the Court's position as the ultimate organ of "the supreme Law of the Land" in that vast range of legal problems, often strongly entangled in popular feeling, on which this Court must pronounce. The Court's authority—possessed neither of the purse nor the sword—ultimately rests on sustained public confidence in its moral sanction. Such feeling must be nourished by the Court's complete detachment, in fact and in appearance, from political entanglements and by abstention from injecting itself into the clash of political forces in political settlements. . . .

The notion that representation proportioned to the geographic spread of population is so universally accepted as a necessary element of equality between man and man that it must be taken to be the standard of a political equality preserved by the Fourteenth Amendment—that it is, in appellants' words "the basic principle of representative government"—is, to put it bluntly, not true. However desirable and however desired by some among the great political thinkers and framers of our government, it has never been generally practiced, today or in the past. . . .

Although the District Court had jurisdiction in the very restricted sense of power to determine whether it could adjudicate the claim, the case is of that class of political controversy which, by the nature of its subject, is unfit for federal judicial action. The judgment of the District Court, in dismissing the complaint for failure to state a claim on which relief can be granted, should therefore be affirmed.

[Mr. Justice Frankfurter had written the opinion in *Colegrove* v. *Green* so, again, this may be an example of loyalty to Court precedents.]

Dissenting opinion of Mr. Justice Harlan, whom Mr. Justice Frankfurter joined:

The dissenting opinion of Mr. Justice Frankfurter, in which I join, demonstrates the abrupt departure the majority makes from judicial history by putting the federal courts into this area of state concerns—an area which, in this instance, the Tennessee state courts themselves have refused to enter.

It does not detract from his opinion to say that the panorama of judicial history it unfolds, though evincing a steadfast underlying principle of keeping the federal courts out of these domains, has a tendency, because of variants in expression to becloud analysis in a given case. With due respect to the majority, I think that has happened here.

It is at once essential to recognize this case for what it is. The issue here relates not to a method of state electoral apportionment by which seats in the *federal* House of Representatives are allocated, but solely to the right of a State to fix the basis of representation in its *own* legislature. Until it is first decided to what extent that right is limited by the Federal Constitution, and whether what Tennessee has done or failed to do in this instance runs afoul of any such limitation, we need not reach the issues of "justiciability" or "political question" or any of the other considerations which in such cases as *Colegrove* v. *Green*, 328 U.S. 549, led the Court to decline to adjudicate a challenge to a state apportionment affecting seats in the federal House of Representatives, in the absence of a controlling Act of Congress. . . .

I can find nothing in the Equal Protection Clause or elsewhere in the Federal Constitution which expressly or impliedly supports the view that state legislatures must be so structured as to reflect with approximate equality the voice of every voter. Not only is that proposition refuted by history, as shown by my Brother Frankfurter, but it strikes deep into the heart of our federal system. Its acceptance would require us to turn our backs on the regard which this Court has always shown for the judgment of state legislatures and courts on matters of basically local concern. . . .

RELATED CASES:

Wood v. Broom: 287 U.S. 1 (1932). Opinion: Hughes, C.J. No dissent.

A statute that expressed the intention of Congress on the composition of Congressional districts prevented the Court from ruling on state action involving the gerrymandering of districts.

Gomillion v. Lightfoot: 364 U.S. 339 (1960). Opinion: Frankfurter, J. No dissent.

A state statute which changes the boundaries of a city in order to eliminate from the city all but four or five of its 400 Negro voters without eliminating any of its white voters is unconstitutional under the Fifteenth Amendment for depriving Negroes of their right to vote on account of race. This case arose in Tuskegee, Alabama.

Scholle v. Hare: 369 U.S. 429 (1962). Per Curiam. Dissenting: Harlan, J. Abstaining: Frankfurter, J.

Question of state senatorial apportionment under Michigan State Constitution is a proper question for the State Supreme Court to consider.

Gray v. Sanders: 372 U.S. 368 (1963). Opinion: Douglas, J. Dissenting: Harlan, J.

Georgia's county-unit system as a basis for counting votes in a Democratic primary election violates the equal protection clause of the Fourteenth Amendment. The practical effect of this system is that the vote of each citizen counts for less and less as the population of his county increases, and a combination of the units from the counties having the smallest population gives counties having one-third of the total population of the state a clear majority of county votes. The statute was designed to give rural minorities control. It applied to statewide offices.

Wesberry v. Sanders: 376 U.S. 1 (1964). Opinion: Black, J. Dissenting: Harlan, Clark, and Stewart, JJ.

The constitutional requirement in Article One, Section 2, that Representatives be chosen by the people of the several states means that as nearly as practicable one man's vote in a congressional election is to be worth as much as another's. This case came out of Georgia.

Wright v. Rockefeller: 376 U.S. 52 (1964). Opinion: Black, J. Dissenting: Douglas and Goldberg, JJ.

It was not shown that the challenged part of the New York state congressional districting act was the product of "state contrivance" to segregate on the basis of race or place of origin, chiefly Negroes and Puerto Ricans.

Reynolds v. Sims: 377 U.S. 533 (1964). Opinion: Warren, C.J. Dissenting: Harlan, J.

The equal protection clause requires that both houses of a bicameral state legislature must be apportioned on a population basis. This case arose in Alabama.

Fortson v. Dorsey: 379 U.S. 433 (1965). Opinion: Brennan, J. Dissenting: Douglas, J.

There is no requirement under equal protection that all districts for representation in a state legislature be single-member districts. This case arose in Georgia.

Burns v. Richardson: 384 U.S. 73 (1966). Opinion: Brennan, J. Abstaining: Fortas, J. No dissent.

Multi-member state legislative districts will constitute an invidious discrimination only if it can be shown that the plan operates to minimize or cancel out the voting strength of racial or political elements of the voting population. Apportionment of districts can be on the basis of the number of voters registered in each. This case came out of Hawaii.

Fortson v. Morris: 385 U.S. 231 (1966). Opinion: Black, J. Dissenting: Douglas, Brennan, Fortas, JJ., and Warren, C.J.

The provision of the Georgia Constitution by which the state legislature is empowered to select the governor from the two candidates with the highest number of votes in an election in which no candidate received a majority vote is not violative of the equal protection clause of the Fourteenth Amendment.

Sailors v. Board of Education of County of Kent: 387 U.S. 105 (1967). Opinion: Douglas, J. No dissent.

The Michigan system for selecting members of the county school board is basically appointive rather than elective. As respects nonlegislative officers, a state can appoint or elect them or combine the elective and appointive systems.

Avery v. Midland County, Texas: 390 U.S. 474 (1968). Opinion: White, J. Dissenting: Harlan, Stewart, and Fortas, JJ. Abstaining: Marshall, J.

The Constitution permits no substantial variation from equal protection in drawing districts for units of local government having general governmental powers over the entire geographic area served by the body. Involved here was a county board.

Kirkpatrick v. Preisler: 394 U.S. 526 (1969). Opinion: Brennan, J. Dissenting: Harlan, Stewart, and White, JJ.

The command of Article I, Section 2 that states create congressional districts which provide equal representation for equal numbers of people (and the "as nearly as practicable" test) permits only the limited population variances which are unavoidable despite a good-faith effort to achieve absolute equality, or for which justification is shown. This case arose in Missouri.

Powell v. McCormack: 395 U.S. 486 (1969). Opinion: Warren, C.J. Dissenting: Stewart, J.

When a person has been elected to the House, the Constitution does not vest in the Congress a discretionary power to deny membership by majority vote. Article I, Section 5 is at most a "textually demonstrable commitment" to Congress to judge only the qualifications set forth in the Constitution. The Court noted that both the intention of the Framers, to the extent that it can be determined, and an examination of the basic principles of our democratic system indicated this.

Kramer v. Union Free School District: 395 U.S. 621 (1969). Opinion: Warren, C.J. Dissenting: Stewart, Black, and Harlan, JJ.

A statutory provision that only such electors as own or lease taxable real property within the school district or are parents of children enrolled in the local public schools can vote in school district elections is void as violating equal protection.

Cipriano v. City of Houma: 395 U.S. 701 (1969). Opinion: Per Curiam. No dissent.

A provision of Louisiana law that only real property taxpayers had the right to vote in elections called to approve the issuance of revenue bonds by a municipal utility was held void as denying equal protection under the Fourteenth Amendment.

Hadley v. Junior College: 397 U.S. 50 (1970). Opinion: Black, J. Dissenting: Burger, C.J., and Harlan and Stewart, JJ.

Trustees of a junior college perform important governmental functions and these powers are general enough to have the "one man, one vote" principle applied to their apportionment for popular elections.

Phoenix v. Kolodziejski: 399 U.S. 204 (1970). Opinion: White, J. Dissenting: Stewart, and Harlan, JJ., and Burger, C.J. Abstaining: Blackmun, J.

Nonproperty owners cannot be barred from voting on the issuance of general obligation bonds. This would violate the equal protection clause of the Fourteenth Amendment.

Oregon v. Mitchell: 400 U.S. 112 (1970). Opinion: Black, J. Dissenting: Burger, C.J., and Harlan, Stewart, and Blackmun, JJ.

Here the original actions involved four states and questioned three provisions of the Voting Rights Act Amendments of 1970. The gist of the opinion was that Congress has the ultimate power of supervision over congressional and presidential elections. The practical effect of this decision was short-lived since the Twenty-sixth Amendment authorizing eighteen-year-old voting in all elections including state and local became a part of the Constitution about six months later.

NOTE:

Baker v. *Carr* represents a basic departure from the time-honored attitude of the Court that questions of redistricting and reapportionment are political questions and not justiciable. The results of the case represent a departure from a policy of judicial restraint in the area of action to force legislative bodies to take positive action. The lower courts have even performed the task of redistricting when the legislature has failed to produce a plan satisfactory to the courts. This represents a virtual revolution in the attitude of the courts toward mandating legislative action.

Recent cases have extended the "one man, one vote" principle to local governments with general governmental power in addition to congressional districting and state legislative districting.

See *WMCA, Inc.* v. *Simon*, 370 U.S. 190 (1962). Also see *Duddleston* v. *Grills*, 385 U.S. 455 (1967), *Branigin* v. *Grills*, 390 U.S. 932 (1968), and *Branigin* v. *Duddleston*, 391 U.S. 364 (1968).

CHAPTER X

CITIZENSHIP

Citizenship is membership in a political state. Such membership is both legally and practically important. To a considerable extent one's citizenship determines the laws to which he will be subject in his daily movements. In international travel the individual's liability and protection are in considerable measure determined thereby. In the United States, most persons possess two types of citizenship, federal and state. The determination of the privileges and the obligations resulting therefrom has been the burden of Supreme Court decisions down to the present time in this area of public law.

United States v. Wong Kim Ark
169 U.S 649; 18 S.Ct. 456; 42 L.Ed. 890 (1898)

(Wong Kim Ark, of Chinese ancestry, was refused readmission to the United States upon his return to San Francisco from a visit to China. He had been born in California of parents who were at the time citizens of China but were permanent residents of the United States. He claimed citizenship of the United States by birth on its soil (*jus soli*) and this was challenged.)

Vote: 6-2

Mr. Justice Gray delivered the opinion of the Court:

... The fundamental principle of the common law with regard to English nationality was birth within the allegiance also called "ligealty," "obedience," "faith," or "power," of the king. The principle embraced all persons born within the King's allegiance and subject to his protection. Such allegiance and protection were mutual —as expressed in the maxim *"Protectio trahit subjectionem subjectio protectionem"* —and were not restricted to natural-born subjects and naturalized subjects, or to those who had taken an oath of allegiance; but were predicable of aliens in amity, so long as they were within the Kingdom. Children born in England of such aliens were therefore natural-born subjects. But the children born within the realm of foreign ambassadors, or the children of alien enemies, born during and within their hostile occupation of part of the King's dominions, were not natural-born subjects, because not born within the allegiance, the obedience, or the power, or, as would be said at this day, within the jurisdiction of the King. . . .

It thus clearly appears that by the law of England for the last three centuries, beginning before the settlement of this country, and continuing to the present day, aliens, while residing in the dominions possessed by the Crown of England, were within the allegiance, the obedience, the faith or loyalty, the protection, the power, and the jurisdiction of the English Sovereign; and therefore every child born in England of alien parents was a natural-born subject, unless the child of an ambassador or other diplomatic agent of a foreign state, or of an alien enemy in hostile occupation of the place where the child was born.

The same rule was in force in all the English Colonies upon this continent down to the time of the Declaration of Independence, and in the United States afterwards, and continued to prevail under the Constitution as originally established. . . .

The foregoing considerations and authorities irresistibly lead us to these conclusions: The Fourteenth Amendment affirms the ancient and fundamental rule of citizenship by birth within the territory, in the allegiance and under the protection of the country, including all children here born of resident aliens, with the exceptions or qualifications (as old as the rule itself) of children of foreign sovereigns or their ministers, or born on foreign public ships, or of enemies within and during a hostile occupation of part of our territory, and with the single additional exception of children of members of the Indian tribes owing direct allegiance to their several tribes. The Amendment, in clear words and in manifest intent, includes the children born within the territory of the United States. Every citizen or subject of another country, while domiciled here, is within the allegiance and the protection, and consequently subject to the jurisdiction, of the United States. . . .

Mr. Justice McKenna, not having been a member of the court when this case was argued, took no part in the decision.

Mr. Chief Justice Fuller dissented, with the concurrence of Mr. Justice Harlan:

. . . The argument is, that although the Constitution prior to that [the Fourteenth] amendment nowhere attempted to define the words "citizens of the United States" and "natural-born citizen" as used therein, yet that it must be interpreted in the light of the English common law rule which made the place of birth the criterion of nationality; that that rule "was in force in all the English colonies upon this continent down to the time of the Declaration of Independence, and in the United States afterwards, and continued to prevail under the Constitution as originally established"; and "that before the enactment of the Civil Rights Act of 1866 and the adoption of the Constitutional Amendment, all white persons, at least, born within the sovereignty of the United States, whether children of citizens or of foreigners, excepting only children of ambassadors or public ministers of a foreign Government, were native-born citizens of the United States." . . .

The English common law rule, which it is insisted was in force after the Declaration of Independence, was that "every person born within the dominions of the Crown, no matter whether of English or of foreign parents, and, in the latter case, whether the parents were settled or merely temporarily sojourning in the country, was an English subject; save only the children of foreign ambassadors (who were excepted because their fathers carried their own nationality with them), or a child born to a foreigner during the hostile occupation of any part of the territories of England." Cockburn on Nationality, 7.

Obviously, where the Constitution deals with common law rights and uses common law phraseology, its language should be read in the light of the common law; but when the question arises as to what constitutes citizenship of the nation, involving as it does international relations, and political as contradistinguished from civil status, international principles must be considered, and, unless the municipal law of England appears to have been affirmatively accepted, it cannot be allowed to control in the matter of construction. . . .

RELATED CASES:

Chirac v. Chirac: 2 Wheat. 259 (1817). Opinion: Marshall, C.J. No dissent.

Congress has the exclusive right to determine the rules of naturalization. States do not share this power, but state courts may be used as a matter of convenience.

Dred Scott v. Sandford: 19 How. 393 (1857). Opinion: Taney, C.J. Dissenting: McLean and Curtis, JJ.

A Negro could not be a citizen of the United States but he could possess state citizenship under the laws of a state. A federal statute (here the Missouri Compromise) cannot deprive a person of property merely because that person goes into a particular area. A slave, not being a citizen, could not bring suit in the federal courts.

Johannessen v. United States: 225 U.S. 227 (1912). Opinion: Pitney, J. No dissent.
Naturalization secured by false or fraudulent statements may be revoked since the citizenship was never rightfully possessed by the individual.

Mackenzie v. Hare: 239 U.S. 299 (1915). Opinion: McKenna, J. Dissenting: McReynolds, J.
Congress may validly provide that a citizen who voluntarily enters into a specified relationship will lose his citizenship. Here a provision of the 1907 act was upheld that declared that an American woman would lose her citizenship by marriage to an alien, here a subject of Great Britain.

Tutun v. United States: 270 U.S. 568 (1926). Opinion: Brandeis, J. No dissent.
Under the naturalization law, an alien has a statutory right to citizenship if the proper court finds that he has fulfilled the requisite qualifications.

United States v. Schwimmer: 279 U.S. 644 (1929). Opinion: Butler, J. Dissenting: Holmes, Brandeis, and Sanford, JJ.
The privilege of becoming a naturalized citizen may be denied to a woman (here a pacifist, fifty years of age) who possesses all other legal qualifications for citizenship, if she refuses to swear that she will bear arms in defense of the United States. See p. 25, above.

United States v. Macintosh: 283 U.S. 605 (1931). Opinion: Sutherland, J. Dissenting: Hughes, C.J., and Holmes, Brandeis, and Stone, JJ.
Under the federal statute governing naturalization, a person (here a Yale divinity professor) may be denied citizenship if he refuses to swear that he will bear arms except in wars that he feels are morally justified. See p. 25, above.

United States v. Bland: 283 U.S. 636 (1931). Opinion: Sutherland, J. Dissenting: Hughes, C.J., and Holmes, Brandeis, and Stone, JJ.
On the strength of *United States* v. *Macintosh*, 283 U.S. 605 (1931), the Court here ruled that a person could be denied application for citizenship who refused to take the oath of allegiance prescribed by Congress to defend the Constitution and laws of the United States against all enemies, etc., except with the written interpolation of the words "as far as my conscience as a Christian will allow." See p. 25, above.

Perkins v. Elg: 307 U.S. 325 (1939). Opinion: Hughes, C.J. No dissent. Abstaining: Douglas, J.
A person born in the United States of naturalized parents does not lose his citizenship by reason of the repatriation of his parents while he is a minor and their return of him to the country of their allegiance, if on attaining majority he elects to retain United States citizenship and returns to the United States.

Regan v. King: 319 U.S. 753 (1943). Opinion: Per Curiam. No dissent.
Here the Supreme Court denied a petition for a writ of certiorari to the Ninth Circuit Court of Appeals. The Circuit Court in a *per curiam* opinion citing *United States* v. *Wong Kim Ark* had affirmed the district court for the Northern District of California which itself had said that the sole question that this case "presents to this court is one which has been definitely decided by the United States Supreme Court: Is a person of Japanese race, born within the United States a citizen? The question has been answered in the affirmative. . . ."

Schneiderman v. United States: 320 U.S. 118 (1943). Opinion: Murphy, J. Dissenting: Stone, C.J. Abstaining: Jackson, J.
In order to revoke naturalization because of fraud, the Government must prove this by "clear, unequivocal, and convincing evidence." Schneiderman was a member of the Communist Party. See p. 74, above.

In re Summers: 325 U.S. 561 (1945). Opinion: Reed, J. Dissenting: Black, Douglas, Murphy, and Rutledge, JJ.

The state of Illinois did not deny religious freedom under due process of law by barring a conscientious objector to military service from the practice of law. Lawyers in Illinois must take an oath to support the Illinois Constitution which requires, at least theoretically, membership of all "able-bodied male persons" in the state militia. See p. 25 above.

Girouard v. United States: 328 U.S. 61 (1946). Opinion: Douglas, J. Dissenting: Stone, C.J., and Reed and Frankfurter, JJ. Abstaining: Jackson, J.

Conscientious objection to military service is no bar to citizenship under the naturalization statute. Here a Seventh Day Adventist refused to swear that he would bear arms, but indicated willingness to serve as a noncombatant. This case reversed *Schwimmer* and *Macintosh*. See p. 25, above.

Savorgnan v. United States: 338 U.S. 491 (1950). Opinion: Burton, J. Dissenting: Frankfurter and Black, JJ. Abstaining: Douglas, J.

A native-born American woman who signed a document in Italian renouncing her United States citizenship in order to marry an Italian, and thereafter resided in Italy, was held to have expatriated herself, even though she claimed not to have understood the document she signed and therefore lacked intent.

Perez v. Brownell: 356 U.S. 44 (1958). Opinion: Frankfurter, J. Dissenting: Douglas, Whittaker, and Black, JJ., and Warren, C.J.

Under its implied power to legislate to regulate foreign affairs, Congress may provide for expatriation for voting in an election or a plebiscite in a foreign state (here Mexico). Such a matter could embarrass the United States government in its conduct of foreign relations. The act of voting must be voluntary but there is no need for desire to relinquish citizenship. This decision was overruled by *Rusk*, below.

Trop v. Dulles: 356 U.S. 86 (1958). Opinion: Warren, C.J. Dissenting: Frankfurter, Burton, Clark, and Harlan, JJ.

Congress cannot provide that desertion in time of war shall result in loss of citizenship. Expatriation can result only from voluntary renunciation or abandonment of citizenship. As punishment for crimes, expatriation is cruel and unusual punishment. Too, there is no reasonable relationship between expatriation and the successful waging of war. The statute was Section 401(a) of the Nationality Act of 1940.

Nishikawa v. Dulles: 356 U.S. 129 (1958). Opinion: Warren, C.J. Dissenting: Harlan and Clark, JJ.

The Government must prove that service in a foreign army (here Japanese) by an American citizen was voluntary on his part before expatriation can result.

Kennedy, Attorney General v. Mendoza Martinez: 372 U.S. 144 (1963). Opinion: Goldberg, J. Dissenting: Stewart, Harlan, White, and Clark, JJ.

A federal statute providing that when a citizen departs from and remains outside the United States in time of war or national emergency for the purpose of evading military service he is to be automatically deprived of his citizenship is void as not affording the procedural safeguards guaranteed by the Fifth and Sixth Amendments.

Schneider v. Rusk: 377 U.S. 163 (1964). Opinion: Douglas, J. Dissenting: Clark, Harlan, and White, JJ.

A federal statutory provision that a naturalized citizen is to lose his citizenship by continuous residence in his country of origin is discriminatory and violative of due process under the Fifth Amendment. It is an impermissible presumption that they are less loyal and reliable. This makes them second-class citizens.

Aptheker v. Secretary of State: 378 U.S. 500 (1964). Opinion: Goldberg, J. Dissenting: Clark, Harlan, and White.

The provision of the Subversive Activities Control Act of 1950 outlawing passports for members of Communist organizations violates the right to travel abroad that is part of the "liberty" guaranteed in the due process clause of the Fifth Amendment.

Zemel v. Rusk: 381 U.S. 1 (1965). Opinion: Warren, C.J. Dissenting: Black, Douglas, and Goldberg, JJ.

The action of the Secretary of State under the Passport Act of 1926 in refusing to allow travel to certain geographical areas, here Cuba, was upheld by the Court as not violative of the First Amendment. Area restrictions on passports were common prior to the 1926 adoption of the legislation and it was this prior administrative practice that Congress presumably had in mind in enacting the statute. Area restrictions involve foreign policy.

United States v. Laub: 385 U.S. 475 (1967). Opinion: Fortas, J. No dissent.

Area restrictions on the use of an otherwise valid passport are not criminally enforceable. See also *Travis* v. *United States*, 385 U.S. 491 (1967).

Afroyim v. Rusk: 387 U.S. 253 (1967). Opinion: Black, J. Dissenting: Harlan, Clark, Stewart, and White, JJ.

The Fourteenth Amendment protects every United States citizen against forcible destruction of his citizenship by Congress. The Court thereby overruled *Perez* v. *Brownell*, 356 U.S. 44 (1958). Citizenship must be relinquished voluntarily. Denaturalization can take place where there has been fraud in acquiring naturalization. Afroyim, a naturalized citizen, had voted in an election for the Israeli parliament.

NOTE:

The *Wong Kim Ark* case clarifies the meaning of citizenship under the Fourteenth Amendment. The two rules governing citizenship throughout the world are *jus soli* and *jus sanguinis*. The United States by statute recognizes both, but *Wong Kim Ark* seems to make *jus soli* basic, as, indeed, does the Fourteenth Amendment on which the case is based.

Toomer v. Witsell
334 U.S. 385; 68 S.Ct. 1157; 92 L.Ed. 1460 (1948)

(South Carolina by statute had regulated commercial shrimp fishing in the three-mile maritime belt off the coast. The statute discriminated against nonresidents of the state so as to make it virtually exclusionary. Suit was brought by five citizens and residents of Georgia and a Florida corporation to restrain the enforcement of the act as a violation of the privileges and immunities provision of the Constitution, Article Four, Section 2.)

Vote: 9-0

Mr. Chief Justice Vinson delivered the opinion of the Court:

. . . As justification for the statute, appellees urge that the State's obvious purpose was to conserve its shrimp supply, and they suggest that it was designed to head off an impending threat of excessive trawling. The record casts some doubt on these statements. But in any event, appellees' argument assumes that any means adopted to attain valid objectives necessarily squares with the privileges and immunities clause. It overlooks the purpose of that clause, which as indicated above, is to outlaw classifications based on the fact of non-citizenship unless there is something to indicate that non-citizens constitute a peculiar source of the evil at which the statute is aimed.

. . . We would be closing our eyes to reality, we believe, if we concluded that there was a reasonable relationship between the danger represented by non-citizens, as a class, and the severe discrimination practiced upon them.

Thus, Section 3379 must be held unconstitutional unless commercial shrimp fishing in the maritime belt falls within some unexpressed exception to the privileges and immunities clause.

Appellees strenuously urge that there is such an exception. Their argument runs as follows: Ever since Roman times, animals *ferae naturae*, not having been reduced to individual possession and ownership, have been considered as *res nullius* or part of the "negative community of interests" and hence subject to control by the sovereign or other governmental authority. More recently this thought has been expressed by saying that fish and game are the common property of all citizens of the governmental unit and that the government, as a sort of trustee, exercises this "ownership" for the benefit of its citizens. In the case of fish, it has also been considered that each government "owned" both the beds of its lakes, streams, and tidewaters and the waters themselves; hence it must also "own" the fish within those waters. Each government may, the argument continues, regulate the corpus of the trust in the way best suited to the interests of the beneficial owners, its citizens, and may discriminate as it sees fit against persons lacking any beneficial interest. Finally, it is said that this special property interest, which nations and similar governmental bodies have traditionally had, in this country vested in the colonial governments and passed to the individual states. . . .

The whole ownership theory, in fact, is now generally regarded as but a fiction expressive in legal shorthand of the importance to its people that a State have power to preserve and regulate the exploitation of an important resource. And there is no necessary conflict between that vital policy consideration and the constitutional command that the State exercise that power, like its other powers, so as not to discriminate without reason against citizens of other states. . . .

Thus we hold that commercial shrimping in the marginal sea, like other common callings, is within the purview of the privileges and immunities clause. And since we have previously concluded that the reasons advanced in support of the statute do not bear a reasonable relationship to the high degree of discrimination practiced upon citizens of other states, it follows that Section 3379 violates Article Four, Section 2, of the Constitution.

Appellants maintain that by a parity of reasoning the statute also contravenes the equal protection clause of the Fourteenth Amendment. That may well be true, but we do not pass on this argument since it is unnecessary to disposition of the present case.

Fifth. Appellants contend that Section 3414, which requires that owners of shrimp boats fishing in the maritime belt off South Carolina dock at a South Carolina port and unload, pack, and stamp their catch (with a tax stamp) before "shipping or transporting it to another state," burdens interstate commerce in shrimp in violation of Article One, Section 8, of the Constitution. . . .

Mr. Justice Frankfurter concurred, and was joined by Mr. Justice Jackson:

. . . While I agree that South Carolina has exceeded her power to control fisheries within her waters, I rest the invalidity of her attempt to do so on the Commerce Clause. The Court reaches this result by what I deem to be a misapplication of the Privileges-and-Immunities Clause of Article Four, § 2, of the Constitution.

. . . A State may care for its own in utilizing the bounties of nature within her borders because it has technical ownership of such bounties or, when ownership is in no one, because the State may for the common good exercise all the authority that technical ownership ordinarily confers.

Mr. Justice Rutledge concurred:

. . . The regulation in question . . . is aimed in terms directly at interstate commerce alone, and thus would seem to be discriminatory in intent and effect upon that commerce. Moreover, in my opinion, it is of such a character that, if applied, for all practical purposes it would block the commerce.

Since it was exactly that sort of state regulation the commerce clause was designed to strike down, I agree that this one cannot stand. The same consideration I also think would be applicable to nullify the license fees levied against nonresidents, since upon the record their transportation of catches would seem to be exclusively in interstate commerce, or practically so.

RELATED CASES:

Corfield v. Coryell: 6 Fed. Cases 3230 (1823). Opinion: Washington, Circuit Judge. No dissent.

A state (here New Jersey) may so regulate the use of oyster beds as to exclude the citizens of other states. This is a matter of the use of the common property of a state and is not a privilege which must be extended to non-residents.

Paul v. Virginia: 8 Wall. 168 (1869). Opinion: Field, J. No dissent.

A corporation is not a citizen in the sense that the privileges and immunities clause ("Comity clause," Article IV, Section 2) includes corporations. Also corporations are not included under self-incrimination.

Ward v. Maryland: 12 Wall. 418 (1871). Opinion: Clifford, J. No dissent.

A state may not, under the privileges and immunities clause, require nonresidents of the state to secure a license in order to sell merchandise by samples.

McCready v. Virginia: 94 U.S. 391 (1877). Opinion: Waite, C.J. No dissent.

A state may restrict the planning of oysters in the beds of streams of the state to its own citizens. Here a property right is involved. Oysters remain in state's inland waters; therefore the case is different from *Toomer*.

McKane v. Durston: 153 U.S. 684 (1894). Opinion: Harlan, J. No dissent.

A citizen of one state while in another state is entitled not to the privileges he possesses in his home state, but only to those extended by the other state to its own citizens. He was denied bail. He claimed other states gave bail in similar circumstances. The case arose in New York.

Geer v. Connecticut: 161 U.S. 519 (1896). Opinion: White, J. Dissenting: Field and Harlan, JJ.

A state may by statute prohibit shipping certain game birds out of the state. This is an exercise of state police power to care for common state property and preserve a valuable food supply. The remote and indirect effect on interstate commerce is not controlling.

Blake v. McClung: 172 U.S. 239 (1898). Opinion: Harlan, J. Dissenting: Brewer, J., and Fuller, C.J.

A state statute (here Tennessee) may not give preference to the claims of resident creditors over those of nonresidents, such as a foreign (out of state) corporation in the distribution of the assets of a bankrupt foreign corporation.

Heim v. McCall: 239 U.S. 175 (1915). Opinion: McKenna, J. No dissent.

Jobs on public works may by statute be restricted to American citizens and preference extended to citizens of the state involved (here New York). This again is a matter of the use of state property.

Asbury Hospital v. Cass County: 326 U.S. 207 (1945). Opinion: Stone, C.J. Dissenting: Black, J. Abstaining: Jackson, J.

A state may prohibit a foreign corporation doing business in that state or even acquiring property therein. Therefore North Dakota could require corporations to dispose of farm lands held by them in the state as long as they were given a fair opportunity of sale. This violated no part of the Fourteenth Amendment. The hospital was chartered in Minnesota. The land had been held for ten years.

Mullaney v. Anderson: 342 U.S. 415 (1952). Opinion: Frankfurter, J. Dissenting: Jackson, J.

A license fee of the territory of Alaska discriminating as to nonresident commercial fishermen is void as contrary to the privileges and immunities clause made applicable to Alaska by Congress by the Organic Act. The state must treat others as its own. Here there was a fifty-dollar fee for nonresidents and a five-dollar fee for local citizens.

NOTE:

Toomer does much to weaken the long-held doctrine that a state owns wildlife within its borders in trust for its citizens. Very probably this means that henceforth the privileges and immunities clause or the commerce power may be invoked to invalidate state statutes discriminating in this area in favor of a state's residents. Certainly there must be some reasonable relationship between the activities of nonresidents and the exercise of state police power. In *Toomer* the locale of the marginal sea was held to distinguish the case from prior decisions.

MEMBERS OF THE SUPREME COURT OF THE UNITED STATES, 1789–1976

Chief Justices	State	Served	Appointed by	Born/Died
John Jay	N.Y.	1789-1795	Washington	1745-1829
John Rutledge	S.C.	1795	Washington	1739-1800
Oliver Ellsworth	Conn.	1796-1800	Washington	1745-1807
John Marshall	Va.	1801-1835	J. Adams	1755-1835
Roger B. Taney	Md.	1836-1864	Jackson	1777-1864
Salmon P. Chase	Ohio	1864-1873	Lincoln	1808-1873
Morrison R. Waite	Ohio	1874-1888	Grant	1816-1888
Mulville W. Fuller	Ill.	1888-1910	Cleveland	1833-1910
Edward D. White	La.	1910-1921	Taft	1845-1921
William H. Taft	Conn.	1921-1930	Harding	1857-1930
Charles E. Hughes	N.Y.	1930-1941	Hoover	1862-1948
Harlan F. Stone	N.Y.	1941-1946	F. D. Roosevelt	1872-1946
Fred M. Vinson	Ky.	1946-1953	Truman	1890-1953
Earl Warren	Calif.	1953-1969	Eisenhower	1891-
Warren Earl Burger	Va.	1969-	Nixon	1907-

Associate Justices	State	Served	Appointed by	Born/Died
John Rutledge	S.C.	1789-1791	Washington	1739-1800
William Cushing	Mass.	1789-1810	Washington	1732-1810
James Wilson	Pa.	1789-1798	Washington	1742-1798
John Blair	Va.	1789-1796	Washington	1732-1800
James Iredell	N.C.	1790-1799	Washington	1751-1799
Thomas Johnson	Md.	1791-1793	Washington	1732-1819
William Paterson	N.J.	1793-1806	Washington	1745-1806
Samuel Chase	Md.	1796-1811	Washington	1741-1811
Bushrod Washington	Va.	1798-1829	J. Adams	1762-1829
Alfred Moore	N.C.	1799-1804	J. Adams	1755-1810
Henry B. Livingston	N.Y.	1806-1823	Jefferson	1757-1823
Thomas Dodd	Ky.	1807-1826	Jefferson	1765-1826
Joseph Story	Mass.	1811-1845	Madison	1779-1845
Gabriel Duval	Md.	1811-1835	Madison	1752-1844
Smith Thompson	N.Y.	1823-1843	Monroe	1768-1843
Robert Trimble	Ky.	1826-1828	J. Q. Adams	1777-1828
John McLean	Ohio	1829-1861	Jackson	1785-1861
Henry Baldwin	Pa.	1830-1844	Jackson	1780-1844
James M. Wayne	Ga.	1835-1867	Jackson	1790-1867
Philip P. Barbour	Va.	1836-1841	Jackson	1783-1841
John Catron	Tenn.	1837-1865	Jackson	1786-1865
John McKinley	Ala.	1837-1852	Van Buren	1780-1852
Peter V. Daniel	Va.	1841-1860	Van Buren	1784-1860
Samuel Nelson	N.Y.	1845-1872	Tyler	1792-1873
Levi Woodbury	N.H.	1846-1851	Polk	1789-1851
Robert C. Grier	Pa.	1846-1870	Polk	1794-1870
Benjamin R. Curtis	Mass.	1851-1857	Filmore	1809-1874
John A. Campbell	Ala.	1853-1861	Pierce	1811-1889
Nathan Clifford	Maine	1858-1881	Buchanan	1803-1881
Noah H. Swayne	Ohio	1862-1881	Lincoln	1804-1884
Samuel F. Miller	Iowa	1862-1890	Lincoln	1816-1890
David Davis	Ill.	1862-1877	Lincoln	1815-1886

Associate Justices	State	Served	Appointed by	Born/Died
Stephen J. Field	Calif.	1863-1897	Lincoln	1816-1899
William Strong	Pa.	1870-1880	Grant	1808-1895
Joseph P. Bradley	N.J.	1870-1892	Grant	1813-1892
Ward Hunt	N.Y.	1872-1882	Grant	1810-1886
Joseph M. Harlan	Ky.	1877-1911	Hayes	1833-1911
William B. Woods	Ga.	1880-1887	Hayes	1824-1887
Stanley Matthews	Ohio	1881-1889	Garfield	1824-1889
Horace Gray	Mass.	1881-1902	Arthur	1828-1902
Samuel Blatchford ˙	N.Y.	1882-1893	Arthur	1820-1893
Lucius Q. C. Lamar	Miss.	1888-1893	Cleveland	1825-1893
David J. Brewer	Kans.	1889-1910	B. Harrison	1837-1910
Henry B. Brown	Mich.	1890-1906	B. Harrison	1836-1913
George Shiras, Jr.	Pa.	1892-1903	B. Harrison	1832-1924
Howell E. Jackson	Tenn.	1893-1895	B. Harrison	1832-1895
Edward D. White	La.	1894-1910	Cleveland	1845-1921
Rufus W. Peckham	N.Y.	1895-1909	Cleveland	1838-1909
Joseph McKenna	Calif.	1898-1925	McKinley	1843-1926
Oliver W. Holmes	Mass.	1902-1932	T. Roosevelt	1841-1935
William R. Day	Ohio	1903-1922	T. Roosevelt	1849-1923
William H. Moody	Mass.	1906-1910	T. Roosevelt	1853-1917
Horace L. Lurton	Tenn.	1909-1914	Taft	1844-1914
Charles E. Hughes	N.Y.	1910-1916	Taft	1862-1948
William VanDevanter	Wyo.	1910-1937	Taft	1859-1941
Joseph R. Lamar	Ga.	1910-1916	Taft	1857-1916
Mahlon Pitney	N.J.	1912-1922	Taft	1858-1924
James C. McReynolds	Tenn.	1914-1941	Wilson	1862-1946
Louis D. Brandeis	Mass.	1916-1939	Wilson	1856-1941
John H. Clarke	Ohio	1916-1922	Wilson	1857-1945
George Sutherland	Utah	1922-1938	Harding	1862-1942
Pierce Butler	Minn.	1922-1939	Harding	1866-1939
Edward T. Sanford	Tenn.	1923-1930	Harding	1865-1930
Harlan F. Stone	N.Y.	1925-1941	Coolidge	1872-1946
Owen J. Roberts	Pa.	1930-1945	Hoover	1875-1955
Benjamin N. Cardozo	N.Y.	1932-1938	Hoover	1870-1938
Hugo L. Black	Ala.	1937-1971	F. D. Roosevelt	1886-1971
Stanley F. Reed	Ky.	1938-1957	F. D. Roosevelt	1884-
Felix Frankfurter	Mass.	1939-1962	F. D. Roosevelt	1882-1965
William O. Douglas	Conn.	1939-1975	F. D. Roosevelt	1898-1975
Frank Murphy	Mich.	1940-1949	F. D. Roosevelt	1890-1949
James F. Byrnes	S.C.	1941-1942	F. D. Roosevelt	1879-1972
Robert H. Jackson	N.Y.	1941-1954	F. D. Roosevelt	1892-1954
Wiley B. Rutledge	Iowa	1943-1949	Truman	1894-1949
Harold H. Burton	Ohio	1945-1958	Truman	1888-1964
Tom C. Clark	Tex.	1949-1967	Truman	1899-
Sherman Minton	Ind.	1949-1956	Truman	1890-1965
John M. Harlan	N.Y.	1955-1971	Eisenhower	1899-1971
William J. Brennan, Jr.	N.J.	1956-	Eisenhower	1906-
Charles E. Whittaker	Mo.	1957-1962	Eisenhower	1901-
Potter Stewart	Ohio	1958-	Eisenhower	1915-
Byron R. White	Colo.	1962-	Kennedy	1917-
Arthur J. Goldberg	Ill.	1962-1965	Kennedy	1908-
Abe Fortas	Tenn.	1965-1969	Johnson	1910-
Thurgood Marshall	Md.	1967-	Johnson	1908-
Harry A. Blackmun	Minn.	1970-	Nixon	1908-
Lewis F. Powell, Jr.	Va.	1972-	Nixon	1907-
William H. Rehnquist	Ariz.	1972-	Nixon	1924-
John P. Stevens	Ill.	1975-	Ford	1920-

THE CONSTITUTION
OF THE UNITED STATES

Adopted September 17, 1787

Effective March 4, 1789

We the people of the United States, in order to form a more perfect union, establish justice, insure domestic tranquillity, provide for the common defense, promote the general welfare, and secure the blessings of liberty to ourselves and our posterity, do ordain and establish this Constitution for the United States of America.

ARTICLE I

SECTION 1.   All legislative powers herein granted shall be vested in a Congress of the United States, which shall consist of a Senate and House of Representatives.

SECTION 2.   1. The House of Representatives shall be composed of members chosen every second year by the people of the several States, and the electors in each State shall have the qualifications requisite for electors of the most numerous branch of the State legislature.

2. No person shall be a representative who shall not have attained to the age of twenty-five years, and been seven years a citizen of the United States, and who shall not, when elected, be an inhabitant of that State in which he shall be chosen.

3. Representatives and direct taxes[1] shall be apportioned among the several States which may be included within this Union, according to their respective numbers, which shall be determined by adding to the whole number of free persons, including those bound to service for a term of years, and excluding Indians not taxed, *three fifths of all other persons.*[2] The actual enumeration shall be made within three years after the first meeting of the Congress of the United States, and within every subsequent term of ten years, in such manner as they shall by law direct. The number of representatives shall not exceed one for every thirty thousand, but each State shall have at least one representative; and until such enumeration shall be made, the State of New Hampshire shall be entitled to choose three, Massachusetts eight, Rhode Island and Providence Plantations one, Connecticut five, New York six, New Jersey four, Pennsylvania eight, Delaware one, Maryland six, Virginia ten, North Caroline five, South Carolina five, and Georgia three.

4. When vacancies happen in the representation from any State, the executive authority thereof shall issue writs of election to fill such vacancies.

[1] See the 16th Amendment.
[2] See the 14th Amendment.

5. The House of Representatives shall choose their speaker and other officers; and shall have the sole power of impeachment.

SECTION 3. 1. The Senate of the United States shall be composed of two senators from each State, *chosen by the legislature thereof,*[3] for six years; and each senator shall have one vote.

2. Immediately after they shall be assembled in consequence of the first election, they shall be divided as equally as may be into three classes. The seats of the senators of the first class shall be vacated at the expiration of the second year, of the second class at the expiration of the fourth year, and of the third class at the expiration of the sixth year, so that one third may be chosen every second year; and if vacancies happen by resignation, or otherwise, during the recess of the legislature of the State, the executive thereof may make temporary appointments until the next meeting of the legislature, which shall then fill such vacancies.[3]

3. No person shall be a senator who shall not have attained to the age of thirty years, and been nine years a citizen of the United States, and who shall not, when elected, be an inhabitant of that State for which he shall be chosen.

4. The Vice President of the United States shall be President of the Senate, but shall have no vote, unless they be equally divided.

5. The Senate shall choose their other officers, and also a president *pro tempore,* in the absence of the Vice President, or when he shall exercise the office of the President of the United States.

6. The Senate shall have the sole power to try all impeachments. When sitting for that purpose, they shall be on oath or affirmation. When the President of the United States is tried, the chief justice shall preside: and no person shall be convicted without the concurrence of two thirds of the members present.

7. Judgment in cases of impeachment shall not extend further than to removal from office, and disqualifications to hold and enjoy any office of honor, trust or profit under the United States: but the party convicted shall nevertheless be liable and subject to indictment, trial, judgment and punishment, according to law.

SECTION 4. 1. The times, places, and manner of holding elections for senators and representatives, shall be prescribed in each State by the legislature thereof; but the Congress may at any time by law make or alter such regulations, except as to the places of choosing senators.

2. The Congress shall assemble at least once in every year, and such meeting shall be on the first Monday in December, unless they shall by law appoint a different day.

SECTION 5. 1. Each House shall be the judge of the elections, returns and qualifications of its own members, and a majority of each shall constitute a quorum to do business; but a small number may adjourn from day to day, and may be authorized to compel the attendance of absent members, in such manner, and under such penalties as each House may provide.

2. Each House may determine the rules of its proceedings, punish its members for disorderly behavior, and, with the concurrence of two thirds, expel a member.

3. Each House shall keep a journal of its proceedings, and from time to time publish the same, excepting such parts as may in their judgment require secrecy; and the yeas and nays of the members of either House on any question shall, at the desire of one fifth of those present, be entered on the journal.

4. Neither House, during the session of Congress, shall, without the consent of the other, adjourn for more than three days, nor to any other place than that in which the two Houses shall be sitting.

[3] See the 17th Amendment.

SECTION 6.   1. The senators and representatives shall receive a compensation for their services, to be ascertained by law, and paid out of the Treasury of the United States. They shall in all cases, except treason, felony, and breach of the peace, be privileged from arrest during their attendance at the session of their respective Houses, and in going to and returning from the same; and for any speech or debate in either House, they shall not be questioned in any other place.

2. No senator or representative shall, during the time for which he was elected, be appointed to any civil office under the authority of the United States, which shall have been created, or the emoluments whereof shall have been increased during such time; and no person holding any office under the United States shall be a member of either House during his continuance in office.

SECTION 7.   1. All bills for raising revenue shall originate in the House of Representatives; but the Senate may propose or concur with amendments as on other bills.

2. Every bill which shall have passed the House of Representatives and the Senate, shall, before it becomes a law, be presented to the President of the United States; if he approves he shall sign it, but if not he shall return it, with his objections to that House in which it shall have originated, who shall enter the objections at large on their journal, and proceed to reconsider it. If after such reconsideration two thirds of that House shall agree to pass the bill, it shall be sent, together with the objections, to the other House, by which it shall likewise be reconsidered, and if approved by two thirds of that House, it shall become a law. But in all such cases the votes of both Houses shall be determined by yeas and nays, and the names of the persons voting for and against the bill shall be entered on the journal of each House respectively. If any bill shall not be returned by the President within ten days (Sundays excepted) after it shall have been presented to him, the same shall be a law, in like manner as if he had signed it, unless the Congress by their adjournment prevent its return, in which case it shall not be a law.

3. Every order, resolution, or vote to which the concurrence of the Senate and the House of Representatives may be necessary (except on a question of adjournment) shall be presented to the President of the United States; and before the same shall take effect, shall be approved by him, or being disapproved by him, shall be repassed by two thirds of the Senate and House of Representatives, according to the rules and limitations prescribed in the case of a bill.

SECTION 8.   The Congress shall have the power

1. To lay and collect taxes, duties, imposts, and excises, to pay the debts and provide for the common defense and general welfare of the United States; but all duties, imposts, and excises shall be uniform throughout the United States;

2. To borrow money on the credit of the United States;

3. To regulate commerce with foreign nations, and among the several States, and with the Indian tribes;

4. To establish a uniform rule of naturalization, and uniform laws on the subject of bankruptcies throughout the United States;

5. To coin money, regulate the value thereof, and of foreign coin, and fix the standard of weights and measures;

6. To provide for the punishment of counterfeiting the securities and current coin of the United States;

7. To establish post offices and post roads;

8. To promote the process of science and useful arts, by securing for limited times to authors and inventors the exclusive right to their respective writings and discoveries;

9. To constitute tribunals inferior to the Supreme Court;

356

10. To define and punish piracies and felonies committed on the high seas, and offenses against the law of nations;

11. To declare war, grant letters of marque and reprisal, and make rules concerning captures on land and water;

12. To raise and support armies, but no appropriation of money to that use shall be for a longer term than two years;

13. To provide and maintain a navy;

14. To make rules for the government and regulation of the land and naval forces;

15. To provide for calling forth the militia to execute the laws of the Union, suppress insurrections and repel invasions;

16. To provide for organizing, arming, and disciplining the militia, and for governing such part of them as may be employed in the service of the United States, reserving to the States respectively, the appointment of the officers, and the authority of training the militia according to the discipline prescribed by Congress.

17. To exercise exclusive legislation in all cases whatsoever, over such district (not exceeding ten miles square) as may, by cession of particular States, and the acceptance of Congress, become the seat of the government of the United States,[4] and to exercise like authority over all places purchased by the consent of the legislature of the State in which the same shall be, for the erection of forts, magazines, arsenals, dockyards, and other needful buildings; and

18. To make all laws which shall be necessary and proper for carrying into execution the foregoing powers, and all other powers vested by this Constitution in the government of the United States, or in any department or officer thereof.

SECTION 9. 1. The migration or importation of such persons as any of the States now existing shall think proper to admit, shall not be prohibited by the Congress prior to the year one thousand eight hundred and eight, but a tax or duty may be imposed on such importation, not exceeding ten dollars for each person.

2. The privilege of the writ of *habeas corpus* shall not be suspended, unless when in cases of rebellion or invasion the public safety may require it.

3. No bill of attainder or *ex post facto* law shall be passed.

4. No capitation, or other direct, tax shall be laid, unless in proportion to the census or enumeration hereinbefore directed to be taken.[5]

5. No tax or duty shall be laid on articles exported from any State.

6. No preference shall be given by any regulation of commerce or revenue to the ports of one State over those of another: nor shall vessels bound to, or from, one State be obliged to enter, clear, or pay duties in another.

7. No money shall be drawn from the treasury, but in consequence of appropriations made by law; and a regular statement and account of the receipts and expenditures of all public money shall be published from time to time.

8. No title of nobility shall be granted by the United States: and no person holding any office of profit or trust under them, shall, without the consent of the Congress, accept of any present, emolument, office, or title, of any kind whatever, from any king, prince, or foreign State.

SECTION 10. 1. No State shall enter into any treaty, alliance, or confederation; grant letters of marque and reprisal; coin money; emit bills of credit; make anything but gold and silver coin a tender in payment of debts; pass any bill of attainder, *ex post facto* law, or law impairing the obligation of contracts, or grant any title of nobility.

2. No State shall, without the consent of the Congress, lay any imposts or

[4] See the 23rd Amendment.
[5] See the 16th Amendment.

duties on imports or exports, except what may be absolutely necessary for executing its inspection laws: and the net produce of all duties and imposts laid by any State on imports or exports, shall be for the use of the treasury of the United States; and all such laws shall be subject to the revision and control of the Congress.

3. No State shall, without the consent of the Congress, lay any duty of tonnage, keep troops, or ships of war in time of peace, enter into any agreement or compact with another State, or with a foreign power, or engage in war, unless actually invaded, or in such imminent danger as will not admit of delay.

ARTICLE II

SECTION 1.   1. The executive power shall be vested in a President of the United States of America. He shall hold his office during the term of four years,[6] and, together with the Vice President, chosen for the same term, be elected as follows:

2. Each State shall appoint, in such manner as the legislature thereof may direct, a number of electors, equal to the whole number of senators and representatives to which the State may be entitled in the Congress: but no senator or representative, or person holding an office of trust or profit under the United States, shall be appointed an elector.

The electors shall meet in their respective States, and vote by ballot for two persons, of whom one at least shall not be an inhabitant of the same State with themselves. And they shall make a list of all the persons voted for, and of the number of votes for each; which list they shall sign and certify, and transmit sealed to the seat of the government of the United States, directed to the president of the Senate. The president of the Senate shall, in the presence of the Senate and House of Representatives, open all the certificates, and the votes shall then be counted. The person having the greatest number of votes shall be the President, if such number be a majority of the whole number of electors appointed; and if there be more than one who have such majority, and have an equal number of votes, then the House of Representatives shall immediately choose by ballot one of them for President; and if no person have a majority, then from the five highest on the list the said House shall in like manner choose the President. But in choosing the President, the votes shall be taken by States, the representation from each State having one vote; a quorum for this purpose shall consist of a member or members from two thirds of the States, and a majority of all the States shall be necessary to a choice. In every case, after the choice of the President, the person having the greatest number of votes of the electors shall be the Vice President. But if there should remain two or more who have equal votes, the Senate shall choose from them by ballot the Vice President.[7]

3. The Congress may determine the time of choosing the electors, and the day on which they shall give their votes; which day shall be the same throughout the United States.

4. No person except a natural born citizen, or a citizen of the United States, at the time of the adoption of this Constitution, shall be eligible to the office of President; neither shall any person be eligible to that office who shall not have attained to the age of thirty-five years, and been fourteen years a resident within the United States.

5. In case of the removal of the President from office, or of his death, resignation, or inability to discharge the powers and duties of the said office, the same shall devolve on the Vice President, and the Congress may by law provide for the case

[6] See the 22nd Amendment.
[7] Superseded by the 12th Amendment.

of removal, death, resignation, or inability, both of the President and Vice President, declaring what officer shall then act as President, and such officer shall act accordingly, until the disability be removed, or a President shall be elected.[8]

6. The President shall, at stated times, receive for his services a compensation, which shall neither be increased nor diminished during the period for which he shall have been elected, and he shall not receive within that period any other emolument from the United States, or any of them.

7. Before he enter on the execution of his office, he shall take the following oath or affirmation:—"I do solemnly swear (or affirm) that I will faithfully execute the office of President of the United States, and will to the best of my ability, preserve, protect and defend the Constitution of the United States."

SECTION 2. 1. The President shall be commander in chief of the army and navy of the United States, and of the militia of the several States, when called into the actual service of the United States; he may require the opinion, in writing, of the principal officer in each of the executive departments, upon any subject relating to the duties of their respective offices, and he shall have power to grant reprieves and pardons for offenses against the United States, except in cases of impeachment.

2. He shall have power, by and with the advice and consent of the Senate, to make treaties, provided two thirds of the senators present concur; and he shall nominate, and by and with the advice and consent of the Senate, shall appoint ambassadors, other public ministers and consuls, judges of the Supreme Court, and all other officers of the United States, whose appointments are not herein otherwise provided for, and which shall be established by law: but the Congress may by law vest the appointment of such inferior officers, as they think proper, in the President alone, in the courts of law, or in the heads of departments.

3. The President shall have power to fill up all vacancies that may happen during the recess of the Senate, by granting commissions which shall expire at the end of their next session.

SECTION 3. He shall from time to time give to the Congress information of the state of the Union, and recommend to their consideration such measures as he shall judge necessary and expedient; he may, on extraordinary occasions, convene both Houses, or either of them, and in case of disagreement between them with respect to the time of adjournment, he may adjourn them to such time as he shall think proper; he shall receive ambassadors and other public ministers; he shall take care that the laws be faithfully executed, and shall commission all the officers of the United States.

SECTION 4. The President, Vice President, and all civil officers of the United States, shall be removed from office on impeachment for, and conviction of, treason, bribery, or other high crimes and misdemeanors.

ARTICLE III

SECTION 1. The judicial power of the United States shall be vested in one Supreme Court, and in such inferior courts as the Congress may from time to time ordain and establish. The judges, both of the Supreme and inferior courts, shall hold their offices during good behavior, and shall, at stated times, receive for their services, a compensation, which shall not be diminished during their continuance in office.

SECTION 2. 1. The judicial power shall extend to all cases, in law and equity, arising under this Constitution, the laws of the United States, and treaties made, or

[8] Superseded by the 25th Amendment.

which shall be made, under their authority;—to all cases affecting ambassadors, other public ministers and consuls;—to all cases of admiralty and maritime jurisdiction;—to controversies to which the United States shall be a party;—to controversies between two or more States; between a State and citizens of another State[9] —between citizens of different States;—between citizens of the same State claiming lands under grants of different States, and between a State, or the citizens thereof, and foreign States citizens or subjects.

2. In all cases affecting ambassadors, other public ministers and consuls, and those in which a State shall be party, the Supreme Court shall have original jurisdiction. In all the other cases before mentioned, the Supreme Court shall have appellate jurisdiction, both as to law and to fact, with such exceptions, and under such regulations as the Congress shall make.

3. The trial of all crimes, except in cases of impeachment, shall be by jury; and such trial shall be held in the State where the said crimes shall have been committed; but when not committed within any State, the trial shall be at such place or places as the Congress may by law have directed.

SECTION 3.   1. Treason against the United States shall consist only in levying war against them, or in adhering to their enemies, giving them aid and comfort. No person shall be convicted of treason unless on the testimony of two witnesses to the same overt act, or on confession in open court.

2. The Congress shall have power to declare the punishment of treason, but no attainder of treason shall work corruption of blood, or forfeiture except during the life of the person attainted.

ARTICLE IV

SECTION 1.   Full faith and credit shall be given in each State to the public acts, records, and judicial proceedings of every other State. And the Congress may by general laws prescribe the manner in which such acts, records and proceedings shall be proved, and the effect thereof.

SECTION 2.   1. The citizens of each State shall be entitled to all privileges and immunities of citizens in the several States.[7]

2. A person charged in any State with treason, felony, or other crime, who shall flee from justice, and be found in another State, shall on demand of the executive authority of the State from which he fled, be delivered up to be removed to the State having jurisdiction of the crime.

3. No person held to service or labor in one State under the laws thereof, escaping into another, shall in consequence of any law or regulation therein, be discharged from such service or labor, but shall be delivered up on claim of the party to whom such service or labor may be due.[10]

SECTION 3.   1. New States may be admitted by the Congress into this Union; but no new State shall be formed or erected within the jurisdiction of any other State, nor any State be formed by the junction of two or more States, or parts of States, without the consent of the legislatures of the States concerned as well as of the Congress.

2. The Congress shall have power to dispose of and make all needful rules and regulations respecting the territory or other property belonging to the United States;

[9] See the 11th Amendment.
[10] See the 13th Amendment.

and nothing in this Constitution shall be so construed as to prejudice any claims of the United States, or of any particular State.

SECTION 4. The United States shall guarantee to every State in this Union a republican form of government, and shall protect each of them against invasion; and on application of the legislature, or of the executive (when the legislature cannot be convened) against domestic violence.

ARTICLE V

The Congress, whenever two thirds of both Houses shall deem it necessary, shall propose amendments to this Constitution, or, on the application of the legislature of two thirds of the several States, shall call a convention for proposing amendments, which in either case, shall be valid to all intents and purposes, as part of this Constitution when ratified by the legislatures of three fourths of the several States, or by conventions in three fourths thereof, as the one or the other mode of ratification may be proposed by the Congress; Provided that no amendment which may be made prior to the year one thousand eight hundred and eight shall in any manner affect the first and fourth clauses in the ninth section of the first article; and that no State, without its consent, shall be deprived of its equal suffrage in the Senate.

ARTICLE VI

1. All debts contracted and engagements entered into, before the adoption of this Constitution, shall be as valid against the United States under this Constitution, as under the Confederation.

2. This Constitution, and the laws of the United States which shall be made in pursuance thereof; and all treaties made, or which shall be made, under the authority of the United States, shall be the supreme law of the land; and the Judges in every State shall be bound thereby, anything in the Constitution or laws of any State to the contrary notwithstanding.

3. The senators and representatives before mentioned, and the members of the several State legislatures, and all executive and judicial officers, both of the United States and of the several States, shall be bound by oath or affirmation to support this Constitution; but no religious test shall ever be required as a qualification to any office or public trust under the United States.

ARTICLE VII

The ratification of the conventions of nine States shall be sufficient for the establihsment of this Constitution between the States so ratifying the same.

Done in Convention by the unanimous consent of the States present the seventeenth day of September in the year of our Lord one thousand seven hundred and eighty-seven, and of the independence of the United States of America the twelfth. In witness whereof we have hereunto subscribed our names.

[Names omitted]

---

[9] See the 14th Amendment, Sec. 4.

AMENDMENTS

Articles in addition to, and amendment of, the Constitution of the United States of America, proposed by Congress, and ratified by the legislatures of the several States pursuant to the fifth article of the original Constitution.

First Ten Amendments passed by Congress Sept. 25, 1789.
Ratified by three-fourths of the States December 15, 1791.

ARTICLE I

Congress shall make no law respecting an establishment of religion, or prohibiting the free exercise thereof; or abridging the freedom of speech, or of the press; or the right of the people peaceably to assemble, and to petition the government for a redress of grievances.

ARTICLE II

A well regulated militia, being necessary to the security of a free State, the right of the people to keep and bear arms, shall not be infringed.

ARTICLE III

No soldier shall, in time of peace be quartered in any house, without the consent of the owner, nor in time of war, but in a manner to be prescribed by law.

ARTICLE IV

The right of the people to be secure in their persons, houses, papers, and effects, against unreasonable searches and seizures, shall not be violated, and no warrants shall issue, but upon probable cause, supported by oath or affirmation, and particularly describing the place to be searched, and the persons or things to be seized.

ARTICLE V

No person shall be held to answer for a capital, or otherwise infamous crime, unless on a presentment or indictment of a grand jury, except in cases arising in the land or naval forces, or in the militia, when in actual service in time of war or public danger; nor shall any person be subject for the same offense to be twice put in jeopardy of life or limb; nor shall be compelled in any criminal case to be a witnesses against himself, nor be deprived of life, liberty, or property, without due process of law; nor shall private property be taken for public use without just compensation.

ARTICLE VI

In all criminal prosecutions, the accused shall enjoy the right to a speedy and public trial, by an impartial jury of the State and district wherein the crime shall have been committed, which district shall have been previously ascertained by law, and to be informed of the nature and cause of the accusation; to be confronted with the witnesses against him; to have compulsory process for obtaining witnesses in his favor, and to have the assistance of counsel for his defense.

ARTICLE VII

In suits at common law, where the value in controversy shall exceed twenty dollars, the right of trial by jury shall be preserved, and no fact tried by a jury shall be otherwise reëxamined in any court of the United States, than according to the rules of the common law.

ARTICLE VIII

Excessive bail shall not be required, nor excessive fines imposed, nor cruel and unusual punishments inflicted.

ARTICLE IX

The enumeration in the Constitution of certain rights shall not be construed to deny or disparage others retained by the people.

ARTICLE X

The powers not delegated to the United States by the Constitution, nor prohibited by it to the States, are reserved to the States respectively, or to the people.

ARTICLE XI

Passed by Congress March 5, 1794. Ratified January 8, 1798.

The judicial power of the United States shall not be construed to extend to any suit in law or equity, commenced or prosecuted against one of the United States by citizens of another State, or by citizens or subjects of any foreign State.

ARTICLE XII

Passed by Congress December 12, 1803. Ratified September 25, 1804.

The electors shall meet in their respective States, and vote by ballot for President and Vice President, one of whom, at least, shall not be an inhabitant of the same State with themselves; they shall name in their ballots the person voted for as President, and in distinct ballots, the person voted for as Vice President, and they shall make distinct lists of all persons voted for as President and of all persons voted for as Vice President, and of the number of votes for each, which lists they shall sign and certify, and transmit sealed to the seat of the government of the United States, directed to the President of the Senate;—The President of the Senate shall, in the presence of the Senate and House of Representatives, open all the certificates and the votes shall then be counted;—The person having the greatest number of votes for President, shall be the President, if such number be a majority of the whole number of electors appointed; and if no person have such majority, then from the persons having the highest numbers not exceeding three on the list of those voted for as President, the House of Representatives shall choose immediately, by ballot, the President. But in choosing the President, the votes shall be taken by States, the representation from each State having one vote; a quorum for this purpose shall consist of a member or members from two thirds of the States, and a majority of all the States shall be necessary to a choice. And if the House of Representatives shall not choose a President whenever the right of choice shall devolve upon them, before the fourth day of March next following, then the Vice President shall act as President, as in the case of the death or other constitutional disability of the President. The person having the greatest number of votes as Vice President shall be the Vice President, if such number be a majority of the whole number of electors appointed, and if no person have a majority, then from the two highest numbers on the list, the Senate shall choose the Vice President; a quorum for the purpose shall consist of two thirds of the whole number of Senators, and a majority of the whole number shall be necessary to a choice. But no person constitutionally ineligible to the office of President shall be eligible to that of Vice President of the United States.

ARTICLE XIII

Passed by Congress February 1, 1865. Ratified December 18, 1865.

SECTION 1.   Neither slavery nor involuntary servitude, except as punishment for crime whereof the party shall have been duly convicted, shall exist within the United States, or any place subject to their jurisdiction.

SECTION 2.   Congress shall have power to enforce this article by appropriate legislation.

ARTICLE XIV

Passed by Congress June 16, 1866. Ratified July 23, 1868.

SECTION 1.   All persons born or naturalized in the United States, and subject to the jurisdiction thereof, are citizens of the United States and of the State wherein they reside. No State shall make or enforce any law which shall abridge the privileges or immunities of citizens of the United States; nor shall any State deprive any person of life, liberty, or property, without due process of law; nor deny to any person within its jurisdiction the equal protection of the laws.

SECTION 2.   Representatives shall be apportioned among the several States according to their respective numbers, counting the whole number of persons in each State, excluding Indians not taxed. But when the right to vote at any election for the choice of electors for President and Vice President of the United States, representatives in Congress, the executive and judicial officers of a State, or the members of the legislature thereof, is denied to any of the male inhabitants of such State, being twenty-one years of age, and citizens of the United States, or in any way abridged, except for participation in rebellion, or other crime, the basis of representation therein shall be reduced in the proportion which the number of such male citizens shall bear to the whole number of male citizens twenty-one years of age in such State.

SECTION 3. No person shall be a senator or representative in Congress, or elector of President and Vice President, or hold any office, civil or military, under the United States, or under any State, who having previously taken an oath, as a member of Congress, or as an officer of the United States, or as a member of any State legislature, or as an executive or judicial officer of any State, to support the Constitution of the United States, shall have engaged in insurrection or rebellion against the same, or given aid or comfort to the enemies thereof. But Congress may by a vote of two thirds of each House, remove such disability.

SECTION 4. The validity of the public debt of the United States, authorized by law, including debts incurred for payment of pensions and bounties for services in suppressing insurrection or rebellion, shall not be questioned. But neither the United States nor any State shall assume or pay any debt or obligation incurred in aid of insurrection or rebellion against the United States, or any claim for the loss or emancipation of any slave; but all such debts, obligations, and claims shall be held illegal and void.

SECTION 5. The Congress shall have power to enforce, by appropriate legislation, the provisions of this article.

ARTICLE XV

Passed by Congress February 27, 1869. Ratified March 30, 1870.

SECTION 1. The right of citizens of the United States to vote shall not be denied or abridged by the United States or by any State on account of race, color, or previous condition of servitude.

SECTION 2. The Congress shall have power to enforce this article by appropriate legislation.

ARTICLE XVI

Passed by Congress July 12, 1909. Ratified February 25, 1913.

The Congress shall have power to lay and collect taxes on incomes, from whatever source derived, without apportionment among the several States, and without regard to any census or enumeration.

ARTICLE XVII

Passed by Congress May 16, 1912. Ratified May 31, 1913.

The Senate of the United States shall be composed of two senators from each state, elected by the people thereof, for six years; and each senator shall have one vote. The electors in each State shall have the qualifications requisite for electors of the most numerous branch of the State legislature.

When vacancies happen in the representation of any State in the Senate, the executive authority of such State shall issue writs of election to fill such vacancies: *Provided,* That the legislature of any State may empower the executive thereof to make temporary appointments until the people fill the vacancies by election as the legislature may direct.

This amendment shall not be so construed as to affect the election or term of any senator chosen before it becomes valid as part of the Constitution.

ARTICLE XVIII

Passed by Congress December 17, 1917. Ratified January 29, 1919.[11]

After one year from the ratification of this article, the manufacture, sale, or transportation of intoxicating liquors within, the importation thereof into, or the exportation thereof from the United States and all territory subject to the jurisdicion thereof for beverage purposes is hereby prohibited.

The Congress and the several States shall have concurrent power to enforce this article by appropriate legislation.

This article shall be inoperative unless it shall have been ratified as an amendment to the Constitution by the legislatures of the several States, as provided in the Constitution, within seven years from the date of the submission hereof to the states by Congress.

ARTICLE XIX

Passed by Congress June 5, 1919. Ratified August 26, 1920.

The right of citizens of the United States to vote shall not be denied or abridged by the United States or by any State on account of sex.

The Congress shall have power by appropriate legislation to enforce the provisions of this article.

ARTICLE XX

Passed by Congress March 3, 1932. Ratified January 23, 1933.

SECTION 1.   The terms of the President and Vice President shall end at noon on the 20th day of January, and the terms of Senators and Representatives at noon on the 3d day of January, of the years in which such terms would have ended if this article had not been ratified; and the terms of their successors shall then begin.

SECTION 2.   The Congress shall assemble at least once in every year, and such meeting shall begin at noon on the 3d day of January, unless they shall by law appoint a different day.

SECTION 3.   If, at the time fixed for the beginning of the term of the President, the President-elect shall have died, the Vice President-elect shall become President. If a President shall not have been chosen before the time fixed for the beginning of his term, or if the President-elect shall have failed to qualify, then the Vice President-elect shall act as President until a President shall have qualified; and the Con-

[11] Repealed by the 21st Amendment.

gress may by law provide for the case wherein neither a President-elect nor a Vice President-elect shall have qualified, declaring who shall then act as President, or the manner in which one who is to act shall be selected, and such person shall act accordingly until a President or Vice President shall have qualified.

SECTION 4.   The Congress may by law provide for the case of the death of any of the persons from whom the House of Representatives may choose a President whenever the right of choice shall have devolved upon them, and for the case of the death of any of the persons from whom the Senate may choose a Vice President whenever the right of choice shall have devolved upon them.

SECTION 5.   Sections 1 and 2 shall take effect on the 15th day of October following the ratification of this article.

SECTION 6.   This article shall be inoperative unless it shall have been ratified as an amendment to the Constitution by the legislatures of three-fourths of the several States within seven years from the date of its submission.

ARTICLE XXI

Passed by Congress February 20, 1933. Ratified December 5, 1933.

SECTION 1.   The Eighteenth Article of amendment to the Constitution of the United States is hereby repealed.

SECTION 2.   The transportation or importation into any State, Territory, or possession of the United States for delivery or use therein of intoxicating liquors in violation of the laws thereof, is hereby prohibited.

SECTION 3.   This article shall be inoperative unless it shall have been ratified as an amendment to the Constitution by conventions in the several States, as provided in the Constitution, within seven years from the date of the submission thereof to the States by the Congress.

ARTICLE XXII

Passed by Congress March 24, 1947. Ratified February 26, 1951.

SECTION 1.   No person shall be elected to the office of the President more than twice, and no person who has held the office of President, or acted as President, for more than two years of a term to which some other person was elected President shall be elected to the office of the President more than once. But this article shall not apply to any person holding the office of President when this article was proposed by the Congress, and shall not prevent any person who may be holding the office of President, or acting as President, during the term within which this article becomes operative from holding the office of President or acting as President during the remainder of such term.

SECTION 2.   This article shall be inoperative unless it shall have been ratified as an amendment to the Constitution by the legislatures of three-fourths of the several States within seven years from the date of its submission to the States by the Congress.

ARTICLE XXIII

Passed by Congress June 16, 1960. Ratified March 29, 1961.

SECTION 1.   The district constituting the seat of Government of the United States shall appoint in such manner as the Congress may direct:

A number of electors of President and Vice President equal to the whole number of Senators and Representatives in Congress to which the District would be entitled if it were a State, but in no event more than the least populous State; they shall be in addition to those appointed by the States, but they shall be considered, for the purposes of election of President and Vice President, to be electors appointed by a State; and they shall meet in the District and perform such duties as provided by the twelfth article of amendment.

SECTION 2.   The Congress shall have the power to enforce this article by appropriate legislation.

ARTICLE XXIV

Passed by Congress August 27, 1962. Ratified January 23, 1964.

SECTION 1.   The right of citizens of the United States to vote in any primary or other election for President or Vice President, for electors for President or Vice President, or for Senator or Representative in Congress, shall not be denied or abridged by the United States or any State by failure to pay any poll tax or other tax.

SECTION 2.   The Congress shall have the power to enforce this article by appropriate legislation.

ARTICLE XXV

Passed by Congress July 6, 1965. Ratified February 10, 1967.

SECTION 1.   In case of the removal of the President from office or of his death or resignation, the Vice President shall become President.

SECTION 2.   Whenever there is a vacancy in the office of the Vice President, the President shall nominate a Vice President who shall take office upon confirmation by a majority vote of both Houses of Congress.

SECTION 3.   Whenever the President transmits to the President pro tempore of the Senate and the Speaker of the House of Representatives his written declaration that he is unable to discharge the powers and duties of his office, and until he transmits to them a written declaration to the contrary, such powers and duties shall be discharged by the Vice President as Acting President.

SECTION 4.   Whenever the Vice President and a majority of either the principal officers of the executive departments or of such other body as Congress may by law provide, transmit to the President pro tempore of the Senate and the Speaker of the House of Representatives their written declaration that the President is unable to discharge the powers and duties of his office, the Vice President shall immediately assume the powers and duties of the office as Acting President.

368

Thereafter, when the President transmits to the President pro tempore of the Senate and the Speaker of the House of Representatives his written declaration that no inability exists, he shall resume the powers and duties of his office unless the Vice President and a majority of either the principal officers of the executive department or of such other body as Congress may by law provide, transmit within four days to the President pro tempore of the Senate and the Speaker of the House of Representatives their written declaration that the President is unable to discharge the powers and duties of his office. Thereupon Congress shall decide the issue, assembling within forty-eight hours for that purpose if not in session. If the Congress, within twenty-one days after receipt of the latter written declaration, or, if Congress is not in session, within twenty-one days after Congress is required to assemble, determines by two-thirds vote of both Houses that the President is unable to discharge the powers and duties of his office, the Vice President shall continue to discharge the same as Acting President; otherwise, the President shall resume the powers and duties of his office.

ARTICLE XXVI

Passed by Congress March 23, 1971. Ratified June 30, 1971.

SECTION 1.   The right of citizens of the United States, who are eighteen years of age or older, to vote shall not be denied or abridged by the United States or by any State on account of age.

SECTION 2.   The Congress shall have power to enforce this article by appropriate legislation.

ARTICLE XXVII

Proposed Amendment passed by Congress March 22, 1972.
Ratification to be by the legislatures of three-fourths of
the several states within seven years from the date of its
submission by the Congress.

SECTION 1.   Equality of rights under the law shall not be denied or abridged by the United States or by any State on account of sex.

SECTION 2.   The Congress shall have the power to enforce, by appropriate legislation, the provisions of this article.

SECTION 3.   This amendment shall take effect two years after the date of ratification.

TABLE OF CASES—Volume II

(Page numbers in boldface type refer to cases given "major" treatment. Page numbers in ordinary type refer to cases treated as "related cases" or to which reference is made.)

369

INDEX—Volume II